WITH THE CORONATION OF CHARLES VII IN THE CATHEDRAL OF RHEIMS,
JOAN OF ARC FELT THAT HER MISSION HAD BEEN FULFILLED.

LANGUAGE, LITERATURE, AND LIFE
A FOREIGN LANGUAGE PROGRAM

FRENCH BOOK ONE

BY

INA BARTELLS SMITH
Formerly of Oak Park and River Forest
Township High School, Oak Park, Illinois

AND

DOROTHY FIELDING ROBERTS
Hyde Park High School, Chicago

PHILIP S. ALLEN, *Directing Editor*
University of Chicago

SCOTT, FORESMAN AND COMPANY
CHICAGO   ATLANTA   DALLAS   NEW YORK

PREFACE

What the Series Is. *Language, Literature, and Life, French Book One* is the first of two books that cover all the reading, grammar, and composition necessary for a two-year modern-language course in high school. Each one of the books furnishes more reading than the requirements of the year for which it is intended.

Advantages of the Series. Three advantages result from welding all the materials of the modern-language course into two books, with one book covering an entire year's work. *First, a very practical saving* for the student in time, cost, and convenience is achieved. Each one of the books takes the place of the several volumes which would be bought and used separately under the usual conditions. *Second,* books in which all reading, grammar, and composition materials are prepared and edited to dovetail into one unified whole make possible *an integration of materials* into a well-balanced single teaching unit. The *third* advantage that this close-knit series offers is *gradation*. From the opening page of *Book One*, the progress from lesson to lesson is apparent in the gradual introduction of integrated material. Such unity, making for the learner's smooth and rapid progress, can be achieved more easily in a well-planned French course than in a confusion of textbooks, unrelated as to level and to context.

The Value of Acquiring a Cultural Background. It is well recognized that one value to be derived from the study of French is not only an acquaintance with the language and literature, but also an understanding of French civilization and its contribution to individual and social culture.

In addition, a truly worth-while aim is this: That, as a result of acquiring some knowledge of France, the pupil may gain, by thoughtful comparison of it and his country, a better understanding of his own country.

As a specific means of accomplishing this end, *French Book One* contains: (*a*) Reading select ons, in French, chosen to show French character through pleasing pictures of folk-ways and customs, through stories of great deeds, persons, and epochs of French history, through an emphasis on the high achievements of French art and literature. (*b*) Twenty separate essays, written in English, and profusely illustrated with specially chosen photographs, that furnish a panoramic view of French activities and background. What high-school boy or girl will not be interested in knowing that his French cousins cycle, motor, and ramble over roads made by a foreign race more than two thousand years ago; that France has as citizens various groups that hundreds of years ago settled within her borders, but that even today cling to the dress and many of the customs of the districts from which they came so long ago; that most French students have to study during their holidays? Such details, and many hundreds of others, are found in essays whose titles range from "How France Was Made" to "French Cooking." The student will therefore have an increased knowledge of the institutions of France and a better understanding of her contributions to modern culture. He will enlarge his sympathy to take in the ideals, aspirations, and traditions of Frenchmen and of Americans of French descent.

Ability to Read. The ability to read with comprehension depends upon a triumvirate of important factors, all of which must be balanced: First, the reading matter must be within the intellectual scope of the reader and must arouse his interest. Second, the vocabulary and idiom content must be recognized and correctly interpreted. Third, the grammatical construction of the material must be unconsciously or analytically recognized. Much of the research during recent years in the modern-language field has particularly emphasized these three points.

From its first page to its last, *French Book One* offers the pupil interesting and varied reading material. The natural experiences of boys and girls, many of them laugh-provoking incidents laid in French towns, descriptions of travel in France, several of La Fontaine's fables, adaptations from *Les Misérables* and *The Song of Roland*, historical anecdotes—these are some of the interesting sketches made available in an attractive, informal style.

But interesting reading alone will not develop in the student the ability to read with moderate ease. He must *have a sufficient amount* of reading. Among the many conclusions reached in the extensive publications of the American and Canadian Committees on Modern Languages is one which states briefly that, in order to increase the reading ability of pupils, the amount of reading must be considerably augmented. *French Book One* has amply provided for this need of more reading. It gives reading material to the equivalent of one hundred and eighty pages of the ordinary grammar or two hundred pages of a reader of the classic type—as much as, or more than, is usually supplied by a beginner's book plus several classics.

But as courses are at present organized, merely adding bulk will not increase the amount of reading that will be done. The only way in which this increased reading can be done is to give the student a large amount of *simple* reading matter, based on previously-learned grammatical constructions and words, and adding only a minimum number of new words. *French Book One* does this exactly. Its increased amount of reading is definitely built on the grammar facts and the vocabulary developed in the preceding lessons, and hence is easier and can be read more rapidly than any material that could be secured from an outside source. Growth in reading ability, as well as joy in the attainment, must follow from such use of an abundance of interesting material in which the student finds few new words and no new grammatical points.

Vocabulary and Idioms. The reliability of word lists compiled on the frequency principle is generally accepted now by teachers and authors as a guide to vocabulary difficulty. The authors are particularly indebted to two publications of the American and Canadian Committees on Modern Languages, the *French Word Book*, by George E. Vander Beke, and the *French Idiom List* compiled by F. D. Cheydleur, for guidance regarding the importance of individual words.

The complete French-English vocabulary of *French Book One* has 180 idioms and 1970 words, 560 being cognates, which reduce the vocabulary load considerably. The 1970 words include (1) articles, common prepositions, pronouns, adverbs derived from adjectives, numerals; (2) the 69 basic items in Part I of the Vander Beke list; (3) 830 of the first thousand words of the Vander Beke list; (4) 80 irregular verb-forms; (5) 40 proper nouns; (6) about 785 words of lower frequency according to the Vander Beke list, the largest group of them being from the second thousand words, the next largest group from the third thousand, etc.; (7) 166 words not found in the Vander Beke list. The last two groups of words, 6 and 7, contain many of the common vocabularies of the schoolroom, the home, weather, time, travel, etc., which are of low frequency or are omitted from the Vander Beke list, since this list is composed of words from printed sources of a wide range of categories of French prose. The remaining words in these two groups are required as part of the passive vocabulary used in the 26 unit reading lessons. Approximately 1300 of the 1970 words comprise what may be called the active vocabulary, that is, the vocabulary that is introduced in the 85 grammar lessons.

Knowledge of Grammar. There is nothing new in requiring a study of grammar in the modern-language course. However, the emphasis on the reading objective during the past five years has been instrumental in altering the viewpoint toward the particular place of grammar in the course. It has been pointed out that over-emphasis in the past on grammar as an end in itself has seriously interfered with the development of real reading with comprehension. Thus, elimination of much of the formalized drill on grammatical forms and points of syntax is considered essential to better training in reading.

French Book One reflects the above viewpoint in three ways:

(*a*) The series distributes the material of the ordinary beginning work over a two-year course in grammar. Definite grammatical lessons will be available not only in the first book, but also in the second, the lessons of *French Book One* carrying the pupil only up to a brief and preliminary presentation of the subjunctive.

(*b*) This slight lessening of the amount of grammatical work in the first-year book is one factor that has made possible the inclusion of so much reading material. The opportunity to make immediate use of newly-acquired grammar in the reading of connected material demonstrates to the student the real necessity of grammar study, and at the same time prevents such study from being an end in itself.

(*c*) In preparing the book, the recurrence of each new grammatical point has been carefully charted through subsequent exercises and reading lessons. As a result, the authors have been able to make certain that each new point is given immediate and frequent application. Much of the repetition necessary to the mastery of grammatical points takes place more or less automatically in connection with the reading exercises, thus minimizing the amount of isolated grammar drill that is necessary.

Provision for systematic review of grammar is made by the inclusion of twenty-two review lessons, appearing approximately every fifth lesson.

Ability to Use the Language Orally. Most people will agree that the burden of teaching pronunciation, more than any other element in the study of French, must fall upon the teacher. *French Book One* provides the tools needed for teaching pronunciation thoroughly. It offers a thorough-going treatment of phonetics and opportunities for such drill on sound elements as teachers may desire to avail themselves of. In their phonetic treatment, the authors of the present book acknowledge with gratitude the guide and counsel given by an outstanding phonetician, Professor John L. Ballif, Jr., of the University of Utah.

Phonetic transcriptions are given in the vocabularies for those teachers desiring to use the symbols. In addition to this ample provision for training in sound elements, the book furnishes abundant opportunity for the oral use of French. Each of the eighty-five grammar lessons contains a *"questionnaire"* of ten to fifteen questions. As these questions cover the important points of the reading material of the lesson, they furnish a convenient test of the pupil's comprehension of his reading at the same time that they afford opportunity for oral practice. Additional provision is made for oral work in many of the *"devoirs,"* where oral exercises are specifically indicated.

Increased Knowledge of English Grammar and Derivation. It is a commonplace with modern-language teachers that pupils come to their study of foreign languages inadequately prepared in English grammar. To aid the pupil to a better understanding of his mother tongue is not to be thought of as a meaningless task but as one of the real contributions of modern-language instruction, which entitles it to an important place in the secondary curriculum. The new principles of grammar are explained in simple language, accompanied by many examples, and with the assumption that the pupil has little previous knowledge of English grammar. Since probably no one has an adequate understanding of the grammar of any language until he has compared it with that of another, *French Book One* provides for such comparison as it presents new points in French grammar.

To encourage the pupil to recognize English equivalents, or cognates, they are set apart in each reading lesson vocabulary, and serve the two purposes of contributing considerably to the simplicity of the reading material and of emphasizing the relationship between French and English in the matter of vocabulary.

French Progress Tests. Due to its accuracy, comprehensiveness, and simplicity, the new-type test is rapidly becoming the standard form for measuring achievement in the foreign languages. Realizing that modern-language teachers have a definite need for objective tests which cover a specific unit of work and which, when administered at frequent intervals, will give them an adequate idea of their students' progress, *French Progress Tests* have been constructed to accompany both *French Books One* and *Two*.

Each set contains twelve tests, including two final semester tests; each test is divided into several parts, stressing several phases of the pupil's work. In addition to the usual pronunciation, grammar, idiom, and vocabulary tests, there are comprehension units that measure the pupil's growing command of French, and cultural material units that test the pupil's information about French life and culture.

Only such vocabulary, idioms, and grammatical constructions as are found in the textbook are used in the tests. Thus, the twelve tests bind more closely the graded material and allow the pupil to follow his own progress more clearly than is possible with unrelated tests and textbooks.

Particularly during the formative stages of the book, the authors have profited by the helpful criticism of Miss Pearl B. Fisher of Los Angeles High School, Los Angeles, California.

Grateful acknowledgment is made to Henry Holt and Company for permission to use copyrighted material from *Chez nous*, by Henri Charles-Edouard David.

THE AUTHORS

SUGGESTIONS TO TEACHERS

Flexibility of the Book. *Language, Literature, and Life, French Book One* is intended for use in the first year of high school. Since two classes of the same grade rarely work with identical speed, it has been the aim of the authors to devise a book usable in every type of class. This book, therefore, may be adapted to the class rather than the class to the book, as is often tried.

The minimum requirements suggested for the first semester are Lessons 1-59, omitting any or all of the seven reading lessons within that group. The requirements for the second semester are Lessons 60-133, omitting any or all of the nineteen reading lessons. In regard to the second semester, the authors wish to emphasize the fact that if *French Book One* is not completed beyond Lesson 109, the pupils will not suffer an irreparable loss, since the grammar contained in these last lessons is reviewed either in the opening grammar lessons of *French Book Two* or shortly thereafter. With the minimum points in mind, teachers will be able to work out a satisfactory course of study for individual classes by adding reading lessons or groups of grammar lessons.

Suggestions for Teaching the Grammar and Review Lessons. Two days may be devoted to each grammar lesson. It is suggested that the last ten minutes of one period be used in reading the new vocabulary and explaining the new grammatical points. The home work for the first day may be the careful reading and study of the story which begins each grammar lesson and the learning of the new grammatical points. The first day's classwork may be the reading of the story, a second explanation of the grammar points, and the answering of the questions based on the reading

(*Questionnaire*). This procedure should leave about ten minutes at the end of the period for the explaining of the following day's work, consisting of such parts of the *Devoir* as the teacher chooses. The teacher is usually free to determine whether the exercises are to be written or prepared orally. The second day's work is devoted to the recitation of these exercises, with the last ten minutes devoted to the explanation of the next lesson, as stated above.

One day is to be devoted to each review lesson. The questions in English cover the previous five lessons plus questions on other important points previously studied. The reviews may be written or oral. If they are to be written, the exercises of the book or other similar ones composed by the teacher may be used. Again the last ten minutes are to be reserved for explaining the following lesson.

The Reading Lessons. With the exception of those classes following the minimum course, each class should be able to read several or all of the reading lessons, either as assigned class work or as outside reading. One day is to be devoted to a reading lesson, which may be assigned wholly or in part. Since the only new problem involved in the reading lessons is that of vocabulary, the lessons should be a source of true encouragement to the beginner. Also, the variety of the reading material should prove attractive to students of French.

Phonetics. The use of phonetics is in most cases a matter of individual choice. The phonetics may be entirely disregarded if another method of teaching pronunciation is preferred.

Translation. The paragraphs of translation may be entirely omitted. Each lesson contains sufficient drill for the average class. The omission of these paragraphs does not impair the unity of the book.

Cultural Essays. The twenty articles in English on a variety of aspects of French culture may be assigned in the order of their appearance. As they appear after each group of five or six lessons and are written in English, the time required for reading them is negligible. The need for adequate cultural material suitable for American boys and girls has been stressed frequently.

CONTENTS

CONTENTS

INTRODUCTION TO PRONUNCIATION

A. FRENCH SOUNDS

1. General Remarks

If we were listening to a Frenchman speak, even though we did not understand him, we would immediately notice several marked differences between his manner of speaking and our own. Some of the important differences are these:

a. French vowels are pronounced more vigorously and energetically than English vowels. This means that the lips and tongue are much more tense in the pronunciation of French than in that of English.

b. Before any French vowel is pronounced, the position of the jaws, lips, and tongue must be taken and must not be changed until the vowel sound has been completed.

c. In general, French vowels are shorter than English vowels.

d. French has no diphthongs.

e. Final consonants are generally silent in French, except c, f, l, and r, which are usually pronounced.

f. When a word ending in a consonant which is ordinarily silent is followed immediately by a closely-related word beginning with a vowel or an inaspirate h, the final consonant of the first word is sometimes sounded in connection with the vowel of the next word (see **Liaison,** page xxvi).

g. In French all the syllables of a word are pronounced with equal force, with the exception of the last syllable, on which there is a slight stress.

2. Table of English Equivalents for French Sounds

Vowels	Consonants
a = a*n*	b = *b*ed
â = *f*ather	ch = *sh*ow
e = th*e* man	d = *d*o (modified)
é = d*a*y	f = *f*ar
è = b*e*d	g = *g*ate
ê = b*e*d	gn = can*y*on (modified)
i = f*ee*t	h—silent in Parisian French
ô = p*o*se	j = plea*s*ure
o = a*w*e (modified)	k = *k*ill
u = no English equivalent	l = *l*et
eu = no English equivalent	m = *m*et
ou = b*oo*t	n = *n*o
ou (before a vowel) = *w*aft	p = *p*ut
oi = *w*aft	r = *r*ow (modified)
i (before a vowel) = *y*earn	s = *s*ee
u (before a vowel) = no English equivalent	t = *t*o
an, in, on, un (nasals) = no English equivalents	v = *v*at
	y = *y*earn
	z = *z*ebra

xiv

3. Table of Spellings and Phonetic Symbols

	SYMBOLS	SPELLINGS	EXAMPLES
FRONT VOWELS:	[i]	i, î, y	fini, île, y
	[e]	é, final ai, ed, er, ez, es (in monosyllables)	été, gai, pied, laver, nez, mes, des
	[ɛ]	è, ai, ei, ê, et (final), e (before a double consonant except *mm*), e (before *s* and a consonant), e (before *il* and *ill*), e (before *x*), e (not final in a syllable)	dès, fait, peine, bête, jouet, elle, est, vermeil, merveille, extrait, mer
	[a]	a, e (before *mm*)	patte, femme
BACK VOWELS:	[ɑ]	â, a (before *s*), a (before *ille* final in nouns)	âme, pas, Versailles
	[ɔ]	o, au (in certain words)	fort, aurai
	[o]	ô, au, eau, o (before *s*), o, os, ot, } final	hôte, haut, eau, chose, écho, clos, sot
	[u]	ou, oû	sou, goût
FRONT ROUNDED VOWELS: (sometimes called mixed or abnormal)	[y]	u, û	une, dû
	[ø]	eu, œu, eû, final or before a silent consonant	feu, nœud, jeûnes
	[œ]	eu, œu, before a pronounced consonant	peuple, sœur
	[ə]	e (final in a syllable)	de, table
NASAL VOWELS:	[ɛ̃]	aim, ain, eim, ein, im, in, ym, yn, ien	faim, sainte, Reims, sein, simple, vin, symbole, syntaxe, bien
	[ɑ̃]	am, an, em, en, aon	camp, dans, temps, dent, paon
	[õ]	om, on	dom, onze
	[œ̃]	um, un, eun	parfum, un, jeun
Sign of length	[ː]		jouːr, aiːde, choːse; grammaiːre

3. Table of Spellings and Phonetic Symbols (Continued)

	SYMBOLS	SPELLINGS	EXAMPLES
SEMI-CONSONANTS:	[j]	y, i, ï, ill (preceded by a vowel), il (final, preceded by a vowel)	yeux, bien, païen, battaillon, bétail
	[ɥ]	u+vowel	cuisine
	[w]	ou+vowel	oui
COMBINATIONS OF SEMI-CONSONANTS AND VOWELS:	[ij]	yi, ii, ill (preceded by a consonant)	payions, priions, pavillon
	[ji]	illi	taillis
	[ɥij]	uy	fuyard
	[wa]	oi, oî	foi, boîte
	[waj]	oy	moyen
	[wɑ]	oi, oî	bois, cloître
	[wɛ̃]	oin	soin
CONSONANTS:	[b]	b, bb	bas, abbé
(explosive)	[p]	p, pp	pas, appeler
	[d]	d, dd	aide, addition
	[t]	t, tt	ton, mette
	[g]	g, gg, gu (before i and e)	aigu, aggraver, guide
	[k]	c, cc, qu	lac, accuser, quand
FRICATIVES:	[v]	v	sève
	[f]	f, ff	fine, effacer
	[z]	z, s (between vowels)	dizaine, vase
	[s]	s, ss, ç, c, sc, t(ion)	son, casse, façade, ceci, scène, nation
	[ʒ]	j, ge, gi	jaune, mangea, gigot
	[ʃ]	ch	vache
NASALS:	[m]	m, mm	mais, femme
	[n]	n, nn	nous, donner
	[ɲ]	gn	digne
TRILLED	[r]	r, rr	gare, arrêt
LATERAL:	[l]	l, ll,	pâle, aller
COMBINATIONS OF CONSONANTS:	[gz]	x	exiler
	[ks]	x	texte

4. Alphabet

The letters of the French alphabet are, in general, the same as those in the English alphabet. The letter *k* occurs only in bookish or foreign words, and the letter *w* occurs only in foreign words such as *wagon*, *Wagner*, etc.

The table below shows in the second and third columns the regular names and the phonetic symbols.

LETTERS	NAMES	PRONUNCIATION OF NAMES
a	a	[ɑ]
b	bé	[be]
c	cé	[se]
d	dé	[de]
e	é	[e]
f	effe	[ɛf]
g	gé	[ʒe]
h	ache	[aʃ]
i	i	[i]
j	ji	[ʒi]
k	ka	[ka]
l	elle	[ɛl]
m	emme	[ɛm]
n	enne	[ɛn]
o	o	[o]
p	pé	[pe]
q	ku	[ky]
r	erre	[ɛːr]
s	esse	[ɛs]
t	té	[te]
u	u	[y]
v	vé	[ve]
w	double vé	[dublə ve]
x	iks	[iks]
y	i grec	[i grɛk]
z	zède	[zɛd]

5. Accents and Orthographic Signs

Accents

Certain marks placed over vowels in French are called accents. These accents have no effect upon stress in pronunciation. They indicate the sound of the vowel or, more rarely, serve to distinguish between words.

1. The acute accent (ˊ), *l'accent aigu*, is used over *e*: **été**.
2. The grave accent (ˋ), *l'accent grave*, is used generally over *e*: **mère**. Occasionally it is used over *a* or *u* to distinguish between words. Then it does not change the sound of the vowel: **la, là; ou, où**.
3. The circumflex accent (ˆ), *l'accent circonflexe*, is used over all vowels except *y*: **hâte, bête, boîte, hôte, goût**.

Other Signs

1. The cedilla (ˌ), *la cédille*, is used under the letter *c* to indicate that ç has the sound of *s*: **garçon.**
2. The apostrophe ('), *l'apostrophe*, shows, as in English, the omission of a vowel: **l'élève, l'histoire.**
3. The diaeresis ("), *le tréma*, is used over the second of two consecutive vowels to show that each vowel is pronounced separately: **naïf.**
4. The hyphen (-), *le trait d'union*, is used, as in English, to connect words: **est-il, porte-monnaie.**

6. Stress or Tonic Accent

In French all the syllables of a group except the last one are spoken evenly   The last one is slightly stressed. If the last syllable is silent, the stress falls on the next to the last.

Spoken language does not consist of isolated words. This is especially noticeable in French, where a series of connected words becomes a single group with but one accent—the tonic accent on the last sounded syllable.

B. THE VOWEL TRIANGLE

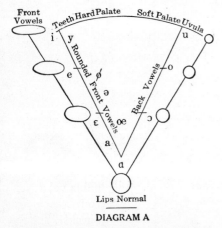

DIAGRAM A

DIAGRAM B

Diagram A represents three things:

(*a*) Rounding or retraction of the lips. Observe that for front vowels the lips are retracted, *i.e.*, drawn back. This retraction is greatest for [i], where the lips are drawn back as in smiling. It is less for [e], less still for [ɛ], while when we come to [ɑ] the lips are practically normal.

For rounded vowels and for back vowels, observe that the lips are rounded like a circle. The rounding is greatest for [y] and for [u]. It is

least for [ɑ], where the lips are only slightly rounded.

(*b*) The elevation of the tongue is indicated by the distance of a symbol on the diagram from the horizontal line at the top. Thus for [i], [y], and [u] the tongue is nearest the roof of the mouth. For [e], [ø], [o], it is next nearest, while for [ɑ] it is farthest away.

(*c*) The angle of the jaws is greatest for [ɑ], and least for [i], [y], and [u].

Diagram B presents words illustrating the various sounds of Diagram A.

C. DRILL ON SOUNDS

The following pages give, in simple, compact form, adequate material for drill on French vowels. It is inadvisable to undertake detailed work on consonants in the first year, though the teacher should always insist on the tenseness of the lips which is necessary for good pronunciation of French consonants.

The sounds are classified according to the standard nomenclature. Under each classification appear, in order, the phonetic symbol, English equivalent, spellings, special directions for pronouncing, and examples (for drill) of each sound. Here, as throughout the book, the phonetic symbols follow the authority of Paul Passy as given in the *International French-English Dictionary*.

1. Front Vowels

[i] = ee in feet

Spellings

i   î   y

The corners of the mouth are drawn back easily as in a smile, and the muscles of the tongue are very tense.

Examples

si [si]	plie [pli]	fils [fis]	fit [fi]
il [il]	fini [fini]	livre [liːvr]	île [il]
dit [di]	ici [isi]	hiver [ivɛːr]	ci-gît [siʒi]
pris [pri]	fille [fiːj]	riche [riʃ]	y [i]

[e] = ay in day

Spellings

é   ai, ed, er, ez (final)   es (final in monosyllables)

Avoid any suggestion of a diphthong.

Examples

ai [e]	été [ete]	lavez [lave]	léger [leʒe]
né [ne]	aimai [ɛme]	bébé [bebe]	pied [pje]
mes [me]	cocher [kɔʃe]	évitez [evite]	des [de]

[ɛ] = e in bed

Spellings

è   ei   ê   et (final)

ai (not final in a syllable)
e (before a double consonant, except **mm**)
e (before **s** and a consonant)
e (before **il** and **ill**)
e (before **x**)

As in [e], avoid any suggestion of a diphthong.

Examples

lève [lɛːv]	fait [fɛ]	espoir [ɛspwaːr]	vermeil [vɛrmɛːj]
après [aprɛ]	peine [pɛn]	jouet [ʒwɛ]	merveille [mɛrvɛːj]
veste [vɛst]	bête [bɛːt]	elle [ɛl]	extrait [ɛkstrɛ]

[a]=a in an

Spellings

a   à   e (before **mm**)

Examples

la [la]	va [va]	il a [i la]	chaque [ʃak]
ma [ma]	face [fas]	patte [pat]	à [a]
ta [ta]	chat [ʃa]	chatte [ʃat]	femme [fam]

2. Back Vowels

[ɑ]=a in father

Spellings

â   a (before **s**)   a (before **ille** final in nouns)

Examples

pâle [pɑːl]	pas [pɑ]	passe [pɑːs]	paille [pɑːj]
pâte [pɑːt]	passé [pɑse]	classe [klɑːs]	Versailles [vɛrsɑːj]

[ɔ] nearly like aw in awe

Spellings

o   au (in certain words)

Make the French sound much more staccato than the English sound **aw**.

Examples

fort [fɔːr]	forte [fɔrt]	roc [rɔk]	cloche [klɔʃ]
dort [dɔːr]	porte [pɔrt]	joli [ʒɔli]	paroles [parɔl]
mort [mɔːr]	morte [mɔrt]	poli [pɔli]	aurai [ɔre]
sort [sɔːr]	sorte [sɔrt]	sonner [sɔne]	saurai [sɔre]

[o]=o in pose

Spellings

ô   au   eau   o (before **s**)   o, os, ot (final

Examples

hôte [oːt]	haut [o]	eau [o]	écho [eko]
au [o]	chaud [ʃo]	chose [ʃoːz]	clos [klo]
aux [o]	peau [po]	pose [poːz]	sot [so]

[u]=oo in boot

Spellings

ou   oû   où

Examples

ou [u]	loup [lu]	avoue [avu]	dessous [dəsu]
bout [bu]	beaucoup [boku]	bouche [buʃ]	voûte [vut]
fou [fu]	moulin [mulɛ̃]	soutenir [sutniːr]	où [u]

3. Front Rounded Vowels

[y]

Spellings

u   û   eu (in forms of **avoir**)

[y] has no English equivalent. While pronouncing [i], move the lips to a whistling position. With the lips tightly rounded and the tongue saying [i], the result should be [y]. There must be no movement of the lips for [y]. Practice changing from *a* to *b* in each pair below.

a. lit [li]	*a.* nid [ni]	*a.* si [si]	*a.* dit [di]
b. lu [ly]	*b.* nu [ny]	*b.* su [sy]	*b.* du [dy]

Examples of [y]

mur [myːr]	**futur** [fytyːr]	**plume** [plym]	**brûler** [bryle]
plus [ply]	**étude** [etyd]	**sucre** [sykr]	**dû** [dy]
sur [syːr]	**étudier** [etydje]	**une** [yn]	**j'eus** [ʒy]

[ø]

Spellings

eu, oeu (final or before a silent consonant)
eû
eu (in the feminine of an adjective which ends in **-eux** in the masculine)

[ø] has no English equivalent. While pronouncing [e], move the lips into position for [o]. The result should be [ø]. The lips should be tense.

Say *a* of each pair below with lips rounded for [o]. The result should be [ø], as spelled in *b*.

a. et [e]	*a.* nez [ne]	*a.* dé [de]	*a.* gai [ge]
b. eux [ø]	*b.* nœud [nø]	*b.* deux [dø]	*b.* gueux [gø]

Examples of [ø]

feu [fø]	**vœu** [vø]	**curieux** [kyrjø]	**joyeux** [ʒwajø]
peu [pø]	**neutre** [nøːtr]	**curieuse** [kyrjøːz]	**milieu** [miljø]
bleu [blø]	**cieux** [sjø]	**heureux** [œrø]	**jeûnes** [ʒøːn]

[œ]

Spellings

eu, œu, œ (before a pronounced consonant)

[œ] can be approximated by the combination of [ɛ] and [ɔ]. While pronouncing [ɛ], move the lips to position for [ɔ]. The result should be [œ].

Say *a* of each pair below with lips rounded for [ɔ]. The result should be *b*.

a. air [ɛːr]	*a.* l'ère [lɛːr]	*a.* Caire [kɛːr]	*a.* sel [sɛl]
b. heure [œːr]	*b.* leur [lœːr]	*b.* cœur [kœːr]	*b.* seul [sœl]

Examples of [œ]

peuple [pœpl]	**voleur** [vɔlœːr]	**vigueur** [vigœːr]	**œillet** [œjɛ]
meurs [mœːr]	**serviteur** [sɛrvitœːr]	**fleur** [flœːr]	**sœur** [sœːr]
œil [œːj]	**rêveur** [rɛvœːr]	**feuille** [fœːj]	**l'œuvre** [lœːvr]

Note: In adjectives ending in **-eux** in the masculine, the sound [ø] is preserved in the feminine, although the **eu** precedes a pronounced consonant.

[ə]

Spelling

e (final in a syllable)

[ə], called mute e, = e in conversational English, as in "I have the book."

Examples

le [lə]	me [mə]	te [tə]
que [kə]	de [də]	je [ʒə]
ce [sə]	ne [nə]	se [sə]

4. Nasal Vowels

Remarks: Keep the tongue down in pronouncing nasals. The sign of the nasalization of a vowel is the tilde, ⌢. A vowel can be nasalized only when the n or m is in the syllable with the preceding vowel. Nn and mm do not nasalize the preceding vowel.

un [œ̃]   une [yn]   an [ã]   année [ane]

[ɛ̃]

Spellings

ain	ein	in	yn	ien
aim	eim	im	ym	

Say [a], trying to make the sound come partly through the nose. Keep the tongue down in pronouncing [ɛ̃]. The sound is similar to the a in the English word rang, although one should be careful not to sound the ng.

Examples

main [mɛ̃]	Reims [rɛ̃:s]	symbole [sɛ̃bɔl]	rien [rjɛ̃]
faim [fɛ̃]	vin [vɛ̃]	synthèse [sɛ̃tɛ:z]	bien [bjɛ̃]
sein [sɛ̃]	chemin [ʃəmɛ̃]	timbre [tɛ̃:br]	mien [mjɛ̃]

[ã]

Spellings

an	am	en	em	aon

Try to say [a], forcing the sound partly through the nose.

Examples

banc [bã]	enfant [ãfã]	parent [parã]	temps [tã]
dans [dã]	champs [ʃã]	prudent [prydã]	paon [pã]

[õ]

Spellings

on	om

Try to say [ɔ], forcing the sound partly through the nose.

Examples

bon [bõ]	oncle [õ:kl]	comprend [kõprã]	nom [nõ]
bonté [bõte]	son [sõ]	nombreux [nõbrø]	ombre [õ:br]

[œ̃]

Spellings

un   um   eun

Pronounce [œ], keeping the tongue down and forcing the breath through the nose.

Examples

un [œ̃]	parfum [parfœ̃]	lundi [lœ̃:di]
humble [œ̃:bl]	emprunter [ɑ̃prœ̃te]	chacun [ʃakœ̃]
jeun [ʒœ̃]	brun [brœ̃]	Verdun [vɛrdœ̃]

5. Semi-Consonants

[j] = y as in yearn

Spellings

y (before a pronounced vowel)   i (before a pronounced vowel)
ill (preceded by a vowel)   il (final, preceded by a vowel)

Examples

yeux [jø]	travail [trava:j]	paille [pɑ:j]	veiller [vɛje]
cahier [kaje]	meilleur [mɛjœ:r]	vieil [vjɛ:j]	panier [panje]
bataillon [batajõ]	lisière [lizjɛ:r]	œil [œ:j]	sixième [sizjɛm]

[ɥ]

Spelling

[y] + a vowel

While pronouncing [y], draw the lips back suddenly and pronounce the following vowel. The [y] glides to the following vowel without noticeable break.

Examples

puis [pɥi]	parapluie [paraplɥi]	puissant [pɥisɑ̃]	détruit [detrɥi]
nuit [nɥi]	nuage [nɥa:ʒ]	épuiser [epɥize]	buis [bɥi]
fuite [fɥit]	bruit [brɥi]	ennui [ɑ̃nɥi]	ruine [rɥin]

[w]

Spellings

ou (before a pronounced vowel)
oi (where sound is [wa])   oy (where sound is [wa])

While pronouncing [u], shift quickly to the next vowel without a break.

Examples

oui [wi]	toile [twal]	nettoyer [netwaje]	loyal [lwajal]
oiseau [wazo]	fois [fwa]	moyen [mwajɛ̃]	moyer [mwaje]

6. Combinations of Semi-Consonants and Vowels

[ij]

Spellings

ill (after a consonant)   yi

Examples

fille [fi:j]	famille [fami:j]	vanille [vani:j]	pavillon [pavijõ]
babille [babi:j]	chenille [ʃəni:j]	gentille [ʒɑ̃ti:j]	payions [pɛijõ]

[ji]

Spellings

illi

Examples

taillis [tɑji]	saillie [saji]	bailli [baji]	failli [faji]

[ɥi]

Spelling

ui

Say [y], passing rapidly to the next vowel.

Examples

puis [pɥi]	suis [sɥi]	cuisine [kɥizin]	conduire [kõdɥiːr]
lui [lɥi]	buis [bɥi]	cuire [kɥiːr]	traduire [tradɥiːr]

[ɥij]

Spellings

uy

Examples

fuyard [fɥijaːr]	fuyant [fɥijã]	bruyant [brɥijã][1]	bruyère [brɥijɛːr][1]

[wa] and [waj]

Spellings

oi   oî   oy

Examples

toi [twa]	fois [fwa]	voisin [vwazɛ̃]	moyen [mwajɛ̃]
moi [mwa]	doigt [dwa]	voisine [vwazin]	joyeux [ʒwajø]
dois [dwa]	boire [bwaːr]	boîte [bwaːt]	voyez [vwaje]

[wɑ]

Spellings

oi, oî (usually preceded by r)

Examples

froid [frwɑ]	roi [rwɑ]	crois [krwɑ]	roide [rwɑd]
trois [trwɑ]	proie [prwɑ]	croyons [krwɑjõ]	broyer [brwɑje]

[wɛ̃]

Spellings

oin

Examples

soin [swɛ̃]	loin [lwɛ̃]	moins [mwɛ̃]	lointain [lwɛ̃tɛ̃]
coin [kwɛ̃]	foin [fwɛ̃]	moindre [mwɛ̃ːdr]	point [pwɛ̃]

[1] This is the preferred pronunciation, although the International Dictionary gives [bryjã] and [bryjɛːr].

7. Difficult Consonants

r

The French **r** is the most difficult of the consonants to pronounce correctly. The other consonants will cause little difficulty if care is taken always to make the lip positions more tense and forward than in English.   But the French **r** is so unlike American **r** that the correct pronunciation of this letter will do more than any other one thing in giving one an acceptable French pronunciation.

There are two correct pronunciations of this letter: (1) that made by vibrating the tip of the tongue against the upper teeth and (2) that made by vibrating the uvula against the tongue.   The uvula, which is the small flap hanging from the roof of the mouth, is vibrated when one gargles.   An effective way to practice this sound is to concentrate on the vibration of the uvula until its muscles can be made to obey at will.

[r]

Exercises

ri [ri]	ré [re]	ra [ra]	ron [rõ]	ru [ry]
ri [ri]	ré [re]	ra [ra]	ron [rõ]	ru [ry]

Examples

roi [rwa]	partie [parti]	Rue de Rivoli [ryd rivɔli]
frère [frɛːr]	regard [rəgaːr]	trois gros rats [trwa gro ra]
parc [park]	servir [sɛrviːr]	grand grain gris [grã grɛ̃ gri]

[ɲ] = ny in canyon

Spelling

gn

Examples

digne [diɲ]	saigner [sɛɲe]	Allemagne [almaɲ]
baigner [bɛɲe]	ignorant [iɲɔrã]	agneau [aɲo]

[ʒ] = s in pleasure

Spellings

g (before e or i)   j (before any vowel)

Examples

âge [ɑːʒ]	gibecière [ʒipsjɛːr]	journal [ʒurnal]
sage [saːʒ]	je [ʒə]	juste [ʒyst]
garage [garaːʒ]	jette [ʒɛːt]	joie [ʒwa]

8. Aspirate and Inaspirate h

Initial **h** is not pronounced in French.   Nevertheless there are two types of **h**'s, aspirate and inaspirate.   As there is no rule indicating which words belong to each of the two groups, each one must be learned separately.   Since it is not a question of pronunciation, the words must be learned because of their influence on the preceding word.

Most **h**'s are inaspirate, i.e., are treated as vowels, thus requiring elision or liaison.

Examples

l'homme [lɔm]	un homme [œ̃nɔm]
l'histoire [listwaːr]	une histoire [yn istwaːr]

The second type, the aspirate **h**, is treated as a consonant. It requires a full stop and complete separation from the definite or indefinite article, no elision or linking taking place. The words in this book which begin with aspirate **h** are:

haïr [aiːr]	héler [ɛle]	honteux [õtø]
les haricots [le ariko]	le héros [lə ero]	le hors-d'œuvre [lə ɔrdœːvr]
la harpe [la arp]	se heurter [sə œrte]	huit [ɥit]
haut [o]	la honte [la õːt]	la huitaine [la ɥitɛn]

D. MUTE SYLLABLES

A mute syllable is a syllable ending in unaccented **e**. In rapid speech the mute **e** is often muted, that is, not pronounced. There are no absolute rules for the muting of **e**, but in the following circumstances mute **e** is usually muted:

1. A mute **e** at the end of a word of more than one syllable is muted.

Examples
table [tabl]   une image [yn imaːʒ]

2. A mute **e** following a vowel sound is muted.

Examples
qu'est-ce que c'est [kɛs kə sɛ]   la leçon [lalsõ]
vous me regardez [vum rəgarde]   c'est cela [sɛ sla]

E. LIAISON

Liaison (linking) is the joining in pronunciation of a word ending in a consonant to the following word beginning with a vowel or inaspirate **h** which is grammatically closely connected to it. The following are instances of the most common liaisons:

1. A noun with an article or adjective modifiers:
les‿élèves [lezelɛːv]
amis‿intimes [amizɛ̃tim]

2. An adjective with a modifying adverb:
bien‿agréable [bjɛ̃nagreabl]
très‿heureux [trɛzœrø]

3. Pronoun subject and verb:
Ils‿ont des‿amis [ilzõ dezami]
vous‿avez‿eu [vuzavezy]

4. Pronoun object and verb.
Il les‿aime [ilezɛːm]

5. Verb and its complement.
Ils sont‿admirés [il sõt‿admire]

6. Auxiliary and participle.
Ils sont‿arrivés [il sõtarive]
Je‿me suis‿amusé [ʒəm sɥizamyze]

7. With prepositions.
chez‿elle [ʃezɛl]

Observe also the following changes which occur in the pronunciation of certain final consonants:

1. *d* becomes *t* prend-il? [prɑ̃til]   2. *f* becomes *v*   neuf heures [nœ vœːr]
3. *g* becomes *k* un long écho [œ̃ lõkeko]   4. *s* or *x* becomes *z* dix élèves [dizelɛːv]

The *t* of the word *et* is never linked. un‿homme et une femme [œ̃nɔm e yn fam]

Liaison is not permitted before an aspirate h (see 8, page xxv), nor before **onze** or **oui**, e. g.,

le onze avril [lə õːz avril]   mais oui [mɛ wi]

F. PHONETIC WRITING

In order to fasten the exact sounds of French words more firmly in your memory, learn to write in phonetic script the French phrases you already know how to spell with the ordinary letters of the alphabet. Just at first it will be a little hard for you to use the phonetic letters properly, and you will make mistakes, but very soon you will learn to write easily with them. No other test indicates so clearly your ability to pronounce French. For your guidance in this exercise a list is here given of the opening sentences of eight lessons, both in ordinary spelling and in phonetic script:

Première Leçon

La maîtresse parle: Voici la classe. Voici la maîtresse. Voici la table. Voici le livre.

la mɛtrɛs parl: vwasi la klɑːs vwasi la mɛtrɛs   vwasi la tabl vwasi lə liːvr

Deuxième Leçon

La maîtresse: Est-ce que je regarde la classe?
La classe: Vous regardez la classe.
La maîtresse: Est-ce que je regarde la table et la chaise?

la mɛtrɛs: ɛs kə ʒə rəgard la klɑːs la klɑːs: vu rəgarde la klɑːs la mɛtrɛs: ɛs kə ʒə rəgard la tabl e la ʃɛːz

Troisième Leçon

Jean: Où est la boîte?
Charles: J'ai la boîte. Vous n'avez pas la boîte; vous avez le livre.

ʒɑ̄: w ɛ la bwaːt ʃarl: ʒe la bwaːt vu nave pɑ la bwaːt vu zave lə liːvr

Quatrième Leçon

La maîtresse parle: Je mets le livre sur la table, et je cherche la boîte. Où est la boîte, Marie?
Marie: Voici la boîte, mademoiselle.

la mɛtrɛs parl: ʒə mɛ lə liːvr syːr la tabl e ʒə ʃɛrʃ la bwaːt w ɛ la bwaːt mari mari: vwasi la bwaːt madmwazɛl

Sixième Leçon

La maîtresse: Je regarde la fenêtre. La fenêtre n'est pas petite. La fenêtre est grande. Voici le store. Le store est vert.

la mɛtrɛs: ʒə rəgard lafnɛːtr lafnɛːtr nɛ pɑ pətit lafnɛːtr ɛ grɑ̄ːd vwasi lə stɔːr lə stɔːr ɛ vɛːr

Septième Leçon

—Bonjour, mes élèves.
—Bonjour, mademoiselle.
—J'ai le stylo. Regardez le stylo. Regardez le tableau et cherchez le mot **stylo**.

bōʒuːr me zelɛːv. bōʒuːr madmwazɛl. ʒe lə stilo rəgarde lə stilo rəgarde lə tablo e ʃɛrʃe lə mo stilo.

Huitième Leçon

Philippe n'est pas en classe. Il est au salon. Maman est au salon aussi. Elle parle avec grand'mère.

filip nɛ pazɑ̄ klɑːs i lɛ to salō mɑ̄mɑ̄ ɛ to salō osi ɛl parl avɛk grɑ̄mɛːr

Neuvième Leçon

Philippe n'est pas en classe. Il est à la maison. Il est au salon avec Marie.

filip nɛ pɑ zɑ̄ klɑːs i lɛ ta la mezō i lɛ to salō avɛk mari

THE SEINE WINDING UNDER PARIS BRIDGES, AS SEEN FROM
THE ROOF OF THE CATHEDRAL OF NOTRE-DAME DE PARIS

PREMIÈRE LEÇON

La Salle de classe

La maîtresse parle: Voici la classe. Voici la maîtresse. Voici la table. Voici le livre. Voici la leçon. Je regarde le livre. Je regarde la table et la chaise. Je regarde le plancher. Je regarde aussi la table. Je regarde aussi la classe. Et vous?

La classe récite: Je regarde la maîtresse. Je regarde la table et la chaise. Je regarde le tableau et aussi la craie.

La maîtresse parle: Où est la craie? Voici la craie. Où est le livre? Voici le livre. Je regarde le livre. J'ouvre le livre. Je regarde la page. Je tourne la page. Je ferme le livre. Où est la chaise? Voici la chaise.

Vocabulaire

la chaise [la ʃɛːz], *the chair*
la classe [la klɑːs], *the class*
la craie [la krɛ], *the chalk*
la leçon [lalsõ],[1] *the lesson*
le livre [lə liːvr], *the book*
la maîtresse [la mɛtrɛs], *the teacher*
la page [la paːʒ], *the page*
le plancher [lə plɑ̃ʃe], *the floor*
la salle de classe [la sal də klɑːs], *the classroom*

la table [la tabl], *the table*
le tableau [lə tablo], *the blackboard*
je[2] [ʒə], *I*
vous [vu], *you*
est [ɛ], *is*
je ferme [ʒə fɛrm], *I close, I am closing, I do close*
j'ouvre [ʒuːvr], *I open, I am opening, I do open*
parle [parl], *speaks, talks*

récite [resit], *recites*
je regarde [ʒə rəgard], *I look at, I am looking at, I do look at, I watch*
je tourne [ʒə turn], *I turn, I am turning*
voici [vwasi], *here is, here are*
aussi [osi], *also, too*
et [e], *and*
où [u], *where*

Grammaire

The Definite Article and the Noun

In English the definite article has but one form. It is *the* before a masculine noun, a feminine noun, or a neuter noun, e.g., *the* boy, *the* girl, *the* house.

In French, however, the form of the definite article varies. Look through the vocabulary above and you will see **le** before some nouns and **la** before others. **Le** is used with a singular masculine noun; **la** with a singular feminine noun:

le tableau   la chaise

Learn each noun with the correct form of the article—**le tableau, le livre, la chaise, la craie,** etc. *Learn the article as a part of the noun.* All nouns in French are either masculine or feminine. There is no neuter gender.

Verbs

In French the ending of a verb depends on the person and number of its subject. In this first lesson we are especially concerned with verbs whose subject is **je** (I), the first person singular pronoun: **je ferme, j'ouvre, je regarde,**

---

[1] Leçon, without the definite article, is pronounced [ləsõ].
[2] In French je is capitalized only at the beginning of a sentence.

etc. You will notice that each of these verbs ends with the letter -e. Try carefully to remember this final -e when you do the **Devoir** (Exercise) below.

Elision

The -e of **je** is elided (is dropped out and replaced by an apostrophe) before a word beginning with a vowel, e.g., **j'ouvre**. This relieves the speaker from having to pronounce two vowel sounds together, and is one of the means by which the French language is made musical and pleasing. On page 48 you will find the rule of elision, telling you what other words may be elided.

Devoir

Study each part of this exercise so carefully that you will be able to give the answers and act them out in class. Study aloud and act as much as you can, for such work will help you greatly in learning this new language.

A. Répondez:

1. Où est la classe? Et la maîtresse?
2. Où est le livre?
3. Où est le plancher? Et la chaise?

B. Change to the correct verb-forms:

1. Je (regarder)[1] la classe.
2. Je (ouvrir) le livre.
3. Je (tourner) la page.

C. Use the correct article (le, la):

1. Voici — salle de classe.
2. J'ouvre — livre.
3. Où est — chaise?

D. Traduction:

1. Where is the teacher?
2. Here is the blackboard.
3. I open the book.

STUDY HELPS

1. French headings. The French words and phrases which head different sections of your book occur over and over again and will soon be familiar to you. They will not usually appear in the vocabularies of the lessons.

In Lesson 1 are these headings:

Première [prəmjɛːr] **leçon,** *first lesson*
La Salle de classe, *the classroom*
La maîtresse parle, *the teacher speaks*
La classe récite, *the class recites*
Vocabulaire [vɔkabylɛːr], *vocabulary*
Grammaire [gramɛːr], *grammar*
Devoir [dəvwaːr], *written* or *oral exercise*
Répondez [repõde], *answer*
Traduction [tradyksjõ], *translation*

2. Vocabulary. The vocabulary groups together the different parts of speech: nouns, pronouns, verb-forms, adverbs, etc. Rewrite the nouns of the first lesson in two columns, placing masculines in the left-hand column and feminines in the right-hand one. *Do not forget the definite article.*

3. The infinitive form of a verb. In section B under the topic **Devoir,** three verbs are given in parentheses in a form which you have not seen before. This form is called the infinitive and is used whenever a verb is mentioned only by name; thus, as we say in English *to open, to turn*—because *to* is the sign of our infinitive—so the Frenchman says **ouvrir, tourner,** because these forms with their particular endings are his infinitives.

4. Footnotes. In your lessons you will occasionally find a small figure ([1]) or ([2]) after a word. This calls your attention to a note at the bottom of the page (a *footnote*). Remember to read these footnotes when they occur.

---

[1] See Study Helps 3. below.

DEUXIÈME LEÇON

Conversation

La maîtresse: Est-ce que je regarde la classe?

La classe: Vous regardez la classe.

La maîtresse: Est-ce que je regarde la table et la chaise?

La classe: Vous regardez la table et la chaise.

La maîtresse: Est-ce que j'ai le livre?

La classe: Oui, mademoiselle, vous‿a-vez[1] le livre.

La maîtresse: Est-ce que j'ouvre le livre?

La classe: Oui, mademoiselle, vous‿ou-vrez le livre.

La maîtresse: Voici la page. Je tourne la page. Est-ce que je ferme le livre?

La classe: Oui, mademoiselle, vous fermez le livre.

(La maîtresse parle, et Marie répond.)

La maîtresse: Où est la boîte?

Marie: Voici la boîte, mademoiselle.

La maîtresse: Avez-vous la boîte?

Marie: J'ai la boîte.

La maîtresse: Regardez-vous la boîte?

Marie: Oui, mademoiselle, je regarde la boîte.

La maîtresse: Ouvrez-vous la boîte?

Marie: J'ouvre la boîte.

La maîtresse: Fermez-vous la boîte?

Marie: Je ferme la boîte.

Vocabulaire

la boîte [la bwaːt], *box*

la conversation [la kõvɛr-sasjõ], *conversation*

mademoiselle [madmwa-zɛl], *Miss*

Marie [mari], *Mary*

j'ai [ʒe], *I have, I do have*

vous avez [vu zave], *you have, you do have*

vous fermez [vu fɛrme], *you close, you do close, you are closing*

vous ouvrez [vu zuvre], *you open*, etc.

vous regardez [vu rəgar-de], *you look at*, etc.

répond [repõ], *answers, replies, responds*

vous tournez [vu turne], *you turn*, etc.

oui [wi], *yes*

est-ce que [ɛs kə], not to be translated. It makes a declarative sentence interrogative (**Est-ce que je regarde la page?** *Am I looking at the page?*)

Grammaire

Verb-Endings

In the first lesson you learned that the verb-ending **-e** is used when the subject is the first person singular pronoun, **je.** In today's lesson you meet the second person pronoun, **vous,** and discover that the verb-ending used with it is **-ez: vous avez, vous fermez, vous ouvrez, vous regardez.** To a slight extent you are familiar with this verb-end change in English also; e.g., you say "I (*or* we) *work*," but "He (she, *or* it) *works*."

As in English the form *you* is used with both singular and plural, so in French **vous** indicates both numbers.

J'ouvre le livre. *I open the book.*

Je ferme la boîte. *I close the box.*

Je regarde la classe. *I look at the class.*

Vous ouvrez le livre. *You open the book.*

Vous fermez la boîte. *You close the box.*

Vous regardez la classe. *You look at the class.*

---

[1] As a help in reading aloud, liaisons have been indicated in the reading of the first twenty-one lessons.

The Interrogative Sentence

In the **Conversation** on page 3 you will note that questions are formed in two different ways. When the French wish to ask a question in which **je** is used, they prefix **Est-ce que** to an affirmative sentence.[1]

Je regarde le livre. *I am looking at the book.* (Affirmative sentence.)
Est-ce que je regarde le livre? *Am I looking at the book?* (Interrogative sentence.)

When **vous** is used, the question may be formed by prefixing **Est-ce que,** as with **je;** but it may be done in another way also—by simply transposing the subject and the verb. (It is in this latter way that you form most of your questions in English, e.g., *Are you there?*)

Vous regardez le livre. *You are looking at the book.* (Affirmative sentence.)
Est-ce que vous regardez le livre? *Are you looking at the book?* (Interrogative sentence.)
　　　　　　　　　　　or
Regardez-vous le livre? *Are you looking at the book?* (Interrogative sentence.)

When the verb is placed before the subject to form a question, we say that *the order is inverted.* When the inverted order is used, a hyphen must be inserted between the verb and the pronoun subject.

Devoir

A. Répondez:

1. Est-ce que vous regardez la classe?
2. Regardez-vous la chaise?
3. Est-ce que je regarde le livre?
4. Ouvrez-vous le livre?
5. Est-ce que je tourne la page?
6. Où est la boîte?
7. Marie, avez-vous la boîte?
8. Fermez-vous la boîte?
9. Est-ce que j'ai la craie?
10. Où est le tableau?

B. Change to the correct verb-forms:

1. Je (ouvrir) le livre.
2. Je (tourner) la page.
3. Vous (ouvrir) la boîte.
4. Je (regarder) le plancher.
5. Vous (fermer) la boîte.
6. Vous (regarder) la chaise.
7. Je (fermer) le livre.

*C. Posez des questions[2]: (Use **je** or **vous** as indicated and watch the agreement of the verb. Begin each sentence with a capital letter and put a question mark at the end of each.)*

1. Vous (regarder) le tableau.
2. Je (regarder) le plancher.
3. Je (fermer) le livre.
4. Vous (ouvrir) la boîte.
5. Je (ouvrir) la boîte aussi.
6. Vous (fermer) le livre.
7. Je (tourner) la page.

Traduction[3]:

1. Where is the teacher, Mary?
2. Have you the chalk?
3. Yes, Charles, I have the chalk.
4. Am I looking at the blackboard?
5. Here is the box.
6. Are you looking at the book?
7. Here is the chair.

---

[1] Two exceptions are ai-je and suis-je, which are used more commonly than Est-ce que j'ai . . . ? and Est-ce que je suis . . . ?
[2] See Study Helps 4, page 5.
[3] Consult the English-French vocabulary if you cannot remember all the words used here.

STUDY HELPS

1. Pronunciation of French sounds. There are two ways of learning how to pronounce French sounds well: (*a*) imitating exactly the pronunciation of the teacher; (*b*) studying on a phonetic chart or in a book the manner in which the sounds are made, and practicing them carefully.

Your teacher may wish you to get your French pronunciation by paying close attention to her lips and the sounds that issue from them. But if she wishes you to get the sounds by learning the mechanical devices used to produce them, she will refer you to particular sections of this book. Probably your teacher will wish you to combine both methods.

2. Review of previous lessons. Your best plan of study is to review Lesson 1 for a few minutes before you start studying Lesson 2, to review Lessons 1 and 2 before beginning Lesson 3, etc. Strengthen your hold each day on what you have learned before.

3. French headings. New headings are: **Deuxième leçon**, *second lesson;*

Conversation, *conversation;* **Marie répond**, *Mary replies;* **Posez des questions**, *make some questions* (of your own).

4. Posez des questions. Before writing the seven French questions asked for in section *C* of the **Devoir**, read over what the Grammar section on page 4 says of the ways in which a French question is formed.

5. The French verb. The most vital part of any sentence, whether English or French, is the verb. Around it is grouped all the rest of the sentence. Since this is true, and since the endings of French verbs are very important, you will need to learn accurately every new form you meet.

6. Pronunciation. Since there is very little time in your lesson period for individual practice in pronunciation, you should work on each new sound at home. An excellent plan is to read the exercises aloud before you write them. In this way you see the spelling of each word and hear the sounds.

Drouet, Nancy

FIRST-YEAR FRENCH IN FRANCE

TROISIÈME LEÇON
La Salle de classe

Jean: Où est la boîte?

Charles: J'ai la boîte. Vous n'avez pas la boîte; vous avez le livre.

Jean: Non, non, je n'ai pas la boîte. J'ouvre le livre, et je tourne la page.

Charles: J'ouvre la boîte. Je regarde la craie.

Jean: Où est la craie?

Charles: La craie est dans la boîte. Le livre n'est pas dans la boîte. Regardez-vous le livre?

Jean: Je ferme le livre. Je mets le livre sur la table.

Charles: Mettez-vous la boîte sur le livre?

Jean: Non, je ne mets pas la boîte sur le livre. Je mets le livre sur la boîte.

Marie: Où est le livre, Jean?

Jean: Voici le livre. Le livre est sur la table.

Marie: N'ouvrez-vous pas le livre?

Jean: Non, je n'ouvre pas le livre. Je regarde le tableau.

Joséphine: Où est la craie, Charles?

Charles: La craie est dans la boîte. J'ouvre la boîte. Voici la craie.

Joséphine: Merci, Charles.

Charles: Il n'y a pas de quoi, Joséphine.

Grammaire
The Negative

The negative *not* requires two words in French. The words are **ne . . . pas**. **Ne** always precedes the verb, and **pas** follows it. The two words really form a frame for the verb.

> Je **ne** ferme **pas** le livre. *I do not close the book.*
> Vous **ne** fermez **pas** le livre. *You do not close the book.*
> **Ne** fermez-vous **pas** le livre? *Don't you close the book?*

When the verb and subject are connected by a hyphen, as in the interrogative, the **pas** follows the verb-subject combination. Words connected by a hyphen cannot be separated, even by **pas**.

The -e of the word **ne** is elided before a word beginning with a vowel.

> Je n'ai pas la craie. *I haven't the chalk.*
> N'avez-vous pas la craie? *Haven't you the chalk?*

Vocabulaire

la salle [la sal], *room*
Charles [ʃarl], *Charles*
Jean [ʒɑ̃], *John*
Joséphine [ʒozefin], *Joséphine*
je mets [ʒə mɛ], *I put, I place, I am putting, I am placing,* etc.

vous mettez [vu mɛte], *you put, you place, you are putting, you are placing,* etc.
dans [dɑ̃], *in, into, to*
sur [syːr], *on, about*
ne . . . pas [nə . . . pɑ], *not*
non [nõ], *no* (adverb)

merci [mɛrsi] (use the person's name[1] or title when making use of this expression), *thank you*
il n'y a pas de quoi [il nja pɑd kwa], *don't mention it; it's a pleasure, you are welcome,* etc.

[1] See Study Helps 3, page 7.

Questionnaire

1. Avez-vous la boîte?
2. Où mettez-vous la boîte?
3. Mettez-vous la chaise sur la table?
4. Est-ce que je regarde la craie?
5. Où est la craie? Et le tableau?
6. Est-ce que je mets la craie sur la table?
7. Est-ce que je ferme le livre?
8. Tournez-vous la page?
9. Où est la salle de classe?
10. Ne regardez-vous pas le tableau? (*Negative answer.*)

Devoir

A. Make these sentences interrogative:

1. J'ouvre le livre.
2. Vous tournez la page.
3. Vous fermez le livre.
4. Je mets le livre sur la table.
5. Vous ne mettez pas le livre dans la boîte. Vous n'avez pas la boîte.
6. Je n'ai pas la craie.

B. Give negative answers to the questions you have formed with A.

C. Complete the verb-forms:

1. Je n'a— pas la craie.
2. Je met— la boîte sur la table.
3. Mett— -vous le livre sur la table?
4. Est-ce que j'ouvr— le livre?
5. Vous av— la boîte.

Traduction:

1. Have you the chalk?
2. No, I haven't the chalk.
3. You do not look at the book.
4. I put the book on the table.

STUDY HELPS

1. **French sentences, word-groups, and idioms.** You learn French, not as a collection of separate words, but as words joined in sentences. That is why each lesson of this book (except special review lessons) begins with a reading lesson which contains only connected French sentences. Learn whole sentences and word-groups as soon as possible. And do not fail to practice expressions like **Il n'y a pas de quoi** until you can say them easily. Such expressions, which are peculiar to the French language, and which we cannot translate literally into English, are called idioms. They are very useful and expressive. Enter them in your notebook if you keep one.

2. **French headings.** The new French heading in this lesson is **Questionnaire**, *Questionnaire*. Hereafter under this heading you will find questions on the reading lesson, which you should always be prepared to answer orally in class, even if your teacher has asked you to write them.

3. **French politeness.** The French take far greater pains to express themselves politely than we ordinarily do. It is wrong when speaking French with another not to use some form of address when saying "Yes" or "No" or "Please" or "Thank you." Remember to say **Oui, mademoiselle; Merci, Joséphine;** etc.

4. **The French negative.** There is nothing difficult about the French negative except that it consists of two words instead of one. If you think you need extra practice in using it, change all the affirmative sentences of Lessons 1 and 2 to negative ones, thus: **La maîtresse parle; La maîtresse ne parle pas;** etc.

QUATRIÈME LEÇON

Conversation

La maîtresse parle: Je mets le livre sur la table, et je cherche la boîte. Où est la boîte, Marie?

Marie: Voici la boîte, mademoiselle.

La maîtresse: Merci, Marie. Je mets la boîte sur la table, et je cherche la craie. Voici la craie. La craie n'est pas rouge. La craie n'est pas rose. La craie est blanche. Est-ce que vous regardez la craie blanche, Charles?

Charles: Oui, mademoiselle, je regarde la craie blanche.

La maîtresse: Je mets la craie dans la boîte, et je regarde le livre. Le livre n'est pas rose. Le livre n'est pas noir. Le livre est rouge. J' ouvre le livre rouge, et je regarde la page. Est-ce que la page est noire, Louise?

Louise: Non, mademoiselle, la page n'est pas noire. La page est blanche. La craie est blanche, et la page est blanche. Est-ce que le papier est blanc?

La maîtresse: Le papier est blanc, Louise. La craie est blanche, et le papier est blanc. Voici la liste:

le livre noir	la boîte noire
le livre rouge	la boîte rouge
le livre blanc	la boîte blanche

Grammaire

Agreement of Adjectives

In French the adjective[1] agrees with its noun in gender and number. This lesson will deal only with gender.

MAS. le papier vert (*green*)   FEM. la craie verte

Most adjectives form their feminine by adding -e to the masculine, as:

noir   noire   vert   verte

If an adjective ends in mute **e** (i.e., **e** without an accent mark [ə]) in the masculine, it does not change for the feminine, as:

rouge   rouge

Some adjectives are irregular, that is, the feminine is not formed in the regular way. Such adjectives must be learned, as:

blanc   blanche

Position of Adjectives

An adjective in French usually follows its noun:

la boîte rouge   le papier blanc

[1] An adjective is a word which limits or describes a noun. It helps to give the picture or image of the noun mentioned.

Vocabulaire

la liste [la list], *list*
le papier [lə papje], *paper*
Louise [lwiːz], *Louise*
je cherche [ʒə ʃɛrʃ], *I look for, I search for*, etc.

vous cherchez [vu ʃɛrʃe], *you look for, you search for*
blanc, blanche [blã, blãːʃ], *white*
noir, noire [nwaːr], *black*

rose, rose [roːz], *pink*
rouge, rouge [ruːʒ], *red*
vert, verte [vɛːr, vɛrt], *green*
mais [mɛ], *but*

Questionnaire

1. Où est-ce que vous mettez le livre?
2. Où est la boîte?
3. Est-ce que je cherche la craie?
4. Est-ce que la craie est blanche?
5. Où est-ce que je mets la craie?
6. Est-ce que vous regardez la boîte?
7. Est-ce que j'ouvre le livre rouge?
8. Est-ce que la page est rose?
9. Avez-vous la boîte blanche?
10. Où est le papier vert?

Devoir

A. Following 1 as a model, prepare similar questions and answers about the nouns in 2, 3, 4, and 5. Use all the colors that you know.

1. Est-ce que le livre est vert? Le livre n'est pas vert; le livre est rouge.
2. la table
3. le papier
4. la boîte
5. le tableau

B. Following 1 as a model, change sentences 2-8 to the negative.

1. Charles regarde la boîte.
   Charles ne regarde pas la boîte.
2. Marie cherche le livre.

3. Je tourne la page.
4. Cherchez-vous la page?
5. J'ouvre la boîte.
6. Joséphine ferme le livre.
7. La maîtresse trouve la chaise.
8. J'ai le livre.

Traduction: *
Are you looking for the chalk, Mary?
Yes, I am looking for the red chalk.
I have the green chalk and the pink chalk, but I have not the red chalk.
No, the red chalk is not in the black box. Charles, have you the chalk?
Thank you, Charles. I have the white chalk, the red chalk, and the green chalk.

STUDY HELPS

1. French adjectives follow their nouns. Does it seem queer to you to learn that French adjectives generally follow their nouns? Then it must seem strange to a French student to discover that English nouns usually follow their adjectives.

2. Noun and adjective agree in gender. This agreement is shown in French by the ending of the adjective, but in English we have no such sign of agreement between the noun and its describing word. Be sure of the gender of your French noun, because otherwise you will not know what form to give the adjective.

If you have become confused as to the gender of any of the French nouns

Note to the Teacher: See page vii.

Branger, Paris

PUPILS FROM A FRENCH LYCÉE

in the first four lessons, turn at once to the vocabularies and review them very carefully. *Always repeat the article with the noun.*

3. **The parts of speech.** French, like English, is made up of several different classes of words: nouns, pronouns, verbs, adverbs, etc. Each class has its one definite work to do: nouns give the name of a thing or a person; pronouns take the place of a noun; adjectives limit or describe a noun, etc. These classes of words are called parts of speech, and together they make up the whole of a language. They do not change as they pass from one language to another; thus the same sort of word is a noun in French as in English, and this is true of all the other parts of speech.

If you do not know the simple facts of English word-usage, you cannot understand these same facts in French. When studying a grammatical point, like the one spoken of in the preceding section, be sure that you know exactly what is meant by the terms "agreement," "noun," "adjective," and "gender."

4. **Pronunciation of French sounds.** Sound is the soul of any language. Be careful to remember all that your teacher tells you in class about French sounds. Compare them with their nearest equivalents in English. Note the difference between the two, and try to discover just what position of the lips, the teeth, or the tongue makes the French sound different from the English one.

CINQUIÈME LEÇON*

Review

A

1. How may an affirmative sentence be turned into an interrogative sentence? Give an example.

2. With what pronoun is **Est-ce que** commonly used? Exceptions?

3. A verb agrees with its subject. Give an example.

4. With what subject is the ending **-ez** used? With what person?

5. If **vous** is used in the question, what pronoun will be used in the answer?

6. If **je** is used in the question, what pronoun will be used in the answer?

7. How many words does it take to make a French sentence negative? What are they?

8. How does one make an affirmative sentence negative? Give an illustration of a negative sentence.

9. What happens to **ne** when it precedes a vowel? Does this occur in words other than **ne**?

10. What is the usual position of an adjective in French?

11. If the noun is feminine, what must be the gender of the adjective that modifies it?

12. How is the feminine of a regular adjective formed?

13. What is the feminine of **rouge?** Give the rule that applies.

14. Mention an irregular adjective.

15. How many ways are there of spelling the sounds [e] and [ɛ]?

16. How do you say, "Thank you" and "You are welcome" in French?

B

I. Supply the correct form of the article with each of the following nouns:

1. — page
2. — table
3. — tableau
4. — papier
5. — boîte
6. — livre
7. — chaise
8. — plancher
9. — salle
10. — liste

II. Change each of the verbs below to agree with its subject:

1. Je (ouvrir) la boîte.
2. (Tourner) -vous la page?
3. Je (fermer) le livre.
4. Vous (chercher) la liste.
5. Vous ne (regarder) pas le tableau.

III. Make these sentences negative:

1. Vous avez la leçon.
2. Je regarde la maîtresse.
3. J'ai le livre.
4. Vous fermez le livre.
5. Je tourne la page.

IV. Make the sentences of III interrogative. Give two forms each for 1 and 4.

V. Supply the correct form of the adjective:

1. Vous ouvrez la boîte (rose).
2. Je tourne la page (blanc).
3. Voici le livre (rouge).
4. Vous avez le papier (blanc).
5. Cherchez-vous la craie (vert)?
6. Où est la chaise (noir)?

---

* *Note to the Teacher:* The aim has been to give in the Review Lessons sufficient material for you to choose the type of exercise best suited to the needs of the class. It is not intended that the class should do every part of every Review Lesson. In the early lessons very little translation from English to French is given; and, since it is always at the end of the "Devoir," it may easily be omitted if desired.

PHONETIC REVIEW*

Practice:

ə, a, y, õ, ɔ, i, ɑ̃, e, ø, ɛ, o, u, œ, ɛ̃,
də, pa, sy, nõ, kɔ, il, dɑ̃, ʒe, ʒø, fɛ, lo, vu, nœ, iːr,
apa, ibi, epe, ɛpɛ.

Pronounce:

[ʃɛːz]	chaise	[mɛte]	mettez
[ʃɛrʃ]	cherche	[roːz]	rose
[blɑ̃ːʃ]	blanche	[vu zave]	vous avez
[il]	il	[paːʒ]	page
[liːvr]	livre	[pɑ]	pas
[vwasi]	voici	[papje]	papier
[mɛrsi]	merci	[plɑ̃ʃe]	plancher
[fɛrme]	fermez	[il nja pɑd kwa]	il n'y a pas de quoi

Read aloud:

1. Voici le livre.   Ouvrez le livre.   Merci, Charles.
   [vwasi lə liːvr.   uvre lə liːvr.   mɛrsi, ʃarl.

   Il n'y a pas de quoi.
   il nja   pɑd   kwa.]

2. Mettez le papier dans le livre.   Fermez le livre.
   [mɛte lə papje dɑ̃ lə liːvr.   fɛrme lə liːvr.]

3. J'ai la rose rouge, mais vous avez la boîte blanche.
   [ʒe la roːz ruːʒ, mɛ vu zave la bwaːt blɑ̃ːʃ.]

4. Je ne mets pas le livre sur le plancher.
   [ʒə nə mɛ pɑ lə liːvr syːr lə plɑ̃ʃe.]

5. Est-ce que vous n'avez pas le papier?
   [ɛs kə vu nave pɑ lə papje?]

*Note to the Teacher: Although special drills on phonetics are added to the first
few Review lessons, it is not expected that they are to be used by all classes.

A FERTILE VALLEY IN THE CEVENNES MOUNTAINS

FRANCE

Though the area of France is but one fifteenth of that of our country, yet in one way the two lands are very much alike: each of them has such a variety of scene and climate that a traveler within the boundaries of either might well think he was passing through many different parts of the world instead of only one.

Because of this variety of scene and climate France is visited every year by great crowds of people from all corners of the earth. Just as in America we do not need to go abroad for new scenes and adventures, just so does the Frenchman find in his own land variety coupled with an admirable civilization. This renowned civilization and this beautiful country have made the French one of the greatest home-loving races.

The boundary lines of France are chiefly those which have been made by nature. When you look at the map on page 18, you see that France is washed on two sides by mighty seas: on the west and northwest by the Atlantic Ocean and the English Channel; on the southeast by the Mediterranean Sea. In the southwest France is shut sharply off from Spain by the Pyrenees Mountains; to the east France is divided from Italy and Switzerland by the towering Alps; the River Rhine is the most important separation between France and Germany.

When you study the map, you notice that on the northeast neither sea nor mountain nor river marks France off from Belgium and Luxembourg. Only an imaginary line exists here, one agreed upon by the three nations.

The long coast of northern and western France is an ever-changing horizon: hills of sand that shift with every breath of wind, stern cliffs of bare rock that rise from shoal water, broad flat plains where contented cattle graze, the thousand quiet bays of the old province of Brittany. Then to the south, quite without warning, green meadows suddenly cease, and as far as his eye can reach, the traveler sees before him nothing but marshland, miles of lonely heather, or mountains of sand that seem to be held together only by pine forests.

A different world indeed is that of France to the southeast. If it is winter time, and you are a tourist, take one last look at dreary Paris from your seat in the famous Blue Train. Next morning you have left winter behind you and wake to a fairyland of red-roofed houses and palm trees, to scarlet flowers that trail the side of a wall beside an azure sea. Or race by motor-car from this land of golden beach and sun to the near-by Alps, and here you find winter again, but not the gray, dreary, cold winter of Paris; no, a world of sparkling snow and dazzling hillside, where from dawn till dark sportsmen ski and slide down steep and curving slopes. Leave these mountains and you quickly find your way to Provence, bordering the Mediterranean, where quaint old towns like Avignon and Nîmes and Arles show

interesting Roman ruins. Except near the Pyrenees Mountains, where it is rocky, the whole Mediterranean region of France is low, sandy, and bordered with lagoons. Look at the map and see where the River Rhône enters the sea. At the mouth of this stream the coast is no longer flat and uninteresting. It is broken by deep bays, which are dotted with islands of unusual beauty.

The map on page 18 shows what France is like when viewed from an airplane. There are six mountain ranges, two of which have been already mentioned—the Alps and the Pyrenees. Two other important ranges, the Jura and the Vosges Mountains, are regarded as a part of the high Alps, for they are a continuation of them. They run almost due north and south, are lower than the great parent range, and gradually decline in height as they get farther away from it. A fifth great range lies in central France and is known as the Cevennes. It is a vast table-land or plateau rather than a real system of mountains. This

Keystone View Co., N. Y.

A ROUGH PASS THROUGH THE ALPS, WHERE THE ROAD MUST
FOLLOW THE COURSE OF THE RIVER

Levasseur, Paris
THE WIDE, PEACEFUL REACHES OF THE SEINE A FEW MILES FROM PARIS

range spreads toward all points of the compass, sloping gradually down until in the north it finally merges with the broad Paris basin. The Ardennes, the sixth range, are very modest mountains indeed, at least so far as elevation is concerned. Perhaps it is better to regard them as an outstanding system of thickly wooded hills.

The two highest of these six mountain ranges, the Alps and the Pyrenees, form boundaries of France and hardly intrude upon the country itself. Fully three-fourths of the Republic is therefore a fairly level plain through which the gay Garonne and the stately Loire Rivers flow to the Atlantic, while the Seine is moving idly on its course toward the English Channel. Each of these great rivers has many tributary streams, most of which are navigable. They are in the main slowly flowing bodies of water, frequently a half-mile in width. The Seine follows a curiously winding course and is most picturesque as it reaches the heart of Paris. Here graceful bridges span its current, quaint wharves border it,

and busy little boats are forever darting about upon its surface. The Loire in its wanderings passes beneath many famous old castles, which are called châteaux in France, and the river is known the world around for the dignity and beauty of its shores. The Garonne district is celebrated for its semitropical vegetation, and the river is justly famous for its unrivaled scenery.

The map shows you a fourth large stream of France, one which sweeps straight southward to the Mediterranean Sea; this is the River Rhône. In many places it plunges ahead so madly that its course is the least navigable of all French streams. The French people, however, have tamed its tempestuous current to their uses and vastly lessened the risks of its navigation by a series of canals. About two hundred fifty years ago shrewd engineers began to build these channels as an aid to national commerce; in fact, the largest canal in all France was dug at that time. This is called the Canal of the South of France —*Canal du Midi*—and joins the Ga-

By Ewing Galloway, N. Y.

AN ANCIENT CANAL, WHERE BOATS ARE NOW TOWED BY TRUCKS
INSTEAD OF BY HORSES

ronne with the Mediterranean. In addition to these four major water-courses (Seine, Garonne, Loire, and Rhône), the map indicates many smaller streams, the principal one of which is the Saône, that empty directly into the sea and for long centuries of the past have played an important part in the growth of French trade and industries.

The natural occupations of France are agriculture and grazing. Vast quantities of wheat are raised in the north. Grapes thrive in the milder climate of the central and southern regions. With but few exceptions districts that are unsuitable for farming have proved admirably fitted to the raising of sheep and cattle. Mining is carried on in the north. Rich coal veins are found in the part of France that borders Belgium. Although present in a much smaller degree, iron mines aid and support the whole manufacturing portion of northern France in its production of metal-wares, cotton and wooien goods, and beautiful laces.

In southern France the city of Lyons is the center of silk manufacturing, because here the mild climate makes profitable the raising of silkworms.

In this relatively small country of France we find seven fairly distinct climatic zones: Brittany has mild and damp weather; Paris is moderately wet and cold in winter, but quite warm in summer; the Vosges have severe winters and heavy rainfall; the weather of the upper Rhône is like that of the Vosges, but drier; the Garonne valley has temperate winters, but hot and rainy summers; the Cevennes is by turns dry and foggy; the Mediterranean has pleasant, gentle winters and warm, dry summers.

Eight hundred years ago poets called troubadours sang of their native land as Sweet France—La Douce France. And to this very day that loving phrase continues. For the world has found in France not only beauty and charm but a sympathy for intellectual and artistic effort which makes her hospitable to men of many nations.

SIXIÈME LEÇON

En classe

La maîtresse: Je regarde la fenêtre. La fenêtre n'est pas petite. La fenêtre est grande. Voici le store. Le store est vert. Je lève[1] le store. Je baisse le store. Où est le store?

Charles: Voilà le store.

La maîtresse: Levez-vous le store?

Charles: Je ne lève pas le store. Je ne baisse pas le store. Je baisse la carte.

La maîtresse: Où est la carte?

Charles: Voici la carte.

La maîtresse: Regardez-vous la carte?

Charles: Oui, mademoiselle, je regarde la carte. Je regarde la France[2] sur la carte. Voici la France. La France n'est pas jaune. La France est rose sur la carte.

Jean: Je regarde la carte dans le livre. Le livre est petit, et la carte est petite. Je cherche la France sur la carte. Voici la France. Je cherche Paris.[2] Voici Paris.

Charles: Oui, voilà Paris sur la carte.

Grammaire

Voici and *Voilà*

In the first lesson you made the acquaintance of the word **voici**. This lesson uses its companion, **voilà**. **Voici** and **voilà** are indicating words. They point out persons or things, **voici** designating what is near at hand, and **voilà** that which is farther away. The noun indicated follows **voici** or **voilà**.

1. Voici la craie. *Here is the chalk.*
2. Voilà la craie. *There is the chalk.*
3. Voici le livre. *Here is the book.*
4. Voilà le livre. *There is the book.*

Vocabulaire

la carte [la kart], *map*
la fenêtre [lafnɛːtr], *window*
le mot [lə mo], *word*
le store [lə stɔːr], *window-shade*
la France [la frãːs], *France*
Paris[2] [pari], *Paris*

je baisse [ʒə bɛs], *I lower, am lowering*, etc.
vous baissez [vu bɛse], *you lower, are lowering*
je lève [ʒə lɛːv], *I raise, am raising*, etc.
vous levez [vu ləve], *you raise, are raising*

grand, grande[3] [grã, grãːd], *large, big, tall, great, noble*
jaune [ʒoːn], *yellow*
petit, petite[3] [pəti, pətit], *small, little*
en classe [ã klɑːs], *in class*
ou [u], *either, or*
voilà [vwala], *there is, there are*

Questionnaire

1. Est-ce que la maîtresse regarde la fenêtre?
2. Où est la fenêtre?
3. Est-ce que la fenêtre est grande?
4. Levez-vous le store?
5. Charles, baissez-vous le store?
6. Est-ce que je regarde la carte?
7. Est-ce que la carte dans le livre est grande ou petite?
8. Avez-vous la carte?
9. Cherchez-vous Paris sur la carte, Charles?
10. Est-ce que la France est rose sur la carte?

[1] Notice the grave accent. It will appear in this and similar verbs when the personal ending is not to be pronounced.
[2] The definite article is regularly omitted before names of cities; but note that it is used with names of countries, e.g., *Je regarde la France sur la carte.*
[3] **Grand** and **petit** precede the noun they modify.

Devoir

A. *Make these sentences negative:*

1. Avez-vous la boîte?
2. Je regarde le mot.
3. J'ai la petite carte.
4. J'ouvre la fenêtre.
5. La carte est petite.

B. *Arrange the following in correct order for French sentences. Begin each with a capital letter and put the proper punctuation at the end.*

1. est la boîte sur verte le livre
2. ouvrez la fenêtre ou vous levez vous le store
3. Chicago voici sur la carte

4. la craie rouge voilà dans la boîte
5. est-ce que cherchez vous le mot

C. *Complete the verb-forms:*

1. Je lèv— le store vert.
2. Charles ne lèv— pas le store.
3. N'av— -vous pas la carte?
4. Je ne baiss— pas la carte.
5. Je n'a— pas la grande boîte.

Traduction:

1. Here is the map, mademoiselle.
2. Thank you, Charles. Here is Paris on the map.
3. France is large on the map.
4. In the book the map is small.

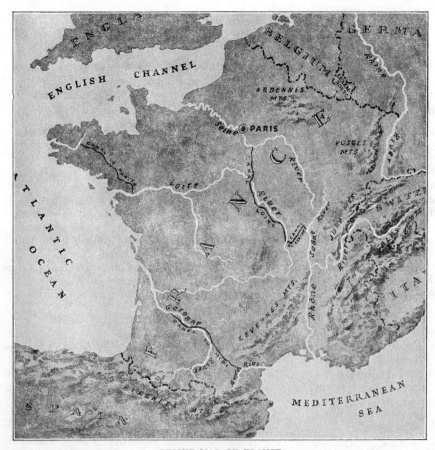

RELIEF MAP OF FRANCE

Note how, by means of rivers and canals, the English Channel is connected with the Mediterranean Sea

SEPTIÈME LEÇON

Conversation

—Bonjour, mes_élèves.

—Bonjour, mademoiselle.

—J'ai le stylo. Regardez le stylo. Regardez le tableau, et cherchez le mot **stylo.** Qu'est-ce que c'est? C'est le **stylo.** Voici le stylo. J'ouvre le tiroir, et je mets le stylo dans le tiroir. Et je ferme le tiroir.

—Voilà la table, Emilie.[1] Qu'est-ce que c'est? C'est la table. Ouvrez le tiroir. Ouvrez-vous le tiroir, Emilie?

—Oui, mademoiselle, j'ouvre le tiroir.

—Cherchez le stylo dans le tiroir. Trouvez-vous le stylo?

—Oui, mademoiselle. Voici le stylo.

Je mets le stylo sur la table avec la grammaire. Le stylo est noir, mais la grammaire est rouge. La gomme est sur la table aussi.

—Merci, Emilie. Charles, où est la gomme?

—Voici la gomme, mademoiselle. J'ai la gomme. Je mets la gomme dans le tiroir.

—Où est le mouchoir, Jean?

—Voici le mouchoir, mademoiselle.

—Est-_il rouge?

—Non, mademoiselle, il est blanc.

—Est-_il sur la table?

—Non, mademoiselle, j'ai le mouchoir.

Grammaire

The Imperative

In giving a command the French use the form corresponding to the one we use in English, the second person plural. In French that means the ending **-ez.** This is called the polite imperative.[2] Generally, in a command, the subject is not expressed either in French or in English.

> Ouvrez-vous le tiroir? QUESTION. *Are you opening the drawer?*
> Ouvrez le tiroir. COMMAND. *Open the drawer.*
> Fermez le livre. *Close the book.*
> Cherchez le stylo. *Look for the fountain-pen.*

Vocabulaire

l'élève[3] [lelɛːv] (m. and f.), *pupil*

la gomme [la gɔm], *rubber, eraser*

la grammaire [la gramɛːr], *grammar*

le mouchoir [lə muʃwaːr], *handkerchief*

le stylo [lə stilo], *fountain-pen*

le tiroir [lə tirwaːr], *drawer*

Emilie [emili], *Emily*

vous trouvez [vu truve], *you find, you are finding,* etc.

mes [me] (plural), *my*

alors [alɔːr], *then, now, so, at that time*

avec [avɛk], *with*

bonjour [bõʒuːr], *good-morning, good-day*

qu'est-ce que c'est? [kɛs kə sɛ], *what is it?*

est-il [ɛtil], *is it?, is he?*

---

[1] The initial sound of Emilie is acute e [e], but an accent is not required with a capital letter.

[2] There are two other imperative forms, but the second person plural is the one to learn first, since it is the most necessary.

[3] The e of le and the a of la are elided before nouns beginning with vowels; e.g., l'élève (m. and f.).

Questionnaire

1. Regardez-vous la fenêtre?
2. Où est le stylo?
3. Est-ce que j'ai le stylo?
4. Où est la carte?
5. Ouvrez-vous le tiroir?
6. Où mettez-vous le stylo?
7. Fermez-vous le tiroir?
8. Est-ce que je mets le livre sur la table?
9. Est-ce que la gomme est blanche?

Devoir

A. Use a different adjective in each blank:

1. J'ai la gomme ——.
2. Le stylo est ——.
3. Vous regardez le livre ——.
4. Voici la fenêtre ——.
5. Avez-vous la boîte ——?
6. Est-ce que je baisse le store ——?

B. Supply a suitable preposition in each of the following blanks:

1. Vous mettez la boîte —— la table.
2. Trouvez-vous le stylo —— le tiroir?
3. La craie est —— la boîte.
4. Je mets le livre rouge —— le livre vert.

5. Le tiroir n'est pas —— la table; le tiroir est —— la table.

C. Change to the imperative:

1. (Chercher) la carte.
2. (Ouvrir) le grand tiroir.
3. (Mettre) la boîte sur la table.
4. (Baisser) le store vert.
5. (Lever) la grande carte, Marie.

Traduction:

1. Here is the black fountain-pen.
2. Open the small drawer, Emily.
3. Have you the red eraser?
4. Look for the green handkerchief.
5. Haven't I the white paper?
6. Here is the red paper.
7. You are welcome, Mary.

HUITIÈME LEÇON

Au salon

Philippe n'est pas en classe. Il est au[1] (*in the*) salon.[2] Maman est au salon aussi. Elle parle avec grand'- mère. Elle est jolie, maman. Grand'- mère tricote le bonnet pour Adèle, la poupée. Marie est au salon aussi. Elle a la poupée. Elle aime la poupée. Philippe n'a pas la poupée. Aimez-vous la poupée?

Philippe a le livre. Il regarde le livre. Il lit le livre. Il aime le livre. Est-ce que vous aimez le livre?

Nous parlons avec maman au salon. Elle ne tricote pas. Nous ne tricotons pas. Maman a le livre rouge. Nous cherchons le livre vert, mais nous ne trouvons pas le livre vert. Maman ferme le livre. Elle n'aime pas le livre. Nous n'aimons pas le livre rouge. Nous parlons.

Grammaire

Personal Pronouns

In French, as in English, a pronoun is a word that takes the place of a noun. The noun to which the pronoun refers is called the antecedent. (*Mother* is sitting down; *she* is tired. *George* is studying; *he* will know the

---

[1] Au is a contraction of à (*in, at, to*) and le (masculine *the*).
[2] Observe and repeat all prepositional phrases, such as au salon. You will find them very easy to learn.

poem.) If the antecedent is masculine, the pronoun is masculine; if the antecedent is feminine, the pronoun must be feminine. You will remember that in French there is no neuter gender.

There are several kinds of pronouns; but it is only those known as personal that need concern you at the present time. Two of these personal pronouns you have been meeting in earlier lessons: je (*I*) and **vous** (*you*). Here are two others:

il, *he* or *it*   elle, *she* or *it*

Papa est là. *Il est là.*   Maman est au salon. *Elle est au salon.*

Le stylo est petit. *Il est petit.*   La table est là. *Elle est là.*

Combining the four forms and adding another, we obtain the following list:

SINGULAR { FIRST PERSON: je, *I*
{ THIRD PERSON: il, elle, *he, she, it*

PLURAL { FIRST PERSON: nous, *we*
{ SECOND PERSON: vous, *you*

All of these personal pronouns are used as subjects of verbs.

Verbs

You have already learned that "in French the ending of a verb depends on the person and number of its subject," e.g., **je ferme; vous fermez.** These marks of identification are called personal endings. To the two verb-forms previously learned (ending in **-e** and **-ez**) you can now add two others, and make most of the present tense of the verb **trouver** (*to find*):[1]

SINGULAR { FIRST PERSON: je trouv **e**   *I find, I am finding, I do find*
{ THIRD PERSON: il, elle, trouv **e**   *he, she, finds, is finding,* etc.

PLURAL { FIRST PERSON: nous trouv **ons**   *we find, are finding,* etc.
{ SECOND PERSON: vous trouv **ez**   *you find, are finding,* etc.

Vocabulaire

le bonnet [lə bɔnɛ], *bonnet, cap*

la grand'mère [la grãmɛːr], *grandmother*

maman [mamã], *mother*

la poupée [la pupe], *doll*

Adèle [adɛl], *Adele*

Philippe [filip], *Philip*

nous [nu], *we*

il, elle, a [il, ɛl, a], *he, she, has*

j'aime [ʒɛːm], *I like, love*

il, elle, aime [il, ɛl, ɛːm], *he, she, likes, loves*

nous aimons [nu zɛmõ], *we like, love*

vous aimez [vu zɛme], *you like, love*

nous baissons [nu bɛsõ], *we lower*

il cherche [il ʃɛrʃ], *he looks for, is looking for*

nous cherchons [nu ʃɛrʃõ], *we look for, are looking for*

il ferme [il fɛrm], *he closes, is closing*

il lit [il li], *he reads, is reading*

nous parlons [nu parlõ], *we talk, are talking*

nous regardons [nu rəgardõ], *we look at, are looking at*

il tricote [il trikɔt], *he is knitting*

nous tricotons [nu trikɔtõ], *we knit, are knitting*

nous trouvons [nu truvõ], *we find, are finding*

au [o] (mas. sing.), *in the, to the;* au salon [o salõ], *in the living-room, to the living-room*

joli[2] [ʒɔli], *pretty*

pour [puːr], *for, in order to*

---

[1] There are verbs that have different endings from these, which you will meet later.
[2] **Joli** precedes the noun it modifies.

Keystone View Co., N. Y.

IN SOUTHERN FRANCE SHEEP GRAZE AMONG THE OLIVE TREES

Questionnaire

1. Où est maman?
2. Où est Philippe?
3. Est-il au salon?
4. Est-ce que maman parle avec Philippe?
5. Est-ce que grand'mère tricote le bonnet pour Philippe?
6. Où est la poupée?
7. Est-ce que Marie a le livre?
8. Aimez-vous la poupée ou le livre?
9. Parlons-nous avec grand'mère?
10. Trouvons-nous le livre vert? Où est le livre?
11. Aimons-nous la boîte blanche?

Devoir

A. Read aloud the last paragraph of "Au salon," on page 20, substituting **vous** *for each noun and pronoun and changing the verb-forms accordingly.*

B. Complete the verb-forms:

1. Nous baiss— le store.
2. Vous lev— le store.
3. Philippe ferm— la fenêtre.
4. Parl— -vous avec Marie?
5. Regard— -nous la chaise?
6. J'ouvr— la boîte.
7. Ferm— la fenêtre.
8. Nous aim— maman.
9. Aim— -vous le livre jaune?
10. Marie cherch— la poupée au salon.

C. Write the negatives of the following:

1. J'ai la craie.
2. Nous regardons la carte.
3. Elle aime la poupée.
4. Vous avez le bonnet **blanc.**
5. Regardez la liste.

Traduction:

We are looking for the book. **We** do not find the book. We talk with mother in the living-room. Mary is in the living-room, too. She has Adele, the pretty doll. We do not like Adele. We like the book. Do you like the book? Philip has the red book. **He** is reading the red book. What is it? It is the map.

NEUVIÈME LEÇON
Le Salon

Philippe n'est pas en classe. Il est à la maison. Il est au (*in the*) salon avec Marie. Marie lit un petit livre rouge. Philippe a un livre. Il regarde le livre. Il tourne les pages, mais il ne lit pas. Il est fatigué.

Il va à une fenêtre. Il tire un rideau rose, et il regarde dans la rue. Où est papa? Il regarde dans la rue, mais il ne voit pas papa. Il n'est pas là.

L'automobile n'est pas là. Une automobile est là, mais elle est verte.

Le salon est joli. Il est gris et rose. Marie est au salon. Elle a une poupée. Marie aime le salon. Elle regarde le tapis gris, les rideaux roses, les chaises confortables, le piano. Elle aime le sofa. Il est gris. Elle est assise sur le sofa. Le sofa est confortable. J'aime un sofa confortable. Et vous?

Grammaire

The Indefinite Article

You have become well acquainted with the definite article, **le, la** (*the*). Now you are going to learn to use the indefinite article (*a, an*). The forms are **un** (masculine) and **une** (feminine), e.g.,

un livre, *a book*

une rue, *a street*

un sofa, *a sofa*

une table, *a table*

The Plural of Nouns

The plural of nouns in French is formed by adding -s to the singular. This -s is always silent except in liaison. (How is the plural of most nouns in English formed?)

la page   les pages

There are some exceptions to this rule for forming plurals in French. If the singular of the noun already ends in **-s,** another -s is not added. If the singular ends in **-au,** the plural is formed by adding **-x.** Find in the vocabulary of this lesson the two words that come under these exceptions.

Agreement of Definite Article and Noun in Number

You now know very well that an article (a kind of adjective) agrees with its noun in gender. It is **le** if the noun is masculine, and **la** if it is feminine.

le livre   la page

The definite article agrees in another way also—number. If the noun is plural, the article must be plural, too.

le livre   la page
les livres   les pages

What do you notice about the formation of the feminine plural of the definite article?

Vocabulaire

l'automobile [lɔtɔmɔbil] (m. or f.), *automobile*
la lampe [la lã:p], *lamp*
papa [papa], *father, papa*
le piano [lə pjano], *piano*
le rideau [lə rido] (pl. les rideaux), *curtain, hangings*
la rue [la ry], *street*
le salon [lə salõ], *living-room, parlor, drawing-room*
le sofa [lə sɔfa], *sofa*

le tapis [lə tapi] (pl. les tapis), *carpet*
assis [asi], *seated*
il lève [il lɛːv], *he raises, is raising*
il regarde [il rəgard], *he looks at, is looking at*
il tire [il tiːr], *he draws, draws aside, takes*
vous tirez [vu tire], *you draw, draw aside, take*
il tourne [il turn], *he turns, is turning*

il va [il va] (inf. aller), *he goes*
il voit [il vwa] (inf. voir), *he sees*
confortable [kõfɔrtabl], *comfortable*
fatigué [fatige], *tired*
gris [gri], *gray*
un, une [œ̃, yn], *a, an, one*
à [a], *at, to, on, with, for, of*
la maison [la mezõ], *house;* à la maison, *at home*
là [la], *there*

Questionnaire

1. Où est Philippe?
2. Avec qui (*whom*) est Philippe?
3. Avez-vous un livre?
4. Tournez-vous les pages?
5. Est-ce que Philippe lit?
6. Où va Philippe?
7. Où est-ce qu'il[1] regarde?
8. Est-ce que le tapis est rouge ou gris?
9. Est-ce que Marie regarde les rideaux et la lampe?
10. Est-ce qu'elle aime le sofa?

Devoir

A. Learn by heart the first two sentences of "Le Salon."

B. Complete the verb-forms:

1. Tourn— les pages de la grammaire.
2. Regard— -vous la lampe rose?
3. Est-ce que je parl— avec vous?
4. Philippe ne li— pas.
5. Je ferm— le tiroir.
6. Vous tir— le rideau.
7. Regard— -nous une automobile?
8. Il voi— le piano dans la salle de classe.
9. Vous n'aim— pas la lampe.
10. Nous trouv—— l'automobile dans la rue.

C. Supply the indefinite article and an adjective with each of the following nouns. Use a different adjective with each noun.

boîte	lampe	stylo
tapis	automobile	tableau

Traduction:

I am looking at grandmother. She is knitting. Mary has Adele. Adele is a doll. Is Philip knitting? Philip has a red book, but he is not reading. He turns the pages, but he does not read. He is tired. Philip goes to a window. He raises the shade. He looks into the street, but he does not see father. Father is not there.

[1] Note the elision here and in 10. What is the reason for it?

DIXIÈME LEÇON

Review

A

1. Name the French personal pronouns you have had that are used as subjects.

2. What verb-ending is found with each of them?

3. How is the negative formed?

4. What does an imperative sentence express?

5. What form of the verb is used in the French imperative?

6. Is the subject of a command expressed in English? In French?

7. What sort of words are **voici** and **voilà**? What do they point out? Does the noun precede or follow them?

8. Why is the grave accent used in the form **lève** (as in **Je ne lève pas le store**)?

9. Give the three forms of the definite article.

10. Give the two forms of the indefinite article.

11. In **les livres rouges** explain the reason for the endings in the definite article and the adjective.

12. How is the plural of most nouns formed in French? Is the final letter of the plural pronounced? Give two exceptions to the rule of adding -s to form the plural.

13. Is there a neuter gender for French nouns?

14. What is elision? Why do we say **j'aime**? What does the apostrophe show?

15. What form of the verb is **cherchez**?

16. How is the feminine of an adjective formed?

17. What two idioms have you learned up to this point? What phrases (preposition and noun)?

B

I. Change each infinitive to the imperative:

1. (Parler), Marie.
2. (Ouvrir) la fenêtre.
3. (Regarder) le tableau.
4. (Tirer) le rideau.
5. (Chercher) l'automobile.

II. Supply a pronoun for each italicized noun:

1. *La poupée* est là.
2. *Philippe* est en classe.
3. *La carte* est petite.
4. *Le rideau* est rose.
5. *Marie* n'est pas là.

III. Use the indefinite article with each of the following nouns:

1. carte   4. sofa
2. rue   5. tiroir
3. gomme   6. livre

IV. Change each noun and its article to the plural:

1. le livre   4. la salle
2. la table   5. l'élève
3. le stylo   6. le rideau

V. Following the first sentence as a model, complete the other three sentences.

1. J'aime l'automobile.
2. Il ——————————.
3. Nous ——————————.
4. Vous ——————————.

VI. Translate the following word-groups. In each translation observe carefully the position and the agreement of the adjective.

1. a pretty doll
2. the gray carpet
3. the small fountain-pen
4. a green window-shade

PHONETIC REVIEW

Practice:

i, ɑ̃, ɔ, u, ɛ, ə, œ, ɛ̃, o, a, y, õ, e, ø,
tri, grɑ̃, stɔ, ʒu, bɛ, lə, œf, bjɛ̃,
mo, pa, ry, bõ, me, rø

Pronounce:

[grɑ̃] grand	[mamɑ̃] maman	[ɑ̃ klɑːs] en classe
[grɑ̃mɛːr] grand'mère	[frɑ̃ːs] France	[lɑ̃ːp] lampe
[muʃwaːr] mouchoir	[dɑ̃] dans	[bõʒuːr] bonjour
[salõ] salon	[mezõ] maison	[blɑ̃] blanc

Read aloud:

Ma grand'mère est en France.
[ma grɑ̃mɛːr etɑ̃ frɑ̃ːs.]

Est-ce que Charles est en France?
[ɛs kə ʃarl etɑ̃ frɑ̃ːs?]

Non, Charles est en classe.
[nõ, ʃarl etɑ̃ klɑːs.]

Où est maman? Est-elle en classe?
[wɛ mamɑ̃? ɛtɛl ɑ̃ klɑːs?]

Non, elle est à la maison.
[nõ ɛ lɛ tala mezõ.]

RUINS OF AN ANCIENT ROMAN THEATER AT ARLES

Archives du Touring-Club de France

A ROMAN BRIDGE IN THE SOUTH OF FRANCE

HOW FRANCE WAS MADE

From the beginning France had no single pure-blooded race for her people, but like many other great nations was a melting pot of humanity. From far and near men wandered westward and northward into ancient France; war, commerce, love of travel and discovery, fertile unoccupied plains for an overpopulated world—these were the prizes that brought great masses of men into her borders. A swift glance into France's past shows us invading hosts on her every horizon. Traces of these foreigners and their customs are still to be found in the land.

For hundreds of years before the birth of Christ, a large portion of what is now France was inhabited by numerous Gallic tribes who called their country Gaul. These men were a tall, strong, fair-haired, and blue-eyed people of high intelligence. Their one great weakness was that they had no central government to bind them together.

Thus, when warlike invasions were aimed at them, the Gauls were helpless before a trained and organized foe. Rome, a strong military nation to the south, had long wished to possess this rich sprawling territory of Gaul, with its well-governed cities and fertile fields, its admirable customs and just laws. This new land was indeed a prize worth fighting for. In the last century before our era, Gaul was successfully overrun and conquered by the Romans.

Conquering foreign soil by war seems cruel, and in most cases wrong, but the invasion of Gaul by the Romans was a fortunate thing for her strength and her progress. The invaders were kind to the Gauls. They gave this people every advantage of the Roman Empire: citizenship, beautiful towns, protection. They built fine roads through the country from north to south, which after two thousand years are still in use. Remains of mighty

Archives du Touring-Club de France

FALAISE CASTLE IN THE LOW HILLS OF NORMANDY WHERE WILLIAM
THE CONQUEROR WAS BORN, 1027

works of Roman construction—temples, theaters, baths, bridges—still dot southern France. Near the quaint city of Avignon stands the almost perfect survival of the greatest of Roman aqueducts, the Pont du Gard. Conquered Gaul grew to be one of the most important parts of the immense Roman Empire.

The Gauls were shrewd enough to know that the civilization the conquerors brought with them was far more advanced than any that had previously existed in western Europe. These Gauls were therefore glad to be called Romans and to adopt the Roman customs, laws, and language in place of their own. This is why the French language today, derived as it is from the speech of Roman officials, soldiers, and colonists, is called a Romanic or Neo-Latin tongue. But perhaps the most important example of Gaul's swift following of Rome's leadership lies in her adoption of Christianity as a state religion soon

after it was firmly established in Italy.

The greatest evil of foreign invasion was that it made the province of Gaul utterly dependent on Rome. So, when early in the fifth century the Roman empire weakened and began to crumble, Gaul could not stand alone in her own strength but became an easy prey for the powerful tribes of barbarians—mainly Franks—who flooded in upon her from German territory. Clovis, a Frankish king, was crowned king of Gaul in the year 481. He made Paris the capital city of this new realm of Gallo-Romans and Franks, and from the latter arose the name by which this country was later to be known—France. By a happy chance this barbarian tribe proved as sensible and broad-minded as the Gauls themselves, and was thus eager to continue without much change the existing customs, laws, and language of the conquered province. Even the Christian religion was by royal decree put in the place of the pagan superstitions until then practiced by the Franks.

The Frankish kings continued in uninterrupted line for more than four centuries. Among them Charlemagne (771-814) was especially famous, and to this very day most Frenchmen consider him their greatest ruler. He extended the empire of France until it included almost as much territory as had once been under the power of Rome. He vastly improved the system of government and legal procedure and did all that could be done to encourage learning and to make his people more civilized than they had ever been before. Although there is no definite proof of the origin of the marvelous church of Notre Dame, it is believed by many that Charlemagne laid the first stone of this beautiful building. Outside the church stands a noble statue of the famous king mounted on the horse he rode to war.

For a thousand years after the reign of Charlemagne, France led a changeful but thrilling existence. Her history, like that of other great nations which have lived through to the present time, is a record of development by force of arms, of the loss of territory and the later regaining of it, of rival powers warring within the country itself in open defiance of the king, and of countless invasions from without. The two most important invasions, judged by their influence on French character, were those of the Britons and the Norsemen. The first of these was the peaceful immigration to the northwest of France of hordes of Britons who were driven from their own home by wild tribes of Angles, Jutes, and Saxons. The region of France occupied by these British fugitives during the fifth and sixth centuries was originally called Armorica, but its name was soon changed to Brittany, and as such continues on the modern maps of France. The other invasion was far less peaceful and was waged by Norsemen from the Scandinavian peninsula, rough sea-rovers and pirates every one. After repeated bloody attacks on France, they finally settled down in the ninth century on a large district about the mouth of the River Seine, which had been granted them in a treaty with the French king. Normandy still remains the name of this district. The spirit of these Norsemen, or Normans as they were now called, was always warlike and willful. England was to feel the weight of it as well as France, for in the year 1066 the Norman duke William (afterwards called William the Conqueror) gained the throne of England by the Battle of Hastings.

In the thrilling centuries that followed the reign of Charlemagne, France grew up. In spite of foreign invasions like the Hundred Years' War and internal struggles over religion, she advanced in art, in literature and learning of every sort. Her language became the most polished tongue of Europe. But a final battle was to be fought before she could emerge a peaceful and happy nation; this was a civil war, an inner conflict that suddenly flamed forth from a small spark of rebellion. Not before the great French Revolution finally burned itself out was France a purified and contented state.

The causes of the Revolution justified it. In the course of the long generations kings and nobles of France had grown richer and more powerful at the expense of the common people. There was no limit to their tyranny and extravagance. By the end of the eighteenth century the greater part of the population was heavily taxed, without a voice in the government, and so poor as to be almost starving to death. The frenzied people burst at last the bonds that held them captive. Their cry was "Liberty, Equality, and Fraternity." Incited by their many courageous leaders, they demanded the execution of their king and queen, of the nobles, and of royal sympathizers. For a year the Reign of Terror lasted, and in this year France was proclaimed a republic.

This first Republic ended in the exile of its ruler and in the establishment of a second Republic. The fault lay not in the idea of democratic government but in the man who governed. This man was a young Corsican named Napoleon Bonaparte, and his life is one of the greatest romances history records. In sixteen years he had conquered nearly every country in Europe and so won the affections of his people that they conferred on him the title Emperor of the French. This was done in spite of the fact that a republic had been proclaimed in France just to do away with kings and emperors.

When the rest of Europe saw that Napoleon was bent on world conquest, they united against him, defeated him decisively at Waterloo, in 1815, and banished him to the island of St. Helena, where he died. One of the most splendid monuments in the world, the Arc de Triomphe, stands today in Paris on the spot where Napoleon began its erection to celebrate his victories of 1805 and 1806. Under the arch is now buried the Unknown Soldier of France (*le soldat inconnu*), whose memory will always be green in the minds of men—just as the Great Emperor will never be forgotten, in spite of his ruined hopes and dreams.

After Napoleon, kings came again briefly to rule in France. But in September, 1870, in the midst of French defeat at the hands of Prussia, the Third Republic was born, and the days of powerful kings and nobles were at an end. At last France is at peace with herself. Born of conquest and invasion, of Roman law and order, France is today a well-knit structure, a great factor in the progress and culture of the world.

By Ewing Galloway, N. Y.

THE GREAT ARCH OF TRIUMPH

ONZIÈME LEÇON

La Famille au salon

La famille sauf papa est au salon. Grand'mère tricote. Maman ne tricote pas. Grand'mère et maman parlent. Elles parlent beaucoup. Philippe a un livre. Il tourne les pages, et il trouve une histoire intéressante. Il lit. Il aime les histoires intéressantes. Il aime aussi les balles et les bicyclettes. Aimez-vous aussi les histoires intéressantes?

Marie a une poupée. Elle joue avec la poupée. Elle aime la poupée. Les petites filles n'aiment pas toujours les poupées, mais Marie aime les poupées. Elle est assise sur le sofa.

—Bonjour, petite poupée. Regardez la lampe rose. N'est-elle pas belle? Aimez-vous le sofa gris? Il est confortable. Nous aimons la petite table aussi. Elle est belle. Nous trouvons toujours une belle chaise au salon. J'aime aussi le beau piano. Maman et papa aiment le piano. Ils aiment beaucoup le piano.

Grammaire

The Present Tense of the Verb *Trouver*

From Lesson 1 on, you have been meeting different forms of the present tense of a verb. If you look back through the reading lessons or the vocabularies, you will see that most of these forms end in -e, -ez, or -ons, regardless of what verb is being used, and that each represents a particular person and number. Now let us collect the forms we have had, add a new one (ending in -ent), and arrange the complete list. Such a list is called a conjugation. As a model we shall use the verb **trouver**.

Conjugation of the Present Tense of *Trouver*

Singular	*Plural*
je trouv e, *I find, am finding, do find*	nous trouv ons, *we find, are finding*, etc.
tu trouv es,[1] *you find, are finding*, etc.	vous trouv ez, *you find, are finding*
il trouv e, *he finds, is finding*, etc.	ils trouv ent, *they find, are finding*
elle trouv e, *she finds, is finding*, etc.	elles trouv ent, *they find, are finding*

In this conjugation of the present tense there is an important new form, the third person plural: ils **trouvent** (masculine) and elles **trouvent** (feminine).[2] The two pronoun forms are obtained by adding an -s in each case to the singulars il and elle. This -s as a mark of the plural is not pronounced. Ils sounds like il, and elles sounds like elle. The verb **trouvent** is pronounced [truv]. The last syllable, -ent, is not sounded. *The third person plural ending of a verb, -ent, is never pronounced.*

[1] The tu form, second person singular, will not be used by the pupils. It is the familiar form used in addressing members of the family, small children, etc. Use tu only in conjugating a verb. The teacher may omit this form if she wishes. The form is pronounced [ty truv].
[2] If one pronoun is used to refer to both masculine and feminine words, ils is used.

The French Infinitive[1]

In an earlier lesson you learned that when we mention a verb by name in French or in English, we use its infinitive form. In English the sign of the infinitive is the preposition *to: to have; to walk; to motor;* etc. The case is different in French, where the sign is an ending only. In the verb you have just been examining, **trouver** is the infinitive and is recognized by its ending **-er**. The infinitive is an important part of the French verb, because from it are made most of the other forms. This is done by dropping the sign of the infinitive and adding the personal endings to the stem. Do you see that this was done in the conjugation of the present tense of **trouver** given on the preceding page? Here are the infinitives of four verbs used in today's reading lesson, "La Famille au salon":

aimer	tourner
tricoter	parler

First Conjugation Verbs

Now there are many verbs in the French language that, like those above, end in **-er**. Such verbs belong to a family called the first conjugation.[2] The personal endings of one will be exactly like those of every other. So from now on when you meet an **-er** verb you will know (unless it is irregular) that its present tense indicative will be formed by dropping the infinitive ending **-er**, and adding to the stem **-e, -es, -e, -ons, -ez,** and **-ent**.

Vocabulaire

la balle [la bal], *ball*
la bicyclette [la bisiklɛt], *bicycle*
la famille [la fami:j], *family*
la petite fille [la ptit fi:j], *little girl*

l'histoire [listwa:r][3] (f.), *story, history*
beau, belle [bo, bɛl], *beautiful, fine, handsome, good*
intéressant [ɛ̃teresã], *interesting*

jouer [ʒwe], *to play*
beaucoup [boku], *very much, a great deal*
toujours [tuʒu:r], *always, still*
sauf [sɔf], *except*

Questionnaire

1. Où est la famille? Avez-vous une famille?
2. Est-ce que maman tricote?
3. Est-ce que grand'mère tricote un bonnet?
4. Est-ce que Marie lit?
5. Jouez-vous avec une poupée?
6. Est-ce que nous aimons les bicyclettes?
7. Est-ce que papa et Philippe jouent?
8. Cherchez-vous une histoire intéressante?
9. Est-ce que la petite fille parle avec la poupée?
10. Aimons-nous beaucoup un livre intéressant?
11. Avez-vous un piano au salon?

---

[1] From now on look up regular verbs of the first conjugation under the infinitive in the French-English vocabulary.
[2] There are two other conjugations, which you will meet later.
[3] Elision occurs here because the **h** is both unpronounced and inaspirate. For an explanation of inaspirate **h**, see page xxv.

ONE OF THE THICK TURRETED WALLS OF AVIGNON, WHICH WERE BUILT
IN THE MIDDLE AGES

Devoir

A. Write the last sentence of "*La Famille au salon*" in phonetic characters.

B. Conjugate these sentences:
1. Je parle avec la petite fille.
2. Je ne joue pas au salon.

C. Supply the indefinite article with each of the following nouns:

store   carte   histoire
mot   fenêtre   famille

D. Supply the definite article and an adjective with each of the preceding nouns.

E. Arrange the following word-groups in proper order for sentences. Begin each sentence with a capital letter, and put the proper punctuation at the end.

1. lit un il livre est-ce que intéressant
2. nous fenêtre petite fermons la
3. boîte la jaune la craie blanche dans voici
4. est bicyclette la rouge et verte est-ce que
5. regardez tapis le dans le salon gris

Traduction:

Philip is not with Mary. Here is Philip. He is reading an interesting story. Mary is playing with Adele. Adele is a small doll. Philip and Emily are not playing with the doll. Emily is seated on the sofa. Philip is not seated on the sofa. Mother goes to the window. She looks into the street. She does not see father.

DOUZIÈME LEÇON

Philippe joue avec le chat

Philippe regarde la petite Marie. Elle joue avec Adèle. Philippe n'aime pas les poupées. Il aime les balles, les locomotives, les bicyclettes, mais pas les poupées. Il aime aussi les livres, les histoires d'aventure.

—Aimez-vous Adèle? dit-il à Marie.

—Beaucoup. Mais j'aime aussi les bicyclettes et les locomotives. Les petites filles aiment beaucoup les bicyclettes. J'ai une bicyclette et vous avez une bicyclette aussi.

Grand'mère parle avec maman.

Marie joue avec la poupée. Papa n'est pas là. Est-il dans la rue? Philippe cherche le chat. Aime-t-il le chat? Oui, beaucoup. Et le chat aime jouer. Philippe tire un bout de ficelle de sa (his) poche. Le chat joue-t-il avec la ficelle? Oui, il court après Philippe, et il joue avec la ficelle. Il aime jouer avec Philippe.

Court-il après Marie? Non. Joue-t-il avec Marie? Non, il joue avec Philippe. Aimez-vous jouer avec le chat?

Grammaire

The Interrogative Form of the Verb

In the second lesson you learned that there are two ways of forming questions in French. One is *to prefix* **Est-ce que** to a declarative sentence. This may be done with any person, and is the *usual form for the first person singular*.

The interrogative form for the other persons corresponds to the English manner of making questions—changing the position of subject and verb. This is called inversion.

> Vous avez, *turned around, is* Avez-vous.
> Il lit, *turned around, is* Lit-il.

What do you see in the interrogative that is not present in the affirmative? Observe that **Est-ce que** requires no change in the order of the affirmative sentence. The inverted form requires verb, hyphen, pronoun-subject.

> Est-ce qu'elle lit l'histoire?
> Lit-elle l'histoire?

If a noun is the subject of an interrogative sentence, a pronoun as well must be used after the verb. This pronoun is, of course, never translated.

> Le livre est ici. *The book is here.*
> Le livre est-il ici? *Is the book here?*
> Le livre n'est-il pas ici? *Isn't the book here?*

The Letter *t* in the Interrogative Verb

The letter *t* often ends the third person singular of a verb, e.g., **Lit-il?** Why is this pronounced [li til]? Observe what happens in an interrogative sentence when there is no final *t* in the verb.

A-t-il le livre?   Trouve-t-il le livre?   Cherche-t-elle la ficelle?

The *t* is added only in the third person singular when the verb does not end in *t* (or sometimes *d*). Can you account for this?

Vocabulaire

l'**aventure** [lavãtyːr] (f.), *adventure*
le **bout de ficelle** [lə bud fisɛl], *piece of string*
le **chat** [lə ʃa], *cat*
la **ficelle** [la fisɛl], *string*

la **locomotive** [la lɔkɔmo-tiːv], *locomotive*
la **poche** [la pɔʃ], *pocket*
il **court** [il kuːr], *he runs, is running,* etc.
il **dit** [il di], *he says,* etc.

sa [sa] (f. sing. poss. adj.), *his, her, its*
après [aprɛ], *after, afterwards*
de [də], *of, from;* (sometimes *for, with, about*)

Questionnaire

1. Marie joue-t-elle avec la poupée?
2. Philippe aime-t-il les poupées?
3. A-t-il un livre?
4. Est-ce qu'il lit une histoire intéressante?
5. Parle-t-il avec Marie?
6. Joue-t-il avec la poupée?
7. Où est le chat?
8. Est-ce que le chat est sur la chaise?
9. Est-ce que le chat aime jouer?
10. Et Philippe, est-ce qu'il joue avec le bout de ficelle?
11. Aimez-vous jouer?

Devoir

A. *Write the last paragraph of "Philippe joue avec le chat" in phonetic symbols.*

B. *Write these sentences in the negative:*

1. Je regarde la locomotive.
2. Vous avez la bicyclette.
3. Elle a la poupée.
4. Il tire le rideau.
5. Il baisse le store.

C. *Write the preceding sentences in the interrogative, giving two forms for all but the first.*[1]

D. *Change to the imperative:*

1. Je regarde la locomotive.
2. Il joue avec la ficelle.

3. Vous ne parlez pas avec papa.
4. Tirez-vous le rideau?
5. Elle cherche l'histoire.
6. Vous baissez la carte.

Traduction:

There is the cat. Mary likes the little black cat very much.[2] I like the cat, too. Philip sees the cat. It is not on the small chair. Philip draws a piece of string from his (**sa**) pocket. The cat runs after Philip. Does the cat run after Mary? Has she the piece of string? The cat likes to play with the string. Do you play with the cat?

---

[1] The first person singular requires Est-ce que.
[2] Remember that in French adverbs follow the verb as closely as possible.

TREIZIÈME LEÇON
Le Journal

Philippe joue avec le chat. Mais voilà papa. Il embrasse maman, grand'mère, Marie, et Philippe. Alors il donne le journal à[1] Philippe. Philippe ouvre le journal. Lit-il? Non, il regarde les illustrations. Marie met la poupée de côté. Marie aime-t-elle les illustrations? Elle aime beaucoup regarder le journal avec Philippe. Ils regardent une illustration. Ils sont assis sur le sofa.

—Qu'est-ce que c'est que ceci? dit Marie.

—C'est un général. Il regarde les soldats. Ils sont fatigués.

—Et qu'est-ce que c'est que cela? Le drapeau américain?[2]

—Oui, c'est le drapeau américain. Voici les soldats, et voilà le général. Est-il beau?

—Il est beau. Voilà un aéroplane. Est-il grand? Il est petit dans l'illustration, mais il est vraiment très grand.

—L'illustration est très petite, mais elle est vraiment intéressante, Philippe.

—Oui, très intéressante. J'aime toujours les soldats, les généraux, les drapeaux, et les aéroplanes. Ils sont intéressants.

Grammaire
Interrogative Forms

There are many interrogative forms in French. Three useful expressions are given below. One of them you have met before.

Qu'est-ce que c'est? [kɛs kə sɛ] *What is it?*
Qu'est-ce que c'est que ceci? [kɛs kə sɛ kə səsi] *What is this?*
Qu'est-ce que c'est que cela? [kɛs kə sɛ kə sla] *What is that?*

Learn to pronounce and write these forms, for you will need them constantly.

Use of *C'est* and *Il est*

The answer to any of the three questions given above should begin with C'est, followed by a noun (called a predicate noun).

C'est le stylo. *It is the fountain-pen.*

The answers to other questions, such as those starting with où, est-ce que, or inverted verbs, as est-il, should begin with il est or elle est, followed by an adjective, adverb, or prepositional phrase.

Où est la boîte? Elle est là. *Where is the box? It is there.*

Est-ce que Marie est grande? Non, elle est petite. *Is Mary large? No, she is small.*

Est-il ici? Il est au salon. *Is he here? He is in the living-room.*

In "Le Journal" find one example of a sentence beginning with c'est, and one beginning with il est or elle est. Note carefully whether a noun, an adjective, an adverb, or a phrase follows each. Repeat the sentences to familiarize yourself with the French forms.

[1] In English we can say, "He gives Philip the paper"; but the French never omit the preposition à in such a case.
[2] Note that the French do not capitalize an adjective made from a proper noun, as we do.

The Plural of *Il est* and *Elle est*

The plurals of **il est** and **elle est** are **ils sont** and **elles sont**.　Learn these new plural forms carefully, as they are frequently used.

Vocabulaire

l'aéroplane [laerɔplan], (m.), *airplane*

le drapeau [lə drapo] (pl. **les drapeaux**), *flag*

le général [lə ʒeneral] (pl. **les généraux**), *general*

l'illustration [lilystrasjɔ̃] (f.), *picture in a newspaper, illustration*

le journal [lə ʒurnal] (pl. **les journaux**), *newspaper*

l'oiseau [lwazo] (m.) (pl. **les oiseaux**), *bird*

le soldat [lə sɔlda], *soldier*

donner [dɔne], *to give*

embrasser [ɑ̃brase], *to kiss*

il met [il mɛ] (inf. **mettre**), *he puts;* **il met de côté** [il mɛd kote], *he puts aside* or *away*

il ouvre [il uːvr], *he opens*

ils sont [il sɔ̃] (inf. **être**), *they are*

américain [amerikɛ̃], *A-merican*

très [trɛ], *very*

vraiment [vrɛmɑ̃], *really, truly*

qu'est-ce que c'est que ceci? [kɛs kə sɛ kə səsi], *what is this?*

qu'est-ce que c'est que cela? [kɛs kə sɛ kə sla], *what is that?*

Questionnaire

1. Papa ouvre-t-il la fenêtre?
2. Donne-t-il le journal à Marie?
3. Est-ce que Philippe lit le journal?
4. Où est-ce que Marie met Adèle?
5. Aime-t-elle regarder l'illustration?
6. Où est le général?
7. Marie voit-elle un oiseau rouge ou un aéroplane?
8. Est-ce que l'aéroplane est petit?
9. Aimez-vous le drapeau américain?
10. Regardons-nous toujours les illustrations?

Devoir

A. Write the nouns in the vocabulary, dividing them into syllables.

B. Complete the verb-forms:

1. Ne jou— pas avec le chat.
2. Regarde— -il les soldats?
3. Marie aim— le journal.
4. Nous donn— le journal à maman.
5. Ils embrass— la petite fille.

C. Prepare to explain in English, and to give examples of, the difference between c'est and il est or elle est.

D. Change these sentences to questions:

1. Vous ne jouez pas en classe.
2. Elle met le stylo de côté.
3. Le salon est joli.
4. Papa ouvre le journal.
5. Je regarde l'automobile.
6. Les soldats sont américains.

Traduction:

"What is this?"

"It is an American flag.　Here is the general, and there are the soldiers."

"We always like to look at the American flag."

"Are you looking at the bird?"

"It is not a bird; it is an airplane. It is not really small.　It is large."

"Is the airplane large?"

QUATORZIÈME LEÇON

La Famille

Papa parle avec maman et grand'-mère. Ils sont au salon. Philippe a toujours le journal. Il lit. Marie regarde les illustrations. Elle ne sait pas lire.

—Qu'est-ce que c'est que ceci?

—Je ne sais pas. Je lis.

—Mais, Philippe, qu'est-ce que c'est que ceci? Une locomotive?

—Oui, Marie, c'est une locomotive électrique. Elle va très vite.

—Qu'est-ce que c'est que cela sur le tapis? dit maman.

—C'est un bout de ficelle, dit Marie.

—Ramassez la ficelle, s'il vous plaît, Philippe.

—Oui, maman. Alors il met le bout de ficelle dans sa poche.

—Regardez la locomotive, Marie. Elle—

Mais voilà la bonne. Elle dit à maman, "Madame est servie."

Grammaire

First Conjugation Endings

You are constantly growing better acquainted with verb-forms. The endings -e, -es, -e, -ons, -ez, and -ent must be familiar by now. They are the personal endings for the present indicative of verbs whose infinitives end in -er—first conjugation verbs. From now on, only the infinitive form of such verbs will appear in the vocabulary.

The Complementary Infinitive

The infinitive is used in French, as it often is in English, to complete the verb. It is then called the complementary infinitive.

Nous aimons **regarder** les illustrations. *We like to look at illustrations.*

There is in today's lesson a verb that is frequently completed by the infinitive, the verb meaning *to know, to know how:*

Je sais parler. *I know how to talk.*
Il sait lire. *He knows how to read.*

When a verb has forms other than those of certain large classes called conjugations, it is irregular. The forms **sais** and **sait,** in the examples above, are irregular. Learn them now.

Vocabulaire

la bonne [la bɔn], *maid, servant*
lire[1] [liːr], *to read*
je lis [ʒə li], *I read*
ramasser [ramɑse], *to pick up, to collect*

je sais[2] [ʒə se] (inf. savoir), *I know (how);* il sait [il se], *he knows (how)*
électrique [elɛktrik], *electric*

vite [vit], *fast, quick*
s'il vous plaît [sil vu plɛ], *if you please* (s' = si, *if*)
madame est servie [madam ɛ sɛrvi], *dinner is served*

[1]Lire is an irregular verb. Learn every form as it is given.
[2]This verb is not used in the sense of knowing a person.

Questionnaire

1. Philippe a-t-il le journal?
2. Marie lit-elle le journal?
3. Qu'est-ce que c'est que cela sur le tapis?
4. Est-ce que maman voit la ficelle?
5. Marie ramasse-t-elle la ficelle?
6. Où Philippe met-il la ficelle?
7. Est-ce que le chat aime jouer?
8. La locomotive va-t-elle vite?
9. Ramassez-vous le bout de ficelle?
10. Est-ce que maman dit "s'il vous plaît," à Philippe?
11. Cherchez-vous toujours les illustrations dans le journal?
12. Qu'est-ce que la bonne dit à maman?

Devoir

A. Learn the last two sentences of "La Famille" by heart.

B. Conjugate these sentences:

1. J'aime jouer.
2. Je regarde la liste.

C. Complete the verb-forms:

1. Nous ne jou— pas au salon.
2. Le chat cour— après Philippe.
3. Philippe sai— jouer avec le chat.
4. Vous tourn— très vite les pages de la grammaire.
5. Ils trouv— le drapeau.
6. Elle di— merci.
7. Je ferm— le tiroir.
8. Charles et Jean ne tricot— pas.
9. Ils n'aim—— pas tricot—.
10. Vous av— la belle poupée.

D. Make the sentences of C interrogative.

Traduction:

Father gives Philip the newspaper. Philip opens the newspaper. He really likes to look at the illustrations. We also like to look at the illustrations. Do you look at the illustrations?

"What is that?" says mother.

"It is a piece of string," answers father.

"Pick up the string, please, Philip," says mother.

Philip picks up the piece of string. Then he puts the string in his pocket. He still has the newspaper. Mary looks at the newspaper. She does not know how to read.

QUINZIÈME LEÇON

Review

A

1. Give the present tense of **trouver**.
2. What are the plural forms of the pronouns **il** and **elle**?
3. Pronounce the form **trouvent**. What part of the third person plural of a verb is never pronounced?
4. What six verb-endings should now be familiar to you?
5. What two letters end the infinitive form of a verb whose present tense ends in **-e, -es, -e, -ons, -ez, -ent**?
6. In English the infinitive is often used to complete a verb. This is also done in French. Illustrate.
7. Translate **je sais parler** and **il sait lire**.
8. Why is it necessary to learn the forms **sais** and **sait**? Can you name another form such as these?
9. With what person is **est-ce que** the required form in an interrogative sentence?
10. What letter is sometimes added in the third person interrogative? Why?
11. Give the French for: *What is it? What is this? What is that?*
12. In answering a question, when is **c'est** used?

13. In answering a question, when is il **est** or elle **est** used?

14. To fill the blank in —— **est le drapeau,** which form do you use?

15. What do you use in —— **est rouge?**

16. What is the plural of elle **est?**

B

I. Conjugate these sentences:

1. Je donne le journal à Philippe.
2. Je n'aime pas lire l'histoire.

II. Make these sentences interrogative:

1. Le chat court après la ficelle.
2. Je ne joue pas avec la poupée.
3. Nous regardons la locomotive.
4. Il a un journal.
5. Ils cherchent la balle.
6. Vous trouvez le stylo.
7. Elles sont petites.
8. Nous trouvons un oiseau.

III. Complete the verb-forms:

1. Je sai— jouer.
2. Il me— la boîte sur la table.
3. Nous regard— les illustrations.
4. Elle voi— les soldats.
5. Elles aim— le drapeau.

IV. Translate:

1. What is this? It is a large flag. It is white.
2. We look at the airplane. It is little.
3. What is that? It is a bird. It is yellow.
4. Pick up the string, please.
5. What is this? It is an illustration. It is pretty.
6. Here is the newspaper.

V. Pretend that you are looking at a newspaper or a magazine, and tell what illustrations you see.

Example: Voici un aéroplane. Il est petit, *etc.*

PHONETIC REVIEW

Practice:

bɔ, bi, be, bɛ, bo, bõ, bã, by, bø, bə, ba, bu, bɛ̃, ba.

pɔ, pi, pe, pɛ, po, põ, pã, py, pø, pə, pa, pu, pɛ̃, pɑ, pa, etc. (Use all other consonants).

Pronounce:

mademoiselle [madmwazɛl]
quoi [kwa]
noir [nwaːr]
maîtresse [mɛtrɛs]
merci [mɛrsi]

moi [mwa]
histoire [istwaːr]
oiseau [wazo]
l'aventure [lavãtyːr]
illustration [ilystrasjõ]
aéroplane [aerɔplan]

Read aloud:

Mademoiselle la maîtresse, la boîte noire est
[madmwazɛl la mɛtrɛs, la bwaːt nwaːr ɛ

sur la table. Fermez la boîte, s'il vous plaît.
syːr la tabl. fɛrme la bwaːt, sil vu plɛ.

La voici. Merci, mademoiselle. Voici l'histoire.
la vwasi. mɛrsi, madmwazɛl. vwasi listwaːr.

La voici. C'est l'histoire de l'oiseau noir.
la vwasi. sɛ listwaːr də lwazo nwaːr.

Regardez les illustrations.
rəgarde le zilystrasjõ.]

A PEASANT FAMILY AT WORK IN THE FIELDS

VIVE LA FRANCE!

We have seen that France makes a home-loving race of her sons and her daughters. They cannot imagine a world in which their native land does not play a leading part; thus the cry *Vive la France* (Long live France) not only expresses their dearest wish that she shall never die, but voices their triumphant faith that so long as the earth lasts France will last.

This love for the *patrie* (native land) is not patriotism alone; it is a true religion without which life itself is unthinkable. An old story known to everyone illustrates this fact very well: A French officer had been tried by a military court and convicted of treason. He attempted to justify his conduct by saying that there was at that time no government left in France, no order, no authority for him to obey. Whereupon the judge reminded him sternly: *"Il y avait encore la France, monsieur!"* (But France herself was still there, my dear sir!)

There is then good reason for the fact that France stamps her people with nationality more than any other nation does: Joffre[1] was first of all a Frenchman—and only after that a famous general. In England, for instance, they say that "blood tells." This means that people of good birth and breeding live as real Englishmen should, but that Britishers who are not well-born and -bred live in a way which cannot rightly represent their country. Such a statement could not be true of France, for here there is less difference between speech and manners than we find in other European countries. There is little to choose in manner and speech between a young girl occupying a humble position and a girl brought up in a wealthy home, clad in the costliest silks; for to both of them has been given a musical language, a happy way of taking life

[1] Marshal Joffre (1852-1931), commander-in-chief of the French army in the Great War from 1914 to 1916.

Photo A. Breger Frères, Paris

A VILLAGE MARKET

as it is, and an equal share in the great heritage of the French past.

In France, as everywhere else in the world, there are of course differences in class; but these depend mostly on the work one does. The old nobility, which constitutes but a small part of the population, upholds the traditions of race and culture for which France is so celebrated. Besides the nobility, the remaining classes of Frenchmen are the middle class, or *bourgeoisie*, the artisans, and the peasants.

The peasants are a simple, hardy folk and do not follow any single type: they may be tall, fair of skin, and blond, as in Normandy; or dark, slight of frame, and lively, as in Provence. Their dress, however, marks them as peasants; for they wear blue smocks over corduroy trousers, often neatly patched, and their clumsy shoes of wood or leather also proclaim them tillers of the soil. Women in plain dark clothes work beside men in the fields, as we see in the pictures of Millet, which show the peasants so vividly. Men and women work very hard in the

fields and live thriftily. They are self-respecting people. As for ambition, each peasant longs to increase his farm by at least one of those ribbon-like fields that impress the traveler in France with the intensive cultivation of the land.

During the week the peasants' dress is as dull as that of brown birds in the thickets, but on Sunday their clothes outshine the rainbow. Each French province (old political division of France) has its own style of dress; so when the rustic is clad in his Sunday-best it is not hard to tell from which district he hails, from Brittany or Alsace or Provence. Even when peasants lay aside their traditional clothes for the prints of the cities, the older women still cling to the head-dress that is typical of their birthplace. The girls strive for urban smartness, but lose thereby some of their quaint dignity.

The artisan class includes mechanics and craftsmen generally. Here is a cabinet maker who slaves for days to restore a piece of fine old furniture to its exact original condition. Alas, this same genius can make the ordinary furniture from a factory look just like real antiques! Here is a skillful furrier who fills the basement shops with rabbit cloaks so like those of seal and ermine that Paris *midinettes* (shopgirls) walk the streets clothed for all the world as if they were ladies of wealth and fashion. A craftsman in a dingy garret turns out artificial flowers that seem an improvement on nature. The silk-weaver at his loom and the maker of *sabots* (wooden shoes) work with a will. A locksmith repairs the hardware on doors and gates of old châteaux as deftly as if he had forged them when first used. The artisan is kindly and well-bred, for he is the aristocrat of wage-earners and considers his trade a highly honorable one. He is always ready to chat with the chance customer, and his talk is as witty and entertaining as that heard in a polite French parlor. The white-collared wage-earner is also classed as an artisan. Of all French citizens he is perhaps the least well-to-do. He is the clerk with small wages who

By Ewing Galloway, N. Y.

WEAVING SILK ON A HAND LOOM

owns nothing and probably never will. His lot is an unhappy one, for he is forced to keep up the appearance of a gentleman, though without sufficient means to live like one.

The French middle class is not quite like that of any other nation, for to be a *bourgeois* one must either own property or have the right to practice a profession. A *bourgeois*, one might say, is born and not made, for he carries on what his father and grandfather began many years before his arrival on earth. He may be a small shop-keeper selling notions, or head of some great commercial enterprise; he may be teacher, doctor, lawyer, government official, or artist. But whether he belong to the high or the low *bourgeoisie*, he has his definite place in the social scheme. He must be an honest citizen and, if married, a good husband and father. He has one real faith which shapes his whole life: France, and the family. He is not given to day-dreams—his family is the solid fact for which all else is sacrificed. Every penny he can scrape together is

By Ewing Galloway, N. Y.

A SABOT-MAKER AT WORK

for his daughter's dowry, so that she can marry well; every influence at his command is pledged for the future career of his son.

There is perhaps on earth no deeper intimacy than the one that exists between a woman of the bourgeoisie and her children. French has a very gracious name for the unselfish middle-class mother: *honnête femme*. These modest home-keepers are countless everywhere throughout France; thus they furnish not only the loveliest type of French womanhood, but the most characteristic one as well. It is true that careless eyes do not always see them; this is because they are found wherever one goes—like light and air; because, too, tireless devotion to their family duties is apt to keep them hidden from public view. For an *honnête femme* is not content to be a good wife only; she remains until death a good daughter, devoted to the family into which she was born, and a firm friend to those of her husband's family. She cherishes her children and guides all the affairs of their lives.

Nor is she content to be an excellent housewife and nothing more: she helps to make life about her a happy thing for all who form part of it, her dependents and servants as well.

But to whichever class he belongs—peasant, artisan, or *bourgeois*—a child born into this nation is essentially a Frenchman. The French spirit of nationality equalizes all classes of men. A pride in his *patrie* (native land) far outweighs any vanity the individual French man or woman may possess. The true Frenchman reserves his tribute not for his fellows but for France as the one greatest separate fact in life. He exalts France's place at the head of civilization and never tires of mentioning her many *gloires*, by which he means her glorious gifts to human progress in science, art, music, and learning. And so long as Frenchmen look upon their country as something apart from them, as something far greater than the sum of all Frenchmen living and dead, so long will France be distinctly different from all other nations of the world.

Photo by Underwood & Underwood

ONE OF THE "GLOIRES" OF FRANCE

SEIZIÈME LEÇON
Au dîner

La famille est servie. Voici la famille dans la salle à manger. A table Philippe est assis à côté de papa. Marie est à côté de maman. Papa découpe le rôti. Philippe découpe-t-il le rôti? Non, c'est papa qui découpe le rôti. Philippe aime beaucoup la viande. Qu'est-ce qu'il n'aime pas? Il n'aime pas les pommes de terre. Marie est petite. C'est maman qui découpe la viande pour Marie.

Où est le petit chat? Est-il dans la salle à manger? Non, non, non. Maman met le petit chat au salon. Là il cherche une chaise confortable.

Philippe regarde la petite fourchette et la jolie petite cuillère de Marie. Qu'est-ce qu'il aime? Il aime les grands couteaux, les grandes fourchettes, et les grandes cuillères. Il a une grande fourchette et un grand couteau. Qu'avez-vous, un grand couteau ou un petit couteau? Papa a une petite cuillère pour le café. Philippe a-t-il une cuillère pour le café? Est-ce que la petite cuillère de Marie est pour le café? Non, le café n'est pas pour les enfants.

Voilà la bonne. Elle apporte à[1] maman la tarte et les assiettes. C'est maman qui coupe la tarte en morceaux. La tarte est bonne. C'est une tarte aux cerises.

Grammaire

Interrogative Pronouns—*Que, Qu'est-ce que*

The interrogative pronoun *what* has several forms in French. The forms used as direct objects of verbs are **que** and **qu'est-ce que**.[2]

> Que lit-il? *What is he reading?*
> Qu'est-ce qu'il lit? *What is he reading?*
> Que mangez-vous? *What are you eating?*
> Qu'est-ce que vous mangez? *What are you eating?*

Note that with **qu'est-ce que** the order of the sentence is not changed. With **que** the inverted order is used.

The Pronoun *Qui*

Qui is a subject pronoun and means *who*. Later you will learn more about it. For the present you will use it only in such cases as:

> C'est maman qui découpe la viande.
> C'est Philippe qui a le bout de ficelle.

Qui is here the subject of the verbs **découpe** and **a**.

---

[1] In English we say "brings mother," with *to* understood; the French do not omit the preposition.
[2] To find the object, in a question, we can change the sentence, as we do in English, to the affirmative: *What is he reading?* becomes *He is reading what*, and shows *what* as the direct object.

Vocabulaire

l'assiette [lasjɛt] (f.), *plate*
le café [lə kafe], *coffee*
la cerise [la səriːz], *cherry*
le couteau [lə kuto] (pl. les couteaux), *knife*
la cuillère [la kɥijɛːr], *spoon*
l'enfant [lãfã] (m. and f.), *child*
la fourchette [la furʃɛt], *fork*
le morceau [lə mɔrso] (pl. les morceaux), *piece*

la pomme de terre [la pɔm də tɛːr], *potato*
le rôti [lə rɔti], *roast*
la salle à manger [la sal a mãʒe], *dining-room*
la tarte [la tart], *pie*
la tarte aux cerises [la tart o səriːz], *cherry pie*
la viande [la vjãːd], *meat*
qui [ki], *who*
apporter [apɔrte], *to bring, to take* (to someone)

couper [kupe], *to cut*
découper [dekupe], *to carve*
il, elle, fait [il, ɛl, fɛ] (inf. faire), *he, she, does, is doing, makes*
manger [1] [mãʒe], *to eat*
bon, bonne [bõ, bɔn], *good*
à côté de [a kote də], *beside*
au dîner [o dine], *at dinner*
en morceaux [ã mɔrso], *in pieces*
en [ã], *in, on*

Questionnaire

1. Où est la famille?
2. Qu'est-ce que papa découpe?
3. Philippe découpe-t-il le rôti?
4. Qu'est-ce que maman coupe pour Marie?
5. Qu'est-ce que la bonne apporte?
6. Maman coupe-t-elle la tarte?
7. Qu'est-ce que Philippe aime?
8. Est-ce que le café est pour les enfants?
9. Est-ce que la cuillère est vraiment très petite?

Devoir

A. *Write the last two sentences of "Au dîner" in phonetic characters.*

B. *Answer the following questions, using a different verb in each answer:*

1. Que fait maman au dîner?
2. Que fait papa au dîner?
3. Que fait la bonne au dîner?
4. Que fait Philippe au dîner?

C. *Give the imperative form of each verb in parentheses:*

1. (Couper) la tarte.
2. (Découper) le rôti.
3. (Regarder) les cerises.
4. (Donner) la cuillère à Marie.
5. (Ramasser) la petite locomotive électrique.
6. (Lever) le store.
7. (Mettre) le mouchoir de côté.
8. (Répondre) à la maîtresse.

D. *Make these sentences interrogative:*

1. Il aime les grandes fourchettes.
2. Elle a une petite fourchette là.
3. J'aime la tarte aux cerises.
4. Philippe n'aime pas les pommes de terre.
5. Vous avez un piano dans la salle à manger.
6. La bonne apporte les assiettes.

Traduction:

At the table Philip is seated beside mother. He is not carving the roast. Father carves the roast. He likes to carve. What does Philip cut? He cuts his (sa) meat, but Mary does not cut her (sa) meat. I cut her meat. The maid brings the plates and the cherry pie to mother. What does mother cut? She cuts the cherry pie. What is this? It is a small fork.

[1] This verb requires the [ʒ] sound of g throughout the conjugation; therefore the g becomes ge before a or o. *Example:* nous mangeons.

DIX-SEPTIÈME LEÇON

A table

La famille est toujours à table.[1] Philippe parle avec grand'mère. Maman coupe la tarte en morceaux.

—Qu'est-ce que vous préférez, la salade ou la tarte, grand'mère? dit Philippe.

—J'aime la tarte et la salade, dit grand'mère.

—Et vous, papa? Qu'est-ce que vous préférez?

—Je préfère la tarte aux cerises.

—Et moi aussi, dit Philippe. J'aime toujours un gros morceau de tarte.

—Et vous‿avez toujours un gros morceau de tarte, dit maman.

La bonne apporte le café. Grand'mère, maman, et papa ont‿une petite tasse de café. Ils‿ont les petites cuillères avec les petites tasses. Les‿enfants ont‿un verre d'eau. Avez-vous toujours l'eau et le café? Nous‿avons toujours l'eau et le café.

Philippe et Marie ne restent pas‿à table. Philippe plie vite sa serviette et passe au salon. Marie plie sa serviette et passe au salon avec Philippe.

Grammaire

Present Tense of *Préférer*

You will readily recognize **préférer** as a verb of the first conjugation. You know the present tense endings so well that they will not trouble you. But note carefully the accent change throughout the singular and in the third person plural. For greater ease in pronunciation the acute accent has been changed to the grave in these four cases. The rule is that a syllable ending in acute **e** (**é**) [e] may not precede a syllable ending in mute **e** [ə].

Present	INTERROGATIVE
je préfère	Est-ce que je préfère?
tu préfères	Préfères-tu?
il préfère [2]	Préfère-t-il?
nous préférons	Préférons-nous?
vous préférez	Préférez-vous?
ils préfèrent	Préfèrent-ils?

Present Tense of *Avoir*, To Have

In English *to have* is a very common and a very useful verb. So it is in French. But as its forms are for the most part irregular, it will be necessary to learn them. Below is given the present indicative of **avoir**. Most of the forms you already know, but you have not previously seen them all together.

j'ai, *I have*	nous avons, *we have*
tu as, *you have*	vous avez, *you have*
il a, *he has*	ils ont, *they have*

---

[1] **à table**, *at the table.*
[2] From this point on, only the masculine form will be given.

Rule of Elision

A vowel is replaced by an apostrophe in the following cases:

VOWEL	IN THE WORDS	BEFORE
y, o, u	never elided	
i	si, *if*	il or ils only
a	la, *the, her*	vowel or mute h
e	ce, de, je, le, me, ne, que, se, te	vowel or mute h

Vocabulaire

l'eau [lo] (f.), *water*
la salade [la salad], *salad*
la serviette [la sɛrvjɛt], *napkin*
la tasse [la tɑːs], *cup*
le verre [lə vɛːr], *glass*

moi [mwa], *I, me*
avoir [avwaːr], *to have*
passer [pɑse], *to pass, to go*
plier [plie], *to fold*
préférer [prefere], *to prefer*

rester [rɛste], *to remain, to stay*
gros, grosse [gro, groːs], *big (usually with the idea of fat or round)*
ici [isi], *here*

Questionnaire

1. Est-ce que Philippe aime la viande?
2. Qu'est-ce que papa préfère?
3. Préférons-nous l'eau ou le café?
4. Qu'est-ce que Philippe aime?
5. Est-ce que le café est pour les enfants?
6. Qu'est-ce que les enfants ont?
7. Où restent grand'mère, maman, et papa?
8. Marie plie-t-elle sa serviette?
9. Et Philippe?
10. Où passe-t-il?
11. Aime-t-il rester à table?

Devoir

A. Learn the last sentence of "A table" by heart.

B. Conjugate the following sentences:
1. Je n'ai pas la cuillère.
2. Est-ce que je passe au salon?

C. Make these sentences interrogative:
1. Ils baissent le store.
2. Nous avons la leçon à la maison.
3. L'oiseau jaune n'est pas ici.
4. Le chat court vite après Philippe.
5. Je tire la ficelle de la boîte.
6. Les enfants restent au salon.
7. Ils jouent avec le chat.
8. Il ne voit pas l'automobile verte.

D. Make a list of the words which group themselves around one of these headings:
1. La salle de classe
2. Le salon
3. La salle à manger

Traduction:
Here is Philip. What does he like? Philip likes meat and pie, but he prefers pie. He likes a large piece of pie. He has a glass of water. Father has a glass of water and a cup of coffee. Mother and father always have two little cups of coffee. Philip does not like to fold his (sa) napkin. Mother looks at Philip, and then he folds his napkin.

By Burton Holmes from Ewing Galloway
A TYPICAL FRENCH VILLAGE STREET

DIX-HUITIÈME LEÇON

Les Adjectifs

Le professeur: Bonjour, mes élèves!

La classe: Bonjour, mademoiselle!

Le professeur: Où sont les fenêtres?

La classe: Voilà les fenêtres, mademoiselle.

Le professeur: Est-ce que les fenêtres sont grandes ou petites?

La classe: Elles sont grandes.

Le professeur: Sont-elles ouvertes?

La classe: Non, mademoiselle, elles ne sont pas ouvertes.

Le professeur: Regardez les phrases: **Elles sont très grandes. Elles ne sont pas ouvertes.** Les adjectifs sont au (*in the*) féminin et au pluriel.

Le professeur: (*Holding up a rose*) Qu'est-ce que c'est que ceci?

La classe: Une rose.

Le professeur: Oui, c'est une rose. C'est une belle rose. La rose est belle; la craie n'est pas belle. Est-ce que la rose est rose?

La classe: La rose est rouge.

Le professeur: Est-ce que vous aimez la belle rose, Robert?

Robert: Pas beaucoup, mademoiselle. Est-ce que l'adjectif précède le substantif?

Le professeur: **Belle** précède, et les autres formes de l'adjectif qui signifie *beautiful* précèdent aussi. Un autre adjectif qui précède?

Joséphine: Petite—la petite Marie.

Le professeur: Bon! Un autre, Philippe, s'il vous plaît.

Philippe: Grand—le grand tableau.

Le professeur: C'est bon! Maintenant écoutez les autres formes de l'adjectif **belle.** Voici le plancher. Le plancher n'est pas beau. Voici le cahier. Le cahier n'est pas beau. Regardez le mot—b, e, a, u. Les roses sont belles. Les cahiers ne sont pas beaux—b, e, a, u, x.

Grammaire

The Plural of Adjectives

In an earlier lesson you learned that an adjective agrees with its noun in gender; since then you have often made use of such agreement:

le papier vert   la craie verte

An adjective agrees in another way also. If the noun is plural, the adjective must be plural. Most adjectives form their plurals in the same way that nouns do, by adding -s to the masculine singular and -s to the feminine singular. This -s is not pronounced.

MASCULINE	FEMININE
le papier vert	la boîte verte
les papiers verts	les boîtes vertes

Position of Adjectives

As a general rule the adjective, in French, follows its noun. There are, however, exceptions.[1] Some short and common adjectives habitually precede the noun. Up to this point you have seen four: **petit, grand, beau, joli.**

The Irregular Adjective *Beau*

The forms of the adjective **beau** are not made in the regular way; it is therefore known as irregular.

MASCULINE	FEMININE
le beau soldat	la belle automobile
les beaux soldats	les belles automobiles

The Pronoun *Qui*, Meaning "Which"

In Lesson 16 you learned that **qui** is used as a subject, and that it means *who*. In this lesson you find it still the subject of a verb, but meaning *which*. **Qui**, then, is a subject pronoun, referring to either persons or things.

Vocabulaire

l'**adjectif** [ladʒɛktif] (m.), *adjective*
le **cahier** [lə kaje], *notebook*
le **féminin** [lə feminɛ̃], *feminine* (gender)
la **forme** [la fɔrm], *form*
la **phrase** [la fraːz], *sentence*
le **pluriel** [lə plyrjɛl], *plural* (number)
le **professeur** [lə prɔfɛsœːr], *professor, teacher*

la **rose** [la roːz], *rose*
le **substantif** [lə sypstɑ̃tif], *substantive, noun*
Robert [rɔbɛːr], *Robert*
écouter [ekute], *to listen to, to pay attention to*
former [fɔrme], *to form, to make*
indiquer [ɛ̃dike], *to point to, to indicate*
précéder [presɛde], *to precede*

signifier [siɲifje], *to signify, to mean* (il **signifie,** *it means*)
ils sont [il sõ] (inf. **être**), *they are*
autre [oːtr], *other*
beau, bel, belle, beaux, belles [bo, bɛl, bɛl, bo, bɛl], *beautiful, fine, good, handsome*
ouvert [uvɛːr], *open*

---

[1]We are not here concerned with differences in meaning according to the position of the adjective.

Questionnaire

1. Les fenêtres sont-elles petites?
2. Que signifie le mot **sont**?
3. Qu'est-ce que le professeur regarde?
4. Est-ce que la rose est jaune?
5. Est-ce que les roses sont toujours rouges?
6. Le petit salon est-il beau?
7. Indiquez le substantif dans la première phrase, s'il vous plaît.
8. Regardez-vous les beaux **tableaux**?
9. Marie regarde-t-elle la belle rue?
10. Est-ce que vous aimez les **belles** illustrations?
11. Donnez-moi un adjectif qui précède le substantif. Un autre. Un autre.
12. Donnez le pluriel de l'adjectif **beau**.

Devoir

A. Write 1 and 2 of the "Questionnaire" in phonetic characters.

B. Use the definite article and an adjective with each of the following nouns:

rideau	bicyclette	chaises
locomotives	bonnets	oiseau
drapeaux	histoire	stylo
aventure	journaux	couteau

C. Complete the verb-forms:

1. Je sai— form— le pluriel.
2. Ferm— la fenêtre, s'il vous plaît.
3. Marie regarde— -elle la fenêtre ouverte?
4. Est-ce que vous aim— une salade?
5. Il ne pli— pas la serviette.
6. Nous trouv— les mouchoirs dans le tiroir.

D. Write the following sentences in the negative:

1. J'ai le cahier.
2. Indiquez la phrase.
3. Regarde-t-il le drapeau?
4. Nous aimons le journal.
5. Avez-vous un chat?
6. A-t-elle le verre?

Traduction:

Look at the teacher. She has a beautiful rose. It is a red rose. Mary likes the beautiful rose. The teacher points to (**indique**) the floor. Is the floor beautiful?

The floor is not beautiful, but look at the beautiful pictures. The pictures are really very beautiful.

In the living-room we have a lamp. It is small, but it is very beautiful. Grandmother has a small yellow bird. What have you? Grandmother kisses Mary. She likes the little girl.

DIX-NEUVIÈME LEÇON
L' Adjectif démonstratif

Le professeur: Regardez la rose aujourd'hui. Est-_elle belle?

La classe: Elle n'est pas belle aujourd'hui.

Le professeur: Cette rose n'est pas belle. Cette rose est fanée. Cette craie est blanche. Cette bibliothèque est petite. Le mot **cette** signifie *this* ou *that*. Ce plancher n'est pas beau. Ce plafond n'est pas beau. Que signifie **ce?**

La classe: **Ce** signifie *this* ou *that*. C'est le masculin.

Le professeur: Bon! Employez **ce** ou **cette**. (*Le professeur indique les objets.*)

La classe: Cette chaise. Cette boîte. Ce tableau. Cette fenêtre. Ce store. Ce stylo.

Le professeur: L'article est **le** au masculin (*in the masculine*), n'est-ce pas?

Et le pluriel est **les**. Le pluriel de **ce**, Marguerite?

Marguerite: Est-ce **ces?**

Le professeur: Oui, Marguerite. Ces livres, ces fenêtres, ces cartes, ces tableaux. Au pluriel la forme est toujours **ces**, au masculin et au féminin. Ces pupitres—Continuez. (*Le professeur indique les objets.*)

La classe: Cette encre. Ce papier. Ces devoirs. Cette carte.

Le professeur: Bon! Regardez ce mot **oiseau**. Il est_au masculin. Cet_oiseau. Oiseau est_au masculin, mais_il commence par une voyelle. Cet_oiseau. Regardez le mot **arbre** —cet_arbre.

Emilie: Est-ce que le pluriel de **cet** arbre est **ces**_arbres, mademoiselle?

Le professeur: Oui, le pluriel de **ce**, **cet**, ou **cette** est **ces**. Ces_arbres.

Grammaire
The Demonstrative Adjective

The demonstrative adjective points out the noun it limits. **It is a sign** which says *this* or *that* (singular) or *these* or *those* (plural).[1] The forms of the demonstrative adjective are:

Singular	*Plural*
MAS. ce livre, *this* (or *that*) *book*	ces livres, *these* (or *those*) *books*
MAS. cet oiseau, *this bird*	ces oiseaux, *these birds*
FEM. cette rose, *this rose*	ces roses, *these roses*

Like all other adjectives, the demonstrative *agrees in gender and number with the noun it limits.*

Cet is used only before a masculine singular noun beginning with a vowel.

Review of the Adjective *Beau*

Review the forms of the adjective **beau** which appeared in the preceding lesson. Observe here the additional form **bel**, that corresponds to **cet**.

le beau livre, *the beautiful book*	les beaux livres, *the beautiful books*
le bel oiseau, *the beautiful bird*	les beaux oiseaux, *the beautiful birds*
la belle rose, *the beautiful rose*	les belles roses, *the beautiful roses*

[1] The more definite way of saying *this* and *that* will be taken up later.

Vocabulaire

l'arbre [larbr] (m.), *tree*
l'article [lartikl] (m.), *article*
la bibliothèque [la bibli-
ɔtɛk], *library, bookcase*
l'encre [lɑ̃:kr] (f.), *ink*
le masculin [lə maskylɛ̃],
masculine (gender)
l'objet [lɔbʒɛ] (m.), *object*
le plafond [lə plafɔ̃], *ceiling*
le pupitre [lə pypitr], *desk*
le singulier [lə sɛ̃gylje],
singular (number)

la voyelle [la vwajɛl], *vowel*
Marguerite [margərit],
Margaret
commencer [kɔmɑ̃se], *to
begin*
continuer [kɔ̃tinɥe], *to continue*
employer [ɑ̃plwaje], *to use,
to employ*
ce, cet, cette, ces [sə, sɛt,
sɛt, se], *this, that, these,
those*

démonstratif [demɔ̃stratif],
demonstrative
fané [fane], *faded*
aujourd'hui [oʒurdɥi], *today*
n'est-ce pas? [nɛs pɑ],
isn't it, doesn't one?
qu'est-ce que c'est que [kɛs
kə sɛ kə], *what is*
par [pa:r], *by, with, through*

Questionnaire

1. Est-ce que cette rose est belle?
2. Regardez-vous cette petite bibliothèque?
3. Que signifie le mot **ce**?
4. Indiquez le store.
5. Indiquez quatre (*four*) objets.
6. Employez une forme de **ce** avec
chaise; avec **chaises**.

7. Employez une forme de **beau**
avec **bibliothèque**; avec **livres**;
avec **arbre**.
8. Est-ce que le singulier est toujours **ce**?
9. Donnez le pluriel de **ce**, de **cet**,
et de **cette**.
10. Parlez-vous en classe?

Devoir

A. *Take one sentence, indicated by the
teacher, and practice it aloud.*

B. *Use the correct form of* **ce** *or* **ce
beau**. *One dash indicates a form
of* **ce**; *two dashes indicate a form
of* **ce beau**.

1. Philippe lit —— journal.
2. Il regarde —— —— illustration.
3. Vous coupez —— tarte.
4. Papa donne —— roses à maman.
5. —— —— chats sont noirs.
6. —— store est vert.
7. Alors la bonne apporte ——
assiettes.
8. Regardez —— oiseau.
9. Je regarde —— —— oiseau.
10. Voilà la petite Marie qui joue
avec —— grande poupée.
11. —— —— automobiles sont ici.
12. Où est —— arbre?
13. Les chats mangent-ils ——
viande?

C. *Go through the reading lessons, pick-
ing out the nouns and saying aloud*
ce livre, cette gomme, cet arbre,
*etc. Be careful both to give the
correct form of the demonstrative
adjective and to pronounce each
sound correctly.*

Traduction:

What is it? It is a bird. No, it is
an airplane. I am looking at the airplane. That airplane is really large.

Charles is looking at those bicycles.
They are large. He likes bicycles.
He is looking at that red bicycle. It
is large.

Father carves the roast. He raises
that large knife and that large fork.
We have these small knives and
these small forks. We have also these
small spoons. Josephine has that
small spoon. What is this? It is a
plate.

VINGTIÈME LEÇON
Review

A

1. What are the present tense endings for a verb of the first conjugation?

2. Use **que** and **qu'est-ce que** in questions.

3. What letter is usually added to form the plural of a noun in French?

4. Is this letter pronounced?

5. Where is the French adjective usually placed, before or after the noun?

6. Can you mention any exceptions to this rule?

7. How does an adjective agree with its noun? Give examples.

8. What is the function of a demonstrative adjective?

9. What are the forms of **ce**?

10. What are the forms of **beau**?

11. How is the negative of a sentence formed in French?

12. What effect has **est-ce que** upon a sentence?

13. Make this sentence interrogative (two ways): **Il court vite après le chat.**

14. What are the forms of the definite article? Of the indefinite article?

B

I. Use the correct form of the demonstrative adjective with each of these nouns:

rose   assiette   oiseau   enfants
rôti   cuillères   livres   professeur

II. Conjugate these sentences:

1. Je n'ai pas le journal.
2. Je continue la phrase.
3. Je préfère cette histoire.

III. Complete the verb-forms:

1. Nous apport— les assiettes.
2. Il découp— le rôti.
3. Vous mang— le dîner.
4. Je pass— le verre.
5. Ils pli— la serviette.
6. Elle aim— la poupée.
7. Ils trouv—— les cahiers là.
8. Nous indiqu—la liste de phrases.
9. Le mot arbre commenc— par une voyelle.
10. Nous ramass— la ficelle.

IV. Make the sentences of III negative.

V. Review the vocabularies of Lessons 1-19 for a written or an oral test. (The teacher may prefer to have a spell-down on the words.)

PHONETIC REVIEW

Practice:

wi, we, wɛ, wa, wɑ, wɔ, wu, wɛ̃
yn, ym, yr, yd, yl, yp, ys, yt
ji, je, jɛ, ja, jɑ, jɔ, jo, ju
ɥi, ɥe, ɥɛ, ɥa, ɥɑ, ɥɔ

Pronounce and write the following words in phonetic symbols:

voici, papier, petite fille, illustration, pluriel, signifier, sur, rue, tiroir, cuillère, serviette, plier, singulier, voyelle, continuer

Read aloud:

Voilà l'assiette. Voici la cuillère. Employez-vous la serviette? N'étudiez pas à table. Fermez votre cahier.

Donnez le singulier de l'article d'un mot qui commence par une voyelle.

Words for Practice in Pronunciation

livre	j'ai	quoi	tableau	serviette	vous
aussi	avez	noir	rose	papier	ou
merci	fermez	voici	maîtresse	dans	rouge
indiquer	ouvrez	mademoiselle	plancher	blanc	sur

Archives du Touring-Club de France

THE RUGGED BRETON COAST

TWO FRENCH PROVINCES

For the better administration of the affairs of its people France is today divided into eighty-nine different *départements* (districts). These *départements* most frequently take their names from the rivers or mountains that intersect them, for example: Seine, Marne, Vosges, Loire, Bouches du Rhône, Jura. But not very long ago each separate region of France was called, not a *département*, but a province. And this region was usually sharply walled off from its neighboring provinces by natural boundaries, so that the special character of its home landscape seems to have reflected itself in the souls of its inhabitants. There were in older days more than thirty such provinces, the most famous of which were Normandy, Brittany, Picardy, Burgundy, Champagne, Touraine, Gascony, Dauphiny, Provence, and Savoy. Therefore, when one wishes to speak of some particular type of Frenchman in terms of his birthplace, one never uses the name of a *département*, which signifies a purely mechanical division, but the name of a province, which helps to explain a Frenchman's racial peculiarities.

Normandy and Brittany are two of the most interesting provinces—Normandy, because of the profound influence it had on the English language, especially after the Norman Conquest (1066); Brittany, because of the important characteristics it received from the Celts, many of whom wandered across the English Channel from Britain after the Saxon Invasion (fifth century). Besides their historical significance, these two provinces in the northwest of France are most often visited by tourists because the simple conditions of life there seem picturesque and quaint.

Although they border on each other, the two provinces are very different.

Brittany is a land of rugged shores and stony fields; Normandy is a garden country.

The history of Normandy is an unusual one. Early in the tenth century men from Scandinavia (called Norsemen or Northmen) invaded the valley of the Seine. They were attracted to that region because of the fertile earth that makes it a stretch of mellow rural countryside today. Its blue skies and mild climate appealed strongly to the adventurers from the cold land of the north. The expedition was led by Rollo the Viking, who was to be an ancestor of dukes of Normandy and of William the Conqueror. To this day Normans of pure race bear the stamp of their Scandinavian forefathers. They are a sturdy race, fair of skin and hair. In disposition they are more akin to the northern peoples than to others of the French race.

By the Battle of Hastings (1066), William the Conqueror became king of the island across the Channel from Normandy. Thereafter many French words became a living part of English speech. Today it is easy to trace the difference between simple Anglo-Saxon terms and later French expressions. Architecture of the Norman fashion also spread with little change across to England. The Norman style of building is, like the people themselves, extremely robust. Size and solidity prevail. The builders erected structures that have stood as lasting monuments of their power.

Normandy has many interesting cities. Rouen, its largest town, is on the Seine, about ninety miles from Paris. It has a commodious port crowded with the ships of all nations. The older section of the city has narrow streets lined with quaintly carved, wood-bound houses. Many of these structures, which run to a point in high gables, date back to the Middle Ages. Their Norman type of building is evident in the strange, toppling appearance of the houses, each of whose stories overhangs slightly the one below it, creating the impression of an inverted flight of steps. The upper stories have white cement walls held

AN OLD HOUSE IN ROUEN

A SMALL PART OF THE BAYEUX TAPESTRY

firm by hewn rafters. The streets are so narrow that lodgers in these uppermost floors might almost shake hands with their neighbors across the way. The market place of Rouen is famous because Joan of Arc, the great heroine of France, was burned at the stake there.

One must not leave Normandy without a rapid glance at Bayeux. This small town of scarcely 8000 inhabitants has attracted world-wide attention because of the so-called Bayeux tapestry, a strip of linen cloth about 214 feet long and twenty inches wide embroidered in colors. This tapestry, believed by some authorities to be the work of the wife of William the Conqueror, is of great historical importance because its figures disclose vivid information regarding the costumes and the methods of waging war common to its day. Its many scenes depict William's conquest of England.

Besides the two ports Havre and Cherbourg, where transatlantic liners come and go, the Norman sea-coast is dotted with summer resorts, which the French—particularly the Parisians —visit in great numbers. Here are fashionable watering-places and humble fishing villages, which offer alike

the recreation and the sunny climate for which Normandy is noted.

Brittany is the great peninsula that you see projecting into the Atlantic at the extreme northwest of France. Here lies the somber and dreary land that, especially in winter, would seem to repel even its own people; for they turn to the sea for their livelihood and become the most marvelous of fishermen. These Bretons are men marked by the gloom of ocean's danger and monotony. Their wives and daughters are as strong and sunburned as the men. They clack about in wooden shoes, as they help with the nets and the boats. The only feminine thing about the Breton woman is the snowy cap, the style of which varies according to locality. Brittany's shores are filled with people whose watchful faces are forever turned seaward. It is only the children who wait for treasures to be washed in with the tide. Older folk are fearful of disaster.

Those Bretons who fear the sea and cling to the soil, in spite of its hostility, depend on grazing for their daily bread. All day long they see only the herds of small cows that keep starvation away. A few cliffs bare of foliage

Keystone View Co., N. Y.

BRETON FISHERMEN

rise here and there across the lonely scene, to break the stretches of heather that meet the far horizon like the purpling waters of another open sea.

Thus there are two distinct zones in Brittany—the maritime coast with its lacework of indented bays, its dangerous reefs, and islets where dwell the famous fishermen; and the inland pastures where men wear brilliant red, blue, or violet waistcoats and women wear the same gay colors in the full skirts of that region. Brittany is one of the really primitive districts of France. Scenes that are familiar enough to us from pictures come suddenly to life: women washing at the river's edge, and dogs harnessed to queer heavy carts.

The British Celts who fled from the invading Saxons to this old province left behind them two definite imprints of their settlement here, fourteen hundred years ago: the name of the land, Brittany, and the Celtic language, that is still spoken in the lower parts of the region today. These British Celts

were a highly imaginative and sensitive people. Because of this Brittany is a land of fairy-wisdom and folklore. Druid stones that served in the sacred rites of ancient priests are a present object of worship to the credulous Bretons. They believe these huge stones are of magic origin. Mount Saint Michael—the rocky crag off the coast on which is built a magnificent monastery—is thought to be a stepping stone hurled into the sea by a French giant to help him reach England when King Arthur needed his aid.

The Bretons are passionate lovers of their homeland. A famous duchess of that province who became queen of France had her heart sent back to Brittany when she died. People here cling to their old customs. They wear the same dress they have worn for centuries. They think much the same thoughts their ancestors thought.

Curiously unlike each other, and yet close together, lie Normandy and Brittany. Both are of uncommon historical interest, both are picturesque.

Keystone View Co., N. Y.

A BRETON WOMAN MENDING A NET

VINGT ET UNIÈME LEÇON*

Raton et les⌣Enfants

Raton, le chat, est dans le jardin. Marcelle est dans le jardin et Pierrot aussi. Raton est très gros. Il aime jouer avec les⌣enfants. Il ne désire pas jouer maintenant. Il ferme ses gros⌣yeux jaunes, et il pense. Oui, Raton pense. Le petit⌣oiseau est dans le jardin. Raton avance.

Voilà le petit⌣oiseau qui chante dans l'arbre. Raton regarde l'oiseau. Pierrot a un morceau de pain. Il parle.

—Petit⌣oiseau, voilà le pain blanc. Il est pour vous.† Cherchez le morceau pour le dîner. J'aime le petit⌣oiseau.

L'oiseau arrive. Marcelle ne bouge pas. Pierrot ne bouge pas. L'oiseau descend de la branche pour manger le morceau de pain.

Regardez Raton. Il bondit. Il a le petit⌣oiseau. L'oiseau crie. Raton est content. Il court. Il sait que Marcelle n'aime pas⌣un chat qui mange les⌣oiseaux. Raton revient. Il a l'air innocent. Il demande des caresses. Il aime les caresses.

—Non, Raton. Je ne vous⌣aime pas. Vous mangez les⌣oiseaux. Je ne vous⌣aime pas.

Raton n'est pas content. Il aime les caresses.

Pierrot avance avec un bout de ficelle. Il a toujours un bout de ficelle dans sa poche. Il joue avec Raton. Raton pense que c'est l'oiseau. Il est fatigué et il monte sur le grand¹⌣arbre. Il est sur la branche. Il ferme les²⌣yeux. Il ouvre les⌣yeux. Il regarde Pierrot.

Pierrot ramasse un petit caillou. Il regarde le caillou. Il regarde la maison. Maman n'est pas là. Il lance le caillou. Raton regarde. Il ne bouge pas.

Oh! le caillou ne touche pas Raton. Pierrot est fort . . . le caillou frappe avec force la fenêtre. Voilà maman qui arrive.

—Pierrot, le dîner est servi. Vous⌣aimez beaucoup la tarte aux cerises. Elle n'est pas pour vous. Elle est pour les⌣enfants qui sont sages.

Vocabulaire

le caillou [lə kaju] (pl. les cailloux), *pebble*

le dîner [lə dine], *dinner*

le jardin [lə ʒardɛ̃], *garden*

la maison [la mezõ], *house*

le pain [lə pɛ̃], *bread, loaf of bread*

les yeux [lezjø] (m.pl.), *eyes*

Marcelle [marsɛl], *Marcella*

Pierrot [pjɛro], *Peter*

Raton [ratõ], there is no English equivalent

il bondit [il bõdi], *he jumps, he leaps*

bouger [buʒe], *to move, to budge*; ne bouge pas [nə buʒ pa], *does not move*

chanter [ʃɑ̃te], *to sing*

désirer [dezire], *to desire, to wish, to want*

frapper [frape], *to strike, to hit*

lancer [lɑ̃se], *to fling*

monter [mõte], *to go up, to rise*

penser [pɑ̃se], *to think, to think of*

il revient [rəvjɛ̃] (inf. revenir), *he returns*

content [kõtɑ̃], *happy, satisfied, glad* (takes de before an infinitive)

fort [fɔːr], *strong*

sage [saːʒ], *good, wise*

qui [ki], *who, which, that*

des [de], *some*

ses [se] (pl.), *his, her, its*

que [kə], *that* (conjunction)

---

* *Note to the Teacher;* See page vii.
† *Note to the Teacher:* To avoid confusion **vous** will be used instead of **tu** until the pupils are more familiar with the language.
¹ This **d** should be pronounced [t].
² Translated as *his* (or *her* or *your*, etc.). In French when there is no doubt as to possession, the definite article is commonly used.

Vocabulaire (Continued)

English Equivalents

The following new words appeared in "Raton et les Enfants," but you were able to read them without help from a vocabulary list because they were exactly like the English words of the same meaning, or were very similar in their appearance.

l'air [le:r] (m.), *air, look, manner*

la branche [la brã:ʃ], *branch*

la caresse [la karɛs], *caress*

la force [la fɔrs], *force, strength*

arriver [arive], *to arrive, to come*

avancer [avãse], *to advance*

demander [dəmãde], *to demand, to ask, to ask for*

il descend [il desã] (inf. **descendre**), *he descends, goes down*

toucher [tuʃe], *to touch*

crier [krie], *to cry*

innocent [inɔsã], *innocent*

VINGT-DEUXIÈME LEÇON

Conversation en classe

(Charles parle à un autre élève. Il parle comme le professeur.)

Charles: Voici la classe. Cette classe est la classe de français. Regardez le plancher, s'il vous plaît. Ce plancher n'est pas beau. Voilà la rose. Cette rose est belle. Ces fenêtres sont petites. Cet arbre est vert. Cette porte est grande.

(Le professeur arrive.)

Le Professeur: Bon. Charles sait les adjectifs démonstratifs. Bonjour, mes élèves.

La Classe: Bonjour, mademoiselle.

Le Professeur: Regardez le verbe au (*on the*) tableau:

Finir

je finis, *I finish, I am finishing*, etc.
tu finis, *you finish*, etc.
il finit, *he finishes*, etc.
nous finissons, *we finish*, etc.
vous finissez, *you finish*, etc.
ils finissent, *they finish*, etc.

Finir est un verbe de la deuxième conjugaison. La terminaison de l'infinitif est -ir. Cherchez les autres terminaisons des verbes en -ir.

La Classe: -is, -is, -it, -issons, -issez, -issent.

Le Professeur: La terminaison de l'infinitif d'un verbe de la deuxième conjugaison est toujours -ir. Les autres terminaisons sont toujours -is, -is, -it, -issons, -issez, -issent. Répondez en français, s'il vous plaît. Finissez-vous l'histoire, Marie?

Marie: Non, mademoiselle, je ne finis pas l'histoire.

Le Professeur: Finissons-nous ce verbe?

Joseph: Nous finissons ce verbe.

Le Professeur: Les élèves finissent-ils le livre vert?

Philippe: Oui, mademoiselle, ils finissent le livre vert.

Le Professeur: Est-ce que Charles finit la leçon?

La Classe: Non, mademoiselle, Charles ne finit pas la leçon.

Charles: C'est le professeur qui finit la leçon.

Grammaire

The Second Conjugation

You have used numerous examples of the first conjugation verbs, whose infinitives end in -er. Now you come to verbs of the second conjugation, whose infinitives have the ending -ir. To form the present tense, indicative mood, of an -ir verb you proceed as you did with verbs of the first conjugation: get the stem, or radical, by dropping the sign of the infinitive (-ir), and then add the personal endings. None of them corresponds to those of the -er verbs. We will take the verb **finir**, *to finish*, as a model.

Present Tense of *Finir*, To Finish

fin ir = infinitive
fin = stem

SINGULAR	PLURAL
je fin **is**, *I finish, am finishing, etc.*	nous fin **issons**, *we finish*
tu fin **is**, *you finish*	vous fin **issez**, *you finish*
il fin **it**, *he finishes*	ils fin **issent**, *they finish*

Vocabulaire

la conjugaison [kɔ̃ʒygɛzɔ̃], *conjugation*
le français [frɑ̃sɛ], *French*
l'infinitif [lɛ̃finitif] (m.), *infinitive*
la porte [pɔrt], *door*

la terminaison [tɛrminɛzɔ̃], *ending, termination*
le verbe [vɛrb], *verb*
Joseph [ʒozɛf], *Joseph*
finir [finiːr], *to finish*
anglais [ãglɛ], *English*

deuxième [døzjɛm], *second*
français [frɑ̃sɛ], *French (adj.)*
comme [kɔm], *like, as, in the manner of*

Questionnaire

1. Chantez-vous en classe?
2. Est-ce que vous parlez à un autre élève?
3. Charles parle-t-il comme le professeur?
4. Qu'est-ce que Charles sait?
5. Est-ce qu'il sait le verbe *finir*?
6. Est-ce que la terminaison de l'infinitif de la deuxième conjugaison est -ir?
7. Finissez-vous toujours la leçon?
8. Grand'mère finit-elle le petit bonnet?
9. Finissons-nous ce verbe?
10. Finissez-vous la deuxième conjugaison?
11. Arrivez-vous en classe avec le professeur ou avec un autre élève?
12. Cherchez dans ce questionnaire un mot qui commence par une voyelle.
13. Avez-vous un petit chat?
14. Charles, sait-il parler français comme le professeur?
15. Donnez les formes de l'adjectif démonstratif.
16. Les élèves aiment-ils le français?

Archives du Touring-Club de France

WOMEN WASHING CLOTHES IN A STREAM IN BRITTANY

Devoir

A. Change to the correct verb-forms:

1. Nous (baisser) le store.
2. Vous (tirer) les rideaux verts.
3. En classe je ne (parler) pas.
4. Ils (avoir) les journaux anglais avec les belles illustrations.
5. Ne (passer) -elle pas au salon?
6. (Préférer) -ils rester dans la salle à manger?
7. Nous (finir) le dîner, et nous (plier) la serviette.
8. (Employer) cette forme de la deuxième conjugaison.
9. Il (finir) ce mot.
10. Ils (finir) ces mots et ils (fermer) les livres.
11. Les soldats (trouver) les objets, n'est-ce pas?
12. Le substantif (précéder) l'adjectif, n'est-ce pas?
13. (Continuer) la conjugaison.
14. (Etre) -elle fatiguée?

B. Complete each of the following sentences by using the correct form of ce *or* ce beau:

1. —— adjectif est démonstratif.
2. —— —— porte est petite.
3. Regardez —— aéroplane dans —— —— illustration.
4. Ne cherchez pas —— mots.
5. J'ai —— —— verres.
6. Qu'est-ce que c'est que —— objet?
7. Elle voit —— —— arbre.

Traduction:

Do you always look for beautiful objects? These illustrations are really beautiful. Look at this red bird. He is very small. He sees another bird. This illustration is very good.

"Give me (moi) the string, please."

"Thank you."

"You are welcome."

VINGT-TROISIÈME LEÇON

Marie et Josette

Marie et Josette finissent la leçon de français. Elles répètent ensemble le verbe **finir**. Elles répètent les formes ensemble. Elles trouvent les formes faciles. Elles sont assises au salon. Maman n'est pas là. Elle est dans la salle à manger avec grand'-mère. Elles tricotent et elles parlent ensemble.

—Je sais la leçon, dit Marie. Les formes de **finir** sont faciles, n'est-ce pas?

—Les formes de **finir** ne sont pas très difficiles, dit Josette, mais je ne sais pas ces formes.

—Finissez vite, dit Marie. Je préfère écouter la T. S. F. Regardez le verbe, Josette. Alors fermez le livre et répétez le verbe.

—C'est ce que je vais faire, dit Josette.

Elle regarde le verbe. Elle ferme le livre. Elle répète le verbe.

—Je sais le verbe, dit Josette. Les verbes ne sont pas vraiment très difficiles. J'aime beaucoup le français.

Les deux jeunes filles sont au salon chez Marie. Elles aiment le salon rose et gris, les jolies lampes électriques, et les chaises confortables. Marie est assise sur le sofa, et Josette est assise sur une belle chaise. Elles écoutent la T. S. F.

—Ecoutez cette musique, dit Josette. Elle est belle, n'est-ce pas? Vous aimez cette musique, n'est-ce pas, Marie?

—J'aime assez cette musique, dit Marie. Mais je préfère danser ou chanter. Voilà la musique que j'aime.

(*Les deux jeunes filles dansent ensemble.*)

Grammaire

The Imperative

The form of the imperative second person plural, for both first and second conjugations, is just the same as the second person plural of the present indicative, omitting the subject pronoun.

	Infinitive	*Present Indicative*	*Imperative*
FIRST CONJUGATION	regarder	vous regardez	regardez
SECOND CONJUGATION	finir	vous finissez	finissez

In answering an imperative sentence in French you may use the phrase **avec plaisir** (*with pleasure*), or sometimes **c'est ce que je vais faire** (*that's what I am going to do*). The answer will, of course, depend on what has been said.

Philippe, répétez la conjugaison de **finir**.
Avec plaisir, mademoiselle.

Josette, pliez la serviette et passez au salon.
C'est ce que je vais faire, maman.

There are other expressions besides these, which you will learn as you go on.

The Use of *N'est-ce pas*

The expression **n'est-ce pas** is so useful that you must be able to use it. **N'est-ce pas** is attached at the end of a declarative sentence, and makes it interrogative. Such a question is used when an affirmative answer is expected, that is, an answer which means *yes*.

J'ai le livre rouge, n'est-ce pas? *I have the red book, haven't I?*
C'est un joli livre, n'est-ce pas? *It's a pretty book, isn't it?*
Ils répètent la phrase, n'est-ce pas? *They repeat the sentence, don't they?*

Observe that **n'est-ce pas** is used with any person of the verb. We have to change in English, but in French the **n'est-ce pas** is invariable.

The Use of *Que*

The word **que** is often a pronoun used as the direct object of a verb. Since the pronoun may refer to persons or things, it may be translated *whom, which, that*. **Que** becomes **qu'** before **il, elle, ils,** or **elles**.

C'est papa qu'il voit. *It is father whom he sees.*
Voilà la musique que j'aime. *That is the music which I like.*

In the first sentence **que** is the direct object of **voit** (he sees *whom*); in the second sentence **que** is the direct object of **aime** (I like *which*).

Vocabulaire

la musique [myzik], *music*
la T. S. F. [te ɛs ɛf], *radio*
télégraphie sans fil [telegrafi sɑ̃ fil] (*wireless telegraphy*) (T. S. F.)
Josette [ʒozɛt], *Josie*
danser [dɑ̃se], *to dance*
remplir [rɑ̃pliːr], *to fill*

répéter [repete], *to repeat*
que [kə], *whom, which, that*
difficile [difisil], *difficult, hard*
facile [fasil], *easy*
assez [ase], *enough, well enough, rather, somewhat*

avec plaisir [avɛk pleziːr], *with pleasure*
ensemble [ɑ̃sɑ̃ːbl], *together*
chez [ʃe], *at, at the house of, at the home of*
c'est ce que je vais faire [sɛs kəʒ ve fɛːr], *that is what I am going to do*

Questionnaire

1. Qu'est-ce que Marie et Josette finissent?
2. Où sont-elles?
3. Qu'est-ce qu'elles répètent?
4. Est-ce que les formes de finir sont très difficiles?
5. Est-ce que Marie préfère répéter les verbes ou écouter la T. S. F.? Et vous, que préférez-vous?
6. Ecoutez-vous la T. S. F. chez Marie?
7. Josette aime-t-elle vraiment cette musique?
8. Aimez-vous danser?
9. Marie et Josette dansent-elles toujours chez Marie?
10. Chantez-vous comme un oiseau?
11. Préférez-vous danser ou préférez-vous chanter?
12. Ecoutez-vous la T. S. F. à la maison ou écoutez-vous la T. S. F. chez Marie?

Devoir

A. Work on the first two sentences of B, below, for the correct pronunciation of each vowel sound.

B. Conjugate:

1. Je répète le verbe. (**Répéter** follows the model of **préférer**.)
2. Je remplis la boîte de morceaux de papier.
3. Est-ce que je finis la leçon sur le pluriel?
4. Je frappe à la porte.

C. Make these sentences interrogative:

1. Il n'aime pas danser dans le jardin.
2. Nous préférons cette bibliothèque.
3. Ils écoutent la musique du piano.
4. J'écoute cette histoire d'aventure.
5. Vous dansez avec Robert.
6. Philippe est assis, et il lit le journal.

7. La bonne apporte la salade avec le pain.
8. Il a sa serviette et un verre d'eau.
9. Il ne voit pas l'encre rouge sur le pupitre.
10. J'ai ces verres jaunes.

D. With each of the following nouns use the correct form of (1) the definite article; and (2) the demonstrative adjective.

1. plafond	9. arbre
2. stores	10. tapis
3. balle	11. gomme
4. élève	12. maîtresse
5. grammaire	13. encre
6. stylo	14. tasses
7. tiroirs	15. tableau
8. automobiles	16. assiette

E. Composition: Write a dialogue in French between a boy and his little sister who are looking at the newspaper.

SOME OF THE MENHIRS OF BRITTANY, MANY OF WHICH ARE
OVER FIFTEEN FEET HIGH

VINGT-QUATRIÈME LEÇON
Le Journal en classe

(*Le professeur et les élèves. Charles a un journal. Il lit le journal. Le professeur regarde Charles.*)

Le professeur: Avez-vous un journal ici, Charles?

Charles: Oui, mademoiselle. Voici le journal. Il est très intéressant. C'est un journal français, *Le Figaro.*

Le professeur: Lisez-vous ce journal?

Charles: Oh, non, mademoiselle, je ne sais pas assez le français pour lire un journal français. Je trouve quelques[1] mots que je sais. Je trouve douze mots que je sais dans cet article. Mais j'ai une question à vous poser. Est-ce que le mot **pour** signifie *to*, mademoiselle?

Le professeur: Le mot **pour** signifie *to* ou *in order to*. Il est employé avec l'infinitif. J'ouvre la grammaire pour chercher ce verbe. Il court à la fenêtre pour regarder l'automobile. Donnez-moi une autre phrase où vous employez le mot **pour**.

Marie: Nous répétons le français pour prononcer comme le professeur.

Le professeur: C'est une bonne phrase. A vous, Philippe.

Philippe: Charles cherche dans le journal français pour trouver les mots qu'il sait.

Le professeur: Bon. A vous, Charles.

Charles: Je mets le journal de côté pour parler avec le professeur.

Grammaire

The Infinitive after *Pour*

When the French wish to express purpose (*in order to*), they use the preposition **pour** and the infinitive. Note that English does not require the literal translation of the purpose phrase.

Il ouvre le tiroir pour chercher le stylo.
He opens the drawer to look for the fountain-pen.

Elle met la poupée de côté pour jouer avec le chat.
She puts the doll aside to play with the cat.

Vocabulaire

le chapeau [ʃapo] (pl. les chapeaux), *hat*
l'orange [lɔrã:ʒ] (f.), *orange*
le présent [prezã], *present* (tense of verb), *present time*
la question [kɛstjõ], *question*
ajouter [aʒute], *to add*

donnez-moi [dɔne mwa], *give me*
vous lisez[2] [vu lize], *you read*
prononcer [prɔnõse], *to pronounce*
j'ai une question à vous poser [ʒe yn kɛstjõ a vu poze], *I have a question to ask you*

douze [du:z], *twelve*
employé [ãplwaje], *used, employed*
quelque [kɛlkə], *some;* quelques [kɛlkə], *few*
à vous [a vu], *you next*
de côté [də kote], *aside*
du [dy] (m. sing.), *of the, from the*
où [u], *where, in which*

---

[1] Although **quelque** (singular) means *some*, the plural, **quelques**, means *few* or *a few*.
[2] **Vous lisez** is a form of the irregular verb **lire**. Learn each form of **lire** as it appears in the lessons.

Questionnaire

1. Qu'est-ce que Charles lit?
2. Trouve-t-il le journal intéressant?
3. Est-ce un journal américain ou un journal français?
4. Qu'est-ce que Charles trouve dans le journal? Trouve-t-il le mot soldat?
5. Sait-il assez le français pour lire le journal?
6. Les bons élèves prononcent-ils comme le professeur?
7. Apportent-ils les grammaires en classe?
8. Lisez-vous le journal en classe?
9. Est-ce qu'ils parlent français en classe?
10. Donnez le présent du verbe aimer.
11. Que signifie le mot serviette?

Devoir

A. *Learn the last sentence of "Le Journal en classe" by heart.*

B. *Conjugate these sentences:*
  1. Est-ce que j'ai un journal américain?
  2. Je tourne la carte.

C. *Complete the verb-forms:*
  1. Vous rest— à la maison.
  2. Ils indiqu— les objets sur la table.
  3. Commenc— -vous la leçon?
  4. Ajout— e à l'adjectif.
  5. Répét— -vous la phrase?
  6. Il a le couteau noir pour coup— l'orange.
  7. Philippe aim— -il les pommes de terre?
  8. Répét— -vous la voyelle a?
  9. Est-ce que je li— cette histoire avec plaisir?
  10. Li— -il cet article dans le journal?

  11. Nous av— une belle lampe rose.
  12. Pass— la viande à maman.
  13. Ferm— -ils les yeux?
  14. Le petit chat aime jou— sur le tapis.
  15. Philippe sai — douze mots dans le journal français.

Traduction:

Philip goes to the open window to look at the automobiles. He sees the green automobile. Mother and grandmother are talking. They are not talking to Philip.

There is father. He says "Good-day." He kisses the family. Then they go (passent) to the dining-room. They eat and talk. We talk a great deal at the table (à table). Do you carve? No, father carves. Mother cuts the meat for Mary. Mary is very small. She has a spoon. What is that? It is the cherry pie.

VINGT-CINQUIÈME LEÇON
Trois garçons

Voici Michel dans la rue. Il va à l'école. Il marche lentement. Pourquoi marche-t-il lentement? Parce qu'il préfère rester à la maison. Pourquoi préfère-t-il rester à la maison? Parce qu'il ne sait pas sa leçon d'algèbre[1] aujourd'hui. Quelquefois il aime aller à l'école, mais pas aujourd'hui.

Voilà Robert et Charles qui passent au coin. Michel voit les garçons. Il court après ces garçons. Pourquoi court-il après ces garçons? Parce qu'il aime aller à l'école avec Robert et Charles. Il court après ces garçons pour aller à l'école avec eux (them).

Michel et Robert et Charles parlent ensemble. Ils regardent les automobiles qui passent. Ils aiment regarder les automobiles. Ils ne discutent pas la leçon d'algèbre parce qu'ils ne trouvent pas la leçon intéressante. Ils préfèrent regarder les autos.

Grammaire
Pourquoi and Parce que

A question containing the word **pourquoi** (*why*) will require an answer giving a reason. Often the answer will contain the conjunction **parce que** (*because*).

Pourquoi ouvrez-vous le tiroir? *Why are you opening the drawer?*
J'ouvre le tiroir parce que je cherche la gomme. *I am opening the drawer because I am looking for the eraser.*

Sometimes instead of **parce que** the French use **pour** with the infinitive.

Pourquoi ouvrez-vous le tiroir? *Why are you opening the drawer?*
J'ouvre le tiroir pour chercher la gomme. *I am opening the drawer to look for the eraser.*

These constructions are very easy because they are similar to the English constructions. Learn the words **parce que** and **pour**. Notice that **parce que** introduces a clause, that is, a group of words containing a subject, verb, etc., while **pour** introduces only an infinitive.

Vocabulaire

l'algèbre [lalʒɛbr] (f.), *algebra*
l'auto [loto] (m. or f.), *auto*
le coin [kwɛ̃], *corner;* au coin, *at the corner, in the corner*
l'école [lekɔl] (f.), *school*

le garçon [garsõ], *boy*
Marthe [mart], *Martha*
Michel [miʃɛl], *Michael*
aller [ale], *to go*
discuter [diskyte], *to discuss*
marcher [marʃe], *to walk*

trois [trwɑ], *three*
lentement [lɑ̃tmɑ̃], *slowly*
parce que [parskə], *because*
pourquoi [purkwa], *why*
quelquefois [kɛlkəfwa], *sometimes*

---
[1] The e of de is elided.

Questionnaire

1. Où est Michel? Où va-t-il?
2. Pourquoi préfère-t-il rester à la maison? Et vous?
3. Où passent Robert et Charles?
4. Pourquoi Michel court-il après ces garçons?
5. Qu'est-ce que les garçons regardent?
6. Qu'est-ce qu'ils discutent?
7. Préférez-vous discuter l'algèbre ou les automobiles?
8. Marchez-vous lentement?

Devoir

A. Write the first three sentences of "Trois garçons" in phonetic characters.

B. Use each of the following words in a sentence. Try to get as much variety as possible in the person and number of your sentences.

ajouter   cahier   jouer
grand'mère   joli   vert

C. Make the declarative sentences interrogative, and make the interrogative sentences declarative.

1. Il ne sait pas la leçon.
2. Avons-nous ces objets que vous désirez?
3. Finissez-vous cette phrase?
4. Vous préférez danser, n'est-ce pas?
5. Ils remplissent le tiroir de gommes.
6. Met-il la tasse de côté?
7. Demande-t-il une belle chaise?
8. Ne commencent-ils pas par cette phrase?
9. C'est ce qu'il va faire.
10. Vous répétez les pronoms démonstratifs.
11. Ils admirent le plafond du salon.
12. Nous ramassons la ficelle sur le plancher.
13. Vous aimez toujours la tarte aux cerises.

Traduction:

Mary is going to school. She walks slowly. There is Martha. Mary sees Martha, who is at the corner. Mary runs after Martha. They do not walk fast, because they are talking. They like to talk. I like to talk, also. They discuss Josephine. They find Josephine pretty. They like Josephine because she is interesting. What do you think (**penser**) of Josephine?

VINGT-SIXIÈME LEÇON

Review

A

1. In what two ways must an adjective agree with its noun? Give two examples.

2. How is the plural of most adjectives formed? Give an example.

3. How is the feminine singular of most adjectives formed? Illustrate.

4. Mention one irregular adjective and give the forms.

5. What is the usual position of an adjective in French?

6. Mention three adjectives that do not follow the regular rule for position.

7. What is the purpose of **ce**, the demonstrative adjective?

8. What forms of **ce** are used with the following nouns: **journal, orange, automobile, chats?**

9. Give three short sentences that show what form of the verb must be used with **nous**.

10. Give the imperative of **finir**.

11. Illustrate the use of **n'est-ce pas.**

12. What is the interrogative form of il a? Of il lit?

13. What endings have you learned for the present tense of first conjugation verbs (-er)?

14. What are the endings in the present tense for verbs of the second conjugation (-ir)?

15. What does the word **pour** express? With what form of the verb is it used?

16. Illustrate the use of the relative pronouns **qui** and **que**.

B

I. Conjugate the following sentences:

1. J'apporte le journal.
2. Est-ce que je finis l'histoire? (*Use the inverted order in the rest of the forms.*)
3. Je ne marche pas lentement.
4. Je ne remplis pas la boîte.

II. Change to the correct verb-forms:

1. Nous (préférer) ce couteau.
2. Je ne (mettre) pas la fourchette sur le tapis.

3. Il (discuter) l'histoire avec Michel et Marthe.
4. (Fermer) la fenêtre, s'il vous plaît, et (rester) là.
5. Ils (aimer) aller chez vous.
6. Vous (manger) une pomme de terre et ce pain.
7. Elles (finir) la tarte.
8. Ils (chercher) un verre.
9. (Continuer) la conjugaison du verbe **crier**.

III. Use each form of the demonstrative adjective **ce** (**ce, cet, cette, ces**) *in a sentence.*

IV. Traduction:

John and Robert like to play with the piece of string, don't they? John finishes the lesson. He listens to the radio.

"This lesson is difficult," he says. "No," says John, "it is not difficult. Finish the lesson quickly."

Robert looks at the book. John plays with the cat. Now Robert closes the book to play. He puts the book aside.

"I know those words," he says.

PHONETIC REVIEW

A. Practice:

ju, jo, jɔ, jɑ, ja, jɛ, je, ji, jə
ʃu, ʃo, ʃɔ, ʃɑ, ʃa, ʃɛ, ʃe, ʃi, ʃə
ʒu, ʒo, ʒɔ, ʒɑ, ʒa, ʒɛ, ʒe, ʒi, ʒə

B. Read aloud:

1. Les yeux de l'enfant sont
   [lezjø   də lɑ̃fɑ̃   sõ
   bleus.
   blø.]
2. Charles revient avec trois
   [ʃarl   rəvjɛ̃   avɛk trwa
   autres garçons.
   zoːtr   garsõ.]
3. Où est le journal français?
   [wɛ   lə ʒurnal   frɑ̃sɛ?]

4. Qu'est-ce que c'est que cela
   [kɛs   kə   sɛ   kə   sla
   sur le tapis?
   syːr lə tapi?]
5. Le garçon est dans le coin.
   [lə garsõ   ɛ   dɑ̃   lə kwɛ̃]

C. Pronounce and write in phonetic characters:

1. Est-ce que les yeux de Raton sont verts?
2. Les autres élèves étudient.
3. Où est-ce que Mme. Gilbert met le rôti?
4. Joséphine et Marguerite écoutent la T. S. F.; et elles dansent.

Photo A. Breger Frères, Paris

HAYING ON A TYPICAL FRENCH FARM

FRENCH PEASANTS AND THE SOIL

An English lady of our acquaintance was recently accused of over-praising the French peasant. Her defense was as follows: "It has been my good fortune to join hands in a round dance with the folk of Anjou (a province southwest of Brittany), old and young footing it under the warm twilight sky; to crown with laurel the little prize-winners of communal schools; to witness signatures in the marriage registers of country churches; and to sit out rustic wedding feasts lasting five hours. Often on market days I have sat down to noon dinner in a country inn whose guests all belonged to one class. Their Sunday suits protected by blue cotton blouses, sparing of words, swiftly bolting whatever food was set before them, these farmers would harness up and drive home the moment that buying and selling was over—because they cared nothing for the attractions of the fair itself. I have enjoyed peasant hospitality on the borders of Spain, within a stone's throw of the German frontier, and in the farmsteads of Normandy, on the banks of the Loire, the Marne, and many a beautiful French river besides, and in remote Breton hamlets. And everywhere, during my twenty-five years in France, I found a cheery welcome and an ungrudging share in all my peasant hosts had to offer."

The French peasant owns France. Many years ago he was no better than a slave—bought and sold with the soil he tilled. But today he is master of his own stretch of farmland. He is the backbone of the French nation— the symbol of loyalty and endurance. He is as deeply rooted in the soil as are the trees that grow in it. True, he may sing mournfully now and then

Le pauvre laboureur
Est toujours tourmenté.
Toujours devant sa porte
Garnison et sergent,
Qui crieront sans cesse,
"Apportez de l'argent!"[1]

[1] *The poor workingman is forever plagued. Forever before his door are troops and sergeant, crying without pause, "Bring some money!"*

but this is only when he is feeling low in his mind, and hopes that the tax collector may overhear him.

It was not until the beginning of the nineteenth century that peasant ownership of land became a reality. For hundreds of years before the French Revolution (1789-1795) these farmers had been practically slaves. So it was only natural for them, when they were permitted to own the soil, to regard it as their most precious birthright. It was the one thing that every peasant in France wanted more than anything else, the object to which he would sacrifice everything. He began to rule his life by the doctrine: Land is Power. And this land signified to him not only security and wealth; it became part of his very being.

In thousands of hamlets all over France you will not meet a single field-laborer who does not own his bit of soil. A French peasant almost never sells any land he owns, unless it is to acquire another field which he considers more fertile and better adapted to his needs. He cultivates every available square inch of ground, so that vacant property is virtually unknown in France—a fact that explains the tidy and well-kept appearance of even the humblest countryside. The peasant is very shrewd in protecting his land from the elements that endanger it. In parts of Provence, in Southern France, for example, rows of cypress trees are planted at intervals of every hundred feet or so as windbreaks against the *mistral*, the cold, dry wind that often blows in furious gusts across that region. These trees are all so bent by the force of it that it is easily seen how without their protection the frailer crops would be destroyed in a few hours.

There are several ways by which a peasant may dispose of his land to his children. The peasant's family is small, it is true, but then the peasant's land-holdings are also small. To divide this modest property into several small parcels is as distasteful to its owner as the sale of such separate pieces would be. So when the oldest son marries, his father ordinarily does one

Archives du Touring-Club de France

MUSICIANS AT A BRETON WEDDING FEAST

By Ewing Galloway, N. Y.
THE THATCH-ROOFED COTTAGE OF A BRETON PEASANT
The roof is so low that the door had to be cut through it.

of two things: either gives him part of the land outright, or demands that his son and daughter-in-law remain with him as fellow-tillers, with the promise that some day they may enjoy part ownership of it. The latter arrangement is often unsatisfactory, for sooner or later the new family is bound to resent its dependence on the older people. But, on the contrary, if the first arrangement should be carried out, and later on when the second son marries, another portion of land be given him also, then as they grow old the parents may well find themselves without sufficient property to insure them against poverty and want. Bitter quarrels among French peasants sometimes result because of this evil situation: children claiming a share in the family land, parents slow to divide a homestead that has been in their family for generations.

But on the other hand one has only to travel through provinces like Normandy or the Ile de France to learn to what extent plots of ground have been divided. It is no uncommon thing to see carefully tilled patches of land which are not more than eight or ten feet in width. Farm ownership thus sometimes means being master of the merest ribbon of soil.

Despite the fact that he is now a free man and a land owner, despite his almost passionate attachment to the homestead, the progress of the peasant is slow. He has more dignity now that he is no longer a slave, but he possesses little more actual knowledge of farming than did his ancestors who were serfs. Scientific training in agriculture has not yet invaded France as thoroughly as it has America, although a good start has been made in this direction. No longer are the ways of his ancestors felt to be good enough for the modern peasant; in all the provinces of France there are now duly-appointed federal professors to teach him farming. Their task is not an easy one, by any means. They must coax the stubborn peasant away from his chores and get him to listen

Les Archives photographiques d'Art et d'Histoire, Paris

THE SHEPHERDESS

From a painting by Millet

to amazing things he has never heard before. He is hard to convince, slow to be won over; but night classes on winter evenings, and Sunday lectures held out of doors are beginning to interest even the most difficult of peasants. New machinery and chemical fertilizers are demonstrated, selected seeds, plants, and roots are exhibited. Curiosity finally leads the hardest headed peasant to ask questions, to study the truth of what is told him.

The peasant and his love for the soil is a subject often treated in French literature.

Painters have found beauty and splendor of a sort in the peasant type. Who does not recall Breton's "Song of the Lark," and Millet's "The Gleaners," and "The Angelus"? Who that has seen his "Shepherdess" can forget the figure of the lonely woman silhouetted against a great plain on which the flock of sheep stretches far? The figure of the shepherd should not be omitted from our record of French country life. Those who have traveled in France doubtless think of him most often as a charming picture passing through the narrow street of a village, with his well-trained dogs guarding the bleating lambs. But this is the shepherd's only contact with civilization. His is a lonely life. He must learn to be content with the company of his thoughts and his gentle animals. For days at a time he sees no human beings, living silently in a shelter of the hills, or on the silent plain. His love for the barren ranges of France is no less real than the peasant's love for fields bursting with life. In a famous painting by Henri Martin we see an old shepherd in his coarse cloak standing among his sheep, his face alight with joy. This same look is on the face of the French peasant as he walks his fields on Sunday, silently approving his own work. As you see him thus, you know he will leave his farm to his children enriched by many weary but happy years of the hardest kind of toil.

VINGT-SEPTIÈME LEÇON*
Les Ballons

La famille est au salon. Grand'mère tricote. Papa lit le journal. Maman écrit une lettre. Jeanne joue avec sa poupée, et le petit Emile amuse le chat.

—Maman!

—Oui, Emile.

—Maman!

—Non, pas encore.

Grand'mère écoute. Elle sait pourquoi Emile parle. Maman va à la ville acheter un costume à Emile et une robe à Jeanne. L'employé va donner des ballons aux[1] enfants. Emile pense aux ballons. Oh! le temps passe lentement. Il joue avec le chat, et maman continue sa lettre.

—Maman.

—Oui, Emile, dans quelques minutes.

Emile met la ficelle dans sa poche. Jeanne met sa poupée sur le sofa. Emile cherche sa casquette, et Jeanne cherche son chapeau.

Voilà maman qui ferme sa lettre. Emile est impatient. Il aime le train. Il aime regarder par la fenêtre. Il voit passer (passing)[2] les maisons, les arbres, les animaux.

Dans le train Emile est à côté de la fenêtre. Jeanne est à côté de sa maman. Elle est grande. Elle ne regarde pas par la fenêtre. Elle parle avec maman.

—Oh! maman, voilà la maison. Elle est petite. Et mon école, je ne vois pas mon école, dit Emile.

Le train va lentement. Il arrive à la ville.

—Mantes! crie l'employé.

La petite famille descend du train. Jeanne et Emile marchent derrière maman.

—J'aime la ville, dit Emile.

—Moi[3] aussi, dit Jeanne, mais je n'aime pas beaucoup les automobiles. J'aime regarder les beaux magasins.

Les magasins sont très grands. Jeanne voit une poupée, et elle pense à sa belle poupée qui est à la maison.

Maman entre dans[4] un grand magasin. Elle achète un beau costume gris à (for) Emile et une belle robe bleue à Jeanne. L'employé donne un beau ballon rouge à Emile et un ballon bleu à Jeanne. Emile est content. Il a un costume et il a un gros ballon. Le ballon est attaché avec un fil.

Quel beau ballon! Il tire le fil, et le ballon descend. Emile aime son ballon. Il oublie qu'il est en ville.

Maman dit:

—Attention, Emile. Garde bien le ballon. Garde bien le fil. Emile réfléchit.

—Pourquoi garder le fil de mon ballon? Je vais voir. Je vais lâcher le fil un peu, un petit peu pour voir. Je ne sais pas. . . .

—Oh! maman, maman, mon ballon, mon ballon! Il monte. Donne-moi mon beau ballon rouge.

—Voilà, Emile, c'est fini. Le ballon est loin.

Emile marche lentement. Il ne pense pas à son beau costume. Il ne pense pas aux bonbons que maman va acheter. Il cherche son ballon.

Voilà Jeanne qui donne son beau ballon bleu à Emile.

—Emile, voilà mon ballon; je suis grande; mais attention, maintenant, n'est-ce pas?

—Merci, merci, Jeanne. Regarde, Jeanne; j'attache le ballon au bouton de mon manteau.

---

*Note to the Teacher: See page vii.
[1] See footnote 1, page 20. Aux is the plural (a +les).
[2] After certain verbs, one of which is voir, to see, the French use an infinitive where we would use an -ing form.
[3] Moi is often used at the beginning or the end of a sentence to intensify the subject je. It is never used as a subject.
[4] Maman entre dans un grand magasin, Mother enters a big store. Observe that in French one says to enter into.

Vocabulaire

la casquette [kaskɛt], *cap*

le fil [fil], *string*

le magasin [magazɛ̃], *store*

le manteau [mɑ̃to] (pl. les manteaux), *coat*

le temps [tɑ̃], *time*

la ville [vil], *city*

Mantes [mɑ̃:t], *Mantes*, a French town

acheter [aʃte], *to buy*

continuer (à) [kɔ̃tinɥe a], *to continue*

il dit [il di] (inf. dire), *he says*

écrire [ekri:r], *to write*

c'est fini [sɛ fini], *that's the end of it, that's finished* (or *done*)

garder [garde], *to hold, to watch, to guard, to keep*

lâcher [laʃe], *to let go, to loosen, to loose*

oublier (de) [ublie də], *to forget*

réfléchir [refleʃi:r], *to think, to ponder, to reflect*

je suis [ʒə sɥi] (inf. être), *I am*

je vais [ʒə vɛ] (inf. aller), *I go, I am going*

je vois [ʒə vwa] (inf voir), *I see, I am seeing*

me [mə], *me, to me*

mon [mɔ̃] (m. sing.), *my*

quel, quelle [kɛl], *what*

son [sɔ̃] (m. sing.), *his, her, its*

bien [bjɛ̃], *well, hard, much*

derrière [dɛrjɛ:r], *behind*

encore [ɑ̃kɔ:r], *again, yet*

loin [lwɛ̃], *far away*

peu [pø], *a little, few; un petit peu, just a little*

aux [o] (m. and f. pl.), *of the, to the, with the*

The French words that are new in this lesson but which resemble their English equivalents are:

les animaux [le zanimo] (pl. of animal) (m.), *animals*

attention [atɑ̃sjɔ̃] (f.), *attention, pay attention*

le ballon [balɔ̃], *balloon*

les bonbons [bɔ̃bɔ̃] (m.pl.), *candy* (used only in the plural)

le bouton [butɔ̃], *button*

le costume [kɔstym], *suit, dress*

l'employé [lɑ̃plwaje] (m.), *employee, clerk, conductor, official*

la lettre [lɛtr], *letter*

la minute [minyt], *minute*

la robe [rɔb], *robe, frock*

le train [trɛ̃], *train*

Jeanne [ʒɑ:n], *Joan, Jean*

amuser [amyze], *to amuse, to entertain*

attacher [ataʃe], *to attach, to fasten*

entrer [ɑ̃tre], *to enter*

bleu [blø], *blue*

impatient [ɛ̃pasjɑ̃], *impatient*

Archives du Touring-Club de France

MANTES, CALLED "LA JOLIE"

VINGT-HUITIÈME LEÇON

Le Champion

Voici Michel dans la rue. Il va à l'école. Pourquoi va-t-il à l'école? Il va à l'école parce qu'il faut aller à l'école. Il marche un peu lentement. Il a une lettre. Il ne faut pas oublier cette lettre de maman (*of mother's*). Il voit une boîte. Voilà. C'est fini. Maintenant il faut aller vite à l'école. Michel est pressé. Il voit Robert et Charles, qui passent au coin. Il court après les garçons.

—Etes-vous pressés?

—Oui, nous sommes pressés.

Les trois garçons vont à l'école ensemble. Ils parlent de[1] football. Ils aiment toujours parler de football. Robert explique pourquoi Jean est le champion de la saison. Les trois garçons parlent des qualités d'un champion. Henri est grand et fort, mais il ne joue pas bien, parce qu'il est très lent. Henri ne joue pas comme Jean.

—Oui, je sais, Henri est assez lourd, dit Charles.

—Mais Jean est grand aussi, et il n'est pas lent. Pourquoi n'est-il pas lourd? dit Robert.

—C'est parce qu'il pense vite. Il faut penser pour jouer au[2] football. J'aime jouer au football, mais je ne suis pas très lourd.

—Etes-vous lent, Charles?

—Oui, je suis lent, dit Charles.

Grammaire

The Use of *Il faut*

Il faut means *it is necessary* or *one has to*. In English we should complete *it is necessary* by using an infinitive, and we do that same thing in French.

Il faut fermer la porte. *It is necessary to close the door.*
Il faut regarder le tableau. *It is necessary to look at the blackboard.*
Il faut écouter papa. *One has to listen to father.*
Il faut faire cela. *One has to do that.*

Vocabulaire

le champion [ʃɑ̃pjõ], *champion*
le football [futbɑːl], *football*
la qualité [kalite], *quality, good quality*
la saison [sezõ], *season*
Henri [ɑ̃ri], *Henry*
vous êtes [vu zɛt] (inf. **être**), *you are*

expliquer [ɛksplike],[3] *to explain*
faire [fɛːr], *to do, to make, to cause*
il faut [il fo], *it is necessary, one has to, one must*
nous sommes [nu sɔm] (inf. **être**), *we are*
je suis [ʒə sɥi] (inf. **être**), *I am*

ils vont [il võ] (inf. **aller**), *they go, they are going, they are on their way to*
fort [fɔːr], *strong*
lent [lɑ̃], *slow*
lourd [luːr], *heavy*
pressé [prɛse], *in a hurry*
vite [vit], *quickly*

[1] de, *about.*
[2] *To play a game* is expressed in French by jouer à followed by the name of the game.
[3] The pronunciation of ex as [ɛks] is given in this book, since it is more elegant than [ɛs], which is given in the International Dictionary.

Questionnaire

1. Où est Michel? Est-il à la maison?
2. Pourquoi va-t-il à l'école?
3. Marche-t-il vite?
4. Qu'est-ce qu'il ne faut pas oublier?
5. Où sont Robert et Charles?
6. Pourquoi Michel court-il après ces garçons?
7. Sont-ils pressés?
8. Parlent-ils de la leçon d'algèbre?
9. Pourquoi Henri ne joue-t-il pas bien?
10. Jean est-il lent?
11. Qu'est-ce qu'il faut faire pour jouer au football?
12. Marie et Adèle jouent-elles au football?

Devoir

A. *Learn the last two sentences of "Le Champion" by heart. Watch the vowel sounds carefully.*

B. *Change to the correct verb-forms:*

1. Je ne (être) pas pressé.
2. Nous (discuter) les qualités de Michel.
3. Il faut (couper) la tarte.
4. Pourquoi ne (lire)-il pas?
5. (Aimer)-elle (aller) quelquefois au théâtre pour la musique?
6. C'est ce que les élèves (aller) faire dans la salle de classe.
7. (Expliquer) cette belle phrase aux élèves.
8. Est-ce que je (lire) le journal américain?
9. (Aller)-elle écrire une lettre?
10. L'adjectif (précéder)-il le substantif?
11. (Etre)-nous pressés?
12. Vous ne (être) pas lent.
13. (Prononcer)-vous les voyelles de l'infinitif?
14. Faut-il (continuer) la conjugaison du présent du verbe employer?

15. (Etre)-ils contents de la lampe?
16. Merci. Il n'y (avoir) pas de quoi.

C. *Using the words below as helps, write a story similar to the one in "Le Champion." You will have to use other words also. Recall words from preceding lessons to add variety to your sentences. Make two paragraphs, as indicated by 1 and 2.*

1. la rue, il faut, lentement, parce que, la leçon d'algèbre.
2. les garçons, discuter, expliquer, le champion, grand et fort, penser, jouer au football.

Traduction:

Sometimes Henry really likes to go to school, but not today. He is going to school because it is necessary to go to school, but he prefers to play. He walks very slowly. There are three boys at the corner. They have a football. Henry runs after the three boys to talk about football. Charles says that it is necessary to think to play football. Have you a football?

P. & A. Photo

FAR TO THE SOUTH THE PYRENEES MOUNTAINS RISE STEEPLY, THEIR
ROCKY SIDES FURNISHING BUT LITTLE PASTURAGE FOR CATTLE

VINGT-NEUVIÈME LEÇON

A l'école

Les trois garçons vont à l'école. Ils arrivent à la porte de l'école. Ils ouvrent la porte et entrent dans[1] l'école. Robert va au bureau. Le bureau est à côté de l'escalier. Il va au bureau pour parler avec le directeur. Charles et Michel ne vont pas au bureau. Ils montent l'escalier. Michel va à la bibliothèque pour rendre un livre. Charles va avec Michel. Alors ils vont au casier de Michel, où il trouve les livres.

Philippe passe. Il voit Michel et Charles.

—Où allez-vous? dit-il.

—Nous allons à la classe d'algèbre. Et vous?

—Je vais à la classe d'anglais. J'aime cette classe, parce que le professeur est très gentil, et nous discutons des choses intéressantes, comme les sports. Aujourd'hui nous discutons la valeur des sports.

—Et nous, nous allons à la classe d'algèbre pour écrire les problèmes au tableau.

—A tantôt.

—Oui, à midi.

Grammaire

The Verb *Aller*

The verb **aller,** *to go,* although it ends in **-er,** is not conjugated like **trouver.** Because it is what is known as an irregular verb you must learn the forms instead of making them according to the endings given for **trouver.**

PRESENT TENSE

je vais, *I go, am going, do go*   nous allons, *we go, are going, do go*
tu vas, *you go, are going, do go*   vous allez, *you go, are going, do go*
il va, *he goes, is going, does go*   ils vont, *they go, are going, do go*

The Contraction of *à* and the Article

The preposition **à,** which means *to* or *at* or *on,* is frequently used with the definite article. When the preposition **à** is used with the forms **le** and **les** we find certain contractions. Observe the following and try to make your own rules.

1. Il parle au garçon.   à+le = au
2. Il parle à l'élève.   à+l' = à l'   (masculine or feminine)
3. Il parle à la petite fille.   à+la = à la
4. Ils parlent aux garçons.   à+les = aux
5. Ils parlent aux élèves.   à+les = aux
6. Ils parlent aux petites filles. à+les = aux

As you will have no difficulty with **à** la, it will not be necessary to work on it; but when in the reading or in questions you come upon **au** or **aux,** observe the expression and say it aloud. Try to make a collection of the expressions using **au** or **aux.**

[1] See footnote 4 on page 75.

Vocabulaire

l'anglais [lɑ̃glɛ] (m.), *English* (language)

le bureau [byro] (pl. les bureaux), *office, desk*

le casier [kɑzje], *locker*

la chose [ʃoːz], *thing*

le directeur [dirɛktœːr], *principal, director, superintendent, manager*

l'escalier [lɛskalje] (m.), *stairs, staircase*

le problème [prɔblɛːm], *problem*

les sports [spɔːr], *athletics, sports* (generally used in the masculine plural)

la valeur [valœːr], *value, worth*

rendre [rɑ̃ːdr], *to return, to give back*

gentil, gentille[1] [ʒɑ̃ti, ʒɑ̃tiːj], *agreeable, kind*

à tantôt [a tɑ̃to], *good-by (for a short time), so long,* literally, *until soon*

à midi [a midi], *I'll see you at noon*

Questionnaire

1. Où est-ce que les garçons arrivent?
2. Est-ce que j'arrive avec les garçons?
3. Où entrent-ils?
4. Pourquoi Robert va-t-il au bureau?
5. Pourquoi Michel va-t-il à la bibliothèque? Qui va avec Michel?
6. Qu'est-ce qu'il va rendre dans la bibliothèque?
7. Alors où va Michel?
8. Qu'est-ce qu'il trouve dans le casier?
9. Que dit Philippe?
10. Pourquoi aime-t-il la classe d'anglais?
11. Pourquoi aime-t-il le professeur?
12. Où vont Charles et Michel?

Devoir

A. Learn the first three sentences of "A l'école" by heart.

B. Write six sentences, using forms of **à** and the definite article. Select nouns from Lessons 11-14.

C. Give two answers for each question, one answer using **parce que** and the other using **pour**:

1. Pourquoi va-t-il au bureau aujourd'hui?
2. Pourquoi va-t-elle à la bibliothèque ?
3. Pourquoi ouvre-t-il ce casier?
4. Pourquoi êtes-vous au tableau?
5. Pourquoi allez-vous à l'école avec Charles?

Traduction:

I am going to the library to return this book. Here is the book. Mary is going with me to the library, because we like to talk together. Then I am going to the locker.

We like the English class very much, because we discuss interesting things like football. Today we are discussing the value of athletics.

"I have a question to ask you. Where are you going?"

"We are going to the algebra class to write these problems on the blackboard."

"So long!"

"See you at noon."

---

[1] Do not forget that il final and ill preceded by a vowel are pronounced [j] like *y* in *yearn.* But ill preceded by a consonant is pronounced [ij].

TRENTIÈME LEÇON
Le petit mot

Après les classes, Michel rentre à la maison. Robert va au parc. Charles et Philippe rentrent chez Philippe. Ils vont après au cinéma, mais Michel rentre à la maison. Il regarde les automobiles. Les personnes en auto[1] vont dans les magasins, dans les théâtres, dans les hôtels. Michel aime toujours regarder les autos.

Le voilà (*There he is*) à la maison. Il ne sonne pas. Il tire la clef de sa poche et ouvre la porte. Maman n'est pas au salon. Michel ôte sa casquette et va vite à la cuisine. Allez-vous quelquefois à la cuisine après les classes? Il ouvre la porte de l'office parce qu'il cherche quelque chose à manger. Voilà la glacière. Il voit un morceau de papier collé à la porte de la glacière. C'est un petit mot de maman.

—N'oubliez pas d'aller chez Mme. Hébert. Elle a un grand livre rouge pour moi.

Pourquoi maman met-elle toujours un petit mot dans la cuisine? Est-ce parce qu'elle sait que Michel va toujours à la cuisine après les classes?

Grammaire
Au and *Aux*

Remember to observe **au** or **aux** whenever you find them in the text. Make a list of the phrases using **à** in combination with an article which are to be found in this lesson.

In writing exercises of the **Devoir** remember:

Masculine	Feminine	Masculine and Feminine
à+le = au	à+la = à la	à+les = aux
à+l' = à l'	à+l' = à l'	

The Preposition *Chez*

The preposition **chez** is always used with a noun or pronoun that represents a person:

chez Philippe, *at the home of Philip; to Philip's home*
chez moi, *at my home*

Aller and the Infinitive

The verb **aller** and its various forms express first of all the idea of motion. When, however, **aller** is used with an infinitive, it has the idea of future time.

Je vais chercher quelque chose à manger. *I am going to look for something to eat.*
Il va jouer avec le chat. *He is going to play with the cat.*
Ils vont chanter. *They are going to sing.*

[1] The definite article is not required when en is used with an unmodified noun.

As this construction is the same in both French and English, you will not need to drill on it.

je vais parler, *I am going to speak*	nous allons parler, *we are going to speak*
tu vas parler, *you are going to speak*	vous allez parler, *you are going to speak*
il va parler, *he is going to speak*	ils vont parler, *they are going to speak*

Other Uses of the Infinitive

In "Le petit mot" you find an infinitive used in a way you are familiar with in English; it follows the verb directly and completes it.

Michel aime regarder les autos. *Michael likes to look at the automobiles.*

You find another infinitive, used also to complete the verb, *but preceded by the preposition* **de:**

N'oubliez pas d'apporter le livre. *Don't forget to take the book.*

In French there are a number of verbs that always require the preposition **de** before the infinitive. **Oublier** is one of them. As these verbs will appear one at a time, learn each with its preposition as it is introduced.

N'oubliez pas de chercher le papier. *Don't forget to look for the paper.*

Vocabulaire

la clef [kle], *key*
le cinéma [sinema], *movies*
la cuisine [kɥizin], *kitchen*
la glacière [glasjɛːr], *re-frigerator*
l'hôtel [lotɛl] (m.), *hotel or large city residence*
Mme., abbreviation for *madame* [madam]

l'office [lɔfis] (f.), *pantry*
le parc [park], *park*
la personne [pɛrsɔn], *person*
le petit mot [pti mo], *note*
le restaurant [rɛstɔrɑ̃], *res-taurant*
le soir [swaːr], *evening*
le théâtre [teaːtr], *theater*

ôter [ote], *to take off*
rentrer [rɑ̃tre], *to return, to re-enter*
sonner [sɔne], *to ring a bell, to ring*
collé [kɔle], *glued, fastened*
quelque chose à manger, [kɛlkə ʃoːz a mɑ̃ʒe], *something to eat*

Questionnaire

1. Où va Robert?
2. Où vont Charles et Philippe?
3. Pourquoi Michel regarde-t-il les autos? Où sont les autos?
4. Qu'est-ce que Michel aime re-garder toujours?
5. Quand Michel arrive à la maison que fait-il? (*does he do?*) Sonne-t-il? Pourquoi tire-t-il la clef de sa poche?
6. Est-ce que je tire la clef de la boîte?
7. Pourquoi va-t-il à la cuisine?
8. Qu'est-ce qu'il voit collé à la porte de la glacière?
9. Qu'est-ce qu'il ne faut pas oublier?
10. Cherchez-vous quelque chose à manger? Mangez-vous un mor-ceau de viande?

Devoir

A. Practice the last paragraph of "Le petit mot" until you can read it without any hesitation.

B. Supply the correct forms of the preposition à and the definite article:

1. Il va —— tableau, n'est-ce pas?
2. Nous ne jouons pas —— cinéma.
3. Il court après moi —— jolie maison.
4. Vous allez —— hôtel avec plaisir.
5. Il aime aller —— bons restaurants.
6. Il faut donner la clef et les couteaux —— bonne.
7. Nous sommes —— salon.

C. Supply a different noun in each of the preceding sentences and use the correct form of à and the article.

D. Make each of the sentences in B, except the first, interrogative.

Traduction:

Michael is at home. He takes off his cap and looks for something to eat. Mother is not in the living-room. She is at Mrs. Gilbert's. Michael goes to the pantry and opens the door. He sees a note from mother. She puts the note there because she knows that Michael always goes to the pantry. We look for something to eat, too, don't we? It is necessary to eat. We like to eat.

Photo A. Breger Frères, Paris

A STREET OF LITTLE SHOPS IN PARIS

TRENTE ET UNIÈME LEÇON

Dans les magasins

Louise ne va pas au cinéma. Louise va au marché pour maman. Elle achète beaucoup de choses. Elle va chez le boucher. Elle y achète six côtelettes de mouton. Elle y achète aussi un kilo de lard. Puis elle entre dans l'épicerie. Elle y achète un kilo de beurre et un kilo de café. A la boulangerie elle achète trois pains. Elle y rencontre Marie, et elles parlent un peu ensemble.

—Vous achetez trois pains? dit Marie. Vous aimez le pain chez vous? Moi,[1] je vais acheter douze petits pains. Ils sont vraiment bons, ces petits pains. Alors Louise va à la pharmacie[2] pour acheter douze timbres-poste. Elle y achète aussi une gomme. Les choses sont lourdes.

Alors elle rentre à la maison. Maman y est avec grand'mère. Elles sont assises sur le sofa, et elles parlent. Louise est contente d'y trouver maman et grand'mère.

Grammaire

The Verb *Acheter*

The verb **acheter** is a verb of the first conjugation; that is, it is conjugated like **trouver, regarder,** etc. There is one thing, however, to observe about this verb—its grave accent.

j'achète, *I buy, am buying, do buy*
tu achètes, *you buy,* etc.
il achète, *he buys*

nous achetons, *we buy*
vous achetez, *you buy*
ils achètent, *they buy*

Before what kind of syllable does the mute **e** become grave? Observe that in French a succession of mute syllables within a word is rare. The first of two mute **e**'s changes to grave **e**, that is, **e** with a grave accent.

The Use of the Word *Y*

Y is an important word in French. It is as short as a word can be, and yet it may take the place of several other words.

Observe these sentences and see if you can tell what words y replaces.

1. Il va à la porte.
He goes to the door.
1a. Il y va.
He goes there (*to the door* or *to it*).

2. Il met les livres sur la table.
He puts the books on the table.
2a. Il y met les livres.
He puts the books there.

3. Nous allons au parc.
We are going to the park.
3a. Nous y allons.
We are going there.

In sentences 1a, 2a, and 3a, **y** replaces the preposition and its object. **Y** may be used *to replace a preposition and its object which denote place.* **Y** always precedes the verb.

[1] See footnote 3, page 75.
[2] In France stamps may be purchased in a tobacco shop, but never in a drug store. This scene takes place in the United States.

A STREET BUTCHER SHOP IN PARIS

Vocabulaire

le **beurre** [bœːr], *butter*

la **boulangerie** [bulɑ̃ʒri], *bakery*

la **côtelette** [kotlɛt], *chop, cutlet*

l'**épicerie** [lepisri] (f.), *grocery store*

le **kilogramme**, le **kilo** [kilɔgram, kilo], *kilogram, about 35 ounces*

le **lard** [laːr], *bacon*

le **marché** [marʃe], *market*

le **mouton** [mutɔ̃], *sheep, mutton*

le **pain** [pɛ̃], *bread, loaf of bread*

le **petit pain** [pti pɛ̃], *roll*

la **pharmacie** [farmasi], *drug store*

le **timbre-poste** [tɛ̃brəpɔst], *postage stamp*

rencontrer [rɑ̃kɔ̃tre], *to meet*

six [sis] ([si] before consonants), *six*

puis [pɥi], *then*

y [i], *there*

chez le boucher [ʃe lə buʃe], *to* or *at the butcher's*

Questionnaire

1. Louise va-t-elle au cinéma?
2. Pourquoi va-t-elle chez le boucher?
3. Pourquoi entre-t-elle dans l'épicerie?
4. Achète-t-elle un kilo de café à la boulangerie?
5. Où rencontre-t-elle Marie?
6. Est-ce que Louise achète douze petits pains?
7. Est-ce qu'elle y achète une tarte aux cerises?
8. Où achète-t-elle les timbres-poste?
9. Est-ce que les timbres-poste sont collés aux lettres?
10. Qu'est-ce qu'elle apporte chez elle?
11. A-t-elle une clef pour ouvrir la porte?

Devoir

A. Write 10 and 11 of the "Question-naire" in phonetic characters.

B. Write five questions to be asked in class whose answers may contain the word **y**. Do not duplicate the sentences given in the grammar – section.

C. In each blank below use the correct form of **à** and the definite article:

1. Les personnes frappent ——— porte.
2. Il lit ——— fenêtre ouverte dans la cuisine.
3. Vous allez ——— théâtre pour la musique.
4. Je ne vais pas ——— magasin à midi pour acheter le costume et le drapeau.
5. Nous rentrons ——— maison pour danser, n'est-ce pas?
6. Je suis ——— pharmacie.

D. Make the sentences in C interrogative whenever possible.

E. Answer the questions in D, using **y** in the answers.

Traduction:

There is Louise. She is going to the grocery store, because mother is at home with grandmother. Louise buys (*there*) a kilogram of coffee and some (**des**) potatoes. Then she goes to the bakery shop. Do you some-times meet Mary there? (Use **Est-ce que.**)

Today Louise meets Mary. What is she buying? Louise is buying three loaves of bread. Mary likes rolls, but Louise likes bread. They talk in the bakery. They buy (*there*) three loaves of bread and twelve rolls, and continue to talk (**à parler**).

TRENTE-DEUXIÈME LEÇON

Review

A

1. What words commonly occur in the answer to a question beginning with **pourquoi?** Give examples of question and answer.
2. What form of the verb is used with **pour?**
3. What must follow **parce que?**
4. What does **il faut** mean? How is it completed?
5. Explain the different forms of the word **ce.**
6. Give the present tense of **aller.**
7. Give the present tense of **trouver;** of **remplir.**
8. What does the word **chez** mean?
9. What kind of object does **chez** require? Illustrate.

10. What word may take the place of **à** and its object or **chez** and its object?
11. If you use **y** in a sentence, where must it be placed?
12. Give a sentence illustrating the use of **y.**
13. How is a grave **e** [è] [ɛ] pro-nounced?
14. In what persons does the grave accent appear in the present of the verb **acheter?**
15. Why is the mute **e** changed to a grave **e** in the verb **acheter?**
16. Give an imperative sentence. What does the imperative express?
17. What forms of **être** do you know?

B

I. Conjugate:

1. Est-ce que je vais à l'école avec Henri?
2. Je n'achète pas le ballon.
3. Je remplis le tiroir.

II. Complete the sentences:

1. Il va au —————
2. Il va à l' —————
3. Il va à la —————
4. Il va aux —————

III. Reply, using y, il, or elle, to replace each italicized word or words in the following sentences:

1. Est-ce que le directeur est *au bureau?*
2. Pourquoi allez-vous *à la fenêtre?*
3. Est-ce que Marie va *chez Joséphine* pour manger les oranges?
4. Est-ce que *la leçon* est difficile?
5. Est-ce que *l'aéroplane* est jaune et noir?

IV. Traduction:

Philip is at home. He is in the living-room. He is seated on the sofa. He is talking with Charles. They have a book. Charles goes to the window and looks into the street. He does not see the little green automobile (*there*). He lowers the shade.

Philip folds and puts aside the American newspaper. He puts this newspaper beside the beautiful gray box on the table. The doll is not far away. It is beside the window behind the curtain. It is a small doll.

Charles is going to look at the stamps now.

The box of stamps is on the floor beside that desk.

V. Write the infinitives of twenty French verbs.

PHONETIC REVIEW

A. Read aloud:

1. Où est-ce qu'il met les illustrations?
   [u   ɛs   kil   mɛ   le   zilystrasjõ?]

2. Il achète le beurre.
   [il aʃɛt lə bœːr.]

3. Mes yeux sont bleus.
   [me zjø sõ blø.]

4. Le substantif précède l'adjectif.
   [lə sypstãtif presɛd ladʒɛktif.]

5. Vos yeux sont beaux.
   [vo zjø sõ bo.]

B. Pronounce and write in phonetic characters:

1. Nous ajoutons les mots.
2. L'épicerie est à côté de la maison.
3. Il demande un kilogramme de beurre.
4. Où est-ce qu'il est?
5. Nous sommes un peu pressés.

FISHER FOLK HAULING IN NETS

FRENCH SEA TOWNS AND INLAND VILLAGES

Very different are the two kinds of French communities—sea towns and inland villages. The one is open in every pore to the sounds and the smells of the sea, is wet with the mist and the spray of it. The other sleeps on in the protecting shade of its plane trees, its quaint houses hidden from view by walls of rough stone and grilled gates of iron.

French sea towns lack the air of separation from the world of reality that is so typical of the country village. They remind the traveler of English Plymouth or of our own Salem. If you have ever lived beside the ocean, a French sea town will have a familiar look to you.

If you are in search of a picturesque harbor, visit Barfleur in Normandy. On its waters swim shoals of one-masted yawls and fishing smacks with red and blue-striped hulls. At low tide they lie on their sides like weary cripples; but when the sea lifts again, every one of them rears itself proudly erect.

A stone quay half encircles the basin of treacherous black rocks. Here are fishermen boiling tar in kettles for calking, or spreading their nets in the sun to dry, or mending lobster-pots. At the back of the quay huddle squat stone houses forever swept by spray-drenched winds.

Of sterner mood is Cancale in Brittany, whose houses stand upon a grim bluff and defy the blasts of ocean. Below the cliffs are oyster beds, submerged when the tide is at full, and near by is a settlement of oystermen, their overturned boats showing wide bottoms and deep keels to the misted sun. The creeping tide, with its odors of pitch and oakum and dead fish, swirls along the shore for miles, and twice a day the oyster beds lie full four fathoms undersea. Brittany has many such fishing villages as Cancale, each perched upon dikes, and with cone-shaped windmills that remind one of Holland.

The sea does not yield its riches

easily to man, but here and there on the French coast are wealthy fishing towns which cause their poorer neighbors to marvel and to envy. Such a town is St. Malo, a tightly-built old fortress on a walled island, once a stronghold of French naval glory. For centuries this ancient town has been a nursery of hardy mariners. It thrusts out into the sea like a buttress, the home of a race whose fierce spirit time and change have been unable to subdue. Five stories in height, its stately houses lift tall chimneys and blue slate roofs above the wall. They are rich in detail, with graceful iron balconies and stone urns under the eaves. Prosperity has defeated the stern melancholy of the sea at St. Malo. Eager visitors fill its church and hunt out its many marvels—although St. Malo is a very small town.

If we journey by motor-car inland away from the sea, we soon find ourselves passing through village after village as like one another as peas in the same pod: serene and still, picturesque clusters of lichen-covered houses, a stone bridge, a parish church, a few tangled gardens, a red-cheeked peasant woman trotting queerly along in wooden shoes—gone forever, and in a twinkling, in the dust that follows the flight of our car! But at noon we are likely to be hungry and tired of motion; so we stop at a market-town. There is time for a quiet stroll on the tree-lined promenade of the old walls. The other streets are only narrow lanes half overgrown with weeds, winding into dark courtways rich in forgotten types of architecture. These lanes, shadowed on each side by houses, are quaintly named: Horses that Dance is the title of one, Path of the Foxes, of another. As we idle along, a stiff old gentleman is entering an ancient mansion with timbered front and high-pitched roof. Three of its stories jut forth one above the other, and we feel as if we were standing below an inverted staircase. This we learn is the spotless home of the retired army officer, known and respected by all.

Here is another house, bearing the coat-of-arms of a proud noble family. A few steps back from the lane is a

ST. MALO

A BAKER'S BOY

stone-paved courtyard — more than that cannot be seen through the high iron grille that bars the pathway of the idler. Here lives the doctor who has turned his spacious dwelling into a hospital. During the late war he was an overworked army surgeon, and his life is still as hard as any that can be easily imagined. He is called at need to lonely and outlying farm-houses where he labors for little or no pay. If there is a château near by, he is summoned there, too. His patients are from every rank of French society. Closely associated with this doctor is the pharmacist who keeps the tidy shop with shining bottles, that stands on the main square. He is a respected citizen of the town, for the title of pharmacist is hard to win and carries with it more than a fair amount of prestige.

Near the market-place the streets are lined with tilted carts, for the horses are stabled for the day. Peasant women in close-fitting white caps have brought in for sale baskets of golden butter. Beneath gayly colored umbrellas plump country girls cry their fresh vegetables and fruits. A line of people is always in front of the busy baker's door. His location is marked by piles of brown furze, a shrub of fine-pointed spines and yellow flowers which is in high demand for purposes of ornament. His shop represents French life more than any other place in town, for everybody goes there to buy, to meet friends, and to hear the latest gossip. The French, for some reason, eat more bread than the people of any other nation do. And so the baker is a sort of directory of the whole district, for he knows not only all the people worth knowing, but all the rest besides; and he delivers his bread, unsweetened rolls, and flour far out into the countryside. His bread he sells by the pound, and his wife will saw you off from her ten-pound loaves any amount you wish.

For cakes you must go to the pastry shop, where the window is filled with great trays of them. Here you may have tea or an ice, choosing your favorite cakes from the tempting array. Each shop makes a specialty of one sort, a masterpiece of the pastry-cook's art. For coffee or another beverage you go to the café, an outdoor restaurant sprinkled with box-trees, wooden tables, footstools—and with pyramids of punch-bowls along the bar. The waiter in black jacket and white apron springs about to obey every nod of the fat proprietor, who watches his trade like a hawk during rush hours, but spends his idle moments playing cards with the auctioneer and a retired soldier or two. Conversation thrives at such gatherings, and the fate of France is decided each day anew by these amateur statesmen of the rural districts.

If we are to stay overnight in this market-town, we turn away at last from the color and gayety of the public square and seek our humble hotel. Its wide-raftered hall is as cheerful as that of an English inn—the great fireplace aflame, its andirons changed into ruddy gold by the warm light. This hall is open away up to its timbered roof, but a balcony reached by a side staircase leads to the bedrooms, each one of which shelters a four-poster bed draped in red, with a small table beside it on which may stand pewter porringers and a tankard.

French inns are of many sorts, some old-fashioned and musty, others up-to-the-minute and showy, with walls striped in mauve and black, and an unnecessary number of serving maids. But one thing you may depend upon. Wherever you spend the night—in a hotel, in the mansion of a great nobleman, or in the modest dwelling of an artisan whose dame flutters about her well-stocked linen cupboard—there is the French bed!

As you climb aboard its several mattresses and put your tired head into a smothering down pillow, you remember the tale of the princess who slept on a pea and felt it through all the bedclothes. But as you sink into hot, dream-haunted slumber, you feel sure the point of the story somehow got turned around: you are not the princess, but the pea that was lost forever in the cushions of a French bed!

Photo A. Breger Frères, Paris

AN INN IN A TINY FRENCH VILLAGE

TRENTE-TROISIÈME LEÇON*
Comment Michel va à l'école

—Vite, vite, dit maman à Michel. Il faut aller à l'école aujourd'hui, Michel. Mademoiselle dit que vous arrivez souvent en retard.

—Oui, maman, mais je suis fatigué. Je n'aime pas aller à l'école.

—Mais, mon Michel, il faut étudier.

Voilà Michel à table avec sa mère et son père. Il mange deux petits pains. Ils sont très bons avec cet excellent beurre, mais Michel n'est pas content. Il plie sa serviette. Maman lui donne ses livres et sa casquette, et voilà Michel dans la rue.

—Il faut marcher vite, dit maman.

Mais Michel ne désire pas marcher vite. Il pense à sa leçon de français. Il aime le français et il aime aussi son professeur, mais il n'aime pas étudier.

Michel passe devant les jolis magasins. Il regarde tous les objets dans le magasin. Il voit des (*some*) livres, des crayons, des stylos, des cahiers. Ce n'est pas intéressant, mais Michel ne désire pas arriver vite à l'école. Il a encore six minutes.

Michel rencontre Charles. Charles est grand. Il ne va pas à l'école comme Michel. Il travaille dans le bureau de son père. Michel pense que Charles est content parce qu'il ne faut pas aller à l'école.

Michel voit des enfants. Il pense aux magasins, aux théâtres, au cinéma. Michel oublie qu'il est là sur le boulevard. Il oublie son école. Mais maintenant Michel écoute.

—Neuf heures, pense Michel, neuf heures! Il ramasse vite ses livres et il court. Oui, vraiment, Michel court maintenant. Il sait qu'il est neuf heures du matin. Il ne voit pas d'enfants maintenant.

Michel arrive à l'école. Il monte l'escalier. Maintenant il faut aller au bureau expliquer pourquoi il est en retard. Que va-t-il dire? Michel commence[1] à regretter.

Michel marche lentement vers le bureau de l'école. Maintenant il pense à sa leçon de français. Il pense à sa leçon d'algèbre. Les théâtres, les automobiles, les magasins, sont loin. Oui, Michel va expliquer sa faute, et demain et toujours maintenant Michel va marcher vite à l'école. Il faut toujours arriver à l'école avant neuf heures, et il faut toujours étudier.

Vocabulaire

le crayon [krɛjõ], *pencil*	**travailler** [travaje], *to work*	**comment** [kɔmã], *how, in what manner, what*
la faute [foːt], *fault, mistake*	**neuf** [nœf], *nine*	
le matin [matɛ̃], *morning*	**neuf heures** [nœvœːr], *nine o'clock*	**demain** [dəmɛ̃], *tomorrow*
la mère [mɛːr], *mother*		**maintenant** [mɛ̃tnã], *now*
le père [pɛːr], *father*	**lui** [lɥi], *him* (ind. obj.)	**souvent** [suvã], *often, frequently*
dire [diːr], *to say, to tell*	**tous** [tu] (pl. of *tout*), *all*	
être [ɛːtr], *to be*	**avant** [avã], *before* (time)	**en retard** [ã rətaːr], *late, tardy*
étudier [etydje], *to study*	**devant** [dəvã], *before* (place)	
penser à [pãse a], *to think of*	**bien** [bjɛ̃], *well*	**vers** [vɛːr], *toward, about, to*

The new French words in this lesson whose meanings you can guess are: **le match** [matʃ], *match, game;* **le boulevard** [bulvaːr], *boulevard;* **regretter** [rəgrɛte], *to regret;* **excellent** [ɛksɛlã], *excellent.*

* *Note to the Teacher:* See page vii.
[1] The verb **commencer** requires **à** to introduce the infinitive.

TRENTE-QUATRIÈME LEÇON
Les Problèmes d'algèbre

Pierre est en classe, mais il n'écoute pas; il ne parle pas; il étudie. C'est l'heure d'étude pour ce groupe d'élèves. Pierre a beaucoup à faire. En ce moment il lit la leçon d'histoire. Il ne commence pas la leçon. Pierre la finit. Il admire Jules César parce qu'il admire toujours les grands généraux. Il aime l'histoire, les aventures, les soldats, les héros.

Mais il a trois problèmes d'algèbre à résoudre. Il faut finir ces problèmes pour la classe d'algèbre.

—Je finis toujours la leçon d'histoire parce que j'aime l'histoire, pense Pierre. Je ne finis pas toujours la leçon d'algèbre. L'algèbre est souvent si difficile!

Il regarde les autres élèves. Ils étudient. Quelques élèves finissent leurs devoirs. Pierre ouvre le livre d'algèbre. Il cherche le douzième problème. Il regarde son devoir. Voilà une faute. Il faut effacer cette faute. Où donc est la gomme, la grosse gomme rouge? Pierre retrouve la gomme. Il efface la faute. Et son stylo? Voici le stylo. Il finit ce problème. Il lit le treizième. Qu'il est facile! Il finit vite le treizième. Et le quatorzième? Il a l'air d'être très difficile, le quatorzième. Pierre réfléchit. Il ne sait pas résoudre ce problème. Il ne finit pas la leçon, parce qu'on sonne. Il va à la classe d'algèbre.

Grammaire
Present Tense of First, Second, and Third Conjugations

French regular verbs are divided into three conjugations. With the first two of these you have already become more or less familiar. Any regular verb ending in -er is formed in the same way, and has the same endings as **aimer**, which you may call the model for the first conjugation. Any regular verb ending in -ir follows the model **finir**.

The third-conjugation verbs are distinguished by the infinitive ending -re. Any regular verb ending in -re follows the model **vendre**, *to sell*. Learn the endings of the present tense of this verb as accurately as you learned the endings of the first two conjugations. Notice that there is no personal ending for the third person singular of **vendre**.[1]

First Conjugation	*Second Conjugation*	*Third Conjugation*
aim **er**	fin **ir**	vend **re**
j'aim **e**	je fin **is**	je vend **s**
tu aim **es**	tu fin **is**	tu vend **s**
il aim **e**	il fin **it**	il vend[1]
elle aim **e**	elle fin **it**	elle vend
nous aim **ons**	nous fin **issons**	nous vend **ons**
vous aim **ez**	vous fin **issez**	vous vend **ez**
ils aim **ent**	ils fin **issent**	ils vend **ent**
elles aim **ent**	elles fin **issent**	elles vend **ent**

[1]If the stem of the verb does not end in -d, add -t, in the third person singular, e.g., il romp t.

Regular and Irregular Verbs

In the French language verbs fall into two great classes—regular and irregular. If a verb follows a pattern, or model, it is regular; if it differs from the pattern, it is irregular. An irregular verb must be memorized, since it often has endings peculiar to itself; but the forms of a regular verb can be made to order when once the endings of its model are known.

Vocabulaire

l'étude [letyd] (f.), *study*
le groupe [grup], *group*
le héros[1] [lə ero], *hero*
l'heure [lœːr] (f.), *hour, time*
l'histoire [listwaːr] (f.), *history, story*
Jules César [ʒyl sezaːr], *Julius Caesar*
Pierre [pjɛːr], *Peter*
avoir l'air d'être [avwaːr lɛːr deːtr], *to seem to be, to look, to appear*

admirer [admire], *to admire*
choisir [ʃwaziːr], *to choose*
effacer [efase], *to erase, to efface*
résoudre [rezudr], *to solve*
retrouver [rətruve], *to find again, to rediscover*
on sonne [õ sɔːn], *the bell rings, someone is ringing the bell*
vendre [vãːdr], *to sell*

douzième [duzjɛm], *twelfth*
quatorzième [katɔrzjɛm], *fourteenth*
treizième [trɛzjɛm], *thirteenth*
leur [lœːr] (pl. *leurs*), *their*
donc[2] [dõːk], *then, now*
ferme [fɛrm], *hard, steadily*
quand [kã], *when*
que [kə], *how;* qu'il est facile [kil ɛ fasil], *how easy it is*

Questionnaire

1. Que fait Pierre?
2. Qu'est-ce qu'il lit?
3. Pourquoi admire-t-il Jules César?
4. Qu'est-ce que Pierre aime?
5. Admirez-vous les soldats?
6. Comment trouve-t-il sa leçon d'algèbre? Et sa leçon d'histoire?
7. Pourquoi ne finit-il pas sa leçon d'algèbre?
8. Qu'est-ce que les autres élèves finissent?
9. Qu'est-ce que vous finissez maintenant?
10. Que fait Pierre quand il trouve une faute?
11. Pourquoi Pierre finit-il si vite le treizième problème?
12. Où va Pierre après l'heure d'étude?
13. Y allez-vous avec Pierre?

Devoir

A. *Write the present tense of* **vendre** *negatively and interrogatively.*

B. *Change to the correct verb-forms:*

1. Nous (écouter) le gentil professeur expliquer et prononcer les verbes des[3] phrases.

2. Je ne (finir) pas le deuxième devoir sur le pluriel des verbes.
3. (Etudier)-vous ferme?
4. (Finir) cette page chez moi, s'il vous plaît.
5. Vous ne (aller) pas résoudre ce problème.

---

[1] The h of héros is aspirate, though not pronounced. See page xxv for an explanation of aspirate h.
[2] Donc is difficult to use correctly. Avoid it, but notice its use each time you meet it.
[3] De plus les forms des.

6. Il (découper) le rôti.

7. Est-ce que les personnes (penser) à l'employé?

8. C'est ce qu'ils (aller) faire à la pharmacie.

9. Elle (vendre) le beurre.

10. Vous (trouver) ce problème assez difficile.

11. Ils (vendre) le costume gris, n'est-ce pas?

12. Vous (jouer) avec la clef.

13. Elle (mettre) la cuillère de côté, n'est-ce pas?

14. Je (choisir) cette viande chez le boucher.

15. Ils (choisir) ces beaux articles ensemble.

16. Nous (être) pressés, mais vous ne (être) pas pressé.

17. Nous (ajouter) la lettre *e*.

18. Ils (avoir) les casquettes et les crayons.

C. In exercise B find another verb besides finir that belongs to the second conjugation, and write its present tense.

D. Use y in answering the following questions:

1. Etudiez-vous les voyelles chez vous?

2. Est-ce que l'eau est dans le verre?

3. Parlez-vous beaucoup en classe?

4. Trouvez-vous un mouchoir de bonne qualité dans le tiroir?

5. Jouons-nous dans le jardin en cette saison?

6. Mettez-vous le manteau sur la chaise?

7. Est-ce que je trouve Josette au coin de la rue?

8. Est-ce que je reste avec elle?

9. Etes-vous au salon?

TRENTE-CINQUIÈME LEÇON

La Leçon d'algèbre

Dans la classe d'algèbre Pierre demande à[1] Robert s'il sait résoudre le quatorzième problème.

—Pas du tout, répond Robert. Ce problème est difficile. Je vais demander à Monsieur Ballu d'expliquer ce problème.

Le professeur fait l'appel. Alors Robert lève la main. —Monsieur le professeur (*sir*), nous trouvons le quatorzième problème très difficile.

—Qui désire résoudre le quatorzième? demande le professeur. Personne? (*No one?*) Eh bien, je vais vous expliquer ce problème, moi. Faites bien attention. Vous êtes ici pour étudier.

Il est exigeant, ce professeur. Mais il sait que ce problème est très difficile.

Il comprend la difficulté du problème. Il va au tableau. Il explique bien. La classe comprend le problème. Le professeur continue. Il donne un autre problème du même genre. Qu'il est facile maintenant!

Les élèves écrivent les autres problèmes de la leçon au tableau. Le professeur corrige les fautes des élèves.

Après il explique la leçon pour demain. Les élèves tournent les pages du livre d'algèbre pour chercher les problèmes.

—Vous allez trouver facile la leçon pour demain, dit le maître. J'ai déjà expliqué (*I have already explained*) les difficultés des problèmes.

La classe finit parce qu'on sonne.

---

[1] demander requires à to introduce the indirect object, i. e., the person.

Grammaire

Contraction of *De* and the Definite Article

The word **de** (*of, from*) has various forms when it is used in connection with **le, la,** and **les.**

1. les phrases du devoir = *the sentences of the exercise.*
2. les phrases de l'exercice = *the sentences of the drill.*
3. les phrases de la leçon = *the sentences of the lesson.*
4. les phrases des devoirs = *the sentences of the exercises.*
5. les phrases des exercices = *the sentences of the drills.*
6. les phrases des leçons = *the sentences of the lessons.*

The word **de** and the article (*of the* or *from the*) form the following combinations:

de+le = du
de+l' = de l' (masculine and feminine)
de+la = de la
de+les = des (masculine and feminine)

Since **de l'** and **de la** offer no difficulty, concentrate on **du** and **des.** When you come upon **du** or **des** in the reading or in the exercises, repeat the whole phrase until you have memorized it. You will not only be adding to your store of correct French, but you will be teaching yourself to avoid troublesome mistakes later.

Verbs Followed by Prepositions

To help you learn the verbs and other parts of speech that are followed by certain prepositions, each example of this kind has been listed as it appeared.

These verbs are followed by **à**:	These verbs are followed by **de**:
commencer **à**	demander **de**
continuer **à**	oublier **de**

Vocabulaire

l'appel [lapɛl] (m.), *roll, roll-call*
la difficulté [difikylte], *difficulty*
l'explication [lɛksplikasjõ] (f.), *explanation*
le genre [ʒãːr], *type, kind, manner*
la main [mɛ̃], *hand*
monsieur [məsjø], *Mr., sir*
Odette [ɔdɛt], *girl's name.* No English equivalent

qui [ki], *who, whom* (interrogative pronoun)
il comprend [il kõprã] (inf. **comprendre**), *he understands*
corriger [kɔriʒe], *to correct*
ils écrivent [il zekriːv] (inf. **écrire**), *they write*
il fait (inf. **faire**) **l'appel** [il fɛ lapɛl], *he calls the roll*
faites (inf. **faire**) **attention** [fɛt atãsjõ], *pay attention*

il sait [il se] (inf. **savoir**), *he knows* (a fact), *he knows how*
exigeant [egziʒã], *strict, exacting*
même [mɛːm], *same*
du tout; pas du tout [dy tu, pɑ dy tu], *not at all, not in the least*
déjà [deʒà], *already*
sans [sã], *without*
si [si], *if*

Questionnaire

1. Pourquoi Robert ne sait-il pas résoudre ce problème?
2. Robert trouve-t-il le quatorzième facile ou difficile?
3. Qu'est-ce qu'il demande à Monsieur Ballu?
4. Qui explique le problème difficile?
5. Pourquoi Monsieur Ballu explique-t-il ce problème?
6. Où écrit-il le problème?
7. Après l'explication, trouvez-vous le problème difficile?
8. Qui corrige les fautes des élèves?
9. Qu'est-ce que les élèves tournent?
10. Qui explique la leçon pour demain?
11. Pourquoi les élèves ne restent-ils pas en classe?

Devoir

A. *Copy the following sentences, crossing out all the* **e**'s *which are muted. Be prepared to read aloud and account for each of the mute syllables.*

1. Marie a encore le livre de Pierre dans la salle à manger.
2. Il n'a pas du tout l'air d'être fort.
3. J'achète les six fourchettes avant les belles cuillères.
4. Nous avons le cahier de ce garçon chez nous.
5. Est-ce que j'achète la viande chez le boucher?

B. *Supply the necessary form of* **de** *and the definite article:*

1. Voici le chapeau —— élève.
2. Voici les casquettes —— élèves. Merci, mademoiselle.
3. Corrigez-vous les fautes —— garçon à l'encre?
4. Je coupe les pages —— livre devant mon casier.
5. Il regarde les illustrations —— histoire.
6. Il ne comprend pas les difficultés —— infinitif.
7. Il faut corriger les mots —— devoir —— gentille petite fille.
8. Le plafond —— salle est blanc, sauf les coins.
9. La rose —— professeur est un peu fanée.
10. La main —— enfant est petite.
11. Je ne vois pas le bonnet —— poupée sur le pupitre.
12. Les douze illustrations —— journal anglais sont grandes.
13. La terminaison —— substantif est -*ion*.
14. Sur le tapis je vois le mouchoir —— élève.
15. Le stylo —— garçon est noir; le stylo —— monsieur est vert.

C. *Pretend that you are the teacher and give five directions to the class (five imperative sentences).*

D. *Answer the five directions in C, using* **Nous allons** *followed by the infinitive in each case.*

Traduction:

Robert goes to class without the fourteenth problem. He finds this problem difficult. He does not like difficult things. He is impatient. Because the teacher knows that the problem is difficult, he writes the problem on the board. He explains the difficulties very well. Now the class understands the difficult problem.

Then the teacher explains the lesson for tomorrow. It is a difficult lesson. He explains the difficulties of the problems. The pupils listen and think (**réfléchir**). Then they look for the problems in the algebra (*book*).

TRENTE-SIXIÈME LEÇON

Dans le parc

Pierre fait une promenade avec Robert. Il aime marcher loin avec Robert, parce qu'il aime marcher assez lentement pour bien regarder[1] les choses qu'il voit. Pierre n'aime pas marcher avec Charles, parce qu'il marche vraiment trop vite.

Les garçons ne vont pas au cinéma. Ils vont souvent au bord du lac. Pour arriver au bord du lac il faut traverser le parc. Pierre aime le traverser. Il regarde les arbres. Robert les regarde aussi, parce qu'il cherche toujours les oiseaux.

—Regardez donc, là-bas, dit-il à Charles. Voyez-vous cet oiseau?

—Oui, je le vois, répond Pierre. C'est un rouge-gorge, n'est-ce pas?

—Oui, qu'il[2] est gros! Ecoutez! Il chante, maintenant.

Le parc est beau. L'herbe est verte. Robert et Pierre l'admirent. Elle est si verte!

—Regardez donc là-bas, dit Robert. C'est Jean.

—Est-ce qu'il nous voit? dit Pierre.

—Non, il ne nous voit pas. Je pense qu'il est très pressé.

Pierre voit un oiseau.

—Voyez-vous cet oiseau? demande-t-il.

—Je le vois. C'est un moineau. Vous savez que le moineau est très commun, continue Robert. Les garçons arrivent au bord du lac.

—Nous voici au lac, dit Pierre.

Grammaire

Pronoun Objects

Here are the personal pronouns used as the direct objects of verbs (accusative case). The forms **nous** and **vous** you already know as subjects (nominative case).

SINGULAR	PLURAL
me, *me*	nous, *us*
te, *you* (familiar)	vous, *you*
le, la, *him, her, it*	les, *them* (m. and f.)
se, *himself*	se, *themselves*

Me, nous, vous are so easy that you cannot make a mistake in using them.

Te is the familiar form of the pronoun *you*. It is much wiser not to use this form until you are proficient in French.

There are, then, only the third-person pronouns that require any thought, and they are not difficult. Note carefully the seven groups that follow:

Pierre traverse le parc. *Peter crosses the park.*
Pierre le traverse. *Peter crosses it.*

Il regarde l'automobile. *He looks at the automobile.*
Il la regarde. *He looks at it.*

Il aime Louise. *He likes Louise.*
Il l'aime. *He likes her.*

[1] Remember that **regarder** (*to look at*) takes a direct object in French.
[2] qu'il=que il. **Que** here means *how*.

Il aime la maison. *He likes the house.*   Il aime les roses. *He likes the roses.*
Il l'aime. *He likes it.*   Il les aime. *He likes them.*

Il aime les restaurants. *He likes the*   Aime-t-il le parc? *Does he like the park?*
restaurants.   L'aime-t-il? *Does he like it?*
Il les aime. *He likes them.*   Il l'aime. *He likes it.*

Any one of the third-person pronouns, le, la, l', les, may be used in speaking of persons or things. When the pronouns represent persons, there is no doubt about gender or number. When the pronoun represents a thing, it is, of course, the gender and number of the noun that determines the gender and number of the pronoun. *A pronoun agrees with its antecedent in gender and number.*

Position of the Pronoun Object

A most important thing to be observed in the use of the personal pronoun object is its position. What is the position of all the noun objects in the seven examples preceding? What is the position of the personal pronoun objects? *A personal pronoun object precedes the verb which governs it.*

Vocabulaire

le bord [bɔːr], *shore, bank*
l'herbe [lɛrb] (f.), *grass, herb*
le lac [lak], *lake*
le moineau [mwano] (pl. les moineaux), *sparrow*
le rouge-gorge [ruʒ gɔrʒ] (pl. les rouges-gorges), *robin*
arriver à [arive a], *to reach, to happen*

faire une promenade [fɛːr yn prɔmnad], *to take a walk*
il fait une promenade [il fɛ tyn prɔmnad], *he takes a walk*
mentionner [mɑ̃sjɔne], *to mention, to name*
vous savez [vu save] (inf. savoir), *you know*

traverser [traverse], *to cross, to go across*
vous voyez [vu vwaje] (inf. voir), *you see;* ils voient [il vwa], *they see*
commun [kɔmœ̃], *common*
bien [bjɛ̃], *well, thoroughly*
trop [trɔ], *too, too much*
là-bas [la bɑ], *down there, over there, yonder*

Questionnaire

1. Avec qui Robert fait-il une promenade?
2. Pourquoi aime-t-il marcher assez lentement?
3. Pourquoi n'aime-t-il pas marcher avec Charles?
4. Où vont les garçons?
5. Pour arriver à l'école, faut-il traverser le parc?
6. Qu'est-ce que Robert cherche toujours?
7. Mentionnez deux oiseaux que les garçons voient au parc.
8. Qu'est-ce que les garçons admirent?
9. Jean voit-il les deux garçons Pierre et Robert?
10. Voyez-vous les oiseaux au parc?
11. Est-ce que les oiseaux aiment les chats?
12. Les chats aiment-ils les oiseaux?

THE PARK OF BUTTES-CHAUMONT, PARIS

Yvon, Paris

Devoir

A. *Rewrite these sentences, using a pronoun instead of the italicized words in each:*

1. Vous mettez *les assiettes* dans la glacière.
2. Vous admirez *ce sofa confortable.*
3. Il n'aime pas du tout regarder *l'aéroplane.*
4. Vous voyez *les grands arbres* devant la pharmacie.
5. Je répète *ce mot.*
6. Il écrit *le douzième devoir* sur les objets chez vous.
7. *La classe* comprend *l'explication.*
8. Nous achetons *les oranges et les côtelettes* au marché.
9. Il tire *la ficelle* de sa poche pour l'attacher au chat.
10. Ils discutent *cette question de la valeur des sports.*
11. Nous amusons *le chat.*
12. Vous regardez *les animaux.*
13. Ils corrigent *ces fautes.*
14. J'indique *le mouton noir.*
15. Pliez-vous toujours *la serviette* après le dîner?

B. *Write or prepare to give in class a brief account of a walk in the park. Use the French words that you know. Make your sentences short. Try to use pronouns to avoid unpleasant repetition. You might begin thus:*

Je traverse le parc pour aller au bord du lac. Au parc je vois, *etc.*

Traduction:

Peter does not like to take a walk with Charles, because Charles walks too fast. How do you walk? When Peter sees the trees and the birds, he likes to look at them. Robert looks at them, too. They see a fat robin and a sparrow. Robert says that the other birds do not like the sparrow.

The boys are going to the lake shore. You go there sometimes, don't you? It is necessary to cross the park to go there. It is beautiful now. The grass is very green, and the trees are green, too. We like this park. What is that over there? It is a sparrow.

TRENTE-SEPTIÈME LEÇON

Les Mouettes

Au bord du lac Robert et Pierre se reposent (*are resting*). Ils regardent le lac. Il est bleu. Les vagues sont petites. Ils les comptent pour savoir si la septième vague est la plus grande (*largest*).

Ils regardent voler les mouettes. Elles ne chantent pas. Ces oiseaux sont blancs et grands. Ils aiment l'eau. Quand ils sont fatigués, ils ne volent pas. Ils flottent sur les vagues. Aimez-vous regarder les mouettes? Les garçons aiment les regarder.

Enfin ils se lèvent pour rentrer à la maison. Une automobile passe. Quelqu'un crie, "Rentrez-vous maintenant?"

C'est Charles. Les deux garçons montent dans l'automobile. Ils ne regardent pas les oiseaux. Ils ne les regardent pas. Les mouettes ne sont pas là, et les garçons les oublient. Ils parlent des vacances.

—Je vais chez vous, dit Charles à Pierre. Ma mère prend le thé chez vous.

—Nous voici à la maison. Descendons, dit Pierre. Ils descendent.

—Je vois ma mère et les autres dames sous la véranda. Les voyez-vous?

—Je les vois, mais où donc est ma mère? répond Charles. N'y[1] est-elle pas?

—Mais si, je la vois dans le coin, près de la porte, dit Pierre. Elle parle à Marie.

—Je la vois aussi maintenant, répond Charles.

Grammaire

The Personal Pronouns

The personal pronouns you have used thus far are given in the following lists. Be sure that you are well acquainted with each of the forms.

Subject		Direct Object	
SING.	PLU.	SING.	PLU.
je	nous	me	nous
tu	vous	te	vous
il	ils	le	les
elle	elles	la	les
		se	se

A pronoun object always precedes the verb of which it is the object.

Je la vois. *I see her.*
Il va le faire. *He is going to do it.*
Vous ne l'avez pas. *You haven't it.*

Present Tense of *Répondre*

The present tense of another regular verb of the third conjugation is given on the next page. The infinitive of the third conjugation must end in what?

---

[1] The e of **ne** is elided before **y** used as a vowel.

Affirmative	*Interrogative*
je répond **s**, *I reply*, etc.	Est-ce que je réponds?
tu répond **s**, *you reply*, etc.	Réponds-tu?
il répond **-**, *he replies*, etc.	Répond-il?
nous répond **ons**, *we reply*	Répondons-nous?
vous répond **ez**, *you reply*	Répondez-vous?
ils répond **ent**, *they reply*	Répondent-ils?

What does the blank after the third person singular indicate? Observe the interrogative third person singular of the verb. The final *d* in this form is pronounced *t*.

Vocabulaire

la dame [dam], *lady*
l'été [lete] (m.), *summer*
la mouette [mwɛt], *sea gull*
le thé [te], *tea*
les vacances [vakɑ̃:s] (f. pl.), *vacation, holidays*
la vague [vag], *wave*
la véranda [verɑ̃da], *porch*
Hélène [elɛn], *Helen*
compter [kõte], *to count, to intend*
descendons [desɑ̃dõ] (inf. descendre), *let's get out*
vous faites [vu fɛt], *you do, you make*

flotter [flɔte], *to float*
ils se lèvent [il sə lɛ:v] (inf. se lever), *they get up, they rise*
elle prend le thé [ɛl prɑ̃ lə te], *she is having tea*
répondre [repõ:dr], *to answer, to reply*
ils se reposent [il sə rəpo:z] (inf. se reposer), *they are resting*
savoir [savwa:r], *to know, to know how*
voler [vɔle], *to fly*

septième [sɛtjɛm], *seventh*
le plus grand, la plus grande [lə ply grɑ̃, la ply grɑ̃:d], *largest*
quelqu'un [kɛlkœ̃], *someone, somebody*
enfin [ɑ̃fɛ̃], *finally, at last*
près de [prɛ də], *near*
sous [su], *under, on*
si [si], *yes* (as an affirmative answer to a negative question). **mais si,** *why yes, of course*

Questionnaire

1. Est-ce que le lac est vert?
2. Pourquoi les garçons comptent-ils les vagues?
3. Que regardent les garçons?
4. Qu'est-ce que les oiseaux aiment?
5. Que faites-vous en été?
6. Qui est dans une automobile?
7. Pourquoi les garçons oublient-ils les mouettes?
8. Où va Charles?
9. Où est la mère de Charles?
10. Qu'est-ce qu'elle fait?
11. Qui ne la voit pas?
12. Pourquoi Charles ne sonne-t-il pas?
13. Rentrez à la maison après la classe, s'il vous plaît.
14. Que signifie "c'est ce que je vais faire"?

Devoir

A. Use pronouns to replace the italicized words:

1. *Robert et Pierre* sont au bord du lac.
2. *Le petit lac* est bleu aujourd'hui, n'est-ce pas?
3. *Les vagues* sont très petites aujourd'hui.
4. Ils comptent *les vagues*.
5. Il comprend *les difficultés*.
6. Je fais *l'appel*.
7. Nous mettons *le lard* dans la cuisine ou dans l'office.
8. Je vais dire *bonjour*.
9. Il n'aime pas du tout lire *les histoires*.
10. Nous regardons *les trois chats* à l'épicerie.

B. *Prepare five questions, similar to the model below, to ask in class. Use a different verb and person of the verb in each of the five questions.*

MODEL

Je regarde les garçons.
Est-ce que Louise les regarde?

C. *Change to the correct verb-forms:*

1. Je (répondre) toujours au professeur.
2. Vous ne (rendre) pas le livre à la bibliothèque.
3. Marie (répondre) -elle en français à Monsieur Michel?
4. Nous (monter) lentement, mais nous (descendre) très vite.
5. Marie et Hélène (acheter) le pain et (continuer) à parler.
6. (Descendre) -ils du même train?
7. (Répondre) -vous toujours aux lettres de grand'mère?

8. Nous (rendre) notre devoir corrigé sur un beau morceau de papier blanc.
9. Je ne (être) pas pressé.
10. Emile (avoir) -il beaucoup de choses dans sa poche?
11. Nous ne (être) pas forts.
12. (Etre) -ils contents?

Traduction:

We are not going to the theater. We are going to the lake. We arrive there late. We look at it. It is very blue, isn't it? We count the waves. Then we watch (**regarder**) the sea gulls. I do not count them, because I see too many (**trop de**) sea gulls. They are large and white. We talk about summer. In summer we have vacation, and we often watch the birds. What do you prefer to do in summer? Do you go to your (**votre**) grandmother's?

TRENTE-HUITIÈME LEÇON
Review

A

1. What is the most vital part of a sentence? Why? (See Study Helps 5, page 5.)
2. What is meant by the expression, "an irregular verb"?
3. Give the infinitive and the present tense of any irregular verb.
4. What is meant by the expression, "a regular verb"?
5. What is the distinguishing mark of an infinitive of the first conjugation?
6. Give as many examples of verbs of the first conjugation as you can recall, together with their meanings.
7. What is the distinguishing mark of an infinitive of the second conjugation? Give an example of a second-conjugation verb.

8. What is the distinguishing mark of an infinitive of the third conjugation?
9. What are the contractions of de and the definite article?
10. Give examples for each form of de and the definite article.
11. When is l' used before a noun?
12. What word beside de contracts when it is used with the definite article? Give examples.
13. What does a pronoun replace?
14. In what ways must a pronoun agree with its antecedent? Illustrate.
15. In French where is the pronoun object placed? Give a sentence showing the position of a noun used as direct object. Change the sentence to show the pronoun direct object.
16. Give the list of subject pronouns. Also direct-object pronouns.

B

I. Give the masculine singular of each of the following adjectives:

cette, ces, facile, verte, treizième, fanée, blanche, rouge

II. Answer the following ten questions, using pronouns to replace italicized words:

1. Voit-il *ces enfants?*
2. Où sont *les clefs?*
3. Entrent-ils *dans le magasin?*
4. Où vont *Hélène et Adèle?*
5. Oublie-t-il *le mot?*
6. Est-ce que *le mouchoir* est *dans le tiroir?*
7. Nous écoutons *l'explication,* n'est-ce pas?
8. Est-ce que *l'explication* est claire?
9. Ne cherchent-ils pas *les soldats?*
10. Sont-ils *dans le parc?*

III. Conjugate these three sentences:

1. Je ne réponds pas.
2. Je choisis cette balle.
3. Je ne désire pas parler.

*IV. Supply the correct form of **de** and the definite article:*

1. Il joue au bord —— lac.
2. Les magasins —— rue sont ouverts.
3. Ils tournent les pages —— journaux.
4. La porte —— école est fermée.
5. Il est à la porte —— cinéma.

V. Use the following forms in sentences:
au, à la, à l', aux.

VI. Use the following nouns in questions. Try to have a different verb or at least a different form of the verb for each question.

le store   les chaises
la carte   la rue
la T. S. F.   la bicyclette

VII. Review the vocabularies of Lessons 22-37 for a test, oral or written.

PHONETIC REVIEW

A. Read aloud:

1. Le héros parle aux élèves.
   [lə ero parl o zelɛːv.]

2. L'herbe est verte maintenant.
   [lɛrb ɛ vɛrt mɛ̃tnã.]

3. Nous choisissons un ballon.
   [nu ʃwazisõ œ̃ balõ.]

4. C'est un bel hôtel.
   [sɛ tœ̃ bɛl ɔtɛl.]

5. Il lit la lettre lentement.
   [il li la lɛtr lãtmã.]

B. Pronounce and write in phonetic characters:

1. Le héros du match est intelligent.
2. Ils achètent un aéroplane.
3. L'herbe devant l'hôtel est belle.
4. Il mange un petit pain et un morceau de chocolat.
5. Nous avons une heure de grammaire.

Meurisse, Paris

A TYPICAL MORNING SCENE ON FOCH AVENUE, NEAR THE BOIS

FRENCH CHILDHOOD

Childhood affords a briefer span of happiness in France than with us, for very early in life a French boy must turn his thoughts to the serious problems of school and his career. Formerly the French girl had to retire into seclusion to await her marriage. Now, however, French girls are seeking economic freedom in the professions and trades, just as girls do in America.

But those few gay early years are never forgotten. On fine days, as in summer, Paris children spend their play hours on the stately boulevards of the Bois—a great park. Little girls in short dresses above bare brown knees, wide straw hats with streamers flying in the breeze, chase their hoops merrily up and down the winding paths. Little boys in short trousers and wide open jackets, flat woolen caps perched on their tousled hair, whip their tops in the way of idling pedestrians. Sometimes the news spreads along these pleasant bypaths that Guignol

is showing on the next street. This is a puppet play quite like our familiar Punch and Judy. Then the children run madly to join the young audience which has already gathered under broad shade trees, and they wait with breathless eagerness to see the curtains part and to hear the squeaky voices of the puppets as they play a drama that seems more real than life itself. Sometimes, for a rare treat, nurse takes the children for a stroll on more exciting highways, along the banks of the Seine, where striped umbrellas are the only roofs of open bookstalls. Here are marvelous picture books on sale for a franc or two; and these always seem more delightful than costly presents bought at a regular shop. In winter time, every few years there is the thrill of unexpected snow and a spell of freezing weather. Ice skates are brought hurriedly forth from their long retirement, and the lagoons of the

Bois are dotted with bright-colored sweaters and sports costumes.

In the country, where there are no parks to play in, the children are not so easily found, but the motoring tourist often flashes by groups of strange small figures in quiet, out-of-the-way hamlets. Without exception these figures are clad in black frocks, or checkered blue ones, that reach nearly to their shoe-tops; they scamper along the road past the great stone château, pausing to gape at the turkeys that strut in the barnyard, giggling loudly as the fat geese cackle. If you peer under their wide-brimmed hats, to your surprise you find that half at least of these odd beings have the bright, lean faces of little French boys. It is still the custom in rural villages for boys and girls alike to wear these long, serviceable smocks, and the only distinctive marks the children bear are the braids of hair and earrings that bespeak the girls.

But all too soon, for youngsters in both town and country, life becomes a serious thing indeed. At the country crossroads the boys and girls part, for in France they are taught in separate schools. In the city, too, the carefree days of gay companionship are gone—never again are the girls playmates of boys until they are grown-up young ladies ready for marriage, and by that time they must follow a hundred social rules that prevent easy and simple association. Meanwhile, school tasks leave little chance for happy play, whether these be studied in a school of primary instruction, which poorer children attend until they are thirteen years of age, or in a *lycée*, attended by children whose parents can afford to give them a better education.

The communal schools are most interesting in the rural districts, where they are old-fashioned and quaint. On long unpainted benches, that have no backs to lean against, the small urchins wriggle uncomfortably through the school day.

Photo A. Breger Frères, Paris

VILLAGE SCHOOLS
At the left is the school for boys, and at the right, the one for girls.

LYCÉE HENRI IV, PARIS   Photo A. Breger Frères, Paris

The schoolroom is often provided with a small organ, maps hang along the walls, and in the big cabinets weights and measures of various sorts mingle with stuffed birds and collections of minerals. The session lasts from eight to four, with two hours at noon for dinner and a nap. Most pupils who attend these rural communal schools have lost all semblance of childhood long before they graduate at thirteen. Usually they then return to the soil, to become hardened tillers of it, like their ancestors before them, and schooling soon gets to be only a blurred recollection of their early days. But a few families manage to send their sons to a secondary school which teaches a trade, or to a normal school where teachers are prepared for the communal schools.

The *lycée*, which serves the richer young people in France, keeps its students until their sixteenth or seventeenth year, when they are required to pass a stiff examination called the baccalaureate. If successful, they receive a certificate which is as valuable to them as our high-school diploma is to us; because without it they are barred from entering any of the higher schools of education. Passing this examination means success in life, for the more prosperous types of French youth are ambitious to train for some profession, that they may become important citizens.

So, when the time comes for his baccalaureate, the French boy packs his traveling bag. Nervous and pale he sits through his last luncheon and gulps down what he can of his eggs, crisp salad, Roquefort cheese, and fruit. He pecks at his mother's cheek dutifully, and then with cap pulled down to hide the moisture in his eyes, he hurries to the shabby station, unmindful of the gay signs and scenic posters which line its dusty walls. Here he secures a third-class ticket and starts for the city in which the district examination is to be held. The train flashes him by rolling fields of golden wheat and crowded little towns. Often a château looms on a hilltop, its slate-roofed towers and serried ramparts gleaming in the sun. The boy looks dismally at this relic of feudal warfare, its moat and keep, and with sinking heart remembers his history books. Will he ever pass his examination?

Practical are the day-dreams of the French schoolboy: of soldiers in white gaiters and gloves and with red epaulets on parade at the Polytechnic School; of youths who capture the "Prize of Rome" at the School of Fine Arts and are sent to study at government expense at the Villa Medicis in Rome. The earnest schoolboy knows that he must toil from childhood on, if he would bring such glory as this to his paternal home. It is the rule in France for a boy to be studious, and not the exception, as it often is with us. At sixteen the French pupil is as far advanced as the American student at nineteen, although the subjects that they study are very much the same. Especially in his ability to speak foreign languages does the French pupil outstrip his American rival.

French girls, too, can now prepare for the same examinations as their brothers. More and more, the French girl is finding her place beside her brother. The professions are open to her. She may become a successful lawyer, doctor, or pharmacist, while innumerable positions are available to her as secretary, typist, or post-office employee. Naturally, as the center of fashion, Paris dressmaking establishments have hundreds of young girls in their employ. Marriage is no longer the only career open to French girls. However, in the wealthy families, young girls rarely or never appear in public unchaperoned, and marriage is considered practically the only aim.

In contrast to an indulged American youth, the French boy or girl has practically nothing. But because this rôle of seriousness and maturity must descend upon the child at an early age, the period of joyous blissful babyhood is very beautiful. So gracious is the memory of it that the tradition will go on unbroken for centuries— little girls, bare-kneed, short-skirted, chasing the rolling hoops, and little boys, in knickerbockers, spinning their painted tops in the Bois.

A SCENE IN THE BOIS DE BOULOGNE

TRENTE-NEUVIÈME LEÇON

Voici l'été

Voici l'été! André et Monette sont contents. Ils ne vont pas à l'école maintenant. André et Monette aiment aller à l'école. Ils étudient bien, mais pendant les vacances ils aiment jouer.

Les parents d'André et de Monette vont passer l'été dans un petit village près d'un lac. Il faut prendre le train et voyager pour y arriver.

Les enfants sont impatients. Papa achète les billets pour la petite famille. Noiraud, le chien d'André, va aussi aller à la campagne.

La locomotive est grande, et le train marche vite. Maman a une surprise pour les enfants. Elle a une grande boîte blanche. A midi elle ouvre la boîte. Voilà un bon petit repas, des sandwichs, des petits gâteaux, des fruits, et deux tablettes de chocolat pour les enfants. Noiraud demande aussi quelque chose à manger. Il mange du pain, et quand maman ne regarde pas, André lui donne un morceau de gâteau. Noiraud aime cela.

Enfin la famille arrive à la campagne. André et Monette courent dans la maison pour regarder leurs chambres. Les chambres ne sont pas très grandes, mais elles sont très jolies. André et Monette aiment leurs chambres. Après ils vont dans le jardin. Au bout du jardin est le lac. Il est si bleu!

—Maman, nous désirons nager.

—Oui, s'il vous plaît, maman.

—Bien, répond maman. Vos costumes sont dans vos chambres. Papa va avec vous parce que les vagues sont hautes aujourd'hui.

Les enfants courent vers le lac. L'herbe est si verte! Papa arrive après les enfants. Les enfants sont déjà dans le lac.

—O papa, c'est amusant, crie Monette. Je suis contente.

Papa regarde nager les enfants. Après quelque temps les enfants sont fatigués. Ils arrivent à côté de papa, et ils regardent les vagues.

—Voilà des mouettes, crie André.

—Oui, répond papa. Regardez comme elles volent. Quand elles sont fatiguées, elles flottent sur les vagues.

—J'aime regarder les mouettes, dit Monette. Elles sont très belles.

Les enfants font souvent des promenades avec leurs parents. Ils traversent le bois. Ils regardent les arbres et ils cherchent les oiseaux. Après la promenade ils rentrent à la maison. Les enfants sont fatigués parce que la promenade est longue. Qu'est-ce qu'il faut faire après une longue promenade? Il faut manger quelque chose.

Papa comprend bien les enfants. Il sait bien les amuser. Il cherche un livre et il lit une histoire amusante aux enfants. Ils oublient qu'ils sont fatigués.

André et Monette aiment aussi jouer[1] au tennis. Quelquefois ils invitent les enfants de la maison voisine, et alors la petite bande joue au tennis, court dans le bois, ou nage dans le lac.

Noiraud joue aussi. Il est content de jouer avec les enfants. André jette un bout de bois, et Noiraud le cherche. Il aime cela. Papa et maman regardent jouer les enfants. Ils sont contents aussi.

[1] See note 2 for Lesson 28, page 77.

Vocabulaire

le billet [bijɛ], *ticket, note*

le bois [bwɑ] (pl. les bois), *wood*

le bout [bu], *piece, end, bit*

la campagne [kɑ̃paɲ], *country*

le chien [ʃjɛ̃], *dog*

le gâteau [gɑto] (pl. les gâteaux), *cake*

la promenade [prɔmnad], *walk, excursion*

le repas [rəpɑ] (pl. les repas), *meal*

la tablette [tablɛt], *tablet, bar*

André [ɑ̃dre], *Andrew*

Monette [mɔnɛt], there is no English equivalent

Noiraud [nwaro], *Blackie*

courir [kuriːr], *to run*

il jette [il ʒɛːt] (inf. jeter), *he hurls, he throws*

ils font des promenades [il fõ de prɔmnad] (infinitive faire), *they take walks*

nager [naʒe], *to swim*

prendre [prɑ̃ːdr], *to take, to obtain*

haut [o], *high*

voisin, voisine [vwazɛ̃, vwazin], *neighboring*

vos [vo] (plural), *your*

cela [səla], *that*

comme [kɔm], *how*

au bout de [o bu də], *at the end of, at the bottom of*

si [si], *so*

pendant [pɑ̃dɑ̃], *during*

The following list of words you were able to read without vocabulary help because of their exact likeness or similarity to English words:

la bande [bɑ̃ːd], *band, group*

la chambre [ʃɑ̃ːbr], *chamber, room*

le chocolat [ʃɔkɔla], *chocolate*

le fruit [frɥi], *fruit*

les parents [parɑ̃] (m. pl.), *parents*

le sandwich [sɑ̃dwitʃ], *sandwich*

la surprise [syrpriːz], *surprise*

le tennis [tɛnis], *tennis*

le village [vilaːʒ], *village*

inviter [ɛ̃vite], *to ask, to invite*

voyager [vwajaʒe], *to travel, to take a trip*

amusant [amyzɑ̃], *amusing*

long, longue [lõ, lõːg], *long*

MONCEAU PARK, ONE OF THE MOST BEAUTIFUL PLACES IN PARIS

QUARANTIÈME LEÇON
Les Enfants dans le parc

Papa et les deux enfants, Raoul et Virginie, sont dans le parc. Papa lit, et les enfants jouent. Les enfants ont chaud parce qu'ils courent. Papa n'a pas chaud parce qu'il ne court pas. Il est assis sur un banc. Il a envie de lire, mais les enfants ont envie de courir. Avez-vous envie de lire ou de courir?

Papa lit. Puis il met le journal de côté et ferme les yeux.

Virginie voit un grand chien brun. Elle court vite vers papa parce qu'elle a peur de ce chien.

—Qu'as-tu?[1, 2] dit papa.

Virginie rougit. Elle a honte, mais elle répond:

—Je n'aime pas les chiens, tu sais.

—Il ne faut pas avoir peur d'un chien, dit papa.

Il appelle le chien, qui est dans le parc avec son maître. Le chien court et saute de joie. Il n'est pas méchant.

Il aime jouer. Papa et Raoul jouent avec le chien pour montrer à Virginie qu'il n'est pas méchant. Comme les enfants, ce chien aime beaucoup jouer. Enfin le chien part[3] avec son maître.

—Papa, nous avons faim, dit Raoul, qui sait bien que papa a une tablette de chocolat.

—Oui, papa, nous avons très faim, répète Virginie, qui aime toujours le chocolat.

Papa donne un gros morceau de chocolat à Virginie et un gros morceau de chocolat à Raoul. Ils mangent le chocolat de bon appétit.

Comme ce chocolat est bon!

—Que c'est bon! dit Raoul. Maintenant j'ai soif. Je vais à la fontaine pour chercher de l'eau, papa.

—J'ai soif aussi. J'y vais avec Raoul, dit la petite fille, qui imite toujours son frère.

Grammaire
Idioms with *Avoir*

The verb **avoir** is so important in French that you should know it perfectly. Are you sure that you can use the forms of the present tense?

j'ai, *I have*	nous avons, *we have*
tu as, *you have*	vous avez, *you have*
il a, *he has*	ils ont, *they have*

In French there is a group of idioms which depend on **avoir** to furnish the verb. Most of such expressions deal with physical sensations or emotions, or with physical states, e.g.,

avoir froid = *to be cold*	avoir sommeil = *to be sleepy*
avoir chaud = *to be hot*	avoir peur = *to be afraid*
avoir faim = *to be hungry*	avoir envie de (followed by infinitive) = *to wish*
avoir soif = *to be thirsty*	avoir honte = *to be ashamed*

The whole list is not given here. Learn these expressions and be on the alert to find others of the same kind.

[1] Qu'as-tu? *What is the matter with you?*
[2] Beginning with this lesson, the familiar form **tu** will be used. However, in translating *you* into French, the pupils should use **vous**.
[3] From the irregular verb **partir**.

Vocabulaire

l'appétit [lapeti] (m.), *appetite;* **de bon appétit** [də bõ napeti], *with relish*
le banc [bɑ̃], *bench*
la fontaine [fõtɛn], *fountain*
le frère [frɛːr], *brother*
le maître [mɛːtr], *master, teacher*
le sac [sak], *sack, bag*
Raoul [raul], *Ralph*
Virginie [virʒini], *Virginia*
appeler [aple], *to call*
il appelle[1] [il apɛl] (inf. appeler), *he calls*
montrer [mõtre], *to show, to point out*

il part [il paːr] (inf. *partir*), *he leaves*
rougir [ruʒiːr], *to blush, to become red*
tu sais [tyse] (inf. *savoir*), *you know, you know how*
sauter [sote], *to jump;* **sauter de joie** [soted ʒwɑ], *to jump for joy*
avoir chaud [avwaːr ʃo], *to be hot, to be warm*
avoir envie de [avwaːr ɑ̃vi də], *to wish*
avoir faim [avwaːr fɛ̃], *to be hungry*
avoir froid [avwaːr frwɑ], *to be cold*

avoir honte [avwaːr õːt], *to be ashamed*
avoir peur [avwaːr pœːr], *to be afraid, to fear*
avoir soif [avwaːr swaf], *to be thirsty*
avoir sommeil [avwaːr sɔmɛːj], *to be sleepy*
brun [brœ̃], *brown*
chaud [ʃo], *warm, hot*
féroce [ferɔs], *fierce, ferocious*
méchant [meʃɑ̃], *wicked, bad, naughty, mischievous*
que c'est bon [kə sɛ bõ], *how good this is, how good it is*

Questionnaire

1. Où sont papa et les enfants?
2. Qu'est-ce que papa a envie de faire?
3. Qu'est-ce que les enfants ont envie de faire?
4. Papa a-t-il chaud?
5. Pourquoi Virginie court-elle vers papa?
6. Pourquoi rougit-elle?
7. Que fait papa quand il voit que la petite fille a peur de ce chien?
8. Pourquoi le chien saute-t-il?
9. Pourquoi papa et Raoul jouent-ils avec le chien?
10. Qu'est-ce que papa donne aux enfants, quand ils ont faim?
11. Raoul où va-t-il et pourquoi?
12. Qui y va avec Raoul?

Devoir

A. Supply the necessary words:

1. S'ils ont ———, ils cherchent quelque chose à manger.
2. Il prend un verre d'eau parce qu'il a ———.
3. Quand un enfant court il a ———.
4. Le héros n'a pas ———.
5. Nous avons ——— de voyager.
6. Je rougis quand j'ai ———.
7. Le beau petit garçon n'étudie pas, parce qu'il a ———.
8. Vous avez ——— de nager.
9. J'ai ——— d'écouter la T. S. F.

B. Use these expressions in sentences with the indicated pronouns:

il (avoir) honte
je (avoir) peur
nous (avoir) chaud
elles (avoir) froid
vous (avoir) sommeil
ils (avoir) envie de

C. Conjugate these sentences:

1. Je remplis le sac.
2. J'appelle le petit garçon.
3. Je ne vole pas comme un oiseau.
4. Je n'ai pas l'air fatigué.

[1] Notice the doubling of the consonant to prevent a succession of mute syllables within a word. In what person will the change in spelling occur?

Traduction:

Are you hungry?

Yes, I am hungry, but I know that father has a bar of chocolate. He is going to give a piece of chocolate to Ralph, because he likes (le) chocolate.

I am going to the fountain because I am thirsty. Are you not thirsty?

I wish to go there, too. I am hot. When I am hot, I am always thirsty.

Look at that dog. I am afraid of dogs.

One should not (**Il ne faut pas**) be afraid of dogs. This dog is not fierce. He wishes to play, and he jumps for joy when you call him.

QUARANTE ET UNIÈME LEÇON

Le Chapeau retrouvé

Virginie et Raoul racontent à maman les aventures de l'après-midi.

—Papa a lu le journal, dit Virginie, mais Raoul et moi, nous avons joué. D'abord, nous avons été au parc où nous avons joué seuls, mais après nous avons joué au bord du lac avec un chien, un gros chien.

—Comment! (*What!*) Vous avez joué avec ce chien!

—Oui, papa et moi nous avons joué avec ce chien. J'ai jeté la balle, et le chien a attrapé la balle. Il a attrapé la balle presque chaque fois, n'est-ce pas, Raoul?

—Il a attrapé la balle chaque fois et il a rapporté la balle presque chaque fois. Et tu sais, maman, nous n'avons pas perdu la balle. Nous l'avons ici, n'est-ce pas? a dit Raoul. Et après, maman, nous avons presque perdu le chapeau de Virginie. Elle a eu si peur! Elle a ôté son chapeau, et elle a oublié de donner son chapeau à papa. Tout à coup elle a crié:

—Où donc est mon chapeau? Nous avons cherché partout, mais nous ne l'avons pas trouvé. Enfin Virginie a dit à papa qu'elle avait perdu (*had lost*) son chapeau. Il a vu quelque chose très loin, et nous avons couru pour le ramasser. Virginie a sauté de joie quand elle a retrouvé son chapeau.

Grammaire

The Past Indefinite

So far you have learned to use one tense in French—the present; and you have also learned to express the approximate future by using **aller** and the infinitive. Now you are going to become acquainted with the most common of all the past tenses in French. It is used in speaking and writing of an act completed in the past. This tense is called the *past indefinite*.

To form the past indefinite we use the present tense of the verb **avoir,** *to have,* and the past participle of the verb in question. (Because **avoir** gives this kind of assistance to other verbs, it is known as an auxiliary, or helping, verb. It is so called in English also, where it does the same sort of work: I *have* looked at the book.)

Je regarde le livre, *I am looking at the book,* etc.
J'ai regardé le livre, *I looked* (*have looked, did look*) *at the book.*

The usual translation for the past indefinite corresponds to the simple past in English: *I looked at the book.*

You know the present tense of **avoir** so well that you will have no difficulty with the auxiliary of the past indefinite. As for the past participle, it is easy enough in regular verbs. Learn the endings from the following table:

	Infinitive		*Past Participle*	
FIRST CONJUGATION	er	jouer	é	joué
SECOND CONJUGATION	ir	finir	i	fini
THIRD CONJUGATION	re	répondre	u	répondu

A few irregular past participles are used in "Le Chapeau retrouvé." Be sure to learn them one by one as you come upon them. It is surprisingly easy to learn them this way.

Past Indefinite

FIRST CONJUGATION

Singular	*Plural*
j'ai joué, *I played, have played,* etc.	nous avons joué, *we played, have played,* etc.
tu as joué, *you played, have played,* etc.	vous avez joué, *you played, have played,* etc.
il a joué, *he played, has played,* etc.	ils ont joué, *they played, have played,* etc.

SECOND CONJUGATION

j'ai fini, *I finished, have finished,* etc.	nous avons fini, *we finished, have finished,* etc.
tu as fini, *you finished, have finished,* etc.	vous avez fini, *you finished, have finished,* etc.
il a fini, *he finished, has finished,* etc.	ils ont fini, *they finished, have finished,* etc.

THIRD CONJUGATION

j'ai répondu, *I replied, have replied,* etc.	nous avons répondu, *we replied, have replied,* etc.
tu as répondu, *you replied, have replied,* etc.	vous avez répondu, *you replied, have replied,* etc.
il a répondu, *he replied, has replied,* etc.	ils ont répondu, *they replied, have replied,* etc.

Vocabulaire

l'après-midi [laprɛmidi] (m.), *afternoon* or *in the afternoon*

la fois [fwa], *time* (in the sense of occurrence)

attraper [atrape], *to catch*

couru [kury] (p.p. of **courir**), *run*

dit [di] (p.p. of **dire**), *said*

été [ete] (p.p. of **être**), *been*

eu [y] (p.p. of **avoir**), *had*

fait [fɛ] (p.p. of **faire**), *made, done*

jeter [ʒəte], *to throw, to throw away*

lu [ly] (p.p. of **lire**), *read*

perdre [pɛrdr] (p.p. **perdu**), *to lose*

raconter [rakõte], *to tell, to recount*

rapporter [rapɔrte], *to bring, to bring back*

vu [vy] (p.p. of **voir**), *seen*

chaque [ʃak], *each, every*

seul [sœl], *alone, only*

d'abord [dabɔːr], *at first, first*

presque [prɛskə], *almost, nearly*

partout [partu], *everywhere*

tout à coup [tu ta ku], *suddenly, all at once, all of a sudden*

Questionnaire

1. A qui parlent les enfants?
2. Où ont-ils été?
3. Est-ce qu'ils ont joué seuls?
4. Qui a jeté la balle?
5. Qu'est-ce que le chien a fait avec la balle?
6. A-t-il rapporté la balle?
7. Les enfants ont-ils perdu la balle?
8. Où est la balle?
9. Qui a eu si peur?
10. Qu'est-ce que Virginie a oublié de donner à papa?
11. Où les enfants ont-ils cherché le chapeau?
12. Qui a vu le chapeau?
13. Pourquoi Virginie a-t-elle sauté de joie?

Devoir

A. What is the past participle of each of the following verbs?

réfléchir	faire	courir
rendre	avoir	répondre
baisser	être	finir
lire	dire	voir

*B. Give the past indefinite negative of each of the verbs in A. Put **ne** before and **pas** after **avoir**.*

C. Change the verbs in the following sentences to the corresponding forms of the past indefinite:

1. Nous finissons cette leçon.
2. Vous trouvez la page sur l'article défini, n'est-ce pas?
3. Lit-il le journal avant le dîner?
4. Est-ce que je perds souvent quelque chose?
5. Les bonnes sont au marché.
6. Il ne voit pas le banc.
7. Il ne fait pas ce devoir.
8. Nous mangeons ces pommes de terre.
9. Courez-vous pour attraper la balle?
10. Etudient-ils la leçon?

D. Conjugate these sentences:
1. Je n'ai pas perdu le ballon à midi.
2. J'ai vu le chien.
3. J'ai eu peur.

Traduction:

We played in the park this afternoon. We saw (*there*) a big brown dog. We threw the ball to the dog, and he brought back the ball. Sometimes he caught the ball. Afterwards we played alone. Virginia almost lost her (**son**) hat. She took her hat off, but she forgot to give it to father. She looked for her (**son**) hat, but she did not see it. Father saw the hat **far** away, and we ran to get it.

Wide World Photos, Paris

FOCH AVENUE, NEAR THE BOIS

QUARANTE-DEUXIÈME LEÇON
Une Explication

Hélène reste après la classe pour parler avec le professeur.   Hélène n'a pas compris ce que le professeur a expliqué en classe.

Hélène: Je suis très bête, mademoiselle, mais je n'ai pas compris l'explication en classe.   Voulez-vous (*will you*) la répéter?

Le professeur: Avec plaisir, Hélène. Mais pourquoi n'avez-vous pas compris cette explication?

Hélène: Je ne sais pas, mademoiselle. J'ai fait attention à tout ce que vous avez dit chaque fois.

Le professeur: Bon! Regardez donc. Je mets ce crayon dans le tiroir.   Le crayon, c'est quelque chose; alors je mets quelque chose dans le tiroir. J'ouvre l'autre tiroir.   Est-ce que j'y mets quelque chose?

Hélène: Non, mademoiselle.

Le professeur: Bon! Je ne mets rien dans ce tiroir.   Je vais écrire cette phrase au tableau.   Regardez maintenant.   Quel mot précède le verbe?

Hélène: Le mot **ne** précède[1] le verbe. Mais pourquoi, mademoiselle?

Le professeur: Traduisez la phrase.

Hélène: I don't put anything into the drawer.

Le professeur: C'est bien.   *I don't put anything* or *I put nothing.*   La phrase est au négatif.   Voilà pourquoi le petit mot **ne** précède le verbe.   Remarquez que le mot **rien** est traduit *not anything* et aussi *nothing.*   Que signifie **jamais?**

Hélène: Le mot **jamais** signifie *never.*

Le professeur: Est-ce un mot négatif?

Hélène: Oui, mademoiselle.   Est-ce que **ne** précède le verbe?

Le professeur: Bien sûr.   Que signifie le mot **personne?**

Hélène: No one, et **ne** précède le verbe.

Le professeur: C'est ça.   Vous avez compris cette fois.   Employez le mot **personne** dans une phrase.

Hélène: **Personne** n'est assis.   Je n'y vois **personne**.   Je comprends maintenant.   Merci, mademoiselle.

Grammaire
Negative Words

The negative expression which you already know very well is **ne . . . pas.** In "Une Explication" you learn three other useful ones:

ne . . . personne, *no one, not anyone*
ne . . . rien, *nothing, not anything*
ne . . . jamais, *never, not ever*

The words **personne, rien,** and **jamais** are known as negative words.   Whenever a negative word is used in a sentence, **ne** must precede the verb.   When **personne, rien,** or **jamais** is used alone, the word **ne** is omitted.

Qui a appelé?   Personne n'a appelé.
Qui a appelé?   Personne.

Que mange-t-il?   Il ne mange rien.
Que mange-t-il?   Rien.

Quand y allez-vous?   Je n'y vais jamais.
Quand y allez-vous?   Jamais.

[1] **précéder**—je précède, il précède, **vous précédez.**   Observe the change of accent.

Archives du Touring-Club de France

A TYPICAL INLAND VILLAGE, CONNECTED WITH THE OUTER WORLD BY A WINDING
MOUNTAIN ROAD

Observe that three of the negative words have as antonyms (opposites) words which are easily grouped, as below:

Negative	Affirmative
jamais, *never*	quelquefois, *sometimes*
rien, *nothing*	quelque chose, *something*
personne, *no one, nobody*	quelqu'un, *anyone*

Chantez-vous quelquefois? *Do you sing sometimes?*
Je ne chante jamais. *I never sing.*

Avez-vous quelque chose? *Have you something?*
Je n'ai rien. *I have nothing.*

Voyez-vous quelqu'un? *Do you see anyone?*
Je ne vois personne. *I see no one (or I don't see anyone).*

Vocabulaire

la **banane** [banan], *banana*
ça [sa] (contraction of **cela**), *that*
c'est ça [sɛ sa], *that is it, that is correct, that's right*
je comprends [ʒə kõprɑ̃] (inf. **comprendre**), *I understand*
compris [kõpri] (p.p. of **comprendre**), *understood*

remarquer [rəmarke], *to notice*
traduit [tradɥi] (p. participle of **traduire**), *translated*
vous voulez [vu vule] (inf. **vouloir**), *you wish, you will, you want*
ce que [sə kə], *what, that which*
bête [bɛ:t], *stupid*

négatif, -ve [negatif, negati:v], *negative*
jamais [ʒamɛ], *never*
personne [pɛrsɔn], *no one, nobody*
rien [rjẽ], *nothing*
sûr, bien sûr [sy:r, bjẽ sy:r], *sure; of course, certainly*
voilà pourquoi [vwala purkwa], *that is the reason, that is why*

Questionnaire

1. Pourquoi Hélène reste-t-elle après la classe?
2. Qu'est-ce que le professeur a répété?
3. Qu'est-ce qu'Hélène a fait en classe?
4. Qu'est-ce que le professeur met dans le tiroir?
5. Ne met-elle rien dans l'autre tiroir?
6. Pourquoi le mot **ne** précède-t-il le verbe?
7. Comment le mot **rien** est-il traduit en anglais?
8. Ne voyez-vous personne ici?
9. N'avez-vous jamais faim?

Devoir

A. *Complete these sentences by using the correct forms of the past indefinite:*

1. Il —— remarqué l'illustration.
2. Vous —— mangé trois bananes.
3. Ils ont (lire) et (traduire) quelques pages de l'histoire.
4. Je —— continué ma phrase.
5. Elle a (faire) le devoir à l'école.
6. Elles ont (comprendre) ce qu'elle —— dit à la boulangerie.
7. J'ai (voir) cet arbre.
8. Il a (courir) à l'aéroplane.
9. Nous avons (avoir) soif.
10. Ils ont (être) au marché.

B. *Change the verbs to the present tense:*

1. Voilà pourquoi il a vu l'auto.
2. Est-ce que j'ai compris l'explication?
3. Vous avez rendu ce manteau.
4. Ils ont presque fini le discours.
5. Nous avons mangé de bon appétit.

C. *Answer the following questions in the negative, using* **jamais, rien,** *or* **personne.**

1. Etudiez-vous quelquefois?
2. Ont-ils quelque chose?
3. Voyez-vous quelqu'un?
4. Dansons-nous quelquefois?
5. Qui a fait l'appel?

QUARANTE-TROISIÈME LEÇON

Le Passé indéfini

Le professeur: Bonjour, mes élèves. Aujourd'hui nous allons parler du passé indéfini.

La classe: Nous l'avons déjà étudié, mademoiselle.

Le professeur: Nous avons commencé l'étude du passé indéfini. Nous ne l'avons pas finie. Qui sait les noms des deux parties du passé indéfini?

Marie: L'auxiliaire et le participe passé.

Le professeur: Quel est l'auxiliaire?

Joseph: L'auxiliaire est le présent du verbe **avoir,** et le participe passé est un mot qui se termine (*ends*) toujours par e aigu.

La classe: Pas toujours. Quelquefois le participe passé se termine par u.

Louise: Et quelquefois par i.

Claire: Et quelquefois le participe passé est irrégulier.

Le professeur: Bon! Organisons[1] un peu ces renseignements! Quand le participe passé se termine-t-il par e aigu? Charles, savez-vous?

Charles: Toujours.

Le professeur: Pas toujours, Charles. Qui est-ce qui sait?

Adèle: Quand l'infinitif se termine par er, le participe passé se termine par e aigu.

Le professeur: Bon! C'est ça. Quelles sont les autres terminaisons du participe passé?

La classe: i, si l'infinitif se termine par ir et u si l'infinitif se termine par re.

Le professeur: C'est bien ça. Aujourd'hui nous allons employer le pronom régime avec le passé indéfini. Donnez les pronoms.

La classe: **me, te, le, nous, vous, les.**

Claire: Et aussi **la.**

Le professeur: Vous avez raison.[2] Il ne faut pas oublier le féminin. Regardez bien ces phrases.

J'ai fermé la porte. Je l'ai fermée.

Il a fermé la porte. Il l'a fermée.

Nous avons fermé les fenêtres. Nous les avons fermées.

Nous avons choisi la robe. Nous l'avons choisie.

Quel mot changez-vous?

Robert: Le participe passé change.

Le professeur: Pourquoi ce changement?

Joseph: Le participe passé s'accorde toujours avec le régime.

Le professeur: Pas toujours, Joseph. (*Le professeur indique la phrase—* J'ai fermé la porte.) Le mot **fermé** ne s'accorde pas avec **la porte.**

Joseph: Je comprends, mademoiselle.

Le professeur: Le participe passé d'un verbe conjugué avec **avoir** s'accorde avec le régime direct, si le régime précède le verbe. Avez-vous compris? Oui? C'est bien, alors.

---

[1] **Organisons,** *Let us collect,* or *let us organize.*
[2] Add **avoir raison** to the list of idioms using **avoir.** See if you can remember any of them before turning to page 112, on which they are given.

Grammaire

The Agreement of the Past Participle

In Lessons 41 and 42 you saw a number of sentences which contained direct objects following the complete verb, that is, the auxiliary and the past participle. Such sentences are very simple:

Le chien a attrapé la balle. *The dog caught the ball.*
Nous avons regardé les chiens. *We looked at the dogs.*

The case is somewhat different when a personal pronoun, instead of a noun, is the direct object. Look carefully at the following:

1. Il a regardé Marie. *He looked at Marie.*
2. Il l'a regardée. *He looked at her.*

1. Nous avons regardé les chiens. *We looked at the dogs.*
2. Nous les avons regardés. *We looked at them.*

What has happened in the sentences numbered 2? The personal pronoun objects, **la** and **les,** come before the verb (the auxiliary). This does not surprise you, since you learned in Lesson 36 that "a personal pronoun object precedes the verb that governs it." But notice the endings of the past participle. Instead of the pure form **regardé**, we find **regardée** and **regardés.** The rule is easy: When a personal pronoun is the direct object, *it precedes the auxiliary,* which is considered the verb; and the past participle *agrees in gender and number with the object.*

The case is not different when the sentence is negative. **Ne** and **pas** take their regular positions, **ne** before the verb (the auxiliary) and **pas** after it. Remember that **ne** and the pronoun must precede **avoir.**

Nous n'avons pas regardé les chiens. *We have not looked at the dogs.*
Nous ne les avons pas regardés. *We have not looked at them.*

Vocabulaire

l'auxiliaire [lɔksiljɛːr](m.), *auxiliary*
le changement [ʃãʒmã], *change*
le nom [nõ], *name*
le participe [partisip], *participle*
la partie [parti], *part, rôle, portion*
le passé indéfini [pase ɛ̃defini], *past indefinite*
le pronom [pronõ], *pronoun*
la raison [rɛzõ], *reason*
le régime [reʒim], *object*
la règle [rɛgl], *rule, ruler*

le renseignement [rãsɛɲmã], *information;* plural, *pieces* or *bits of information*
le résultat [rezylta], *result, answer to a problem, score*
le sujet [syʒɛ], *subject*
Claire [klɛːr], *Clara*
avoir raison [avwaːr rɛzõ], *to be right*
il s'accorde [il sakɔrd], *it agrees*
conjuguer [kõʒyge], *to conjugate*

écrit [ekri] (p.p. of **écrire**), *written*
il se termine [il sə tɛrmin], *it ends*
aigu, aiguë [ɛgy], *sharp, acute*
direct [dirɛkt], *direct*
régulier, -ière [regylje, regyljɛːr], *regular*
irrégulier, -ière [iregylje, iregyljɛːr], *irregular*
c'est bien ça [sɛ bjɛ̃ sa], *that's exactly right; that's very good*
quoi [kwa], *what*

Questionnaire

1. De quoi ont parlé les élèves et le professeur?
2. Est-ce que nous avons fini l'étude du passé indéfini?
3. Quelles sont les deux parties du passé indéfini?
4. Quel auxiliaire est employé au (*in the*) passé indéfini?
5. Par quoi se terminent les participes passés des verbes réguliers?
6. Quels sont les pronoms régimes?
7. Qu'est-ce que le pronom régime précède?
8. Est-ce que le participe passé s'accorde toujours avec le régime direct?
9. Quand le participe passé s'accorde-t-il avec le régime direct?
10. Est-ce que les élèves ont compris l'explication?
11. L'avez-vous comprise?

Devoir

A. Answer the following questions, substituting pronouns for the italicized words:

1. Est-ce que vous avez remarqué *ces phrases?*
2. A-t-il écrit *le devoir?*
3. Avons-nous vu *les garçons?*
4. *Me* regardez-vous d'abord?
5. Avez-vous regardé *le sujet?*
6. Vous avez rencontré *les enfants* dans le parc, n'est-ce pas?
7. Est-ce que j'ai raconté *l'histoire?*
8. A-t-elle traduit *ces lettres?*
9. Avez-vous attaché *la ficelle?*
10. Ont-ils perdu *les billets?*
11. N'est-ce pas que j'ai fait *ces bonnets* seule?
12. Est-ce que j'ai cherché *les journaux* partout?
13. Avez-vous ajouté *e aigu?*
14. Avons-nous répété *la règle?*
15. A-t-il expliqué *le problème?*
16. Ont-elles répété *la phrase?*

B. Use the contractions of à or de and the definite article where necessary in the following sentences:

1. Nous n'allons jamais seuls —— magasin.
2. Je tourne les pages —— livre.
3. Il n'a vu personne —— école.
4. Vous voulez regarder les illustrations —— journal.
5. Ils ne rendent pas les livres —— bibliothèque chaque fois.
6. Il a écrit —— tableau le résultat —— problème.
7. La mère —— enfants a toujours été gentille.
8. Le chien —— petite fille ne trouve rien —— épicerie.

QUARANTE-QUATRIÈME LEÇON

Review

A

1. Give a list of idioms with the verb **avoir**.

2. What two tenses have you learned to use?

3. What does the past indefinite express?

4. Of what parts is the past indefinite formed?

5. What is the ending of the past participle of a regular verb of the first conjugation? Give three examples.

6. What is the ending of the past participle of a regular verb of the second conjugation? Give two examples.

7. What is the ending of the past participle of a regular verb of the third conjugation? Give three examples.

8. Give an example of an irregular present tense.

9. Give three examples of irregular past participles.

10. Which part of the past indefinite is considered the verb?

11. Account for the difference in spelling of the two past participles below:

Nous avons rendu les bonnets.
Nous les avons rendus.

12. Does the past participle always agree with the direct object?

13. When a negative word is used in a French sentence, what word must precede the verb?

14. Learn the first sentence of the last paragraph on page 120 by heart, pronouncing each word with care.

B

I. Change the verbs to the past indefinite:

1. Papa découpe le rôti.
2. Nous coupons la viande.
3. Philippe regarde-t-il cette petite fourchette?
4. La bonne remplit les verres.
5. Ils finissent le bon dîner.
6. Je vends le pain.
7. Vous avez la cuillère.

II. Write the sentences of I in the past indefinite, changing the direct objects to pronouns.

III. Write questions using the forms **quelque chose, quelquefois, quelqu'un.** *Answer in the negative.*

IV. Write the first three sentences of "Les Enfants dans le parc," on page 112, in phonetic characters.

V. Answer, using idioms with **avoir:**

1. Pourquoi ouvrez-vous la fenêtre?
2. Pourquoi désire-t-il un verre d'eau?
3. Pourquoi fermez-vous les yeux?
4. Pourquoi courez-vous quand vous voyez le chien?
5. Pourquoi achetez-vous la tablette de chocolat?
6. Pourquoi cherchez-vous ce livre?
7. Pourquoi ont-ils fermé la petite fenêtre?

VI. Conjugate:

1. Je n'ai vu personne.
2. Je l'ai bien comprise.
3. Est-ce que je n'ai pas eu honte?

Jiès, Paris

A DOCK FOR SMALL BOATS ON THE SEINE

VACATION DAYS OF FRENCH YOUTH

All over the world boys and girls feel just the same about vacation days. But in no other country than ours perhaps, and certainly not in France, do young people enjoy the long seasons of rest and of freedom from study that American youth has come to regard as its right. At the turn of each year French schools close for a single week, when textbooks may be flung aside and the dull grind of recitation forgotten, but French Christmas is not gay like ours; gifts are not so frequently exchanged, the air does not smell of evergreen and holly, Santa Claus is unknown, the holiday spirit is not abroad in the land. The Easter season brings to French boys and girls a two weeks' vacation, but their freedom at this time is much encroached upon by religious duties, and they often feel they have only traded their school burdens for tasks of another sort. It is therefore in the months of August and September alone that French vacation days are

really memorable, and then, just as is the case in America, French youth is as happy as the pocketbook and the generosity of its family permit.

Most Parisians of the middle class remain in the city during the whole summer to take advantage of the hordes of tourists who descend upon them at this time. The travels of a bourgeois family thus largely consist of trips to the environs of their town. On a hot evening when their stuffy flats grow unbearable, Parisians go to the Seine and from the docks there embark on small steamboats headed down the river. In almost no time they have passed the Eiffel Tower, the Trocadero palace, whose continuous open galleries skirt the river front, the small copy of Liberty Enlightening the World, the beautiful bridge of Point-du-Jour.

A soft cool breeze begins to sweep between the wooded hillsides of the river banks, soothing weary eyes and resting tired spirits. After a short gay stop or two, the boat comes to the suburban town of Bas-Meudon, and there they descend: *bon bourgeois* and his wife and a child or two. In a moment they are at a railing of the upper balcony of a great white restaurant facing the Seine, and seated at a spotless white table decorated with flowers. As they linger over a perfectly cooked dinner, they see the dying glory of day above the western hills, watch its rose-gold reflections in the water, look down as in a dream on little boats which glide silently past to vanish in the shadows of night.

Later on, when their simple meal is finished, the family will ride in the cable-train up to the pavilion that looms on the heights above. And there the older folk will sip their coffee, and the children their *sirop*— a sweet and sticky beverage made from the juices of fruit. They will stare eagerly at the fashionable crowds, sway their heads to the dancing rhythms of the orchestra, and look across the darkening landscape far below them to where mysterious Paris is beginning to twinkle with her million lights. Late that night the family will return to the stuffy flat and tumble into bed to dream, not of the morrow's work in the shop, but of vacation nights beside a shining river.

French boys and girls who really get away from town spend a very different vacation from ours. Many American parents believe their children require a complete rest from school work in the summer. But French fathers and mothers believe it bad for children to lose entire touch with the duties of term time; so during his summer holiday the French child reviews those subjects in which he has shown weakness during the school year, or does advance work in preparation for the coming year. It matters not how well-off the family is. Should they go to show-places like Biarritz, St. Jean, Pougues-les-Eaux, Contrexéville; should they motor in Provence, tramp the valley of the Loire, cruise the Oise in power boats, cycle in the once solitary forests of Fontainebleau, fly to the Swiss moun-

Meurisse, Paris

BICYCLING THROUGH MOUNTAINOUS COUNTRY

SCHOOL-BOYS WITH THEIR PRIZE BOOKS

tains, the Scotch moors, or the Norwegian fiords—all one! The mornings of French children will be largely devoted to home work.

In England the possession of a town house and a country house usually indicates wealth and social position. This is not the case in France. There, as in America, members of the upper middle class may own a simple dwelling in the city and a small cottage in some rural countryside. But most often the French city family has relatives in the country, where the children at least may go for their summer vacation. French marriages create further connections, and you have read enough about family life in France to know how close such ties are to the hearts of these people. So French children are quite sure to have at least one set of grandparents who live in the country and are eager for the company of their little ones during the hot months of each year.

There the children win back the rosy cheeks they have lost in the schoolroom. Let us visit with them a grandmother who has such a charming old farm!

She lives several miles from the railroad station. The young people have been at the farm many times now; so they know by heart every tree and turning on the wide white road traveled by the stage in which we are riding—an ancient automobile that meets each of the few trains that stop at the small station. The road follows the river, whose banks are shaded with trees as far as the eye can reach. The third village through which we pass is the one nearest the grandmother's farm. The kindly chauffeur drives us to the far end of the village, and from there it is but five minutes' walk to the walled court that incloses the buildings familiar to your memory. Soon we see grandmother standing in the road, her hand shielding her eyes from the glare of the bright sun. So she stood and watched their departure when last the children left the farm. Beside her is Bijou, who seems to know all about their coming, although he is only a half-blind old black poodle. Now grandmother is embracing them and asking to see the red-bound volumes their mother wrote her about: the books won as prizes on the last night of school and awarded for general excellence in scholarship. We steal a look into the farmyard through the great arched gate—no, not a thing has changed! The house with its half-opened shutters stands to the right, then come the barns and lofts forming a wide half-circle of pink. This will be the children's world for two months.

French youth has many splendid playgrounds that in the summer time it uses to the full: great rural districts cut everywhere by a network of navigable streams. These rivers, even the smallest of them, are splendid for travel by punt or canoe, because their course has been straightened and made easy to follow by canals and by systems of locks. Few French boys, however, have boats of their own in which to set off on a summer's adventuring; the one unfailing companion of their vacation trips to unknown places is the bicycle. And this network of navigable streams is a great help to such journeys awheel or afoot; for along the bank of every

French river, no matter how unimportant it may look, runs a towpath which is a well-beaten dirt road, and sometimes a smoothly paved highway, that is of much value to the cyclist and the tramper: in fact, district maps refer to these trails as cycle-paths.

French youths whose purse is limited believe there is nothing like the bicycle to assist their travels: a boat is forever in need of care and coaxing, whereas a wheel can be thrust aside at a moment's notice. It permits French boys to dawdle slowly amid scenes that are pleasant and full of beauty, or to whiz like lightning past less attractive spots. Thus it comes about that in July and August one sees as many French youths pedaling provincial poplar-lined roads as there are locusts in the wheat fields. And as to which sort of living creature— boy or locust—is the merrier, none may surely judge. For by the sounds they make and by their general conduct, both seem to be in high good humor.

Photo A. Breger Frères, Paris

A TYPICAL FARM-YARD
On such a farm as this many French children spend their vacations.

Jiès, Paris

THE BEACH AT BIARRITZ

QUARANTE-CINQUIÈME LEÇON

Le bon chien Pataud

Les enfants aiment beaucoup les animaux. Roger n'est pas une exception. Il demande souvent à son père de lui donner un chien, mais son père hésite. Enfin il pense que Roger est assez grand maintenant pour soigner un chien. Il prépare une petite surprise.

Un soir le père de Roger entre dans la salle à manger. Il porte une grande boîte. Il offre la boîte à Roger.

—Tu[1] m'as apporté des bonbons, papa. Merci. J'aime les bonbons; mais la boîte est si grande . . . et si lourde! Je vais dire que ——.

Roger entend quelque chose. Non, ce n'est pas une boîte de bonbons. Qu'est-ce que c'est? Il ouvre la boîte.

—Papa, un joli petit chien, brun et noir! Merci, merci. Je vais l'appeler Pataud. Il est si gros.

Roger met le petit chien par terre. Il court dans tous les coins de la salle à manger. Il joue avec Roger. Roger lui donne quelque chose à manger. Roger est content maintenant. Il a un chien.

* * * * *

Maintenant Pataud est grand. Il a sa niche sous l'escalier. Il garde bien la maison de Roger. Roger et Pataud sont amis.

Un jour la petite cousine de Roger arrive à la maison. Roger a envie d'amuser la petite fille, mais elle a peur de Pataud. Pataud court dans le jardin, et il arrive devant Jacqueline pour demander des caresses. La petite Jacqueline ne le touche pas.

—Pataud a envie de jouer, Jacqueline.

—Oui, mais j'ai peur. Il est si grand. J'ai honte, mais j'ai peur.

[1] As the familiar form **tu** is used only in addressing members of one's family or in speaking to one's pets, you will not need it. Always use **vous** for *you*. You must, however, be able to understand **tu** in your reading.

—Pataud, mon ami, il faut montrer à Jacqueline que tu[1] l'aimes. Donne[1]-lui la patte. Elle a peur. Montre[1] que tu es un bon chien.

Pataud offre la patte. Jacqueline la prend timidement. Elle est si grosse, cette patte noire. Pataud regarde Jacqueline. Jacqueline trouve qu'elle est stupide d'avoir peur.

Pataud reste devant Jacqueline. Il regarde sa poche. Jacqueline a un morceau de chocolat dans sa poche. Pataud n'a pas faim, mais il est très gourmand. Jacqueline lui donne un petit morceau de chocolat, et Pataud saute de joie. Il est amusant.

—Désires-tu monter sur son dos? demande Roger. Désires-tu faire une petite promenade?

—Oui, j'aime Pataud maintenant. Roger aide la petite fille à monter sur le large dos de Pataud. Pataud reste tranquille. Il sait que Roger le regarde. Il marche doucement dans le jardin. Pataud n'est pas bête.

* * * * *

Maman a mis une assiette devant la niche de Pataud. Il y a des pommes de terre et un morceau de viande dans l'assiette. Raton, le chat, arrive. Il saute sur la viande.

—Méchant Raton! Donne la viande à Pataud. Elle n'est pas pour toi. Tu es méchant.

C'est Jacqueline qui parle, mais Raton est loin avec la viande. Il n'écoute pas Jacqueline. Jacqueline caresse la tête de Pataud.

—Pauvre Pataud! Il faut manger les pommes de terre. Tu es bon. Tu n'aimes pas les disputes. Alors, c'est toi[2] que je préfère chaque fois.

Vocabulaire

l'ami [lami] (m.), *friend*
le dos [do], *back*
le jour [ʒuːr], *day;* **un jour,** *one day*
la niche [niʃ], *kennel*
la patte [pat], *paw*
la terre [tɛːr], *earth, land, ground*
par terre [paːr tɛːr], *on the ground, on the floor*

la tête [tɛːt], *head*
Jacqueline [ʒaklin], *Jacqueline*
Pataud [pato] (from *patte*), hence, *"large paws"*
Roger [rɔʒe], *Roger*
entendre [ɑ̃tɑ̃ːdr], *to hear, to listen to, to understand*
mis [mi] (p.p. of **mettre**), *put*

il offre [il ɔfr] (inf. **offrir**), *he offers*
soigner [swaɲe], *to care for, to look after*
toi [twa], *you* (disjunctive)
gourmand [gurmɑ̃], *greedy, gluttonous*
pauvre [poːvr], *poor*
doucement [dusmɑ̃], *gently, smoothly*

In this lesson the French words with English equivalents are:

le cousin, la cousine [kuzɛ̃, kuzin], *cousin*
la dispute [dispyt], *dispute*
l'exception [lɛksɛpsjɔ̃] (f.), *exception*
aider [ede], *to aid, to help*

caresser [karese], *to caress, to pet*
hésiter [ezite], *to hesitate, to falter*
préparer [prepare], *to prepare*

large [larʒ], *broad, large, wide*
stupide [stypid], *stupid, dull*
tranquille [trɑ̃kil], *quiet, tranquil, calm*
timidement [timidmɑ̃], *timidly*

---

[1] See footnote on preceding page.
[2] See Lesson 118, page 324, for the use of disjunctive pronouns.

QUARANTE-SIXIÈME LEÇON

Grand-père

Tout le monde est content, parce que grand-père va arriver aujourd'hui. Ce n'est pas tous les jours que grand-père arrive. Papa va à la gare. Gauthier a demandé la permission de rester à la maison cet après-midi, mais maman a dit:

—Gauthier, il ne faut pas manquer la classe et il ne faut pas être en retard aujourd'hui.

Gauthier aime beaucoup grand-père et aussi ses cadeaux et ses histoires. La dernière fois il n'a pas joué avec Gauthier. Il a raconté des histoires. Après Gauthier les **a racontées** à ses amis.

Grand-père aime aussi faire une longue promenade l'après-midi. Il est rarement trop fatigué pour marcher ou pour raconter des histoires. Il comprend aussi qu'un petit garçon a souvent faim, et qu'il n'a pas tou-jours envie de manger des tartines, mais qu'il préfère des friandises. Bien sûr, il est très indulgent, grand-père.

Personne ne gronde grand-père quand il arrive en retard pour les repas. Une fois ils ont fait une longue promenade jusqu'à une fabrique. Ils ont trouvé la fabrique si intéressante qu'ils ont oublié l'heure. Tout à coup ils ont entendu le coup de sifflet qui annonce l'heure de déjeuner pour les ouvriers.

—Nous allons être en retard pour le déjeuner, a dit Gauthier. Maman va nous gronder, mais que voulez-vous?[1]

—Nous n'allons pas être très en retard, a répondu grand-père, et une fois (*once*) dans la rue, il a hélé un taxi.

En dix minutes les voilà à la maison pour l'heure du déjeuner. Personne ne les a grondés.

Grammaire

Tout le monde

Tout le monde means "everyone." **Tout le monde** is used with a singular verb, as *everyone* is in English.

Remember that **ne** must precede the verb in a negative sentence.

> Personne **ne** gronde grand-père. *No one scolds grandfather.*
> Rien **n'**arrive pour moi. *Nothing comes for me.*

Review of the Past Indefinite

You will recall that the past indefinite requires two parts—the auxiliary **avoir** and the past participle. In the negative **ne** precedes and **pas** follows **avoir**.

> Je **n'**ai **pas** vu les enfants. *I have not seen the children.*
> Je **ne** les ai **pas** vus. *I have not seen them.*

Remember also that the past participle must agree with the direct object if the direct object precedes the verb.

---

[1] **que voulez-vous?**, *what can I do about it?*

Vocabulaire

le **cadeau** [kado] (pl. les cadeaux), *gift*

le **coup de sifflet** [kud siflɛ], *blowing of the whistle, sound of the whistle*

le **déjeuner** [deʒœne], *luncheon*

la **fabrique** [fabrik], *factory*

la **friandise** [friɑ̃diːz], *delicacy, dainty, tidbit*

la **gare** [gaːr],[1] *railway station*

le **grand-père** [grɑ̃pɛːr], *grandfather*

l'**ouvrier** [luvrie] (m.), *workman*

la **permission** [pɛrmisjɔ̃], *permission*

la **tartine** [tartin], *slice of bread and butter* or *jam*

le **taxi** [taksi], *taxi*

Gauthier [gotje], *Walter*

annoncer [anɔ̃se], *to announce, to portray, to advertise*

gronder [grɔ̃de], *to scold*

héler [ele], *to hail*

manquer [mɑ̃ke], *to be absent from, to miss*

tout le monde [tul mɔ̃ːd], *everyone*

dix [dis] ([di] before consonants), *ten*

dernier, dernière [dɛrnje, dɛrnjɛːr], *last, final*

indulgent [ɛ̃dylʒɑ̃], *indulgent, lenient*

rarement [rarmɑ̃], *rarely*

tous les jours [tu le ʒuːr], *every day*

jusqu'à [ʒyska], *up to, until, as far as*

les voilà [le vwala], *there they are, there they were*

Questionnaire

1. Pourquoi tout le monde est-il content?
2. Où papa va-t-il?
3. Quand grand-père va-t-il arriver?
4. Qu'est-ce que Gauthier aime?
5. Qu'est-ce que grand-père raconte à Gauthier?
6. Et après, qu'est-ce que Gauthier fait?
7. Comment savez-vous que grand-père est indulgent?
8. Qui gronde grand-père?
9. Pourquoi grand-père et Gauthier ont-ils oublié l'heure?
10. Qu'est-ce que Gauthier a dit quand il a entendu le coup de sifflet?
11. Pourquoi grand-père a-t-il hélé un taxi?

Devoir

A. Change to the correct verb-forms:

1. Ils (trouver) une fabrique.
2. Nous (aller) à la gare à midi.
3. Il ne faut jamais (arriver) en retard.
4. Vous avez (attraper) la balle au bord du lac.
5. Il (avoir) etudié les histoires.
6. Ils les ont (raconter) à leur mère.
7. Bien sûr, nous avons (faire) une promenade au bois.
8. Je (faire) une promenade.
9. Nous (finir) la banane.
10. Il a (manquer) son déjeuner.
11. Vous ne (répondre) rien.
12. Vous avez (répondre) à la question sur l'e aigu.
13. Nous avons (voir) les automobiles tout à coup.
14. J'ai (regarder) le résultat avec attention.
15. Vous avez (traduire) ces pages.
16. L'adjectif (s'accorder) avec son substantif.

Traduction:

Grandfather and Walter took a long walk. They found the factory so interesting that they forgot the time. When they heard the sound of the whistle, they said, "We are going to be late." Walter said, "Mother is going to scold us." In the street they saw a taxi. Grandfather hailed it, and in ten minutes there they were at home, seated on the sofa.

---

[1] Although [gaːr] is given in the International Dictionary, [gaːr] is preferable.

QUARANTE-SEPTIÈME LEÇON

Les Drapeaux

Grand-père et Gauthier font une promenade presque tous les jours après la classe. Quelquefois grand-père va chercher Gauthier à l'école. Le petit garçon est fier de grand-père. Il a l'air si distingué! Et grand-père est fier de son petit-fils parce qu'il a l'air si intelligent.

Cet après-midi, grand-père a fait une promenade avant d'aller chercher (*going after*) Gauthier à l'école. Il n'a pas marché très vite, et il est un peu en retard. Quand Gauthier l'a vu, il a commencé à courir vers lui.

—Où allons-nous aujourd'hui? a dit grand-père.

—A la bibliothèque, s'il te plaît[1] (*please*), grand-père. Mon ami Jean m'a parlé d'un bon livre. Je veux le chercher à la bibliothèque.

Grand-père et Gauthier ont marché sans trouver rien d'intéressant (*without finding anything interesting*), quand tout à coup les voilà devant une boutique. Grand-père et Gauthier ont hésité un instant devant la vitrine, une vitrine pleine de drapeaux et de cartes. A ce moment[2] ils ont oublié la bibliothèque. Que les cartes sont intéressantes, et les drapeaux aussi!

Gauthier n'a pas beaucoup étudié la géographie. Il n'a jamais trouvé les cartes très intéressantes; mais les drapeaux, il les adore.

—Je vois le drapeau espagnol, rouge, jaune, et pourpre (*purple*), dit-il; et le drapeau anglais, bleu, blanc, et rouge; et le drapeau français, bleu, blanc, et rouge aussi. Voici trois nations qui ont les mêmes couleurs dans leurs drapeaux—la Grande-Bretagne, la France, et les Etats-Unis. Ce sont trois beaux drapeaux, mais je préfère le drapeau américain.

—Nous avons lu l'histoire du drapeau américain et de Betsy Ross à l'école. Est-ce que les autres drapeaux ont aussi des histoires intéressantes?

—Très intéressantes. Un jour (*some day*) je vais raconter l'histoire du drapeau français. Je sais que tu as envie de l'entendre.

Grammaire

Prepositions

There are no rules for the use of prepositions, yet they are most essential in the study of French. Your best plan will be to observe carefully each preposition as you meet it.

Many of the simple prepositions have a number of different translations. If you are in any doubt as to the correct translation in any case, consult the French-English Vocabulary at the back of your book, beginning on page 384.

The two commonest prepositions, à and de, are often used after certain verbs to introduce an infinitive or after certain adjectives to introduce a noun or a pronoun. The verbs listed on page 97 should be familiar to you now. Several more have appeared since then. **Make a complete** list of the verbs and adjectives used with **à and de that you have had thus far.** Make several sentences using these expressions in order to **help yourself learn** them.

---

[1] Familiar form.

[2] A ce moment, just then.

Vocabulaire

la **boutique** [butik], *small shop*

la **classe** [klɑːs], *class, session, school*

la **couleur** [kulœːr], *color*

la **géographie** [ʒeɔgrafi], *geography*

l'**instant** [lɛ̃stɑ̃] (m.), *instant, moment*

le **moment** [mɔmɑ̃], *moment*

la **nation** [nɑsjõ], *nation*

le **petit-fils** [pti fis], *grandson*

la **vitrine** [vitrin], *shop-window, show-window*

les **Etats-Unis** [lezeta zyni], (m. pl.), *the United States*

la **Grande-Bretagne** [grɑ̃ːd brɔtaɲ], *Great Britain*

adorer [adɔre], *to adore, to love*

ils **font** [il fõ] (inf. **faire**), *they make, they do, they take*

il **prend** [il prɑ̃] (inf. **prendre**), *he takes*

je **veux** [ʒə vø] (inf. **vouloir**), *I wish, I want, I desire*

distingué [distɛ̃ge], *distinguished*

espagnol [ɛspaɲɔl], *Spanish*

fier, fière [fjɛːr], *proud*

intelligent [ɛ̃teliʒɑ̃], *intelligent*

Questionnaire

1. Que font grand-père et Gauthier l'après-midi?
2. Pourquoi Gauthier est-il fier de grand-père?
3. Pourquoi grand-père est-il fier de Gauthier?
4. Pourquoi grand-père est-il en retard cet après-midi?
5. Pourquoi vont-ils à la bibliothèque?
6. Trouvent-ils d'abord quelque chose d'intéressant?
7. Pourquoi ont-ils oublié la bibliothèque?
8. Comment est la vitrine de la boutique?
9. Quels drapeaux est-ce que Gauthier a vus dans la vitrine?
10. Quelles nations ont des drapeaux de mêmes couleurs?
11. Qu'est-ce que Gauthier a lu à l'école?
12. Qu'est-ce que grand-père va raconter à Gauthier?

Devoir

A. *Change the italicized nouns to pronouns:*

1. *Grand'mère* tricote *le bonnet.*
2. *Philippe* n'aime pas *les poupées.*
3. *Philippe et Marie* regardent *les animaux.*
4. *La bonne* apporte *la tartine.*
5. *Papa* prend *son café* au dîner.
6. *Marie* rapporte *le verre.*
7. *Vous* faites *la robe* seule.
8. Il voit *les oiseaux* d'abord.
9. *Philippe* achète *une géographie* dans la boutique.

B. *Change the sentences of A to the past indefinite, using pronoun objects.*

C. *List all the prepositional phrases used in "Les Drapeaux." With the teacher's help discover whether*

each preposition has its own meaning or whether it is needed with certain words, e. g., **fier de.**

D. *Put each of the following prepositions into a sentence. Use a noun as the object of each preposition.*

sur   pour

dans   après

Traduction:

Every day grandfather takes a walk. When he meets Walter, they walk slowly. One day they found an interesting shop-window. In this window they saw many (**beaucoup de**) maps and flags. Walter saw the Spanish flag, the English flag, the French flag, and the American flag. He said to his grandfather, "I prefer that flag."

QUARANTE-HUITIÈME LEÇON

Le Drapeau tricolore

Grand-père et Gauthier ont quitté la bibliothèque. Gauthier a trouvé son livre, et les voilà au parc en route pour la maison. C'est grand-père qui parle. Il parle du drapeau français, et le petit garçon l'écoute.

—Le drapeau français que nous avons vu est un drapeau moderne, le drapeau tricolore. C'est le drapeau de la Révolution française, le drapeau républicain. On a changé le drapeau avec les changements de gouvernement. Le drapeau le plus ancien (*oldest*) est l'oriflamme (*the King's special banner*). Le nom indique la couleur, n'est-ce pas?

—Est-elle rouge? a dit Gauthier.

—Oui, rouge semé de flammes d'or— le drapeau de Charlemagne. L'oriflamme a été la bannière de bataille des rois. On peut voir aujourd'hui une reproduction de cette bannière dans l'abbaye de Saint-Denis.[1]

—Le vrai drapeau des rois de France est blanc et porte en or les fleurs de lis. C'est aujourd'hui le drapeau des royalistes, qui préfèrent une monarchie à une république. Tous ces renseignements, Gauthier, sont importants.

—Mais grand-père, n'est-ce pas que la France est une république comme les Etats-Unis?

—Pas tout à fait comme les Etats-Unis, mais c'est une république. Après la Révolution on a établi une république.

—C'est comme chez nous (*i.e., in this country*), grand-père. Après la Révolution on a établi les Etats-Unis.

—Oui, mais il ne faut pas oublier la grande différence entre la Révolution française et la Révolution américaine. Nous parlons en ce moment du drapeau. Les couleurs de la ville de Paris sont bleu et rouge. Pendant la Révolution les républicains ont décidé de marier le drapeau de Paris et le drapeau des rois. Ils l'ont fait, et les Français ont aujourd'hui le drapeau tricolore, le drapeau bleu, blanc, et rouge que nous avons vu. Les Français aiment beaucoup leur drapeau tricolore, sauf les royalistes, qui espèrent rétablir la monarchie et le drapeau blanc aux (*with*) lis d'or.

—Mais la France est une république, grand-père; tu l'as dit.

—Oui, la France est aujourd'hui une république, et on ne va pas changer le gouvernement, a répondu grand-père.

[1] **L'abbaye de Saint-Denis** is a famous church in the town of St. Denis, a few miles north of Paris. It is the historic burial place of the kings of France. See page 152 for pictures of exterior and interior.

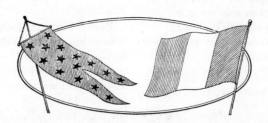

Grammaire

Review of *à* and the Definite Article

You have learned that the preposition **à** and the definite article contract in the following ways:

Il donne le livre au garçon.   Il donne les livres aux garçons.
Il donne le livre à l'élève.   Il donne les livres aux élèves.
Il donne le livre à la petite fille. Il donne les livres aux petites filles.

Use of *On*

The French word **on** is used to express an indefinite person or even an indefinite number of persons. It corresponds to the English indefinite pronoun *one* (or *they*, or *we*, or *you*, when not referring to specified persons). We say, "One never regrets a good deed." **On** is always used with a singular verb.

On dîne dans la salle à manger. *One eats* (or *we eat*), etc.
On ne dîne pas en classe. *One does* (or *we do*) *not eat*, etc.

On and the active voice are frequently used in French instead of the passive voice and are to be translated into English by passive forms.

On a établi une république. *A republic was established.*
On a marié les deux drapeaux. *The two flags were joined.*

Vocabulaire

l'abbaye de Saint-Denis [labeji də sɛ̃ dəni], *abbey of Saint Denis*

la bannière [banjɛːr], *banner*

la bataille [bataːj], *battle*

la différence [diferɑ̃ːs], *difference*

la fille [fiːj], *daughter, girl*

la flamme [flaːm], *flame*

la fleur de lis [flœːr də liːs], *fleur-de-lis, lily* as an emblem

les Français [frɑ̃sɛ], *French people, Frenchmen*

le gouvernement [guvɛrnəmɑ̃], *government*

l'homme [lɔm] (m.), *man*

le lis [liːs], *lily*

la monarchie [mɔnarʃi], *monarchy*

l'oriflamme [lɔriflaːm] (f.), *king's special banner (flame of gold)*

l'or [lɔːr] (m.), *gold*

la reproduction [rəprɔdyksjõ], *reproduction*

la république [repyblik], *republic*

la révolution [revɔlysjõ], *revolution*

le roi [rwa], *king*

le royaliste [rwajalist], *royalist*

le drapeau tricolore [drapo trikɔlɔːr], *tricolor*

dîner [dine], *to dine, to eat dinner*

espérer [ɛspere], *to hope*

établir [etabliːr], *to establish*

marier [marje], *to marry, to join, to ally*

porter [pɔrte], *to bear, to have, to wear, to strike*

vous pouvez [vu puve] (inf. **pouvoir**), *you can, you may, you are able*

quitter [kite], *to leave, to leave off*

rétablir [retabliːr], *to reestablish*

semé [səme] (p.p. of **semer**), *semé* (with a pattern of small figures), *strewn*

on [õ], *one, we, you, they* (indefinite reference)

Charlemagne [ʃarləmaɲ], *Charlemagne*

ancien, ancienne [ɑ̃sjɛ̃, ɑ̃sjɛn], *ancient, former, old*

moderne [mɔdɛrn], *modern*

républicain [repyblikɛ̃], *of the republic*

vrai [vrɛ], *true, real*

en route pour [ɑ̃ rut puːr], *on the way to*

entre [ɑ̃ːtr], *between, into*

pas tout à fait [pa tu ta fɛ], *not exactly, not entirely, not altogether*

Questionnaire

1. Qu'est-ce que Gauthier a trouvé dans la bibliothèque?
2. Pendant que (*while*) grand-père parle, que fait son petit-fils?
3. Comment Gauthier écoute-t-il?
4. De quoi parle grand-père?
5. Qu'est-ce que c'est que (*what is*) le drapeau tricolore?
6. Pourquoi a-t-on changé le drapeau français?
7. De quelle couleur est le drapeau des rois de France?
8. Quel est le gouvernement de la France?
9. Pourquoi les Français ont-ils un drapeau bleu, blanc, et rouge?
10. Qui n'aime pas le drapeau tricolore?
11. Qu'est-ce que les royalistes espèrent rétablir?

Devoir

A. Practice reading aloud the first paragraph of "Le Drapeau tricolore" until you can read it without hesitation.

B. Change to the past indefinite:

1. Ils parlent de l'aéroplane français.
2. Bien sûr je comprends cette histoire.
3. Avez-vous le lis?
4. Je vois la dernière reproduction.
5. Ils la font.
6. Répondons-nous souvent à cette question?
7. Continue-t-elle à répéter cette raison?
8. Grand-père ne lit pas le journal.
9. Elles appellent la maîtresse.
10. Ils les trouvent dans l'assiette.

C. Fill in each of the blanks in the following sentences with the definite article or the definite article contracted with à*:*

1. —— père a été —— parc avec —— mère.
2. —— homme donne ce drapeau —— petite fille.
3. On passe —— salon.
4. Ils ne parlent de rien —— ouvriers.
5. Ils parlent —— enfant distingué.
6. Nous pouvons acheter ces friandises —— gare.
7. —— oiseau rouge et jaune chante —— fenêtre.
8. J'ai montré cette illustration —— ami de Jeanne.

Traduction:

The French flag is the tricolor. We have the same colors. The French government is a republic. It was established (**On l'a établie,** etc.) after the Revolution.

Our (**notre**) republic was also established after a revolution.

We saw a reproduction of the oriflamme at the abbey of Saint Denis. We admired the banner very much.

The flag of the kings of France is white with (**aux**) gold lilies. The royalists hope to re-establish a monarchy and this flag.

QUARANTE-NEUVIÈME LEÇON

Le Cousin Hippolyte

Quand grand-père est à la maison on parle souvent des parents et des anciens[1] amis. On parle de beaucoup de personnes que Gauthier n'a pas vues. C'est ennuyeux pour le petit garçon! Des noms et des noms! Il est difficile de dire si on parle du père ou du fils; de la mère ou de la fille. On comprend qu'on parle de l'oncle Robert, quand on dit, "Vous savez que Robert a acheté une maison près du parc."

Il n'y a pas de doute. On ne parle pas du petit cousin. Mais quand on dit, "Françoise est intelligente," comment savoir (*how is one to know*) si c'est la tante ou la petite cousine?

La tante, c'est la sœur de papa ou de maman. C'est maman qui l'a dit (*who said so*). Quand on parle de la tante Emilie que Gauthier n'a jamais vue, il demande à maman:

—Est-ce votre sœur, maman, ou la sœur de papa?

—Ni l'une, ni l'autre, répond maman. Votre tante Emilie est ma belle-sœur, la femme de mon frère.

Alors Gauthier a compris qu'une tante c'était (*was*) la sœur de papa ou de maman, ou que c'était la femme d'un oncle.

Gauthier pensait (*always thought*) qu'un cousin c'était toujours un enfant. Sa cousine Marie est petite, ses cousins Robert, Raoul, et Jean sont petits. Hier on a mentionné le cousin Hippolyte.

—C'est un savant qui a fait une découverte importante, a dit grand-père.

—Tiens, tiens, un petit garçon a fait une découverte! dit Gauthier.

—Mais non, Gauthier, le cousin Hippolyte n'est pas un petit garçon. Il est aussi (*as*) âgé que (*as*) moi, a dit papa. Pourquoi as-tu pensé qu'Hippolyte était (*was*) un petit garçon?

—Parce que c'est le cousin Hippolyte. J'ai pensé que les cousins étaient (*were*) toujours des petits garçons. C'est difficile—tous ces renseignements—presque aussi difficile qu'un problème. Vous pouvez comprendre cela, n'est-ce pas? J'ai vraiment tant de parents!

Grammaire

Review of *De* and the Definite Article

You will remember that the word **de** contracts with the article:

le père du garçon, *the boy's father*   le père de l'élève, *the pupil's father*
le père de la jeune fille, *the girl's father*   le père des garçons, *the boys' father*

Adverbs of Quantity

In the French language there are some adverbs which, because they denote *how much*, are known as *adverbs of quantity*. These words are as follows:

> beaucoup [boku], *much, a great many, a great deal*
> peu [pø], *little, few, not much*
> tant [tã], *so much, so many*
> assez [ase], *enough*
> trop [trɔ], *too much, too many*
> combien [kõbjɛ̃], *how much, how many*

[1] *old,* that is, *of long standing.*

Adverbs of quantity require the preposition **de** before a noun, whether the noun is singular or plural.

> J'ai **beaucoup de** papier. *I have much paper.*
> J'ai **beaucoup d'**amis. *I have a great many friends.*
> J'ai **peu de** papier. *I have little paper.*
> J'ai **peu d'**amis. *I have few friends.*
> J'ai **tant de** papier. *I have so much paper.*
> J'ai **tant d'**amis. *I have so many friends.*
> Ils ont **assez de** roses. *They have enough roses.*
> Ils ont **assez de** drapeaux. *They have enough flags.*
> Ils ont **trop d'**élèves. *They have too many pupils.*
> Ils ont **trop de** drapeaux. *They have too many flags.*
> **Combien de** chocolat avez-vous? *How much chocolate have you?*
> **Combien de** cousins avez-vous? *How many cousins have you?*

Note that the negative **pas**+**de**+noun (corresponding to *no*+noun in English) has the same construction. For example:

> Il n'a pas de cousins. *He has no cousins.*

Vocabulaire

la **belle-sœur**[1] [bɛl sœːr], *sister-in-law*
la **découverte** [dekuvɛrt], *discovery*
le **doute** [dut], *doubt*
la **femme** [fam], *woman, wife*
le **fils** [fis] (pl. **les fils**), *son*
le **neveu** [nəvø] (pl. **les neveux**), *nephew*
la **nièce** [njɛs], *niece*
l'**oncle** [lõːkl] (m.), *uncle*
le **parent** [parã], *relative*
le **savant** [savã], *learned person, scholar*

la **sœur** [sœːr], *sister*
la **tante** [tãːt], *aunt*
Françoise [frãswɑːz], *Frances*
Hippolyte [ipɔlit], *Hippolyte*
apprendre [aprãːdr] (p. p. **appris**), *to acquire, to learn, to teach*
âgé [ɑʒe], *old*
ennuyeux,-se [ãnɥijø, ãnɥijøːz], *boring, tiresome*
important [ɛ̃pɔrtã], *important*

jeune [ʒœn], *young*
votre [vɔtr], *your*
combien [kõbjɛ̃], *how much, how many*
hier [jɛːr], *yesterday*
ni ... ni [ni, ni], *neither, nor*
beaucoup de [boku də], *many*
aussi...que [osi kə], *as...as*
tant [tã], *so much, so many*
tiens [tjɛ̃], *say, look here, well*
mais non [mɛ nõ], *no indeed, why no, not at all*

Questionnaire

1. De qui parle-t-on chez Gauthier?
2. Pourquoi est-ce ennuyeux pour Gauthier?
3. Pourquoi a-t-il compris qu'on parlait (*they were talking*) de l'oncle et non pas du cousin quand on a dit, "Robert a acheté une maison près du parc"?
4. Combien de neveux avez-vous?
5. Expliquez le mot **belle-sœur**.
6. Qu'est-ce que c'est qu'une grand'mère?
7. Qu'est-ce que c'est qu'un oncle?
8. Qu'est-ce que le cousin Hippolyte a fait?
9. Est-ce que le cousin Hippolyte est distingué?
10. Pourquoi Gauthier a-t-il pensé que le cousin Hippolyte était (*was*) petit?

[1] Can you give the word for *brother-in-law?*

Devoir

A. Learn the first sentence of "Le Cousin Hippolyte" by heart.

B. Explain in French:

cousin	neveu
tante	nièce

C. Use the correct forms of the words in parentheses:

1. Le père (de) enfants est l'oncle de (ce) jeune fille.
2. Tout le monde parle (de) homme qui a parlé (à) élèves.
3. Vous pouvez aller (à) bord du lac pour voir les oiseaux.
4. J'apporte tous les jours des tartines (à) ouvrier.
5. Ce sont les amis de (ce) garçons.
6. Madame Ruche est une (ancien) amie de ma mère.
7. (Ce) histoire n'a pas l'air facile.
8. Voilà pourquoi nous avons mentionné le nom de (ce) dame.
9. Elle a été (bon) et (indulgent).
10. (Ce) oiseau chante tout à coup.

D. Change to the correct verb-forms:

1. L'adjectif (s'accorder) avec son substantif.
2. Combien de participes irréguliers les élèves ont-ils (étudier) pour aujourd'hui?

3. Vous avez (répondre) à Louise.
4. J'ai (voir) tant d'oiseaux hier. Les avez-vous (voir) aussi?
5. Il ne faut pas (manquer) la classe de géographie.
6. Si vous voulez bien réciter, (étudier) beaucoup d'heures.
7. Nous l'avons (dire) à ce monsieur.
8. Il a (faire) trop de fautes.
9. Ils (avoir) annoncé le sujet de la leçon hier.
10. Les parents de Céline (compter) héler un taxi.

Traduction:

When grandfather talks with mother and father, Walter learns that he has many relatives. They (**On**) talk of persons whom Walter has not seen. He learns a great deal from these conversations. Yesterday he learned a great deal about his (**ses**) relatives. The day before yesterday (**avant-hier**) he learned that a cousin is not always small. Cousin Hippolyte, who has made an interesting discovery, is almost as old as father, but nobody thinks he is old. He is distinguished. Have you many distinguished relatives?

A FAVORITE SPOT FOR BOATING IN THE BOIS DE BOULOGNE

CINQUANTIÈME LEÇON
Review

A

1. What form of the verb is used with **tout le monde?**

2. Instead of a passive verb what form is frequently used in French?

3. What preposition is used with the adjective **fier?** Use the phrase in a sentence.

4. Give the rule for the agreement of the past participle.

5. Give the past participles of **voir, faire, comprendre, avoir, être.**

6. What are the infinitive endings of regular verbs of the three conjugations?

7. What are the endings of the past participles of regular verbs of the three conjugations?

8. Give the present indicative of **choisir** (to choose).

9. Give the present indicative of **entendre** (to hear, to understand).

10. Give the present indicative of **plier** (to fold).

11. Give the past indefinite of **entendre.**

12. Give ten words that group themselves around **les parents.**

13. Mention six words that group themselves about **le drapeau.**

14. Use these adverbs in sentences: **peu de, beaucoup de, assez de, tant de, combien de, trop de.**

B

I. *Use the correct forms of the words in parentheses:*

1. Personne n'a (établir) une monarchie.

2. Les hommes et les femmes (manquer) le déjeuner.

3. La bataille n'est pas (finir).

4. Vous pouvez (porter) les pains.

5. Nous ne (quitter) jamais l'école entre neuf et dix heures.

II. *Supply the correct forms of **de** and the article:*

1. Il met les livres à côté —— lampe.

2. Elle est assise au bord —— lac.

3. Grand-père écoute les histoires —— petit garçon.

4. Nous ne savons pas l'histoire —— drapeaux.

5. Le gouvernement —— homme change.

III. *Answer, using a pronoun for each italicized word or words:*

1. Pourquoi allez-vous *dans la rue?*

2. De la fenêtre voyez-vous *le coin?*

3. Où est *l'école?*

4. Avez-vous perdu *votre casquette?*

5. Aimons-nous *cette saison?*

6. A-t-il discuté *les qualités du champion?*

7. Ont-ils fini *le problème?*

8. *Les clefs* sont là, n'est-ce pas?

9. Va-t-il *au théâtre?*

10. Va-t-elle ôter *ce beau manteau?*

IV. *Conjugate:*

1. Je vais au parc.

2. J'entends ces mots.

3. J'espère voir ce tableau.

V. *Use each of the following expressions in a question to be asked in class:*

avoir froid, avoir chaud, avoir faim, avoir soif, avoir peur, avoir sommeil, avoir envie, avoir honte, avoir raison, avoir l'air de.

VI. *Use these expressions in sentences:*

la géographie   la vitrine
cette invitation   les boutiques
ce petit-fils   la couleur
votre drapeau   leur roi
ma nièce   notre découverte

AN OLD ROMAN ARENA IN PARIS, WHERE SPECTATORS WATCHED GAMES
TWO THOUSAND YEARS AGO

SCENES IN PARIS

PART ONE

Paris has behind her nearly two thousand years of uninterrupted civilization. Her history has been a stirring and a noble one. Today she is a most beautiful city and a center of knowledge and of art.

We first hear of her in the days of Julius Caesar, whose legions conquered a town known as Lutetia in the year 58 B.C. This was a settlement on two small islands in the River Seine, inhabited by fishermen of the small Gallic tribe called Parisii. For four hundred years the old name Lutetia continued, but when a later Caesar, Julian the Apostate, established his residence there and built a splendid palace for this new capital of the West, the name was changed by the Romans to *Parisea civitas*, which in our language means City of Paris. When the Franks under Clovis took Gaul from the Romans, the town remained as capital of the Frankish empire, and so it has continued to our

day. For centuries the two small islands in the Seine were the home of court and church, and this is why so many splendid buildings of historical significance are now to be found on the Ile de la Cité.

The Paris of our time is the fifth largest city in the world. It has left the two islands far behind and spread across fields and into the near-by hills. But the heart of this great mass is still the Ile de la Cité. And the inhabitants of the city are important for other reasons than their number and the buildings in which they dwell. Paris has always had more than her share of world-famous people within her walls.

So often a river which runs through a city becomes more a part of it than the solid foundation on which it stands! London and the Thames— Florence and the Arno—New York and the Hudson—Vienna and the Blue Danube: Paris and the Seine. The left bank and the right bank of the River Seine are known everywhere as symbols of the two Parises: art and jollity on the left, fashion and power on the right.

The stream is a central artery. Sooner or later all people come to gaze with pleasure on its gentle beauty. Many of its bridges are works of art: the Pont Royal is a wonderful creation; the single span of the Pont d'Alexandre III is a thing of joy to even the most critical mind. The boats that pass constantly beneath them look like mechanical toys as they chug up and down the broad current.

The banks of the Seine are lined with bookstalls that seem to stretch for miles. There they have been for almost three hundred years. In 1650 these stalls were moved from the Pont Neuf to the parapets of the *quais*, where they are today. In the eighteenth century it was the habit of men of letters to browse among the books and old curiosities exposed for sale

there. Now it is the fashion for tourists to walk that way. But in spite of the fact that modern tourists are not as much in tune with the quaint atmosphere of the stalls as were the gay spirits of the last century, the *quais* still wear an air of antiquity and charm.

Paris has been planned with great forethought. Houses conform in height to the width of the street, and those which front on fine avenues or squares had to be built after the pattern made by the architect who planned that section of the city. There is nothing left to chance in Paris. Walk along the Avenue Champs-Elysées at the far end, where white mansions stand, or drive down Avenue Hoche, where somber gray apartments form a vast stone wall of equal height, and you will be impressed by the severity and restraint that marks Parisian taste in building. Trolley cars are barred from the central parts of the city and relegated to outlying districts. A fine system of underground railways helps

Yvon, Paris

A VIEW OF THE ILE DE LA CITÉ SHOWING NOTRE DAME AT THE RIGHT AND THE PONT NEUF IN THE CENTER

BOOKSTALLS ON A PARIS QUAY Yvon, Paris

solve the traffic problem, which is made so difficult by madly-dashing hordes of blue, yellow, and scarlet taxicabs.

Telephone and telegraph wires are underground. No disfiguring poles line the avenues. For a city of its size, Paris is very clean and well kept. Strict rules and ordinances make this possible: for example, on nearing the city, trains are required to consume their own smoke or to change from steam to electric engines. It is worth while taking such precautions, for Paris is filled with monuments and statues designed to make the city attractive. Because these are clean, her buildings fresh, and her gardens fragrant, this amazing city conveys the impression of youthful charm, in spite of its age of two thousand years and its many memorials.

Because of their size and the famous monuments they contain, the four important squares of Paris are the Place de la Concorde, the Place de l'Etoile, the Place de la Bastille, and the Place Vendôme. The first of these is a congress of lamps at night,

the most spectacular square in any city. This Place of Peace (*Concorde* means peace) has two great fountains that are rushing sounds of happiness and eight perfectly proportioned statues of heroic size to remind the Frenchman of the eight cities which warrant his firm faith in the future of his native land. It is hard for him to realize that this restful square marks the spot where, in the Revolution, king, queen, and hundreds of famous beings perished in a debauch of blood. Where the guillotine once stood rises a slender column of stone that in ancient days fronted the great temple of Thebes. It is sometimes called one of Cleopatra's three needles.

In the Place de l'Etoile (or meeting-place of converging ways) is the famous arch built by the first Napoleon to commemorate his victories. This *Arc de Triomphe* is the largest monument of its kind anywhere. It is adorned with sculptures portraying Napoleon's campaigns. In the year 1921 the body of France's unknown soldier was placed beneath the center of the archway. Each day the tomb is covered with fresh flowers. The simple inscription that graces the last resting-place of the *Soldat Inconnu* profoundly stirs each reader: He Died for His Country. Twelve wide avenues radiate from this square and explain its name. They are streets of distinction, like Avenue Hoche, where aristocratic Paris dwells, or Passy, where the English colony is at home, or Bois de Boulogne (now called Foch Avenue), about which songs are written and where children roll their hoops, or other boulevards whose names you could not fail to recognize.

Closer to the heart of the Frenchman than any other square is the Place de la Bastille. Here until the close of the eighteenth century stood the most feared and hated prison fortress of the whole world. From the stirring story of the French Revolution by Charles Dickens, *A Tale of Two Cities*, you will remember that the Bastille was a prison in which were held without trial, often until their death, many hundreds of political offenders. Their only fault was that they had displeased a despotic king or a cruel government official. Therefore one of the happiest dates in French history is that of the fall of the Bastille at the hands of a com-munist mob who took it by storm, killed the guards, and freed its unhappy inmates. Later the republican government ordered the Bastille to be completely demolished; its key was sent to America during the presidency of George Washington, as a grateful gift of France to a sister republic. In the center of the Place de la Bastille, close to the site of the hated prison, stands today the *Colonne de Juillet*, a lofty bronze pillar resting on a base of white marble. Surmounting this column is a beautiful statue representing Liberty. The anniversary of the taking of the Bastille, July 14, is now celebrated in France as a national holiday.

The monument in the Place Vendôme, the fourth principal square of Paris, is called the *Colonne Vendôme* and was built under the direction of the first Napoleon. Encircling the column is a broad spiral of bronze, three hundred yards in length, which details the story of many of Napoleon's victories. Surmounting the whole is a statue of the Corsican who made of Europe, for a short moment, a plaything and an idle toy.

The plan of these four famous squares is indicated below—a description of the avenues that connect them will be found on page 159.

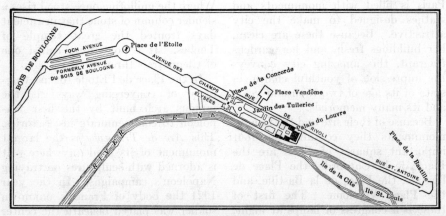

DIAGRAM OF THE FOUR PRINCIPAL SQUARES IN PARIS

CINQUANTE ET UNIÈME LEÇON

La petite paysanne

Marie est une petite paysanne de douze ans. Elle habite un très joli petit village près d'un beau château. Le village compte (*contains*) douze maisons. Alors vous voyez qu'il n'est pas grand du tout. Les paysans qui habitent ce village travaillent dans les champs du château.

Marie a passé six ans à la petite école du village. Elle y a bien travaillé; sa maîtresse était (*was*) fière d'elle, et il faut ajouter que les parents de Marie étaient (*were*) fiers aussi. Marie est assez âgée maintenant pour aider ses parents. Elle n'est plus une petite fille. Son père, comme les autres paysans du village, travaille dans les champs du château.

Voulez-vous savoir ce que Marie fait? Ecoutez donc. Tous les jours il faut mener les beaux moutons blancs aux champs. Marie ne reste pas seule. Pas du tout. Noiraud, le vieux chien noir de Marie, l'accompagne. Noiraud est vieux, mais pas trop vieux pour garder les moutons. C'est un chien très intelligent qui a vraiment l'air de comprendre les paroles de sa jeune maîtresse. Il trouve toujours quelque chose à faire; il court après les moutons, il saute dans l'herbe.

Marie ne perd pas son temps aux champs. Aujourd'hui elle va tricoter comme tous les jours. Elle fait une jolie robe bleue. Elle tricote vite, et la robe avance. Marie est assise sous un bel arbre. Noiraud est là, assis à côté de sa jeune maîtresse. Tout à coup Marie met la robe de côté. Elle met la main dans sa poche et en tire (*takes out*) un petit pain. Noiraud le voit, et ses beaux yeux indiquent qu'il a envie de manger un morceau du petit pain.

—Mon vieux Noiraud, dit Marie.

Je n'oublie jamais que tu aimes les petits pains, n'est-ce pas? Il ne faut pas être si pressé. Un instant, Monsieur Noiraud.

Noiraud attrape les morceaux que Marie lui jette. Il les mange vite. Il a vraiment l'air d'avoir toujours faim, ce vieux Noiraud. Quand ils ont fini de manger le petit pain, Marie continue à tricoter. Après quelque temps elle se repose (*rests*) pour admirer les petites fleurs des champs et le beau ciel si bleu.

Elle pense aussi à son amie Jeanne qui habite la grande ville. Jeanne passe peut-être beaucoup de temps à jouer, mais elle aide aussi sa mère comme une bonne petite fille. Elle va au marché. Bien sûr, Jeanne travaille aussi.

—Tiens, Noiraud, dit tout à coup la jeune fille. N'est-ce pas maman qui nous appelle, là-bas?

Noiraud saute de joie. Oui, bien sûr, c'est maman qui appelle pour annoncer l'heure du dîner. Marie pousse un cri de joie. Elle cherche son chapeau qu'elle trouve dans l'herbe à la même place où elle l'a mis. Elle le prend et le met. Voilà la jeune fille qui va rentrer parce que sa mère l'a appelée.

—Vite, les moutons, Noiraud, dit Marie. Nous allons rentrer à la maison. La robe n'est pas terminée, mais ce soir après le dîner je vais trouver peut-être un peu de temps pour la finir. Maintenant en route pour la maison.

La jeune fille marche derrière Noiraud et les moutons. On avance lentement vers le village. D'autres paysans rentrent aussi. Ils pensent à leurs femmes et aux enfants qu'ils vont retrouver à la maison.

Vocabulaire

l'an [lɑ̃] (m.), *year*
le champ [ʃɑ̃], *field*
le ciel [sjɛl], *sky, heaven*
la fleur [flœːr], *flower*
la joie [ʒwa], *joy*
la parole [parɔl], *word;*
　les paroles [parɔl], *talk,*
　words

le paysan [peizɑ̃], *peasant*
la　paysanne　[peizan],
　peasant girl or *woman*
comprendre [kɔ̃prɑ̃ːdr], *to*
　understand
habiter [abite], *to live in*
mener [məne], *to take, to*
　lead, to drive

pousser [puse], *to utter,*
　to push
vieux, vieille [vjø, vjɛːj],
　old
peut-être [pətɛːtr], *per-*
　haps, maybe
ne . . . plus [nə . . . ply],
　no longer, no more

French words in this lesson whose English equivalents have similar or identical spellings are:

le château [ʃato], *château,*
　castle

le cri [kri], *cry, shout*
la place [plas], *place, spot*

accompagner [akɔ̃paɲe], *to*
　accompany, to go with
terminé [tɛrmine], *finished*

CINQUANTE-DEUXIÈME LEÇON

Les Parties du corps

Nous allons faire aujourd'hui la connaissance d'un autre parent de Gauthier. C'est un jeune homme qui fait ses études de médecine. Gauthier admire énormément ce cousin. Le petit garçon veut l'imiter. Parce qu'on dit qu'il faut commencer très jeune, Gauthier veut commencer tout de suite ses études.

—Bon! dit le cousin Georges. Qu'est-ce que vous[1] savez du corps humain?

—Je sais les noms de toutes les parties du corps, dit Gauthier fièrement.

—A la bonne heure! Vous pouvez m'instruire. Nous étudions en ce moment les nerfs, et je ne sais pas les noms de tous les nerfs.

—Vous vous[2] moquez (*you are making fun*) de moi, dit Gauthier. Je sais les noms des parties principales du corps, mais pas les noms des nerfs.

—Dites-moi, par exemple, ce que c'est que ceci, demande le grand cousin Georges. (*Il indique la tête.*)

—C'est la tête. Voici la figure. Voici le front, les yeux, les joues, le nez, la bouche, et le menton.

—Qu'est-ce qu'on fait avec les yeux? demande Georges.

---

[1] **Vous** is used in this lesson for drill on practical recurrent forms.
[2] The first vous is the subject; the second is the object. (You will learn about this construction when reflexive verbs are taken up.)

—On voit avec les yeux. On mange avec la bouche.

—C'est plutôt avec la langue et les dents qui sont dans la bouche, n'est-ce pas?

—Oui, monsieur le critique, vous avez bien raison, mais on parle aussi avec la langue et les dents et les lèvres. On sent avec le nez; et on entend avec les oreilles.

—C'est bien ça! Qu'est-ce que c'est que ceci, mon enfant?

—C'est le bras. Voici la main, et voici les doigts et le pouce.

—Combien de bras avez-vous?

—J'ai deux bras.

—Et combien de mains?

—J'ai deux mains.

—Et combien de pouces?

—J'ai deux pouces.

—Est-ce que vous avez aussi deux doigts?

—J'ai plus de deux doigts, monsieur le docteur. J'ai quatre doigts et un pouce à chaque main. Quatre et quatre font huit.

—Est-ce que vous marchez sur les mains?

—Seulement pour rire (*for fun*). Je marche sur les deux pieds. Ils sont attachés aux jambes.

—C'est bien, mon ami. C'est assez pour aujourd'hui. Maintenant je vais écrire une lettre avant le déjeuner.

Vocabulaire

la **bouche** [buʃ], *mouth*

le **bras** [bra], *arm*

la **connaissance** [kɔnɛsã:s], *acquaintance*

le **corps** [kɔ:r], *body*

le **critique** [kritik], *critic*

la **dent** [dã], *tooth*

le **docteur** [dɔktœ:r], *doctor*

le **doigt** [dwa], *finger*

la **figure** [figy:r], *face*

le **front** [frõ], *forehead*

la **jambe** [ʒã:b], *leg*

la **joue** [ʒu], *cheek*

la **langue** [lã:g], *tongue, language*

la **lèvre** [lɛ:vr], *lip*

la **médecine** [metsin], *medicine*

le **menton** [mãtõ], *chin*

le **nerf** [nɛ:r], *nerve*

le **nez** [ne], *nose*

l'**œil** [lœ:j] (m.), *eye* les **yeux** [lezjø], *eyes* (Note the difference between the singular and the plural.)

l'**oreille** [lɔrɛ:j] (f.), *ear*

la **physiologie** [fizjɔlɔʒi], *physiology*

le **pied** [pje], *foot*

le **pouce** [pus], *thumb*

le **texte** [tɛkst], *text*

Georges [ʒɔrʒ], *George*

dites-moi[1][dit mwa], *tell me*

faire ses études [fɛ:r se zetyd], *to pursue one's studies, to be studying*

instruire[2] [ɛ̃strɥi:r], *to instruct*

il peut [il pø] (inf. **pouvoir**), *he can, he may*

rire [ri:r], *to laugh*

sentir [sãti·r], *to smell*

il veut [il vø] (inf. **vouloir**), *he wishes*

huit [ɥit], *eight*

humain [ymɛ̃], *human*

principal [prɛ̃sipal], *principal*

toutes [tut] (f. pl. of tout), *all, every*

énormément [enɔrmemã], *greatly*

fièrement [fjɛrmã], *proudly*

seulement [sœlmã], *only*

à la bonne heure [a la bɔ nœ:r], *good!* or *that's good!*

par exemple [pa:r egzã:pl], *as an illustration, for instance, for example*

plus [ply], *more*

plus de [ply də], *more than*

plutôt [plyto], *rather*

que [kə], *than*

A good plan, in acquiring a vocabulary, is to try to group words. There are various ways of doing this, but in the case of words dealing with the body the best way is to take small units, **la tête**, for instance, and group all the parts around it. Learning the words with a diagram will help to fix them in your mind.

---

[1] Imperative of **dire**.

[2] Instruire is irregular; do not now use any form except the infinitive.

Questionnaire

1. Avec qui[1] parle Gauthier?
2. Que fait ce jeune homme?
3. Comment sait-on que Gauthier admire son cousin?
4. Quand est-ce que Gauthier veut commencer ses études?
5. Mentionnez les parties de la tête.
6. Que fait-on avec les yeux?
7. Et avec la bouche?
8. Avec quelles parties de la bouche parle-t-on?
9. Qu'est-ce qu'on fait avec les oreilles?
10. Combien de doigts avez-vous?
11. Que fait-on avec les doigts?
12. Combien de pouces a-t-on?
13. Où sont attachés les pieds?
14. Que va faire le cousin de **Gauthier** avant le dîner?

Devoir

A. *Learn the first sentence of "Les Parties du corps" by heart.*

B. *Rewrite the following sentences, using pronouns in place of the italicized words:*

1. Il a fait *ses études* ici.
2. On commence *la leçon de physiologie* cet après-midi.
3. J'ajoute *les noms des articles*.
4. Voilà pourquoi nous étudions *un nerf très important*.
5. Il peut indiquer *la figure*.
6. Voici *le front*.
7. Voici *les yeux*.
8. Je regarde *cette belle main*.
9. Vous continuez *la leçon sur l'e aigu*.
10. Ils ne mangent pas *la tarte* à midi.

C. *Change the first five sentences of B into questions, using the past indefinite.*

D. *Answer the questions of C, using pronouns.*

E. *Continue this list, adding all the verbs that you know:*

1. On écrit avec les doigts.
   On touche avec les doigts, *etc.*
2. On parle avec la bouche.

F. *Complete these sentences:*

1. J'espère faire tant —— découvertes.
2. Le jeune savant travaille trop —— heures chaque jour.
3. La sœur et le neveu ont beaucoup —— or.
4. Combien —— jeunes filles sont là?
5. On établit peu —— monarchies.

Composition: Ecrivez une leçon de physiologie d'après (imitating) *le texte. Expliquez les parties du corps à une personne plus jeune* (younger) *que vous.*

Exemple: Nous allons apprendre les parties principales du corps. Voici la tête, *etc.*

[1] qui, *whom*

CINQUANTE-TROISIÈME LEÇON
L'Ange et le Démon

Grand-père a toujours le temps d'écouter Gauthier. Papa va au bureau. Il est très occupé. Maman est occupée[1] aussi. Elle fait beaucoup de choses, mais grand-père n'est pas occupé. Il n'a pas beaucoup à faire. Nous sommes très occupés. Nous allons à l'école; nous étudions; nous jouons.

Gauthier a répété la leçon de physiologie à grand-père. Il a bien récité. Il a parlé du corps, de la figure, des bras, des doigts, des jambes, des pieds.

—A la bonne heure! a dit grand-père. Cette leçon de physiologie me fait penser à l'histoire que ma mère racontait autrefois (*used to tell me*).

Il y a (*There are*) dans le cœur de chaque enfant deux peintres qui travaillent du matin jusqu'au soir. Un de ces peintres est un bel ange blanc aux ailes d'or; l'autre est un vilain démon aux ailes noires et rouges et aux yeux de flammes. Chaque fois qu'il (*that there*) vient une bonne pensée à l'esprit de l'enfant, l'ange lui peint sur la figure une expression douce. Mais chaque fois qu'il lui vient une mauvaise pensée, c'est le démon qui prend la brosse et qui lui trace une vilaine expression, maussade et cruelle. Quel (*what a*) changement!

Quand l'enfant devient homme les deux artistes s'en vont (*go away*) ensemble, l'ange et le démon. Leur travail est fini. L'expression reste. Elle est douce et belle si les pensées ont été bonnes; cruelle et méchante si les pensées ont été mauvaises. Il est trop tard pour changer.

Gauthier n'a pas trop aimé cette histoire. Il l'a trouvée un peu ennuyeuse, mais il ne l'a pas vite oubliée. Ces histoires n'amusent pas beaucoup les enfants.

Grammaire
Review of the Present Tense of *Etre*

In French the verb **être** (*to be*) is very important. Before you learn more about this verb, it will be well to review here its present tense and to learn two new forms, in the imperative.

je suis, *I am*	nous sommes, *we are*
tu es (familiar form), *you are*	vous êtes, *you are*
il est, *he is*	ils sont, *they are*

A New Form of *Etre*—the Imperative

sois, *be* (familiar form); soyez, *be;* soyons, *let us be*

Notice the form **soyons** and its translation. All regular French verbs form the first person plural imperative in the same way—i.e., by omitting the subject pronoun of the first person plural of the present indicative. The form **soyons** expresses in one word the idea given in three English words, *let us be.* No matter what verb is used, the first two words of the translation of the first person plural imperative are *let us.* The first person plural imperative of **parler** is **parlons**, *let us speak;* of **finir** is **finissons**, *let us finish;* of **répondre** is **répondons**, *let us reply.*

[1] Past participles may be used as adjectives, and, as such, follow the rules for the agreement of adjectives.

The Feminine of Certain Adjectives

The feminine of the adjective does not present great difficulties. As given in an earlier lesson, the general rule for forming the feminine is *to add e to the masculine.*

There are some exceptions to this rule:

1. **Ennuyeux** has the feminine form **ennuyeuse.** Adjectives ending in **eux** change the **x** into **se** to form the feminine.

2. **Cruel** has the feminine form **cruelle.** Adjectives ending in **el** form their feminine by adding **le.**

3. **Doux, douce** is entirely irregular.

You can readily see that it is very necessary to learn the forms of adjectives which are not formed in the regular way. In your reading watch for examples of them.

Vocabulaire

l'aile [lɛl] (f.), *wing*

l'ange [lɑ̃:ʒ] (m.), *angel*

l'artiste [lartist] (m. and f.), *artist*

la brosse [brɔs], *brush*

le cœur [kœ:r], *heart*

le démon [demõ], *demon*

l'esprit [lɛspri] (m.), *mind, spirit, intelligence*

l'expression [lɛkspresjõ] (f.), *expression*

le peintre [pɛ̃:tr], *painter, artist*

la pensée [pɑ̃se], *thought*

le travail [trava:j], *work*

il devient [il dəvjɛ̃] (inf. devenir), *he becomes*

il peint [il pɛ̃] (inf. peindre), *he paints*

me fait penser [mə fɛ pɑ̃se], *makes me think*

tracer [trase], *to trace*

il vient [il vjɛ̃] (inf. venir), *he comes, there comes*

aimable [ɛmabl], *amiable, pleasant, kind*

cruel, cruelle [kryɛl], *cruel*

doux, douce [du, dus], *sweet, gentle*

maussade [mosad], *cross, disagreeable*

mauvais [mɔvɛ], *bad, unpleasant*

occupé [ɔkype], *busy, occupied*

un, une [œ̃, yn], *one*

vilain [vilɛ̃], *ugly*

autrefois [otrəfwa], *formerly*

du matin jusqu'au soir [dy matɛ̃ ʒysko swa:r], *from morning till night*

trop tard [trɔta:r], *too late*

Questionnaire

1. Qui a toujours le temps d'écouter Gauthier?

2. Pourquoi papa n'a-t-il pas le temps d'écouter Gauthier?

3. Que fait maman?

4. Chez vous que fait maman?

5. Avons-nous quelque chose à faire?

6. A qui Gauthier a-t-il répété sa leçon de physiologie?

7. De quoi a-t-il parlé?

8. A quoi grand-père a-t-il pensé?

9. Qu'y a-t-il dans le cœur de chaque enfant?

10. Qui est-ce qui travaille dans le cœur de chaque enfant?

11. Faites une description des deux peintres.

12. Quand le démon prend la brosse, quelle est l'expression de l'enfant?

13. Quand l'ange prend la brosse, quelle est l'expression de l'enfant?

14. Quand s'en vont les artistes?

15. Comment Gauthier trouve-t-il cette histoire?

16. Va-t-il l'oublier bien vite?

17. Ces histoires amusent-elles les enfants?

18. Les écoutent-ils avec beaucoup de plaisir?

Devoir

A. *In the following sentences use the correct forms of the words in parentheses:*

1. (ce) bouche n'est pas (grand).
2. L'expression du démon est (cruel).
3. On a parlé de (ce) ami anglais.
4. L'histoire ancienne n'est pas (ennuyeux).
5. Il a l'air (doux) aussi.
6. Je ne trouve pas les enfants (méchant).
7. Ils ont (voir) les peintres.
8. Marie a les yeux (brun).
9. N'avez-vous rien entendu de cette histoire? Moi, je ne l'ai pas (entendre).
10. C'est ça, les grandes personnes (être) toujours (occupé).
11. (Etre)-vous (occupé), Joséphine?
12. Ils (faire) leurs études.
13. Je veux une amie (distingué), (intelligent), et (doux).

B. *Continue the conjugation:*

1. Bien sûr, je suis américain.
2. J'ai les yeux bleus.
3. Je vais lire les journaux.
4. Je n'ai pas eu l'air aimable.
5. Je fais l'appel.

C. *Using 1 as a model, give the feminine of sentences 2-8.*

1. Le cousin Joseph est grand.
   La cousine Joséphine est grande.
2. C'est un jeune garçon aimable.
3. Il n'est jamais cruel.
4. Sont-ils bons?
5. Bien sûr, Jean est fatigué.
6. Mon oncle est occupé.
7. L'homme travaille au bureau.
8. L'ancien maître mange de bon appétit.

D. *Use each of these phrases in a sentence:*

1. espérer
2. vous pouvez
3. en route
4. pas tout à fait
5. le neveu
6. la femme
7. le roi
8. les Etats-Unis
9. la vitrine
10. le fils

Yvon, Paris

PLACE VENDÔME

THE FAÇADE

THE CRYPT

THE ABBEY OF ST. DENIS, NEAR PARIS

CINQUANTE-QUATRIÈME LEÇON

Joseph rentre à la maison

Papa et maman sont inquiets parce que Joseph n'est pas rentré. Il est allé faire une promenade en auto avec la famille d'un ami. Ils sont partis le matin, et ils ne sont pas encore rentrés.

—Ne sois pas inquiète, dit papa à maman, mais il regarde sa montre.

—Ils sont allés à Beloit sans doute, répond maman, mais elle regarde par (*looks out of*) la fenêtre.

—M. Renaud sait bien conduire une auto, dit papa.

—Oui, très bien, répond maman, mais elle a l'air bien inquiet.

Tout à coup on entend une corne.

—Les voilà, crie maman. Elle va pour la dixième fois à la fenêtre. Elle voit une automobile bleue; et elle sait bien que l'auto des Renaud[1] est verte.

—Ce n'est pas leur auto, dit maman, et elle prend un livre. Elle va oublier que Joseph n'est pas rentré. Elle va lire. Elle regarde son livre; elle voit les mots; elle tourne les pages; mais elle ne lit pas. C'est-à-dire qu'elle ne comprend pas ce qu'elle lit.

Papa prend un livre aussi. Il ne va pas à la fenêtre pour voir si l'auto arrive. Il dort un peu; après il ouvre son livre. Il le trouve intéressant, si intéressant qu'il oublie son inquiétude.

Tout à coup la porte s'ouvre (*opens*). C'est Joseph qui entre, qui les salue, qui parle des aventures de la promenade, et qui annonce qu'il a faim. Papa et maman sont très contents de voir Joseph. Ils ne le grondent pas.

[1] Family names do not add an s in the plural.

Grammaire

The Past Indefinite of Verbs Conjugated with *Etre*

THE VERB *être* AS AN AUXILIARY

You have noticed that two parts are necessary to form the past indefinite tense. There must always be the auxiliary and the past participle. The verbs whose past indefinite you have already studied are conjugated with **avoir,** but now you are going to have a few verbs that are conjugated with **être.** Four common ones, all verbs of motion without specifying the kind of motion, are **aller, partir, retourner,** and **arriver.** Below is given the past indefinite of **aller.**

Singular

je suis allé(e), *I went, I did go, I have gone*
tu es allé(e), *you went, etc.* (familiar)
il est allé, *he went*
elle est allée, *she went*

Plural

nous sommes allés(ées), *we went*
vous êtes allé(s) (ée) (ées), *you went*
ils sont allés, *they went*
elles sont allées, *they went*

Learn the first of the rules that follow, and review the second:

1. The past participle of a verb conjugated with **être** agrees with the subject in gender and number, e.g.,

Il est parti.   Ils sont partis.
Elle est partie.   Elles sont parties.

2. The past participle of a verb conjugated with **avoir** agrees with the direct object in gender and number if the direct object comes before the verb, e.g.,

Elle a cherché les mouchoirs.
Elle les a cherchés.
Quelle lettre avez-vous lue?

Vocabulaire

le bassin [basɛ̃], *pond*
la corne [kɔrn], *horn*
l'éléphant [lelefã] (m.), *elephant*
l'inquiétude [lɛ̃kjetyd] (f.), *anxiety*
l'intérêt [lɛ̃terɛ] (m.), *interest*
le lion [ljõ], *lion*
la montre [mõ:tr], *watch*
l'ours [lurs] (m.), *bear*
le poisson [pwasõ], *fish*

M., abbreviation for **Monsieur**
avoir l'air inquiet [avwa:r lɛ:r ɛ̃kjɛ], *to seem worried*
conduire [kõdɥi:r], *to conduct, to drive, to take*
il dort [il dɔ:r] (inf. **dormir**), *he sleeps*
faire une promenade en auto [fɛ:r yn prɔmnad ãnoto], *to take a ride*

partir [parti:r], *to leave*
pris [pri] (p.p. of **prendre**), *taken*
saluer [salɥe], *to greet*
inquiet [ɛ̃kjɛ], *anxious, uneasy*
sauvage [sova:ʒ], *savage, wild*
c'est-à-dire [sɛ ta di:r], *that is to say*
pas encore [pɑ zãkɔ:r], *not yet*

Questionnaire

1. Pourquoi maman est-elle inquiète?
2. Avec qui est allé Joseph?
3. Comment savez-vous que papa est inquiet?
4. Et maman?
5. Quel air a maman?
6. Qu'est-ce qu'elle entend?
7. Comment sait-elle que ce n'est pas l'auto des Renaud?
8. Que fait maman pour oublier que Joseph n'est pas rentré?
9. Lit-elle?
10. Que fait papa?
11. Qui entre?
12. Que fait-il?
13. Pourquoi papa et maman sont-ils contents?
14. Joseph parle-t-il des aventures de la promenade en auto?

Devoir

A. Conjugate:
1. Je suis parti.
2. Je ne suis pas rentré.
3. Je suis arrivé avec Jean.

B. Change the verbs to the past indefinite. Do not forget the agreement of the past participle.

Les enfants vont au parc avec papa. Ils voient beaucoup de choses intéressantes. Ils regardent avec intérêt les animaux sauvages. Ils préfèrent le lion. Quand papa et les enfants arrivent au grand bassin, ils voient les ours blancs. Un homme jette beaucoup de poissons aux ours blancs. Les ours blancs les attrapent. Les enfants vont voir aussi les éléphants et les oiseaux. Après cela papa et les enfants rentrent à la maison.

C. Write five imperative sentences to be given orally in class.

*D. Give as many words as you can that group themselves around **le drapeau tricolore**.*

E. Make a list of the parts of the body.

Traduction:

Father is sleeping; mother is reading a book. She does not understand what (**ce que**) she is reading. She looks worried because Joseph has not returned. He left in the morning to take an automobile ride with a friend's family. Joseph finally arrives. He enters, greets his mother and father, and talks about his adventures. His parents adore him. They are indulgent. They are proud of Joseph.

PLACE DE LA BASTILLE

Yvon, Paris

CINQUANTE-CINQUIÈME LEÇON

La Promenade de Joseph

Au dîner, dans la grande salle à manger, Joseph parle de sa promenade en auto avec les Renaud.

—Nous avons décidé d'aller plus loin (*farther*) parce que M. Renaud a dit qu'il avait vu (*had seen*) un joli endroit pour un pique-nique. Nous sommes allés à cet endroit, mais nous y avons trouvé trois personnes. Alors nous sommes allés plus loin, et nous avons trouvé un bon endroit. Marcel et moi, nous avons ramassé beaucoup de bois, et nous avons allumé un beau feu. Mme. Renaud a fait cuire un bifteck. Nous l'avons mangé de bon appétit parce que nous avions (*were*) très faim. Après le déjeuner, M. Renaud a parlé de sa jeunesse. Et puis il a dormi, Mme. Renaud a lu, et Marcel et moi, nous avons pris nos livres pour étudier.

—Vous n'avez pas étudié, vous deux, dit papa; vous avez regardé un livre, mais c'est tout.

—Non, papa, nous avons étudié. Nous sommes restés près de Monsieur et de Madame Renaud, et nous avons repassé quarante lignes de latin.

—A la bonne heure! dit papa. Je vois que vous avez vraiment étudié. Je suis content de vous.

—Et après, êtes-vous allés plus loin? dit maman.

—Non, nous sommes restés longtemps dans le bois. Puis nous sommes partis pour rentrer chez nous. Que (*what*) nous avons passé une belle journée!

Grammaire

Verbs Conjugated with *Etre*

The verbs conjugated with **être** are intransitive, that is, they are verbs which do not take an object. Learn this list of **être** verbs, or learn each one when you come to it.

arriver	entrer	rester
aller	rentrer	retourner
partir	monter	mourir (*to die*)
sortir (*to go out*)	descendre	naître (*to be born*)

Do not forget that the past participle of a verb conjugated with **être** agrees with the subject in number and in gender.

The Comparative of the Adverb

In English when we wish to show adverbial comparison we do one of two things: we add *-er* to the positive form of the adverb or prefix *more: fast, faster; quickly, more quickly.* The French form their comparative in the second way. They say, **vite, plus vite.** The word **plus** is added to form the comparative of an adverb. Look in the reading above for an adverb used in this way.[1]

[1]This subject is treated more fully in Lessons 116 and 117, pages 320, 322, and 323.

Vocabulaire

le **bifteck** [biftɛk], *beef-steak*

l'**endroit** [lɑ̃drwɑ] (m.), *place*

le **feu** [fø], *fire*

la **jeunesse** [ʒœnɛs], *youth*

la **journée** [ʒurne], *day (duration of time)*

le **latin** [latɛ̃], *Latin*

la **ligne** [liɲ], *line*

Madame [madam], *Mrs.;* abbreviation, **Mme.**

le **pique-nique** [piknik], *picnic*

allumer [alyme], *to light (a fire)*

cuire[1] [kɥiːr], **faire cuire** [fɛːr kɥiːr], *to cook*

dormir [dɔrmiːr] (p.p. **dormi**), *to sleep*

ouvrir [uvriːr] (p.p. **ouvert**), *to open*

repasser [rəpɑse], *to go over, to review*

heureux, -se [œrø, œrøːz], *happy*

que [kə], *what*

longtemps [lõtɑ̃], *a long time, for a long time, long*

Questionnaire

1. De quoi parle Joseph?
2. Avec qui a-t-il fait sa promenade?
3. Pourquoi sont-ils allés plus loin?
4. Qu'est-ce qu'ils ont trouvé?
5. Qu'est-ce que Marcel et Joseph ont ramassé?
6. Qu'est-ce qu'ils ont mangé?
7. Qui a parlé de sa jeunesse?
8. Qu'est-ce qu'il a fait après?
9. Qu'est-ce que les garçons ont fait?
10. Combien de lignes repassent-ils?
11. Qu'est-ce que Mme. Renaud a lu?
12. Où sont-ils restés?
13. Pourquoi Joseph est-il heureux au dîner?

Devoir

A. In the second paragraph of "La Promenade de Joseph" change the verbs you find in the past indefinite to the third person plural of the same tense.

B. Change the infinitives to the past indefinite:

1. Ils (écouter) le garçon de treize ans.
2. Ils (aller) aux bois.
3. (Etre)-vous avec vos amis?
4. (Lire)-vous la leçon de latin?
5. Je (partir) ce matin.
6. Elle (entrer) dans la boutique pour acheter un bifteck.
7. Nous (finir) l'étude de l'auxiliaire.
8. Nous (rester) chez ma tante du matin jusqu'au soir.
9. Je (ramasser) beaucoup de bois.
10. Vous (rentrer) avec nous.
11. Elles (dormir) hier un instant.
12. Ils (décider) d'aller l'aider aussi.

13. (Entendre) -ils la corne?
14. Est-ce que je (accompagner) le peintre âgé?
15. Ne (employer) -vous pas ces verbes au passé indéfini?

C. Be prepared[2] to write in class the present and past indefinite tenses of these verbs:

partir, rester, lire, ouvrir, avoir

*D. Complete these sentences with **de** or contractions of **de** and the definite article:*

1. La jeune fille ennuyeuse a peu —— amis.
2. Il n'y a pas —— doute.
3. La découverte —— savant est importante.
4. Combien —— nièces avez-vous?
5. Hier nous avons lu tant —— articles.

[1] cuire is irregular. Do not use any form except the infinitive.
[2] For any forms of which you are doubtful see the section on irregular verbs, pages 371-379.

E. Arrange these words to make correct sentences. Begin each sentence with a capital letter and put the proper punctuation at the end.

1. s'il dites-moi peut m'instruire
2. nous études faisons nos de médecine
3. veut république rétablir seulement il la
4. quelques parties les jambes sont les joues le menton le nez les oreilles les pieds du corps

Traduction:

They did not arrive at Mary's, because they stayed in the woods. We saw them there. The boys studied, Mrs. Renaud read, and Mr. Renaud slept. We left, but they remained a little longer. I want to stay in the woods in order to build a good fire and to cook a steak. I am going to stay there tomorrow. I like to eat in the woods. I always have a good appetite (*there*).

A SECTION OF THE LOUVRE

CINQUANTE-SIXIÈME LEÇON

Review

A

1. What is the general rule for the formation of the feminine of an adjective?

2. What is the feminine form if the adjective ends in **eux**?

3. What other adjectives given in the preceding lessons form their feminine irregularly?

4. Give the feminine plural of **beau, blanc, ennuyeux, heureux.**

5. Write from memory a list of ten parts of the body.

6. Give the present tense of the verb **être.**

7. How is the present tense of **être** used in forming the past indefinite?

8. With what class of verbs is **être** used as an auxiliary?

9. What other auxiliary verb is there in French besides **être**?

10. What is the rule for the agreement of the past participle of a verb conjugated with **être**? Of a verb conjugated with **avoir**?

11. Give two sentences which illustrate the past indefinite of verbs conjugated with **avoir**; two for verbs conjugated with **être.**

12. What are the personal endings of the present tense of the first conjugation?

13. What are the personal endings of the present tense of the second conjugation?

14. What are the personal endings of the present tense of the third conjugation? Give the present tense of **entendre.**

15. What form of the verb is used after **il faut**? Give an example.

16. What are the present interrogative third person singular forms of **avoir, allumer, perdre, repasser?**

17. In which form of the verb is it sometimes necessary to insert **t**? Why? Give two illustrations.

18. How is the comparative of an adverb or adjective formed?

B

I. Change the verbs in the following sentences to the past indefinite. (One cannot be changed. Find this verb and tell why it cannot be changed.)

1. Nous attrapons la balle.
2. Ils la perdent.
3. Je vois ces friandises.
4. Assis au salon Jean lit quarante lignes de latin.
5. Vous réfléchissez peu de temps.
6. Rapportez les bonbons, s'il vous plaît.

II. In the blanks below use the correct forms of **ce:**

1. —— lèvres sont rouges.
2. J'admire —— tête de l'artiste.
3. N'est-ce pas que —— dents sont blanches?
4. —— aile d'or est belle.

III. Form the feminine of these adjectives and use them in sentences:

> heureux (*happy*)
> content (*glad*)
> maussade (*disagreeable*)
> cruel (*cruel*)
> doux (*sweet, gentle*)

IV. Use the following expressions in negative sentences:

1. avoir chaud	7. avoir soif
2. avoir froid	8. avoir sommeil
3. avoir faim	9. avoir l'air fatigué
4. avoir peur	
5. avoir honte	10. avoir l'air inquiet
6. avoir raison	

PLACE DE LA CONCORDE

Agence Rol, Paris

SCENES IN PARIS

PART TWO

The Place de l'Etoile and the Place de la Concorde, two of the famous squares of which you were told on page 143, are connected by the loveliest avenue in Paris and perhaps in all Europe. This is the Avenue Champs-Elysées, a name taken from Greek mythology. Its fitting title of Elysian Fields signifies a roomy space of great contentment and delight. Anyone who has really lived in Paris will tell you that the Avenue Champs-Elysées is one spot on the earth's surface where one is filled with a sense of happy lightness and joy. Whether you are bound for the house of Madame Jenny, the famous *couturière* (dressmaker), or are dashing along this sophisticated pathway for tea at the new Lido, the Champs-Elysées will make your pulses quicken.

If New York had only had the vision to make Fifth Avenue as wide as this splendid boulevard of France, what a glory of living would have been added to the capital of American power and influence! For this broad Paris artery of world fashion is over two hundred fifty feet in width, and a mile and a half long, extending from the *Arc de Triomphe* to the *Place de la Concorde*. It is a blessing that this imposing promenade does not break off abruptly or terminate in some ugly byway; its noble beginning and its satisfying end lend the final touch of distinction to a really great drive.

If we leave the Arch of Triumph in the opposite direction, we are at once on the avenue that forms the approach to the famous park, the *Bois de Boulogne*. "I walked along the *Bois de Boulogne* with an independent air," runs the old music-hall song that describes exactly the feeling of the tourist who takes his happy-go-lucky way toward the spot that is like fairyland. The park comprises over 2220 acres and was formed by Napoleon from a forest. Hither flock the inhabitants of the great city, to ride in delightful avenues, to ramble along winding paths, or under a gayly-striped umbrella to chat across the table of an outdoor café. In winter, if the weather permits, the lagoons are covered with skaters. All day long and every day, people throng the *Bois de Boulogne* during the hours when American parks are apt to be empty. For with us the great business world commands the presence of its ambitious citizens, but Parisians have learned the gentle art of idling for certain periods of each work day, sure that they will labor all the better for these moments of recreation.

From the Place de la Concorde, by way of the Rue de Rivoli, one can continue in almost a straight line to the Place de la Bastille. Here is a gallery of attractive shops. Jewels flash—Sulka's windows cry forth the last word in men's fashions—the old Continental Hotel rears its proud head —the wise tourist pauses at Rumpelmayer's for tea and a caviar sandwich.

Across the street the Tuileries gardens are stately and fragrant, forming a fine outlook for the artist studios that are high in buildings on the Rue de Rivoli. It is an enchanting street for the stranger in Paris, and a very tempting one to shoppers.

You will wish to know of certain buildings that have outlasted time and continue to lead a charmed life. Paris has more than twenty cathedrals, but the *one* is Notre Dame. Its foundation stone on the Ile de la Cité was laid in 1163. It fulfills the three requirements of a really great cathedral: it holds many people—seven thousand at a time; so sound is its construction that it has endured for twenty-five generations of humanity; it is a thing of beauty—a poem in stone, frozen music. It lends its unique touch to a thousand paintings and etchings of Paris: a familiar subject of popular art is Notre Dame with its far-flung flying buttresses, in the background the bookstalls of the Seine *quais.*

THE PALAIS DE JUSTICE
Sainte Chapelle is at the left.

L'HÔTEL DES INVALIDES
The tomb of Napoleon is under the great central dome.

The most perfect piece of Gothic architecture in the world is Sainte Chapelle, built in three years (1245-1248). It is hard to imagine that so short a space of time could complete a work which is amazing in the beauty of its materials, the purity of its lines, and the variety of its details. This church was erected for the king of France known as Saint Louis, to inclose sacred relics he had brought back from the Holy Land. The interior of the chapel is a breathtaking marvel of beauty. Its stained-glass windows are very lovely.

Next to Notre Dame, the oldest as well as the first object of historic interest in Paris is the Louvre Museum. Originally built in the thirteenth century as a royal fortress, many later kings have contributed to its enlargement and ennobling. This palace is now the richest treasure-house of art the modern world knows. It contains uncounted thousands of rare paintings, sculptures, bronzes, and pieces of jewelry from ancient times to the day of which we write. To enrich this unrivaled French museum many expeditions to explore and excavate have been sent to far parts of the earth. It requires many days just to see the wonders of the Louvre, but yet it happily is in the power of the visitor for a short hour only to achieve much. He can go from the radiant splendor of the Venus of Milo against her glowing curtain of scarlet to the deathless Winged Victory, to Mona Lisa of the mysterious smile—and in a few brief moments envision the objects that have called forth centuries of critical study and inspiration.

A most interesting hospital for aged and wounded soldiers was built in Paris in the year 1670. It is called the Hôtel des Invalides. It now contains a notable collection of armor and weapons, and memorials of Napoleon. Its church is a center of attraction, for it contains the impressive tomb of Napoleon, whose inscription reads, "I wish my ashes to repose by the banks of the Seine, in the midst of

CAFÉ DU DÔME

Yvon, Paris

the French people I have loved so well."

This love of the picturesque Seine is typical of the Parisian. The river somehow marks even the lives of the people who live beside it. The Left Bank (*Rive Gauche*)! These words are enough; one need not add "of the Seine," or "in Paris." Here lives the world of carefreeness; the amusing long-haired artists who eat bread and ham at the Two Maggots and talk long afternoons away. Here is the wild jungle of cabarets on Montparnasse— as The Jockey, whose walls are plastered with posters, newspapers, photographs, sheet-music, whose dusky shadows hide the extreme youth of its pleasure-seekers, whose hideous din fails quite to drown the American accents of most of its dancers. Then there is the Café du Dôme, where artists and writers, real and pretended, drink coffee far into the night, discussing hedonism—which means the pursuit of pleasure as an end in life— and other "isms" that are even less simple to understand. Out of these

sordid cabarets have come only a few geniuses, but one is apt to forgive the thousand others for not being great. The Left Bank has privileges that no other spot may ever hope for.

The music-halls of Paris are far renowned. The stage effects gained by lighting and color in the Paris houses are attained nowhere else. The Opéra of Paris is world-famous. It has the support of the government, which also has under its wing the Comédie Française, where the classic plays are presented. High points in the dramatic season are of course the revivals of Molière—the French Shakespeare— and the grand opera.

Paris is full of a dozen phases of life we know little about. The world of dressmakers—*couturiers*, as they are called—is a fascinating study. There are social functions far more brilliant than any in our knowledge, as— for instance—the Steeplechase at Auteuil, polo at Bagatelle, the Bal de la Couture in the Opéra. Paris will always be a combination of the enchanting new and the arrogant old.

CINQUANTE-SEPTIÈME LEÇON

Les Vacances sont finies

Que c'est ennuyeux! (*How annoying it is!*) Les vacances sont finies! L'école commence lundi (*Monday*). La campagne est si calme! Avec leurs nouveaux camarades, Charles et Louis ont fait de longues promenades à travers les champs. Les yeux vifs de Louis deviennent (*become*) tristes à la pensée de leur retour à Paris. Il parle ainsi à sa mère:

—Maman, où est notre (*our*) nouvelle maison?

—Rue de la République.

—Avons-nous un jardin?

—Non, mon enfant, mais un jardin public est à côté de la maison.

—Pas de jardin (*No garden*) chez nous!

—Nous avons six grandes chambres: trois chambres à coucher, une salle à manger, un salon, et—

—Et une cuisine et une office?

—Bien sûr; une office avec une porte qui ferme à clef.

Charles devient triste à la pensée de rentrer à Paris. Louis devient triste. Ils sont chez tante Françoise depuis trois semaines. Après leur retour à Paris, qu'est-ce qu'ils vont faire? La nouvelle maison n'a pas de jardin— seulement une cuisine avec une office, qui ferme à clef. C'est dur, vraiment.

Les petits voleurs (*thieves*)

Monsieur et Madame Lefèvre ne sont pas à la maison. Marie, la bonne, est sur le pas de la porte. Charles et Louis sont au lit.

—Charles?

—Quoi?

—Dors-tu déjà?

—Oui. Qu'est-ce que tu désires?

—Je sais où sont les gâteaux. Ils sont dans l'office.

—Je n'ai pas faim. L'office ferme à clef.

—Je sais où est la clef. Elle est dans la chambre de maman.

—Naturellement.

—Charles, désires-tu du chocolat?

—Non, non, laisse-moi tranquille

(*don't bother me*). Bonne nuit!

—Tu ne désires pas de tarte?

—De la tarte aux cerises?

—Oui. J'y vais. Viens. (*Come on.*)

A la fin de cette conversation les garçons se lèvent (*get up*). Sans bruit ils sortent de leur chambre. Louis cherche la clef. Ils descendent (*go down*) l'escalier. Louis ouvre la porte de l'office. Charles ferme la porte. Silence.

Sur le pas de la porte, Marie parle avec la voisine.

—Monsieur et Madame ne sont pas à la maison. Les enfants dorment comme des anges.

—A la bonne heure! C'est bien.

Dans l'office

Les enfants sont dans l'office. Voici les gâteaux, le chocolat, la tarte aux cerises, et les bananes.

—Du chocolat! Voilà mon affaire (*That's what I want*), dit Charles.

—Donne-moi des gâteaux.

—Du bruit! Qu'est-ce que c'est?

—Rien. C'est bon, n'est-ce pas?

—Très bon. Ne mange pas trop de gâteaux.

—Encore un. C'est le tour de la tarte. Donne-moi un couteau.

—En voici un. Coupe de grands morceaux, s'il te plaît.

—Quel gourmand! Des bananes maintenant?

—Non, c'est assez pour moi. Et toi?

—Moi aussi. Retournons (*Let's go back*) à la chambre.

Charles et Louis rentrent dans leur chambre. Pas de lumière, pas de bruit.

—Charles, dors-tu?

—Non, et toi?

—Moi non plus (*Nor I either*).

—Oh!

—Quoi!

—Ça va mal! (*Something is the matter!*) Les gâteaux et la tarte aux cerises!

—J'ai mal au cœur! (*I have a stomach-ache!*)

—Marie! Marie! Marie!!

Qui est-ce qui bat les tapis?

Marie monte vite dans la chambre des enfants.

—Qu'est-ce qu'il y a? (*What is the matter?*)

—Je suis malade, dit Charles.

—Je suis malade aussi, dit Louis.

—Oh, oh, crie Marie, je vais appeler le docteur.

Le docteur qui était (*was*) libre arrive. Il sait que les enfants ne sont pas dans un état grave (*serious*).

—Ah! voici deux grands gourmands. Ils sont déjà punis.

—On va me gronder, dit Marie.

Quelque temps après, les parents rentrent. Ils posent des questions.

—C'est Louis qui est coupable.

—Non, c'est Charles.

—Louis a cherché la clef.

—Charles a pris le chocolat.

—Oui, mais c'est Louis qui a pris les gâteaux.

Les explications cessent, mais l'affaire n'est pas encore terminée. Le lendemain matin un voisin dit à Madame Lefèvre—Qui est-ce qui bat les tapis chez vous?

Elle répond: C'est Monsieur Lefèvre . . . mais ce ne sont pas les tapis qu'il bat!

Vocabulaire

le bruit [brɥi], *noise*

la chambre à coucher [ʃɑ̃:brə kuʃe], *bedroom*

l'état [leta] (m.), *state, condition*

la fin [fɛ̃], *end*

le lit [li], *bed*

la lumière [lymjɛ:r], *light*

la nuit [nɥi], *night*

le pas [pɑ], *step*

le retour [rətu:r], *return*

la semaine [səmɛn], *week*

le tour [tu:r], *turn, trip*

le voisin, la voisine [vwazɛ̃, vwazin], *neighbor*

battre [batr], *to beat, to strike*

laisser [lɛse], *to let, to leave*

punir [pyni:r], *to punish*

sortir [sɔrti:r], *to go out, to get out, to leave, to come out*

deux [dø], *two*

dur [dy:r], *hard*

libre [libr], *free*

malade [malad], *sick*

nouveau, nouvelle [nuvo, nuvɛl], *new*

triste [trist], *sad*

vif, vive [vif, vi:v], *bright, clear, quick*

ainsi [ɛ̃si], *thus*

depuis [dəpɥi], *since, for*

à travers [a travɛ:r], *across, through*

English Equivalents

l'affaire [lafɛ:r] (f.), *affair, matter*

le camarade [kamarad], *comrade*

le silence [silɑ̃:s], *silence*

calme [kalm], *calm, quiet*

public, -que [pyblik], *public*

naturellement [natyrɛlmɑ̃], *naturally, of course, certainly*

CINQUANTE-HUITIÈME LEÇON
Etienne cherche son stylo

Il est l'heure d'aller à l'école, mais Etienne n'est pas encore prêt. Il va arriver en retard, et le professeur va le retenir après la classe. Pauvre Etienne! Mais il est un peu coupable. Il n'est pas prêt parce qu'il égare ses affaires. Il court partout pour les chercher. Il trouve sa serviette dans sa chambre, et il y trouve aussi trois livres, mais où donc est son stylo? Il le cherche sur la table dans sa chambre; puis il le cherche au salon.

—Maman, dit-il, tu n'as pas vu mon stylo?

—Tu n'es pas encore prêt, Etienne? Tu vas arriver en retard. Non, je n'ai pas vu ton stylo.

Elle commence à le chercher aussi.

—Marie-Louise ne perd pas ses affaires, continue maman. Pourquoi perds-tu toujours ton stylo?

—J'ai mis mon stylo avec mes livres et ma serviette, répond Etienne. Et ce matin il n'est pas là.

Sa sœur, Marie-Louise, entre. Etienne explique ce qu'ils cherchent.

—Quel complet as-tu porté hier? dit Marie-Louise. Le bleu, n'est-ce pas? Le stylo est peut-être dans la poche de ton veston bleu.

Etienne court chercher son veston bleu. Voilà le stylo.

—Le voici, crie Etienne. Je ne l'ai pas mis avec mes livres. Je l'ai mis dans ma poche. Il prend sa serviette et son stylo et descend l'escalier.

—Je ne vais pas être si bête la prochaine fois. Maman et papa ne perdent pas leurs affaires. Je ne vais rien perdre, non plus. Je ne vais jamais rien perdre. Je vais mettre chaque chose à sa place, annonce-t-il.

—Nous l'espérons, dit maman, mais maintenant, vite, vite (*hurry up*)! Si tu arrives en retard le professeur va te gronder.

—Oui, maman, dit Etienne. Au revoir, maman. A tantôt!

Vocabulaire

les **affaires** [lezafɛːr] (f. pl.), *things, belongings, business*

le **complet** [kõplɛ], *suit*

les **lunettes** [le lynɛt] (f.), *spectacles*

la **serviette** [sɛrvjɛt], *brief-case*

le **veston** [vɛstõ], *coat* (of a boy's or man's suit)

Etienne [etjɛn], *Stephen*

Marie-Louise [marilwiːz], *Mary Louise*

égarer [egare], *to mislay, to misplace*

retenir [rətniːr], *to retain, to keep in*

coupable [kupabl], *to blame, at fault*

prêt [prɛ], *ready*

prochain [prɔʃɛ̃], *next, neighboring*

sévère [sevɛːr], *severe, stern*

au revoir [o rəvwaːr], *good-by*

non plus [nõ ply], *neither, either*

Grammaire
Review of the Past Indefinite

You will recall that the past indefinite in French consists of two parts, the auxiliary **avoir** or **être** and the past participle. In the negative, **ne** must precede **avoir** or **être**, and if pronoun objects are used, they, too, must precede the auxiliary verb. If you have forgotten the rules for the agreement of the past participle, consult Lessons 43, page 121, and 54, page 153.

The Possessive Adjective

If you look in "Etienne cherche son stylo" for words that express possession, you will find the forms **mon, ma**, etc. These are possessive adjectives.
Here is the complete list of possessive adjectives, singular and plural:

SINGULIER		PLURIEL
Masculin	*Féminin*	*Masculin et Féminin*
mon, *my*	ma	mes
ton, *your*	ta	tes
son, *his, her, its*	sa	ses
notre, *our*	notre	nos
votre, *your*	votre	vos
leur, *their*	leur	leurs

Notice that the possessive adjective, like a descriptive adjective, agrees in
gender and number with the noun it modifies.

> son stylo (le stylo de Robert), *his fountain-pen*
> sa lettre (la lettre de Robert), *his letter*
> son stylo (le stylo de Marie), *her fountain-pen*
> sa lettre (la lettre de Marie), *her letter*
> leur journée, *their day*
> leurs journées, *their days*

Questionnaire

1. Pourquoi Etienne n'est-il pas prêt?
2. S'il arrive en retard, qu'est-ce que le professeur va faire?
3. Où court-il?
4. Qu'est-ce qu'il ne trouve pas?
5. Où cherche-t-il son stylo?
6. Est-ce que maman l'a vu?
7. Qu'est-ce qu'elle fait?
8. Qui ne perd pas ses affaires?
9. Où est-ce qu'Etienne dit qu'il a mis son stylo?
10. Qui aide Etienne à trouver son stylo?
11. Où le trouve-t-il?
12. Qu'est-ce qu'Etienne va faire?
13. Où va Etienne après avoir dit "Au revoir!" à sa mère?
14. Que fait le professeur si un élève arrive en retard?

Devoir

A. Conjugate:

1. Je finis ma géographie.
2. J'ai perdu mes billets.
3. Je cherche chaque raison.
4. Je suis allé à la gare.

B. Complete by using possessive adjectives:

1. Je cherche —— mouchoir dans —— poche.
2. La mère gronde —— fils parce qu'il perd —— affaires.
3. Les élèves préparent —— devoirs sur l'adjectif démonstratif à la maison; ils ont —— livres et —— cahiers.
4. Met-elle —— tasse près de —— verre?
5. Voulez-vous —— mouchoirs verts et bleus?

6. Avez-vous perdu —— gomme et —— crayons?

7. Je n'ai pas apporté (*my*) clefs.

8. Il n'a pas invité —— amis anglais à dîner avec —— famille non plus.

9. Nous avons parlé de —— travail.

10. Joseph a donné —— fruits à —— mère.

C. Change the italicized words to pronouns and rearrange the order of the sentences when necessary. Do not forget the agreement of the past participle.

1. Nous sommes allés *à la fabrique.*

2. Nous avons trouvé *la fabrique* intéressante.

3. J'aime appeler *le chien.*

4. *Notre tante* est arrivée hier.

5. Vous avez grondé *les méchants garçons.*

6. Écrivez-vous *la lettre?*

D. Give the imperative first and second person plural of these verbs:

1. espérer		5. quitter
2. établir		6. rétablir
3. comprendre		7. manquer
4. porter		8. partir

E. Complete these sentences:

1. Le peintre est occupé —— matin jusqu'au soir.

2. Ses pensées ne sont ni (vilain) ni (cruel).

3. Il peint avec une (gros) brosse.

4. Elle vient effacer une seule (mauvais) expression.

5. Le cœur et l'esprit (aider) l'artiste dans son travail.

Traduction:

My grandfather often mislays his spectacles. He puts them aside and forgets where he has put them. One day he looked for them in his bedroom and in the living-room; then he found them in his pocket.

Giraudon, Paris

THE ODÉON

CINQUANTE-NEUVIÈME LEÇON

Le Professeur sévère

Etienne a couru aussi vite que possible, mais on avait déjà sonné (*but the bell had already rung*) quand il est arrivé à l'école. Il a trouvé la porte de la salle de classe fermée et il a hésité un peu devant cette porte fermée. Ouvrir la porte, entrer dans la classe sous le regard sévère du professeur!

Vous pouvez comprendre pourquoi il a hésité, n'est-ce pas? Mais il n'a pas hésité longtemps. Il a ouvert la porte doucement. Le professeur a regardé son élève, mais il n'a rien dit. Etienne est allé à sa place, et tout le monde a ri (*laughed*) parce que ce n'était (*was*) pas la première fois qu'il est arrivé en retard, ni la deuxième.

Le professeur a regardé ses élèves, et ils ont continué la leçon. Etienne a récité plusieurs fois. Il avait (*had*) étudié longtemps hier soir. Il avait étudié sa leçon et écrit son devoir. Les élèves de cette classe préparent toujours leurs leçons, parce que le professeur est exigeant. Il a demandé à Georges d'écrire plusieurs phrases au tableau.

Georges a fait beaucoup de fautes.

—Pas très bien! a dit le professeur. Corrigez les fautes dans vos phrases.

Georges a corrigé ses fautes, et il est retourné à sa place.

Joséphine et son amie Marianne ont fini le devoir. Elles ont bien travaillé. Elles étaient (*were*) heureuses. Leurs fautes n'étaient pas graves.

Après la classe Georges et Etienne ont parlé ensemble.

—Monsieur est très sévère, ont-ils dit.

—Je vais rester après les autres cet après-midi. Je sais, pourtant, qu'il faut arriver à l'heure (*on time*), a dit Etienne.

—Et moi, j'ai fait trop de fautes dans mes phrases, a dit Georges. Si nous corrigeons[1] nos fautes, monsieur le professeur n'est pas trop sévère. Je n'ai pas assez étudié, hier soir. Mon oncle et ma tante sont arrivés de Boston, et je n'ai pas étudié mes leçons. Est-ce que vous étudiez toujours vos leçons le (*in the*) soir?

—Oui, mon vieux, a répondu Etienne. Il le faut chez nous. Et maintenant, si vous êtes aimable, accompagnez-moi à la pharmacie.

Grammaire

The Possessive Adjective

To review the possessive adjectives read through the following list, and then recite it without looking at the book:

SINGULIER		PLURIEL
Masculin	*Féminin*	*Masculin et Féminin*
mon	ma	mes
ton	ta	tes
son	sa	ses
notre	notre	nos
votre	votre	vos
leur	leur	leurs

[1]From the verb **corriger**. The **e** is added to keep the soft *g* sound.

The adjectives **mon, ton,** and **son** are used with feminine nouns if the nouns begin with vowels.

Masculin	*Féminin*
mon ami Jean, *my friend John*	mon amie Jeanne, *my friend Joan*
mon élève Louis	mon élève Louise
son ami Jean	son amie Jeanne
son élève Louis	son élève Louise

In the plural, the masculine and the feminine possessive adjectives have the same form:

Masculin	*Féminin*
mes amis	mes amies
mes élèves	mes élèves

Vocabulaire

le regard [rəga:r], *look, glance*
mon vieux [mõ vjø], *old chap, old man, my dear fellow* (colloquial form of address used between men and boys)

la voix [vwa], *voice*
Marianne [marjan], *Marianne*
réciter [resite], *to recite*
ri [ri] (p.p. of **rire**), *laughed*
grave [gra:v], *grave, serious, solemn*

plusieurs [plyzjœ:r], *several*
possible [pɔsibl], *possible*
premier, première [prəmje, prəmjɛ:r], *first*
pourtant [purtã], *however, nevertheless*

Questionnaire

1. Comment Etienne est-il allé à l'école?
2. Où a-t-il hésité?
3. Comment a-t-il ouvert la porte?
4. Qu'est-ce que le professeur a dit quand Etienne est arrivé?
5. Qu'est-ce que les autres élèves ont fait?
6. Qui a fait beaucoup de fautes?
7. Est-ce que Joséphine et Marianne ont fait beaucoup de fautes?
8. Pourquoi Georges n'a-t-il pas étudié ce soir?
9. Quel air a le professeur si vous n'étudiez pas vos leçons?
10. Pourquoi Etienne étudie-t-il toujours le soir?

Devoir

A. Use the correct form of the possessive adjective in each of the blanks below:

1. Nous avons perdu —— lunettes.
2. Il gronde toujours —— fils.
3. Elle aime —— fils et —— fille.
4. Il est allé jusqu'au bois avec —— ami.
5. En route elle a acheté —— encre.
6. Les dames ont acheté —— fleurs hier au bord du lac.
7. J'ai décidé d'allumer —— feu là, à cet endroit, a dit Charles.
8. —— belle-sœur parle beaucoup à —— amie du résultat du match.
9. André et moi, nous avons préparé —— déjeuner.
10. Il peint —— tableaux avec intérêt.
11. Je suis parti chercher —— montre d'or.
12. Pendant la journée nous avons parlé de —— heureuse jeunesse.

13. Il ne faut pas encore faire cuire —— dernières côtelettes.

14. Avez-vous trouvé un bon endroit pour —— pique-nique?

B. *Use each of the following expressions in a question to be addressed to the pupils:*

1. mon sujet
2. mes raisons
3. notre gare
4. nos cadeaux

5. leurs ouvriers
6. notre vitrine
7. son neveu
8. leur bassin
9. vos tartines
10. sa fabrique
11. son déjeuner
12. ses friandises
13. ma banane
14. leur boutique
15. mes doutes
16. mon inquiétude

C. *Préparez-vous à raconter de vive voix (aloud) l'histoire du texte. Racontez-la à la première personne.*

SOIXANTIÈME LEÇON

Les Devoirs d'Etienne

Etienne est dans sa chambre. Il va étudier cet après-midi, parce qu'il pleut et on ne peut pas jouer dehors quand il pleut. Etienne se met à la table. Il prend son livre d'algèbre. Dort-il? Non. Il travaille avec intérêt. Il ne s'ennuie pas, parce qu'il comprend ces problèmes, et il les résout sans trop de difficulté. Moi, je m'amuse en travaillant (*while working*) si je travaille avec succès. Travaillez-vous tous les jours?

La leçon d'algèbre finie, Etienne se lève pour s'amuser un peu. Il tourne les pages de son album de timbres-poste. Mais après quelques minutes il se met de nouveau à la table pour continuer son travail. La leçon de latin! Vingt lignes à écrire! Et le professeur trouve beaucoup de fautes

dans ses devoirs! Nous ne nous amusons pas si nous pensons que notre travail n'est pas bien fait.

Un coup de téléphone. Etienne, heureux de cesser d'étudier, va au téléphone. On demande son père. Pauvre Etienne! Il continue sa leçon de latin. Il s'applique à cette leçon, et après une heure, il ferme son livre avec satisfaction. Voilà une leçon finie et bien préparée.

La leçon de sciences—Etienne ne l'étudie pas beaucoup et c'est pourtant la leçon qu'il préfère. On parle de tant de choses dans cette classe, et les devoirs sont presque toujours intéressants. Etienne ne s'ennuie pas dans la classe de sciences. Il y pense, il y récite, il ne s'y repose pas. Il n'a jamais envie d'y dormir.

Grammaire

The Reflexive Verb

A reflexive verb, in French, is one that always has a personal pronoun direct object that refers to the same person as the subject. You make use of such a verb occasionally in English: I cut *myself*. You burned *yourself*. He hurt *himself*. In French reflexives are much more common than in English. Some of the most necessary verbs are of this kind. **S'amuser,** *to amuse oneself* (*to have a good time*), **se coucher,** *to go to bed*, and **se lever,** *to get up*, are verbs no one can omit from his speech and writing. You will have no trouble in recognizing a reflexive in the vocabulary, because the pronoun **se** always appears directly before the infinitive.

Observe that every verb-form has the pronoun, though the pronoun is not necessarily translated into English.

The reflexive pronoun varies for the different persons:

je	me	il	se		nous	nous		ils	se
tu	te	elle	se		vous	vous		elles	se

s'amuser, *to have a good time*   **se lever,** *to get up*   **se mettre,** *to place oneself*

je m'amuse	je me lève	je me mets
tu t'amuses	tu te lèves	tu te mets
il s'amuse	il se lève	il se met
nous nous amusons	nous nous levons	nous nous mettons
vous vous amusez	vous vous levez	vous vous mettez
ils s'amusent	ils se lèvent	ils se mettent

In the negative the old rule of pronoun object directly before the verb must be followed.

Je ne me lève pas. *I do not get up.*

In the interrogative the same rule prevails. The pronoun object directly precedes the verb.

Vous levez-vous? *Do you get up?*
Se lève-t-il? etc. *Does he get up?* etc.

Vocabulaire

l'album [lalbɔm] (m.), *album*

le coup de téléphone [kud telefɔn], *ring of a telephone bell*

la satisfaction [satisfaksjõ], *satisfaction*

les sciences[1] [sjã:s] (f.pl.), *science*

le succès [syksɛ], *success*

s'amuser [samyze], *to have a good time*

s'appliquer [saplike], *to apply oneself*

cesser [sɛse], *to stop, to cease, to end*

se couper [sə kupe], *to cut oneself*

s'ennuyer[2] [sãnɥije], *to be bored*

se lever [sə ləve], *to get up, to rise*

se mettre [sə mɛtr], *to put, to place oneself, to go*

il pleut [il plø] (inf. **pleuvoir**), *it is raining*

dehors [dəɔːr], *out of doors*

de nouveau [də nuvo], *again*

à droite [adrwɑt], *at the right*

Questionnaire

1. Pourquoi Etienne va-t-il étudier cet après-midi?
2. Quand ne peut-on pas jouer dehors?
3. Où se met Etienne?
4. Pourquoi ne s'ennuie-t-il pas?
5. Qu'est-ce qu'il résout?
6. Que fait Etienne pour se reposer?
7. Où garde-t-il ses timbres-poste?
8. Qu'est-ce qu'Etienne entend?
9. Pourquoi continue-t-il son travail?
10. Pourquoi préfère-t-il la classe de sciences?
11. Qu'est-ce qu'il y fait?
12. Quand vous amusez-vous?
13. Quand s'ennuie-t-on?
14. Travaillez-vous avec intérêt?
15. Savez-vous conduire une auto?

[1] When it refers to the physical or biological sciences, **science** is used in the plural form only.
[2] Wherever **y** precedes a mute **e**, **y** becomes **i**. See if you can find examples in "Les Devoirs d' Etienne."

Devoir

A. *Write the present tense, indicative, of the following verbs:*
1. se reposer—*negative*
2. s'amuser—*interrogative*
3. s'appliquer—*affirmative*

B. *Supply the necessary forms of the possessive adjective:*
1. J'ai —— cahier où se trouve —— leçon.
2. Nous nous amusons en lisant —— histoire des Etats-Unis.
3. Vous vous mettez à —— (*my*) droite dans le taxi.
4. Il prend —— brosse et —— gomme.
5. Ils mettent —— album de côté.
6. Nous avons cherché —— chien partout dehors.
7. J'ai compris toutes —— leçons et j'ai écrit tous —— devoirs.
8. Je dis bonjour à —— tante.
9. L'homme ne vient pas non plus dire au revoir à —— fils.
10. Je n'égare pas souvent —— affaires.
11. La prochaine fois je ne vais pas retenir —— amis maussades.
12. Voilà pourquoi nous avons voulu faire —— (*your*) connaissance d'abord.
13. Elle a acheté —— chapeau à Paris.
14. Il a répondu à —— question (de M. Martin).
15. Elle a cherché —— amie Jeanne.

C. *Use the following verbs in questions and write appropriate answers.*
1. se mettre
2. se lever
3. s'appliquer
4. s'amuser
5. se reposer
6. s'ennuyer

D. *Using these sentences as models, make others about parts of the body.*
Que fait-on avec la tête?
On pense avec la tête.

E. *Give five names of animals.*

Traduction:

When I have studied hard, I like to get up and go into the living-room to talk with my mother. Sometimes I eat something, but I do not stay there too long. I return to my room, place myself at the table, and continue my work. Sometimes I am bored; sometimes I have a good time. When my brother works successfully (**avec succès**) he enjoys himself. He always works as quickly as possible. Several times he has recited very well. We are to blame if the teacher scolds, aren't we? He doesn't scold us if we apply ourselves.

L. Derepas, Sr., Paris

L'HÔTEL DE VILLE, PARIS
A view from the Seine.

SOIXANTE ET UNIÈME LEÇON
Le Soir et le Matin

Etienne a fini ses leçons ce soir. Il s'est levé de sa chaise. Il était (*was*) fatigué. Il est allé au salon pour parler un peu avec maman et papa. Après il est allé dans la salle à manger pour chercher une pomme. Il mange presque toujours une pomme, le soir.

Après avoir dit bonne nuit (*after he had said good-night*) à ses parents, Etienne est rentré dans sa chambre pour se coucher. Il s'est vite déshabillé. Il se déshabille toujours vite, mais il s'habille très lentement. Il a ouvert le lit (*turned back the covers*); il a éteint la lumière; et il a ouvert la fenêtre. Le voilà dans son lit confortable. Il s'est endormi tout de suite.

Le lendemain matin maman l'a réveillé. Le pauvre Etienne s'est levé. Il s'est lavé, et il s'est habillé, mais pas très vite. Qu'il est lent le matin!

Maman est arrivée. Elle lui a dit:

—Vite, Etienne. Tu vas arriver en retard ce matin. Es-tu arrivé à l'heure, hier?

—Non, maman, a répondu Etienne, je suis arrivé en retard, mais ce matin je vais arriver à l'heure, bien sûr. Je ne vais pas manger mon petit déjeuner. Je vais courir comme—

—Il faut manger quelque chose, a dit maman, mais tu peux te dépêcher de manger. Tu peux porter ce complet.

Etienne s'est dépêché. Il s'est lavé. Il s'est habillé. Il a mangé son petit déjeuner, et il s'est mis en route pour l'école.

Grammaire
The Past Indefinite of the Reflexive Verb

In the preceding lesson you made the acquaintance of reflexive verbs. You saw that each reflexive verb must have a pronoun object referring to the same person as the subject:

il **se** lève   nous **nous** levons, *etc.*

All the reflexive verbs you have met were used in the present tense. Reflexive verbs have, however, as many tenses as other verbs.

The past indefinite is formed from the present of the verb **être** and the past participle of the verb. The pronoun object must precede the auxiliary.

je me lève, *I get up*   elle se lève, *she gets up*
je me suis levé, *I got up*   elle s'est levée, *she got up*

Learn that the past participle of a reflexive verb agrees with the direct object if it precedes the verb.[1]

Commit to memory the past indefinite of **s'amuser**.

je me suis amusé (e) hier   nous nous sommes amusés (es) hier
tu t'es amusé (e) hier   vous vous êtes amusé (s) (e) (es) hier
il s'est amusé hier   ils se sont amusés hier
elle s'est amusée hier   elles se sont amusées hier

[1] This is a necessary point to learn, as you will see later, the reflexive pronoun is sometimes the indirect and not the direct object.

Vocabulaire

le petit déjeuner [pti de-ʒœne], *breakfast*
le lendemain [lãdmɛ̃], *the next day*
la pomme [pɔm], *apple*
Charlotte [ʃarlɔt], *Charlotte*
se coucher [sə kuʃe], *to go to bed*
déjeuner [deʒœne], *to have breakfast, to have lunch*

se dépêcher [sə depeʃe], *to hasten, to hurry*
se déshabiller [sə dezabije], *to undress*
s'endormir [sãdɔrmiːr], *to fall asleep* (conjugated like **dormir**)
éteint [etɛ̃] (p.p. of **éteindre**), *extinguished, put out*
s'habiller [sabije], *to dress*

se laver [sə lave], *to wash* (oneself)
se mettre en route [sə mɛtrã rut], *to start off*
tu peux [ty pø] (inf. **pouvoir**), *you can, you may*
réveiller [revɛje], *to wake, to waken*
d'ordinaire [dɔrdinɛːr], *ordinarily*
à l'heure [a lœːr], *on time*

Questionnaire

1. Pourquoi Etienne est-il fatigué?
2. Pourquoi est-il allé au salon?
3. Pourquoi est-il allé à la salle à manger?
4. Qu'est-ce qu'il mange le soir?
5. Pourquoi Etienne est-il rentré dans sa chambre?
6. Comment s'est-il déshabillé?
7. Est-ce que les petits enfants se déshabillent seuls?
8. Qu'est-ce qu'Etienne a ouvert?
9. Vous endormez-vous tout de suite d'ordinaire?
10. Et hier soir?
11. Qui a réveillé Etienne?
12. Qu'est-ce qu'il a fait?
13. Qu'est-ce que maman a dit à Etienne?
14. A-t-il mangé beaucoup pour le petit déjeuner?
15. Pourquoi vous dépêchez-vous le matin?

Devoir

A. Conjugate:

1. Je me suis dépêché.
2. Je ne me suis pas couché.

B. Change these sentences to the past indefinite:

1. Trois garçons vont à l'école.
2. Ils ouvrent la porte.
3. Ils l'ouvrent le lendemain.
4. Nous allons à la classe.
5. Quand nous récitons, nous nous levons.
6. Vous manquez le taxi.
7. J'y déjeune d'abord.
8. Je me mets à côté de Charlotte.
9. Après la classe je rentre chez moi.
10. Charlotte et Philippe égarent leurs affaires.
11. Personne ne rapporte ma règle.
12. Voilà pourquoi je finis la géographie.
13. Marie ne reste pas avec nous.
14. Elle va repasser de nouveau la leçon avec ces jeunes filles.
15. Voyez-vous ces mouchoirs?
16. Les voyez-vous en route?
17. Ils se lavent le matin.
18. Je fais mes études.
19. Quelquefois nous nous ennuyons.
20. Vous amusez-vous au bord du lac?

Traduction:

Peter finished his lessons. He said good-night to his parents and went to his room. He undressed quickly because he was (**était**) tired. He turned back the covers.[1] He turned out the light. He raised the shade and opened the window. He went to bed and fell asleep immediately.

[1] See idiom in "Le Soir et le Matin."

SOIXANTE-DEUXIÈME LEÇON

Review

A

1. Give the complete list of French possessive adjectives.

2. Explain why the form **mon amie** is correct, although at first glance **mon** seems to be masculine with **amie** feminine.

3. Give an example of a reflexive verb in English.

4. Mention three reflexive verbs in French.

5. Give the present indicative of **se laver.**

6. Explain the necessity of the grave accent in certain forms of the present tense of **se lever.**

7. What auxiliary is used with reflexive verbs?

8. What is the rule for the agreement of the past participle of reflexive verbs?

9. Give the past indefinite of **se coucher.**

10. Give the past indefinite negative of **s'ennuyer.**

11. Write in six sentences the principal events of the day: **Je me lève,** etc.

12. When is **il est** used? When is **c'est** used?

13. In a negative sentence what word must precede the verb? Mention four negative words.

14. What interrogative words can you mention?

15. Give the list of subject pronouns.

16. Give the list of direct object pronouns.

B

I. Conjugate these sentences:

1. J'ai vu mon cousin.
2. Je choisis mes amis.
3. Je ne me couche pas.
4. Je me suis bien amusé.

II. Use the following words in sentences:

ma	notre
mes	nos
ses	votre
sa	leur

III. Translate:

1. When I looked for my fountain-pen, I did not find it. No one has found it.
2. I do not like to mislay my belongings, but I have mislaid that pen.
3. I had a good time yesterday, but Mary and Josephine were bored (s'ennuyer).
4. He is going to bed because he is tired.
5. The next day they got up very late.

IV. If you cannot recall three suitable adjectives for each of the following nouns, look back through the lessons to find some.

chien	poissons
femme	endroit
maison	petite fille
figure	yeux

V. Find a picture of a head in a book or magazine and label in French all the parts you know.

PROMENADE DES ANGLAIS, NICE   Yvon, Paris

INTERESTING CITIES OF FRANCE

As long as France keeps Paris, so long will the nations outside her come a-visiting. But even if Paris should somehow be lost to France, the world would still flow through her doors for a glimpse at least of the other towns and cities of this ancient nation. For men would never be content until they had seen her playgrounds, her busy ports, her sleepy old-world cities that hark back to half-forgotten things of Greece and Rome.

The Gold-Coast towns of France —Nice, Cannes, and Monte Carlo— entertain each winter the gayest and youngest of visitors. Nice, with its pink villas, white walls, and green shutters, glows with energy and life. Its palm-lined Promenade des Anglais is thronged with royalties and million-aires, with newly-married couples and photographers. Cannes, which calls itself the smartest of the three cities, boasts purple mountains crowned with snow and a crescent avenue lined with the shops of famous Paris *couturiers* (dressmakers) and grand hotels that bear kingly names. Monte Carlo, while not quite so noble in demeanor, has a more vivid personality.

A ride of a few hours from Monte Carlo on the luxurious Blue Train utterly changes any previous idea our visitor on the Gold Coast may have had. For he has reached the River Rhône, on whose banks are the towns of Arles, Avignon, and Nîmes, and these contain well-preserved ruins which date from the period of Roman supremacy.

Arles was founded long before the birth of Christ and is one of the oldest settlements in all France. Its chief relic of antiquity is a magnificent arena built to hold thirty thousand spectators. In the outlying district of Nîmes stands the impressive Roman aqueduct called the Pont du Gard. Bridging the River Gard, its stout masonry spans the great space between two wooded hills; engineers from everywhere come to study the marvels of its construction. Within the city proper are endless remains of an ancient Roman civilization, which endure in almost perfect condition. Nîmes contains also some interesting old baths, two Roman gates, and a large structure called the Maison Carrée.

Avignon is rich in historical landmarks, chief of all, no doubt, the palace of the Popes, which reminds us that in the fourteenth century the papal home was here. The building is a rhythm of lines in gray stone, containing within it the court of justice—a vast empty hall with Gothic ceiling and a single pyramid of steps which fairly flows into the gray floor, so perfect are its curved lines.

Other interesting relics of the dim past Avignon has in plenty. But they all pale in importance beside the famous bridge which people used only as a dance floor because they thought it had been bewitched and was impassable—until one day a thoughtless person actually crossed it.

Near Avignon is one of the most strange and thrilling sights that France has to offer: the city of Les Baux. It is no longer an actual place of human habitation, but a shapeless mass of stone fragments which remind the onlooker of the ruins of Pompeii.

Above all this desolation is a castle carved entirely out of rock. It rears itself high against the sky, even as the rocky cliff was lifted high ages before man came to hew his home from it. The sharp slope of the stone-faced hill below it fortifies the castle against possible attack more surely than if it were surrounded by impassable ramparts. Hereabouts are found not only survivals of Roman days but those of prehistoric times, for many flint implements and chippings of pottery from those far-off days have been uncovered on the brow of the cliff in the wind-swept place that faces the sea and fronts southward. This old castle is so rich in history and legend that its tale cannot even begin to be told here. But once seen it will never be forgotten, crouching like some prehistoric monster washed up by the sea, its battered limbs lifted aloft in mute protest at its evil fate.

Farther to the west is Carcassonne, a double city: one city on a hill and another on the plain, each an ancient settlement. The River Aude divides

LES BAUX

Yvon, Paris

CARCASSONNE

the two towns. It is crossed by a bridge with a quaint little chapel beside it. From this bridge a view of upper Carcassonne—*la Cité*, as it is called—bursts on the sight. It stands on a height about 125 feet above the Aude, and this height has two peaks, one occupied by the citadel, the other by the cathedral of St. Nazaire.

The whole of this *Cité* is surrounded by walls and towers that have been carefully restored to their original condition. So in the France of today we have before us a fortified town of the Middle Ages that looks just as it did nine centuries ago.

There are cities in France famed for their industries. Everyone has heard of Cluny lace, and of the marvelous handwork of the women of Valenciennes and Le Puy. Rouen and many cities of Normandy and Brittany are known for their potteries with quaint peasant decorations. Strasbourg, Limoges, and Sèvres have acquired world renown because of their beautiful porcelains. Grasse is the center of the perfume industry, and hundreds of visitors motor over every day during the season from the Riviera, to inspect the great factories there. You can easily guess without being told how the tiny towns of Camembert and Roquefort, and the district of Brie received their reputation.

Another interesting category of cities includes the ports of France. Marseilles in the extreme south, on the eastern shore of a bay of the Mediterranean, is chief of them all. It was already a Gallic city of much importance when captured by the Greeks about 600 years B.C. Considering the wealth and splendor of this ancient town, it is strange that we find nowhere in it any ruins of its prehistoric founders. But in its voyage of three thousand years through life, Marseilles has been plundered of every fragment of these treasures. Every stone of her old tombs and temples has been stolen for the construction of newer houses and buildings. She has passed through twenty fires and as many sieges. Taken, sacked, plundered, Marseilles has been rebuilt over and over again, always hurriedly, always without respect for her historic associations.

Behind Marseilles to the east rises an amphitheater of hills, so that from the sea the city seems to lie peacefully at the foot of a protecting guardian. But once on her streets the illusion of quiet vanishes, for this is the one exciting, busy town of the south with quays and wharves without end, old-fashioned schooners and modern freighters, and swarms of natives from every port in the known world. The splendid modern street, Canne-bière, runs along the site of the old docks of the Greeks. Here a few years ago was found an old galley still containing, as part of her cargo, coins of the age of Julius Caesar.

Bordeaux is a fine city of south-western France, situated on the River Garonne, sixty miles from the sea. It is the fourth port of France. Its harbor can house and shelter twelve hundred ships. Bordeaux is known for its beautiful boulevards built in a semicircle and lined with plane trees, yet close by its wharves are low white tenement houses and swarthy sailors from the merchant marine. This city exports many products.

The second seaport of France in importance is Le Havre—which means simply "the harbor."

The building of a city is perhaps the most wonderful task to which man may set his hand, whether the work was done centuries before our era, or was begun only yesterday. The very reason for the location of a city may be the cause of its flourishing or its decay. Each city seems to have a personality of its own—sometimes expressed in gayety and beauty (as in Paris), or again by soft voices singing *Sur le Pont d'Avignon* (as in the deserted residence of the Popes).

A VIEW OF THE OLD PORT, MARSEILLES

SOIXANTE-TROISIÈME LEÇON
L'Histoire d'Etienne Mayran

Etienne Mayran est un jeune garçon français de quinze ans. Son père qui a été si longtemps malade vient de (*has just*) mourir. Il laisse sa jeune femme et Etienne seuls au monde avec très peu de fortune. Pour dire la vérité, le mari laisse à sa famille la petite somme de trois mille francs. Maintenant que le père est mort, Etienne sait qu'il va être obligé de travailler beaucoup pour pouvoir gagner des prix. Pour ceux qui gagnent des prix, l'école est gratuite (*free*) en France.

Etienne sait que le professeur d'une grande école de Paris est à l'hôtel du village, et il a l'intention d'aller le voir le lendemain matin. Puisque le garçon n'a personne pour le présenter, il hésite un peu, mais il sait que le professeur cherche un élève capable de gagner des prix. Quelle chance pour Etienne s'il est choisi!

Le lendemain Etienne va à l'hôtel. Il sent battre son cœur quand il entre dans la chambre, mais il faut être brave. Etienne avance vers le gros monsieur grave assis près de la fenêtre. Il cherche les paroles qu'il veut prononcer. Sa voix tremble un peu.

—Monsieur, je m'appelle (*my name is*) Etienne Mayran. Mon père vient de (*has just*) mourir, et je veux aller à Paris dans une grande école. Voulez-vous me permettre d'entrer dans vos classes?

Le professeur, qui par le ton de la voix d'Etienne sait qu'il dit la vérité, regarde le jeune homme. Il remarque son regard vif et intelligent.

—Mon petit, savez-vous quelque chose?

—Je peux (*I can*) apprendre, monsieur.

—Pouvez-vous apprendre le latin en un an?

Etienne réfléchit.

—Est-ce que quelqu'un a déjà appris le latin en un an?

—Oui, on l'a déjà fait.

—Alors je peux le faire aussi, dit Etienne. Ce n'est pas chose impossible.

Le jeune homme pousse un cri de joie et dit—Monsieur, voilà un livre de Jules César que je porte dans ma poche. Choisissez-y un passage.

Il présente le vieux livre au professeur, qui indique un passage, rend le livre au garçon, se lève, et fait quelques pas vers la fenêtre. Etienne lit. Quand il rencontre un mot qu'il ne sait pas, il le devine si juste que le gros monsieur devant la fenêtre commence à rire de plaisir.

—Tiens, pense-t-il. Quelle chance! L'affaire semble bonne. Il me semble que j'ai là un garçon qui peut réussir.

Etienne cesse de lire.

—C'est bien, dit le professeur. Mon intention n'était (*was*) pas de décider ce matin. Il se lève de nouveau et donne la main à Etienne. Allez annoncer la bonne nouvelle à votre mère. Nous partons demain.

Etienne, le chapeau à la main, dit merci de tout (*all*) son cœur et descend vite l'escalier pour aller retrouver sa mère qui, depuis une heure, pense à son fils qui a tant envie de faire ses études à Paris.—*d'après Taine*

Vocabulaire

le **mari** [mari], *husband*
le **monde** [mõːd], *world, people*
la **nouvelle** [nuvɛl], *news*
le **plaisir** [pleziːr], *pleasure*
le **prix** [pri], *prize, price*
la **somme** [sɔm], *sum*
la **vérité** [verite], *truth*
ceux [sø] (m.pl.), *those*

Vocabulaire (*Continued*)

deviner [dəvine], *to guess,*
  to divine
gagner [gaɲe], *to win, to*
  earn, to gain
mourir [muriːr], *to die*

mort [mɔːr] (p.p. of mou-
  rir), *dead, died*
réussir [reysiːr], *to succeed*
sembler [săble], *to seem*
sentir [sătiːr], *to feel*

mille [mil], *thousand*
quinze [kɛ̃ːz], *fifteen*
juste [ʒyst], *correctly,*
  exactly, just
puisque [pɥiskə], *since*

English Equivalents

la chance [ʃăːs], *luck*
la fortune [fɔrtyn], *fortune*
l'intention [lɛ̃tãsjõ] (f.),
  intention
le passage [pasaːz], *passage*
le ton [tõ], *tone*

obliger [ɔbliʒe], *to oblige*
permettre [pɛrmɛtr], *to*
  permit
présenter [prezãte], *to*
  present
trembler [trăble], *to tremble*

brave [braːv], *brave, good,*
  fine
capable [kapabl], *capable,*
  able, fit
impossible [ɛ̃pɔsibl], *im-*
  possible

SOIXANTE-QUATRIÈME LEÇON
Dans les magasins

Ce matin Hélène est allée en ville avec sa mère. Elles sont allées acheter un manteau pour Hélène. Elles sont allées en ville dans l'autobus. Hélène a regardé tous les bâtiments avec intérêt. Elle a vu tout le monde dans les rues. Elle a regardé tous les manteaux. Une fois, elle a vu un joli manteau, et elle a dit—Je vais chercher un manteau comme ce manteau brun.

Elles sont descendues de l'autobus, et elles sont entrées dans un magasin. Elles sont montées dans l'ascenseur au rayon des manteaux pour jeunes filles. Elles ont regardé tous les manteaux bruns et, ensuite, tous les manteaux verts. Hélène a essayé tous ces manteaux, et elle a trouvé un joli manteau vert. La mère a demandé le prix. Elle a examiné tout le manteau, la fourrure, les boutons. Elle a pris ce manteau pour Hélène.

Après, elles sont allées au rayon des chapeaux. Elles ont passé par le rayon des robes. Elles ont regardé toutes les jolies robes.

Arrivées au (*When they arrived at the*) rayon des chapeaux, elles ont examiné tous les chapeaux verts. Hélène a essayé un joli petit chapeau, mais maman a dit—Je n'aime pas tout ce ruban. On a trouvé un autre chapeau. Hélène a dit—Je l'aime beaucoup.

—Eh bien, a dit la mère, nous allons prendre ce chapeau.

Alors elles sont allées au rayon des soies. Elles ont trouvé une pièce de crêpe brun.

—C'est une occasion, a dit la mère, mais il faut prendre toute la pièce. Je n'ai pas besoin de tout ce crêpe. Elle a cherché une autre pièce, et Hélène est allée regarder toutes les autres soies. Elle les a trouvées très jolies.

Grammaire
The Use of *Tout*

The adjective tout is so important that it must be especially emphasized. It is, however, like all adjectives in French in that it agrees with its noun in gender and number. It has consequently four forms:

	Singular	*Plural*
MASC.	tout	tous
FEM.	toute	toutes

Examples

tout le rôti, *all the roast*
toute la tarte, *all the pie*

tous les rôtis, *all the roasts*
toutes les tartes, *all the pies*

Observe that the article (**le**, **la**, etc.) corresponds to the English article in *all the.*

The Use of *Tout le monde*

Tout le monde generally means *everyone.* As in English, this expression is used with a third person singular verb.

Tout le monde est content. *Everyone is glad.*
Tout le monde est arrivé tard. *Everyone arrived late.*

Tous les deux means *both.* What would **tous les trois** mean? *Can **tous les** be used with other numerals?*

Vocabulaire

l'ascenseur [lasãsœːr] (m.), *elevator*
l'autobus [lɔtɔbys] (m.), *autobus*
le bâtiment [batimã], *building*
le crêpe [krɛːp], *crêpe*
la jeune fille [ʒœn fiːj], *young girl, girl*

la fourrure [furyːr], *fur*
l'occasion [lɔkazjõ] (f.), *bargain*
le rayon [rɛjõ], *department (of a store), shelf*
le ruban [rybã], *ribbon*
la soie [swa], *silk*
avoir besoin [avwaːr bəzwɛ̃], *to need*

essayer[1] [esɛje], *to try, to try on*
examiner [egzamine], *to examine*
charmé [ʃarme], *charmed*
clair [klɛːr], *clear, bright, light*
ensuite [ãsɥit], *afterwards, then*

Questionnaire

1. Où est allée Hélène?
2. Pourquoi?
3. D'où est-ce qu'Hélène a regardé les bâtiments?
4. Où est-ce qu' Hélène et sa mère sont descendues?
5. Où sont-elles entrées?
6. Comment sont-elles montées au rayon des manteaux?
7. Pourquoi y sont-elles allées?
8. Qu'est-ce qu'elles ont regardé?
9. Qu'est-ce qu'elles ont choisi?
10. Qu'est-ce qu'elles ont fait au rayon des robes?
11. Et au rayon des chapeaux?
12. Pourquoi la mère n'a-t-elle pas aimé le premier chapeau?
13. Qu'est-ce qu'elles ont trouvé au rayon des soies?
14. Pourquoi la mère n'a-t-elle pas pris la première pièce de soie?
15. Qu'est-ce qu'Hélène a fait?

Devoir

*A. Use the correct form of **tout le** in each of the following sentences:*

1. —— —— raisons ne sont pas assez claires.
2. —— —— boulevard est beau.
3. —— —— peintres sont venus.

4. D'ordinaire je trouve —— —— leçon d'algèbre aussi difficile que la leçon de latin.
5. On a donné un dîner à l'école pour —— —— champions de football.

[1] This verb changes the **y** to **i** before **e** [ə].

6. Nous avons mangé —— —— petits pains.

7. —— —— deux se sont endormis à l'heure.

8. —— —— cinq restent à la maison.

9. Il est occupé par —— —— travail.

10. Du matin jusqu'au soir son esprit est occupé par —— —— pensées de sa jeunesse.

11. Il vient instruire —— —— hommes.

B. *Use the following adjectives in sentences:*

1. doux	5. sauvage
2. vilain	6. charmé
3. prêt	7. occupé
4. méchant	8. inquiet

C. *Change these sentences to the past indefinite:*

1. Michel va à l'école.
2. Il se dépêche.
3. Il marche fièrement.
4. Michel court après les méchants garçons.
5. Ils s'amusent ensemble à l'école.
6. Ils ne restent pas dehors.
7. Nous expliquons l'aventure.
8. Ils comprennent bien (**comprendre**) son succès.
9. Vous aidez Marie.
10. Je l'aide aussi.
11. Elles partent pour le grand bâtiment.
12. Elle choisit le chien.
13. Mangez-vous tout le gâteau au dîner?
14. Parlons-nous français en classe?

Archives du Touring-Club de France

THE PONT DU GARD, NEAR NÎMES

SOIXANTE-CINQUIÈME LEÇON

Le Déjeuner

Après cette matinée bien remplie, la jeune fille et sa mère sont allées déjeuner dans un restaurant. Le garçon a indiqué une petite table, et il a donné la carte du jour à chacune.

—Comme (*how*) j'ai faim, a dit Hélène. J'ai envie de manger toutes ces bonnes choses.

—Tu ne peux pas manger tout cela, a répondu sa mère. Je vais prendre un potage au poulet, une salade, des petits pains, et du café.

—Et moi, a décidé Hélène, je vais prendre la même chose, sauf le café. Je vais prendre du lait.

La mère a commandé le déjeuner. Le garçon a apporté de l'eau. Il a apporté aussi des assiettes, des couteaux, des fourchettes, et des cuillères.

Hélène a regardé autour d'elle. Elle a admiré des roses sur une autre table.

—Maman, pourquoi n'avons-nous pas de roses? a demandé Hélène.

—Tu vois des roses sur cette grande table parce qu'elle est dressée pour une fête.

La jeune fille a regardé tout le monde. Elle a trouvé des dames charmantes et des messieurs distingués. Elle n'a pas vu d'enfants.

Le garçon a servi d'abord sa mère. Il a apporté le potage, la salade, des petits pains, du café, et du lait. Il n'a pas apporté de beurre. Il a oublié d'apporter du beurre. Quand la mère d'Hélène a demandé du beurre, il en a apporté pour toutes les deux. Elles ont mangé tout le déjeuner.

Après le repas la mère d'Hélène a payé l'addition, et elle a laissé de l'argent pour le garçon. Elle a laissé un pourboire.

Grammaire

The Partitive Article

When the French wish to speak of *all* or the *whole* of something, they use, as you know, the word *tout*. When they wish to speak of a *part* of something they use a construction known as the *partitive*. You already know the forms, but you will need to grow acquainted with these new meanings for them.

Singulier: J'ai acheté du papier. *I bought some paper.* (de+le=du)
               J'ai acheté de l'encre.[1] *I bought some ink.*
               J'ai acheté de la craie. *I bought some chalk.*

Pluriel: J'ai acheté des crayons. *I bought some pencils.* (de+les=des)
               J'ai acheté des gommes. *I bought some erasers.*

To express the partitive idea in French, therefore, we shall use the word **de**+*the definite article*. The form of the definite article depends, of course, upon the number, gender, and initial letter of the noun.

        J'ai acheté du papier. *I bought some paper.*
        J'ai acheté de l'encre. *I bought some ink.*
        J'ai acheté de la craie. *I bought some chalk.*
        J'ai acheté des crayons. *I bought some pencils.*
        J'ai acheté des gommes. *I bought some erasers.*

---

[1] **de l'** is used before a masculine or a feminine word that begins with a vowel.

In the negative the form of the partitive is always **de** (or **d'**).

Je n'ai pas acheté de papier. *I have not bought any paper.*
Je n'ai pas acheté d'encre. *I have not bought any ink.*
Je n'ai pas acheté de craie. *I have not bought any chalk.*
Je n'ai pas acheté de crayons. *I have not bought any pencils.*
Je n'ai pas acheté de gommes. *I have not bought any erasers.*

Vocabulaire

l'addition [ladisjõ] (f.), *bill* (in a restaurant or hotel)
l'argent [larʒã] (m.), *money, silver*
la carte du jour [kart dy ʒuːr], *menu, bill of fare*
la fête [fɛːt], *holiday, birthday, birthday party, festival*
le garçon [garsõ], *boy, waiter*
le lait [lɛ], *milk*

la matinée [matine], *morning* (duration), *matinee*
le monsieur, les messieurs [məsjø, mesjø], *gentleman, gentlemen*
le potage [pɔtaːʒ], *soup*
le poulet [pulɛ], *chicken*
le pourboire [purbwaːr], *tip*
commander [kɔmãde], *to order*
dresser [drɛse], *to arrange, to prepare, to decorate*

payer[1] [pɛje], *to pay (for)*
servir [sɛrviːr] (irregular), *to serve*
chacun, chacune [ʃakœ̃, ʃakyn], *each one, every one*
charmant [ʃarmã], *charming*
tous les deux, toutes les deux [tu le dø, tut le dø], *both*
autour de [otuːr də], *about, around*

Questionnaire

1. Pourquoi Hélène et sa mère sont-elles entrées dans un restaurant?
2. Qu'est-ce que le garçon a donné à chacune?
3. Qu'est-ce que la mère d'Hélène a demandé comme déjeuner?
4. Est-ce qu'Hélène a demandé les mêmes choses?
5. Qu'est-ce que le garçon a apporté à Hélène et à sa mère avant le déjeuner?
6. Ont-elles admiré les cuillères?
7. Qu'est-ce que la jeune fille a vu sur une autre table?
8. Comment a-t-elle trouvé les messieurs?
9. A-t-elle vu des enfants?
10. Qu'est-ce que le garçon a oublié d'apporter?
11. Qu'est-ce que la mère a laissé après le repas?
12. Avec quoi payez-vous l'addition?
13. Vous amusez-vous quand vous allez dîner au restaurant?

Devoir

*A. Use the correct forms of **tout** in these sentences:*

1. Le garçon a indiqué —— le bifteck.
2. La jeune fille a regardé —— les messieurs.
3. Il a rarement perdu —— l'argent.
4. L'enfant a pris —— l'eau.
5. Nous avons conjugué —— les verbes au passé indéfini.

B. Change the sentences of A to the negative and use the partitive.

C. Give the opposite of each word in this list:

monter	petit
arriver	travailler
noir	perdre
quelquefois	lentement
rien	marcher lentement
jamais	ment (one verb)

[1] Either the **y** or the **i** form of this verb is correct before **e** [ə].

Traduction:

The little boy said to his father, "I am so hungry and thirsty! I want to eat a large luncheon."

"Very well," said the father to his son. "We are going into this restaurant for lunch."

A waiter indicated a table and brought a menu.

The father ordered a good luncheon.

The little boy took some chicken, some potatoes, a salad, and some pie. He did not take any coffee. He took milk, but his father took coffee. They both took water. The waiter served them.

The father left some money for the waiter. Then he paid the bill. The waiter looked for his tip; and when he found it, he put it in his pocket.

SOIXANTE-SIXIÈME LEÇON

Le Goûter

Arnaud et Raoul ont joué dans le parc cet après-midi. Ils sont rentrés chez Arnaud pour chercher quelque chose à manger. Ils n'y ont trouvé personne, ni la mère d'Arnaud, ni la bonne.

Les deux garçons sont allés à l'office. Ils ont ouvert la glacière.

—Je ne vois pas grand'chose, a dit Arnaud. Voici des pommes de terre froides, des œufs, du fromage, de la crème, de la viande froide, et du potage. Voulez-vous des sandwichs?

—Je crois bien, a répondu Raoul. J'aime toujours les sandwichs, et j'ai grand faim.

Arnaud a trouvé du pain, du beurre, du sel, du poivre, de la laitue, et de la moutarde. Il a trouvé un couteau pour couper le pain et un couteau pour découper le rôti. Ils ont fait six gros sandwichs. Arnaud en a mangé trois, et Raoul en a mangé trois. Ils ont bu du lait. Chacun en a bu deux verres.

Enfin ils ont aussi mangé des biscuits.

Après leur repas ils ont lavé la vaisselle. Ils ont laissé tout en ordre.

Quand maman a commencé à préparer le dîner parce que c'était (*it was*) le jour de congé de la bonne, elle a cherché la viande froide pour faire un bon ragoût. Elle a vu un très petit morceau de viande. Elle a appelé Arnaud.

—As-tu mangé tout le rôti? a-t-elle demandé.

—Non, maman, nous n'avons pas mangé tout le rôti. Nous en avons mangé un peu. Raoul et moi nous avons fait des sandwichs et nous avons mangé de la viande. Un peu, pas tout.

—Un peu, a répété maman. Toute la viande! Je n'en ai pas assez pour faire un ragoût. Il faut faire cuire (*I must cook*) des œufs pour le dîner. Raoul et son père n'aiment pas les œufs pour le dîner.

Grammaire

The Partitive Article

The partitive article has the following forms:

du
de l'
de la } *some, any*
des

pas de, *not any*

The Partitive Pronoun

The French have a very useful little word, **en**. It is known as the partitive pronoun, because it denotes a part as distinguished from the whole. **En** means *some* or *any*, *some* or *any of them*, or *some* or *any of it*, as the case may be. Its position is directly before the verb.

> J'ai des livres. En avez-vous?
> *I have some books. Have you any?*

> Avez-vous du gâteau? Je n'en ai pas.
> *Have you any cake? I have none. (I have not any.)*

> Nous avons quatre chevaux. Ils en ont cinq.
> *We have four horses. They have five (of them).*

> Il a deux chapeaux. Il en a deux.
> *He has two hats. He has two (of them).*

En, as you notice, never changes. It is invariable, no matter what may be the gender or number of its antecedent. It does not affect the past participle.

In English we may omit the expressions *of it* and *of them*. *In French* **en** *is never understood. It is always expressed.*

> J'en ai un morceau. *I have a piece (of it).*
> J'en ai quatre. *I have four (of them).*

Vocabulaire

le biscuit [biskɥi], *biscuit*
le congé [kõʒe], *day out, short holiday, leave*
le fromage [frɔmaːʒ], *cheese*
le goûter [gute], *tea, snack*
la laitue [lɛty], *lettuce*
la moutarde [mutard], *mustard*
l'œuf [lœf] (m.) (pl. **les œufs** [lezø]), *egg*

le poivre [pwaːvr], *pepper*
le ragoût [ragu], *stew*
le sel [sɛl], *salt*
Arnaud [arno], *Arnold*
boire [bwaːr] (p.p. **bu**), *to drink*
je crois bien [ʒə krwa bjɛ̃], *I should say so; I think so; why, yes indeed, certainly, of course*

laver la vaisselle [lave la vɛsɛl], *to wash the dishes*
froid [frwa], *cold*
mince [mɛ̃ːs], *scanty, thin*
en [ã], *of it, of them, some, any*
en ordre [ã nɔrdr], *in order*
grand'chose[1] [grãʃoːz], *much, a great deal*

Questionnaire

1. Où les garçons ont-ils joué?
2. Pourquoi sont-ils rentrés chez Arnaud?
3. Qui est-ce qu'ils ont trouvé à la maison?
4. Qu'est-ce qu'Arnaud a vu dans la glacière?
5. Qu'est-ce qu'il a demandé?
6. Pourquoi a-t-il cherché du pain, du beurre, et de la viande?
7. Faites-vous la même chose?
8. Aimez-vous les sandwichs minces ou les gros sandwichs?
9. Combien de sandwichs ont-ils mangés?
10. Qu'est-ce qu'ils ont bu?
11. Pourquoi maman a-t-elle grondé Arnaud?
12. Qu'est-ce que papa a mangé pour le dîner?
13. Aimez-vous le sel et la moutarde?

[1] In this book **grand'chose** is to be used only in negative sentences.

Devoir

A. Find words in the lesson which contain these sounds and repeat each word five times: [y], [ø], [ã].

B. Supply the correct form of the partitive article in each of the following sentences:

1. Avez-vous acheté —— friandises?

2. Vont-ils lire —— histoires?

3. Nous n'allons pas encore demander —— renseignements.

4. Est-ce que l'enfant a bu —— lait à la gare?

5. Les ouvriers ne fument[1] jamais —— cigarettes à la fabrique.

6. A-t-elle besoin —— ruban clair, —— soie, et —— fourrure?

C. Answer the questions in B, using the partitive pronoun in each case.

D. Rewrite the fifth paragraph of the story in the first person where it is suitable. Write as if you were Arnold talking to one of his friends—J'ai trouvé du pain, du beurre, et de la viande; et nous avons fait, etc.

SOIXANTE-SEPTIÈME LEÇON

La Queue du lapin

Joséphine a un petit frère. Il aime écouter les histoires, surtout les histoires de bêtes. Il adore toutes les histoires de bêtes. Quand Joséphine raconte une histoire, il préfère une histoire qu'il connaît bien. Si elle change des détails, c'est lui qui la corrige. —L'autre fois vous avez dit *un cheval noir* ou *trois moutons*, etc.

Ce soir-là Joséphine a raconté une histoire à son petit frère, parce que[2] maman et papa sont sortis. Elle a mentionné toutes les histoires que son petit frère aime.—Je veux l'histoire du petit lapin qui a perdu sa queue, dit-il.

—Mais, Jacques, tu la connais.

—Je crois bien. C'est pourquoi je l'aime, a répondu le petit.

—Un matin le lapin a rencontré son ennemi le renard qui avait (*had*) à la main des poissons enfilés sur une corde. Le lapin a regardé les poissons avec envie.

—Bonjour, Monsieur le Renard, où avez-vous pêché ces beaux poissons? Vous en avez beaucoup.

—Dans le petit lac, a répondu le renard. J'en ai vu beaucoup. Mettez-vous au bord du lac, votre longue queue dans l'eau. Passez-y la nuit, et le matin vous allez trouver des poissons au bout de votre queue.

Le lapin a suivi toutes ces instructions. Quel froid au bord du lac, la queue dans l'eau! Il a bu tout le café chaud dans son thermos, mais il a presque gelé vif.

Enfin, voici le jour! Il a tiré pour ramener les poissons attachés à sa queue. Que les poissons lui ont fait mal! (*How the fish hurt him!*) Il s'est retourné et a vu que sa belle queue était restée (*had stayed*) dans la glace. Il a perdu pour toujours sa belle queue. Tu n'as jamais vu un lapin avec une longue queue. Ni moi non plus! Les lapins ont tous une petite queue.

—Que j'aime cette histoire! Tu as ajouté une chose, le café à cause du[3] froid, a dit Jacques. Merci, ma bonne sœur. J'aime beaucoup cette histoire. J'aime surtout le petit lapin.

---

[1] Don't look up this word in the vocabulary. Get it from the meaning of the sentence, the context.
[2] Parce que introduces a clause. There must be a verb in the group of words which it introduces.
[3] A cause de is a compound preposition. It takes a noun or pronoun as its object.

Grammaire

The Demonstrative Adjective

The demonstrative adjective **ce**, as you saw in Lesson 19, may be translated as either *this* or *that*. Since at times the meaning would be doubtful, the French add a word to make it absolutely clear. When the meaning is *this*, **-ci** is added to the noun indicated; when it is *that*, **-là** is added. The suffix, or ending, **-ci** comes from **ici**. The ending never changes, since it is really an adverb. Likewise the ending **-là** is unchanging. Notice the hyphen joining the words.

ce poisson-ci, *this fish*	cette histoire-ci, *this story*
ces poissons-ci, *these fish*	ces histoires-ci, *these stories*
ce poisson-là, *that fish*	cette histoire-là, *that story*
ces poissons-là, *those fish*	ces histoires-là, *those stories*

Vocabulaire

la bête [bɛːt], *animal, beast*
le cheval [lə ʃəval], *horse*
le conte [kõːt], *short story*
la corde [kɔrd], *cord, rope*
le détail [detaːj], *detail*
l'ennemi [lɛnmi] (m.), *enemy*
l'envie [lãvi] (f.), *envy, desire*
la glace [glas], *ice*
l'instruction [lɛ̃stryksjõ] (f.), *instruction, direction*
le lapin, la lapine [lapɛ̃, lapin], *rabbit*
le paquet [pakɛ], *package, parcel, packet*
la queue [kø], *tail*

le renard [rənaːr], *fox*
le thermos [tɛrmɔs], *Thermos bottle*
Jacques [ʒaːk], *James*
blesser [blɛse], *to wound*
il connaît [il kɔnɛ] (inf. connaître), *he knows, is acquainted with;* tu connais [ty kɔnɛ], vous connaissez [vu kɔnɛse], *you know, are acquainted with*
décrire [dekriːr], *to describe, to draw*
geler [ʒəle], *to freeze*
geler vif [ʒəle vif], *to freeze to death*
pêcher [pɛʃe], *to fish, to catch fish*

ramener [ramne], *to bring, to bring out*
renfermer [rãfɛrme], *to shut in*
se retourner [sə rəturne], *to turn around*
suivre [sɥiːvr] (p.p. **suivi**), *to follow*
court [kuːr], *short*
enfilé [ãfile], *threaded, strung*
surtout [syrtu], *above all, especially*
à cause de[1] [a koːz də], *because of*
ni moi non plus [ni mwa nõ ply], *nor I either*

Questionnaire

1. Qu'est-ce que Jacques aime?
2. Comment savez-vous qu'il écoute avec attention?
3. Pourquoi sa sœur a-t-elle raconté une histoire ce soir?
4. Quel conte a-t-il choisi?
5. Pourquoi l'a-t-il choisi?
6. Pourquoi le lapin a-t-il regardé les poissons avec envie?
7. Qu'est-ce qu'il a demandé au renard?
8. Où est-ce que le renard a vu des poissons?
9. Quelles sont les instructions que le renard a données au lapin?
10. Les a-t-il suivies?
11. Quand il a tiré pour ramener les poissons, où sa queue est-elle restée?
12. Qu'est-ce que vous n'avez jamais vu?
13. Décrivez la queue d'un lapin.

[1] See footnote 3 on the preceding page.

Devoir*

A. Find four words in "*La Queue du lapin*" which contain the sound [ɛ̃]. What are the ways of spelling this sound?

B. Change the italicized words to personal pronouns, or to **y** or **en:**
1. Nous sommes allés *à l'ascenseur.*
2. *Le directeur* parle avec *Mme. Renard.*
3. Ils ont parlé *des sports.*
4. *Le problème* se trouve *à la dernière page* à droite.
5. Ils vont expliquer *les raisons.*
6. Il peint *le tableau.*
7. Vous connaissez *mon frère et moi.*
8. Elles ont trouvé *ces jolies robes de soie.*
9. Il jette *la casquette* de côté.
10. Grand-père est resté *chez elle.*
11. Ils ont parlé *du cheval.*
12. Elle a acheté dix *timbres-poste.*
13. *A la boulangerie* on achète le pain et les biscuits.
14. Alors nous avons donné un morceau *de chocolat* au chien.
15. Nous avons préparé ce repas pour *vous et pour Jean.*

C. What is the difference between:
1. ces boutiques-ci *and* ces boutiques-là?
2. cette poupée-là *and* cette poupée-ci?
3. ce drapeau-ci *and* ce drapeau-là?

D. Complete the following sentences, using the necessary forms of **de, de l', du, de la, des.**
1. Elle commande —— poulet, —— potage, et —— lait.
2. Nous servons peu —— messieurs, surtout pendant la matinée.
3. Il a laissé —— argent pour le pourboire —— garçon.
4. Je demande —— sel, —— moutarde, et —— poivre.

E. Composition: *Write the conversation between le lapin and la lapine when he returned without his long tail. You might begin as follows:*

La lapine: Où avez-vous passé la nuit?
Le lapin: Au bord du lac.
La lapine: Pourquoi? *etc.*

Note to the Teacher: As a variation from the exercises or for extra credit, allow the pupils who can draw to make a sketch illustrating "La Queue du lapin." They should label in French all the objects in the picture.

Levasseur, Paris
CANNES

SOIXANTE-HUITIÈME LEÇON
Review

A

1. Write a sentence to illustrate each form of the word **tout**.

2. What does the partitive construction express?

3. Give the forms of the partitive article.

4. When is **de l'** used?

5. What is the negative of **J'ai du papier?**

6. What is the partitive pronoun?

7. Explain what is meant by the statement, "The partitive pronoun is invariable."

8. With what person and number of the verb is **tout le monde** used?

9. Mention at least six verbs that are conjugated with **être**.

10. Write three sentences to show the agreement of the past participle of a verb conjugated with **être**.

11. What form of the verb is used with **pour?**

12. What are the two ways of answering a question beginning with **pourquoi?**

13. Give the interrogative form of the present of **aller**.

14. Write the past indefinite of **aller**.

15. Write the past indefinite of **ramener**.

16. What is the difference in meaning between:

   (*a*) cette brosse-ci and cette brosse-là?

   (*b*) ces noms-ci and ces noms-là?

   (*c*) ce travail-ci and ce travail-là?

B

I. In the seven sentences that follow, in the next column, supply the correct forms of the partitive.

1. Il a —— argent tous les jours.
2. Ils ont bu —— lait.
3. Nous avons commandé —— œufs.
4. L'homme a donné —— détails.
5. Vous cherchez —— friandises.
6. Elle achète —— sel.
7. Elle achète —— rubans clairs.

II. Write the seven sentences of I, preceding, in the negative.

*III. Write the sentences of I, changing the partitive phrase in each case to the pronoun **en**.*

IV. Write the first paragraph of Lesson 31, page 85 (except the first two sentences), changing the verbs to the past indefinite.

V. Conjugate these sentences:

1. Je me couche à l'heure.
2. Je ne m'habille pas de soie.
3. Le lendemain je me suis mis en route.
4. Je ne me suis pas dépêché.
5. J'ai rapporté les poissons.
6. Je n'ai pas payé l'addition.

VI. Translate:

Ralph has lost some money. He has not lost all his money. Charles has some. He gives some to Ralph. They stay at school after lunch because they have (*some*) classes. The boys study their lessons. They have problems to prepare for tomorrow. They need to study.

Charles has no ink. He buys some. He does not buy any chalk, because he does not need any. He buys some chocolate in that large building.

SOIXANTE-NEUVIÈME LEÇON

Une Lettre de Paris

Paris, le 12 septembre (*September*)
Cher Roger,

Puisque vous gardez toujours le silence pendant si longtemps quand je vous envoie de Paris une lettre un peu courte, j'ai l'intention ce matin de vous écrire tous les détails de notre magnifique promenade d'hier. Si je ne vous parle pas en termes ordinaires (*ordinary*), c'est que ce que nous avons vu n'était pas ordinaire.

Maman m'a accompagnée puisqu'elle était (*was*) libre. A cause de son grand intérêt personnel dans l'histoire de l'art français, elle m'a aidée par ses explications à comprendre ce que j'ai vu. C'était hier mon anniversaire, et mon grand désir était d'aller à la cathédrale (*cathedral*) de Notre-Dame[1] et au Louvre.[2]   Les divers monuments que j'ai déjà vus représentent si bien l'esprit français que j'ai grande envie d'en connaître (*to know*) d'autres.

A la cathédrale de Notre-Dame nous sommes tombées juste au moment où le soleil éclairait (*was lighting up*) les vitraux (*stained glass windows*). La scène à l'intérieur était d'une grande beauté—une lumière douce reposait sur tout l'intérieur. Nous nous sommes assises au fond de la cathédrale pour l'admirer.   Pour pouvoir (*to be able*) emporter un peu de cette beauté, je l'ai bien regardée. Il me semble que j'ai bien fait. Même (*Even*) aujourd'hui mon impression reste très vive, et celle de maman aussi.   Elle a vu la cathédrale plusieurs fois déjà, mais elle est toujours frappée par sa grande beauté.

Une heure après nous nous sommes dirigées vers le Louvre. Naturellement, j'ai eu envie de tout voir (*to see*),

et à cause de mon désir de tout voir (*to see*), il m'est arrivé un petit accident, pas grave du tout. Je suis tombée dans la rue. La rue était pleine de monde. Vous devinez bien que j'ai eu honte. On est arrivé de partout. Rien de grave—merci—un léger accident. J'ai fait un faux pas. Voilà tout. Enfin le mal n'était pas grave, et j'ai réussi, il faut le dire, à continuer la promenade.

En quelques minutes nous étions au Louvre, ce musée (*museum*) d'art, unique au monde.   On y voit des tableaux (*pictures*) de toutes les époques. Les Français considèrent l'art et la beauté en toute forme aussi nécessaires que la liberté. Vraiment, nous devons aller souvent au Louvre, chaque mois, chaque année, deux ou trois fois. Je sais que vous, Roger, vous vous intéressez beaucoup aux armes, anciennes et modernes, à cause de votre grand'père qui en a de si vieilles. Je regrette de devoir vous dire que nous n'en avons pas vu.

Un de ces jours je vais vous envoyer quelques illustrations des tableaux que nous avons admirés ou plutôt, puisque je ne sais pas ce que vous préférez, dressez une liste des tableaux que vous voulez et envoyez-moi la liste. Je peux (*can*) en faire un paquet très léger que je peux donner à mon oncle le mois prochain, au moment de son retour à Lyon.

A la fin de l'après-midi nous sommes rentrées. Nous avons suivi cette fois des rues qui nous ont menées dans des coins de Paris que je n'avais pas (*had*) encore vus. Enfin nous avons pris l'autobus qui nous a ramenées à la maison à l'heure du dîner. Toutes

[1] The famous Gothic cathedral in Paris.
[2] A world-famous art museum in Paris.

les deux nous étions contentes de notre journée. Nous en avons beaucoup parlé pendant le dîner, et papa espère pouvoir (*to be able*) nous accompagner la prochaine fois. Alors, vite votre liste, cher ami.

Tout le monde vous embrasse de tout cœur.

Votre camarade qui ne vous oublie pas,

Louise Bender

Vocabulaire

l'année [lane] (f.), *year*

l'anniversaire [laniverse:r] (m.), *birthday*

l'époque [lepɔk] (f.), *time, period, epoch*

le fond [fõ], *back, background, bottom*

le mal [mal], *harm, evil, damage*

le mois [mwɑ], *month*

le soleil [sɔlɛ:j], *sun*

celle [sɛl] (f.), *the one*

s'asseoir [saswa:r] (p.p. assis), *to sit down*

devoir [dəvwa:r], *ought, must, owe, to be obliged, should*

nous devons [nu dəvõ], *we should, we ought, we must*

se diriger vers [sə diriʒe vɛ:r], *to go toward*

éclairer [eklɛre], *to light up*

emporter [ãpɔrte], *to take away, to carry off*

envoyer [ãvwaje], *to send*

tomber [tõbe], *to fall*

cher, chère [ʃɛ:r], *dear, expensive*

divers [divɛ:r], *various, different*

faux, fausse [fo, fo:s], *false*

léger, légère [leʒe, leʒɛ:r], *light, slight*

plein, -e [plɛ̃], *full*

English Equivalents

l'accident [laksidã] (m.), *accident*

les armes [le zarm] (f. pl.), *arms, weapons*

l'art [la:r] (m.), *art*

la beauté [bote], *beauty*

le désir [dezi:r], *desire, wish*

l'impression [lɛ̃presjõ] (f.), *impression*

l'intérieur [lɛ̃terjœ:r] (m.), *interior, inside*

la liberté [liberte], *liberty*

la scène [sɛ:n], *scene*

le terme [tɛrm], *term, end, period*

considérer [kõsidere], *to consider*

s'intéresser à [sɛ̃terese a], *to be interested in*

représenter [rəprezãte], *to represent*

magnifique [maɲifik], *magnificent*

nécessaire [nesesɛ:r], *necessary*

personnel, -le [pɛrsɔnel], *personal*

unique [ynik], *unique, only*

SOIXANTE-DIXIÈME LEÇON*

Les Souris

Première partie

Monsieur, Madame, et Bébé ont faim. Il est l'heure de déjeuner, mais ils ne trouvent rien à manger dans la maison. Ils ont cherché partout, et ils n'ont rien trouvé du tout. Monsieur part et sa femme l'attend. Elle l'attend avec impatience. Elle est seule avec Bébé. Bébé s'amuse.

Monsieur traverse la salle à manger. Il n'y voit rien à manger. Il se glisse dans l'office. Oh, que ça sent bon! Un gros fromage! Vous savez, n'est-ce pas, que Monsieur et Madame sont deux petites souris, et vous savez assurément que les souris aiment beaucoup le fromage.

Monsieur dévore un gros morceau de fromage, et il n'oublie pas Madame et Bébé. Il rapporte un gros morceau de fromage à Madame, qui le mange de bon appétit, je vous assure.

Quand Madeleine, la cuisinière, entre dans l'office, elle voit tout de suite qu'une souris a mangé un gros morceau de fromage. Elle cherche la souricière, et elle met dedans un morceau tentant, un morceau de fromage grillé. Elle sait bien que les souris aiment le fromage.

Madame mange vite son fromage, mais elle a toujours faim. Monsieur part, et il rentre bientôt pour raconter ce qu'il a trouvé dans l'office. Il y a senti quelque chose de très bon (*something very good*), du fromage, mais on a mis ce fromage dans une drôle de petite maison. Il est rentré pour demander conseil à sa femme. Il raconte tout.

Elle dit qu'il ne faut pas y toucher. Les femmes sont toujours prudentes.

Son mari part pour la troisième fois, décidé à ne pas regarder, à ne pas sentir le fromage grillé. Mais, hélas! Il touche le fromage, et clic!

Madeleine entend le bruit. Elle appelle le gros chat. Vous pouvez comprendre pourquoi Madame la Souris ne voit plus son mari. Et elle le pleure, la pauvre veuve.

Vocabulaire

le **bébé** [bebe], *baby*
le **conseil** [kõsɛ:j], *advice*
la **cuisinière** [kɥizinjɛ:r], *cook*
une **drôle de petite maison** [yn dro:l də ptit mezõ], *a funny little house*
l'**impatience** [lɛ̃pasjã:s] (f.), *impatience*
la **souricière** [surisjɛ:r], *mouse-trap*

la **souris** [suri], *mouse*
la **veuve** [vœ:v], *widow*
assurer [asyre], *to assure*
attendre [atã:dr], *to await, to wait for*
dévorer [devɔre], *to devour, to eat up*
se glisser [sə glise], *to creep, to slip*
pleurer [plœre], *to weep, to weep for*

grillé [grije], *toasted*
prudent [prydã], *wise, prudent*
tentant [tãtã], *tempting, enticing*
assurément [asyremã], *surely, doubtless*
bientôt [bjɛ̃to], *soon*
dedans [dədã], *within, inside*
hélas! [ela:s], *alas!*

*Note to the Teacher: This lesson develops no grammatical principle. It is suggested that the teacher work with the students to help them read without translating. There is enough action to make reading for comprehension easy. The questionnaire checks on the pupil's comprehension, but it is even better for the teacher to ask many simple questions during the development of the lesson and the reading of the story.

Questionnaire

1. Qui sont Monsieur et Madame?
2. Qu'est-ce qu'ils ont?
3. Qu'est-ce que Monsieur va chercher?
4. Où trouve-t-il quelque chose?
5. Pourquoi dévore-t-il un gros morceau de fromage?
6. Qu'est-ce qu'il rapporte à sa femme?
7. Pourquoi Madeleine a-t-elle cherché la souricière?
8. Qu'est-ce qu'elle met dedans?
9. Pourquoi Monsieur sort-il la deuxième fois?
10. Pourquoi rentre-t-il si vite?
11. Pourquoi n'a-t-il pas rapporté ce fromage qu'il a senti?
12. Quel conseil est-ce que Madame a donné?
13. Pourquoi?
14. Est-ce que Monsieur a écouté les conseils de sa femme?
15. Pourquoi Madame pleure-t-elle?

Devoir

A. Pronounce **fromage.** *Find examples of the four nasals in "Les Souris."*

B. Rewrite paragraphs three and four of "Les Souris" in the past indefinite.

*C. Rewrite paragraph three in the approximate future (**aller** with a complementary infinitive).*

D. Use the correct verb-forms in the following sentences:

1. Il (s'ennuyer) hier.
2. Je (être) charmé de faire la connaissance de la jeune fille.
3. Nous allons (essayer) la fourrure.
4. Vous ne (avoir) pas besoin de cette occasion.
5. Hier l'ascenseur du bâtiment (marcher) de nouveau.
6. (Apporter) la carte du jour, s'il vous plaît.
7. Ils (payer) l'addition en argent français.
8. Les messieurs (être) assis autour de la table dressée pour la fête.
9. Voulez-vous (laver) la vaisselle?
10. Ils (commander) du sel, du poivre, de la laitue, de la moutarde, et des œufs.
11. Les lapins (avoir) gelé vifs à cause du froid.
12. Ni moi non plus je ne (avoir) pas vu la glace.

Traduction:

The little mice are hungry because they have nothing to eat. They like cheese very much. Mr. Mouse (**Monsieur**) finds a large cheese in the pantry. He eats a piece of cheese and takes another piece (*of it*) to his wife. She eats it with relish. He goes to the pantry the second time and returns without the toasted cheese. The third time he touches the cheese in the mouse-trap which the cook prepared. Click! Mrs. Mouse never sees her husband again (**ne . . . plus**).

SOIXANTE ET ONZIÈME LEÇON
Les Souris
Deuxième partie

La petite souris habite avec sa mère dans une petite maison non loin de la salle à manger. Elle est jolie, la petite bête aux yeux bruns, au poil soyeux, et à la queue longue et gracieuse. Sa mère l'aime bien. Elle lui a appris à éviter l'office et à redouter le fromage. Elle comprend bien ces dangers. La petite souris ne sort jamais seule. C'est la mère qui sort chercher leur nourriture. Elle la cherche partout excepté dans l'office, mais elle ne trouve pas beaucoup de nourriture. Elles ont toujours faim, ces deux. La mère n'est pas courageuse. Elle est prudente, et elle a faim.

Ce soir elle est souffrante. Elle ne peut pas sortir pour courir partout. La petite souris lui a dit—Je vais sortir aujourd'hui. Je comprends les dangers. Tu m'as appris à faire attention aux chats et aux souricières.

Tu m'as appris aussi à éviter l'office. Je vais être très prudente, maman.

Elle sort. Elle va dans le salon. Elle cherche partout, mais elle ne trouve rien à manger. Que faire? Elle a très faim. Elle va dans la salle à manger. Elle y trouve un paquet de biscuits. Elle commence à ronger. Elle mange quelques morceaux, et elle rentre pour inviter sa mère à dîner. Elles sortent, toutes les deux, et elles mangent beaucoup de biscuits.

Le matin Madeleine voit le paquet, et elle dit—Encore des souris (*more mice*)! Elle cherche la souricière, elle met dedans un morceau de fromage grillé. Elle met la souricière dans la salle à manger.

Vous voulez savoir le dénouement? Il est trop triste. Une pauvre souris sans mari, sans enfant. La voilà seule, et elle pleure.

Grammaire

Verbs

As you know, French verbs are divided into two great classes, regular and irregular. How can you distinguish between them?

What is the infinitive ending of first-conjugation verbs? Of second? Of third? How is the stem, or radical, found? How is the present tense of a regular verb formed?

The Verb *Prendre*

You find in this lesson an important irregular verb—important because it is much used and because several other verbs are derived from it. Learn the present tense of the verb **prendre**, *to take.*

je prends le livre, *I take the book.*	nous prenons le livre
tu prends le livre	vous prenez le livre
il prend le livre	ils prennent[1] le livre

Give the present tense of the following derived verbs: **apprendre**, *to learn;* **comprendre**, *to understand;* **entreprendre**, *to undertake;* **surprendre**, *to surprise.*

The past participle of **prendre** is **pris.** What is the past participle of each of the infinitives given above?

---

[1] In French there is rarely a succession of mute syllables within a word. In **prennent** the n is doubled, thus changing the first mute e to [ɛ]. What other change in spelling have we found made for the same purpose?

Vocabulaire

le **danger** [dãʒe], *danger*
le **dénouement** [denumã], *outcome*
la **mort** [mɔːr], *death*
la **nourriture** [nurityːr], *food, nourishment*
le **poil** [pwal], *fur*
la **vie** [vi], *living, life*
Madeleine [madlɛn], *Madeline*
entreprendre [ãtrəprãːdr], *to undertake*
éviter [evite], *to avoid, to escape*

faire attention [fɛːr atãsjõ], *to pay attention*
gagner [gaɲe], *to earn, to gain, to win*
gagner sa vie [gaɲe sa vi], *to earn one's living*
redouter [rədute], *to dread, to fear*
ronger [rõʒe], *to gnaw*
surprendre [syrprãːdr], *to surprise*
courageux, -se [kuraʒø, kuraʒøːz], *brave, courageous*

gracieux, -se [grasjø, grasjøːz], *graceful, gracious, kind, agreeable*
précédent [presedã], *preceding*
souffrant [sufrã], *ill, sick, indisposed*
soyeux, -se [swajø, swajøːz], *soft, silky*
évidemment [evidamã], *evidently*
excepté [ɛksɛpte], *except*

Questionnaire

1. Où habite la petite souris?
2. Pourquoi est-elle jolie?
3. Qu'est-ce que la mère a appris à la petite?
4. Qu'est-ce qu'elle comprend?
5. Pourquoi la mère ne trouve-t-elle pas beaucoup à manger?
6. Comment est la mère?
7. Pourquoi ne sort-elle pas ce soir?
8. Où va la petite souris?
9. Qu'est-ce qu'elle trouve au salon?
10. Qu'est-ce qu'elle trouve dans la salle à manger?
11. Qu'est-ce qu'elle commence à faire?
12. Que voit Madeleine le matin?
13. Qu'est-ce qu'elle fait?
14. Pourquoi Madame est-elle très triste?
15. Est-il difficile de gagner sa vie?

Devoir

A. Write the story of the mice. Before beginning, review "Les Souris," page 194. Then write a summary, using the seven points below as suggestions for a unified whole, not for separate sentences. Write the story without looking up words. Leave a space if you forget a word, and continue. Then look up the words, fill in the blanks, and copy your story. Tell:

1. Ce que le père cherche.
2. Pourquoi il le cherche.
3. Ce qu'il trouve. Où ça?
4. Ce qu'il apporte à la souris et à la petite souris.
5. Ce que Madeleine fait. Pourquoi?
6. Ce que le père trouve la deuxième fois.
7. Ce qu'il fait la troisième fois.

B. Use the correct form of the adjective with each noun:

1. (beau) la laitue, la vaisselle, l'œuf, l'endroit, les cordes, le cerisier.
2. (gros) le poulet, le renard, la lapine, les pourboires, la bête.
3. (heureux) les journées, la matinée, la jeunesse, l'homme, le dénouement.

Levasseur, Paris

CHÂTEAU WALZIN
From its lofty crag this château overlooks a gentle river valley.

CHÂTEAUX AND PALACES

Historically, two types of château live on in France today. The older type is the fortified feudal castle built in the Middle Ages, especially the thirteenth century, which ordinarily remains to us only as a desolate ruin. The newer type of château, built in the sixteenth century, is the royal palace or proud castle which still dominates the vast country estate of some landed proprietor.

The first type of fortified château was usually built on a high place. It was surrounded by moats and thick walls; flanked by towers and defended by works. An elevated keep of solid construction was its center of defense. Its entrance was guarded by a drawbridge overlooked by turrets and patrolled by soldiers of the watch. Famous examples are Coucy, Loches, and Pierrefonds. The second type of beautiful palace for king and noble is quite perfectly illustrated to our modern world by Azay-le-Rideau and Chenonceaux.

There is perhaps even in France nothing quite worthy to rank with Pierrefonds, for it gives us at once so gracious and so powerful a picture of medieval splendor. It was completely restored in 1862 and looks today as it did when Louis d'Orléans, its royal builder, in 1390 climbed the height above the town to enter it.

The castle has eight huge towers and walls fifteen to twenty feet thick, which soar well over a hundred feet into the air. One tower at each corner of the ramparts and one in the middle of each side render defense easy. Around the walls are double fighting-platforms for soldiery, one above the other. The keep of the castle occupies the southern angle. A study of its many rooms shows the kind of life a rich and powerful French lord was able to live during the late Middle Ages. That he was inclined to satisfy his slightest whim is told us at Pierrefonds by the glorious paintings and decoration everywhere.

The valley of the Loire in Touraine is a pleasant place of broad and peaceful landscapes. The winds are mild here and days are sunny. Amid the orchards and vineyards French peasants find life easier than elsewhere. This valley is rich in the older feudal style of fortress we have described above: as in the great walled château at Angers and ruined Plessis-les-Tours. But side by side with such fortified castles of the earlier period, there sprang up along the poplared Loire, when French life was at the summit of its luxury, those palaces of kings and courtiers which are now known as the châteaux of Touraine. Up and down the long line of this valley, from the fifteenth century on, Frenchmen lived in these favored spots an unbelievably happy life of cultured ease and leisure. Let us consider this point of view in Azay-le-Rideau and Chenonceaux.

The first of these châteaux is a pure creation of early French Renaissance art. About it flow the clear waters of the little Indre, gay with yellow lilies. No fortress home is this. Some of the forms of military stronghold are preserved, as if in play: high-pitched roof, for example, turrets, and buttressed windows. But that this pretense is for the sake of beauty alone is indicated by the sculptured bands that frame the windows, and by other delicate embroideries of stone. Doors, roof-tops, chimney-pieces, and circular stone stairways are half inclosed by sculptures. This château has become the property of the French government.

Chenonceaux is a jewel of a building, set astride the River Cher upon the piles and massive masonry of an old mill. One tower, preserved for ornament, is all that is left of the age when a fortified castle occupied what is now an open court.

Chenonceaux is a lofty Renaissance pile with graceful lines, given character and charm by turrets where towers may once have been, and by gables, pinnacles, and dormers at unexpected places. The little Cher offers it one of the most exquisite natural settings in the world. Wherever you walk in the grounds of this palatial mansion,

PIERREFONDS, BUILT 1390, AS IT LOOKS TODAY

CHENONCEAUX

you come upon beauty: an old well, or a splendid tree exactly duplicated in Nature's water-mirror of the moat. Chenonceaux is now again private property; but, as it is seldom used for residence, it is more a brilliant show-place than anything else.

Another part of France, beside the Loire valley, is rich in old castles and fortifications. In the southwest is a great stretch of land known as a *pays perdu* (lost country). Find on an old map Limousin, Perigord, Cantal, Quercy; and you will see that from the mountains of Auvergne—the so-called Little Switzerland of France—a vast plateau reaches westward and southward. This is as savage and silent as ever it was in the Middle Ages when its castles were first built. Distant mountain peaks are like a sharply pointed wall that guards the heather-covered hillsides of the plateau; torrents rush in cascades down slaty gorges; deep caverns are filled with treacherous pools and waste swamp lands. The most human thing about this *pays perdu* is the imprint of history it

bears, the marks of other times than ours: Gallic forts, Roman temples like that to Diana, the strongholds of Beynac and Laroque. This wild plateau was the land of the Troubadours, those minstrels who sang brave songs to Richard the Lion-Hearted.

The most famous of French royal palaces is Versailles, one of the wonders of the world (see pages 204, 207, and 210). Situated twelve miles southwest of Paris, its construction was started by Louis XIV after he had grown tired of all other existing court residences. He gathered around him the best architects of his time, and through many years spent enormous sums of money to create the palace and its magnificent environment. Hundreds of spacious and beautifully designed rooms housed the royal treasures. The stables held twenty-five hundred horses. A vast garden was laid out and filled with marble statues, conventional hedges, and hundreds of fountains—more than were ever gathered together before or since in any one place in the world. A park encircled the garden, and this in turn was surrounded by a vast forest.

Today the palace is one of the show places of France. Thousands of tourists visit it every year, to view the state apartments of Louis XIV and of Marie Antoinette, the marvelous art galleries, the unbelievable gardens. One great gallery is completely lined with mirrors—here at the end of the Great War the Treaty of Versailles was signed on June 29, 1919.

Perhaps the greatest interest of Versailles lies in two charming houses built in its grounds, the Grand Trianon and the Petit Trianon, which are symbols of the intimate and real existence of royalty. Near the gardens of Versailles the visitor finds a one-story building entirely faced with colored marbles, the five windows of which face a court with an arcade that opens on a lovely garden. Within the house, the walls are covered with plaques and ornaments of blue-and-white earthenware, which explains the name Trianon of Porcelain. With its shining gold roof, it is like a diminu-

tive fairy palace. This Grand Trianon was used as a gay refreshment pavilion for the ladies of the court. It was Louis XV who erected the Petit Trianon, a creation of equal loveliness. A picturesque hamlet of rustic cottages was installed in the gardens for Marie Antoinette, who became queen in 1774. There she and her ladies-in-waiting played at butter-making and living the simple life, on the eve of the French Revolution.

The only other French palace which can remotely compare with Versailles either in extent, magnificence, or historical importance is Fontainebleau, thirty-seven miles southeast of Paris. Its park is world-famous, and its forest contains no less than 42,500 acres. In its villages of Barbizon, Chailly, and Marlotte the modern French school of landscape painters have lived and produced their masterpieces. The palace of Fontainebleau, which incloses six great courts, was from the Middle Ages a chief residence of the kings of France, and the favorite home of Napoleon I.

AZAY-LE-RIDEAU
Publishers' Photo Service, N. Y.

SOIXANTE-DOUZIÈME LEÇON

Les Jours de la semaine

Marie-Louise est fière. Vous voulez savoir pourquoi? C'est parce qu'elle sait parler français. Elle parle très peu, il faut l'avouer, mais elle est évidemment fière de ses quelques (*few*) mots.

Ce matin quand la nouvelle femme de ménage est arrivée, Marie-Louise était (*was*) enchantée. Elle est Belge, la femme de ménage, et elle parle très peu d'anglais. Maman la comprend avec peine. Elle a dit à maman —Madame ne parle pas français? Maman a dit que non, mais elle a dit à Marie-Louise que voilà l'occasion de parler un peu le français.

La femme de ménage a compris ce que la jeune fille lui a dit. La Belge a parlé trop vite d'abord, mais après elle a commencé à parler très lentement.

Elle a appris à Marie-Louise les noms des jours. Elle les a prononcés et elle les a écrits: lundi, mardi, mercredi, jeudi, vendredi, samedi, dimanche. Bientôt Marie-Louise les a appris.

—Pas si vite, a prié Marie-Louise. Vous parlez trop vite pour moi.

Elle a répété les noms, et Marie-Louise les a appris. Elle a quitté la maison.

Elle est arrivée à l'école. Elle a raconté à ses amies qu'elle a parlé français et qu'elle a appris les jours. Elles ont trouvé ce récit très intéressant à cause de leurs études.

Dans la classe de français quand le professeur a dit—Aujourd'hui nous allons apprendre les noms des jours, les amies de Marie-Louise se sont mises à sourire.

—Qu'avez-vous, Dorothée? a demandé le professeur.

—Je n'ai rien; mais Marie-Louise sait déjà les noms des jours.

—Tant mieux, a répondu le professeur. Voulez-vous écrire ces noms au tableau, Marie-Louise?

La jeune fille s'est levée, est allée au tableau, et a écrit les noms. Elle les a bien écrits. Elle n'a fait qu'une faute. Elle était fière de son travail.

Le professeur a corrigé la faute, et la classe a récité et a copié la liste des sept jours:

le lundi [lœ̃di], *Monday*
le mardi [mardi], *Tuesday*
le mercredi [mɛrkrədi], *Wednesday*
le jeudi [ʒødi], *Thursday*
le vendredi [vɑ̃drədi], *Friday*
le samedi [samdi], *Saturday*
le dimanche [dimɑ̃:ʃ], *Sunday*

Grammaire

The Days of the Week

Learn the French names of the days of the week so that you can pronounce and write them without hesitation. Note that the French do not capitalize these words.

In French, the name of a day of the week used with the article has a slightly different meaning from the same name used without the article. Thus **dimanche** and **le dimanche** have somewhat different meanings.

Observe the sentences given on the top of the next page, and then form your own conclusions.

Le dimanche, je vais à l'église. *On Sunday I go to church.*
Dimanche je suis allé à l'église. *Sunday I went to church.*

Le samedi, je m'amuse. *On Saturday I have a good time.*
Samedi je vais aller au théâtre. *Saturday I am going to go to the theater.*

dimanche, *Sunday, one special Sunday*
le dimanche, *Sundays in general*

samedi, *Saturday, one special Saturday*
le samedi, *Saturdays in general.*

Note that no preposition is used with the days of the week, as we use it in English. With divisions of time within the day, a preposition may be used but is not required.[1] The use of the article in this case is identical with that explained above: it adds the idea of frequency.

Le matin je travaille. *In the morning I work.*
A midi je déjeune. *At noon I have lunch.*
Je vais y aller dans l'après-midi. *I am going there in the afternoon.*

Vocabulaire

Belge [bɛlʒ] (m. and f.), *Belgian*
l'église [egliːz] (f.), *church*
la femme de ménage [fam də menaːʒ], *charwoman, cleaning-woman*
l'occasion [lɔkazjõ] (f.), *occasion, chance, bargain, opportunity*
la peine [pɛn], *effort, difficulty, trouble*
le récit [resi], *tale, story, recital of facts*

Dorothée [dɔrɔte], *Dorothy*
avouer [avwe], *to admit, to affirm, to avow*
copier [kɔpje], *to copy*
faire le ménage [fɛːr lə menaːʒ], *to do housework, to keep house*
se mettre à [sə mɛtr a] (+infinitive), *to begin*
sourire [suriːr], *to smile*
qu'avez-vous? [kave vu], *what's the matter with you?*

je n'ai rien [ʒe ne rjɛ̃], *nothing (is the matter with me)*
Maman a dit que non [mamã a di kə nõ], *Mother said that she didn't*
enchanté [ãʃãte], *delighted*
sept [sɛt], *seven*
tant mieux [tã mjø], *so much the better*
ne ... que [nə kə], *only*
tout de suite [tut sɥit], *immediately*

Questionnaire

1. Pourquoi Marie-Louise est-elle fière?
2. Qui est arrivé chez Marie-Louise ce matin?
3. Comment maman la comprend-elle?
4. Quelle langue (*language*) la femme de ménage parle-t-elle?
5. Est-ce qu'elle a compris Marie-Louise?
6. Pourquoi Marie-Louise n'a-t-elle pas compris tout de suite?
7. Qu'est-ce que la femme de ménage a appris à Marie-Louise?
8. Qu'est-ce qu'elle a raconté à ses amies?
9. Pourquoi ses amies se sont-elles mises à sourire en classe?
10. Qui a écrit les noms au tableau?
11. L'a-t-elle bien fait?
12. Qu'est-ce que la classe a fait?
13. Récitez les sept jours de la semaine.

[1] **Dans** is frequently used with divisions of time.

Devoir

A. *Conjugate:*

1. J'ai bien compris le récit.
2. Je n'ai pas été courageux.
3. Je suis sorti dimanche.

B. *Change the italicized nouns in the following sentences to pronouns:*

1. *Les garçons* vont à *l'école* à l'heure.
2. Ils portent *les livres* dans leurs serviettes.
3. Voilà pourquoi *Marie et Joséphine* ne portent pas *de lunettes.*
4. Voulez-vous aller avec *mon ami et avec moi?* (Use one pronoun.)
5. J'entends *le coup de sifflet.*
6. Il vient regarder *l'église.*
7. Elle aime faire *le ménage.*
8. Nous allons *chez le docteur.*
9. Ils n'ont pas entendu *la voix de la veuve.*
10. Il a égaré *son complet.*
11. Elle a ouvert *la fenêtre* pour dire au revoir.
12. Il a dormi longtemps *chez lui.*
13. Ils lavent *la vaisselle* et laissent tout en ordre.

C. *Explain the difference between* **le jeudi** *and* **jeudi**. *Write two sentences to show the difference.*

D. *Write a brief outline of your week's work, e.g.,*

Le dimanche je........, *etc.*

Traduction:

The cleaning-woman speaks very little English. She works at Mary Louise's on Thursdays and Fridays. She earns her living. She is delighted to speak French with the girl. Mary Louise understands fairly well. At first the woman spoke too rapidly, but now she speaks slowly. It is an opportunity to hear and to speak French.

Mary Louise told her friends the tale when she arrived at school. They found her tale very interesting.

THE GARDENS AT VERSAILLES

Publishers' Photo Service, N. Y.

SOIXANTE-TREIZIÈME LEÇON

Marthe se trompe de jour

Marthe s'est réveillée. Elle a regardé sa montre. Huit heures! (*Eight o'clock!*) Elle a sauté du lit, et elle s'est mise à s'habiller vite. Elle a trouvé son linge propre sur la chaise où elle l'avait (*had*) mis le soir. Elle s'est vite habillée. Elle a pris ses bas pour les mettre. Elle a mis le droit. Elle a mis le gauche. Oh! Il y a un grand trou dans le bas gauche.

Elle a jeté ces bas de côté, et elle a couru chercher une autre paire de bas dans son tiroir. Elle l'a trouvée. Elle a mis les bas. Elle a mis ses souliers et elle s'est précipitée dans la salle de bains pour se laver.

Elle n'a entendu personne dans la maison. Personne n'était (*was*) réveillé. Elle est entrée dans la chambre de sa sœur.

—Odette, il est presque huit heures! Lève-toi vite.

Odette s'est réveillée. Elle a regardé sa sœur.

—Nous allons être très en retard bien sûr, a continué Marthe.

Odette, tout à fait réveillée, a demandé à sa sœur—Tu as oublié que c'est aujourd'hui dimanche?

—Mais c'est vrai, s'est exclamée Marthe; je me suis trompée de jour. Quel ennui! Mais tant mieux! Je ne veux pas me coucher de nouveau. Je vais me mettre à étudier avant le petit déjeuner.

Elle est rentrée dans sa chambre. Elle a pris son livre, et elle a appris à compter jusqu'à vingt.

0	zéro [zero]
1	un [œ̃], une [yn]
2	deux [dø]
3	trois [trwɑ]
4	quatre [katr]

5	cinq [sɛ̃:k]
6	six [sis]
7	sept [sɛt]
8	huit [ɥit]
9	neuf [nœf]
10	dix [dis]
11	onze [õ:z]
12	douze [du:z]
13	treize [trɛ:z]
14	quatorze [katɔrz]
15	quinze [kɛ̃:z]
16	seize [sɛ:z]
17	dix-sept [disɛt]
18	dix-huit [dizɥit]
19	dix-neuf [diznœf]
20	vingt [vɛ̃]

Regardez la prononciation:

six hommes [sizɔm]
six chats [si ʃa]
sept chats [sɛ ʃa]
huit chats [ɥi ʃa]
neuf chats [nœ ʃa]
dix chats [di ʃa]
un élève [œ̃ nelɛ:v]
deux élèves [dø zelɛ:v]
trois élèves [trwɑ zelɛ:v]
quatre élèves [katr elɛ:v]
cinq élèves [sɛ̃:k elɛ:v]
six élèves [si zelɛ:v]
sept élèves [sɛ telɛ:v]
huit élèves [ɥi telɛ:v]
neuf élèves [nœ velɛ:v]
dix élèves [di zelɛ:v]
onze élèves [õ:zelɛ:v]
douze élèves [du:zelɛ:v]
treize élèves [trɛ:zelɛ:v]
quatorze élèves [katɔr zelɛ:v]
quinze élèves [kɛ̃:zelɛ:v]
seize élèves [sɛ:zelɛ:v]
dix-sept élèves [disɛ telɛ:v]
dix-huit élèves [dizɥi telɛ:v]
dix-neuf élèves [diznœ velɛ:v]
vingt élèves [vɛ̃ telɛ:v]

Grammaire

Numerals

CARDINAL NUMERALS

In French, as in English, numerals are divided into two kinds—ordinals and cardinals. Cardinal numerals are used to express the number of persons, things, units, etc. This lesson gives you the first twenty cardinals. If the numeral limits another word it is called a cardinal adjective, e.g., **quatre livres.**

Observe in the list on the preceding page that the pronunciation often varies according to the next word. If the next word begins with a vowel, what happens to the preceding final consonant? Does this preceding final consonant ever change in sound when it is carried over to the next word? Give examples.

POSITION OF CARDINAL ADJECTIVES

You have seen in the list on page 205 that the cardinal adjective precedes the noun as it does in English.

AGREEMENT OF CARDINAL ADJECTIVES

With the exception of **un** the cardinals are invariable. **Un** has a feminine form, **une.** The others do not change for gender and, of course, not for number.

un homme, *one man*   deux hommes, *two men*
une femme, *one woman*   deux femmes, *two women*

Vocabulaire

le bas [bɑ], *stocking*
la salle de bains [sal də bɛ̃], *bathroom*
l'ennui [lɑ̃nɥi] (m.), *boredom, weariness*
le linge [lɛ̃:ʒ] (singular only), *linen (household or personal)*

la paire [pɛ:r], *pair*
le soulier [sulje], *shoe*
le trou [tru], *hole*
s'exclamer [sɛksklame], *to exclaim*
se précipiter [sə presipite], *to rush, to hasten, to hurry, to throw oneself into*

se tromper (de) [sə trõpe], *to be mistaken*
gauche [goːʃ], *left, clumsy*
propre [prɔpr], *clean*
quel ennui [kɛl ɑ̃nɥi], *what a bore, what a nuisance*
tout à fait [tu ta fɛ], *completely, entirely*

Questionnaire

1. Qu'est-ce que Marthe a regardé?
2. Pourquoi a-t-elle sauté du lit?
3. Qu'est-ce qu'elle s'est mise à faire?
4. Qu'est-ce qu'elle a trouvé sur la chaise?
5. Pourquoi a-t-elle jeté de côté le bas gauche?
6. Où est-elle allée trouver une autre paire de bas?
7. Où s'est-elle précipitée?
8. Qui est-ce qu'elle a entendu?
9. Pourquoi Odette ne s'est-elle pas levée quand Marthe l'a réveillée?
10. De quoi Marthe s'est-elle trompée?
11. Qu'est-ce qu'elle a fait avant le petit déjeuner?
12. Avez-vous appris à compter?
13. Comment dit-on *one pair* en français?

Devoir

A. How are *il* and *ill* pronounced?

B. Be able to write or give orally the numerals in the following sentences:

1. Marie a (1) stylo; moi, j'ai (2) stylos. Nous avons (3) stylos.
2. J'ai écrit (2) mots ici et (5) mots là. J'ai écrit (7) mots.
3. Mon frère a acheté (6) bananes, et ma sœur a acheté (6) oranges.

C. Write three groups like the preceding ones, using these words:

crayons   autos
gommes   jolies lampes

D. Answer in as many ways as you can: Où est le piano? *Use such words as* **voici, ici,** *etc.*

E. Use *il, ils, elle, elles,* or *ce* to complete the following sentences:

1. Je ne vois pas le petit livre. Est-—— avec le gros livre?
2. Nous avons parlé avec grand'mère. —— est bonne pour nous.
3. Je n'ai pas traduit mes devoirs. —— sont trop longs.
4. Les dames sont parties seules, —— ne sont pas ici tous les jours.

F. Write sentences, about members of the family, containing these forms of the possessive adjective:

son   notre   leur
sa   vos   mon
ma   (2 *ways*)

Traduction:

Martha looked at her watch. She jumped out of bed. She dressed herself hurriedly. She put on her shoes. She hurried into the bathroom to wash (*herself*). She heard no one. She went into her sister's bedroom. She woke her sister with difficulty.

"We are going to be late. Quick, quick, Odette! You have only a few minutes."

Odette did not get up. She said, "You have made a mistake, Martha. Today is Sunday. What is the matter with you?"

Martha went back to her room to study. She learned to count to twenty before breakfast. She hopes that all the pupils are going to recite well. The teacher rarely scolds. He is lenient if everybody pays attention.

Publishers' Photo Service, N. Y.

THE HALL OF MIRRORS, VERSAILLES

SOIXANTE-QUATORZIÈME LEÇON
Review

A

1. Give six idiomatic expressions which belong in the group with **avoir chaud.**

2. What form of the verb is used to complete another verb (e.g., **aller, il faut**)? Illustrate.

3. Give the present and the past indefinite of **entreprendre.**

4. Give the present and the past indefinite of **se tromper.**

5. Point out differences between the past indefinite of **entreprendre** and that of **se tromper.**

6. Name the days of the week.

7. Explain the difference between **samedi** and **le samedi.** Use each in a sentence.

8. Mention four words denoting divisions of time within the day.

9. Give the numerals up to 20.

10. Pronounce: **dix élèves, dix bâtiments,** and **J'en ai dix.**

11. When do we use **il** and when **ce** as subjects of the verb **est?**

12. Use **voici** in two sentences, in the first sentence with a noun and in the second with a pronoun. Do the same with **voilà.**

13. How is the plural of a noun ordinarily formed in French? Give an example.

14. Give an exception to the above rule. Give an example.

15. Make these statements into questions in at least three ways:

1. Robert a une belle bannière semée de lis.
2. Il prend la pomme.
3. Il se glisse dedans.

B

I. Conjugate these five sentences:

1. Je comprends la physiologie.
2. J'ai appris et compris la leçon.

3. Je m'applique, pourtant.
4. Je cesse de dormir.
5. Je me suis couché à l'heure.

II. Conjugate these sentences, changing the possessive adjectives so that they agree with the subjects:

1. Je prends ma brosse.
2. J'apprends ma leçon par cœur.
3. J'attends mes parents.
4. Je fais mes études.

III. Give the numeral in each of the following sentences:

1. Nous avons (1) père et (1) mère.
2. Nous avons (2) grand-pères et (2) grand'mères.
3. Nous avons (3) tantes.
4. Nous avons (5) oncles.
5. Nous avons (6) cousins.
6. Nous avons (4) cousines.

IV. Write the diary of a boy's fountain-pen for the week, following this model:

Lundi—Je travaille. J'écris beaucoup de devoirs.

Mardi—Je reste à la maison. Robert m'a laissé sur la table dans sa chambre.

V. Write four sentences, each beginning with "Je vais" and using the following forms:

au, à l', à la, aux

VI. Complete these sentences, using suitable nouns:

1. Je prends ce ——-ci et ce ——-là.
2. Il prend cet ——-ci et cet —— -là.
3. Elle fait ces ——-ci et ces —— -là.
4. Vous faites cette ——-ci et cette ——-là.

VII. Study the vocabularies of Lessons 56-73.

JEAN BART STRIKES RIGHT AND LEFT.

SOIXANTE-QUINZIÈME LEÇON

Quand Jean Bart veut

Jean Bart est un des héros les plus intéressants de l'histoire de France. C'était (*He was*) un homme de beaucoup de courage qui a aidé son roi Louis Quatorze à sauver le pays pendant les grandes guerres de l'époque. Jean Bart n'est pas comme les autres grands hommes de son siècle. Il a des manières très simples, aussi simples que ses vêtements. Il n'hésite pas à dire ses pensées, et c'est parce qu'il est si brave qu'on l'aime tant.

Jean Bart vient de Dunkerque,[1] pays très froid. C'est peut-être parce que l'air de son pays est si froid que Jean Bart a presque toujours sa pipe à la bouche. A cause de son grand courage, Louis Quatorze lui offre une place dans la Marine (*navy*). A ce moment Jean Bart n'est plus très jeune. Il ne peut pas changer ses vieilles habitudes. Il ne peut pas à son âge supporter de changements dans sa vie. S'il doit venir (*come*) à la cour du roi, il faut l'accepter, tel qu'il est, avec tous ses défauts.

Un jour Jean Bart arrive à la cour du roi. Il veut demander au roi de lui accorder une grâce, pas pour lui, mais pour un de ses hommes qui a tué (*killed*) un camarade en duel (*in a duel*). Celui qui a été tué est un des anciens soldats de Jean Bart. Le brave Jean Bart est là, dans l'antichambre (*antechamber*). Il a sa pipe à la main et attend avec tous ceux qui désirent parler au roi. A cause de sa pipe qu'il a allumée, celui qui est chargé de présenter les gens au roi refuse de le laisser entrer.

[1] A French port on the North Sea.

—Monsieur, lui dit le soldat d'un ton qui indique la colère, le roi ne peut pas vous recevoir.

—Pourquoi donc, répond Jean Bart. Dites-lui que j'attends.

Jean Bart n'a pas l'air inquiet. Il allume de nouveau sa pipe. Il n'est pas en colère parce qu'il sait qu'il va obtenir ce qu'il veut. S'il doit attendre un peu, tant pis, il peut attendre; il a beaucoup de temps.

Le soldat, chargé de présenter les gens au roi, va trouver Louis Quatorze. Le roi n'a pas de peine à deviner qui veut lui parler, et il se met à sourire.

—Si je ne me trompe pas, c'est Jean Bart qui attend. Oui, je veux bien le voir.

Jean se précipite dans la chambre du roi. Il entre, salue son roi, et parle de l'homme qu'il espère sauver.

—C'est bien, Jean Bart, répond le roi. Le mal est grand, mais votre homme ne va pas mourir. Vous voyez que la France n'a pas oublié les services que vous lui avez rendus.

Heureux de son succès, Jean Bart sort de la chambre. Il ne peut pas cacher son plaisir et se met à crier "Vive (*Long li e*) le roi!" Tout de suite on vient autour de lui pour lui poser des questions. On veut surtout savoir comment il est sorti de Dunkerque pendant le siège de cette ville.

—Vous voulez savoir cela? dit-il. Vous voulez savoir comment je suis sorti de Dunkerque ayant (*having*), devant moi, vos ennemis, les Anglais (*the English*)? Ce n'est pas difficile à raconter. Ecoutez bien. Vous êtes la flotte (*fleet*) anglaise. Vous me menacez. Je représente la flotte française. Je ne vois pas de passage. Alors que faut-il faire pour sortir?

Et voilà notre Jean Bart qui commence à donner des coups à droite et à gauche. En quelques instants il réussit à s'ouvrir un passage, il se dirige vers la porte, et un moment après il est dehors dans la cour du château.

Vocabulaire

la colère [kɔlɛːr], *anger*

le coup [ku], *blow, hit, punch*

la cour [kuːr], *court, yard*

le défaut [defo], *fault (of character)*

les gens [ʒã] (m. and f. pl.), *people*

la guerre [gɛːr], *war*

l'habitude [labityd] (f.), *habit*

le pays [pei], *country*

le siècle [sjɛkl], *century*

le siège [sjɛːʒ], *siege*

les vêtements [vɛtmã] (m. pl.), *clothes*

celui [sǝlɥi] (m. sing.), *the one*

cacher [kaʃe], *to hide*

charger [ʃarʒe], *to charge, to load*

il doit [il dwa] (inf. devoir), *he must, ought, has to, owes*

obtenir [ɔptǝniːr], *to obtain*

recevoir [rǝsǝvwaːr] (p.p. reçu), *to receive*

rendre [rãːdr], *to render, to return (something)*

sauver [sove], *to save*

supporter [syporte], *to put up with, to stand for*

tuer [tɥe], *to kill*

tant pis [tã pi], *all the worse, never mind*

tel, telle [tɛl], *such*

English Equivalents

l'âge [lɑːʒ] (m.), *age*

le courage [kuraːʒ], *courage*

la grâce [grɑːs], *favor, grace*

la manière [manjɛːr], *manner, way*

la pipe [pip], *pipe*

le service [servis], *service*

accorder [akɔrde], *to accord, to grant*

menacer [mǝnase], *to menace, to threaten*

refuser [rǝfyze], *to refuse, to deny*

simple [sɛ̃ːpl], *simple*

SOIXANTE-SEIZIÈME LEÇON

Les Nombres

Première partie

Le professeur tâche d'apprendre aux élèves à compter. Ils savent les adjectifs numéraux jusqu'à vingt. Ils regardent les colonnes au tableau.

1. un	11. onze
2. deux	12. douze
3. trois	13. treize
4. quatre	14. quatorze
5. cinq	15. quinze
6. six	16. seize
7. sept	17. dix-sept
8. huit	18. dix-huit
9. neuf	19. dix-neuf
10. dix	20. vingt

Le professeur a écrit une autre colonne au tableau. Les élèves la regardent pour bien comprendre les nouveaux mots.

21. vingt et un[1] [vɛ̃ te œ̃]
22. vingt-deux [vɛ̃t dø]
23. vingt-trois [vɛ̃t trwa]
24. vingt-quatre [vɛ̃t katr]
25. vingt-cinq [vɛ̃t sɛ̃:k]
26. vingt-six [vɛ̃t sis]
27. vingt-sept [vɛ̃t sɛt]
28. vingt-huit [vɛ̃t ɥit]
29. vingt-neuf [vɛ̃t nœf]
30. trente [trɑ̃:t]
31. trente et un [trɑ̃t e œ̃]

Le professeur prononce les mots, et les élèves les prononcent après lui.

—Monsieur, pourquoi n'y a-t-il pas de trait d'union entre le mot *vingt* et le mot *un?* demande Richard.

—On n'a pas besoin d'un trait d'union, répond le professeur. Observez un peu et dites-moi pourquoi.

—C'est à cause du mot *et,* annonce Richard après un moment.

—Parfaitement. Cherchez un autre nombre où on n'a pas besoin d'un trait d'union.

—Trente et un, répondent les élèves. Le mot *et* remplace le trait d'union.

—C'est cela. Remarquez les autres formes où le mot *et* remplace le trait d'union.

Les élèves regardent les autres formes au tableau. Ils tâchent de bien comprendre.

40. quarante [karɑ̃:t]
41. quarante et un [karɑ̃t e œ̃]
50. cinquante [sɛ̃kɑ̃:t]
51. cinquante et un [sɛ̃kɑ̃t e œ̃]
60. soixante [swasɑ̃:t]
61. soixante et un [swasɑ̃t e œ̃]
70. soixante-dix [swasɑ̃t dis]
71. soixante et onze [swasɑ̃t e õ:z]

Les élèves apprennent ces nombres. Puis après le professeur indique les fenêtres.

—Voilà la première fenêtre, dit-il; voilà la deuxième fenêtre; voilà la troisième fenêtre; voilà la cinquième fenêtre; et voilà la sixième fenêtre.

Il ouvre un livre. Il tourne les pages—Voici la vingtième page; voici la vingt et unième page. Voici le trente-huitième exercice; et voici le quarante et unième exercice. Qui est-ce qui comprend?

Quelques élèves comprennent.

—Tant mieux! Expliquez, s'il vous plaît, Joséphine, dit le professeur.

—La terminaison i, è, m, e [jɛm] est comme la terminaison *th* en anglais.

—Bon! la terminaison de l'adjectif ordinal en francais, c'est i, è, m, e, excepté dans le mot **premier.**

---

[1] The t of **vingt** is pronounced in the forms **vingt et un,** etc., up to trente.

Grammaire

Cardinal Numerals Beyond Twenty

Beyond twenty, cardinal numerals are very easy. As in English, numerals are in groups of ten. The multiple of ten identifies the group of nine which follows. When you have learned **vingt, trente, quarante, cinquante, soixante, soixante-dix**, you should have no difficulty in arranging each group that follows.

Remember that when the word **un** is used in combination with another numeral the words are connected by **et: trente et un**. Otherwise the parts of a compound numeral are connected only by a hyphen: **trente-deux**.

Ordinal Numerals

The cardinals express the number of persons, things, units, etc. Ordinals express the order or the arrangement in relation to other persons, things, or units.

Cardinals	*Ordinals*
la page deux, *page two*	la deuxième page, *the second page*
l'exercice vingt et un, *exercise twenty-one*	le vingt et unième exercice, *the twenty-first exercise*
le problème quinze, *problem fifteen*	le quinzième problème, *the fifteenth problem*

Cardinal+*ième* = ordinal[1]

Examples: six +ième = sixième
                      sept+ième = septième
                      huit+ième = huitième

The order of numerals in French will be easy for you, because it is the same as in English. Place the French numeral where you would place the English numeral:

(les) trois pages	(la) page trois	la troisième page
(*the*) *three pages*	*page three*	*the third page*

Vocabulaire

la colonne [kɔlɔn], *column*
l'exercice [legzɛrsis] (m.), *exercise*
le nombre [nõ:br], *number*
le trait d'union [trɛ dynjõ] *hyphen*
observer [ɔpsɛrve]. *to observe*

remplacer [rãplase], *to replace*
ils savent [il sa:v] (inf. **savoir**), *they know* (a fact), *they know how*
tâcher (de) [taʃe də], *to try, to endeavor*

numéral [nymeral], *numeral*
ordinal [ɔrdinal], *ordinal*
parfaitement [parfɛtmã], *perfectly, exactly*
c'est cela [sɛ sla], *that's right, that is it, that's that*

---

[1] The only exception is the word **premier**, first. In **vingt et unième, trente et unième**, etc., there is no exception to the rule. **Cinq** adds **u** before -**ième**, and the **f** of **neuf** becomes **v** before -**ième**, thus, **cinquième** and **neuvième**.

Questionnaire

1. Qu'est-ce que les élèves savent?
2. Savez-vous la même chose?
3. Qui a écrit les nombres au tableau?
4. Qu'est-ce qu'il y a entre le mot vingt et le mot **un**?
5. Où a-t-on besoin d'un trait d'union?
6. Comptez de dix à vingt.
7. Comptez de vingt à trente.
8. Quelle est la terminaison de l'adjectif ordinal en français?
9. Quelle est l'exception?
10. Qu'avez-vous remarqué sur la position de ces mots avec un substantif?

Devoir

A. Write in phonetic characters:

vingt-sept	soixante-six
trente-cinq	soixante et onze
cinquante-huit	quarante-neuf

B. Following problem 1 as a model, solve and read aloud problems 2-6:

1. $\begin{array}{r} 23 \\ +44 \\ \hline 67 \end{array}$ (Vingt-trois et quarante-quatre font soixante-sept)

2. $\begin{array}{r} 16 \\ +37 \end{array}$ 3. $\begin{array}{r} 19 \\ +44 \end{array}$ 4. $\begin{array}{r} 55 \\ +8 \end{array}$ 5. $\begin{array}{r} 65 \\ +10 \end{array}$ 6. $\begin{array}{r} 22 \\ +18 \end{array}$

C. Continue this series to **dimanche:**

Lundi est le premier jour de la semaine.

Mardi est, *etc.*

D. Explain in one sentence in French:

1. la chambre à coucher
2. la bibliothèque
3. la peine
4. le conseil
5. la glacière
6. la fête
7. le détail

Traduction:

Mary set the table (**mettre le couvert**) this morning. She laid the cloth (**mettre la nappe**). She put a napkin (**la serviette**) at each place. She put a plate at each place. At the left she put a fork, at the right a knife and two spoons. She put glasses on the table, also, three for the others and the fourth in front of her place. It is only the fifth time that Mary has set the table, but she did it well.

THE KING'S BEDROOM, AZAY-LE-RIDEAU

SOIXANTE-DIX-SEPTIÈME LEÇON*

Les Nombres

Deuxième partie

On a sonné. La classe est entrée. Les élèves sont allés à leurs places, mais pas de (*no*) professeur! Il n'est pas arrivé. Faut-il commencer sans le professeur? Assurément; et on a choisi un élève de la classe pour le remplacer. Le professeur a fait ces arrangements en cas d'absence.

La classe a choisi André comme remplaçant. Maintenant il s'est levé; il s'est mis près de la table et il a demandé à Marthe de compter jusqu'à vingt. Après il a écrit au tableau quelques problèmes d'addition:

$$\begin{array}{ccc} 20 & 16 & 59 \\ +19 & +35 & +11 \end{array}$$

Tout à coup la porte s'est ouverte, et une dame est entrée dans la salle.

—Je suis la remplaçante, a-t-elle dit. Elle a ôté son manteau et son chapeau. Elle a regardé les problèmes.

—Apprenez-vous l'arithmétique ici?

—Non, mais nous étudions les nombres, ont répondu les élèves.

—Ah! je comprends. Repassez les nombres que vous avez étudiés.

Ils ont récité les nombres.—Soixante-dix, soixante et onze, soixante-douze, soixante-treize, soixante-quatorze, soixante-quinze, soixante-seize, soixante-dix-sept, soixante-dix-huit, soixante-dix-neuf—Ils se sont arrêtés.

—Vous ne savez pas continuer? Comment dit-on "twenty"?

—Vingt.

—Parfaitement! Et comment dit-on "four"? a continué la remplaçante.

—Quatre.

—Bon! Comprenez-vous **quatre-vingts**? Elle a écrit au tableau, quatre-vingt-un, quatre-vingt-deux, etc.

—N'est-ce pas que vous vous êtes trompée? a demandé Robert, qui aime corriger les fautes des autres. Vous avez oublié le s dans quatre-vingt-un et le reste.

—Non! a-t-elle répondu, quatre-vingts est la seule forme qui prenne[1] s.

—Quatre-vingt-dix signifie 90. Maintenant continuez jusqu'à cent (100).

Les élèves ont continué, quatre-vingt-onze, quatre-vingt-douze, quatre-vingt-treize, quatre-vingt-quatorze, quatre-vingt-quinze, quatre-vingt-seize, quatre-vingt-dix-sept, quatre-vingt-dix-huit, quatre-vingt-dix-neuf, cent.

—Ce n'est pas difficile, a dit Charles.

—Pas du tout, a répondu la remplaçante. Mais il faut répéter les nombres pour les employer facilement. Nous allons compter les choses ici.

—Je vois trois manteaux, a dit Jean.

—Et combien de gilets? a demandé la remplaçante à Maurice.

—Je vois un gilet, a-t-il répondu.

—Je vois cinquante-six souliers, a dit Jean, et des jupes, et des pantalons.

La remplaçante a demandé à Adèle de continuer.

—Un instant, s'il vous plaît. Je compte les livres. Je vois soixante-sept livres. Non, j'ai oublié les six livres sur la table. Cela fait soixante-treize.

—A la bonne heure! a dit Mademoiselle, et la classe a ri parce qu'Adèle est toujours si exacte.

---

*Note to the Teacher: The explanation (*Grammaire*) is really included in the reading lesson.

[1] *takes.* Subjunctive of **prendre.** Subjunctive mood after **la seule.**

Grammaire

The Grouping of Cardinals

Numerals fall so readily into similar groups that they are easy to learn.
From sixty add by ones up to eighty:

$$60+ 1 = 61 \quad \text{soixante et un}$$
$$60+10 = 70 \quad \text{soixante-dix}$$
$$60+11 = 71 \quad \text{soixante et onze}$$
$$60+19 = 79 \quad \text{soixante-dix-neuf}$$

From eighty add by ones to 100:

$$80+ 1 = 81 \quad \text{quatre-vingt-un}$$
$$80+15 = 95 \quad \text{quatre-vingt-quinze}$$

Only in **quatre-vingts** is the s used, never when another numeral follows.

Cardinals up to One Hundred

0. zéro	14. quatorze	28. vingt-huit
1. un	15. quinze	29. vingt-neuf
2. deux	16. seize	30. trente
3. trois	17. dix-sept	31. trente et un
4. quatre	18. dix-huit	32. trente-deux
5. cinq	19. dix-neuf	40. quarante
6. six	20. vingt	50. cinquante
7. sept	21. vingt et un	60. soixante
8. huit	22. vingt-deux	70. soixante-dix
9. neuf	23. vingt-trois	71. soixante et onze
10. dix	24. vingt-quatre	80. quatre-vingts
11. onze	25. vingt-cinq	81. quatre-vingt-un
12. douze	26. vingt-six	90. quatre-vingt-dix
13. treize	27. vingt-sept	100. cent

The Use of *Demander de* and *Demander à*

The verb **demander** means *to ask* or *to ask for*. Observe the construction
which it requires.

La remplaçante a demandé **à Marie de continuer.**

What preposition introduces the person one asks? What preposition introduces the infinitive?

Learn these sentences. They will help you to use **demander** correctly.

Demandez à quelqu'un de faire quelque chose. *Ask someone to do something.*
Je demande à Marie. *I ask Mary.*
Je demande à Marie de continuer. *I ask Mary to continue.*

Vocabulaire

l'absence [lapsɑ̃:s] (f.), *absence*

l'addition [ladisjõ] (f.), *addition*

l'arithmétique [laritmetik] (f.), *arithmetic*

l'arrangement [larɑ̃ʒmɑ̃] (m.), *arrangement*

la blouse [blu:z], *blouse (middy), smock*

le cas [kɑ] (pl. les cas), *case*

le gilet [ʒilɛ], *vest*

la jupe [ʒyp], *skirt*

le pantalon [pɑ̃talõ], *pair of trousers, pantaloons*

le remplaçant, -e [rɑ̃plasɑ̃], *substitute*

le reste [rɛst], *remainder, rest*

Maurice [mɔris], *Maurice*

nous pouvons [nu puvõ] (inf. pouvoir), *we can, we shall be able, we may*

nous voyons [nu vwajõ] (inf. voir), *we see*

exact [egzakt], *exact, punctual, accurate*

facilement [fasilmɑ̃], *easily, readily*

Questionnaire

1. Pourquoi le professeur n'a-t-il pas commencé la leçon?
2. Qui a-t-on choisi pour le remplacer?
3. Qu'est-ce qu'André a fait pour commencer?
4. Quand la porte s'est ouverte, qui est arrivé?
5. Qu'est-ce qu'ils ont fait après soixante-dix-neuf?
6. Qu'est-ce que Robert aime faire?
7. Quelle forme prend s?
8. Pour employer les nombres facilement qu'est-ce qu'il faut faire?
9. Combien de manteaux avez-vous?
10. Combien de souliers faut-il porter (*wear*)?
11. Est-ce que Philippe porte une jupe?
12. Pourquoi les élèves ont-ils ri quand Adèle a répondu?
13. Savez-vous compter?

Devoir

A. *Prepare to give these problems in class, according to the model in Lesson 76, page 213:*

$$\begin{array}{ccccc} 70 & 69 & 58 & 80 & 84 \\ +15 & +30 & +27 & +13 & +16 \end{array}$$

B. *Continue this story.* (*Marie parle*): Hier j'ai mis un peu d'ordre dans ma chambre. J'ai mis mon linge propre à sa place, etc. (7 items).

C. *Continue the conjugations in the present tense, changing the possessive adjective to agree in person with the noun it modifies.*

1. Je choisis ma place.
2. Je n'ai pas mes souliers.
3. Je ne prends pas mon chien.
4. Je vais compter mes fautes.

D. *Find in "Les Nombres" four examples of words which do not form the plural by adding s.*

Traduction:

Philip likes to look at the illustrations in the newspaper. He does not read many articles. He always looks for the seventh page, however, because the sporting articles (articles sur les sports) are to be found there.

One day Philip asked his mother to give him (lui) an interesting problem in arithmetic. She asked him (lui) to count the words in the newspaper. Philip laughed and began to count the words in a line (ligne). He found five words. Then he counted the lines in a column. He found one hundred lines in the column. Then he counted the columns on each page. Then he counted the pages.

THE INTERIOR OF NOTRE-DAME DE PARIS

MONT SAINT MICHEL

CATHEDRAL TOWNS OF FRANCE

People who live in a French cathedral town are always conscious of the ancient church which rises in their midst. They mark their day by the chiming bells of its high towers. When its spires are hidden by dark storm-clouds, the townspeople are depressed; but they are gay when the sun shines, turning its rose-windows into a glory of flame.

Because skyscrapers like ours have not yet appeared on the continent of Europe, the heaven-aspiring towers of old churches are peculiarly impressive, as they rise high above the lowly French villages clustered about their base. French cathedral towns attract great crowds of tourists from our shores, first of all because of their rare beauty, and also because these churches are monuments of medieval times, true survivals of an age that the western hemisphere did not yet know.

On an island just off the north-western coast of France is one of the most frequently visited cathedrals of the Continent, the monastic fortress of Mont St. Michel. At sea-level it is defended by lofty ramparts behind which huddles the village; but above these rise, tier over tier, the huge fortified walls of the monastery, so rugged that they seem but part of the lonely cliff which faces the open Atlantic. High on the crown of this pyramid of rock stands the gloomy, forbidding church of granite, which, once seen, remains forever after in the beholder's mind, a thing apart. On its topmost tower, wrapped in chill sea-mists, is the fierce figure of the warrior archangel Michael.

It is in a cathedral such as this that we find one main trend of the French medieval spirit held captive for the ages that followed. Like the Normans who built it, the architecture of Mont St. Michel is very robust.

Size and massiveness prevail. Even after they adapted Gothic forms for their vast churches, the craving of the Normans for weight is noticeable. They wished their cathedrals to be lasting monuments to their sturdiness and brutal power. And so it is that Mont St. Michel lives on as a clear symbol of those troubled days at the close of the eleventh century when William of Normandy was a forbidding and an arrogant figure.

Not gloom alone typified the Middle Ages; there were joy and gladness, too, as exemplified in the cathedral of Chartres. This city, located fifty-five miles southwest of Paris, is far out of the world of commerce and trade. Chartres is in the center of a rich pastoral district. The spires of its cathedral are visible for many miles over the wheatfields that surround it. The gentle River Eure flows near by. The church and part of the town stand on an elevation far different from the perpendicular rock which Mont St. Michel surmounts. Most of the church that survives today is of twelfth- and

thirteenth-century construction, but the lower crypts go back to the time of Bishop Fulbert in 1020. That was the heyday of Chartres' greatness, when all Europe was going to school there, and the fame of this city was wider than that of Rheims, Orléans, and Paris combined. Wherever one looks from the winding streets of the little town, there is the church, its spires shining in the sun. The original plan of the building called for no less than nine towers, but, like most of the ancient churches of France, Chartres has never been completed. So only two of the nine towers exist, and these have a unique appearance because they are so unlike in their design. The southern tower was built much earlier than its fellow, and its lines are simple and delicately proportioned. The north tower is much more fanciful, its flying buttresses and pinnacles contrasting sharply with the restraint of the other one.

The cathedral of Chartres seems to be nearly all windows. The glass for the windows was made in the thir-

CHARTRES
A side view of the cathedral

RHEIMS CATHEDRAL

Yvon, Paris

The statue in front of the cathedral is of Joan of Arc.

teenth century, brilliantly stained by a process which the world has since lost, and is very harmonious in pattern. The west rose-window is known everywhere for its happy combination of color and design. Mont St. Michel gains its power from gloom and threatening shadow, but Chartres is a stronghold of happiness and beauty, emphatic of radiance and light. Its soaring arch seems to lift the body of him who stares up at it through the haze of the vast vaulted nave. Fifty pillars within the church give the beholder an idea of amazing strength; yet some long-forgotten artist has wreathed the top of each of these pillars with most delicate stone carvings: oak leaves, clusters of thistle, clover, daisy, rose, and holly.

Left behind is the sunny fertility of the Chartres region as the traveler approaches the battle-scarred country east of Paris and comes to the cathedral of Rheims. Like all else around it, this church has recently suffered

the wounds of war. Perhaps just because it has been maimed and scarred in so terrible a way, the building seems somehow like a breathing human thing. Its first appearance is inspiring. Though it does not stand upon a hill, it is on a higher level than its surroundings, with a broad bare stretch of ground in front of it, so that not even the tiniest shop or house obstructs the view. It dawns suddenly upon its beholder with theatrical, almost regal, splendor; it startles him more than any other cathedral of all Europe.

The west front is the most elaborate of any of the more famous cathedrals —with its three immense portals, its colossal figures, and its huge rose-window. The wealth of detail here is overwhelming, even though thousands of statues, brackets, pinnacles, and gargoyles were demolished not long since by the enemy's cannon. The ill-fated church of Rheims has lost some of its most beautiful parts,

PYTHAGORAS
A carving from the interior of Chartres

but these are being slowly replaced, in so far as it lies in the skill of man to do so. Modern artists have restored the shattered rose-window, but plain glass still fills most other openings which knew the glory of medieval stained work.

Rheims is a cathedral of surpassing historical interest. From Philip II (1180) to Charles X (1824) the kings of France were crowned at its altar. Here in 1429 Joan of Arc crowned her sovereign for whom she had won France from the British invader. In the open space before the church is the statue of a thrilling young Joan astride her warlike charger. It is a beautiful interpretation of her, for in spite of the heavy armor she wears the figure is that of a young woman, and the expression on her face is one of spiritual joy.

Enchanting Paris itself contains a fourth church, sometimes hailed as the one perfect example of Gothic architecture that has come down to us.

In a most romantic setting, Notre Dame looms high above the Seine. The colorful life of the capital city of the world surrounds it, barges and steamboats almost graze its mighty walls in passing. The famous bookstalls of Paris line the banks of the river close by. Here are sold every year thousands of etchings which picture the cathedral rising peaceful and serene into the upper air, telling all men of a life greater than any led upon this earth.

In the eighteenth century, a certain Pierre Levieil had its priceless stained windows destroyed and in their place plain glass with monograms and borders of fleur-de-lis inserted. Modern artists have restored these ruined windows to something like their original beauty, and the effect of this national cathedral of France is therefore as gorgeous as in days of yore. Though part of the charm of antiquity has gone from the church forever, eager visitors find it still inspiring.

GARGOYLE
From the parapet of Notre-Dame de Paris

SOIXANTE-DIX-HUITIÈME LEÇON
L'Heure
Première partie

1 2 3 4 5

Henriette est heureuse aujourd'hui, parce qu'elle a une jolie petite montre. C'est un cadeau de la part de grand-père. La montre est en or. Les amies d'Henriette l'ont beaucoup admirée avant la classe.

En classe on a parlé de l'heure et Henriette a eu l'occasion de regarder souvent sa montre. Elle s'est dit—Je vais apprendre l'heure en regardant (*by looking at*) ma jolie montre. Chaque fois que je la regarde, je vais tâcher de dire l'heure en français.

Le professeur a montré une pendule aux élèves. Il a tourné les aiguilles. Les élèves ont regardé la pendule avec attention. (See 1, above.)

—Il est une heure, a dit le professeur. Il a tourné la grande aiguille. Il a demandé aux élèves de bien regarder. (See 2.)

—Il est une heure cinq.

Il a tourné l'aiguille de nouveau.

—Quelle heure est-il? (See 3.)

—Il est une heure dix, ont répondu les élèves.

—Maintenant il est une heure et quart. (See 4.)

—Est-ce qu'on dit aussi deux heures et quart, monsieur? a demandé Richard.

—Parfaitement; mais remarquez la différence. (*Le professeur écrit au tableau.*)

Il est une heure et quart.

Il est deux heures et quart.

Il est trois heures et quart.

Excepté avec une le mot **heure** est au pluriel.

—**Quart**, c'est comme le mot *quarter*, n'est-ce pas? a dit Rosalie, qui cherche toujours le mot anglais.

—C'est ça. Quelle heure est-il maintenant?

—Il est une heure vingt, ont répondu les élèves. Ils savent bien.

—Bon! Et il est maintenant une heure et demie. (See 5.)

(*Le professeur écrit au tableau.*)

Il est une heure et demie.

Il est deux heures et demie.

Henriette a regardé sa montre.—Il est onze heures vingt-neuf, a-t-elle pensé. Qu'il est facile de dire l'heure!

—Nous déjeunons à midi, a continué le professeur, et nous devons être couchés[1] (*asleep*) à minuit.

—A quelle heure rentrez-vous chez vous, Adèle?

—En général, je rentre chez moi à trois heures, mais aujourd'hui je rentre à quatre heures, parce que je prends ma leçon de musique le jeudi.

—Rentrez-vous à quatre heures exactement, Adèle?

—Non, monsieur, il est quelquefois quatre heures dix, quelquefois quatre heures vingt, a répondu la jeune fille.

—Alors, on dit "Je rentre après quatre heures." Tiens, on sonne. Nous pouvons aller déjeuner. J'ai si faim que je vais dévorer mon déjeuner.

[1] Observe that the word **couchés** is used as an adjective. That explains why the verb is not reflexive.

Grammaire

Telling Time in French

THE HOUR

Since you know the numerals, it will be a simple matter for you to learn to tell time in French. You can start with the word **heure** as a center, and with the aid of the numerals swing around the entire circle.

The word **heure** is singular with **une,** and plural with every other numeral. Note that the French do not say *twelve o'clock* for either noon or midnight.

une heure, *one o'clock*	sept heures, *seven o'clock*
deux heures, *two o'clock*	dix heures, *ten o'clock*
trois heures, *three o'clock*	onze heures, *eleven o'clock*
quatre heures, *four o'clock*	midi, *twelve o'clock* (noon)
cinq heures, *five o'clock*	minuit, *twelve o'clock* (*midnight*)

When the French are mentioning the hour only, in telling time, the order of the sentence is the same as in English:

Il est une heure. *It is one o'clock.*   Il est midi. *It is noon.*
Il est onze heures. *It is eleven o'clock.* Il est minuit. *It is midnight.*

TELLING THE HOUR UP TO HALF PAST

Suppose now that you wish to add minutes to the hour. Simply place the number of minutes directly after the hour (just the opposite of English). The word **minutes** is very often omitted, but the word **heure** never is.

une heure cinq (minutes), *five minutes past one,* or, *one-five*
deux heures dix, *ten minutes past two,* or, *two-ten*
huit heures dix-sept, *seventeen minutes past eight,* or, *eight-seventeen*

THE USE OF "QUART" AND "DEMI"

For ordinary purposes the people in France as well as in America say "a quarter past" and "half past." But when special accuracy is needed (for trains, theaters, etc.), the exact number of minutes is given.

quatre heures et (*or* un) quart, *a quarter past four*
quatre heures quinze, *fifteen minutes past four,* or, *four-fifteen*

cinq heures et demie, *half past five*
cinq heures trente, *thirty minutes past five,* or, *five-thirty*

Observe that **demie** is feminine, to agree with **heure.** **Demi** is the form to be used with **midi** and **minuit:**

Il est midi et demi.
Il est minuit et demi.

The preposition **à** is used in such expressions as:

à sept heures, *at seven o'clock*
à minuit. *at midnight*

Vocabulaire

l'aiguille [legɥiːj] (f.), *needle, hand of a clock*
midi [midi], *noon*
minuit [minɥi], *midnight*
le quart [kaːr], *quarter*
Henriette [ãrjɛt], *Henrietta*

Rosalie [rozali], *Rosalie*
demi, demie [dəmi], *half*
en [ã], *of, made of, in*
exactement [egzaktəmã], *exactly, punctually*

de la part de [də la paːr də], *from, on behalf of*
en général [ã ʒeneral], *generally, in general, usually*

Questionnaire

1. Qui a donné cette montre à Henriette?
2. Décrivez la montre.
3. Qu'est-ce que les amies d'Henriette ont fait quand elles ont vu la montre?
4. Pourquoi Henriette a-t-elle regardé sa montre en classe, et qu'est-ce qu'elle a dit?
5. Qu'est-ce que le professeur a montré aux élèves?
6. Pour indiquer les minutes, qu'est-ce qu'il a tourné?
7. Quand emploie[1]-t-on le mot *heure* au pluriel?
8. Pourquoi Adèle va-t-elle rentrer après quatre heures?
9. A quelle heure déjeunez-vous?
10. A quelle heure vous couchez-vous?
11. A quelle heure vous mettez-vous en route pour l'école?

Devoir

A. Recite the hours around the clock in order to drill on the word **heure.**

B. Read aloud and then write in full:

(1)	1:08	(6)	9:30
(2)	2:10	(7)	12:25 A.M.
(3)	3:15	(8)	12:00 P.M.
(4)	8:20	(9)	6:12
(5)	7:16	(10)	5:27

C. Write simple sentences, using each of the following words in the form indicated. Do not use the verb **est** *in more than one sentence. Choose words from the vocabularies of Lessons 16 and 17 for these sentences.*

(1)	ces	(5)	beaux
(2)	cette	(6)	belle
(3)	cet	(7)	quel
(4)	beau	(8)	quelle

D. Use the correct forms of the words in parentheses:

1. Elle a l'air (inquiet) à cause de son regard (sévère).
2. Il (savoir) conduire l'auto. C'est à dire qu'il (aller) conduire.
3. Il vient allumer un feu pendant la (froid) journée.
4. Les ours blancs du grand bassin (nager) du matin jusqu'au soir.
5. Ils ont été (maussade) et (sauvage) pendant plusieurs jours.
6. Elle n'est pas (prêt) non plus à l'heure.
7. Ils ne (saluer) pas encore le drapeau.

Traduction:

We learned to tell time in class to-day. Now when I look at my watch I say—*une heure,* or *trois heures vingt,* etc. The watch is a gift from grandfather. I am going to think in French when I look at it.

When I arrived home today I found my friend Charles. We talked until (jusqu'à) a quarter past five. He left because they (on) have dinner every day at six o'clock.

---

[1] This is the present of the verb **employer**, in which the y changes to i before a mute e. It differs from a regular first conjugation verb in this respect only.

SOIXANTE-DIX-NEUVIÈME LEÇON

L'Heure

Deuxième partie

Quand Henriette est arrivée chez elle l'après-midi, sa mère a dit—Tu ne sais pas qui va dîner ici ce soir!

—Est-ce Joséphine que tu as invitée?

—Non, ce n'est pas Joséphine. C'est M. Baker. Il a donné un coup de téléphone.

—Que je suis contente, s'est exclamée Henriette. De tous les amis de papa, je préfère M. Baker. Cette fois il va parler français avec moi.

M. Baker n'est pas arrivé en retard. Il a demandé à Henriette de lui montrer sa montre.

—C'est une très jolie montre, mais vous ne savez pas dire l'heure en français.

—Mais si (*yes, I do*), monsieur, nous l'avons appris en classe ce matin. J'ai bien compris. Il est—

Elle s'est arrêtée. Elle a rougi.

—Je ne sais pas dire cette heure-ci.

—Vous savez les autres? C'est ce qu'on dit toujours.

—Mais c'est vrai, monsieur. Nous avons appris une heure, deux heures, et une heure et quart, etc. Nous n'avons rien appris après "demi."

—Il est six heures moins vingt-cinq, a expliqué M. Baker. Nous disons "twenty-five minutes to six" en anglais. En français on dit "six o'clock less twenty-five." Dites-moi quelle heure il est maintenant.

—Il est six heures moins vingt et une, a répondu Henriette.

M. Baker a expliqué qu'on porte une montre, qu'on a une pendule dans la maison, et qu'on regarde une horloge à l'extérieur d'un bâtiment.

Tout à coup il a demandé à Henriette—Quelle heure avez-vous?

—Six heures moins seize, a dit Henriette. Je comprends maintenant.

Alors M. Baker a continué à parler de l'heure. Il a expliqué qu'en France ou en Europe on a un excellent système pour les chemins de fer, etc. Sept heures peut signifier sept heures du matin ou sept heures du soir. Parce que ce n'est pas clair, on a aussi une autre façon de le dire en France. On dit sept heures ou dix-neuf heures, onze heures ou vingt-trois heures. On commence à une heure du matin et on continue jusqu'à minuit. On n'a besoin ni de A.M. ni de P.M. Il a dressé une petite liste pour Henriette, qui a écouté avec grand intérêt.

1 P.M.	13 heures	6 P.M.	18 heures
2 P.M.	14 heures	10 P.M.	22 heures

Agence Rol, Paris

A TWENTY-FOUR-HOUR CLOCK

—Alors il faut dire qu'il est maintenant dix-huit heures, a dit Henriette.

—Mais non. Il a expliqué que les formes exactes sont pour les affaires (*business*) ou pour les chemins de fer. La forme générale pour la conversation c'est une heure, deux heures, sept heures, etc. C'est dans les affaires qu'on emploie la forme exacte.

Quand maman est entrée au salon, M. Baker n'a pas continué à parler en français, mais Henriette n'a pas oublié ce qu'il a dit, je vous assure. Elle est trop contente de savoir dire l'heure.

Grammaire

Telling Time after the Half Hour

In the preceding lesson you learned to tell time as far as the half hour. Up to that point minutes are added to the hour. After the half hour the case is just the reverse—*minutes are subtracted from the next hour*. In English we use the word *to;* the French use the word **moins** (*less*).

trois heures moins vingt, *twenty minutes to three*
cinq heures moins dix, *ten minutes to five*
sept heures moins un (*or* le) quart, *a quarter to seven*

Where special accuracy is needed, the French use the form that has grown very common in America (*three forty-five, five fifty-two*, etc.):

trois heures quarante-cinq   cinq heures cinquante-deux

Vocabulaire

le chemin de fer [ʃmɛd fɛːr], *railroad*
l'extérieur [lɛkstɛrjœːr] (m.), *outside, exterior*
la façon [fasõ], *way, fashion, manner*
l'horloge [lɔrlɔːʒ] (f.), *clock*
le système [sistɛːm], *system*

l'Europe [lœrɔp] (f.), *Europe*
nous disons [nu dizõ] (inf. **dire**), *we say, we are saying, we tell*
donner un coup de téléphone (à) [dɔne œ̃ kud telefɔn a], *to telephone (to)*

général [ʒeneral], *general*
moins [mwɛ̃], *less, to* (in telling time)
chez elle [ʃe zɛl], *at her house, to her house, at home*
de bonne heure [də bɔn œːr], *in good time, early*

Questionnaire

1. Qui va dîner chez Henriette?
2. Est-ce qu'elle l'aime?
3. Quand est-il arrivé?
4. Qu'est-ce que M. Baker a admiré?
5. Qu'est-ce qu'Henriette a fait quand elle s'est arrêtée?
6. Pourquoi a-t-elle rougi?
7. Quels sont les trois mots que M. Baker a expliqués?
8. Est-ce que la jeune fille a compris toute l'explication?
9. De quoi a-t-il parlé à Henriette?
10. Pourquoi quatorze heures est-il préférable à deux heures pour un train?
11. Faut-il dire quinze heures dans la conversation?
12. Quand a-t-on besoin d'une forme exacte?

Devoir

A. Read aloud in French and then write in full the following phrases. Give them in ordinary conversational form in French as well as in the form indicated:

(1) 3:20
(2) 4:30
(3) at nine o'clock
(4) a quarter past seven
(5) a quarter to eleven
(6) twenty minutes to ten
(7) ten minutes to four
(8) 5 p.m.
(9) 6:20 p.m.
(10) 8:45 p.m.

B. Write a schedule for a typical day, following this form:

A sept heures je me lève, *etc.*

C. Write or read the paragraph asked for in B in the past indefinite, beginning:

Hier je me suis levé, *etc.*

Traduction:

Mr. Baker is always interesting. He has traveled a great deal. He talked about Henrietta's watch. He thought (**trouver**) it pretty. He said that in Europe one sometimes sees the words "17 heures" or "20 heures." This system is good. It is good for business because it is clear.

Mr. Baker explained that one wears a watch, one has a clock in the living-room, and one looks at the large (**gros**) clock on the outside of a building.

We are happy now because we can tell time.

STRASBOURG
Here, as in many other cities, the cathedral is the dominant building

QUATRE-VINGTIÈME LEÇON
Review*

A

1. Give an example in English of a cardinal numeral and of an ordinal numeral.

2. How is the ordinal formed?

3. Give five examples of numerals in which the word **et** is used.

4. In compound numerals where the word **et** is not used, how are the parts connected?

5. Write the following numerals in words: 15, 16, 31, 71, 80, 81, 94.

6. Translate this sentence and explain the constructions: *I ask Charles to read.*

7. Explain the system of telling time, up to the half hour.

8. What word is used with **quart, demie**?

9. After the half hour what word is used?

10. Translate: *What time is it?*

11. Answer by telling the actual time as you write this lesson.

12. What system is used in Europe whenever the exact time is necessary?

13. Make this sentence interrogative in as many ways as possible: **Charlotte remarque le changement.**

14. Give the French for these words: *noun, pronoun, object, subject, participle, it agrees, it ends, infinitive.*

B

I. Use the correct form of each adjective in parentheses with the nouns that follow:

1. (*beau*) la jeunesse, l'enfant, les enfants, le résultat, l'homme

2. (*premier*) la pharmacie, les mots, les fautes, l'occasion, le rayon, le bâtiment

3. (*grand*) les généraux, le héros, la brosse, le roi, l'esprit (m.)

4. (*ce*) la pomme, le groupe, l'étude (f.), les difficultés, l'exercice (m.), le cœur, la pensée, la découverte, le bruit

5. (*heureux*) le monsieur, la femme, les garçons, les amies, le neveu

II. Read aloud, or write, in French:

9:30	5:45
4:15	12:30 P.M.
18 hrs.	8:00
2:38	1:20

III. Use these partitives in sentences: du, de la, de l', des, pas de, en. In order to review vocabulary at the same time try to use some of these words in your sentences: les billets, le thé, la paille, les souris, la tête, les oreilles, les pouces, la soie, la fourrure.

IV. Write these sentences in the past indefinite:

1. La Belge se dépêche.

2. Je m'habille à l'heure.

3. Nous nous lavons dans la salle de bains.

4. Vous tâchez de réveiller de bonne heure votre sœur.

5. Nous essayons le gilet clair.

6. Ils payent l'addition avec de l'argent.

7. Il commande du potage, du poulet, du lait, du pain, et surtout des fruits.

8. Je me précipite dans l'endroit.

Note to the Teacher: Make the review of numerals a game. Most teachers have some favorite device. These two games will suggest others.

1. Call a number in French and have the pupils turn to that page in their books. The pupil who finds the page first will raise his hand and, as the teacher asks him, will give the first word on the page.

2. Use some variation of the game "Buzz."

QUATRE-VINGT-UNIÈME LEÇON

La Surprise

Voilà une aventure qui est arrivée à un de mes camarades et à moi pendant un voyage (*trip*) dans un pays dont on dit les gens très méchants. Cette histoire va suffire à vous dire la vérité sur ce peuple qu'on a si mal (*badly*) jugé. Je dois (*I must*) vous dire d'abord que mon ami ne veut jamais voir (*to see*) le mal chez les autres. Il voit toujours le bon côté de ceux chez qui il est. Il s'intéresse aux gens, et de cette façon l'idée de les juger ne lui vient jamais à l'esprit.

Or, cette nuit-là nous perdons notre chemin. Nous marchons à travers le bois dans l'espoir de trouver une maison où passer la nuit. A ce moment nous voyons une vieille maison se dresser (*rise up*) sur notre chemin à gauche. Nous frappons à la porte, et on nous ouvre tout de suite. Là nous trouvons toute une famille qui nous prie (*asks*) d'entrer.

Je me mets à examiner le lieu. Tout y est en ordre, mais partout je vois des couteaux, de longs et de courts. Ils semblent remplir toute la maison. Je fais un léger mouvement pour sortir, mais mon camarade se met à parler et à rire avec ses nouveaux amis. Je suis obligé d'abandonner mon projet de partir puisque mon ami ne semble pas avoir peur. Il parle de sa jeunesse, de ses plaisirs d'autrefois, et n'a pas du tout l'air inquiet.

On nous invite à dîner, et une fois le dîner terminé (*after dinner*), on nous montre un lit pas trop dur dans le grenier (*garret*) où on voit attachées sur des cordes des provisions (*supplies*) de viande pour toute l'année. Nos nouvelles connaissances nous quittent. Lorsqu'elles sont parties, mon ami se met à enlever ses vêtements, et se couche. Puisque je sais que je ne vais pas dormir, je n'enlève pas mes affaires. Bientôt la famille se couche, et le bruit en bas cesse.

La nuit semble longue. J'entends sonner trois heures, quatre heures, cinq heures. J'entends bientôt qu'on se lève en bas. J'entends le mari parler à sa femme, et les paroles du mari qui m'arrivent jusqu'à l'oreille sont, "Enfin, faut-il les tuer tous les deux?" A quoi la femme répond un simple "oui."

Mes cheveux se dressent (*stands up*) sur la tête. Est-il nécessaire de dire que je tremble? Comment trouver le moyen d'échapper de ce lieu? Comment nous défendre? Comment obtenir des armes? Où trouver le secours nécessaire pour nous sauver? Si je fais un mouvement, on va monter nous tuer dans nos lits. Je n'ose pas appeler mon ami. Je regarde la fenêtre. Elle est haute. Si je tombe dans la cour . . .

Au bout d'un quart d'heure j'entends quelqu'un dans l'escalier. On monte, et par la porte ouverte j'observe la femme qui éclaire l'escalier. Elle porte une lampe à la main dont elle cache un peu la lumière de ses doigts. Son mari monte doucement devant elle. Je me lève et me mets derrière la porte. Le mari, un couteau dans les dents, pousse un peu la porte et vient près du lit de mon pauvre ami. D'une main l'homme prend son couteau et de l'autre . . . ah! chers amis, comment vous dire . . . de l'autre main il saisit un jambon (*ham*), en coupe un gros morceau, et quitte doucement la chambre, sa femme derrière lui. Vous imaginez-vous dans quel état d'esprit j'étais (*was*)!

Au moment où le soleil se lève,

"I STOOD BEHIND THE DOOR."

toute la famille vient frapper à la porte. On nous invite à descendre. Le déjeuner est prêt. Sur la table je vois deux magnifiques poulets. Quand j'ai vu ces deux poulets, j'ai compris enfin les mots, "Faut-il les tuer tous les deux?" Maintenant, avant de (*before*) dire du mal de quelqu'un, je vous assure que je réfléchis longtemps. Une telle aventure ne doit pas vous arriver deux fois.

d'après P. L. Courier

Vocabulaire

le chemin [ʃəmɛ̃], *road, way*
les cheveux [ʃəvø] (m. pl.), *hair*
le côté [kote], *side*
l'espoir [lɛspwaːr] (m.), *hope*
le lieu [ljø], *place*
le moyen [mwajɛ̃], *means, way*

le secours [səkuːr], *help*
défendre [defãːdr], *to defend, to protect, to forbid*
échapper [eʃape], *to escape*
enlever [ãlve], *to take off*
juger [ʒyʒe], *to judge*
oser [oze], *to dare*
saisir [seziːr], *to seize*
sonner [sɔne], *to strike*

suffire [syfiːr], *to be enough, to suffice*
pauvre [poːvr], *poor*
dont [dõ], *of which, whose*
lorsque [lɔrskə], *when*
quoi [kwa], *what, which*
or [ɔːr], *well*
en bas [ã ba], *downstairs, below*

English Equivalents

l'idée [lide] (f.), *idea, thought*
le mouvement [muvmã], *movement*

le peuple [pœpl], *people, populace*
le projet [prɔʒɛ], *project, plan*

abandonner [abãdɔne], *to abandon*
s'imaginer [simaʒine], *to imagine*

QUATRE-VINGT-DEUXIÈME LEÇON

Le Calendrier

Vous vous rappelez Marie-Louise, la jeune fille qui a parlé avec la blanchisseuse belge; la jeune fille qui a appris les jours de la semaine? Hier elle a appris quelque chose de nouveau. Quand la blanchisseuse est arrivée, elle a demandé à voir Marie-Louise.

—Mais vous savez, Marie-Louise est à l'école, a expliqué la mère.

Quand la jeune fille est rentrée, la blanchisseuse l'a priée de venir dans la cuisine.

—J'ai quelque chose pour mademoiselle.

Elle a déroulé un calendrier français.—Mais c'est tout en français! s'est exclamée Marie-Louise. Merci bien! C'est merveilleux!

Elle a commencé à tourner les pages, et elle a lu chaque mois—janvier, février, mars, avril, mai, juin, juillet, août, septembre, octobre, novembre, décembre.

—Les noms sont presque les mêmes en anglais et en français.

—N'est-ce pas? Mademoiselle peut les apprendre facilement.

Marie-Louise a regardé ce calendrier avec intérêt.—Je connais les jours et les nombres. Je dois apprendre les mois. Je ne peux pas donner les dates sans savoir les noms des mois.

—Quel est le mois qui est très court? a demandé la blanchisseuse.

—C'est février. Il n'a que vingt-huit jours, ordinairement. Quelquefois il en a vingt-neuf. C'est une année spéciale. Comment dit-on "leap year" en français?

—Mais je ne sais pas, mademoiselle. Je n'en sais rien du tout, a répondu la blanchisseuse très embarrassée.

Marie-Louise a expliqué et tout de suite la femme a souri.—Vous voulez dire l'année bissextile, l'année où il y a trois cent soixante-six jours!

—Et comment donne-t-on la date? a continué Marie-Louise. Elle a indiqué une date dans le calendrier.

—C'est le vingt juin. Et ça c'est le mercredi vingt et un juin.

—Et ceci?

—C'est aujourd'hui le premier février. Mais maintenant il faut que mademoiselle m'excuse. Il faut que je repasse le linge pendant l'après-midi, ou Madame va être fâchée. Mais est-ce que mademoiselle veut apprendre ces vers?

Trente jours ont septembre
Avril, juin, et novembre.
De vingt-huit il y en a un,
Les autres en ont trente et un.

Grammaire

The Months of the Year

The months are easy to learn because the French and English names are for the most part similar. Observe that, as in the case of the days of the week, names of months in French begin with a small letter.

janvier [ʒɑ̃vje]	mai [mɛ]	septembre [sɛptɑ̃:br]
février [fevrie]	juin [ʒɥɛ̃]	octobre [ɔktɔbr]
mars [mars]	juillet [ʒɥijɛ]	novembre [nɔvɑ̃:br]
avril [avril]	août [u]	décembre [desɑ̃:br]

Dates

Observe the following dates, and by answering the questions below them try to make your own rules for dates:

(1) le premier mars   (4) le vingt-quatre juin
(2) le deux mars   (5) le trente et un octobre
(3) le quinze avril   (6) le lundi quatorze novembre

1. What is the single exception to the rule that cardinal numerals are used in dates?
2. Where is the numeral always placed, before or after the month?
3. What is usually the first word of a date?
4. Does this vary if the day of the week is included in the date?

In using the name of the month without the day of the month these two forms are correct:

en[1] avril, *in April*   au mois d'avril, *in the month of April*
en mai, *in May*   au mois de mai, *in the month of May*
en juin, *in June*   au mois de juin, *in the month of June*
en août, *in August*   au mois d'août, *in the month of August*

The Use of *Il y a*

We have in English the expressions *there is*, *there are*. These expressions do not indicate place but rather existence. Their purpose is merely to introduce the important factors in the sentence, the nouns. Observe, in the sentences below, the corresponding form in French, **il y a**, which precedes either a singular or a plural noun. It is translated *there is* or *there are*, depending on the number of the noun that follows.

Il y a une maison près d'ici. *There is a house near here.*
Il y a vingt maisons près d'ici. *There are twenty houses near here.*
Il y a une petite fille dans la famille. *There is one little girl in the family.*
Il y a quatre garçons dans la famille. *There are four boys in the family.*

Vocabulaire

l'année bissextile [lane bi-sɛkstil] (f.), *leap year*
la blanchisseuse [blãʃi-sø:z], *washerwoman, laundress*
le calendrier [kalãdrie], *calendar*
la cathédrale [katedral], *cathedral*
la tour [tu:r], *tower*
les vers [vɛ:r], *verse*
dérouler [derule], *to unroll*
je dois [ʒə dwa] (inf. devoir), *I must, I should, I ought*
excuser [ɛkskyze], *to excuse*

patiner [patine], *to skate*
je peux [ʒə pø] (inf. pouvoir), *I can, I may*
prier [prie], *to ask, to pray, to invite*
se rappeler [sə raple], *to recall, to remember*
repasser [rəpase], *to iron*
souri [suri] (p.p. of sourire), *smiled*
venir[2] [vəni:r], *to come*
voir [vwa:r], *to see*
vous voulez dire [vu vule di:r], *you mean*
il y a [ilja], *there is, there are*

embarrassé [ãbarase], *confused, embarrassed*
merveilleux, -se [mɛrvɛjø, mɛrvɛjø:z], *marvelous, wonderful*
spécial [spesjal], *special*
ordinairement [ɔrdinɛr-mã], *ordinarily*
merci bien [mɛrsi bjɛ̃], *thank you very much* (Use person's name or title)
je n'en sais rien du tout [ʒə nã se rjɛ̃ dy tu], *I know nothing at all about it*

[1] En is used with a noun if it is unqualified, i.e., not modified by an adjective.
[2] Very irregular. Use only the infinitive until other forms are given.

Questionnaire

1. Avec qui a parlé Marie-Louise?
2. Qu'est-ce qu'elle a appris?
3. Quand Marie-Louise est rentrée où est-elle allée?
4. Qu'est-ce que la blanchisseuse a dit?
5. Qu'est-ce qu'elle a donné à Marie-Louise?
6. Expliquez le mot *calendrier*.
7. Qu'est-ce qu'il faut savoir pour donner la date?
8. Combien de jours y a-t-il en février?
9. Qu'est-ce que c'est qu'une année bissextile?
10. Combien de jours y a-t-il dans une année ordinaire?
11. Combien de jours y a-t-il au mois de décembre?
12. Récitez les vers que la jeune fille a appris.
13. Donnez la date et l'heure.

Devoir

A. Study this phrase carefully:
   Que voulez-vous dire?

B. Make a list of the months and what we do in each month, following this form: "Au mois de janvier on patine."

C. Explain the difference between il y a and voilà in the following sentences:
1. Dans cette salle il n'y a que trente vitres.
2. Voilà deux vitres.
3. A Strasbourg il y a une belle cathédrale.
4. Voilà la tour espagnole.

D. Use the correct forms of tout in the blanks below:
1. Personne n'a sonné à —— les portes.
2. —— ce groupe est charmé.
3. —— les personnages de ce conte sont fiers.
4. Les jeunes filles vont finir —— leurs études au mois de juillet.
5. Le dernier ouvrier a effacé —— les couleurs.

E. Use these prepositions in sentences:
1. pour
2. à
3. chez
4. près de
5. sur
6. en
7. dans
8. entre

Traduction:

When we arrived home, we found a package. When we opened it, we saw a French calendar. We liked it very much, and we learned the names of all the months. In January there are thirty-one days. In September there are only thirty days, and in February there are only twenty-eight days ordinarily. In leap year there are twenty-nine days in the month of February.

We have learned the names of the months. Now we are going to write the date in French every day.

QUATRE-VINGT-TROISIÈME LEÇON
Les Saisons

Cinq garçons sont assis sur la pelouse devant la maison de Charles. Pour être exact trois garçons sont étendus sur l'herbe et les deux autres sont assis. Tous les cinq parlent du lendemain, le lendemain fatal où il faut rentrer en classe.

—Je préfère l'été, dit Thomas. En été je peux faire tout ce que j'aime faire. Il fait beau. Il fait doux. Il ne fait jamais froid en été. Je peux jouer au golf; je peux nager ou ramer.

—C'est vrai qu'il ne fait pas froid en été, mais il fait quelquefois très chaud. En été nous avons tous les fruits à manger, a murmuré Henri dans l'herbe.

—Ecoutez Henri, dit Jérôme. Il parle, bien entendu, de quelque chose à manger. Mais nous avons aussi des fruits en automne, n'est-ce pas? Moi, je préfère l'automne. En été je suis paresseux. Je ne veux ni travailler ni jouer quand il fait chaud. En automne j'ai beaucoup de force.

—C'est en automne qu'on joue au football, dit Charles.

—Et qu'on rentre en classe, dit Jérôme.

—Vous savez bien que nous sommes ordinairement contents de rentrer en classe, répond Henri.

—Pas tout à fait. C'est difficile, même désagréable pour quelques jours, mais après deux semaines nous sommes accoutumés à la vie scolaire.

—Et aussi je n'aime pas penser aux longues vacances en hiver, continue Thomas. Il fait noir et mauvais. On peut patiner, mais c'est le seul sport en plein air.

—Moi, je suis philosophe, annonce Philippe, qui se relève. J'aime toutes les saisons. J'aime le printemps, l'été, l'automne, et l'hiver. Je suis content de faire des choses différentes au printemps, en été, en automne, et en hiver. Mais il est presque l'heure de dîner. A demain! Je me suis amusé énormément. Nous pourrons (*shall be able*) parler encore demain.

Grammaire

The Verb *Faire*

You have had most of the forms of the present indicative of the verb **faire**, but the forms have been found here and there in different lessons. Familiarize yourself now with the whole of the present tense of this most necessary verb.

Present

je fais, *I make, I do*	nous faisons, *we make, we do*
tu fais, *you make, you do*	vous faites, *you make, you do*
il fait, *he makes, he does*	ils font, *they make, they do*

The third person singular of **faire** is used in a group of idiomatic expressions. See if you can label this group[1] by saying, "**Il fait** is used in expressions of . . ."

Il fait froid. *It is cold.*	Il fait noir. *It is dark.*
Il fait chaud. *It is hot.*	Il fait clair. *It is bright.*
Il fait frais. *It is cool.*	Il fait mauvais. *It is disagreeable.*
Il fait doux. *It is mild.*	Il fait beau. *It is pleasant (weather).*

[1] Notice that the group is arranged in a series of opposites. Learn the opposites in groups of two.

The Seasons

Here are the names of the four seasons.   Note that they are all masculine.

le printemps, *spring*   l'automne (m.), *autumn*
l'été (m.), *summer*   l'hiver (m.), *winter*

Observe and learn these prepositional phrases:

au printemps, *in spring*   en automne, *in autumn*
en été, *in summer*   en hiver, *in winter*

The Use of *Jouer à*

The verb **jouer** means *to play*. When used in connection with a game or a sport, the verb takes **à** or a contracted form of **à**+the article before the name of the sport:

Je joue au golf. *I play golf.*
Je joue à la balle. *I play ball.*
Je joue aux cartes. *I play cards.*

Vocabulaire

l'automne [loton] (m.), *autumn*
l'hiver [livɛːr] (m.), *winter*
la pelouse [pluːz], *lawn*
le printemps [prɛ̃tɑ̃], *spring*
le sport [spɔːr], *sport*
Jérôme [ʒeroːm], *Jerome*
Thomas [tɔma], *Thomas*
murmurer [myrmyre], *to murmur*
ramer [rame], *to row*
se relever [sə rəlve], *to get up, to rise again*

accoutumé [akutyme], *accustomed*
désagréable [dezagreabl], *disagreeable*
énergique [enerʒik], *energetic*
étendu [etɑ̃dy], *stretched out*
fatal [fatal], *fatal*
frais, fraîche [frɛ, frɛːʃ], *fresh, cool*
paresseux, -se [paresø, paresøːz], *lazy, idle*

philosophe [filɔzɔf], *philosophical*
scolaire [skɔlɛːr], *academic*
en plein air [ɑ̃ plɛ̃ nɛːr], *out of doors*
même [mɛːm], *even*
où [u], *when* (after a word indicating time)
avoir beaucoup de force [avwaːr bokud fɔrs], *to be strong, to be energetic*
bien entendu [bjɛ̃ nɑ̃tɑ̃dy], *of course, naturally*

Questionnaire

1. Où se trouvent les cinq garçons?
2. Qu'est-ce qu'ils discutent?
3. Quel temps fait-il en été?[1]
4. Qu'est-ce qu'on fait en été?
5. Pourquoi Henri aime-t-il l'été?
6. Pourquoi Jérôme préfère-t-il l'automne?
7. Joue-t-on au football en été? Pourquoi pas?
8. Est-il difficile de rentrer en classe après les vacances?
9. Pourquoi Thomas n'aime-t-il pas l'idée des vacances en hiver?
10. Pourquoi Philippe est-il content de toutes les saisons?
11. Pourquoi part-il?
12. Quelle saison préférez-vous?
13. Nommez les quatre saisons.

[1] *What kind of weather do we have in summer?*

Devoir

A. *Drill on* [y]. *Find in "Les Saisons" and pronounce five words in which the letter* **u** *appears.*

B. *Write a list of the twelve months, dividing them into four groups. Label each group with the name of a season.*

C. *Conjugate these sentences:*
   1. Je ne fais pas attention.
   2. Je me rappelle[1] ces yeux.
   3. Je finis presque tout le poisson.
   4. Je descends la rue jusqu'à la boutique.
   5. Je suis parti de bonne heure.

D. *Conjugate 1, 2, 3, of C in the past indefinite.*

E. *Use these partitive forms in sentences:*

du	de la	pas de
de l'	des	en (*pronoun*)

Traduction:

(*Three boys speak of the next day.*)

Thomas: I don't like to go back to school. I like (*the*) vacation. I like to stay out of doors.

Charles: I like to play golf and tennis, but if it is cold, I don't have a good time (**s'amuser**) in the park. After two weeks we are accustomed to classes. We have (*the*) afternoons and (*the*) Saturdays for sport.

Thomas: We really like to go back to school because we see (*there*) all our friends. We like to meet them and speak of (*the*) vacation. We have a good time at school. In the winter when it is dark and cold and disagreeable, we are glad (**content**) to go there. We need to study.

[1] A form of **se rappeler.** To prevent a succession of mute syllables within a word the l is doubled before a mute **e.** This verb is conjugated like **appeler.**

Yvon, Paris

APPLE-BLOSSOMS IN NORMANDY
The cows are very small

QUATRE-VINGT-QUATRIÈME LEÇON*

Les Affiches

Alice est allée à la bibliothèque chercher un livre. Il a fallu chercher le numéro dans le catalogue. Il est fatigant de regarder ces cartes blanches, et Alice a regardé le mur d'en face. Elle a vu, un peu à gauche, quatre grandes affiches des chemins de fer de la France.

Alice oublie la bibliothèque. Elle est charmée par ces quatre affiches, qui suggèrent les quatre saisons et les quatre parties de la France. Dans la première on voit une belle route de Normandie. C'est le printemps. Le long de la route on voit des pommiers fleuris. Qu'il fait beau au printemps!

La deuxième affiche montre la Bretagne. C'est évidemment l'été, parce que les arbres sont verts. On voit dans la baie les petits bateaux à voiles. La mer est bleue. Beaucoup de personnes vont en Bretagne en été. Quand il fait chaud à Paris, il fait frais en Bretagne. Si quelquefois il fait un peu chaud, on peut se baigner dans la mer.

La troisième affiche représente Paris. C'est l'automne. Il fait assez sombre. Il fait froid aussi. Quelques feuilles restent sur les branches. On les voit dessinées sur un ciel gris. La cathédrale de Notre-Dame se dessine grise sur ce ciel gris. Il fait mauvais en automne, mais tout le monde rentre à Paris pour retourner à son travail.

La quatrième affiche est peut-être la plus belle. C'est une affiche qui annonce les sports d'hiver à Chamonix. Qu'il y fait froid! Regardez le Mont-Blanc qui se dresse couvert de neige. Toutes les autres montagnes sont blanches, parce qu'en hiver même les petites montagnes sont d'ordinaire couvertes de neige. Il y a tant de monde qui va à Chamonix pour les sports d'hiver. Qu'il fait beau dans les Alpes!

* Note to the Teacher: There is no new grammatical point developed in this lesson. The time in class ordinarily spent in the development of a new point may be used either for drill or for beginning or continuing an acquaintance with the map of France. The vocabulary of the lesson should offer the pupil little difficulty.

Vocabulaire

l'affiche [lafiʃ] (f.), *placard, poster*

la baie [bɛ], *bay*

le bateau [lə bato], *boat;* le bateau à voile [bato a vwal], *sailboat*

le catalogue [katalɔg], *catalogue*

le devoir [dəvwaːr], *duty, work*

la feuille [fœːj], *leaf*

la mer [mɛːr], *sea*

la montagne [mõtaɲ], *mountain*

le mur [myːr], *wall*

la neige [nɛːʒ], *snow*

le pommier [pɔmje], *apple-tree*

la route [rut], *road*

les Alpes [lezalp] (f. pl.), *Alps Mts.*

la Bretagne [brətaɲ], *Brittany*

Chamonix [ʃamɔni], *Chamonix*

le Mont-Blanc [mõ blõ], *Mont Blanc*

la Normandie [nɔrmãdi], *Normandy*

Notre-Dame [nɔtr dam], *Notre Dame Cathedral*

couvert [kuvɛːr] (p.p. of couvrir), *covered*

dessiner [desine], *to draw*

se dessiner [sə desine], *to stand out*

se dresser [sə drɛse], *to rise, to stand*

il a fallu [il a faly] (past indefinite of il faut, inf falloir), *it was necessary*

suggérer [sygʒɛre], *to suggest*

fatigant [fatigã], *tiring*

fleuri [flœri], *in bloom*

sombre [sõːbr], *dark, gloomy*

en face [ã fas], *opposite*

le long de [lə lõ də], *all along*

Questionnaire

1. Où est-ce qu'Alice a vu ces affiches?
2. Pourquoi oublie-t-elle la bibliothèque et le livre?
3. Qu'est-ce que les quatre affiches suggèrent?
4. Dans quelle saison faut-il voir la Normandie?
5. Que voit-on le long de la route?
6. Pourquoi va-t-on en Bretagne en été?
7. Que voit-on dans la baie?
8. En quelle saison sommes-nous dans la troisième affiche?
9. Quelle cathédrale s'y trouve?
10. Pourquoi rentre-t-on à Paris en automne?
11. Quel temps y fait-il?
12. Mentionnez une haute montagne.
13. De quoi est-elle couverte?
14. Pourquoi va-t-on à Chamonix en hiver?
15. Quel temps y fait-il?

Devoir*

A. Change to the correct verb-forms:

1. (Repasser) ces lignes.
2. Je (trouver) la faute la semaine dernière.
3. Nous ne (être) pas paresseux.
4. Le lendemain ils vont (annoncer) le résultat.
5. Elle (partir) pour Boston lundi dernier dans l'autobus.
6. (Se mettre) près de votre amie gracieuse.
7. Vous (faire) toujours attention.
8. Maintenant il (savoir) sa leçon.
9. (Savoir) -ils le reste?
10. Il (voir) les bateaux sur le lac.
11. L'année dernière il (voir) les mêmes bâtiments.
12. Voilà pourquoi nous (s'amuser) chez vous hier soir.
13. Vous (mettre) cette robe de crêpe hier.
14. Ils (aller) à la campagne en été pour (se reposer).
15. Assurément elles (finir) d'examiner les lettres hier matin.

B. Substitute pronouns for the italicized words:

1. *La petite bête* a été blessée par la corde, assurément.
2. *Les poissons enfilés à la corde* sont tombés *sous la glace*.
3. *Les lapins* ont des queues très courtes et des poils soyeux.
4. Dans le récit la veuve pleure *son mari*.
5. *La cuisinière* a glissé *un morceau de fromage grillé* dedans.
6. *Le pain grillé* est tentant.
7. *La femme de ménage* n'a fait que le ménage.
8. La blanchisseuse a mis *des bas sans trous* dans mon tiroir.

Traduction:

We admire these posters. I prefer the poster which shows Mont Blanc in the winter. The mountains are covered with snow. It is cold and clear. In Brittany it is cool in summer when it is hot in Paris.

Note to the Teacher: As an alternative to some part of the lesson or for written work, allow the pupils to make sketches suggested by the four posters described in the text or posters in the classroom. Have them label these sketches or diagrams in French. French railway posters may be secured at small cost from the Office français du tourisme, 4 East Fifty-second Street, New York.

MONT BLANC   "L' Illustration," Paris

QUATRE-VINGT-CINQUIÈME LEÇON
Les Trains

La tante Héloïse est arrivée chez les Robert[1] cet après-midi. Tout le monde est enchanté, et tout le monde veut l'entendre parler, mais personne ne l'écoute. La mère, le père, et les enfants parlent. Ils veulent exprimer leur plaisir. Alors (*therefore*) ils parlent.

Mais après dîner Charles veut entendre quelque chose sur la France.

Il demande à sa tante de lui raconter une histoire.

—Je veux bien, répond la tante. Qu'est-ce que vous voulez?

—Nous voulons une histoire de locomotive, répond vite le petit Jean.

—Je vais vous parler des chemins de fer français, mais ce n'est pas une histoire, explique la tante.

—Les locomotives, pour la plupart, ne sont pas grandes. J'en ai vu de grandes, mais pas souvent. Mais ces petites locomotives tirent beaucoup de wagons. Vous avez vu des photographies de ces wagons divisés en compartiments, n'est-ce pas? Chaque compartiment a une portière. Les wagons pour les longs voyages sont les wagons à couloir. Les couloirs ne se trouvent pas au milieu des wagons comme chez nous. Ils se trouvent à l'extérieur des compartiments.

—N'est-ce pas qu'il y a beaucoup de portes dans ce couloir? demande Charles.

—Oui, il y a une portière pour chaque compartiment. Si vous ne voulez pas rester assis dans le compartiment, vous vous mettez dans le couloir pour voir le paysage. Souvent les messieurs fument dans ce couloir.

Dans un compartiment il y a six ou huit places—six places en première et huit places en deuxième. Les places de coin sont très confortables, et il faut réserver ces places d'avance.

[1] Observe that in the plural of a family name, only the article is pluralized. The noun remains unchanged.

Il y a trois classes dans presque tous les trains: la première, la deuxième, et la troisième. Beaucoup de personnes voyagent en deuxième, mais les places en première sont plus confortables, et il n'y a que *(there are only)* six personnes dans un compartiment.

En troisième, vous êtes assis sur des bancs en bois. Il n'y a pas de ressorts, pas de coussins, dedans en général.

—C'est plus confortable de voyager ici? demande la mère.

—Oui, plus confortable, mais cela coûte plus cher *(more)*.

Grammaire

The Verb *Vouloir*

The verb **vouloir**, *to wish, to want,* is so important and so irregular that it demands special consideration. Its past participle is **voulu**. Learn each form.

vouloir, *present tense*

je veux ce livre	nous voulons ce livre
tu veux ce livre	vous voulez ce livre
il veut ce livre	ils veulent ce livre

Review of the Plural of Nouns

For most nouns: Singular form+s=plural. Examples: la classe+s=les classes; le train+s=les trains.

For most nouns ending in **u**: Singular form+x=plural. Examples: le milieu+x=les milieux; le bateau+x=les bateaux.

For most nouns ending in **al**: Singular form minus al+aux=plural. Example: le cheval minus al+aux=les chevaux.

For nouns ending in **s, z,** *or* **x**: Singular form=plural form. Examples: le bas, les bas; la voix, les voix; le nez, les nez.

SUMMARY

To form the plural most nouns add **s** to the singular.

Exceptions: Most nouns ending in **u** in the singular add **x** to form the plural. Most nouns ending in **al** drop the **al** and add **aux**. A noun ending in **s** or **x** does not change for the plural.

Vocabulaire

le compartiment [kõpartimã], *compartment*

le couloir [kulwaːr], *aisle (of a train), narrow corridor*

le ooussin [kusẽ], *cushion*

le milieu [miljø], *middle*

le paysage [peizaːʒ], *landscape*

la photographie [fotografi], *photograph*

la plupart [plypaːr], *most part;* **pour la plupart**, *for the most part*

la portière [portjɛːr], *small door*

le ressort [rəsɔːr], *spring (used in upholstery)*

la valise [valiːz], *valise, traveling bag*

le voyage [vwajaːʒ], *trip, journey, traveling*

le wagon [vagõ], *railroad car, coach*

Héloïse [eloiːz], *Eloise*

coûter [kute], *to cost*

exprimer [ɛksprime], *to express*

fumer [fyme], *to smoke*

réserver [rezɛrve], *to reserve*

se trouver [sə truve], *to be, to be found*

vouloir [vulwaːr], *to wish, to want*

je veux bien [ʒə vø bjẽ], *willingly*

déchiré [deʃire], *torn*

divisé [divize], *divided*

énorme [enɔrm], *enormous*

d'avance [davãːs], *in advance*

Questionnaire

1. Qui est-ce que tout le monde veut entendre?
2. Pourquoi est-ce que tout le monde parle quand la tante Héloïse est chez les Robert?
3. Qu'est-ce que Charles demande après le dîner?
4. Pourquoi le petit Jean demande-t-il une histoire de locomotive?
5. Qu'est-ce que les locomotives tirent?
6. Comment sont les wagons d'un train français?
7. Où se trouve le couloir dans un train français?
8. Où fument souvent les messieurs?
9. Combien de places y a-t-il dans un compartiment de première classe?
10. Pourquoi faut-il réserver les places de coin d'avance?
11. Pourquoi les places en troisième ne sont-elles pas confortables?
12. Dans un wagon où aimez-vous vous mettre?
13. Quand préférez-vous voyager?

Devoir

A. Practice for perfect pronunciation:

Il y a trois classes dans presque tous les trains. Beaucoup de personnes voyagent en deuxième, mais les places en première sont plus confortables, et il n'y a que six personnes dans un compartiment. Ce système est bon.

B. Supply the correct form of à or de+ the article in each blank below:

1. Nous allons —— *Etats-Unis.*
2. Ils veulent réserver —— billets d'avance.
3. Le dimanche elle est allée —— *église* pour apporter —— *fleurs.*
4. Ils sont sortis à six heures exactes acheter —— *œufs.*
5. Vous avez vu plusieurs cartes —— jour.
6. Il n'y a pas —— *chats* ici.
7. Le monsieur a joué —— golf.
8. C'est l'horloge —— église.
9. Nous jouons —— balle.
10. Il fait froid —— Canada.

C. Write sentences 1, 3, 4, and 6 of B, using pronouns to replace the italicized phrases.

D. In the following sentences use the correct forms of the words in parentheses:

1. La pomme est (gros).
2. C'est le (même) cadeau.
3. Elles sont (déchiré).
4. (Ce) (oiseau) sont (bleu).
5. Ses (poulets) ne sont pas (cher).
6. Leurs (nez) sont énormes.
7. Cette partie est (irrégulier).
8. Cette femme est (exigeant).

E. Conjugate this sentence. Be sure to change the possessive adjective.

Je veux mon mouchoir.

Traduction:

There are two women in the car. They do not want to open the window. When a window is open, they are always cold. It is hot in the car. I want some air. I stand (*place myself*) in the corridor. I see another man in the corridor. We wish to talk. He wants to place himself beside me, but there is a large valise near me. I go over to this man (*place myself beside this man*). We admire the landscape.

QUATRE-VINGT-SIXIÈME LEÇON

Review

A

1. Name the days of the week in French.

2. Name the divisions of time in a day—*morning*, etc.—in French.

3. Give five idiomatic expressions using **il fait**.

4. Why must we say
Je joue *à* la balle?
Je joue *au* tennis?

5. Name the months of the year.

6. What are the four seasons? Give the preposition used with each.

7. What does **il y a** mean? What is the negative of **il y a**?

8. Give four rules for the formation of the plural in French.

9. Give one example for each rule in 8, trying to get a word not used as an example for the rule in Lesson 85.

10. Count to twenty in French.

11. Count to one hundred by tens.

12. Explain the difference between these sentences:
a. J'ai froid.　b. Il fait froid.

13. Name the subject pronouns.

14. Name the direct-object pronouns.

15. What is the regular position for a pronoun as direct object?

B

I. Conjugate these sentences:

1. Je ne lave jamais la vaisselle.
2. Je veux le remplacer.
3. Je prends l'addition.
4. Je m'applique à l'exercice.
5. Je ne me suis pas ennuyé.

II. Complete these sentences, using one of the idioms with **il fait** *in each case:*

1. On ne nage pas s'il ——.
2. J'ai ouvert la fenêtre parce qu'il —— dans la salle.
3. Levez le store. Il ——.

4. J'ai besoin d'un manteau de fourrure parce qu'il ——.

5. Il ne —— pas —— à Chicago au mois de janvier.

6. En hiver il ne —— pas —— le soir.

7. Nous sommes allés déjeuner au parc parce qu'il —— si ——.

III. Answer, using pronouns for italicized words:

1. Avez-vous vu *la cathédrale?*
2. N'est-ce pas que *la cathédrale* est merveilleuse?
3. Sommes-nous entrés *dans le théâtre* le premier janvier?
4. A-t-il parlé *de la tour?*
5. Voyez-vous *ces affiches?*
6. Ordinairement faut-il chercher *la route* sur la carte?
7. N'aimez-vous pas *les pommes de Normandie?*

IV. Write or give orally the numbers and dates in French:

March 4	February 22	eighty-five
June 30	October 12	fifty
July 14	April 15	fifteen
August 1	eighty	twenty-one

V. Complete these sentences, using the partitive whenever possible:

1. Nous commandons —— poulet, —— laitue, et —— lait.

2. Elle a fait cuire —— pommes et —— tartes toute la matinée.

3. Nous avons —— dents, —— doigts, —— nez, —— oreilles, et —— pieds.

4. Portez-vous —— lunettes?

5. Je n'achète pas grand'chose; seulement —— sel, —— poivre, et —— moutarde.

6. Comme nourriture la jeune fille souffrante a pris —— potage.

7. Quel ennui! Je me suis trompé. Ce sont —— côtelettes.

Yvon, Paris

A NORMAN FARM-HOUSE BUILT LONG AGO

THE FRENCH HOME

There is no French word which takes just the place of our tenderly cherished word *home*. But it is equally important for us to remember that English has no single term which exactly corresponds to the intimate French *foyer*. Two French phrases (*chez soi* and *à la maison*) indicate that one is in his own house, or at home, but the fine shades of meaning that dwell in *foyer* sum up a Frenchman's passionate devotion to his home and its inmates in a way that often seems strange to an English-speaking person.

By the irony of fate, the term "foyer" has come into English usage meaning a spacious and empty public hall through which chance visitors pass. As thus applied, the word brings to mind the brilliant antechambers of French theaters, and, in general, the vaulted lobby of any theater, particularly since movie palaces have adopted the word.

But to the French mind *foyer* no more means this sort of thing than the English word *home* signifies a furnished kitchenette flat, with combination ice-box and oven, and in-a-door bed. The original meaning of *foyer* conveys the true sense of it to Frenchmen. It is the chimney, the hearthstone; the core of domestic life; the place where the family gathers complete in itself, distinct from any other group in this confused and restless world.

So, if we Americans think the French do not know what is meant by "home," the Frenchman is very sure we cannot know what he means by *foyer*. In a land like ours where children are early weaned away from family life by travel, absence at school, visits at summer camps, we are not as likely to love one particular sacred spot where family is all in all and undivided. In a modern world like ours where young people are often allowed to make their own plans without family counsel, we perhaps do not know very much of that close-knit family sense that binds a French home together.

Examples of this French feeling for the family can be realized only by one who lives in France for a season and makes his friends there. Such a one finds that little things which are mere matters of politeness to him take on the character of genuine feeling in France. If at home an acquaintance asks after the health of our family, we feel this is only a careless act of courtesy. But in France this interest in our relatives (even those that have never been seen) is not just a gesture of good manners. It is based rather on the belief that our close kin must be cherished in our minds, as their close relatives are in theirs.

The unity of the family group in France is carried even into the business world. A small dressmaking shop will be run by father and mother, and all the children will have some part in it. In such a case, the father procures patterns and materials, the mother and older daughter do the sewing, and the younger girl, who has studied English at school, discusses prices with the American tourists.

Another interesting phase of family life in France is the endless chain of connections it sets up. If one can claim acquaintance with a distant branch of the family, he is welcomed into all other parts of it. An adventure which recently befell an American illustrates this perfectly.

Just as he was to leave a French town where he had stopped over night, this tourist tore his only coat very badly. It was too early in the morning for the shops to be open; so the American hurried to the flat of a small tailor who lived next door to his hotel. The obliging tailor fell to work at once; his wife turned away from the song bird she was feeding and began to heat the irons that would soon be needed to finish her husband's task. Meanwhile she was full of polite chatter: Where did monsieur come from?

Branger, Paris

INTERIOR OF A PEASANT HOME LIKE THE ONE SHOWN ON PAGE 243

By Ewing Galloway, N. Y.

VILLAGE HOMES OF THRIFTY FRENCH PEOPLE

America? Then of course he spoke Spanish!

Monsieur said regretfully that he hailed from North America, and not from South America, where Spanish was spoken.

Oh, that was a great pity! Herself, she spoke Spanish, in fact she had been in Gibraltar.

So had monsieur, a short time before.

The good wife looked up eagerly. By any chance, had monsieur stayed at the Hôtel de l'Univers?

It so happened that the American had been a guest at that particular hotel, and upon his affirmative answer Madame beamed like the sun, and exclaimed, "That is the hotel my uncle keeps! Oh, how happy we are to be of service to one whom my uncle knows!"

Immediately the tailor's work was interrupted by a cry that the customer was a dear friend of their dear uncle. When the time came to pay the tailor, neither he nor his wife would accept

a cent from the American: Owe! Nonsense, he owed nothing! Was he not the intimate friend of her uncle? Was he not a friend of the family?

And so, to the tourist's great dismay, he found himself paying for the mended coat with thanks instead of money.

This story illustrates as well as anything could the intensity of family feeling in all classes of French people. In this case it completely overcame the thrifty impulse to demand payment, no matter how small, which is characteristic of French tradesmen. Further, the tale also shows how utterly a French family regards itself as a unit. The Gibraltar innkeeper was uncle not of the busy tailor, but of his wife. The tailor worked for nothing, because the uncle of one of his family was the uncle of all of it. The relationship was not a separate fact; it was a family matter, and the husband would have acted just as he did without any urging on the part of his wife.

Many instances could be given to show the intimate knowledge one member of a French family has of all other members. There is the tale of the grandmother who ruled a household of granddaughters with all the airs of an ancient and powerful autocrat. She insisted on reading every letter they wrote or received, and discussing the contents of it, although the youngest of the girls was old enough to be a school teacher and to devote her salary to the expenses of the household. Another tale is of an American boy studying in Paris. He was not succeeding very well, for he found the work he had chosen did not fit in with his ideas as he had hoped it would. So when he got an opportunity to change to another type of effort which seemed more suitable, he gave up what he was doing and switched over to the new line of study. Only after his decision was made, did he write home to tell his parents in America of the change.

On hearing this story, French people condemned the boy's conduct as highly undutiful and even cruel to his parents. They sympathized with the latter because they had not been consulted in a matter as important as the professional future of their son. If such a change had confronted a French youth, he would have laid the whole affair before his father and mother.

In France the most lasting of all human ties is that of parentage, of common blood. For generations the French race has persistently followed this idea of family as a closed corporation, or clan. The family is a unit larger than the mere sum of separate individuals who belong to it—it is an institution, and not just a collection of relatives. All must be sacrificed to its needs, supreme devotion must be paid to it. This fact makes of the French *foyer* a thing sacred and beautiful almost beyond our power to understand.

Keystone View Co., N. Y.

THE COUNTRY HOME OF A WELL-TO-DO FRENCH FAMILY

QUATRE-VINGT-SEPTIÈME LEÇON
Des Fables de La Fontaine

C'est La Fontaine, auteur français du dix-septième siècle, qui a écrit les fables que vous allez lire. Pendant toute sa vie il a composé des fables charmantes. Il a réussi à nous présenter en quelques lignes des personnages de toutes sortes, dont la plupart sont des animaux. Mais il connaît aussi très bien la nature humaine.

Dans toutes ses fables il réunit en général plusieurs personnages afin de nous montrer les divers traits de leur caractère à (*with*) l'aide de quelques mots très précis. Ses fables sont vraiment de petites pièces de théâtre. Il y a des actes et des scènes où on peut suivre les différents personnages qui sont quelquefois forts et quelquefois faibles. Lisez ces fables pour comprendre sa manière d'écrire.

I. Le Loup, la Chèvre, et le Chevreau
(*The Wolf, the Goat, and the Kid*)

La Chèvre, qui a l'habitude de sortir l'après-midi afin de chercher quelque chose à manger, dit à son petit Chevreau d'ouvrir la porte seulement à ceux qui répètent la phrase, "Au diable (*the devil take*) le Loup."

La Chèvre dit ensuite au revoir à son petit Chevreau et se dirige vers la ville. Or, pendant cette conversation le Loup est caché sous les feuilles sous la fenêtre. Il cherche le moyen de pénétrer dans la maison. Le Loup regarde s'en aller la Chèvre; dès qu'il ne peut plus la voir, il s'approche de la porte, frappe doucement, et dit d'une voix charmante:

"Ouvre vite, mon petit, au diable le Loup."

—Tiens, dit le Chevreau. On frappe. Et le petit Chevreau appelle par la fenêtre: C'est bien de dire "au diable le Loup," mais il faut montrer patte blanche aussi.

Bien entendu, les loups n'ont pas les pattes blanches. Le Loup, en colère parce qu'il ne peut saisir le petit Chevreau ni par la porte ni par la fenêtre, se met en route pour le bois. Il garde l'espoir de revenir un autre jour et avec plus de succès.

Cette histoire montre bien qu'il vaut mieux réfléchir avant d'agir.

d'après La Fontaine

II. Perrette et le pot (*jar*) au lait

Perrette porte un pot au lait sur sa jolie tête. Elle va au village pour vendre son lait, et pour y arriver sans accident, elle a mis des souliers simples et une robe courte. Ainsi habillée (*dressed*), elle compte dans sa pensée la somme d'argent qu'elle va recevoir au village.

—C'est bien, dit Perrette. Je vais vendre mon lait à un bon prix. Avec cet argent je peux certainement acheter cent œufs. Je peux élever des poules (*chickens*) autour de la maison. L'argent des poules va me permettre d'acheter un cochon (*pig*). A la fin de l'hiver je peux le vendre au marché. Quel bonheur pour moi! Ce qu'on donne à manger à un cochon ne coûte pas cher (*much*). Il va être gros! Je vais remplacer le cochon par une vache (*cow*) au printemps, et en été je peux mener la vache aux champs. Ah! le bon lait de la vache!

Perrette s'imagine qu'elle est déjà aux champs. Elle saute de joie, et aux mouvements de sa tête le pot au lait tombe. Perrette se rappelle trop tard pour le sauver. Pauvre Perrette! Quel coup pour elle! Elle perd tout!

d'après La Fontaine

III. Le Renard et le Bouc
(*The Fox and the Billy-goat*)

Il fait chaud, et Maître Renard fait une promenade avec son voisin le Bouc. Le pauvre Bouc ne voit pas plus loin que son nez, mais Maître Renard est intelligent et ne manque jamais l'occasion de montrer combien il est supérieur aux autres. Tous les deux ont soif, et pour boire ils sont descendus dans un puits (*well*) qui se trouve près du chemin.

Lorsqu'ils ont fini de boire, le Renard dit au Bouc:—C'est bien de boire de cette eau froide, mais il faut sortir d'ici. Mets tes pieds là et lève la tête. De cette façon, je peux monter sur ton dos et sortir, après quoi je peux certainement trouver le moyen de t'aider.

—J'avoue que tu es intelligent, cher ami, lui répond le Bouc. Tu as toujours des secrets que tu me caches. Tant mieux pour moi! En cas de besoin, tu es toujours là. Je suis faible. Tu es fort. J'ai de la chance (*am lucky*) d'avoir un ami comme toi.

Le Renard sort du puits et y laisse son camarade sans secours et sans espoir d'échapper de ce mauvais lieu sombre. Il exprime ainsi ses pensées au Bouc:

—Tu as le grand défaut, mon cher ami, de toujours croire (*believe*) ce qu'on te dit. Il faut savoir juger toi-même. Il vaut mieux réfléchir avant de faire une telle chose. Il faut toujours considérer la fin avant d'agir. Au revoir, je vais à mes affaires.

Et le Renard abandonne sa victime au fond du puits.

d'après La Fontaine

IV. Le Corbeau et le Renard
(*The Crow and the Fox*)

Maître Corbeau est là sur une branche d'arbre. Il est heureux parce qu'il a trouvé un gros morceau de fromage. Les gros morceaux de fromage ne sont pas faciles à trouver. Il a fallu chercher longtemps. Voilà Maître Renard qui arrive. Le fromage sent si bon. Maître Renard a une idée.

—Tiens, Monsieur Corbeau, lui dit le Renard. Vraiment vous êtes un bel oiseau. Si j'ose le dire, je vous préfère à tous les autres oiseaux du bois. Vous avez des traits de caractère charmants.

Notre personnage dans l'arbre entend avec plaisir ces paroles. Il veut exprimer son bonheur. Il se met à dire "merci"; et le fromage, vous le devinez, n'est-ce pas, tombe par terre. Le Renard saisit vite le beau morceau.

—Tant pis pour vous, lui dit le Renard. C'est bien triste, ce qui est arrivé, mais cette leçon va suffire à vous montrer qu'il vaut mieux réfléchir avant de parler. Tôt ou tard il faut l'apprendre. Je suis sûr que vous allez retenir mes paroles.

d'après La Fontaine

V. La Cigale et la Fourmi

(The Grasshopper and the Ant)

La Cigale, ayant *(having)* chanté
  Tout l'été,
Se trouva fort dépourvue *(unprovided)*
  Quand la bise fut venue.[1]
Pas un seul *(single)* petit morceau
De mouche *(fly)* ou de vermisseau
  (worm).
  Elle alla *(went)* crier famine
  Chez la Fourmi, sa voisine,
  La priant *(begging)* de lui prêter
Quelque grain *(kernels)* pour subsister
  (to get along)
Jusqu'à la saison nouvelle.
  "Je vous paierai *(shall pay)*, lui
  dit-elle

Avant l'août, foi d'animal,[2]
  Intérêt et principal."
La Fourmi n'est pas prêteuse *(lender)*.
C'est là son moindre défaut.[3]
  "Que faisiez-vous *(did you do)* au
  temps *(weather)* chaud?"
Dit-elle à cette emprunteuse
  (borrower).
—Nuit et jour, à tout venant[4]
Je chantais *(sang)*, ne vous déplaise.[5]
—Vous chantiez *(sang)*? J'en suis
  fort aise.[6]
Eh bien, dansez, maintenant.

La Fontaine

[1] *When winter had come.*
[2] *on my faith*
[3] *That is her least fault.*

[4] *for everyone*
[5] *I hope you are not displeased.*
[6] *Very good.*

Vocabulaire

le bonheur [bɔnœːr], *happiness, good fortune*
le trait [trɛ], *feature, trait*
agir [aʒiːr], *to act*
s'en aller [sãnale], *to go away, to go off*
élever [elve], *to raise, to rear*

prêter [prɛte], *to lend*
réunir [reyniːr], *to unite, to collect, to join*
revenir [rəvniːr] *(p.p. revenu), to return, to come back*
il vaut mieux [il vo mjø] *(inf. valoir), it is better*

faible [fɛːbl], *feeble, weak*
afin de [afɛ̃ də], *in order to*
dès que [dɛ kə], *as soon as, when*
tôt [to], *soon, early*
tard [taːr], *late; trop tard* [trɔ taːr], *too late*

English Equivalents

l'acte [lakt] (m.), *act*
l'aide [lɛːd] (f.), *aid, help*
le caractère [karaktɛːr], *character*
la nature [natyːr], *nature*
le personnage [pɛrsɔnaːʒ], *personage, character*
la pièce [pjɛs], *piece, part, play*

le secret [səkrɛ], *secret*
la sorte [sɔrt], *sort, kind*
la victime [viktim], *victim, dupe*
s'approcher de [saprɔʃe də], *to approach, to draw near*
composer [kõpoze], *to compose*

considérer [kõsidere], *to consider*
pénétrer [penetre], *to penetrate*
précis [presi], *precise, exact*
supérieur [syperjœːr], *superior, upper*
certainement [sɛrtɛnmã], *certainly*

QUATRE-VINGT-HUITIÈME LEÇON
Voyage en chemin de fer

—Qu'est-ce que vous voulez aujourd'hui? a demandé tante Héloïse aux deux petits garçons.

—Un voyage! Nous voulons l'histoire d'un voyage en France, ont-ils répondu.

—Bon! Nous voici en taxi, en route pour la gare. Quand nous y arriverons, un porteur en blouse bleue prendra nos bagages. Nous paierons le taxi, et nous chercherons notre porteur et nos bagages. Et voilà, nous entrerons dans la gare. Nous ne chercherons pas le guichet où on prend les billets. Nous les aurons déjà pris. Nous ne chercherons pas la salle d'attente, parce que le train partira dans un quart d'heure. Nous ne chercherons pas le buffet parce que nous aurons pris (*we shall have had*) notre petit déjeuner à l'hôtel de bonne heure.

Nous trouverons la porte qui donne sur le quai. Nous montrerons nos billets à l'employé, et nous donnerons au porteur les billets qui indiquent les numéros des places réservées.

Il cherchera la porte qui donne sur le quai où se trouve notre train. Le voilà—"Direction de Lyon." A côté de l'écriteau est une pendule qui indique l'heure du départ.

Le porteur trouvera facilement nos places. Il montera les bagages, et nous nous installerons dans nos coins. Nous regarderons par la portière. Voilà beaucoup de porteurs qui attendent l'arrivée d'un train. Voilà les employés de chemin de fer. Voilà sans doute le chef de gare.

Nous écouterons quelqu'un qui crie, —En voiture! Nous écouterons les portières qu'on ferme. Nous écouterons la locomotive qui siffle, et tout doucement nous partirons.

Le contrôleur arrivera plus tard (*later*) pour prendre les billets. Il nous laissera une partie du billet pour montrer à la gare où nous descendrons.

Après, nous entendrons une cloche. C'est l'employé qui annonce le déjeuner. Il faudra prendre bientôt les places pour le déjeuner. Si nous demandons trois places, il nous donnera trois billets, et de cette façon nous aurons des places dans le wagon-restaurant.

A. Braunstain, Paris

A SECOND-CLASS CARRIAGE ON A FRENCH RAILWAY TRAIN

Grammaire

The Future Tense

You know how to form and use the present and the past indefinite tenses. Today you are going to add to your knowledge by learning how to form the future tense. You have used the approximate future—*I am going to*, but now you have the real future, corresponding to the English *shall* and *will* forms. The future in French is simple to make and easy to use.

regarder, *to look at*

je regarderai le bateau, *I shall look at the boat*
tu regarderas le bateau, *you will look at the boat*
il regardera le bateau, *he will look at the boat*
nous regarderons le bateau, *we shall look at the boat*
vous regarderez le bateau, *you will look at the boat*
ils regarderont le bateau, *they will look at the boat*

Observe first the stem of the future, and you will see that it is the whole infinitive, **regarder**. Then notice the endings. They are like the present tense of the verb **avoir**. *The infinitive + the endings of the present tense of* **avoir** = *future tense*. This formula holds true with any regular verb.

finir, *to finish*

je finirai, *I shall finish*	nous finirons, *we shall finish*
tu finiras, *you will finish*	vous finirez, *you will finish*
il finira, *he will finish*	ils finiront, *they will finish*

The seeming exception in the third conjugation is a change we should expect. What is the exception? Why should we expect it?

rendre, *to return*

je rendrai le livre, *I shall return the book*
tu rendras le livre, *you will return the book*
il rendra le livre, *he will return the book*
nous rendrons le livre, *we shall return the book*
vous rendrez le livre, *you will return the book*
ils rendront le livre, *they will return the book*

The endings of the future are always the same for all three conjugations.

Singular	Plural
ai	ons
as	ez
a	ont

Even if the verb is irregular, the endings do not change. Learn the first person singular of the future of an irregular verb, and the rest will be easy.

avoir, *to have*

j'aurai, *I shall have*	nous aurons, *we shall have*
tu auras, *you will have*	vous aurez, *you will have*
il aura, *he will have*	ils auront, *they will have*

Vocabulaire

les bagages [baga:ʒ] (m. pl.), *baggage*

le buffet [byfɛ], *restaurant in a station*

le chef de gare [ʃef də ga:r], *station master*

la cloche [klɔʃ], *bell*

le contrôleur [kõtrolœ:r], *conductor, inspector*

le départ [lə depa:r], *departure*

l'écriteau [lekrito] (m.), *sign, bill, poster*

le guichet [giʃɛ], *small window*

le porteur [pɔrtœ:r], *porter*

le quai [ke], *station platform*

la salle d'attente [sal datã:t], *waiting-room*

le wagon-restaurant [vagõ restɔrã], *dining-car*

donner (sur) [dɔne sy:r], *to open (upon), to face*

il faudra [fodra] (future of falloir), *it will be necessary, one must, etc.*

s'installer [sɛ̃stale], *to settle*

obéir [ɔbei:r], *to obey*

nous paierons [nu pɛjrõ] (f. of payer), *we shall pay*

siffler [sifle], *to whistle, to whistle to*

réservé [rezɛrve], *reserved*

faire un voyage [fɛːr œ̃ vwaja:ʒ], *to take a trip*

Direction de Lyon [dirɛksjõ də ljõ], *for Lyons, a city in southern France*

en voiture! [ã vwaty:r], *all aboard!*

sans doute [sã dut], *without doubt, undoubtedly*

Questionnaire

1. Pourquoi les deux garçons veulent-ils l'histoire d'un voyage en France?
2. Qui prendra les bagages à la gare?
3. Pourquoi ne chercherons-nous pas la salle d'attente?
4. Aurons-nous des billets?
5. Quelle porte chercherons-nous?
6. Pourquoi donnerons-nous les billets au porteur?
7. Qu'est-ce qui indique l'heure de départ du train?
8. Qu'est-ce que le groupe de porteurs attend?
9. Qu'est-ce que nous entendrons?
10. Comment dit-on "All aboard"?
11. Pourquoi le contrôleur laissera-t-il une partie du billet?
12. Pour entrer dans le wagon-restaurant qu'est-ce qu'il faudra avoir?

Devoir

A. Change the verbs to the future:

1. Il répond au chef de gare.
2. Nous ne partons qu'à midi.
3. Le train siffle avant son départ.
4. J'ai deux œufs.
5. Vous vous installez sur le sofa.
6. Ils gagnent leur vie.
7. Le chien obéit à son maître.
8. Je laisse tout en ordre.
9. Elles ne montrent pas les valises.
10. Ils mettent leur travail de côté.

B. Conjugate these sentences:

1. Je vendrai mes terres. (*I shall sell my land.*)
2. J'aurai un congé.

C. Use these expressions in sentences or in a connected paragraph:

1. en été
2. il fait frais
3. donner sur
4. les vacances
5. s'amuser
6. avoir chaud

Traduction:

We shall be cold if we go to the park today. Even the boys will not have a good time, because they will be cold.

In summer we shall like to play tennis in the park. We shall not be cold then. This boy will play with us. We shall return home on the bus. We shall look at the lake. There will be many people on the shore. There will be many automobiles, too.

QUATRE-VINGT-NEUVIÈME LEÇON

La Poste

Je ne vais pas souvent à la poste à Paris, parce qu'il y a partout dans la ville des boîtes aux lettres. Mais aujourd'hui j'irai à la poste parce que j'ai un colis à envoyer. C'est-à-dire, j'irai à un bureau des Postes et Télégraphes, et j'irai de bonne heure.

Je trouverai sans peine ce bureau, parce que je chercherai l'écriteau "Bureau National des Postes et Télégraphes." J'entrerai dans le bureau de poste. J'y trouverai beaucoup de guichets, un employé derrière chaque guichet. Je lirai les écriteaux au-dessus des guichets—

"Poste-Restante." Non, ce n'est pas ce guichet, parce que "poste restante" veut dire "General Delivery." "Vente de Timbres."—Non, je ne sais pas combien de timbres il faudra pour le colis. "Poste Recommandée." Voilà le guichet où j'irai.

Une fois j'y suis allée, et j'ai donné mon colis à l'employée. Elle l'a pesé et elle m'a dit "vingt-quatre francs." J'ai pensé que ce colis était (was) trop léger pour exiger tant de timbres. C'était (it was) un colis pour une amie de Bordeaux.

—Je me suis trompée, mademoiselle, a dit l'employée. Ce colis n'est pas pour l'étranger.[1] Alors de cette façon il ne faut que sept francs.

Le facteur apporte les lettres à la maison. Il est habillé de noir. Comme les facteurs chez nous[2] il porte les lettres dans un sac. On est toujours content de voir le facteur.

Grammaire

The Future Tense

What is the radical for the future tense? What are the endings? How is it translated in English? The future of two irregular verbs is given below. The first person singular is the one to learn. The other forms follow:

aller, *to go*

j'irai, *I shall go*
tu iras, *you will go*
il ira, *he will go*
nous irons, *we shall go*
vous irez, *you will go*
ils iront, *they will go*

être, *to be*

je serai, *I shall be*
tu seras, *you will be*
il sera, *he will be*
nous serons, *we shall be*
vous serez, *you will be*
ils seront, *they will be*

Vocabulaire

la boîte aux lettres [bwaːt o lɛtr], *letter-box*
le colis [kɔli], *package*
le facteur [faktœːr], *postman*
le franc [frɑ̃], *franc (value about four cents)*
la poste [pɔst], *post-office, post*

Postes et Télégraphes[3] [pɔst e telegraf], *post and telegraph office*
la poste recommandée [pɔst rəkɔmɑ̃de], *registered mail*
la poste restante [pɔst rɛstɑ̃ːt], *general delivery*
la vente [vɑ̃ːt], *sale*

envoyer [ɑ̃vwaje], *to send, to send away*
exiger [egziʒe], *to require, to need*
offrir [ɔfriːr] (p.p. offert), *to offer*
peser [pəze], *to weigh*
vider [vide], *to empty*
au-dessus [odsy], *above*

[1] *for a foreign country.*
[2] i.e., in the United States.
[3] They are always together in France.

Questionnaire

1. Pourquoi n'allez-vous pas souvent à la poste à Paris?
2. Pourquoi irez-vous à la poste ce matin?
3. Pourquoi trouverez-vous ce bureau sans difficulté?
4. Quand vous entrerez dans la poste, qu'est-ce que vous y trouverez?
5. Pourquoi lirez-vous les écriteaux au-dessus de chaque guichet?
6. Pourquoi n'irez-vous pas au guichet, "Vente de timbres?"
7. Pourquoi l'employée a-t-elle dit "Vingt-quatre francs"?
8. S'est-elle trompée?
9. Qu'est-ce que vous avez payé?
10. Qui apporte les lettres à la maison?
11. Où porte-t-on ces lettres?
12. Quel jour est-ce aujourd'hui?
13. Quelle heure est-il?

Devoir

A. *Conjugate these sentences:*

1. Je ne serai pas là.
2. Je rougirai de honte.
3. J'achèterai[1] des bas et des souliers.
4. Je viderai la boîte aux lettres.
5. J'irai à la poste.

B. *Here are expressions which may serve as answers. Write a sentence which might logically precede each one. It may be a question. It may be an exclamation.*

1. N'est-ce pas?
2. Merci beaucoup.
3. Je veux bien.
4. Pas du tout.
5. Bien sûr.
6. Je n'ai rien.
7. Ni moi non plus.
8. A cause de vous.
9. En plein air.
10. En voiture!

C. *Use a pronoun in the answer to each of these questions, to replace the italicized word or words:*

1. Ont-ils trouvé *les trous?*

2. Avons-nous parlé *de la vente?*
3. Ont-ils vu *l'ennemi?*
4. Elle cherche *Jean et vous,* n'est-ce pas?
5. Elle a parlé *du récit,* n'est-ce pas?
6. Est-ce que la maison a deux *salles de bains?*
7. Allez-vous quelquefois *à la poste?*
8. *Philippe et Madeleine* se sont précipités dehors, n'est-ce pas?
9. *Grand'mère* a-t-elle envoyé *ce colis* pour *Jean et pour moi?*
10. Cherchera-t-il bientôt *son linge propre?*

D. *Give in French:*

1. It is 10:30.
2. It is noon.
3. It is a quarter to eight.
4. It is a quarter after five.
5. It is twelve o'clock.

Composition: Write five questions as different as possible from those in the "Questionnaire" and yet based on "La Poste," or write a dialogue giving the main points of "La Poste."

[1] Observe the accent to prevent a succession of mute syllables.

QUATRE-VINGT-DIXIÈME LEÇON

Une Visite

Quelqu'un a donné un coup de téléphone à maman. Elle rentre au salon et elle dit à tante Héloïse:—Madame Alexandre vient nous rendre visite.

Maman est charmée. Elle aime Madame Alexandre, qui vient lui rendre visite assez souvent. Quelquefois Monsieur et Madame Alexandre viennent ensemble. Les enfants ne les voient pas, parce que quand ils viennent ensemble, ils viennent le soir. C'est-à-dire, après huit heures.

Quand Madame Alexandre arrive, elle embrasse tante Héloïse et maman.

—Je comprends pourquoi vous n'êtes pas venue me voir la semaine dernière, dit Madame Alexandre. C'est parce que votre sœur est chez vous. Quelle joie pour vous de l'avoir auprès de vous pendant deux semaines!

—Je suis charmée de rester ici, a dit tante Héloïse. Avant mon arrivée, j'ai fait des projets de visites, mais maintenant je suis si contente ici que je ne veux pas partir.

—Etes-vous venue par New York? a demandé Madame Alexandre.

—Oui, je suis venue par New York. Je viens toujours par New York, parce que les trains sont bons.

—N'est-ce pas? En été, quand nous revenons de la campagne, nous disons toujours—Je préfère un voyage à New York à ce voyage de Syracuse.

—Mais l'été passé[1] vous êtes revenus en auto, n'est-ce pas? a dit maman. Le trajet est plus intéressant en auto, et on n'a pas d'ennuis.

La bonne a apporté le thé. Les enfants ne sont pas venus. Ils sont restés dans la cuisine avec la bonne. Elle a donné du lait et des biscuits aux garçons. Ils ont bu le lait.

Quand Madame Alexandre est partie, elle a dit—N'oubliez pas. C'est pour vendredi. Je vous prie de venir.

—Oui, chère madame, nous viendrons vendredi sans faute, a répondu maman. Nous serons enchantées de venir.

Grammaire

The Verb *Venir*

In this lesson you find a verb which has been constantly lacking in your work until now, the verb **venir,** *to come.* It is difficult to write or speak without using this verb. Observe that it can be added to the list of verbs conjugated with **être.**

venir, *to come*

PRESENT TENSE

je viens, *I come*
tu viens, *you come*
il vient, *he comes*

nous venons, *we come*
vous venez, *you come*
ils viennent, *they come*

PAST INDEFINITE

je suis venu (e), *I came*
tu es venu (e), *you came*
il est venu, *he came*
elle est venue, *she came*

nous sommes venus (es), *we came*
vous êtes venu (s) (e) (es), *you came*
ils sont venus, *they came*
elles sont venues, *they came*

[1] *last summer*

All verbs derived from **venir** are also conjugated with **être**. Find one, in "Une Visite," on the preceding page.

FUTURE

je viendrai, *I shall come*	nous viendrons, *we shall come*
tu viendras, *you will come*	vous viendrez, *you will come*
il viendra, *he will come*	ils viendront, *they will come*

Vocabulaire

l'antichambre [lɑ̃tiʃɑ̃:br] (f.), *entrance-hall, reception-room*

le trajet [traʒɛ], *route, trip* (usually shorter than is implied by **voyage**)

la visite [vizit], *visit;* **rendre visite** [rɑ̃:dr vizit], *to visit*

venir [vəni:r], *to come*

assez souvent [ase suvɑ̃], *fairly often, often enough*

auprès de[1] [oprɛ də], *with, near*

par [pa:r], *by way of, through, by*

sans faute [sɑ̃ fo:t], *without fail*

Questionnaire

1. Qui a donné un coup de téléphone à maman?
2. Pourquoi est-elle charmée?
3. Qui vient assez souvent?
4. Quand viennent Monsieur et Madame Alexandre?
5. Que fait Madame Alexandre quand elle arrive?
6. Quels projets est-ce que tante Héloïse a abandonnés?
7. Pourquoi vient-elle toujours par New York?
8. Qu'est-ce que Madame Alexandre préfère?
9. Comment est-elle revenue l'été passé?
10. Qu'est-ce que la bonne a apporté?
11. Qu'est-ce qu'elle a donné aux garçons?
12. Où iront maman et tante Héloïse, vendredi?
13. Est-ce que les enfants vont les accompagner?

Devoir

A. *Practice aloud the present and future tenses of* **venir.**

B. *Write in the future tense these questions from the "Questionnaire":*
1, 2, 3, 4, 7, 8, 10.

C. *Give five different answers to this question:*
Où allez-vous?

D. *Use the correct form of the present tense of each verb in the following sentences:*
1. Nous (être) prudents.
2. Vous le (faire) parfaitement.
3. Je (mettre) cette robe de soie.
4. Ils (aller) à New York à minuit.
5. Nous (réfléchir) longtemps.
6. Elle (répéter) l'exercice.
7. Ils (avoir) beaucoup de projets.
8. Elle (venir) dans la matinée.
9. (Essayer) un peu de ce poulet.
10. Nous (venir) voir les gilets.

Traduction: Write this paragraph first in the present. Then write it in the future.

He always comes on time. When he enters the house, he puts his hat in the hall. We talk and take tea. Then he leaves. He never stays very long except on Sundays. He earns his living.

[1] The object of this preposition must always be a personal pronoun or a person's name.

QUATRE-VINGT-ONZIÈME LEÇON

Review

A

1. Explain the formation of the future in French.

2. Write the future, underlining the endings, of: **avoir, être,** and **venir.**

3. Are most verbs regular or irregular in the future?

4. Give a list of the personal pronoun direct objects.

5. Give the dates for today and yesterday.

6. Give four rules for the formation of the plural of nouns in French.

7. Write one question on the point which gives you most difficulty in French. (This may be a question which you cannot answer.)

8. What is the position of most adjectives in French?

9. Can you give any exceptions to this rule?

10. What is the rule for the agreement of the past participle of a verb conjugated with **avoir?**

11. Give an example illustrating the rule in 10.

12. What is the rule for the agreement of the past participle of a verb conjugated with **être?**

13. Give an example illustrating the rule in 12.

14. With what auxiliary are reflexive verbs conjugated?

15. How does the past participle of a reflexive verb agree?

B

I. *Use the correct forms of the verbs in each sentence below:*

1. Il (faire) beau hier, mais il ne (faire) pas beau aujourd'hui.

2. Elles ne (aller) pas au guichet aujourd'hui, mais elles (aller) demain.

3. Nous (remplir) le thermos.

4. Ils ne (avoir) pas faim à ce moment, à cause du goûter.

5. Ils (avoir) faim plus tard.

6. Vous ne (venir) pas hier.

7. Il (perdre) toujours ses affaires.

II. *List at least twenty words that you could use in writing about a restaurant.*

III. *Answer negatively:*

1. Avez-vous vu quelque chose?

2. Qui a parlé à trois heures?

3. A-t-elle fait un voyage en France?

4. Aimez-vous dîner dans le wagon-restaurant?

5. Qu'avez-vous?

IV. *Rewrite the third paragraph of Lesson 88, using* **elle** *instead of the pronoun* **nous,** *and making all necessary changes.*

V. *Complete these sentences, using de, du, de la, de l', or des:*

1. Nous avons commandé et dévoré le goûter. Il y a eu —— sandwichs minces.

2. La bonne n'a pas bu —— lait pendant son congé.

3. Je n'ai pas pris grand'chose: seulement —— ragoût, —— sel, —— poivre, et —— laitue.

4. Elle a assez —— potage, et trop —— poulet.

5. Bientôt elle a entendu —— bruit.

6. La cuisinière fait —— tartes.

7. La remplaçante se met à copier —— phrases.

8. La blanchisseuse va venir repasser —— linge.

9. Au milieu du magasin on vend —— coussins.

10. Je ne veux pas —— garçons paresseux ici!

QUATRE-VINGT-DOUZIÈME LEÇON

Boum-Boum

L'enfant est là étendu sur son petit lit blanc. Ses traits sont tirés, et ses yeux semblent immenses sous ses beaux cheveux noirs. La mère vient s'asseoir auprès de son fils malade. Elle essaye de ne pas pleurer, mais comment son âme peut-elle être en paix devant le spectacle de la mort qu'elle croit (*believes*) voir? Son mari, un brave ouvrier, est revenu de son travail, le cœur gros. Un enfant de l'âge de son petit François ne doit pas être malade. Comment le bon Dieu peut-il le laisser souffrir ainsi?

Voilà un mois (*A month ago*) qu'on l'a ramené de l'école, la tête lourde, les mains chaudes. Et depuis ce temps il est là, le regard fixé sur ses petits souliers que la mère a placés dans un coin.

—On peut jeter les souliers, dit l'enfant à voix basse. Petit François ne les mettra plus. Il n'ira plus à l'école. Jamais, jamais.

Les parents, inquiets, l'air grave, réussissent mal (*badly*) à cacher leur peine. L'enfant est si faible. Ils ne se trompent pas; l'enfant est dans un très mauvais état.

Le médecin, âme noble, ne réussit pas non plus à tirer l'enfant de cet état lorsqu'il vient lui rendre visite. Enfin il parle aux parents en ces termes:

—C'est pourtant votre enfant. Vous l'avez élevé, et vous le connaissez mieux que moi. Il va certainement devenir plus faible encore et peut-être mourir. Je ne peux rien promettre. Il ne s'intéresse à rien. Il faudra vite trouver quelque chose qui amuse son esprit si nous voulons éviter tout danger. Il faut agir vite. Alors, cherchez!

Aussitôt après le départ du médecin les parents tâchent de se rappeler ce que l'enfant aimait (*liked*)—les belles promenades, les jardins publics, les animaux. Non, vraiment, il ne s'intéresse à rien. Il refuse tout et reste comme avant. Il ne veut pas vivre. Et pourtant il est si jeune. Il faut trouver quelque chose afin de le sauver. Il faut trouver le secret de son mal. On ne peut plus supporter cet état de choses.

Tout à coup l'enfant lève la main et dit à voix basse:

—Je veux Boum-Boum. Je veux Boum-Boum.

Que signifient ces mots "Boum-Boum?" L'enfant est sans doute perdu. Mais tout à coup le père se met à sourire un peu. Oui, il se rappelle maintenant. Un dimanche il a assisté au cirque (*circus*) avec son fils, et là le petit François a admiré un beau clown en costume rouge et jaune. Chaque fois que le clown faisait un tour (*did a trick*), il prononçait (*pronounced*) un énorme Boum-Boum. Ce clown marchait (*walked*) la tête en bas et les pieds en l'air. Comme le petit François a ri ce jour-là! Ce personnage faisait son bonheur (*delighted him*).

Le père se précipite dehors. Il court aussi vite que possible au cirque demander où demeure le beau clown. On lui donne son adresse et son nom. On n'a pas de temps à perdre. On ne peut pas attendre au lendemain. Pour être tranquille, il vaut mieux y aller tout de suite puisque l'enfant est menacé de mort. Dès que le père se trouve en présence du clown, il tremble, mais M. Moreno, le clown, est charmant.

"BOUM-BOUM, MY DEAR BOUM-BOUM, IT IS YOU!"

—Ah! c'est pour votre enfant malade? Bien sûr. J'accepte avec plaisir. Je viendrai tout de suite. Vous demeurez?

Une demi-heure après il pénètre dans la chambre de François, s'approche de l'enfant, et s'installe à côté du lit. François ne fait pas du tout attention à M. Moreno. Il ne le salue même pas.

—François, voilà ton Boum-Boum. Il faut lui parler, dit la pauvre mère.

—Ce n'est pas Boum-Boum, murmure l'enfant à voix basse, et il tourne le front vers le mur.

—Il a raison, dit M. Moreno. Attendez, je vais revenir. Et il sort de la chambre pour enlever ses vêtements ordinaires.

Un quart d'heure après il rentre de nouveau, cette fois en costume de cirque, un petit bonnet rouge sur la tête, des couleurs aux bras et aux jambes. Il salue l'enfant.

Cette fois l'enfant ouvre de grands yeux et les fixe sur Boum-Boum, la figure éclairée par la joie.

—Boum-Boum, mon cher Boum-Boum, c'est vous. Et il saisit les mains de Boum-Boum.

Quant à la mère et au père, ils pleurent, mais cette fois de joie. Leur enfant va peut-être vivre.

Une semaine après le médecin qui a assisté à ce spectacle permet à l'enfant de se lever. A la prochaine visite de M. Moreno, le père lui demande:

—Qu'est-ce que je vous dois, Monsieur, pour le grand service que vous nous avez rendu? Notre fils va vivre.

—Soyez tranquilles. Rien du tout, mes chers amis, rien du tout, toujours pas d'argent. Pourtant, vous pouvez peut-être m'accorder une chose: c'est-à-dire l'honneur de mettre sur mes cartes de visite (*visiting cards*): Boum-Boum, médecin ordinaire (*family doctor*) du petit François.

d'après Jules Claretie

Vocabulaire

l'âme [lɑːm] (f.), *soul*
Dieu [djø] (m.), *God, Lord*
le médecin [metsɛ̃], *doctor*
la paix [pɛ], *peace*
assister à [asiste a], *to be present at*
demeurer [dəmœre], *to live in or at, to remain*

devenir [dəvniːr] (p.p. devenu), *to become*
souffrir [sufriːr] (p.p. souffert), *to suffer*
tirer [tire], *to draw*
vivre [viːvr] (p.p. vécu), *to live, (to be alive)*

bas, basse [bɑ, bɑːs], *low;*
à voix basse [a vwa bɑːs], *in a low voice*
aussitôt [osito], *immediately*
mieux [mjø], *better*
quant à [kɑ̃ta], *as for*

English Equivalents

l'adresse [ladrɛs] (f.), *address*
l'honneur [lɔnœːr] (m.), *honor*
la présence [prezɑ̃ːs], *presence*

le spectacle [spɛktakl], *spectacle*
accepter [aksɛpte], *to accept*
fixer [fikse], *to fix, to fasten, to set (the day)*

placer [plase], *to place, to put*
promettre [prɔmɛtr] (p.p. promis), *to promise*
immense [imɑ̃ːs], *immense*
noble [nɔbl], *noble*

QUATRE-VINGT-TREIZIÈME LEÇON

Les Paysans français

Les paysans français constituent peut-être la partie la plus importante de la population de la France. Avant la Révolution française, c'est-à-dire, vers la fin du dix-huitième siècle et bien avant encore, cette partie de la population ne possédait (*possessed*) rien, ni terres ni maisons. Les paysans étaient (*were*) des sortes d'esclaves (*slaves*). Ils étaient obligés de travailler la terre pour les seigneurs (*lords*).

Peu à peu les paysans sont devenus plus forts, et ils ont obtenu des morceaux de terre. On trouve souvent des familles de paysans qui habitent la même ferme depuis des années. Aux Etats-Unis nous n'avons pas vraiment une idée très exacte de la façon dont les paysans sont attachés à leur terre. Leur âme est dans leur bout de champ. Ils ont été obligés de tant souffrir pour obtenir quelque chose que (*so that*) posséder un champ est leur plus vif désir.

Ce sentiment est sans doute si fort parce qu'ils ont payé si cher le droit de posséder un morceau de terre.

Et avec le droit de posséder est venu aussi la liberté politique et personnelle. C'est grâce à la Déclaration des Droits de l'Homme (notre "Declaration of Independence") que les paysans français sont devenus libres.

On a raison de considérer les paysans comme une des parties principales de la population. Ils n'ont pas le moindre désir d'abandonner la campagne pour s'en aller à la ville. Leur seul désir c'est de gagner assez pour pouvoir acheter un second ou un troisième bout de terre afin de laisser à leurs enfants une petite ferme qui rapportera assez pour vivre. Ils espèrent produire assez pendant leur vie pour être assurés qu' à leur mort les enfants ne manqueront pas d'avoir chacun une petite terre. Leur bonheur c'est de travailler pour la famille, mais ils veulent aussi que les enfants les aident. Ils travaillent en commun, et ils connaissent tous la fatigue; mais ils acceptent cette fatigue dont ils sont fiers puisque, grâce à elle, ils peuvent (*are able*) produire et vivre.

OXEN AT WORK By Ewing Galloway, N. Y.

Quand ceux qui connaissent la France pensent aux paysans français, ils pensent en (*at the*) même temps à leurs beaux champs de blé (*wheat*), ce blé dont on fait ce bon pain français. En France on met le pain au-dessus de tout, puisque pour les paysans français le pain constitue la partie la plus importante d'un repas.

Les paysans mènent une vie très simple. Ils se lèvent tôt et se couchent tôt aussi. Au printemps et en été on les voit de bonne heure, c'est-à-dire dès que le soleil se lève, conduire leurs bœufs (*oxen*) aux champs. La nuit on garde les bœufs dans la cour de la ferme. La maison des paysans est d'ordinaire une maison basse. C'est dans la grande chambre où il y a du feu qu'on passe le plus de temps, surtout en hiver quand, après le repas du soir, toute la famille est réunie autour de la grande table, sous une seule (*single*) lumière, chacun avec un petit travail. On cause, on raconte les dernières nouvelles du village et des voisins, on raconte toutes sortes d'histoires amusantes, et même on chante quelquefois. On est pénétré d'un sentiment de bonheur puisqu'on est là, à la maison, assis auprès d'un bon feu; on est content de sa journée, et après ce dur travail dans les champs on a l'âme en paix.

La Normandie et La Bretagne

On a envie de croire (*believe*) quand on fait un voyage en Normandie ou en Bretagne que ces deux jolies provinces ont été faites pour notre plaisir et pour notre bonheur. Cela est en partie vrai, mais il ne faut pas croire (*believe*) que la beauté de ces provinces constitue le seul côté qu'on admire. Elles sont très différentes, ces deux provinces.

La Normandie est comme un immense jardin, avec de belles fermes et des routes magnifiques où on peut rouler en voiture et en auto à travers un pays charmant. Le long des routes on voit de petits villages où demeurent les paysans qui travaillent dans les champs. Impossible de ne pas admirer la beauté tranquille de la campagne. On supporte bien mal (badly) le bruit des villes quand on se trouve en présence de cette nature calme. Il faut la voir au printemps toujours si doux si on veut fixer dans son esprit tout son charme (charm). Aussitôt après l'hiver c'est une vraie fête, c'est la nature en fleurs. Dans la partie de la Normandie près de la Seine, des côtes se dressent le long de la rivière (river), pas très hautes, mais juste assez pour protéger (protect) les champs et les maisons du vent froid qui vient souvent de la Bretagne qui se trouve à l'ouest (to the west).

Il fait plus froid en Bretagne, et on y voit moins le soleil à cause de la mer et des vents froids qui viennent jusqu'aux côtes. En hiver il fait sombre, mais l'été y est doux. On trouve des fermes en Bretagne aussi, mais elles sont un peu moins belles que les fermes de la Normandie. On y élève surtout des vaches (cows), de petites vaches qui peuvent vivre de l'herbe des champs. C'est au marché des grandes villes qu'on les envoie pour les vendre.

C'est de la Bretagne que viennent la plupart des marins (sailors) français.

C'est une race très forte, qui accepte la vie telle qu'elle est, bonne ou mauvaise. Les jeunes gens (young men) quittent de bonne heure la maison pour accompagner leur père au loin. Ils passent de longs mois en bateau où malgré le vent et malgré le froid, ils attrapent des poissons. Ils donnent un excellent exemple de courage à ceux qui restent à la maison puisque c'est grâce à leur travail si dur qui semble souvent dépasser toute force humaine qu'ils gagnent leur vie. Le retour à la maison dans leur bateau léger est plein de danger. Le secours leur manque, et ils ont souvent de la chance (are lucky) de rentrer.

Après leur retour c'est une fête préparée d'avance par leurs femmes qui les attend. Tout le village va au bord de la mer pour attendre les bateaux. Quant aux femmes, ce sont des cris de joie qu'elles poussent quand elles voient paraître les bateaux au loin. Leurs maris et leur fils vont revenir, et elles remercient le bon Dieu d'avoir (for having) laissé échapper cette fois encore leurs hommes à la mer en colère, cette mer qui prend souvent des victimes. Pour ceux qui ont assisté à ce spectacle du retour, c'est une scène de joie et de bonheur qui dépasse l'imagination.

Vocabulaire

la **côte** [koːt], *coast, low hill*
le **droit** [drwɑ], *right*
la **ferme** [fɛrm], *farm*
le **vent** [vɑ̃], *wind*
la **voiture** [vwatyːr], *carriage, car*
causer [koze], *to chat, to talk*

dépasser [depɑse], *to exceed, to surpass*
paraître [parɛːtr], *to appear*
produire [prɔdɥiːr], *to produce*
remercier [rəmɛrsje], *to thank*
rouler [rule], *to roll along*

moindre [mwɛ̃ːdr], *least*
malgré [malgre], *in spite of*
au loin [o lwɛ̃], *in the distance, far off*
grâce à [grɑːs a], *thanks to*
peu à peu [pø a pø], *little by little, gradually*

English Equivalents

l'**exemple** [legzɑ̃ːpl] (m.), *example*
la **fatigue** [fatig], *fatigue, weariness*

le **sentiment** [sɑ̃timɑ̃], *sentiment, feeling*
constituer [kɔ̃stitɥe], *to constitute*

posséder [pɔsede], *to possess, to own*
politique [pɔlitik], *political*
second [səgɔ̃], *second*

QUATRE-VINGT-QUATORZIÈME LEÇON

Le Chien Bijou

Trouvez-vous la tante Héloïse ennuyeuse? J'espère que non,[1] parce qu'elle est toujours chez les Robert, et les garçons demandent toujours "une histoire." La tante est enchantée.

Ils ont vu un chien dans une de ses photographies, et ils demandent l'histoire de la petite bête.

—Ce chien s'appelle Bijou.

—Pourquoi s'appelle-t-il Bijou? demande Charles.

—Parce qu'en France on donne souvent aux chiens le nom de Bijou, et aussi parce que cette famille aime le petit chien. Il est blanc et très intelligent. Son poil est très soyeux. Il sait faire beaucoup de tours. Je vous dirai comme il est intelligent. Il sait compter. Quand Suzanne lui dit, "Compte," il compte. Il ne dit pas un, deux, trois; mais il aboie. Il sait compter jusqu'à sept.

Bijou sait aussi jouer à la balle. Suzanne jette la balle dans le jardin, et Bijou court la chercher. Il l'attrape et il la rapporte à Suzanne. Il lui rapporte toujours la balle. Quand Madame jette la balle, il lui rapporte aussi la balle, et elle lui donne du chocolat. Quand il lui rapporte la balle, elle lui donne un morceau de chocolat comme récompense.

—Qui lui apprend ces tours? demande Charles.

C'est Suzanne qui lui apprend ces tours. Son frère va lui donner un autre chien. Elle va apprendre des tours aux deux chiens. Elle va leur apprendre des tours.

—Avez-vous le temps de commencer l'histoire du chat? demande maman. Vous nous avez raconté cette histoire. Je l'ai trouvée très amusante.

—Je vais leur raconter cette histoire plus tard. Maintenant il est presque l'heure de partir pour aller prendre le thé chez Mme. Alexandre. Elle nous attend, et il faut être à l'heure.

Grammaire

The Indirect Object

In English you are constantly using indirect objects. They are nouns or pronouns which receive the benefit or effect of the action of the verb:

I gave her an apple.

The thing you gave away was an apple. To whom did the benefit of receiving the apple go, or to whom was the apple given? (To) *her*. *Her* is the indirect object.

We wrote them a letter.

The thing you wrote was a letter. Who benefited by your writing? The persons represented by *them*. To whom did the letter go? (To) *them*. *Them* is the indirect object.

The French use indirect objects in the same manner that we do. Learn the list of personal pronouns used as indirect objects. Which of them are identical in form with the direct-object pronouns?

[1] *I hope not*

Personal Pronoun Indirect Objects

me, (*to* or *for*) *me*	nous, (*to* or *for*) *us*
te, (*to* or *for*) *you*	vous, (*to* or *for*) *you*
lui, (*to* or *for*) *him, her, it*	leur, (*to* or *for*) *them*

In "Le Chien Bijou," on page 263, pick out all the indirect-object pronouns. What is the position of direct-object pronouns? What is the position of the indirect objects in the story? When you have answered these questions it will be easy for you to make a rule: *When there is only one pronoun object, whether direct or indirect, it immediately precedes the verb.* Observe that the past participle does not agree with the indirect object.

Marie l'a donné à Jeanne.	(*Direct*)	*Mary gave it to Jane.*
Marie lui a donné le livre.	(*Indirect*)	*Mary gave her the book.*

In the following sentences explain the use of the direct and the indirect objects. (See the paragraph above.)

Je lui prête ce livre. *I lend him this book.*
Nous leur avons parlé. *We spoke to them.*
Ils me donnent la boîte. *They give me the box.*
Elle vous répète les vers. *She repeats the verses to you.*

The Future of *Faire*

One more verb whose future you will need is **faire**. Notice both the pronunciation and the spelling of the following forms:

Singular	*Plural*
je ferai [fəre], *I shall do, make*	nous ferons [fərõ], *we shall do, make*
tu feras [fəra], *you will do, make*	vous ferez [fəre], *you will do, make*
il fera [fəra], *he will do, make*	ils feront [fərõ], *they will do, make*

Vocabulaire

Bijou [biʒu], *Bijou* (the name means *jewel*)
le tour [lə tuːr], *trick*

aboyer [abwaje], *to bark, to bay, to yelp*
faire des tours [fɛːr de tuːr], *to do tricks*

s'appeler [saple], *to be named, to be called*

Questionnaire

1. Qu'est-ce que les garçons demandent toujours à tante Héloïse?
2. Qu'est-ce qu'ils ont vu d'intéressant dans une photographie?
3. Comment le chien s'appelle-t-il?
4. Décrivez ce chien.
5. Que fait ce chien?
6. Est-il stupide?
7. Qu'est-ce qu'il sait faire?
8. Qu'est-ce que ce chien fait avec une balle?
9. Quelle est la récompense de Bijou?
10. Qui lui apprend ces tours?
11. Qu'est-ce que Suzanne va faire avec les deux chiens?
12. Préférez-vous les chiens aux chats?

Devoir

A. *Use pronouns instead of the italicized phrases in the following:*

1. Nous lisons le récit *aux enfants.*
2. Je vais donner un coup de téléphone *à Marie.*
3. Gagnez-vous *votre vie?*
4. Parlez-vous *à Marie et à Claire?*
5. J'offre du chocolat *à Bijou.*
6. Il envoie ce colis *à Joséphine et à moi* de bonne heure.
7. Je veux bien donner la carte *aux enfants.*

B. *Give three words formed from the adjective* **quelque.**

C. *Give the negatives of the three words you used in B.*

D. *Write sentences using the negatives of C.*

E. *Conjugate these sentences:*

1. Je le ferai sans peine.
2. Je suis resté auprès de cette dame souffrante.
3. J'ai eu cette difficulté.
4. Je ne suivrai que mon ami.

F. *Write sentences using the partitive article with the following nouns. Some of the sentences should be negative:*

drapeaux	paix
franc	feuille
glace	fourrure
poivre	soie
thé	légumes

Traduction:

When our father came home, he brought us a dog. We asked him to give us a name for the dog. He suggested Bijou. We called the dog Bijou. We bought him a collar (**collier,** m.). He did not like it. He unfastened it (**détacher**). He carried the collar to us. We are teaching him some tricks. He has learned several (*of them*). He devours many large pieces of meat. His food is good.

(*Add three sentences to this translation. Use "Le Chien Bijou" for suggestions.*)

Branger, Paris

A BRETON BAY WHERE FISHING-BOATS ARE SAFELY SHELTERED

CHAMONIX, THE CENTER OF WINTER SPORTS IN FRANCE

FRENCH SPORTS AND AMUSEMENTS

France has no traditional national sport like English cricket or American baseball. The explanation of this lies in the psychology of the French people. A game cannot be popular unless it creates widespread enthusiasm among all classes of society, and the average Frenchman is not deeply interested in the efforts of anyone but himself.

This does not mean that France is quite without sports. The wealthy classes are learning that sports help greatly in the pursuit of elegant leisure; schools are learning that athletic games are both healthful and exhilarating; so the great pastimes of England and America are slowly taking root in French soil. Every boys' *lycée* now has its football team; sporting clubs and athletic societies have organized others. And yet football has no special importance in French schools, as it has in those of the United States. The vast crowds that crash the gates of college bowls and stadia on Saturday afternoons in late autumn remain a mystery to the visiting Frenchman.

No such thing is possible in France. There, games are played between the *lycées* of rival cities, but the crowds at such events are small; and Sunday contests in the towns are attended only by those whose walks lead past the athletic field—they are rarely the object of such walks.

Gymnastic exercises are an important part of the study program in French *lycées*, which also give credit for outdoor games as do our American schools: tennis, for instance, is included in their schedule and is becoming very popular. It is now being played by lower middle-class youth as well as by the wealthy—and the number of public and private courts is rapidly increasing. Golf is still played mainly by the rich and cannot hope to become a poor man's game in France until the present number of public links is multiplied many times. Another pastime that is almost exclusively for the well-to-do is fencing. This is an unfortunate situation, because fencing appeals to the French mind for two reasons: first, it strengthens the muscles, develops their graceful activity, and demands an amazing quickness of eye; second, it is a sport for the single man, with the control of the situation dependent upon individual skill—very different from a mass game like football, where individual prowess is subordinate to the technic of teamwork and group effort.

Hunting, oddly enough, is the pastime that in one modest form or another belongs to all Frenchmen. The moment the open season begins, townsmen as well as country dwellers are to be found oiling their fowling-pieces and studying the likely haunts of small game such as hares, ducks, and partridges. Those whose fortunes permit ride to hounds, a colorful chase in which dogs, horses, and men show their skill in running to bay the fox, and sometimes the stag or boar. Many châteaux maintain their own stocked preserves of game.

It is true that one part of France—the Riviera—tends to give foreigners the impression that the French race is a sporting nation. This is because during the winter months of each year the Azure Coast of southern France is known the world round for its sporting events. But this does not mean the French have become athletes. It only proves them a shrewd race of shop-keepers and hotel-owners who stage tournaments and regattas at their winter resort for the English who flock to the Riviera bringing their sports with them, and for the legions of Americans who follow in their wake. France's part in all this open-air amusement is purely an economic one —to provide the scenery and the equipment. The tourist may join in the babel of tongues in Nice, may spend a fortune for a suite facing the sea at Cannes, or may rent a modest room in some villa at Antibes. But no matter where he stays, all about him are opportunities for outdoor sport of the most vigorous kind: tennis, swimming, golf, motoring, yachting, motor-boat racing, and polo—all in the soft golden air. Although the French recently won the world championship in tennis, few Frenchmen are seen taking advantage of the Riviera playground.

A TYPICAL RIVIERA SCENE

Yvon, Paris

SHRIMPING

There is a distinction between exercise and sport. France has as yet no great interest in the latter, but of exercise alone there is a great deal. Every Frenchman rich or poor walks a great deal. No small town is ever without its promenade. Usually this occupies the site where fortifications or city walls once stood. These have now been leveled and replaced by a broad strolling-ground bordered with shade trees.

Compared with our excessive number of cars, automobiles in France are regarded as articles of luxury. Those who own motor cars, however, may leave town with family and friends for a delightful run in almost any direction, for French roads are excellent. It takes almost no time at all for the city-dweller to reach lovely countrysides in France. Bicycles are the means by which every class of French citizen enjoys these trips into picturesque lanes that lead to places of romantic beauty or of historical interest. Wayside inns appear in most unexpected places, where for a small sum cyclists are served a delicious dinner of local dishes. Many Frenchmen spend their vacation pedaling through the provinces. The railroads favor such cyclists, carrying them and their wheels for a low fare. The hardest spots of uphill riding may thus be avoided without inconvenience.

During the summer months many French families abandon the city to visit mountain resorts or the seashore, where even the poorer people find cheaply-priced lodgings. The French do not go camping for pleasure, since they are not as fond of the out of doors as are Americans and English. Centuries of snug living, and an inherited taste for neat homes, make them regard open-air housekeeping with horror. When at the seashore of course they picnic, swim, go boating, bask in the sun, play tennis—and when the tide recedes, a favorite occupation of French youth is shrimping. Knee-deep at the ocean's edge they stand, and carefully scrape their nets along the sandy bottom until the small mollusks reward their patient effort.

In amusements, as opposed to sports, the theater ranks first. In Paris alone there are a hundred, the most famous of them enjoying government support. Many of excellent reputation have been founded by successful actors and actresses. Here is amusement at every price and for all tastes. The *Comédie Française*, a government theater, produces the great plays of Racine, Corneille, and Molière, thus keeping alive the French classics. Other houses of international fame are the *Odéon*, which is subsidized by the state, and the *Renaissance*, where the best social comedies are staged, the *Vaudeville* and the *Gymnase* which present modern farce, light comedy, and *opéra bouffe*. In the field of music loom the majestic *Opéra*, the *Opéra Comique*, and several impressive concert halls. Throughout France the theater has a large share in the spreading of social reforms. And despite the invasion of the movie, there is no French town of thirty thousand inhabitants or more which does not own its theater and during the season sponsor the production of operas, light operas, classical and modern plays.

Will it come to the reader as a shock of comical surprise to find listed among favorite French amusements that one which interests the Frenchman most, that one in which his nation most excels: Conversation? For centuries this high art of good talking was fostered by the *salon*, that drawing-room conference at which intellectual leaders of France gathered to discuss subjects of literary and artistic interest. This salon has a modern survival in the "at home" of many French households, at which no other entertainment than conversation is provided for the guest. Even French children have learned the art of speaking well, and a conversation with any French person is thus apt to prove a pleasing experience. Whether he be peasant, artisan, or bourgeois, the Frenchman shows invariable taste in the choice of his words, and astonishes the stranger by the correctness of his speech, which is pleasantly free from slang.

THE OPERA, PARIS

Agence Rol, Paris

QUATRE-VINGT-QUINZIÈME LEÇON

Le Chat Minou

Les Français adorent les chats et les chiens. J'aime beaucoup les chiens, mais en général je n'aime pas trop les chats. Mais ce gros chat noir chez les Roger est si intelligent et si beau que je l'aime autant qu'un chien.

Il y a quelques amies de Madame Roger qui détestent les chats. Alors quand Madame a son jour,[1] quand elle reçoit ses amies, elle dit à la cuisinière:

—Gardez Minou dans la cuisine. Je ne le veux pas au salon. La cuisinière répond:

—Je ferai de mon mieux, Madame, mais Madame sait que Minou n'est pas bête. Ce n'est pas un chat ordinaire. Il ne redoute rien.

La cuisinière donne à Minou des miettes tentantes de gâteaux secs. Elle lui en donne beaucoup. Elle lui dit qu'il faudra rester ici. Il ne faudra pas entrer au salon cet après-midi. Elle le lui dit plusieurs fois. La femme de chambre le lui dit aussi, et le chat leur répond. Il comprend, ce chat, je l'avoue.

Quand les amies de Madame arrivent, il entend le bruit au salon. Il sent les bons petits gâteaux faits au beurre. Ils sont pour le goûter. Il veut des gâteaux. La cuisinière lui en a donné, mais pas assez.

Il sort par la porte de service. Il descend l'escalier. Il traverse la cour. Il se met près de la porte de l'appartement. Quand une amie de Madame arrive, il ne lui dit rien, mais quand la porte est ouverte, il se glisse dans l'appartement. Il est dans l'antichambre. Il entend les dames qui parlent. Il ne leur dit rien. Il va tout doucement vers le salon. Oh, les bons gâteaux! Il ne demande pas de gâteaux à ces dames. Il ne leur demande pas de gâteaux. Il attend. Il voit une dame qui a un gâteau. Il s'approche d'elle. Il lui demande très poliment du gâteau. Elle aime les chats. Elle lui en donne un morceau. Il voit une autre dame. Il lui demande aussi du gâteau. Elle déteste les chats. Elle ne lui donne rien.

Madame le voit. Elle lui dit—Tu es méchant. Elle sonne la bonne. La bonne arrive. Elle le porte à la cuisine. Elle lui parle sévèrement. Il ne lui répond pas. Il attend l'occasion de répéter sa visite au salon.

Grammaire

The Position of Pronoun Objects

In Lesson 94 you learned that when there is only one pronoun object we put it before the verb, whether it is direct or indirect. When there are two pronoun objects, we put them both before the verb. There accordingly arises the question of precedence—the question of which goes first.

The diagram on the next page gives the arrangement of pronoun objects before the verb. You will find the position of pronoun objects easy if you remember how this diagram looks. In the past indefinite, pronouns come before **avoir** or **être.**

[1] her day at home, i.e., for entertaining

POSITION OF PRONOUN OBJECTS BEFORE THE VERB

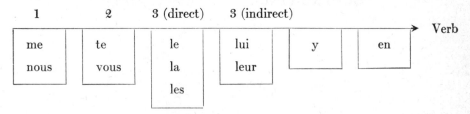

Observe:

A. The first person precedes the second or third and the second precedes the third, regardless of whether they are direct or indirect. The arrangement is 1, 2, 3.

B. When there are two objects in the third person, the direct precedes the indirect. Remember the alphabet—*d* (direct) precedes *i* (indirect).

Apply these simple rules in the examples given below:

Charles me le donne. *Charles gives it to me.*
Charles vous le donne. *Charles gives it to you.*
Charles le lui donne. *Charles gives it to him.*
Charles le lui a donné. *Charles gave it to him.*

Vocabulaire

l'appartement [lapartəmɑ̃] (m.), *suite of rooms, apartment*
la femme de chambre [fam də ʃɑ̃:br], *chambermaid*
le gâteau sec [gɑto sɛk], *cooky*
le jeu [ʒø], *play, game, fun*
la miette [mjɛt], *crumb*

la porte de service [pɔrt də sɛrvis], *back door*
Minou [minu], no English equivalent
détester [detɛste], *to detest*
faire de son mieux [fɛːr də sɔ̃ mjø], *to do one's best*
mériter [merite], *to merit, to deserve*

il reçoit [il rəswa] (inf. **recevoir**), *he receives*
ordinaire [ɔrdinɛːr], *ordinary, usual*
autant que [otɑ̃ kə], *as much as*
poliment [pɔlimɑ̃], *politely*
sévèrement [sevɛrmɑ̃], *severely*

Questionnaire

1. Aimez-vous un chat autant qu'un chien?
2. Pourquoi Madame Roger ne veut-elle pas son chat au salon?
3. Qu'est-ce qu'elle dit à la cuisinière?
4. Qu'est-ce que la cuisinière répond?
5. Pourquoi est-il difficile de garder ce chat dans la cuisine?
6. Qu'est-ce que la cuisinière donne au chat?
7. Qu'est-ce qu'il sent?
8. Où va-t-il?
9. Comment un chat marche-t-il?
10. Pourquoi la première dame lui donne-t-elle du gâteau?
11. Que fait la deuxième?
12. Comment la bonne parle-t-elle à ce chat?
13. Qu'est-ce qu'il attend?
14. Mérite-t-il des gâteaux?
15. Donnez la date en français.
16. Donnez les saisons en français.

Devoir

A. Practice reading the first paragraph of "Le Chat Minou" aloud. Pay special heed to vowel sounds and stress.

B. Change italicized words to pronouns:
1. Il reçoit *l'énorme gâteau.*
2. Nous vous donnons *ces affiches.*
3. J'offre *le gâteau aux porteurs.*
4. Vous pèserez *le colis.*
5. Vous racontez *cette histoire à la femme de ménage belge.*
6. Ils finissent *le jeu.*
7. *Le train* siffle souvent.
8. Je ne mérite pas *cette récompense.*
9. Les enfants rapportent *les œufs.*
10. Elle perd *le paquet sur le quai.*
11. Je vous lis *la carte du jour.*
12. Je vous parle *de l'appartement* dans l'ascenseur.

13. Ils ne nous donnent que trois *pommes.*
14. Vous montrez *la carte à Marie* en classe.

C. Write the first five sentences of B, using pronoun objects, in the past indefinite.

Traduction:

I sent Jane a large (**gros**) package. The postman did not bring it to her. She spoke to him. He said that he had (**avait**) not seen it.

She went to the post-office. She explained the loss (**la perte**) to two employees. She explained it to them. Did she speak to you of it? She spoke to me of it. She also told the story to my mother later. She told it to us in the afternoon.

QUATRE-VINGT-SEIZIÈME LEÇON

Les Agents de police

Parce qu'il a fait beau aujourd'hui, nous avons pu visiter un ancien quartier de Paris. Nous y sommes allés pour voir d'anciens hôtels. Nous en avons vu beaucoup. Quand nous avons fini notre promenade dans ce quartier, nous avons cherché un autobus. Maurice m'a demandé:

—Voyez-vous un autobus ou un taxi?

—Non, Maurice.

Nous avons vu un agent de police. Nous sommes allés lui demander où il faut attendre l'autobus. Nous le lui avons demandé. Les agents de police sont presque toujours polis. Ils sont assez beaux, habillés de bleu foncé avec des képis galonnés et de petites capes bleu foncé. Les agents de police qui sont dans les rues peuvent beaucoup aider les piétons. Ils leur donnent l'occasion de traverser la rue sans danger. Les agents de police portent un bâton blanc. Ils peuvent arrêter les voitures. Quand ils étendent le bâton, les voitures s'arrêtent. Il faut attendre le barrage pour traverser la rue. Les piétons savent cela.

Nous avons attendu le barrage hier. Nous avons demandé à l'agent où il faut prendre l'autobus. Il nous a répondu poliment. Il nous a indiqué le coin. Nous l'avons remercié.

J'ai dit à Maurice:

—Quand j'arriverai chez moi, je pourrai dire que j'ai trouvé les agents de police très gentils. Oui, nous pourrons le dire. Ils sont très polis, et ils aident beaucoup les étrangers.

Grammaire

Position of Pronoun Objects

If necessary, refer to the explanation and diagram in the preceding lesson to answer these questions.

1. What is the rule for the position of pronoun objects?
2. Give a sentence to illustrate the rule.
3. If there are two pronoun objects in the third person, which precedes?
4. Where is the pronoun en always found?
5. In the past indefinite, before which part of the verb do you place the pronouns?

Present, Past Indefinite, and Future Tenses of the Verb *Pouvoir*

Learn the following tenses of another necessary verb, **pouvoir,** *to be able.* You have met various persons of the present. Here you have the whole tense.

PRESENT INDICATIVE

Singular	*Plural*
je peux, *I am able, I can*	nous pouvons, *we are able, we can*
tu peux, *you are able, you can*	vous pouvez, *you are able, you can*
il peut, *he is able, he can*	ils peuvent, *they are able, they can*

PAST INDEFINITE

j'ai pu, *I was able, I could*	nous avons pu, *we were able, we could*
tu as pu, *you were able, you could*	vous avez pu, *you were able, you could*
il a pu, *he was able, he could*	ils ont pu, *they were able, they could*

FUTURE

je pourrai, *I shall be able*	nous pourrons, *we shall be able*
tu pourras, *you will be able*	vous pourrez, *you will be able*
il pourra, *he will be able*	ils pourront, *they will be able*

Vocabulaire

l'agent de police [laʒɑ̃d pɔlis] (m.), *policeman*
le barrage [baraːʒ], *signal* (for the traffic to stop and the pedestrians to cross)
le bleu[1] [blø], *blue*

la cape [kap], *cape*
l'étranger [letrɑ̃ʒe] (m.), *stranger, foreigner*
le képi [kepi], *military cap*
le piéton [pjetõ], *pedestrian*
le quartier [kartje], *district, quarter*

pouvoir [puvwaːr] (p.p. pu), *to be able, can, may*
foncé [fõse], *deep, dark*
galonné [galɔne], *trimmed with gold braid or lace*
habillé [abije], *dressed*
poli [pɔli], *polite*

[1] Names of colors are always masculine.

Questionnaire

1. Où sommes-nous allés?
2. Pourquoi?
3. Après la promenade, qu'avons-nous cherché?
4. Avons-nous vu beaucoup de taxis?
5. Pourquoi sommes-nous allés parler à l'agent de police?
6. Comment sont-ils habillés, les agents de police?
7. Comment peuvent-ils aider les piétons?
8. Qu'est-ce qu'il faut attendre pour traverser la rue?
9. Comment l'agent de police nous a-t-il répondu?

Devoir

A. In "Les Agents de police" change the verbs that are in the past indefinite (except **avons vu**) *to the present.*

B. Answer, using pronouns for the italicized words:

1. Avez-vous demandé *ces renseignements sur l'horloge?*
2. A-t-il pu donner beaucoup *de raisons exactes?*
3. Qui a fait *le changement?*
4. Avez-vous vu *les bâtiments?*
5. Est-ce que les animaux sauvages ont peur *du feu?*
6. Est-ce qu'ils viennent *près du feu?*
7. A-t-il vidé *la boîte aux lettres?*
8. Lui avons-nous parlé *de ce jeu?*

9. Leur a-t-il donné *ce conseil?*
10. Nous ont-ils donné *cette occasion* avant-hier?
11. Y a-t-il *des couloirs* au milieu?
12. Combien coûtent *ces coussins?*
13. Au printemps que font *les garçons?*
14. *Le trajet* a été court, n'est-ce pas?
15. Sait-il faire *des tours?*
16. En a-t-il fait *au parc?*

Composition: Write a dialogue embodying as much of "Les Agents de police" as possible. It might begin as follows:

Jeanne: Regardez cet hôtel là-bas.
Maurice: Il est très ancien, *etc.*

A PARIS POLICEMAN

QUATRE-VINGT-DIX-SEPTIÈME LEÇON

Progress Test

Review

A

1. Write the list of direct-object pronouns.

2. Write the list of indirect-object pronouns.

3. Write the list of object pronouns, showing position and order.

4. Write questions and use these pronoun groups in the answers: **la lui, me le, nous les, le leur.**

5. Give the future tense of these verbs: **avoir, être, faire, pouvoir, aller.**

6. Give ten nouns which indicate parts of the body.

7. Give the rule for the agreement of the past participle of a verb conjugated with **avoir.** Illustrate.

8. Give the rule for the agreement of a verb conjugated with **être.** Illustrate.

9. Give the past participles of the following verbs: **ouvrir, faire, mettre, lire, dire, avoir, être, courir, finir, vendre, boire, pouvoir, vouloir.**

10. What are the contractions of the preposition **à** and the article?

11. What is the use of the word **y**?

12. What is the use of the word **en**?

13. Give three adjectives which do not form their feminine by adding **-e** to the masculine.

14. How is the ordinal numeral formed?

15. Count to one hundred by fives in French.

16. Give in French: *It is twenty minutes to ten.*

17. Name ten words which group themselves around **le train.**

B

I. Answer, using pronouns for direct and indirect objects:

1. Est-ce qu'il écrit le récit à Charles?

2. Est-ce que je vous ai mentionné cette famille?

3. Avez-vous trouvé les bas?

4. Allez-vous remplacer la colonne?

5. Pourquoi ôte-t-il son képi galonné de cette façon?

6. Elle nous a chanté ce morceau, n'est-ce pas?

7. Quand pourrons-nous donner ce paquet aux garçons?

8. Est-ce qu'il a envoyé les aiguilles à sa mère?

II. Conjugate:

1. Je ne peux pas jouer au tennis.

2. Je tâcherai d'y aller.

3. Je me suis levé facilement.

4. Je suis américain.

5. Je gagnerai ma vie.

6. Je viendrai de bonne heure.

III. Change the infinitives to the future tense:

1. Je (être) là demain sans faute.

2. (Indiquer)-il le coin à gauche?

3. Ils (rendre) visite à l'étranger.

4. Nous (avoir) des gâteaux.

5. Vous (finir) l'article bientôt.

6. Il (être) très méchant.

7. Ils (faire) des tours gracieux.

8. Vous (venir) chez nous sans faute.

IV. Review the words in the vocabularies of Lessons 76-96.

QUATRE-VINGT-DIX-HUITIÈME LEÇON

Les Misérables[1]: Première partie

I. Le crime de Jean Valjean

Jean Valjean à l'âge de vingt-neuf ans a volé un pain pour les sept enfants de sa sœur dont le mari était (*had*) mort. Il est arrêté et condamné (*condemned*) à cinq ans de prison. Parce qu'il a essayé plusieurs fois d'échapper de prison, les cinq ans sont devenus dix-neuf ans. Un jour il a entendu ces paroles étranges (*strange*): "Tu es libre." Oui, on lui a donné sa liberté, mais il possède un passeport jaune.[2]

II. Dans la petite ville de Digne

Dans les premiers jours du mois d'octobre de l'année 1815 (dix-huit cent quinze), un homme mal (*badly*) habillé entre à pied dans la petite ville de Digne. Il a l'air sombre. Son visage montre des traits durs. Personne ne le connaît; c'est donc un étranger. Dans la rue principale il tourne à gauche et se dirige aussitôt vers une auberge (*inn*). Dans la grande salle on entend rire et causer. L'aubergiste (*inn-keeper*) au fond de la salle, sans paraître regarder l'homme qui est entré, prépare un bon dîner.

—Que veut monsieur?

—Manger et dormir, répond Jean Valjean. J'ai de l'argent.

L'aubergiste cette fois fixe son regard sur l'homme et lui dit:

—Tenez, assez de paroles, je vous connais. Vous vous appelez Jean Valjean. Il faut quitter ce lieu. Il vaut mieux vous en aller tout de suite; il me faudra appeler les agents de police si vous ne partez pas.

Malgré sa faim et malgré sa fatigue, l'homme sort. Le vent et le froid le font souffrir. Il marche droit devant lui, l'air triste. Il fait encore quelques pas et puis trop fatigué pour continuer son chemin, il se couche par terre dans un endroit obscur près de l'église.

A ce moment-là une vieille femme sort de l'église, s'approche de l'endroit où Jean Valjean est étendu, et lui dit:

—Que faites-vous là, mon ami?

L'homme répond avec colère:

—Vous le voyez, je me couche.

—Il est impossible de passer ainsi la nuit.

—J'ai frappé à toutes les portes.

—Avez-vous frappé à celle-là, là-bas, à côté de l'église?

—Non.

—Frappez-y.

III. Chez l'évêque

Or, ce soir-là, Monsieur l'évêque de Digne est resté assez tard dans sa chambre assis à sa table de travail. Il y a une lampe sur la table. Un assez bon feu est allumé. Un silence tranquille remplit la chambre. Tout à coup on frappe à la porte un coup assez fort.

—Entrez, dit l'évêque d'un ton calme.

Un homme entre. C'est celui que nous avons vu près de l'église. Le feu éclaire le visage de l'évêque, ce beau visage au (*with*) front haut et aux yeux tranquilles.

—Voici, dit l'homme. Je m'appelle

---

[1] Well-known masterpiece of the French writer, Victor Hugo (1802-1885).
[2] A yellow passport indicates that the holder is a former convict.

"I GAVE YOU THE SILVER CANDLESTICKS ALSO."

Jean Valjean. J'ai passé dix-neuf ans en prison. Je meurs de faim et de fatigue, car j'ai marché beaucoup. J'ai de l'argent que j'ai pu gagner en prison. Je payerai. Voulez-vous que je reste?

L'évêque se retourne et dit à Madame Magloire, la servante (*servant*):

—Préparez la table.

L'homme, au lieu d'attendre une réponse, ajoute:

—Tenez, avez-vous compris? J'ai été en prison.

—Madame Magloire, dit l'évêque, dont le visage aux (*with*) traits fins indique une grande paix, préparez un lit.

Peu à peu l'expression sombre et dure de Jean Valjean change.

—Ah! dit-il, vous êtes aubergiste (*inn-keeper*), n'est-ce pas?

—Je suis, dit l'évêque, sans paraître surpris, un prêtre (*priest*) qui demeure ici.

—Vous êtes humain, monsieur. Je vous remercie.

Pendant ce temps Madame Magloire place sur la table deux beaux flambeaux (*candlesticks*) d'argent dont la forme parfaite (*perfect*) fait la joie (*delights*) du vieux prêtre. A côté des assiettes elle met les lourdes cuillères d'argent. L'homme d'un regard rapide les remarque et les juge de grande valeur.

Après le dîner l'évêque offre un des flambeaux à Jean Valjean.

—Vous avez sommeil, sans doute. Je vais vous conduire à votre chambre, lui dit-il.

La maison est ainsi composée que, pour passer dans la petite chambre où doit dormir Jean Valjean, il faut traverser la chambre de l'évêque. Au moment où Jean Valjean traverse cette chambre, Madame Magloire met les cuillères d'argent dans un placard (*cupboard*) qui se trouve près du lit de l'évêque.

Une fois dans la chambre l'homme tombe de fatigue sur ce lit sans même enlever ses vêtements. Vers le milieu de la nuit il se réveille. Quelque chose a changé dans son âme depuis sa jeunesse. Autrefois les sentiments nobles et l'honneur étaient tout pour Jean Valjean; maintenant l'honneur ne compte plus et les beaux sentiments non plus. Il se lève, se glisse doucement dans la chambre de l'évêque, prend les cuillères d'argent, et quitte la maison.

Le lendemain matin Madame Magloire court trouver l'évêque.

—Nos belles cuillères, c'est l'homme qui les a volées, et il est parti!

—Madame Magloire, il y a erreur. Ces cuillères sont aux pauvres. Qui était cet homme? Un pauvre, évidemment.

Quelques instants après on frappe à la porte. Un groupe étrange (*strange*) est là. Trois hommes, des agents de police, tiennent (*hold*) Jean Valjean par les bras.

—Ah! vous voilà, lui dit l'évêque, les yeux fixés sur le visage de Jean Valjean. Je vous ai donné les flambeaux d'argent aussi. Pourquoi ne les avez-vous pas emportés avec les cuillères? Vous en aurez bien pour mille francs.

—Quant à vous, messieurs les agents de police, vous n'avez pas besoin de tenir cet homme puisque vous êtes chargés d'arrêter ceux qui ont volé, et cet homme n'a rien pris. Vous pouvez vous en aller.

Après leur départ, l'évêque offre les flambeaux à Jean Valjean et lui dit à voix basse:

—Jean Valjean, je ne vous reproche rien, mais n'oubliez pas que vous avez promis d'employer cet argent à devenir honnête. Je suis sûr que vous ne tomberez plus en erreur, car c'est votre âme que je vous achète, et je la donne à Dieu.

d'après Victor Hugo

Vocabulaire

l'**évêque** [levɛːk] (*m.*), bishop
le **visage** [vizaːʒ], *face*
arrêter [arɛte], *to arrest, to stop*
je **connais** [kɔnɛ] (inf. **connaître**), *I know* (a person)

je **meurs** [mœːr] (inf. **mourir**), *I am dying; I die*
tenez [tǝne] (pres. imp. of **tenir**), *look here, I say, listen*

tenir [tǝniːr], *to hold, to have, to keep*
fin [fɛ̃], *handsome, fine, clever*
car [kaːr], *for*
au lieu de [o ljø dǝ], *instead of*

English Equivalents

l'**erreur** [lɛrœːr] (f.), *error, mistake*
reprocher [rǝprɔʃe], *to reproach*

honnête [ɔnɛːt], *honest*
obscur [ɔpskyːr], *obscure, dark, not clear*

rapide [rapid], *rapid, quick, fast*

QUATRE-VINGT-DIX-NEUVIÈME LEÇON

Les Misérables : Seconde partie

I. Monsieur Madeleine

Vers la fin de l'année 1815 (dix-huit cent quinze) un homme, un étranger, était (*had*) venu à la petite ville de Montreuil-sur-Mer. Parce que cet homme avait (*had*) sauvé deux enfants du feu, on ne lui a pas demandé son passeport.[1] Depuis ce temps-là il s'appelle le père Madeleine.

Il y a dans la petite ville une seule (*single*) fabrique qui emploie presque tous les ouvriers de la ville. Quand le père Madeleine est arrivé à Montreuil-sur-Mer, il a eu l'idée de changer quelques détails du travail. Cette nouvelle manière de faire a amené des résultats heureux, et les gens de la ville ne savent pas assez remercier celui qui a causé ce changement dans leur vie d'ordinaire si difficile.

Au lieu de réduire leur salaire (*wages*), il peut élever le prix (*amount*) de leur semaine. C'est ainsi que peu à peu les conditions de vie changent, et que tout le monde se trouve dans un état plus heureux (*happier*). En moins de (*less than*) trois ans, le père Madeleine était (*had*) devenu riche (*rich*), ce qui est bien ; et il avait (*had*) tout fait riche autour de lui, ce qui est mieux. Grâce aux changements rapides, Montreuil-sur-Mer est devenu une ville assez importante.

Le père Madeleine fait peu à peu sa fortune, mais il semble penser beaucoup aux autres, chose assez étrange pour un simple homme tel que le père Madeleine. Dans toutes les petites villes on cause beaucoup. En 1820 (dix-huit cent vingt), par exemple, on sait qu'il a placé 600,000 (six cents mille) francs à Paris. La vérité c'est qu'il a réservé plus d'un million pour les pauvres de la ville. Les services de toutes sortes rendus à la ville étaient (*were*) énormes, et on a prié le père Madeleine de devenir maire (*mayor*). Il finit par accepter, et ainsi par degrés le père Madeleine est devenu Monsieur le maire, ce qui (*a fact which*) a causé le bonheur de tout le monde.

Monsieur Madeleine reste aussi simple qu'avant. Il parle peu. Il prend ses repas seul avec un livre devant lui. Il aime les livres, qui sont des amis froids et sûrs. On remarque que ses manières sont plus douces et qu'il parle en termes mieux choisis.

On sait qu'il a toujours les poches pleines quand il sort et qu'il ne lui reste rien quand il rentre. On a l'idée qu'il a vécu (*lived*) autrefois de la vie des champs, car il a toutes sortes de secrets pour les paysans. Le soir il pénètre chez les pauvres gens et y laisse de petites sommes. Quand on veut le remercier, il leur dit doucement :—Taisez-vous, mon ami, ce n'est rien.

Il exerce une excellente influence sur les gens de la ville qui sans ce chef, juste et bon, mèneraient (*would lead*) une vie bien triste. Au lieu de chercher à réduire leur vie, il essaye de les soutenir, de leur offrir le moyen de changer l'état malheureux (*unfortunate*) dans lequel ils vivent (*live*), et tout cela sans la moindre idée de gain (*benefit*) personnel.

[1] See footnote 2, page 276.

JEAN VALJEAN TEACHING COSETTE TO READ

II. Arrêté pour la seconde fois

Quand Jean Valjean a quitté l'évêque de Digne, il a rencontré sur son chemin un petit garçon. Cet enfant assis à côté de Jean Valjean a laissé tomber une pièce de deux francs. Jean Valjean, parce que l'impression causée par l'évêque a été si forte, met son pied sans le savoir sur la pièce et ne fait pas attention aux cris de l'enfant.

L'enfant s'en va (goes off) à la ville raconter son histoire aux gendarmes (police). De nouveau on cherche Jean Valjean pour vol (theft), et on le retrouve plusieurs années après à Montreuil-sur-Mer. Il est arrêté, mais réussit pourtant à échapper de prison; et il revient chercher Cosette une petite fille dont la mère, maintenant morte, a travaillé dans la fabrique de M. Madeleine. Naturellement, il est obligé de disparaître avec l'enfant puisqu'on le cherche toujours.

III. Cosette et Jean Valjean s'installent à Paris

Jean Valjean juge nécessaire de choisir à Paris quelques chambres dans une vieille maison dans une rue obscure où les voitures sont rares. C'est là qu'il porte la petite Cosette, enfant de huit ans, et qu'il commence sa nouvelle vie. Cosette accepte sa vie avec cet homme si bon et ne demande rien. La joie de Jean Valjean dépasse tout espoir, et il considère que la vie lui a accordé une faveur spéciale en lui envoyant (by sending him) cette enfant.

Quelque chose a changé dans l'âme de Jean Valjean. L'évêque lui a montré le chemin de la vertu. Cosette va peut-être l'aider à éviter pour toujours le mal. Jean Valjean passe toute la journée auprès de la petite fille à considérer son visage aux traits si fins et à la regarder jouer. Les jours deviennent (*become*) des semaines.

Un jour Jean Valjean a l'idée d'apprendre à lire à Cosette. Il se rappelle que c'est en prison qu'il a appris à lire dans l'espoir que cela l'aiderait (*would help*) à en échapper plus tôt (*sooner*). La vie, dès qu'il se trouve ainsi occupé avec la petite fille, semble pleine d'intérêt. Des jeux divers et le travail constituent toute sa vie. Jean Valjean et Cosette recommencent avec le même plaisir tous les jours. L'homme n'ose pas croire à tant de bonheur. Dans sa pensée il ne reproche plus rien à personne (*anything to anyone*), car la présence de l'enfant lui cause de la joie et du bonheur. Grâce à Jean Valjean, Cosette peut marcher dans la vie. Grâce à l'enfant, il peut continuer dans la vertu.

d'après Victor Hugo

Vocabulaire

amener [amne], *to bring about, to bring (someone) along*
disparaître [disparɛ:tr], *to disappear*

réduire [redɥi:r] (p.p. **réduit**), *to reduce*
soutenir [sutni:r] (p.p. **soutenu**), *to sustain, to support*

taisez-vous [tɛze vu] (inf. **se taire**), *be quiet, hush, be silent*
lequel [ləkɛl], *which, which one*

English Equivalents

le chef [ʃef], *chief, leader*
la condition [kõdisjõ], *condition, state*
le degré [dəgre], *degree, step*

la faveur [favœ:r], *favor*
le million [miljõ], *million*
la vertu [vɛrty], *virtue*
causer [koze], *to cause*

exercer [egzɛrse], *to exercise*
recommencer [rəkɔmãse], *to begin again*

CENTIÈME LEÇON*
Le Jardin potager

En arrivant dans le jardin potager, Jean trouve le vieux jardinier Christophe en train de planter des pommes de terre. Le jardin potager, situé, derrière la maison au soleil, n'est pas très grand, mais il fournit de bons légumes. Christophe travaille pour la famille Bouchard depuis très longtemps. Il aime beaucoup ses patrons, qui sont bons pour lui. En voyant travailler Christophe, Jean veut l'aider. Le jardinier lui donne un petit sac contenant des graines de radis. Jean plante ces graines sous la direction de Christophe. En travaillant il demande au jardinier s'il est content de son jardin. Christophe répond que ses patrons sont très heureux quand il apporte des pommes de terre, des navets, des choux, des épinards, des carottes, des petits pois, des haricots . . .

—Et des radis, ajoute Jean, en agitant son sac de graines.

Grammaire
The Present Participle

To form the present participle omit only -ons of the first person plural of the present indicative and add -ant. This ending corresponds to the English -ing.

EXAMPLES: parlons − ons + ant = parlant, *talking*
finissons − ons + ant = finissant, *finishing*
répondons − ons + ant = répondant, *answering*

The present participles of être and avoir are étant and ayant.

The present participle is never used in forming a verb tense in French. It may be used independently or with the preposition en, which is the only preposition with which it may be used. En is translated as *on, while, upon, in, by.*

Vocabulaire

la carotte [karɔt], *carrot*
le chou [ʃu] (pl. les choux), *cabbage*
les épinards [le zepina:r] (m. pl.), *spinach*
la graine [grɛ:n], *seed*
les haricots [le ariko] (m. pl.), *beans* (sometimes *kidney-beans*)
le jardin potager [ʒardɛ̃ pɔtaʒe], *vegetable garden, kitchen garden*

le jardinier [ʒardinje], *gardener*
le légume [legym], *vegetable*
le navet [navɛ], *turnip*
le nid [ni], *nest*
le patron [patrɔ̃], *employer*
le pois [pwɑ], *pea*
le radis [radi], *radish*
Christophe [kristɔf], *Christopher*
agiter [aʒite], *to shake, to wave*

fournir [furni:r], *to furnish*
planter [plɑ̃te], *to plant*
contenant [kɔ̃tnɑ̃], *containing*
situé [sitɥe], *placed, situated*
au soleil [o sɔlɛ:j], *in the sunshine*
depuis très longtemps [dəpɥi trɛ lɔ̃tɑ̃], *for a long time*
en train de [ɑ̃ trɛ̃ də], *in the act of*

Questionnaire

1. Qui est-ce que Jean voit en arrivant dans le jardin?
2. Que plante Christophe?
3. Où est le jardin potager?
4. Qu'est-ce que Jean désire faire?
5. Que voyez-vous en allant au jardin?
6. Que dit Jean en agitant son sac?
7. En quel mois plante-t-on les légumes?

Note to the Teacher: To allow ample time for reading, drill, and review, some of the lessons from here on are shorter than the preceding ones.

Devoir

A. Write the present participle of each of the following verbs, using the correct preposition:

arriver   acheter   venir
entendre   faire   traverser
pouvoir   agiter   rougir

B. Change to the correct verb-forms:

1. Le participe présent se (terminer) en *ant*.
2. Nous ne (être) pas dans la salle d'attente.
3. Hier nous (planter) des pommes de terre et des haricots.
4. En (faire) une promenade ce matin, nous (rencontrer) un vieux monsieur très poli.
5. (Aller) chercher des légumes au jardin.
6. (Avoir) -il envie de faire une promenade demain?
7. Je (répondre) à la lettre hier soir.
8. Elle (partir) pour New York la semaine dernière sans doute.
9. Demain la pauvre veuve (porter) un gros manteau à cause du froid.
10. Ni moi non plus je ne (vouloir) pas pêcher.
11. Le vilain renard a (geler) vif.
12. Il a (rapporter) les poissons enfilés à la corde.
13. La souris prudente (se glisser) dans l'office pour chercher le pain grillé.
14. J'ai (lire) ce conte avec plaisir, excepté le dénouement.
15. Nous nous sommes (précipiter) dans le trou.
16. Nous ne (pouvoir) acheter ni des jupes bleues, ni des gilets.

C. Write, using pronouns instead of nouns, these sentences from B:

    2, 3, 6, 9, 12, 13, 15

Traduction:

While working in the garden, John found a nest. Christopher, the gardener, admired the nest containing the eggs. Christopher was (**était**) in the act of planting the seeds when John showed it to him.

There are many vegetables in the garden—carrots, cabbages, potatoes, and turnips. By bringing vegetables to his employers the gardener shows that he works.

In winter upon arriving from the market, the maid prepares the vegetables.

CENT UNIÈME LEÇON

Le Jardin d'agrément

Je veux vous montrer notre jardin d'agrément. Nous y arriverons en montant deux marches. Il est situé sur une belle terrasse, bien exposé aux chauds rayons du soleil. Il y fait beau en été. Vous trouverez une table et des chaises sous le vieux marronnier; en prenant le thé au jardin nous pouvons regarder les fleurs et le ciel. Il y a trois grands arbres dans ce petit jardin, un chêne, un bouleau, et un marronnier. Même en été il fait frais sous ces arbres. Au printemps le marronnier est tout fleuri.

Les allées du jardin sont bien soignées. C'est Christophe qui s'en occupe. Au milieu du jardin il y a une jolie fontaine qui rafraîchit l'air en été. En arrosant chaque jour les fleurs, les géraniums, les pétunias, et les roses, on peut les conserver longtemps. Ma mère aime beaucoup les fleurs, et elle en met dans toutes les chambres.

Grammaire

Pronouns after Verbs

Every now and then you must learn something new about French pronouns. They are very different from English pronouns and will puzzle you when you try to read unless you understand their usage and position. In Lesson 95 you studied the general plan for pronouns before the verb. Now you are going to learn about the pronouns after the verb. The pronoun object follows a verb in the *affirmative* imperative. In the negative all former rules apply.

Regardez les fleurs. *Look at the flowers.*
Regardez-les. *Look at them.*

Apportez sûrement les fleurs à Lucie. *Be sure to take the flowers to Lucy.*
Apportez-les-lui sûrement. *Be sure to take them to her.*

Apportez-moi les fleurs. *Bring me the flowers.*
Apportez-les-moi. *Bring them to me.*
Ne me les apportez pas. *Don't bring them to me.*

Observe that the third person direct object stays close to the verb. You might imagine that the verb is like a magnet and that the third person direct object is the most strongly attracted.

Observe, too, that the indirect objects, **me** and **te,** become **moi** and **toi** after the verb.*

Notice that the verbs and pronouns are connected by hyphens.

Vocabulaire

l'agrément [lagremã] (m.), *pleasure*
le jardin d'agrément [ʒardɛ̃ dagremã], *flower garden, pleasure garden*
l'allée [lale] (f.), *passage, path, walk*
le bouleau [bulo], *birch*
le chêne [ʃɛːn], *oak*
le géranium [ʒeranjɔm], *geranium*

la marche [marʃ], *step, track, walking*
le marronnier [marɔnje], *French chestnut tree*
le pétunia [petynja], *petunia*
la terrasse [tɛras], *terrace, terracing*
arroser [aroze], *to water, to sprinkle*

conserver [kõsɛrve], *to save, to make last*
exposer [ɛkspoze], *to expose*
s'occuper de [sokype də], *to take care of*
rafraîchir [rafreʃiːr], *to refresh*
soigné [swaɲe], *taken care of, cared for*

Questionnaire

1. Où est situé le jardin d'agrément?
2. Qu'y a-t-il sous le marronnier?
3. Combien d'arbres y a-t-il dans le jardin?
4. Que voit-on en prenant le thé?
5. Où fait-il frais en été?
6. Comment est le marronnier?
7. Comment sont les allées?
8. Qui s'en occupe?
9. Quelles fleurs y a-t-il dans le jardin?
10. Qui aime beaucoup les fleurs?
11. Qu'y a-t-il au milieu du jardin?
12. Que fait-on chaque jour pour conserver les fleurs?

---

* Note to the Teacher: The use of **me** or **m'en** is given, though not explained, in Lesson 111, page 307.

Devoir

A. *Complete these sentences, using a present participle and a preposition where necessary:*

1. —— à l'école, j'ai rencontré Bijou, le chien.
2. Elle a une boîte —— des fleurs.
3. —— les fleurs on les conserve.
4. —— le chien aboie fort.
5. —— au cinéma je le trouverai.
6. —— elle est tombée.
7. Il le lui donnera —— chez elle.
8. —— le thé dans le jardin, j'ai regardé les fleurs bleu foncé.

B. *Change the italicized nouns to pronouns:*

1. Arrosez assez *les légumes.*
2. Montrez-moi *l'écriteau au-dessus du guichet.*
3. Coupez-lui *les roses rouges.*
4. Conservez sans faute *cette allée.*
5. N'évitez pas *le soleil.*
6. Lisez-moi *le journal.*
7. Ne demandez pas *le cadeau.*
8. Racontez *les aventures* à votre ami.

C. *Give the feminine of:*

merveilleux	cher
embarrassé	déchiré
accoutumé	doux
fatigant	occupé
dernier	cruel
sombre	jeune

Traduction:

Our pleasure garden is not very large, but it is well situated. There are four old trees there. We have tea under the oak tree, and while watching the pretty fountain, we often talk together.

By watering the flowers every day the gardener can make them last all summer. Do you like flowers?

Composition: Ecrivez une composition sur votre jardin. Dites:

(1) où il est situé
(2) s'il est grand ou petit
(3) s'il y a des fleurs ou des légumes
(4) qui s'en occupe
(5) comment il conserve les fleurs
(6) pourquoi vous aimez le jardin

CENT DEUXIÈME LEÇON

Les Commissions

En allant en ville aujourd'hui, Marie va faire des commissions pour ses parents. Avant d'aller aux grands magasins du Printemps, elle va à la poste pour acheter des timbres-poste. Après avoir acheté les timbres elle se met en route pour les grands magasins du Printemps. Devant la porte elle regarde sa montre. Il est huit heures et demie, et avant neuf heures elle ne peut pas entrer dans le magasin. Elle traverse la rue pour regarder la vitrine d'une librairie et, pendant qu'elle la regarde, Berthe arrive. Elle sourit.

—Bonjour, Marie.

—Bonjour, Berthe. J'attends l'ouverture du magasin.

—Mais vous savez que vous avez une demi-heure à attendre. Venez faire une courte promenade avec moi. J'ai une question à vous poser.

Après avoir marché une demi-heure, Marie quitte son amie et retourne au magasin. Cette fois elle trouve les portes ouvertes. Après avoir traversé le magasin, elle arrive aux ascenseurs. Avant de monter, elle consulte sa liste d'achats. Il ne faudra pas en oublier. Elle espère trouver des occasions au rayon des soies.

LES GRANDS MAGASINS DU PRINTEMPS "L'Illustration," Paris

Grammaire

The Perfect Infinitive

In French the only preposition that can be used with a present participle is **en**.

In French there is only one way of translating *after speaking* and *after having spoken*, namely by the preposition **après** plus the perfect infinitive. To form the perfect infinitive the auxiliary verb **avoir**, or **être**, is used with the past participle. Most verbs taking direct objects use **avoir**, and verbs which do not take objects use **être**. See Lessons 54 and 55, pages 153 and 155.

> après avoir rencontré, *after meeting*, or *after having met*
> après être allé, *after going*, or *after having gone*

Notice that the opposite of **après avoir attendu** is **avant d'attendre**, and that the opposite of **après être allé** is **avant d'aller**.

The simple prepositions **avant** and **devant** must be followed by nouns or pronouns. **Avant de**, however, is used with the infinitive.

Il faut arriver avant neuf heures. *It is necessary to arrive before nine o'clock.*
Avant de monter elle consulte sa liste. *Before going up she consults her list.*

Vocabulaire

l'achat [laʃa] (m.), *purchase*
la commission [kɔmisjõ], *errand;* faire des commissions [fɛːr de kɔmisjõ], *to do some errands*

les grands magasins du Printemps [grã magazɛ̃ dy prɛ̃tã] (m. pl.), *the Printemps,* one of the large department stores in Paris

la librairie [librɛri], *bookseller's shop, publishing house*
l'ouverture [luvɛrtyːr] (f.), *opening*
avant de [avã də], *before*

Questionnaire

1. Pourquoi Marie va-t-elle en ville?
2. Que fait-elle avant d'aller au magasin?
3. Après avoir acheté les timbres où va-t-elle?
4. Pourquoi ne peut-elle pas y entrer?

5. Que regarde-t-elle?
6. Qu'attend Marie?
7. Avant de monter dans l'ascenseur que fait-elle?
8. Qu'est-ce qu'elle espère trouver?
9. Quel jour du mois choisirez-vous pour aller en ville?
10. Donnez les mois en français.

Devoir

A. Supply the missing word or words:
1. —— en ville elle voit son amie.
2. Après —— les timbres Marie traverse la rue.
3. Après —— la vitrine elle rencontre Berthe.
4. —— monter elle consulte sa liste d'achats.
5. Après —— monté je fais mes commissions.
6. Avant —— en classe il étudie les vers.

B. Write the first paragraph of "Les Commissions" in the first person singular.

C. Write a sentence for each of the following expressions:
1. avant de
2. en (et le participe présent)
3. après (et l'infinitif passé)
4. Je vous prie de (et l'infinitif)

5. en plein air
6. je veux bien
7. merci bien
8. s'occuper de

D. Use pronouns in place of the italicized words:

1. *La blanchisseuse paresseuse* ne repasse pas *le linge.*
2. Réservez *des places* au milieu.
3. Apportez *les affiches à votre sœur.*
4. En hiver *les gens* ne font pas beaucoup *de promenades,* à cause du froid.
5. Ramenez-moi *ce garçon paresseux.*
6. *Le guichet* donne sur le quai.
7. *Le chef de gare* et *le contrôleur* disent "En voiture!"
8. Je ferai *le trajet* tout seul.
9. *Le facteur* a pesé *le colis.*
10. *L'épicerie* fournit *des choux et des haricots.*

CENT TROISIÈME LEÇON

Review

A

1. How is the present participle formed? Is it used in forming a French verb tense? Must it be used with a preposition? With what preposition may it be used? What meanings may this preposition have?

2. How is the perfect infinitive formed? When is **avoir** used in making it? Give examples.

3. When is **être** used in constructing the perfect infinitive? Give examples.

4. With what preposition is the perfect infinitive used in French? How may it be translated into English?

5. How would you express the opposite of **après être venu?** How is it formed? How may it be translated?

6. Are **après** and **avant de** always followed by verbs? By what parts of speech other than verbs may **après** be followed?

7. By what must **avant** and **devant** be followed? How can you determine which to use?

8. May **avant** be followed directly by an infinitive?

9. List the direct-object pronouns.

10. Write five sentences, using a different object pronoun in each sentence.

11. Give the French for:
   (a) April first
   (b) August seventh
   (c) July fourth

B

I. Give the present participle of:

regretter	rendre	être
étudier	avoir	répondre
fournir	exprimer	ramer

II. Give the perfect infinitive of:

finir	avoir	agiter
descendre	venir	planter
aller	partir	vouloir

III. Give the opposite of:

1. avant de mentionner
2. avant de choisir
3. avant de voir
4. avant d'entrer
5. avant de me coucher
6. avant de faire
7. avant d'être
8. avant de se rappeler
9. avant de sortir
10. avant de se rafraîchir

*IV. Complete the following sentences, using a present participle, a perfect infinitive, or **avant de** plus an infinitive:*

1. —— (me coucher) je vais chercher les graines de radis.
2. —— (visiter) la bibliothèque nous irons dans le jardin d'agrément.
3. —— (attendre) mon oncle, elle répondra aux lettres.
4. —— (aller) voir le paysage, j'ai rencontré mon amie.
5. Elle est arrivée —— (chanter).
6. —— (les regarder) ils en ont parlé.
7. —— (réserver) des places à l'avance, elle en a de bonnes.
8. —— (patiner) nous viendrons vous chercher près de l'école.
9. —— (rendre) visite à ma tante j'ai continué mon trajet au théâtre.
10. —— (répéter) ce vers je l'ai appris.
11. Elle est venue —— (pleurer).

Courtesy of Dr. Dunbar Rowland, State Historian of Mississippi

FRENCH EXPLORERS LANDING NEAR THE MOUTH OF THE MISSISSIPPI RIVER
From a painting in the Mississippi Hall of Fame.

EARLY FRENCH ADVENTURE IN AMERICA

In the sixteenth century America was still a land of wonder. Each powerful country of Europe longed to win for itself this fabled wilderness of romance, adventure, and gold.

Spain was already reaping huge rewards from her trade with "the Indies," and Francis I wished to have a share of the riches for France. He sent an Italian navigator called John Verrazzano to seek for a passage westward to the rich kingdom of Cathay.

On January 17, 1524, the navigator set sail in a caravel for the western world. After forty-nine days he and his comrades reached a low shore near the present site of Wilmington, N. C. "A new land," Verrazzano wrote, "never before seen of any man either ancient or modern."

Verrazzano's next port of call was the bay of New York. Rowing in his boat through the Narrows under the steep bluffs of Staten Island, he saw the inner harbor dotted with canoes, in which the feathered natives put off from shore to welcome him. He then coasted the shores of Long Island to Newport, and up the rugged coasts of New England.

Verrazzano followed the seaboard to Newfoundland, whence for more than twenty years French codfishers had been bearing home bountiful provision. He returned to France without finding the passage to Cathay, but he had explored the American coast from the thirty-fourth to the fiftieth degree, and written the earliest known description of the shores of the United States.

In 1562 Jean Ribaut, a seaman of Dieppe, set sail for America in two antiquated ships with high poops and tublike hulls. With him, besides his crew, were a band of veteran soldiers and not a few adventurous noblemen. Seventy-one days later they sighted the coast of Florida.

The next morning they found themselves off the mouth of a great river. Riding at anchor on a sunny sea, they lowered their boats, crossed the bar that obstructed the entrance, and floated on a basin of sheltered water. Indians were running along the beach, beckoning. The Frenchmen—sailors, soldiers, and eager young nobles— pushed their boats ashore and knelt to give thanks to Him who had guided their course to a land of promise. Seated gravely under the neighboring trees, the Indians looked on in silent respect, thinking the strangers worshiped the sun. Ribaut gave the chief a robe of blue cloth, worked in yellow with the royal fleur-de-lis. The French sought and soon found a suitable haven, where they built a small fort and named it Port Royal.

It had been their plan to explore and not to settle, but the adventurers were so enthusiastic over what they saw in their roamings that thirty remained to hold Port Royal for the French king. De Pierria was left in command; Ribaut embarked and spread his sails for France. From the beach the little company saw the receding ships grow less on the expanse of blue, dwindle to faint specks, and disappear. They were alone in these fearful solitudes. From the North Pole to Mexico there were no white men but them.

Alas, their thought was not of food and shelter—but of gold! Of the thirty, the greater number were soldiers and sailors, with a few gentlemen: men of the sword and nobles who had never worked or traded in France. They barely stopped to finish building their fort, and then set gayly forth in quest of adventure.

Good will from the Indians was their fortune. Village chieftains never failed to provide them with maize and beans and hominy. It was not to Indian war-clubs that the infant colony owed its ruin. It destroyed itself by quarrels and petty conspiracies. The rude buildings of their fort grew hateful to the weary eyes of the Frenchmen. They dreamed of the home they had left in Dieppe. So trees were hewn down, and the building of a ship begun. At this they worked with zeal, calking the seams with long moss hanging from near-by trees, getting pitch from the pines, sewing bedding and shirts together for sails.

They laid in what store of provisions they could and put to sea. A fair wind filled the patchwork sails and bore them from the hated coast. Day after day they held their steady course, until they were caught in a glassy waste of calm. Florida was far behind, France yet farther before. Food and fresh water failed, one man after another sickened and died. Finally, an English bark reached the water-logged vessel and its dying survivors, who were carried as prisoners to England. Thus closed another scene of woe at the stormy dawn of American history.

French colonists in America sprang in large part from soldiers more interested in forest warfare than in settlement. The French were spurred by the excitement of new scenes but unwilling to make enduring homes there. France was always in the van, daring and indomitable. Foremost on this bright roll of forest chivalry stands the half-forgotten name of Samuel de Champlain.

The Jesuit missionaries did much to aid exploration and fur-trading. Lawless as the traders were—they were called *coureurs des bois* or forest-rangers—they helped greatly to extend French influence and to subdue the western continent to white man's rule. As the *coureurs des bois* pushed ever more deeply into the wilderness of the

Courtesy of Chicago Historical Society

FRENCH EXPLORERS SAILING UP THE ST. LAWRENCE RIVER, 1534

Great Lakes, they brought back tales of a mighty western river where ferocious Sioux Indians dwelt. On the eighth of December, 1672, under orders from Governor Frontenac of New France, a young Quebec merchant, twenty-seven years of age, by name Louis Joliet, reached the mission house of Jacques Marquette. The message young Joliet brought to this place on the north side of the Strait of Mackinac was that Marquette and he had been commanded to find the Mississippi River. He found Marquette eager to visit the Indian nations on the remote stream.

In two birch canoes, with a supply of smoked meat and Indian corn, the Frenchmen set out with five men, May 17, 1673. By day they traveled and explored—at night they sat beside a flickering fire over a meal of bison flesh or venison before falling asleep in the vast wilderness. On June 17 the travelers first saw the wide and rapid current of the river that they sought.

For a month thereafter they paddled and floated down the stream. Time and again they were threatened by hostile red men, but their fearlessness, a peace-symbol given them by a friendly Illinois chieftain, and the burning eloquence of Marquette saved the party from death or torture. Near the mouth of the Arkansas, however, they barely escaped massacre. They took counsel and decided they had gone far enough to establish the fact that the Mississippi flows into the Gulf of Mexico. If they went farther, they feared they might be captured and the results of their discovery lost. So they turned back to Canada.

In spite of the courage of her explorers and the tenacity of her settlers, the efforts of France toward colonization were everywhere less successful than those of England. To learn the particular historical and political reasons for France's loss of power reference must be made to detailed studies of the building of our nation.

From a painting by E. S. Paxson in the Capitol, Helena, Montana

A "COUREUR DES BOIS"

CENT QUATRIÈME LEÇON

Les Explorateurs français en Amérique

Samuel de Champlain

En 1603[1] Samuel de Champlain a quitté la France pour explorer le Nouveau Monde. Il est arrivé au Saint-Laurent avec un marchand de St. Malo. Il a rencontré quelques Algonquins, mais il n'a pas réussi à découvrir les lacs et les rivières qui existaient (*were to be found*) au sud.

Cinq ans plus tard[2] Champlain a entrepris une nouvelle expédition. Cette expédition est très importante, parce que l'explorateur a fondé la ville de Québec. Cette ville est encore aujourd'hui très française.

En 1609[3] Champlain a entrepris le voyage qu'il méditait depuis longtemps.[4] En compagnie des Hurons et des Algonquins il est allé vers le sud. Il a donné son nom au lac qu'il a découvert—le Lac Champlain qui est si pittoresque.

Ce n'est pas tout. Toute sa vie Champlain a voyagé. En 1611[5] il a fondé une autre ville, Mont Royal, appelée aujourd'hui Montréal.

Deux ans plus tard Champlain a été blessé[6] dans un combat avec les Peaux-Rouges, mais ses aventures ont cessé seulement avec sa mort en 1635.[7] En 1615[8] il a découvert le Lac Huron.

Une grande partie du Canada est restée française à cause des expéditions et du travail courageux de Champlain.

Jacques Marquette

C'est sous le règne de Louis XIV que beaucoup d'explorateurs français sont allés en Amérique. Le père Marquette, prêtre jésuite, accompagné par Joliet, est parti de Mackinaw à la recherche d'une grande rivière. Leur voyage a commencé en 1672.[9]

Après une semaine de voyage les deux explorateurs ont découvert le Mississippi. La variété du paysage leur a fait une impression agréable.

Il y avait (*were*) des forêts, des rochers, des plaines où errait (*wandered*) le buffle. Le voyage de retour était (*was*) difficile. Le courant du grand fleuve était (*was*) fort.

Marquette, après son retour, a fondé une mission sur les bords de la rivière Illinois. Il était (*was*) très courageux, mais après une longue maladie il est mort sur les bords du Lac Michigan en 1675.[10]

Sieur de La Salle

Joliet et Marquette ont découvert le Mississippi; mais c'est La Salle qui a utilisé leur découverte au profit de la France. De tous les explorateurs français il est le plus grand.[11]

Voici les projets de La Salle. Le gouverneur Frontenac, envoyé par Louis XIV, a donné des terres à La Salle. Mais La Salle désire autre chose aussi. Il veut coloniser les plaines fertiles du Mississippi. Il désire convertir les Peaux-Rouges. Il désire réunir la vallée du Mississippi au royaume de France. Il va réussir.

---

[1] en seize cent trois
[2] *later*
[3] en seize cent neuf
[4] *of which he had been thinking for a long time*
[5] en seize cent onze
[6] *was wounded*
[7] en seize cent trente-cinq
[8] en seize cent quinze
[9] en seize cent soixante-douze
[10] en seize cent soixante-quinze
[11] *the greatest*

Le roi de France autorise La Salle à aller au sud. Henri de Tonti, officier italien, l'accompagne dans ses voyages. En 1678[1] La Salle fait construire un bateau,[2] le *Griffon*. Le voyage est difficile. Il y a des orages. Les Peaux-Rouges attaquent les blancs. La Salle est courageux, mais il est obligé de retourner au Canada.

En 1681[3] une nouvelle expédition est organisée. La Salle veut descendre le Mississippi jusqu'au Golfe du Mexique. Cette fois La Salle réussit. Il arrive au golfe, et en l'honneur de son roi, Louis XIV, La Salle donne le nom de Louisiane à tout le vaste territoire.

La Salle établit ensuite un poste à Fort St. Louis. Il retourne au Canada, mais le nouveau gouverneur le reçoit mal. La Salle repart pour la France. Le roi lui donne quatre vaisseaux, et plein d'espoir La Salle retourne au Golfe du Mexique. Malheureusement il ne trouve pas l'embouchure du Mississippi. Accompagné par plusieurs hommes, il décide de traverser les vastes plaines pour aller au Canada.

Ses hommes ne l'aiment pas, parce qu'il est si brave et si courageux. Ils le tuent, lui et ses fidèles compagnons. Mais La Salle reste par son grand courage un des héros de notre histoire.

Vocabulaire

les **blancs** [blɑ̃] (m. pl.), *the whites*
le **buffle** [byfl], *buffalo*
l'**embouchure** [lɑ̃buʃyːr] (f.), *mouth* (of a river)
le **fleuve** [flœːv], *river*
le **golfe** [gɔlf], *gulf*
la **maladie** [maladi], *illness*
l'**orage** [lɔraːʒ] (m.), *storm*
les **Peaux-Rouges** [poruːʒ] (m. pl.), *redskins*
le **poste** [pɔst], *station, body of men*
le **prêtre** [prɛːtr], *priest*
la **recherche** [rəʃɛrʃ], *search*

le **rocher** [rɔʃe], *rock*
le **royaume** [rwajoːm], *kingdom*
le **sud** [syd], *south*
le **vaisseau** [vɛso] (pl. les **vaisseaux**), *vessel, ship*
l'**Amérique** [lamerik] (f.), *America*
le **Golfe du Mexique** [gɔlf dy mɛksik], *the Gulf of Mexico*
la **Louisiane** [lwizjan], *Louisiana*
St. Malo [sɛ̃ malo], *St. Malo, a port in northern France*

construire [kɔ̃strɥiːr], *to construct*
découvrir [dekuvriːr], *to discover*
errer [ɛre], *to wander, to err*
rechercher [rəʃɛrʃe], *to seek again*
repartir [rəpartiːr], *to set out again*
fidèle [fidɛl], *faithful*
jésuite [ʒezɥit], *Jesuit*
pittoresque [pitɔrɛsk], *picturesque, beautiful*
mal [mal], *badly*
malheureusement [malœrøzmɑ̃], *unhappily*

Words with English Equivalents

le **combat** [kɔ̃ba], *combat*
le **compagnon** [kɔ̃paɲɔ̃], *companion*
le **courant** [kurɑ̃], *current*
l'**expédition** [lɛkspedisjɔ̃] (f.), *expedition*
l'**explorateur** [lɛksploratœːr] (m.), *explorer*
le **gouverneur** [guvɛrnœːr], *governor*
l'**impression** [lɛ̃prɛsjɔ̃] (f.), *impression*
la **mission** [misjɔ̃], *mission*
le **profit** [prɔfi], *profit*

le **règne** [rɛɲ], *reign*
la **rivière** [rivjeːr], *river*
le **territoire** [tɛritwaːr], *territory*
la **vallée** [vale], *valley*
la **variété** [varjete], *variety*
Québec [kebɛk], *Quebec*
le **Saint-Laurent** [sɛ̃ lɔrɑ̃], *the St. Lawrence River*
attaquer [atake], *to attack*
autoriser [ɔtɔrize], *to authorize*
coloniser [kɔlɔnize], *to colonize*

convertir [kɔ̃vɛrtiːr], *to convert*
exister [ɛgziste], *to exist*
explorer [ɛksplore], *to explore*
fonder [fɔ̃de], *to found*
méditer [medite], *to meditate, to think of*
utiliser [ytilize], *to utilize*
agréable [agreabl], *agreeable, pleasant, enjoyable*
italien [italjɛ̃], *Italian*
vaste [vast], *vast*

---

[1] en seize cent soixante-dix-huit
[2] *had a boat built*
[3] en seize cent quatre-vingt-un

LA SALLE BUILDING THE "GRIFFON"
From an account of La Salle's voyage published in France in 1704

CENT CINQUIÈME LEÇON

Des héros français

Pierre l'Ermite

Les Turcs possèdent Jérusalem. Ils sont très méchants et maltraitent souvent les chrétiens. Les chrétiens sont très malheureux.

Pierre l'Ermite est moine. Il va à Jérusalem. A son retour en France il parle des Turcs. Il voyage partout en France, dans les grandes villes, et dans les petits villages. Il dit qu'il faut aller à Jérusalem. Il faudra en chasser les Turcs, qui sont méchants.

Il parle aux chrétiens. Il les décide à partir pour Jérusalem. Tous les chrétiens portent des croix. On appelle croisades les guerres des chrétiens contre les Turcs.

Le voyage des chrétiens est long. Il faut traverser toute la France et beaucoup d'autres pays. Les pauvres sont obligés de marcher pendant des semaines. Chaque fois que les voyageurs voient une ville, ils espèrent que c'est Jérusalem.

Beaucoup de ces pauvres gens meurent. Ils meurent de faim, de fatigue, ou de maladie. D'autres n'arrivent pas à leur destination parce que les Turcs les attendent et les massacrent.

Pierre l'Ermite accompagne Godefroy de Bouillon dans sa croisade. Malheureusement les Turcs sont forts. Les Français ne réussissent pas à prendre Jérusalem. Le voyage est trop difficile. Une fois seulement ils prennent la ville, et ils arrivent au tombeau de Jésus-Christ. Godefroy de Bouillon est roi de la ville. Mais les Turcs attaquent Jérusalem, et malheureusement la ville tombe de nouveau entre leurs mains.

Saint Louis et la Sainte-Chapelle

SAINTE-CHAPELLE

absence sa mère est morte. Le jeune roi organise maintenant son royaume, et il est très aimé (*much loved*).

Les Turcs sont toujours à Jérusalem. Saint Louis veut les chasser. En 1270[1] il entreprend la huitième et dernière croisade. Le roi décide de partir pour Tunis. Il veut convertir le sultan au christianisme. Le bon roi Saint Louis tombe malade et meurt à Carthage.

Saint Louis a fait construire[2] la Sainte-Chapelle à Paris. La chapelle est très petite, mais elle est très belle. C'est un chef-d'œuvre d'architecture gothique.

La Sorbonne a été fondée par Saint Louis aussi. C'est une des meilleures[3] universités du monde.

Louis IX, ou Saint Louis, est un très bon roi. Sa mère, Blanche de Castille, règne à sa place quand il est très petit. Sa mère est très pieuse, et son fils, qui est très beau, veut être bon comme sa mère. Il écoute bien ses professeurs parce qu'il aime beaucoup travailler.

Le jeune roi est très charitable. Il invite les pauvres dans son palais. Il leur donne à manger, et tout le monde aime le roi. Il est très simple. Il aime les pauvres gens. Il leur parle volontiers.

Saint Louis apprend que la Terre-Sainte est tombée entre les mains des Turcs. Il y va, mais il est fait prisonnier. Il rachète sa liberté. Pendant son

Jiès, Paris
CHURCH OF THE SORBONNE

[1] en douze cent soixante-dix
[2] *had built*
[3] *one of the best*

Bertrand Du Guesclin

C'est en 1330[1] que le petit Bertrand Du Guesclin joue au soldat avec ses petits amis. Il aime se battre. Ses parents ne l'aiment pas, parce qu'il est très laid; mais il devient[2] général dans les armées du roi.

Il attire l'attention du roi pendant le siège de Vannes. Il se bat avec courage contre les Anglais et tombe ensuite entre les mains des Anglais en 1364,[3] mais on le libère.

Il est à la tête des Grandes Compagnies. Il va en Espagne. On l'emprisonne, mais il rachète sa liberté.

Ensuite, n'ayant (*not having*) plus besoin des Grandes Compagnies, il débarrasse la France de ces bandes de ravageurs.

A son retour en France il est nommé connétable. Il réussit à chasser presque tous les Anglais de France. Il meurt devant Châteauneuf-de-Randon en 1380.[4]

Tous les enfants français admirent le connétable Du Guesclin. Il est fils d'un petit seigneur (*lord*), mais par son grand courage il devient un grand héros.

Vocabulaire

le **chef-d'œuvre** [ʃɛdœːvr], *masterpiece*

le **chrétien** [kretjɛ̃], *Christian*

le **connétable** [kɔnetabl], *commander-in-chief, constable*

la **croisade** [krwɑzad], *crusade*

la **croix** [krwɑ] (pl. les **croix**), *cross*

l'**ermite** [lɛrmit] (m.), *hermit*

le **moine** [mwan], *monk*

les **pauvres** [poːvr] (m. and f.pl.), *poor people, paupers*

le **ravageur** [ravaʒœːr], *ravager, spoiler*

le **tombeau** [tõbo], *tomb*

l'**Allemagne** [lalmaɲ] (f.), *Germany*

les **Grandes Compagnies** [grɑ̃ːd kõpaɲi] (f. pl.), rough bands of mercenary soldiers

Du Guesclin, Bertrand [dy gɛklɛ̃, bɛrtrɑ̃], a French hero

l'**Espagne** [lɛspaɲ] (f.), *Spain*

Pierre l'Ermite [pjɛːr lɛrmit], *Peter the Hermit*, a monk of the early twelfth century

la **Sainte-Chapelle** [sɛ̃t ʃapɛl], a Gothic chapel in Paris

la **Sorbonne** [sɔrbɔn], the University of Paris

la **Terre-Sainte** [tɛːr sɛ̃t], *the Holy Land*

le **Turc** [tyrk], *Turk*

attirer [atire], *to attract, to draw*

se **battre** [sə batr], *to fight*

chasser [ʃase], *to drive out, to hunt, to chase*

croire [krwɑːr], *to believe*

débarrasser [debarase], *to free*

libérer [libere], *to set free*

il **meurt** [il mœːr] (inf. **mourir**), *he dies;* ils **meurent**, *they die*

posséder [pɔsede], *to possess*

racheter [raʃte], *to buy back, to ransom*

régner [reɲe], *to reign*

laid [lɛ], *ugly*

volontiers [vɔlõtje], *freely, willingly, gladly*

English Equivalents

l'**architecture** [larʃitɛktyːr] (f.), *architecture*

la **chapelle** [ʃapɛl], *chapel*

le **christianisme** [kristjanism], *Christianity*

la **destination** [dɛstinasjõ], *destination*

le **palais** [palɛ], *palace*

le **sultan** [syltɑ̃], *sultan*

l'**université** [lynivɛrsite] (f.), *university*

le **voyageur** [vwajaʒœːr], *traveler, voyager*

emprisonner [ɑ̃prizɔne], *to imprison, to put in prison*

maltraiter [maltrete], *to mistreat, to maltreat*

massacrer [masakre], *to massacre*

charitable [ʃaritabl], *charitable*

gothique [gɔtik], *Gothic*

pieux, -se [pjø, pjøːz], *pious*

---

¹ treize cent trente
² *becomes;* **devenir** is conjugated like **venir**
³ en treize cent soixante-quatre
⁴ en treize cent quatre-vingt

CENT SIXIÈME LEÇON
Dans la ferme

Autrefois Eve et Jean passaient leurs vacances à la campagne dans une ferme. Ils jouaient toute la journée en plein air. Quelquefois les enfants de la ferme voisine venaient jouer avec Eve et Jean. Ils faisaient ensemble de longues promenades à pied ou à bicyclette. Chaque fois qu'ils faisaient de petites excursions, la mère d'Eve et de Jean leur préparait un panier qui contenait de bonnes choses à manger. Assis à l'ombre d'un grand arbre, ils dévoraient les sandwichs et les gâteaux. Quelquefois, même, ils s'endormaient, parce que la promenade les fatiguait. En revenant, ils s'arrêtaient toujours pour cueillir des fleurs pour leur mère. Tout de suite en arrivant à la maison, ils cherchaient leur mère pour les lui donner. Leur mère les embrassait pour les remercier. Les enfants étaient fatigués. Ils se mettaient toujours sur l'herbe, sous un grand chêne, et parlaient de leur agréable journée, en se reposant. Ils aimaient tant parler ainsi ensemble.

Grammaire
The Past Descriptive

To form the past descriptive tense drop **-ant** of the present participle and add the past descriptive endings.

chercher		finir	
PRESENT PARTICIPLE: cherch **ant**		PRESENT PARTICIPLE: finiss **ant**	
je cherch **ais**	nous cherch **ions**	je finiss **ais**	nous finiss **ions**
tu cherch **ais**	vous cherch **iez**	tu finiss **ais**	vous finiss **iez**
il cherch **ait**	ils cherch **aient**	il finiss **ait**	ils finiss **aient**

There is but one set of past descriptive endings for *all* regular and irregular verbs. The ending **aient** is pronounced [ɛ].

Use of the Past Descriptive

The past descriptive tense is used to describe *repeated* action in the past.[1] It is very simple to know when to use this tense. Ask yourself, "Did this action occur one or more times in the past?" If the answer is "more than once," use the past descriptive. This tense is translated into English as follows:

Nous allions à la campagne. *We went to the country* (implying more than once), or *We used to go to the country.*

Used to indicates that the act was customary or habitual. Would such words as *often, sometimes, always, every year*, help to decide what tense is to be used?

Vocabulaire

l'excursion [lɛkskyrsjõ] (f.), *excursion*
l'ombre [lõːbr] (f.), *shade*

le panier [panje], *basket*
Eve [ɛːv], *Eva*
contenir [kõtniːr], *to contain*

cueillir [kœjiːr], *to pick, to gather*

[1] See Lesson 107, page 300, for other functions.

Questionnaire

1. Où allaient Eve et Jean autrefois pendant les vacances?
2. Qui venait jouer avec les enfants?
3. Que faisaient les enfants ensemble?
4. Que trouvaient-ils dans le panier?
5. Pourquoi s'endormaient-ils quelquefois?
6. Pourquoi les enfants s'arrêtaient-ils en revenant?
7. Qui cherchaient-ils en arrivant à la maison?
8. Que faisaient-ils pour se reposer?

Devoir

A. Read "Dans la ferme" aloud, substituting **nous** for **Eve et Jean.**

B. Conjugate:
  1. Je m'amusais toujours.
  2. Je ne remplissais pas le panier.
  3. Je pouvais le faire.
  4. J'étais heureux.

C. Change the verbs in the following sentences to the past descriptive:
  1. Il vient souvent chez moi.
  2. Vous êtes arrivés à midi.
  3. Ils font souvent des promenades.
  4. La mère leur donne un panier.
  5. Je vais à l'école à huit heures un quart.

6. Nous ne pouvons pas nous reposer.
7. Eve remercie son frère du livre.
8. Jean s'est arrêté sous le grand marronnier.

Traduction: Explain what tense you use and why.

1. They often gave me flowers. 2. She used to take a walk every day. 3. Sometimes they went to the country on foot. 4. You used to study a great deal. 5. Every day he fell asleep under the trees. 6. We often looked for our books. 7. The children from the neighboring farm used to play with us every afternoon.

CENT SEPTIÈME LEÇON

L'Invitation

Je marchais dans la rue ce matin avec ma sœur. En passant devant un grand magasin, nous avons rencontré une amie. Elle était toute souriante, et elle avait l'air très heureux. Je lui ai demandé pourquoi elle avait l'air si content.

—J'étais en route pour aller vous voir quand je vous ai rencontrées.

—En quoi puis-je[1] vous servir?

—Vous vous rappelez notre ancien professeur de français, Mademoiselle Costet, n'est-ce pas, celle (*the one*) qui avait de si beaux cheveux noirs et qui était si gentille pour nous? Elle traversait la rue tout à l'heure et elle m'a reconnue. Je lui ai parlé en français, et elle avait l'air tout heureux. J'ai demandé à ma mère de l'inviter à déjeuner, et Mlle. Costet a accepté l'invitation avec plaisir. Je voulais venir vous voir pour vous inviter aussi.

—Pour quand est votre aimable invitation?

—Pour jeudi prochain, à une heure.

—Je vous en (*for it*) remercie. J'accepte avec plaisir. Alors, à jeudi?

—Oui, à jeudi.

[1] Irregular interrogative form of **pouvoir.**

Grammaire

The Past Descriptive

In the preceding lesson you learned that the past descriptive tense is used to express *repeated action* in the past. It has two other uses. One of these is to express continued action in the past. To translate this use into English the *past progressive*[1] tense is used. For example:

> j'allais, *I was going*
> nous finissions, *we were finishing*
> il lisait, *he was reading*

The third use of this tense is to express *a physical state, a state of mind*, or *a state of the weather* in the past.

> il avait[2] faim, *he was hungry* (physical state)
> j'étais heureux, *I was happy* (state of mind)
> il faisait beau, *it was nice weather* (state of the weather)

The three possible translations for this tense are illustrated below:

> nous fournissions, *we used to furnish, we furnished, we were furnishing*

Vocabulaire

l'invitation [lɛ̃vitasjɔ̃] (f.), *invitation*

le temps [tã], *weather, time* (not occurrence)

reconnaître [rəkɔnɛːtr] (p.p. reconnu), *to recognize*

ancien, ancienne [ãsjɛ̃, ãsjɛn], *former*

souriant [surjã], *smiling*

tout à l'heure [tu ta lœːr], *a few minutes ago, in a few minutes*

Questionnaire

1. Où marchiez-vous ce matin?
2. Qui était toute souriante?
3. Pourquoi avait-elle l'air content?
4. Comment était le professeur de français?
5. Où allait-elle?
6. Lui avez-vous parlé en anglais ou en français?
7. Qui l'a invitée à déjeuner?
8. Pour quel jour est l'invitation?
9. Quand je vous ai rencontré ce matin, où alliez-vous?
10. Que faisiez-vous pendant vos vacances, quand vous étiez petit?
11. Quel temps faisait-il hier?
12. Quel temps fait-il aujourd'hui?
13. Que faisiez-vous quand vous étiez très petit?
14. Aviez-vous souvent envie de travailler quand vous étiez jeune?
15. Que faisiez-vous hier matin à onze heures?
16. Vous ennuyiez-vous en jouant à la balle hier?
17. Savez-vous danser?
18. Savez-vous nager?
19. Pourquoi ne nagez-vous pas au mois de janvier?

---

[1] Progressive tenses in English indicate continued action. They always contain a form of the verb *to be* and a present participle.

> *Example:* He reads. Simple Present.
> He is reading. Present Progressive.
> He read. Simple Past.
> He was reading. Past Progressive.

[2] The past descriptive of **avoir** is **j'avais**, etc.

Devoir

A. *Illustrate each use of the past descriptive by two sentences.*

B. *Change the present participle to the past descriptive in each of the following sentences:*

1. Nous (étant) fatigués après la promenade.
2. Je (choisissant) ce livre quand il m'a rencontré.
3. Ils (répondant) toujours aux questions.
4. Vous (étudiant) toujours vos leçons.
5. Nous vous (voyant) souvent.
6. Il ne (pouvant) pas y aller, parce qu'il (étant) malade.
7. Elles ne (travaillant) pas souvent au jardin.
8. Autrefois (écoutant) -vous avec intérêt?

Traduction:

Before translating these sentences, ask yourself the following questions:

1. Did the action occur more than once? 2. Do I wish to express a state in the past? 3. Do I wish to express a continued action in the past?

If the answer is "yes," use the past descriptive. If the answer is "no," use the past indefinite.

We were walking in the park yesterday afternoon when we met our friends. They seemed very happy. I asked why they were smiling. They answered that they wished to invite us to their house (**chez eux**). They used to live in the country. Now they live in a large house near the park. After leaving (**quitter**) our friends, we went to the lake.

Les Archives photographiques d'Art et d'Histoire, Paris

THE CORONATION OF CHARLEMAGNE
A painting by Lévy in the Pantheon

CENT HUITIÈME LEÇON
Dans le magasin

Ce matin je suis allée faire des commissions pour ma mère. J'achetais la viande quand il a commencé à pleuvoir. Je voulais retourner à la maison, mais je n'avais pas de parapluie. Le boucher, que nous connaissons depuis longtemps, m'a permis de rester dans le magasin. Je n'étais pas très contente. La pluie tombait très fort. Je portais mes souliers neufs, et je ne voulais pas les abîmer en marchant dans l'eau. Pendant que j'attendais, beaucoup de personnes qui portaient des manteaux de pluie ou des parapluies entraient pour acheter de la viande. Il y avait des côtelettes de mouton, des rôtis, du veau, et des biftecks. Une dame a acheté un rôti de bœuf de deux kilos, parce qu'elle disait qu'elle allait avoir du monde à déjeuner.

Je commençais[1] à être inquiète. Le ciel devenait plus noir. Je regardais tristement par la fenêtre quand j'ai vu mon cousin. Il portait un grand parapluie. J'ai frappé sur la vitre. Il m'a reconnue, et il est venu immédiatement chez le boucher. Je suis partie avec lui, mais vous savez, mes souliers neufs étaient abîmés!

Grammaire

The Difference between the Past Indefinite and the Past Descriptive

The past indefinite is used to describe action which occurred only *once* in the past. Remember that the past descriptive is used to express *repeated* action, *continued* action, or a *state* in the past. Go through the passage above and justify the use of each tense according to these rules.

The past indefinite may be translated as follows:

nous sommes arrivés $\begin{cases} we\ arrived\ \text{(implying once)} \\ we\ did\ arrive \\ we\ have\ arrived \end{cases}$

The past descriptive is translated in the following ways:

nous arrivions $\begin{cases} we\ arrived\ \text{(implying repeated action)} \\ we\ were\ arriving \\ we\ used\ to\ arrive \end{cases}$

Vocabulaire

le **bœuf** [bœf], *beef, ox*
le **boucher** [buʃe], *butcher*
le **manteau de pluie** [mãtod plɥi], *raincoat*
le **parapluie** [paraplɥi], *umbrella*
le **veau** [vo], *veal, calf*

la **vitre** [vitr], *window-pane*
abîmer [abime], *to ruin*
nous **connaissons** [nu kɔnɛsõ] (inf. **connaître**), *we know* (a person)
frapper [frape], *to knock*

neuf, -ve [nœf, nœːv], *new*
tristement [tristəmã], *sadly, sorrowfully*
du **monde** [dy mõːd], *company, guests*
pendant que [pãdã kə], *while*

---

[1] Notice the cedilla in je **commençais**. Can you think of a reason for using it? Do all six forms in this tense need it?

Questionnaire

1. Où êtes-vous allée ce matin?
2. Qu'est-ce que vous achetiez quand il a commencé à pleuvoir?
3. Pourquoi n'êtes-vous pas retournée à la maison?
4. Qu'est-ce que vous portiez?
5. Qu'est-ce qu'une dame a acheté?
6. Qui avez-vous vu par la fenêtre?
7. Qu'avez-vous fait?
8. Faisait-il beau?
9. Que faisiez-vous hier à une heure?

Devoir

A. *Look at the following sentences carefully. You will find in each of them an indication of the tense to be used. Change the infinitive to the correct tense, either the past indefinite or the past descriptive.*

1. Ce matin je (envoyer) une lettre à ma grand'mère.
2. Il (faire) beau toute la journée hier.
3. Nous (aller) souvent à la campagne en été.
4. Ma mère (acheter) des côtelettes de veau pour le dîner ce soir.
5. Mes amis (étudier) leurs leçons quand je (arriver) chez eux.
6. En regardant par la fenêtre nous (voir) quelquefois des automobiles.
7. Hier Jean (être) heureux parce que son père (revenir).

B. *Write in full the time given in parentheses:*

1. Quelle heure est-il? Il est (9:00).
2. Le train part à (10:30).
3. Il arrive à (11:15).
4. Nous déjeunons à (12:00).
5. On couche le bébé à (1:20).
6. Je retourne à la maison à (3:40). (*Two ways.*)
7. Nous prenons le thé à (4:45). (*Two ways.*)
8. Je reviens du théâtre à (12:00). (*Two ways.*)

Traduction:

Be sure that you can explain why you use each tense.

One day Charles went to the butcher shop for his mother. He liked to make purchases for her. He was crossing the street when he met his friend Roger. Roger asked him to go home with him. Charles replied that he was on his way (**en route**) to the butcher shop. Roger went with him, and while they were buying the meat, it began to rain. Roger had his umbrella. He went home with Charles, and Charles's mother invited him to lunch. They played in the afternoon.

CENT NEUVIÈME LEÇON

Review

A

1. Explain how the past descriptive tense is formed.
2. What are the endings of the past descriptive tense? How is the third person plural ending pronounced?
3. Give the past descriptive of **avoir**.
4. Spell the first person plural past descriptive of **commencer**.
5. Give the past descriptive negative of **être**.
6. When is the past descriptive used?
7. How would you translate the past descriptive of **venir** to show you were thinking of continued action?

8. What adverbs may help in determining the tense to be used?

9. What three translations can you give for the past descriptive? Use **nous étudiions**.

10. How is the past indefinite of a transitive verb formed?

11. How is the past indefinite of most intransitive verbs, i.e., verbs not requiring objects, formed?

12. Give the past participles of **avoir, voir, mettre,** and **prendre**.

13. With what does the past participle of verbs conjugated with **avoir** agree? Illustrate. Of reflexive verbs? Illustrate. Of verbs conjugated with **être**? Illustrate.

14. What simple test can you apply to determine whether you must use the past indefinite or the past descriptive?

15. What three translations may be given for the past indefinite? Translate **ils sont allés**.

16. When and in what order do pronouns follow the verb? Give two examples.

B

I. Conjugate:

1. Je finissais mes leçons.
2. Je ne pouvais pas y aller.
3. Je n'avais pas mes affaires.
4. Je n'étais pas content.

5. Je ne faisais pas attention.
6. Je suis arrivé à l'école.
7. Je les ai étudiés hier soir.
8. Je me suis couché à neuf heures.

II. Change to the past descriptive:

1. Nous finissons les sandwichs.
2. Elle chante tous les jours.
3. Ils vont acheter des gâteaux.
4. Vous avez la viande.
5. Il ne fait pas beau.
6. Ils sont beaux.

III. Write the following sentences in the past, being careful to use the correct past tense in each case:

En arrivant à la gare je commence tout de suite à chercher mon amie. C'est très difficile parce qu'il y a tant de monde qui va et vient, et avec cela il fait très noir. Enfin, après avoir cherché plusieurs minutes, je la trouve, et nous retournons ensemble à la maison.

IV. Read aloud these nouns, using the definite article before each one:

blanchisseuse	tour	mur
fleuve	feuille	route
appartement	cloche	façon
montagne	couloir	wagon
paysage	miette	écriteau
portière	nid	porteur
ouverture	croix	boutique

CENT DIXIÈME LEÇON

La Chanson de Roland

I. Le Roi Marsile

Marsile, le roi des Sarrasins, est fatigué de sa longue guerre avec Charlemagne. Il demande conseil à ses barons. C'est le baron Blancandrin qui le lui donne.

—Allez trouver Charlemagne, lui dit-il. Promettez-lui de le suivre en France et de devenir chrétien. Après son départ nous oublierons notre promesse.

Marsile choisit deux barons qui sont fidèles. Les deux barons se mettent immédiatement en route. Marsile leur promet de l'or, de l'argent, et des terres s'ils réussissent auprès de Charlemagne.

II. L'Empereur Charlemagne

L'empereur et toute sa cour s'amusent à Cordoue.[1] Ils ont pris la ville. Tous les païens sont morts ou chrétiens. Les soldats sont assis sur des tapis blancs. Charlemagne les regarde. Sa tête est blanche, sa barbe longue. Les barons du roi Marsile arrivent. C'est Blancandrin qui parle.

—Marsile veut devenir chrétien. Il vous donnera beaucoup de ses trésors. Il vous prie de retourner en France. Il promet de vous suivre.

L'empereur baisse la tête et réfléchit. Enfin il promet de donner une réponse le lendemain après avoir demandé conseil à ses barons. Le lendemain Roland, que Charlemagne aime de tout son cœur, prie l'empereur de ne pas écouter Marsile.

—C'est un traître. La dernière fois il a dit la même chose. Continuez la guerre et montrez que vous êtes fort.

Tous les Français sont silencieux. Enfin Ganelon prend la parole.[2]

—Ce n'est pas juste, dit Ganelon. Marsile vous offre la paix, et vous refusez. Il serait (*it would be*) mal de lutter davantage. Allez trouver Marsile, et dites-lui que vous acceptez.

Charlemagne accepte et cherche un baron qui portera ce message à Marsile. Il pense à Roland, son neveu, mais les barons trouvent que Roland est trop fier. Enfin Roland suggère Ganelon. Ganelon est en colère, parce qu'il sait que c'est une mission très dangereuse; mais il faut obéir à son empereur.

III. Ganelon le Traître

Ganelon monte à cheval. Son corps est beau, mais son regard est méchant. Sa colère est grande. Blancandrin accompagne Ganelon au roi Marsile.

—Sire, dit-il, Charlemagne va rentrer en France. Il laissera l'avant-garde, qui est peu nombreuse, derrière lui. Roland y sera avec son ami Olivier. Tuez ces deux-là, et Charlemagne n'aura plus envie de vous faire la guerre.

Marsile réfléchit. Oui, il veut tuer Roland, ce baron courageux. Si Roland meurt, Charlemagne perdra son bras droit, et l'Espagne sera libre. Marsile commence à ouvrir ses trésors pour en donner à Ganelon, qui les accepte sans hésiter.

IV. La Bataille

Roland et son ami Olivier voient venir l'immense armée des païens. Il n'y a que peu de soldats dans l'avant-garde. Olivier pense à Ganelon.

—Roland, mon compagnon, il faut sonner votre olifant pour demander secours à Charlemagne. L'armée de l'ennemi est très grande. Nous sommes en danger.

—Non, répond Roland. J'ai ma bonne épée, Durandal.

—Roland, mon compagnon, sonnez votre olifant, et l'empereur viendra.

L'armée des païens avance, et Roland arrive à Roncevaux.[3] Il est sur son bon cheval. Son visage est beau. Il oublie que l'armée de l'ennemi est grande, et que lui, Roland, n'a que peu de soldats.

Les soldats de Roland se battent avec courage. Ils tuent beaucoup de païens, mais les païens sont trop nombreux. Roland appelle Olivier.

—Olivier, mon compagnon, je sonnerai l'olifant. Charlemagne viendra.

—Il est trop tard, répond Olivier.

L'archevêque Turpin arrive.

—Si, Roland, sonnez. Charlemagne arrivera trop tard, mais ainsi les chiens ne nous mangeront pas.

[1] Cordoue, Cordova, Spain
[2] *takes the floor*

[3] Roncevaux, Roncesvalles, a valley or pass at the foot of the Pyrenees Mountains.

ROLAND BLOWS HIS HORN WITH ALL HIS STRENGTH

V. Roland sonne l'olifant

Roland sonne de toutes ses forces. Charlemagne l'entend, et il est inquiet.

—Il faut partir au secours de Roland, dit-il.

—Il n'y a pas de bataille, dit Ganelon le traître.

Encore une fois Roland sonne. L'empereur et ses hommes vont au secours de Roland, mais ils arriveront trop tard. Charlemagne fait saisir Ganelon et le fait mettre en prison.

Olivier est blessé, et il meurt. Les Sarrasins attaquent Roland. Ils veulent prendre sa chère épée, Durandal; mais ils ne réussissent pas à la prendre des mains de Roland.

La mort est proche. Roland va sous un arbre et se couche sur l'herbe. Il met sous lui l'olifant et l'épée, Durandal. Il pense à la douce France et à Charlemagne. Sa tête tombe sur son bras. Roland est mort.

Vocabulaire

l'avant-garde [lavã gard] (f.), advance-guard, vanguard

la barbe [barb], beard

la chanson [ʃãsõ], song

l'épée [lepe] (f.), sword

l'olifant [lɔlifã] (m.), horn

le païen [pajɛ̃], pagan, unbeliever

le secours [səkuːr], help

le traître [trɛːtr], traitor

lutter [lyte], to fight

sonner [sɔne], to sound, to blow (a horn)

chrétien [kretjɛ̃], Christian

nombreux, -se [nõbrø, nõbrøːz], numerous

davantage [davãtaːʒ], more, any more

mal [mal], bad, evil

proche [prɔʃ], near

English Equivalents

l'armée [larme] (f.), army

le baron [barõ], baron

l'empereur [lãprœːr] (m.), emperor

le message [mesaːʒ], message

la promesse [prɔmɛs], promise

le sire [siːr], sire, sir

les Sarrasins [Sarazɛ̃] (m. pl.), Saracens

CENT ONZIÈME LEÇON
Les Repas des Français

Les Français prennent générale-ment quatre repas par jour. Le petit déjeuner, qui est souvent servi dans la chambre à coucher, est très simple— une tasse de café au lait ou un verre de lait, des petits pains, et du beurre.

A midi le repas est plus copieux. On prend un hors-d'œuvre, de la viande, des pommes de terre, et un autre légume. On mange ensuite du fromage, du camembert ou du roquefort, qui sont des fromages très (*highly*) estimés. Pour terminer le repas on prend des fruits, qui sont excellents en France.

L'après-midi vers quatre heures on goûte. On prend des tartines de beurre ou des gâteaux secs, et quel-quefois du thé.

Le souper est souvent servi entre sept et huit heures. On commence par la soupe. Elle est bonne et nour-rissante. On mange ensuite des lé-gumes ou un pâté. On prend encore une fois du fromage. Pour le des-sert on prend une crème au caramel ou au chocolat, ou même une bonne tarte. Si on reçoit des amis, le dessert est toujours excellent.

Grammaire
Pronoun Objects with the Imperative

You have already found that the third-person direct object stays close to the verb. Today you are going to make another discovery. Here are the examples. You must do the thinking.

Donnez-lui du café. Donnez-lui-en.
Donnez-leur du café. Donnez-leur-en.
Donnez-moi du café. Donnez-m'en (m' = me).

Make a rule about the position of **en** when it is used after the verb.

The Relative Pronoun *Qui*

The relative subject pronoun **qui** is translated as *who* if its antecedent is a person, and as *which* if its antecedent is a thing. Remember that it is a *subject* pronoun. If the relative pronoun is followed by a verb, use **qui**.

Les enfants qui étudient sont intelligents.
Le pâté qui a coûté cher est excellent.

Vocabulaire

le camembert [kamãbɛːr], *Camembert cheese*
le caramel [karamɛl], *car-amel*
la crème au caramel [krɛːm o karamɛl], *cara-mel pudding*
la crème au chocolat [krɛːm o ʃokɔla], *choco-late pudding*

le dessert [deseːr], *dessert*
le hors-d'œuvre [ɔrdœːvr], *hors-d'œuvre, appetizer*
le pâté [pɑte], *meat-pie, pasty*
le roquefort[rɔkfɔːr],*Roque-fort cheese*
goûter [gute], *to have tea, to taste, to eat some-thing*

copieux, -se [kɔpjø, kɔ-pjøːz], *hearty, copious*
estimé [ɛstime], *esteemed, prized*
nourrissant [nurisã], *nour-ishing, nutritious*
encore une fois [ãkɔːr yn fwa], *again, once again*
généralement [ʒeneralmã], *generally*

Questionnaire

1. Combien de repas les familles françaises prennent-elles par jour?
2. Où le petit déjeuner est-il souvent servi?
3. Que mange-t-on le matin?
4. Que mange-t-on à midi?
5. Que prend-on à quatre heures?
6. Quand mange-t-on de la soupe?
7. Aimez-vous le fromage?
8. Quel dessert prend-on le soir?
9. Quand dînez-vous chez vous?

Devoir

A. *Look through "Les Repas des Français" to determine whether the relative pronoun* **qui** *is followed by a verb in each case.*

B. *Change the italicized words to pronouns:*

1. Prenez *des petits pois*.
2. Passez-moi *des pommes*.
3. Lisez-nous *cet article* tout à l'heure.
4. Lisez-lui *cet article*.
5. Apportez *des graines à Louis et à Charles* sans faute.
6. Conservez *les roses*.
7. Occupez-vous *de la terrasse*.
8. Montez *ces marches*, s'il vous plaît.
9. Regardez *ses beaux cheveux*.

C. *Give the future of the verbs in these sentences:*

1. Il faut s'y installer.
2. Il y en a trop.
3. Le buffet donne sur la rue.
4. Ils ont tant de vêtements.
5. Vous faites un long voyage.
6. Nous avons raison encore une fois.
7. Je le mets au-dessus de ma tête.
8. La vente est pour les étrangers.
9. Le patron est en train de planter des radis.
10. La fontaine arrose les fleurs.

Traduction:

1. The meal which is served at noon is called (the) luncheon.
2. The vegetables which come from the garden are excellent.
3. The French eat a great deal of cheese.
4. (The) Camembert and (the) Roquefort, which are highly esteemed, are excellent.
5. The cook, who has worked all morning, has prepared a hearty meal.
6. Madame Bouchard, who went to market with her basket at ten o'clock, bought the meat.
7. The children who are eating the chocolate pudding look happy.

Composition:

Ecrivez une courte composition au sujet d'un dîner chez votre grand'mère.
Dites:

1. A quelle heure vous êtes arrivé.
2. Qui étaient les autres invités.
3. Qui a préparé le dîner.
4. Qui l'a servi.
5. Ce que vous avez mangé.
6. De quoi vous avez parlé.
7. Ce que vous avez dit à votre grand'mère en partant.
8. Pourquoi vous aimez dîner chez votre grand'mère.

THE FAMOUS "PONT D'AVIGNON" OF DANCE AND SONG

FOLK SONGS AND PEASANT DANCES

To appreciate the real beauty of French folk song, you should not only read it from the printed page—you should hear it sung. And then you really understand it. The French poet André Theuriet says: "I shall always remember with a thrill that moment when the charm of French popular poetry was first made clear to me. It was in a small town of Poitou. One summer morning at dawn I was asleep by an open window, when I was rudely awakened by the voice of a lad who was leading his horses down to the river for their morning drink and bath. He was singing with all the strength of his young lungs:

Elle a son doux berger
Qui vient la voir souvent.

Hé! levez-vous, bergère.
Hé! levez-vous, car il est jour.

Les moutons sont en plaine,
Le soleil luit partout.[1]

But the words are nothing without the music. You should hear this air, dragging at first and with the rhythm of plainsong, then all at once soaring away in light, clear, happy notes like so many larks. It seemed to me at that very instant that I saw the sky grow bright and heard the earth sing."

In all the provinces of France, folk songs like the one heard by Theuriet have been sung for uncounted generations, and no living man knows where they all come from. They contain simple sentiments that are common to all human beings. Such songs live on and on in much the same way that popular superstitions do. Each generation teaches them to the next. Absent sons return from travel and work away from home, with new melodies. Many folk songs sung by city people tell of the pleasures of country life; rustic verses are apt to treat of the delights of town.

[1] *She has her charming shepherd, who often comes to see her. Oh, rise now, shepherdess. Oh, rise, for it is day. The sheep are in the meadows, the sun shines all around.*

Folk songs are divided into several kinds according to their subjects. There are verses for almost anything that can happen to a person in this life. Important are the lullabies with which baby is rocked or trit-trotted off to sleep; for these are the songs first learned and longest remembered. Then there are songs for small children, who dance while singing them, and songs for different seasons of the year, notably for May and for harvest time. Other verses are intended for the fiancée, for the bride, the young soldier on his departure for military service. A large group of melodies whose rhythm fits the movements of laborers make up the work-songs: reaping couplets, sailors' chanteys, choruses for wood-choppers, porters, miners, millers, workers at anvil and forge; marching songs for soldiers. Teasing songs, intended to make friendly mock of people, are as numerous as flies in summer: dairymen who water the milk, grocers who give short weight, innkeepers who add another cross to the slate when their guest is not looking, millers who absent-mindedly put the best flour into their own sacks, tailors who make coats of fag-ends of cloth. All such tradesmen are immortalized in popular ballads that reflect the kindly malice of their authors.

If we compare French folk songs with those of other European nations, we are struck at once by the fact that the story element in the French is much weaker, that the whole tone of the narrative is much less important. It is the lyrical element that is strong in these popular ballads. Love is the subject of most of them—a tender love tinged with melancholy, typical of the Romantic spirit.

French folk songs are often combined with folk dances. The commonest form of popular ballad in which dancing has a part is called the round. One of the most famous of these is danced to the old tune, "Sur le Pont d'Avignon," which you will find on page 312. It is performed mainly by children, though older folk in their moments of outdoor play often share in its joys. The action of a

DANCING THE ROUND, "SUR LE PONT D'AVIGNON"   Drouet, Nancy

DANCING THE FARANDOLE

round is simple: singing and holding hands, the dancers fly about in a circle, now from left to right, now from right to left, faster and faster, ever more madly until breath and sense are gone, and feet and words are hopelessly mixed. Nor can they pause in their career before the magic word agreed on is spoken—and then they sink exhausted to the ground. In the round of "Sur le Pont d'Avignon" and some others, the dancers imitate the steps and gestures of the people of the song. Riotous laughter is the reward of that dancer whose mimicry is the most absurdly true to life.

On Sunday, or on a holiday or a market day, peasants meet to trip their measures in the public square. In France, as in our country, the older dances are disappearing in surrender to the wild capering of couples stirred by bands bleating ragtime and jazz. But at stated festivals one still sees group dancing that has been handed down from time immemorial, such as the *bourrée* of Auvergne. In this the gay steps follow one another like light,

while the hands of the dancers clap the rhythm for each step and figure, and urge on the bagpipe players.

Another old dance which is occasionally revived at various festivities is the Farandole. This popular dance comes from Provence and is usually executed out of doors, often to most informal or impromptu music. There are various figures in the Farandole, which is based on a circle or long line of dancers sometimes facing alternately in and out, with hands clasped.

The occasion when one is sure to witness old-fashioned peasant dances is the wedding celebration. Singing and merry dancing never fail at such festivals. Fiddle, flute, and drum furnish continual din—songs are sung to the wedding couple, old ballads all of them, but slyly changed here and there to fit the needs of the moment. Dancers are all in their traditional provincial costumes. Gay movement and singing continue until all are exhausted. Then they sleep and rest up, for the morrow will bring its usual work.

SUR LE PONT D'AVIGNON

Old Round

Sur le Pont d'A - vi - gnon L'on y pas - se, l'on y dan - se;

Sur le Pont d'A - vi - gnon L'on y dan - se tout en rond.

1. Les beaux mes - sieurs font comme ça, Et puis en - core comme ça.
2. Les braves sol - dats font comme ça,
3. Les ga - mins font comme ça,

Sur le Pont d'A - vi - gnon L'on y pas - se, l'on y dan - se;

FINE

Sur le Pont d'A - vi - gnon L'on y dan - se tout en rond.

CENT DOUZIÈME LEÇON

A la gare

Nous sommes arrivés à la gare à huit heures un quart. Il y a deux salles d'attente au milieu de la gare. La grande est réservée aux voyageurs de première et de seconde classes, et l'autre aux voyageurs de troisième classe. Nous avons attendu dans la salle réservée aux voyageurs de troisième pendant que mon père est allé chercher les billets. Il les a pris au guichet. Deux porteurs, qui étaient très forts, sont venus chercher nos bagages pour les enregistrer dans la salle des bagages. Ma mère m'a donné de l'argent pour acheter des provisions au buffet de la gare. Les sandwichs que j'y ai achetés étaient très bons. Mon père, qui avait les billets à la main, nous a appelés. Nous sommes allés à la porte qui donnait sur les quais. Un employé que mon père connaissait lui a pris les billets. En allant à notre wagon nous avons vu la grosse locomotive, que le chauffeur inspectait avant le départ du train. Nous sommes montés dans un compartiment de troisième, où nous avons installé nos petits bagages. Après quelques minutes le chef de gare, que nous pouvions voir par la portière, a sifflé après avoir crié "En voiture!"; et notre train est parti.

Grammaire

The Relatives *Qui* and *Que*

The relative object pronoun **que** means *whom* if its antecedent is a noun and *which* or *that* if its antecedent is a thing. You learned in the preceding lesson that **qui** must be followed by a verb. **Que** *must be followed by a noun or pronoun.* Look through "A la gare" to ascertain whether **qui** and **que** follow these rules.

Vocabulaire

le **chauffeur** [ʃofœːr], *engineer, chauffeur*

la **provision** [prɔvizjɔ̃], *something to eat;* les **provisions** [prɔvizjɔ̃], *supplies, food*

la **salle des bagages** [sal də bagaːʒ], *baggage-room*

enregistrer [ɑ̃rəʒistre], *to check* (baggage)

inspecter [ɛ̃spɛkte], *to inspect*

installer [ɛ̃stale], *to put, to place*

second [səgɔ̃], *second*

pendant que [pɑ̃dɑ̃ kə], *while*

Questionnaire

1. A quelle heure êtes-vous arrivés à la gare?
2. Combien de salles d'attente y a-t-il, et pourquoi?
3. Qui a acheté les billets?
4. Où avez-vous acheté les sandwichs, et comment étaient-ils?
5. Qui vous a appelés?
6. Qui connaissait votre père, et où était-il?
7. Que faisait le chauffeur?
8. Qui avez-vous vu par la portière?
9. Qu'est-ce qu'il a crié?
10. Aimez-vous voyager?
11. Que faut-il avoir pour pouvoir faire des voyages?
12. Que préférez-vous, les trains ou les bateaux?
13. Avez-vous été à Paris?

Devoir

A. *Supply the correct relative pronouns and complete the sentences:*

1. Les enfants —— étaient à la gare ——
2. Mon père, —— l'employé connaît, ——
3. Le veau —— le boucher a préparé tout à l'heure ——
4. La locomotive —— le chauffeur inspectait ——
5. La porte —— donnait sur le quai ——
6. Nos bagages —— le porteur a pris ——
7. Les voyageurs —— étaient à la gare ——
8. Les petits pains —— nous avons achetés ——
9. Les souliers neufs —— j'ai abîmés ——

B. *Change the verbs to the past indefinite. Remember the past participle.*

1. Ma petite cousine (venir) visiter notre jardin d'agrément.
2. Elle nous (rendre) visite.
3. Je ne la (voir) pas.
4. La lettre que je (écrire) à la librairie était très longue.

5. Quels amis (rencontrer) -vous?
6. Je (acheter) les livres, mais je ne les (lire) pas encore.
7. Nous nous (lever) à sept heures.
8. (S'amuser) -elle assez bien?
9. Les enfants souriants (reconnaître) la dame aux cheveux noirs.

C. *Give these dates in French:*

July 6	April 12
February 1	August 19
November 23	June 15

*Traduction: (If the sentence contains a relative pronoun, determine by the word following whether you must use **qui** or **que**.)*

My little sister, whom I love very much, went to the country. My aunt went with her. My father, who is my aunt's brother, bought the tickets. The box containing the sandwiches which my mother prepared was on the seat of the coach. The engineer, whom we could see, was inspecting his locomotive. When the station master blew the whistle (**siffler**), the train left.

Copyright by Wide World Photos, Paris

THE GARE DU NORD, PARIS

CENT TREIZIÈME LEÇON
Review

A

1. What tenses of the French verb have you studied?

2. How is the past participle of regular verbs of the first, second, and third conjugations formed?

3. Give the present tenses of **ve-nir, pouvoir,** and **vouloir.**

4. In what ways may the present tense be translated into English? Use **ils parlent** in your answer.

5. How is the future tense formed?

6. Give the future tense of **aller, prendre,** and **faire.**

7. Give the infinitives of four reflexive verbs.

8. Name five verbs conjugated with **avoir.**

9. Name five conjugated with **être.**

10. Name three reflexive verbs. With what auxiliary are they conjugated?

11. In what three ways may the past indefinite be translated? Use **nous avons lu** in your answer.

12. Before which of the two parts of the past indefinite tense are pronoun objects placed?

13. With what does the past participle of verbs conjugated with **avoir** agree? Verbs conjugated with **être?** Reflexive verbs?

14. How is the past descriptive formed?

15. How may the past descriptive be translated into English? Use **vous veniez** in your answer.

16. What are the three rules governing the use of the past descriptive? Illustrate each rule.

17. What is irregular about the past descriptive of **commencer?**

18. If an action occurred *once* in the past, what tense would you use in French?

19. If in an English sentence the form "was beginning" is used, by what tense must it be translated into French and why?

20. If you saw the English sentence "We went to the theater" standing alone, would you be certain which tense you were to use in translating it into French? Explain why not.

21. How is the present participle formed? Is it used in forming verb tenses in French? If it is used with a preposition, what must that preposition be?

22. How is the perfect infinitive formed? In what two ways may **après m'être levé** and **après avoir étudié** be translated? How would the opposite idea of these constructions be translated into French?

23. Explain the use of **qui** and **que** and give an example of each.

B

I. Give the future third person plural of:

chanter	aller	faire
remplir	avoir	venir
descendre	être	pouvoir

II. Give the past indefinite of the verbs in (I), second person plural.

III. Give the past descriptive of the verbs in (I), first person plural.

IV. In the following sentences replace the italicized words by pronouns:

1. Elle a enregistré *les bagages.*
2. Nous avons dévoré *les épinards.*
3. Ils ont regardé *les locomotives.*
4. Vous n'avez pas fait *de voyage.*
5. Je pourrai acheter *les légumes.*
6. Elles n'ont pas réuni *les bagages.*
7. Ils ont acheté *les petits pois et les haricots.*
8. Nous paierons *la nourriture* après avoir mangé *au buffet de la gare.*
9. Apportez *les bas à Marie.*
10. Vendez-moi *la corde.*

CENT QUATORZIÈME LEÇON
Louis Pasteur et Jupille

—Un chien enragé! Un chien enragé! Avez-vous entendu ce cri terrible? Avez-vous peur d'un chien enragé? Oui, certainement, tout le monde en a peur, mais maintenant on ne meurt pas si on est mordu. Ecoutez bien cette petite histoire.

Un jour un garçon de quatorze ans, nommé Jupille, garde comme d'ordinaire ses moutons dans la montagne. Tout à coup on crie—Un chien enragé!

—Courez, vous autres, courez, dit-il. Je vais rester ici. Je tuerai la bête.

Jupille prend son fouet et attaque la bête enragée. La lutte est terrible; mais le garçon tue la bête. Malheureusement il est cruellement mordu.

C'est en 1885.[1] Vous savez que la morsure d'un chien enragé cause une maladie très sérieuse. On en meurt. Mais il y a un homme qui fait des merveilles. C'est Louis Pasteur.

Le brave petit Jupille va peut-être mourir. Mais non, le bon Monsieur Pasteur invite l'enfant chez lui (*to his home*). Il y va, et grâce à la découverte de M. Pasteur l'enfant est sauvé, et il peut retourner auprès de ses parents.

Toute sa vie Pasteur a travaillé dans son laboratoire. Il a fait des découvertes magnifiques. Par ses découvertes cet homme si modeste, qui a tant travaillé, mérite notre reconnaissance.

Madame Curie

Madame Curie est née à Varsovie[2] en 1867.[3] C'était une jeune fille très intelligente. Elle aimait les sciences et les mathématiques. Pendant quelques années elle était gouvernante dans une famille. Elle a économisé tout son argent, parce qu'elle voulait retourner à l'école.

Sa sœur était à Paris. En 1891[4] la jeune Marie Skladowska est partie pour rejoindre sa sœur. Elle travaillait dur à l'école.

En 1893[5] elle rencontre Pierre Curie, jeune physicien. En 1895[6] leur mariage a lieu. Ils sont très heureux ensemble. Ils travaillent dans leur modeste petite maison près de Paris. C'est en 1898[7] que Madame Curie découvre un nouvel élément, le radium.

En 1906[8] au moment où les Curie comptent prendre une maison et un laboratoire un peu mieux installé[9] il arrive un déplorable accident. Pierre Curie est écrasé par un camion.

Mais Madame Curie est courageuse. C'est à ce moment-là que l'Université de Paris fait une chose extraordinaire. Pour la première fois une femme est nommée professeur à la Sorbonne. Elle prend la place de son mari.

Pendant la guerre Madame Curie continue son travail, aidée par ses filles. Tous les pays désirent lui offrir des décorations. L'Amérique aussi prend part à ce mouvement. En 1921[10] Mme. Curie est allée à Washington pour recevoir un gramme de radium, cadeau de ses admiratrices américaines.

Voici ce qu'elle dit:—Ce gramme de radium représente une énorme somme d'argent. Ce n'est pas pour moi; c'est pour la science. Après ma mort ce gramme de radium sera donné à l'Institut de Radium à Paris.

En octobre, 1929,[11] Madame Curie a visité l'Amérique pour recevoir un second gramme de radium.

---

[1] dix-huit cent quatre-vingt-cinq
[2] in Warsaw
[3] dix-huit cent soixante-sept
[4] dix-huit cent quatre-vingt-onze
[5] dix-huit cent quatre-vingt-treize
[6] dix-huit cent quatre-vingt-quinze
[7] dix-huit cent quatre-vingt-dix-huit
[8] dix-neuf cent six
[9] *a little better equipped*
[10] dix-neuf cent vingt et un
[11] dix-neuf cent vingt-neuf

Vocabulaire

l'admiratrice [ladmiratris]
(f.), *admirer*
le camion [kamjõ], *truck,*
dray
le fouet [fwɛ], *whip*
la gouvernante [guvɛrnã:t],
governess
la lutte [lyt], *struggle, fight,*
contest

la merveille [mɛrvɛ:j], *mar-*
velous thing, marvel
la morsure [mɔrsy:r], *bite*
la reconnaissance [rəkɔ-
nɛsã:s], *gratitude*
avoir lieu [avwa:r ljø], *to*
take place
écraser [ekraze], *to run*
over, to crush

mordre [mɔrdr], *to bite*
naître [nɛ:tr] (p.p. **né**),
to be born
nommer [nɔme], *to name,*
to appoint
enragé [ãraʒe], *mad*
cruellement [kryɛlmã], *cru-*
elly, sadly
dur [dy:r], *hard*

English Equivalents

l'accident [laksidã] (m.),
accident
le cri [kri], *cry*
la décoration [dekɔrasjõ],
decoration (awarded for
distinguished work)
l'élément [lelemã] (m.),
element, metal
le gramme [gram], *gram* (a
very small unit of weight)
l'institut [lẽstity] (m.), *in-*
stitute

le laboratoire [labɔra-
twa:r], *laboratory*
le mariage [marja:ʒ], *mar-*
riage
la mathématique [mate-
matik], *mathematics*
le physicien [fizisjẽ], *phy-*
sician
le radium [radjɔm], *radium*
la science [sjã:s], *science*
il arrive [il ari:v], *there*
happens, there occurs

économiser [ekɔnɔmize],
to save, to economize
rejoindre [rəʒwẽ:dr], *to join,*
to rejoin, to catch up with
déplorable [deplɔrabl],
sad, deplorable
modeste [mɔdɛst], *modest,*
simple, plain
sérieux, -se [sɛrjø, sɛr-
jø:z], *serious*
terrible [tɛribl], *terrible,*
frightful

CENT QUINZIÈME LEÇON

Charlemagne

Charlemagne est le roi des Francs. C'est un homme très simple. Il n'aime pas les cérémonies. Il est très grand. Il est bon aussi. Il fait venir ses fermiers, et il leur parle ainsi:—Vous travaillez mes champs. Les paysans travaillent aussi. Je veux que tout le monde travaille. Si vous travaillez, vous aurez des poules (*chickens*) et des oies dans vos fermes. Vous n'aurez jamais faim. Vous serez contents.

Charlemagne aime la chasse. Un jour de fête après la messe il appelle ses seigneurs. Charlemagne s'habille très simplement d'une blouse ou d'une peau de mouton. Ce jour-là il porte la peau de mouton. Tous les seigneurs ont des vêtements de soie brodés d'or. Il les invite à la chasse. On part.

Pendant la chasse il pleut. Les seigneurs sont malheureux, parce que leurs vêtements sont mouillés.

—Insensés, leur dit Charlemagne, regardez-moi. Ma peau de mouton me préserve bien de la pluie, tandis que vous avec vos vêtements de soie, vous êtes mouillés. C'est stupide, cela.

Charlemagne est un conquérant. Il fait la guerre aux peuples qui ne croient pas en Jésus-Christ. Il va en Espagne se battre avec les Sarrasins.[1] Après quelque temps Marsile, le roi des Sarrasins, demande la paix. A cause du traître Ganelon, Charlemagne perd son neveu Roland. Tout le monde connaît cette histoire du grand Charlemagne et de son neveu courageux, Roland.

---

[1] See Lesson 110, page 305, for details.

Charlemagne et les Ecoles

Charlemagne a une école dans son palais à Aix-la-Chapelle.[1] Il visite souvent l'école pour voir si les enfants travaillent bien. Un jour il entre dans la classe pour écouter les leçons. Il y a là des enfants pauvres et des enfants riches. Ils sont assis sur les mêmes bancs. Le professeur est un prêtre. Il demande aux élèves de donner leurs devoirs à l'empereur.

Charlemagne lit les devoirs. Il remarque que les devoirs des enfants pauvres sont excellents. Les devoirs des enfants riches sont pleins de fautes.

Charlemagne parle aux enfants pauvres.—Je vous félicite, mes enfants. Vous avez bien travaillé. Je suis très content de vous. Vous êtes très intelligents. Vous serez un jour très instruits. Je ne vous oublierai pas. Quand vous serez grands, vous serez contents d'avoir travaillé.

Maintenant l'empereur regarde les enfants riches. Il est fâché.—Vous êtes paresseux, leur dit-il. Si vous voulez quelque chose de moi, il faut travailler. Vous ne pouvez pas tout acheter avec votre argent. Je n'aime que les enfants qui travaillent bien. Ne l'oubliez pas.

L'empereur veut fonder des écoles partout. Il veut que les enfants sachent lire et écrire.[2] La fête des écoles c'est la Saint-Charlemagne, le 28 janvier. Ce jour-là tous les enfants français pensent au grand empereur qui a encouragé les enfants qui travaillent bien.

Le Chevalier sans peur et sans reproche

C'est le grand héros, Bayard, qui porte le nom de Chevalier sans peur et sans reproche.

Bayard aide trois rois français. Il est très brave et très généreux. Il se couvre de gloire, et même ses ennemis l'admirent pour son grand courage.

Les Français font la guerre en Italie. Un jour l'armée française est au bord d'une rivière, le Garigliano. L'armée de l'ennemi est de l'autre côté. Les armées sont séparées par un pont. L'ennemi désire traverser le pont, mais le brave Bayard est là. Il monte vite sur son cheval, et il arrive de l'autre côté du pont au moment où l'ennemi va le traverser.

Voilà le grand Bayard seul contre l'ennemi, mais il n'a pas peur. Il tire son épée. Il frappe à droite et à gauche. Les soldats italiens que Bayard tue tombent dans l'eau. Il y a beaucoup de soldats qui attaquent Bayard. Va-t-on le tuer?

Voilà une troupe de soldats français qui arrive. Ils trouvent Bayard seul sur le pont, et ils l'aident à tuer l'ennemi. Depuis ce moment on appelle Bayard le Chevalier sans peur et sans reproche.

* * * * *

Une autre fois encore Bayard montre son grand courage. François Ier est roi. Il est jeune et beau. C'est pendant une bataille en Italie. On se bat[3] très longtemps. C'est la nuit. Le combat cesse. Bayard est seul au milieu de ses ennemis. Il veut retourner chez son roi, qui a besoin de ses services. Il avance doucement. Il arrive sain et sauf, et il va trouver son roi.

François Ier est content.—Je suis

---

[1] a city in Germany.
[2] *He wants the children to know how to read and write.*

[3] *they fight.*

fier de vous, Bayard, lui dit-il. Je n'ai pas été armé chevalier. Vous allez m'armer chevalier.

Bayard hésite. Que faire? Armer son roi chevalier? Il faut obéir. Le roi se met à genoux devant Bayard. Bayard prend son épée. Que fait-il? Il touche l'épaule de son roi. C'est la cérémonie qu'il faut faire pour l'armer chevalier.

Vocabulaire

le chevalier [lə ʃəvalje], *knight*
le conquérant [kõkerã], *conqueror*
l'épaule [lepoːl] (f.), *shoulder*
la fête des écoles [fɛːt de zekɔl], *school holiday*
la gloire [glwaːr], *glory*
le jour de fête [ʒuːr də fɛːt], *holiday*
le malheur [malœːr], *misfortune*
la messe [mɛs], *mass*
le nord [nɔːr], *north*
l'oie [lwɑ] (f.), *goose*

la peau de mouton [pod mutõ], *sheepskin*
la pluie [plɥi], *rain*
la richesse [riʃɛs], *riches*
le seigneur [lə sɛɲœːr] *lord, squire, nobleman*
se couvrir [sə kuvriːr], *to cover oneself*
faire venir [fɛːr vəniːr], *to send for*
féliciter [felisite], *to congratulate*
se mettre à genoux [sə mɛtra ʒənu], *to kneel*

oser [oze], *to dare*
brodé [brɔde], *embroidered*
insensé [ɛ̃sãse], *foolish*
instruit [ɛ̃strɥi], *learned*
malheureux, -se [malœrø, malœrøːz], *unhappy, unfortunate*
mouillé [muje], *wet*
sain et sauf [sɛ̃ e soːf], *safe and sound*
simplement [sɛ̃pləmã], *simply*
plein de [plɛ̃ də], *full of*
tandis que [tãdi kə], *while*

English Equivalents

la cérémonie [seremɔni], *ceremony*
la chasse [ʃas], *chase, hunting*
l'empereur [lãprœːr] (m.), *emperor*
la tape [tap], *tap, rap*

la troupe [trup], *troop, band, company*
armer chevalier [arme ʃəvalje], *to make* or *dub* (one) *knight*
préserver [prezɛrve], *to preserve, to protect*

généreux, -se [ʒenerø, ʒenerøːz], *generous, liberal*
riche [riʃ], *rich, wealthy, sumptuous*
séparé [separe], *separated, divided*

CENT SEIZIÈME LEÇON

Les Journaux

Il y a beaucoup de journaux à Paris. Ils sont plus petits que les journaux américains. Dans six ou huit pages d'un journal français on trouve autant de nouvelles que dans un journal américain de vingt pages. Il n'y a presque pas d'annonces dans les journaux français. On trouve des nouvelles de Paris à la première page. Les nouvelles moins importantes on trouve à l'intérieur. Il y a aussi des nouvelles commerciales, sportives, et théâtrales. *Le Figaro* est aussi important que *le Matin*. Le facteur apporte les journaux aux habitants des provinces. Il y a des journaux régionaux aussi, mais ils sont souvent moins bons que les journaux parisiens. Je lis aussi quelques journaux étrangers.

Notre facteur ne vient pas si exactement qu'autrefois. Il s'arrête pour causer avec ses amis qui demeurent dans la maison voisine. Je l'aime moins que notre ancien facteur, qui était plus exact. Maintenant que je suis un peu plus âgé je suis impatient de voir le journal pour lire les nouvelles politiques. Quelquefois le journal est perdu. En ce cas je vais en chercher un autre chez le marchand de tabac, qui demeure plus près de chez nous que le marchand de journaux.

Grammaire

The Comparative of the Adjective

All the adjectives used so far have been in the positive degree, **beau, joli, vert,** etc. As you well know, there are two ways of forming the comparative degree in English, either by adding *-er* to the adjective or by using the adverbs *more, less, as,* before it. In French there is but one way of forming the comparative: that is, to add the adverbs **plus, moins, aussi,** or **si** before the adjective. In "Les Journaux," when a comparison is used, one of these four words precedes the adjective, which is followed by **que** if the object to which the noun or pronoun is compared is mentioned.

> beau, *beautiful*
> plus beau que, *more beautiful than*
> moins beau que, *less beautiful than*
> aussi beau que, *as beautiful as*
> si beau que, *as beautiful as* (use **si** after a negative verb)

Remember the agreement of an adjective in French. It must always agree in gender and number with the noun or pronoun it modifies.

The Comparative of the Adverb

To form the comparative of an adverb, add **moins, plus, aussi,** or **si** before it.

> moins vite que, *less quickly than*
> plus loin que, *farther than*
> aussi bien que, *as well as*
> si près que, *as near as* (use **si** after a negative verb)

Vocabulaire

l'annonce [lanõːs] (f.), *advertising, advertisement*
l'intérieur [lɛ̃terjœːr] (m.) *interior, inside*
la province [prɔvɛ̃ːs], *country district, province*

le tabac [taba], *tobacco*
causer [koze], *to chat*
neiger [nɛʒe], *to snow*
commercial [kɔmɛrsjal], *commercial*
parisien [parizjɛ̃], *Parisian*

politique [pɔlitik], *political*
régional, -aux [reʒɔnal, reʒjono], *regional, local*
sportif, -ve [spɔrtif, spɔrtiːv], *sporting* (news)
théâtral [teɑtral], *theatrical*

Questionnaire

Be careful to make the adjective agree in each answer.

1. Les journaux français sont-ils plus petits ou plus grands que les journaux américains?
2. Quels journaux sont moins bons que les journaux parisiens?
3. L'autre facteur était-il plus ou moins exact que le facteur qui vient maintenant?
4. Pourquoi aime-t-on voir venir le facteur?
5. Votre sœur est-elle plus petite ou plus grande que vous?
6. Marchez-vous plus vite ou moins vite que votre ami?
7. Demeurez-vous plus près du marchand de tabac que du marchand de journaux?
8. Y a-t-il moins de nouvelles dans un journal français que dans un journal américain?
9. Pourquoi êtes-vous impatient de voir le journal?

Devoir

A. Complete the sentences, using comparatives:

1. Le journal est —— que le livre.
2. Les articles —— sont à la deuxième page.
3. Notre boucher n'arrive pas —— que l'autre.
4. Notre marchand de journaux est —— que votre marchand.
5. Nous demeurons —— de l'école que possible.

B. Change italicized words to pronouns:

1. Lisez-moi *le récit.*
2. Ne répétez pas *ces mots.*
3. Envoyez-nous *l'écriteau.*
4. Mettez *les assiettes* sur la table.
5. Parlez *de cette affaire à Joséphine.*

C. Change the infinitive to the correct past tense in each of the following:

1. Quand je (rencontrer) mon amie, elle (acheter) des légumes.
2. Le petit garçon (courir) pendant que sa grande sœur (étudier).
3. Hier je (être) heureux, parce que mon père me (apporter) une belle montre.

4. La neige (tomber) fort quand je (sortir).
5. Ils (se promener) souvent quand ils (demeurer) à la campagne.
6. (Avoir)-vous grand peur quand le chien (s'approcher) de vous hier?
7. Ce matin quand Thomas (aller) à l'école, il (faire) mauvais.
8. Après être montée, elle (aller) à sa chambre.
9. Après avoir lu l'article, nous le (comprendre).

Traduction:

The French newspapers are smaller than (*the*) American newspapers. The articles which are less important are on the second page. I like a paper containing sporting news. *Le Figaro* is as popular as *le Matin*. The local newspapers are often not as good as (*less good than*) the Parisian papers. The mail-carrier who brings our paper is not as punctual as our former mail-carrier. If the paper does not arrive, I go to the tobacco-shop near my house to get another.

CENT DIX-SEPTIÈME LEÇON

Les Rues de Paris

Les rues les plus grandes de Paris sont les boulevards, qui sont plantés d'arbres. Souvent les rues les plus pittoresques sont les plus petites et les plus étroites. Elles sont souvent si étroites que deux automobiles ne peuvent pas passer. Les automobiles vont souvent très vite, et les piétons sont obligés de faire attention en traversant les rues. La meilleure façon de connaître Paris est de marcher ou de se promener en autobus. On peut mieux voir si on marche lentement le long des trottoirs.

Les meilleurs magasins sont dans la Rue de Rivoli, mais le Printemps, qui est très bon aussi, est sur le boulevard Haussmann. C'est dans la Rue de la Paix et dans l'Avenue de l'Opéra qu'on trouve les objets du plus grand luxe. Les étrangers aiment mieux les petits magasins. Les rues de Paris sont toujours pleines de monde qui va et vient. Sur l'Avenue des Champs-Elysées on voit une foule élégante se promener à pied ou en auto. Sur les larges trottoirs devant les cafés et les restaurants sont installées des tables et des chaises où on peut prendre une glace ou quelque chose à boire.

Séeberger Frères, Paris

RUE DE LA PAIX, LOOKING TOWARD THE PLACE VENDÔME

Grammaire

The Comparison of Adjectives and Adverbs

To form the superlative of an adjective or of an adverb, add the definite article before the comparative degree.

Comparison of the Adjective Petit

POSITIVE: petit, petite, petits, petites, *small*
COMPARATIVE: plus petit, plus petite, plus petits, plus petites, *smaller*
SUPERLATIVE: le plus petit, la plus petite, les plus petits, les plus petites, *smallest*

Comparison of the Adverb Vite

POSITIVE: vite, *fast*
COMPARATIVE: plus vite, *faster*
SUPERLATIVE: le plus vite, *fastest*

If the adjective follows the noun, as is usually the case, the definite article is repeated before the adjective as well as before the noun.

les rues les plus étroites, *the narrowest streets*

BUT

les plus petits magasins, *the smallest stores*

Often there is no apparent difference between the comparative and the superlative degrees. Thus, **les plus petits livres** may mean *the smaller books* or *the smallest books.*

The only preposition that may be used after a superlative in French is **de.** Consequently it is used to translate the prepositions *in, of.*

Marie est la meilleure élève de la classe.

The comparison of the adjective **bon** is irregular in French.   (Is the comparison of the English *good* regular or irregular?)

> bon, bonne, bons, bonnes, *good*
> meilleur, meilleure, meilleurs, meilleures, *better*
> le meilleur, la meilleure, les meilleurs, les meilleures, *best*

The comparison of the adverb **bien** is irregular in French.   (Is the comparison of the English *well* regular or irregular?)

> bien, *well*   mieux, *better*   le mieux, *best*

Remember that **bon** is an adjective and must modify a noun or a pronoun. **Bien,** an adverb, must modify an adjective, a verb, or another adverb.

Vocabulaire

la foule [ful], *mob, multitude, crowd*
la glace [glas], *ice, ice-cream*
le luxe [lyks], *luxury, richness, splendor*
le trottoir [trɔtwaːr], *sidewalk*

connaître [kɔnɛːtr], *to be acquainted with, to know (a person)*
se promener à pied ou en auto [sə prɔmne a pje u ɑ̃ nɔto], *to walk or to ride in a car*

élégant [elegɑ̃], *elegant, fashionable*
étroit[etrwa],*narrow,strict, tight*
meilleur [mɛjœːr] (adj.), *better*
mieux [mjø] (adv.), *better*

Questionnaire

1. Comment sont les boulevards de Paris?
2. Quelles rues sont les plus pittoresques?
3. Quelle est la meilleure façon de connaître Paris?
4. Les rues ici sont-elles toujours pleines de monde?
5. Où sont les meilleurs magasins?
6. Qu'est-ce que les étrangers aiment mieux?
7. Comment sont les rues de Paris?
8. Que faut-il faire en les traversant?
9. Où peut-on prendre une glace?
10. Où voit-on une foule élégante?

Devoir

Traduction:

1. These streets are the narrowest.
2. We believe (**trouver**) that the best store is the Printemps.
3. Without doubt the foreigners like the smaller stores better.
4. We do not walk as fast as our friends.
5. They can see better by (**en**) walking.
6. The Rue de Rivoli is one of the longest streets in Paris.
7. The small stores are not always better than the large stores.
8. The pedestrians are obliged to be careful while (**en**) crossing the widest streets.

Composition: Ecrivez une composition sur les rues de votre ville.   Dites:

1. Si elles sont larges ou étroites.
2. Si elles sont plantées d'arbres.
3. Si les maisons sont neuves ou vieilles (m. sing. **vieux**).
4. S'il y a beaucoup de grands magasins.
5. S'il y a des tables et des chaises devant les restaurants.
6. Quelle est la meilleure façon de voir une ville.

CENT DIX-HUITIÈME LEÇON

A la poste

—Qui désire aller à la poste avec moi? demande Henri.

—Moi, répond une voix dans le salon. J'écoute votre T. S. F.

—Qui est-ce?

—C'est moi, vous savez bien, répond Jean en arrivant dans la salle à manger.

—Je dois porter ce paquet à la poste pour mon oncle. Lui et moi, nous sommes de très bons amis. Je fais souvent des commissions pour lui.

—Moi, je n'ai pas d'oncle, mais j'ai une tante. Partons (*Let us leave*).

—Ma petite sœur, elle aime sortir. Elle et moi, nous sortons souvent ensemble.

Voilà Henri et Jean dans la rue.

—N'est-ce pas notre professeur de français qui vient vers nous?

—Oui, c'est lui. Je vais lui parler en français. Bonjour, Monsieur Blanchard.

—Bonjour, Henri. Bonjour, Jean. Allez-vous à la poste?

—Oui, Monsieur, Jean et moi, nous portons ce paquet à la poste pour mon oncle.

—Mais ne savez-vous pas que la poste est fermée? Il est midi vingt.

—C'est vrai. Je n'ai pas regardé l'heure avant de partir. Merci, Monsieur. Au revoir, Monsieur.

—Au revoir, mes enfants.

—C'est bête, cela. J'ai oublié que la poste ferme de midi à deux heures. Rentrons (*Let us return*) vite chez moi. Nous pourrons ainsi jouer aux cartes tout à l'heure.

Grammaire

Disjunctive Pronouns

In every lesson you have been meeting the subject and object pronouns; so that now you know them almost as well as their English equivalents. These pronouns, you have noticed, are always joined closely to a verb as either subject or object.

In this lesson you are going to learn about a different kind of pronoun— known as *disjunctive*, because the various forms are disjoined, or separated, from the verb. Note that four of the disjunctive pronouns have the same form as the subject pronouns.

SUBJECT PRONOUNS		DISJUNCTIVE PRONOUNS	
je, *I*	nous, *we*	moi, *I*	nous, *we*
tu, *you*	vous, *you*	toi, *you*	vous, *you*
il, *he*	ils, *they*	lui, *he*	eux, *they*
elle, *she*	elles, *they*	elle, *she*	elles, *they*

Most of the disjunctive pronouns you have met in your reading lessons; but now you are going to learn about them so that you can use them in your French conversation and writing. The disjunctive pronouns can be used in six important ways:

1. As predicate nominative after c'est, est-ce, ce sont:

c'est moi, *it is I*	c'est nous, *it is we*
c'est toi, *it is you*	c'est vous, *it is you*
c'est lui, *it is he*	ce sont eux, *it is they*
c'est elle, *it is she*	ce sont elles, *it is they*

2. With prepositions:

J'y vais avec elle. *I am going there with her.*

Nous avons dîné sans lui. *We dined without him.*

Je veux marcher après toi, grand-père. *I wish to walk after you, grandfather.*

When a disjunctive is used with the preposition **chez,** the meaning is *at the home of:*

ils sont chez nous, *they are at our home*

elle est chez moi, *she is at my home*

3. Alone, as question, reply, or exclamation:

Qui est là? Vous?

Moi.

Il est sorti? Lui!

Lui.

4. In compound subjects and objects. In addition to the disjunctive pronoun, the regular subject pronoun is regularly used also, although it is not to be translated into English:

Lui et moi, nous allons jouer. *We are going to play.*

Toi et lui, vous dansez bien ensemble. *You and he dance well together.*

Je les vois, lui et elle. *I see him and her.*

5. To call attention to a word: In English, when we wish to emphasize a pronoun, we accent it if we are speaking, and underline or put it in a different kind of type if we are writing. The French stress their personal pronouns (or nouns standing for them) by adding a disjunctive pronoun.

Il s'est arrêté, mais moi, je suis entré. *He stopped, but I went in.*

Moi, je voudrais aller au théâtre. *I should like to go to the theater.*

6. In comparisons:

Je suis plus âgé que lui.

Questionnaire

1. Que demande Henri?
2. Qui va avec lui?
3. Que va-t-il faire?
4. Aimez-vous faire les commissions?
5. Qui vient vers les garçons?
6. Lui parlent-ils en anglais?
7. A quelle heure ferme la poste?
8. Qu'est-ce qu' Henri a oublié?
9. Qui vide les boîtes aux lettres?

Devoir

A. *Explain the use of each disjunctive pronoun in "A la poste."*

B. *Use disjunctive pronouns to replace or emphasize the italicized words:*

1. Jeanne et *son amie* vont à la poste.
2. Nous avons envoyé le colis pour *mon oncle.*
3. Je marche plus vite que *Jean.*
4. Est-ce *Louis* qui est venu offrir son auto ce matin?
5. Charles veut faire les commissions chez *le marchand.*
6. *Marie et son frère* iront avec la petite fille.
7. Est-ce que ce sont *vos cousins* qui sont venus?
8. Ce sont *ses cousins.*
9. Ce n'est pas *le chien* qui aboie.

C. *Here are some very familiar expressions. Give a sentence with each one, using as many different tenses as possible.*

1. tout le monde
2. tout à coup
3. tout de suite
4. avoir raison
5. avoir honte
6. faire une promenade
7. se mettre en route
8. faire mauvais
9. au printemps
10. faire de son mieux
11. en train de

Traduction:

I (*stressed form*) cannot go to the post-office. Send Mary. Her little friend will go with her. Isn't it she in the vegetable garden now? She and Mary like to go on errands. When they return (*use future tense*), they can play together. Henry (*stressed form*) can go on an errand, too, but he will not go with them. Has he money? No, give him some.

CENT DIX-NEUVIÈME LEÇON

Le Garçon sage

Jules avait été très sage toute la journée. Il s'était levé quand la bonne l'avait appelé. Il s'était lavé les mains et la figure, et il s'était brossé les dents. Après il était descendu à la salle à manger, où il avait trouvé sa mère. Il lui avait dit bonjour en l'embrassant. Après le déjeuner il avait aidé Christophe, le jardinier, qui était en train d'arroser les fleurs. En général Jules n'aimait pas travailler au jardin, mais aujourd'hui il y était allé tout seul. Christophe l'avait regardé en souriant. Quand il avait fini au jardin il était allé trouver Marthe, la bonne. Il lui a demandé poliment s'il ne pouvait pas faire des commissions pour elle. Non, il n'y avait rien à faire. Elle avait tout fait. L'après-midi Jules était resté dans sa chambre occupé à lire. Pourquoi était-il si sage? C'était son anniversaire et il espérait recevoir de beaux cadeaux après le dîner.

Grammaire

The Pluperfect Tense

To form the pluperfect tense, add the past participle to the past descriptive of the auxiliary verb—**avoir** for transitive verbs and **être** for intransitive and reflexive verbs. All rules for the agreement of the past participle as applied to the past indefinite are also applied to the pluperfect. Remember that **pas** and **rien** follow the auxiliary.

The pluperfect is the simplest of all the compound tenses to use correctly, because it can be translated in only *one* way in English, that is, by the auxiliary *had* and the past participle.

I *had* studied, etc   I *had* remained, etc.   I *had* arisen, etc.

AFFIRMATIVE

j'avais étudié	j'étais resté (e)	je m'étais levé (e)
tu avais étudié	tu étais resté (e)	tu t'étais levé (e)
il avait étudié	il était resté	il s'était levé
nous avions étudié	nous étions restés (es)	nous nous étions levés (es)
vous aviez étudié	vous étiez resté (s) (e) (es)	vous vous étiez levé (s) (e) (es)
ils avaient étudié	ils étaient restés	ils s'étaient levés

NEGATIVE

je n'avais pas étudié, etc.   je n'étais pas resté, etc.   je ne m'étais pas levé, etc.

INTERROGATIVE—AFFIRMATIVE

avais-je étudié,[1] etc.   étais-je resté, etc.   m'étais-je levé, etc.

INTERROGATIVE—NEGATIVE

n'avais-je pas étudié, etc.   n'étais-je pas resté, etc.   ne m'étais-je pas levé, etc.

Vocabulaire

se brosser les dents [sə brɔse le dã], *to brush one's teeth*

tout seul [tu sœl], *of his own free will*

Questionnaire

1. Pourquoi Jules avait-il été très sage?
2. Quand s'était-il levé?
3. Qu'avait-il dit à sa mère?
4. Qui avait-il aidé?
5. Qui était-il allé trouver?
6. Avait-elle tout fait?
7. Qu'avait-il fait l'après-midi?
8. Pourquoi était-il si sage?
9. Quand est votre anniversaire?

Devoir

A. *Choose a transitive, an intransitive, and a reflexive verb from "Le Garçon sage" and write in full (1) the pluperfect negative and (2) the pluperfect interrogative affirmative.*

B. *Change the verbs in the following sentences to the pluperfect:*

1. Elle n'achète pas de choux.
2. Vous allez dans l'antichambre.
3. Ils y ont admiré les affiches.
4. Je m'amuserai.
5. Nous restons à la vente.
6. Marie est toute souriante.
7. Nous ne fournissons pas de navets.
8. Lit-elle assez souvent?
9. Vous ne m'aidez pas.
10. Elles se lavent encore une fois.
11. J'ai abîmé la vitre.
12. Nous avons du monde à dîner.
13. Il se trompe souvent.

C. *Read these nouns, using the correct form of **ce** before each one:*

hiver	panier	lunettes
portière	boucher	bâtiment
cloche	choux	matinée
contrôleur	regard	cheveux
étranger	ascenseur	automne

Traduction: Determine the tense of each verb before writing.

We had played all afternoon with our friends. We played in the shade. They had arrived at three o'clock. Mary, the smallest girl, had gone into the garden to (*in order to*) help Christopher. She had sprinkled the flowers. She always liked them and wished to pick them. We amused ourselves with our dog. At five o'clock Martha came to the garden. She told us that she had prepared something for us in the dining-room while we were playing.

---

[1] The interrogative form with **est-ce que** may also be used in the first person singular.

CENT VINGTIÈME LEÇON

Review

A

1. In what ways should an adjective agree in French?

2. What word must follow the adjective if the object of comparison is mentioned?

3. When is si . . . que used? Give an example?

4. How is the comparative degree of an adjective formed in French?

5. How is the comparative of an adverb formed? Illustrate.

6. Explain how the superlative of an adjective is formed; of an adverb. Give an example of each.

7. When is the definite article repeated? Illustrate.

8. What preposition must follow the superlative in French?

9. Compare **bon** and **bien**.

10. What are the disjunctive pronouns, and why are they so called?

11. When are disjunctive pronouns used?

12. Give one illustration of each rule for using disjunctive pronouns.

13. How is the pluperfect tense formed in French?

14. How is the pluperfect tense translated?

15. What rules for the agreement of the past participle are applicable to the pluperfect tense?

16. In the negative of a compound tense, where are **pas** and **rien** placed?

17. Give the pluperfect of s'installer.

18. Give the pluperfect of **rester**, negatively.

19. Give the pluperfect of **être**, interrogatively.

20. Give the pluperfect of **faire**, negatively and interrogatively.

21. Give the first person plural future of **venir**, **pouvoir**, and **être**.

B

I. *Compare the following adjectives and adverbs:*

grand	pittoresque	vite
souvent	difficile	heureux

II. *Following the first sentence as a model, make other comparative sentences that use these words:*

MODEL

1. a. Les journaux de Paris, petits, les journaux américains
   b. Les journaux de Paris sont plus petits que les journaux américains.

2. Les rues de Paris, pittoresque, les rues de New York

3. Mon automobile, bon, l'automobile de Louise

4. Ma mère, longtemps, ses fleurs, conserver, les autres

5. Ce chauffeur-ci, bon, ce chauffeur-là

6. Cette annonce-ci, intéressante, cette annonce-là

III. *Conjugate:*

1. J'avais laissé chez moi les journaux pour l'étranger.

2. Je m'étais arrêté sur le trottoir.

3. Je n'avais rien perdu.

4. Je ne veux pas me coucher.

5. Je peux patiner en hiver.

6. Je me suis rappelé cette personne.

7. Je suis en train de m'en occuper.

8. Je l'avais reconnu.

IV. *Translate:*

1. the most interesting book
2. the best gift
3. the most difficult lessons
4. the richest man in the city
5. the widest street
6. the most intelligent dog
7. the highest mountain

CAFÉ MARGUERY, PARIS

A. Braunstain, Paris

FRENCH COOKING

French cooking has reached its final state of perfection and from now on must be known as an art. There is a reason for this perfection, which foreigners are almost likely to consider caused by magic. Anyone may know, for instance, how the famous onion soup of France is put together; and yet his onion soup will not taste like what was set before him in Paris. This is because he did not follow his recipe exactly. He thought that grated cheese would do as well as melted cheese. Or he thought the tablespoonful of thus-and-so unnecessary. Or he made his float of toast from white bread freshly baked. It is such carelessness as this that makes American onion soup just plain soup; while French onion soup remains a thing to dream of, to write poems about, to order whenever possible—except for breakfast, as is the custom in France.

Another instance of a French recipe easily obtainable and yet quite impossible to reproduce is *crêpes suzette.*

The chef of one of the finest French steamships presents each passenger with a printed recipe for this glorified pancake. Just think how many newly-weds have rushed from the dock to their three-room flat in order to try this recipe for *crêpes suzette* in their brand-new kitchenette! Alas, in vain! For they do not get their batter thin enough. And they do not pour the batter quickly enough so that it just covers the bottom of an extremely hot wide pan. Thus they cannot fold it over twice, so that it looks like a wedge of pie. And unless it has this shape, it is not *crêpes suzette*—it is just a pancake. Then, too, the recipe demands that the batter be flavored with four separate extracts, each added at exactly the right moment in exactly the right way. What American girl has the patience to follow these directions?

And so it goes. The English housewife who is content to give her family bread and cheese for luncheon cannot compete with the French matron who, swathed in bandanna and white cover-all, cans even vegetables because she has no faith in commercial products from the store. The American bride is likely to trust to the delicatessen shop; the French bride studies her grandmother's recipes and those given her by her husband's family.

No trouble seems too great for a professional chef to take. The story is told of a famous French chef in New York who was unhappy because no guest ever discussed his cooking with him, either to praise or to criticize it. In France he would have been asked a hundred questions: How old was the lamb served at dinner? How big was it? Where was it reared? How long had it hung? How was it cooked? How was the gravy made? The aim of every French cook is to allow no single flavor to dominate a dish; the rest of the world does not bother about such subtlety. And the dream of every chef is to create some special dish that will make his name live among French *gourmets* (or epicures) who eagerly follow new cooks. The genius of

Marguery was blazoned abroad when with his newly-discovered sauce of clams and mushrooms he created "filet of sole Marguery" and so became famous throughout the world. Very often a restaurant will take its name from some one special dish it emphasizes—thus a quaint old place that has served three generations of Parisian *gourmets* is called Bœuf à la Mode, its great specialty being beef larded and braised with spices, vegetables, fine herbs, and wine.

A popular type of grillroom in Paris is the *rôtisserie*, where before a huge open fireplace grilled food is served as a specialty. The best known of these is perhaps the Grill of Queen Pedauque. Anatole France, a famous French writer of our own age, wrote a book entitled *At the Sign of the Queen Pedauque*. Another celebrated *rôtisserie* is the Pied Horse Grill; and the Perigord Grill, called the temple of *gourmets*, is one of the most typically French of all and is named for a district famous for its truffles.

BŒUF À LA MODE

This picture of an "ox in style" hangs on the wall of the restaurant by the same name.

HUNTING TRUFFLES

In the grills many delicious dishes are made from truffles. The truffle is an underground root related to the mushroom. The winter species in France is the most valuable in Europe, because when made into a pasty with goose-liver it gives us *pâté de foie gras*, a delicacy exported all over the world. Truffles are brown or black in color, and are discovered in a unique way: dogs and pigs are trained to dig them up. The sensitive nostrils of the animal detect the faint strawberry-like smell of the truffle. Piggy is rewarded with a piece of cheese by his owner every time he lays bare a proper root; so the game is worth while for the strange hunter.

The menus adopted by the *rôtisseries* are quaint. They consist of a large sheet of paper with comical and colorful drawings to illustrate the name of the restaurant. The menu is usually written down in ink, its headings in informal printed letters, so that the whole gives the effect of an old-fashioned bill of fare from the days when printing was so expensive that few restaurants could afford it.

Another class of eating-place which has grown popular in Paris since the war is the Russian restaurant or tearoom. The best known of this type is *La Petite Maisonnette Russe*. It is a single dark room with seats lining the walls. The food is costly but delicious; the entertainers sing Russian gypsy songs, dance in shining Russian boots, play upon instruments that resemble grotesque accordions. Then for the homesick American traveler there is Sherry's, to surprise college girls abroad with hot-fudge sundaes and the only real sodas that can be found on the Continent; to surprise older souls with coffee that is not as thick and black as ink and does not taste like licorice. And there is also Delmonico's, where food takes on an intimate New York air, where menus are different every day in the week, but always contain a charming drawing that might have popped right out of *Life* or *Judge* or *Vanity Fair*. Strange how after a few weeks of France the American tourist yearns for something that looks and tastes and smells like home!

Leaving Paris, with its many enchanting restaurants, let us go to some remote part of France, where regional cooking is a discovery never to be forgotten. Every small province of France has its particular dish that has been handed down in that district from time immemorial; and this specialty is brought to you in restaurants there even if you do not order it, as for instance in the city of Chartres, where chestnut soufflé is always your dessert unless you protest against it.

Small city restaurants are continually changing hands, because each chef is eager to return to his native district, which appreciates his special dishes more than Paris does. Often in the most remote place there will be a restaurant worthy of the finest boulevard of Paris. Few people may have heard of it outside its own town, yet its food will have been famous for two generations among the wealthy and noble families of the neighborhood.

French thrift is a trait we have all heard about, and one might think it would detract from perfect cooking. This is not the case, however, for economy can be practiced without skimping the butter; the matter of thrift enters into the amount of food that is prepared. A French housewife never has an ice-box filled with left-over fragments; she buys precise amounts to supply the day's meals only. And great French chefs practice the same care. They make everything according to an approved recipe, no matter how costly a process this may be, but they do not prepare too much; and so none is ever thrown away. The Frenchman is an artist at cooking, but he measures his pinch of salt with precision and passion for detail. And the same creative gift that makes French dressmakers known to all the world prompts the chef to conjure up a magic dish or a wonderful recipe from the most ordinary materials.

By Ewing Galloway, N. Y.

THE TREE-TOP RESTAURANT, CHEZ ROBINSON, NEAR PARIS

HENRY IV REJOINS HIS COURTIERS

CENT VINGT ET UNIÈME LEÇON

Le Roi et le Paysan

Henri IV aime la chasse. Il aime profiter des beaux jours pour aller au bois. Un jour il va à la forêt avec ses seigneurs pour chasser le sanglier. Il est à cheval. Il s'éloigne un peu de sa suite pour admirer la beauté du paysage. Il rencontre un paysan assis au pied d'un arbre au bord de la route. Il le regarde et lui parle de cette façon:

—Qu'est-ce que tu attends là? lui demande Henri IV. Pourquoi restes-tu là au pied de l'arbre?

—On m'a dit que le roi va passer ici. J'aime mon roi, et je désire le voir. Voilà pourquoi j'attends ici.

—C'est bien, répond le roi. Si tu veux monter avec moi sur mon cheval, je te conduirai à l'endroit où sera le roi.

—Bien, dit le paysan, et il monte derrière le roi. Mais je ne connais pas le roi. Que ferai-je pour le reconnaître? Je ne l'ai jamais vu et je suis sûr que je ne le reconnaîtrai pas.

—Je te le dirai, répond le roi. Regarde bien toutes les personnes qui seront là. Devant le roi il faut ôter son (*one's*) chapeau. Celui (*the one*) qui gardera son chapeau sur la tête sera le roi. Alors regarde bien tout le monde. Ce ne sera pas difficile.

Le roi arrive bientôt à l'endroit où est son entourage. Tout le monde ôte son chapeau pour le saluer, parce qu'on sait que c'est le roi.

—Eh bien! dit Henri IV au paysan, où est-il, ton roi?

—Ma foi, monsieur, il faut que ce soit vous ou moi.[1] Nous sommes les seuls qui ayons[2] notre chapeau sur la tête!

---

[1] *it must be you or I*   [2] *who have*

Henri IV et Mayenne

Après la bataille d'Ivry entre Henri IV et le duc de Mayenne, ce dernier est obligé de se soumettre.

Mayenne va trouver le roi dans son jardin. Il s'y promène. En arrivant devant le roi Mayenne se met à genoux. Le roi lui dit de se relever tout de suite.

Ils se mettent à marcher. Henri IV marche très vite, car il est agile. Le pauvre Mayenne est petit et très gros. Il commence à avoir très chaud. Il prend son mouchoir. Il est bien malheureux.

Le roi s'arrête. Il regarde le pauvre duc.—Je marche trop vite pour vous? demande-t-il.

—Ma foi, répond Mayenne, j'ai si chaud, et je suis si fatigué! Je ne peux pas continuer la promenade.

Le bon roi Henri IV commence à rire.—C'est bien. Vous êtes assez puni.

Vocabulaire

le dernier [dɛrnje], *the latter, the last*
le duc [dyk], *duke*
l'entourage [lãtura:ʒ] (m.), *attendants, associates*
la foi [fwa], *faith*
ma foi [ma fwa], *upon my word*

le sanglier [sãglie], *wild boar*
la suite [sɥit], *attendants, retinue, followers*
celui [səlɥi] (m. sing.), *the one*
s'éloigner [selwaɲe], *to go away*

se mettre à marcher [sə mɛtr a marʃe], *to start to walk*
soumettre [sumɛtr], *to submit, to surrender*
à cheval [a ʃəval], *on horseback*

English Equivalents

la beauté [bote], *beauty*   **profiter** [prɔfite], *to profit*   **agile** [aʒil], *agile, active*

CENT VINGT-DEUXIÈME LEÇON

Sans Famille

I. L'Enfant trouvé

Je suis un enfant trouvé. C'est mère Barberin, une bonne paysanne, qui m'a élevé. Mère Barberin m'aime, mais son mari ne m'aime pas. Il est méchant. Il ne veut pas me garder chez lui. Il veut m'envoyer à l'hospice, mais mère Barberin ne le veut pas.

—Quel âge a-t-il? dit Barberin.

—Remi a huit ans. C'est un brave enfant. Il travaillera pour nous un jour quand il sera grand.

—Et maintenant il faut travailler pour le nourrir.

—Mais ses parents le chercheront peut-être un jour.

—Ses parents, est-ce qu'il a des parents? Parce qu'il était enveloppé dans des dentelles quand je l'ai trouvé cela ne signifie pas que ses parents sont riches et qu'ils vont le chercher. Il va partir.

A ce moment-là père Barberin prend son chapeau et quitte la maison.

—Maman, me laisseras-tu aller à l'hospice?

—Non, mon petit Remi, non. Et elle m'embrasse doucement. Non, mon enfant, tu n'iras pas. Tu va bien voir. Nous travaillerons.

—Oui, je travaillerai aussi, mais ne me laisse pas aller à l'hospice.

II. La Troupe du Signor Vitalis

Un jour à midi père Barberin me dit de mettre ma casquette. J'ai peur, parce que je crois que c'est pour aller à l'hospice. Nous marchons pendant une heure. Où vais-je? Bientôt nous entrons dans un café.

Dans un coin il y a un grand vieillard qui porte un costume bizarre. Il a sur la tête un chapeau de feutre gris orné de plumes vertes et rouges. Il porte une peau de mouton. Près de lui il y a trois chiens, un caniche blanc, un barbet noir, et une petite chienne grise. Le caniche porte un vieux bonnet de police sur la tête.

Barberin cause avec ses amis. Il leur dit qu'il va m'envoyer à l'hospice.

—C'est cet enfant-là que vous envoyez à l'hospice? lui demande le vieillard. Oui? Donnez-le-moi.

—Vous donner Remi? Pour rien?

—Non, écoutez-moi bien. Je ne vous l'achète pas, mais je vous le loue.

—Et quels services vous rendra-t-il?

—Il prendra place dans la troupe du signor Vitalis. Le signor Vitalis, c'est moi, la troupe, la voici, mes trois chiens et Monsieur Joli-Cœur.

A ce moment il ouvre sa peau de mouton et y prend un animal étrange —un singe.

—Voici ma troupe, M. Joli-Cœur, Capi, Zerbino, et Dolce. Remi fera la bête.[1] Nous voyagerons partout en France. Nous donnerons des représentations. Remi ne sera pas malheureux avec moi. J'aime les enfants.

Barberin accepte l'offre de Vitalis. Me voilà (*There I am*) engagé dans la troupe du Signor Vitalis.

III. Mes Débuts

Nous voilà à Ussel. Vitalis m'achète un costume complet. Mais j'ai l'air d'un garçon italien avec mon chapeau à plumes et mes rubans de couleur. Je ne les aime pas beaucoup, et j'en parle à mon maître.

—Crois-tu qu'on nous regardera si nous sommes habillés comme tout le monde? me demande Vitalis. Demain nous donnerons notre première représentation. Il faut répéter ton rôle maintenant. La pièce a pour titre, *Le Domestique de M. Joli-Cœur.*

Moi, Remi, je suis le nouveau domestique qui remplace Capi, qui est vieux. Il faut mettre la table,[2] mais comment? J'avance la main, la bouche ouverte. Je ne sais pas mettre la table. Vitalis applaudit.—Bravo, dit-il, c'est parfait. Tu es admirable.

Le Domestique de M. Joli-Cœur n'est pas une grande comédie. La représentation dure seulement vingt mi-nutes. J'ai peur, mais Vitalis est bon. Il m'encourage.

Nous cherchons la place publique. Tout le monde nous regarde à cause de nos costumes italiens. Vitalis attache une corde à quatre arbres, et voilà notre salle de spectacle. Il y a beaucoup de spectateurs. Nous présentons nos pièces, qui montrent l'intelligence des animaux et la stupidité du garçon.

Tout va bien. On applaudit. A la fin Capi prend une sébile entre ses dents et fait le tour "de l'honorable société."

Si un spectateur ne veut pas donner de sous, Capi s'arrête et pose les pattes sur sa poche. On ne résiste pas à sa gentillesse.

Après la représentation Vitalis me complimente.

—Tu es un bon comédien, me dit-il. Je suis content de toi.

[1] *will play the fool*
[2] *to set the table*

IV. En Bateau

Mon pauvre maître est en prison. Un agent de police l'a pris prisonnier, parce que les chiens n'étaient pas muselés. Il est condamné à deux mois de prison. Je suis seul avec les animaux. Nous sommes bien tristes sans notre bon maître, mais il faut travailler pour manger. Nous avons faim. J'ai onze sous dans ma poche. A la boulangerie j'achète une livre et demie de pain. Je fais cinq parts égales et je les distribue. Après quelques instants de repos je donne le signal du départ.

Après une heure de marche nous nous arrêtons aux bords d'un canal. Pour ne pas penser à notre tristesse je prends ma harpe et je joue un air gai. Les chiens commencent à valser; c'est pour oublier que nous avons faim et que nous sommes tristes.

—Bravo, bravo, dit une voix d'enfant. Oh, les beaux chiens!

Je me retourne. Je vois un bateau qui ressemble à une jolie maison. Je vois aussi un garçon à peu près de mon âge. Il est couché. A côté de lui il y a une dame.

—Voulez-vous jouer encore? me demande la dame. Elle parle avec un accent étranger.

—Oui, certainement, avec plaisir. Peut-être qu'on nous donnera à manger. Les animaux dansent; nous présentons nos comédies. Le petit garçon applaudit. Il est si pâle. Il est malade sans doute.

—Arthur désire voir les animaux, me dit la dame. Venez sur le bateau.

La dame nous offre à manger. Les animaux se mettent autour de la table. Ils ont si faim. C'est la mère d'Arthur qui nous parle. Elle me pose des questions. Ensuite elle parle avec son petit garçon, mais je ne comprends pas la langue qu'ils parlent.

—Voulez-vous rester avec nous? demande Arthur tout à coup.

—Sur ce bateau?

—Oui, sur ce bateau, répond la mère. Mon fils est malade. Vous resterez avec nous. Vous donnerez des représentations pour amuser Arthur.

—Oh, madame, merci. Nous serons si heureux avec vous.

Je prends ma harpe, et je commence à jouer.

d'après Hector Malot

Vocabulaire

l'**âge** [lɑ:ʒ] (m.), *age;* **quel âge a-t-il?** [kel ɑ:ʒ atil], *how old is he?*
le **barbet** [barbɛ], *water spaniel*
le **bonnet de police** [bɔnɛd pɔlis], *informal military cap*
le **caniche** [kaniʃ], *poodle*
la **chienne** [ʃjɛn], *dog* (f.)
les **débuts** [deby] (m. pl.), *first appearance*
la **dentelle** [dɑ̃tɛl], *lace*
l'**enfant trouvé** [lɑ̃fɑ̃ truve] (m.), *foundling*

le **feutre** [fø:tr], *felt*
la **gentillesse** [ʒɑ̃tijɛs] *pretty tricks*
l'**hospice** [ɔspis] (m.), *poorhouse hospital*
la **livre** [li:vr], *pound*
la **plume** [plym], *feather*
la **salle de spectacle** [sal də spɛktakl], *playhouse*
la **sébile** [sebil], *wooden bowl*
le **singe** [sɛ̃:ʒ], *monkey*
le **sou** [su], *penny*
le **titre** [titr], *title*
la **tristesse** [tristɛs], *sadness*

le **vieillard** [vjɛja:r], *old man*
Remi [remi], *no English equivalent*
élever [elve], *to bring up, to raise*
louer [lwe], *to rent*
museler [myzle], *to muzzle*
nourrir [nuri:r], *to support, to nourish*
valser [valse], *to waltz*
égal [egal], *equal*
orné [ɔrne], *ornamented*
parfait [parfɛ], *perfect*
à peu près [a pø prɛ], *about, approximately*

English Equivalents

l'accent [laksã] (m.), *accent*

le canal [kanal], *canal*

la comédie [kɔmedi], *comedy*

le comédien [kɔmedjɛ̃], *comedian*

l'offre [lɔfr] (f.), *offer*

le rôle [roːl], *rôle, part*

le signal [siɲal], *signal*

la société [sɔsjete], *society*

le spectateur [spɛktatœːr], *spectator*

la stupidité [stypidite], *stupidity*

applaudir [aplodiːr], *to applaud*

complimenter [kõplimãte], *to congratulate, to compliment*

condamner [kõdɑne], *to condemn*

distribuer [distribɥe], *to distribute*

envelopper [ãvlɔpe], *to wrap*

résister [reziste], *to resist, to oppose*

ressembler à [rəsãble a], *to resemble*

admirable [admirabl], *admirable, fine*

bizarre [bizaːr], *bizarre, strange, queer*

complet [kõplɛ], *complete*

engagé [ãgaʒe], *engaged, employed, enlisted*

étrange [etrãːʒ], *strange, odd, queer*

gai [ge], *gay*

honorable [ɔnɔrabl], *honorable*

pâle [pɑːl], *pale*

public,-que [pyblik], *public*

bravo [bravo], *bravo*

CENT VINGT-TROISIÈME LEÇON

L'Anniversaire

Qu'avait-on donné à Jules pour son anniversaire? Tout d'abord Marthe avait fait un magnifique gâteau. Sa mère avait invité quatre de ses amis à dîner, et tous ses amis lui avaient dit en entrant "Tous mes vœux de bonheur à l'occasion de votre anniversaire." Les beaux cadeaux qu'ils lui avaient apportés! Il les avait chaleureusement remerciés. Tout le monde l'avait regardé pendant qu'il ouvrait les paquets. Jean lui avait apporté un beau livre. Charles avait apporté une jolie cravate de soie. Henri avait enveloppé un canif dans une énorme boîte. Comme tout le monde avait ri pendant qu'il cherchait dans les papiers! André était venu lui apporter des mouchoirs. Quels beaux cadeaux ses amis lui avaient donnés! Il n'en avait jamais eu de si beaux.

Après que les garçons avaient joué un bon moment la mère de Jules les avait appelés à table. Là, sur l'assiette de Jules, il y avait une petite boîte ronde. Qu'y avait-il dans cette boîte? Une montre, une belle montre en or de la part de ses parents. Quel bel anniversaire!

Vocabulaire

le canif [kanif], *penknife*

la cravate [kravat], *necktie*

le vœu [vø] (pl. les vœux), *wish, vow*

rond [rõ], *round*

chaleureusement [ʃalœrøzmã], *warmly, ardently*

tout d'abord [tu dabɔːr], *first of all*

un bon moment [œ̃ bõ mɔmã], *for some time*

Questionnaire

1. Qu'est-ce que Marthe avait fait pour Jules?

2. Qui la mère de Jules avait-elle invité?

3. Qu'est-ce que les amis de Jules lui avaient dit en entrant?

4. Quels cadeaux avait-on apportés?

5. Qu'y avait-il dans l'énorme boîte?

6. Pourquoi a-t-on ri?

7. Comment Charles a-t-il remercié ses amis?

8. Qu'est-ce que Jules avait trouvé sur son assiette?
9. Qui lui avait donné cette montre?
10. Avez-vous une montre en or?
11. Que désirez-vous pour votre anniversaire?

Devoir

A. Conjugate:

1. Je veux me reposer.
2. Je me suis couché de bonne heure.
3. Je serai en train de lire.
4. Je pourrai faire ce voyage.
5. J'en aurai besoin, n'est-ce pas?
6. Je n'ai eu ni froid ni chaud.
7. J'attends l'ouverture de la boutique.
8. J'ai été là tout à l'heure.

Traduction: Remember that the plu-perfect is used only to translate had *and a past participle.*

Yesterday was my little sister's birthday. My mother had invited six of her friends, but only five came. The other little girl was sick, and her mother had called the doctor to see her. After having played in the garden, the children went into the dining-room. The prettiest flowers were on the table. There was a beautiful cake on the table. Martha had made it. My little sister was very happy. She was smiling. Her little friends had brought gifts and had put them on the table at her plate. She thanked them.

They said, "Give her the gifts. Give them to her."

Composition: Ecrivez une conversation entre Remi et Arthur.[1]

Arthur demande à Remi:
  (1) Où était sa mère.
  (2) Où travaillait son père.
  (3) Pourquoi il ne voulait pas le garder.
  (4) S'il aimait jouer les rôles dans la comédie.

Remi demande à Arthur:
  (1) S'il aime les animaux.
  (2) Pourquoi il est toujours couché.
  (3) S'il aime voyager.
  (4) Comment il a appris (*learned*) à parler français.

[1] Based on "Sans Famille," pages 334-336.

Yvon, Paris

THE PRINCIPAL STREET OF A FRENCH VILLAGE
In such a square Remi made his debut.

CENT VINGT-QUATRIÈME LEÇON

Une Aventure en Turquie

Quand j'irai en France, je parlerai toujours français. Mon professeur de français a été en France cette année. Ses parents y demeurent. Elle a voyagé en Angleterre, en Italie, en Belgique, et en Hollande. Quand je serai plus âgé, j'espère pouvoir voyager aussi dans ces pays. Il y a beaucoup à voir. Je sais que Paris est la plus grande ville de France, mais moi, je passerai beaucoup de temps en province. J'ai un oncle qui a fait le tour du monde l'année dernière. Il a voyagé en Chine, en Turquie, en Russie, en Grèce, et dans tous les autres pays européens. Quand il est revenu en Amérique, il m'a raconté toutes ses aventures.

En Turquie il lui est arrivé[1] une aventure désagréable. En débarquant du bateau il a cherché sa malle partout. Il ne l'a pas trouvée. Que faire? Il avait besoin de linge. Il est allé à la recherche d'un magasin pour faire ses achats. Il n'a trouvé que des soieries, des pantoufles turques, et des écharpes. Pas de chemises, pas de cols, pas de mouchoirs, pas de cravates. Ne parlant pas turc, il était au désespoir. Finalement, un Américain, voyant son embarras, est venu le tirer d'affaire.

Grammaire

The Future Tense

After the conjunction **quand** the future tense is used in French whenever the future is implied. The present tense is used if habitual action is implied.

> Quand je visiterai la France, je parlerai français.
> Quand j'étudie, je reste dans ma chambre.

En with Feminine Names of Countries

Before the names of most continents and all countries of the feminine gender,[2] singular, the preposition **en** must be used to express *to* or *in*. Learn the following names of countries with their correct preposition:

en Angleterre	en Grèce	en Turquie
en Belgique	en Italie	en France
en Chine	en Russie	en Amérique

Elle a voyagé en Angleterre. *She has traveled in England.*
L'année prochaine j'irai en France. *Next year I shall go to France.*

The French names of the continents with their correct prepositions are:

dans l'Amérique du Nord	en Europe	en Asie
dans l'Amérique du Sud	en Afrique	en Australie

> La France est en Europe.
> Je demeure dans l'Amérique du Nord.

---

[1] *there happened to him.*
[2] The names of countries ending in -e, with the exception of **Mexique**, are feminine.

Vocabulaire

la chemise [ʃəmiːz], *shirt*
le col [kɔl], *collar*
le désespoir [dezɛspwaːr], *despair*
l'écharpe [leʃarp] (f.), *scarf*
l'embarras [lãbarɑ] (m.), *embarrassment*
la malle [mal], *trunk*

la pantoufle [pãtufl], *slipper*
la soierie [swɑri], *silk material*
le turc [tyrk], *Turkish* (language)
débarquer [debarke], *to get off, to disembark, to debark*

tirer d'affaire [tire dafɛːr], *to help out*
européen [œrɔpeɛ̃], *European*
turc, -que [tyrk], *Turkish*
en [ã] (with geographical names), *to, in*

Questionnaire

1. Que ferez-vous quand vous irez en France?
2. Qui a été en France cette année?
3. Dans quels pays a-t-elle voyagé?
4. Quand voyagerez-vous en France?
5. Quelle est la plus grande ville de France?
6. Où passerez-vous beaucoup de temps?
7. Où votre oncle a-t-il voyagé?
8. Qu'a-t-il fait quand il est retourné en Amérique?
9. Quand a-t-il cherché sa malle?
10. Qu'a-t-il trouvé dans les magasins?

Devoir

A. Change the infinitives to the correct tenses:

1. Vous visiterez beaucoup de pays quand vous (aller) en Europe, n'est-ce pas?
2. Hier quand nous (voir) Marie, elle (parler) au facteur.
3. Quand ils (aller) en France, ils m'écriront des lettres.
4. Quand Louise (arriver) devant la vitrine, elle (choisir) ce qu'elle veut.
5. Quand je (finir) mes devoirs, je pourrai jouer au tennis.
6. (Apporter)-les-moi.
7. (Prêter) m'en les plus grands.
8. (Parler) m'en, s'il vous plaît.

B. Write a sentence for each of the following:

débarquer
tirer d'affaire
être au désespoir
faire le tour du monde
l'embarras
faire de son mieux

C. Write these sentences in the past indefinite:

1. Le boucher fournit toute la viande.
2. Nous voulons des épinards.
3. Je veux m'en occuper.
4. Il ne se rappelle pas le patron.
5. Ce colis est pour l'étranger.
6. Vous le voulez autant que moi.
7. Ils ont raison sans doute.
8. Ce matin il fait plus désagréable qu'hier.
9. Je n'abîme pas mon parapluie neuf.
10. Je me tire d'affaire.

Traduction:

Last year my French teacher went to France, to Italy, and to England. She has also been in Holland and in Belgium. I have not yet been in France. When I am older, I shall visit all these countries. My aunts have been in Turkey. When they returned, they told me about (*omit*) their adventures.

THE BIRTHPLACE OF JOAN OF ARC

Branger, Paris

CENT VINGT-CINQUIÈME LEÇON

Jeanne d'Arc

I. Les Voix et le Départ

Jeanne d'Arc est née à Domremy, petit village situé en Lorraine. Ses parents étaient pauvres. C'étaient des paysans. Ils parlaient des malheurs qui affligeaient leur pays. Jeanne pleurait en silence, parce qu'elle aimait son pays et son roi, Charles VII.

Jeanne aimait aller à l'église. Elle quittait souvent ses petits amis pour aller prier dans la chapelle.

Un jour elle était assise occupée à tricoter dans le jardin. Tout à coup elle croyait (*thought*) entendre des voix. Elle pensait que c'était la voix de Saint Michel. Elle écoutait bien. Ces voix lui disaient: "Jeanne, ton pays est en danger. Va trouver ton roi. Tu délivreras la ville d'Orléans."

—Hélas, répond la jeune fille de dix-sept ans, je suis jeune. Je ne suis qu'une fille de paysans. Je ne sais pas monter à cheval. Je ne sais pas faire la guerre. Je ne sais rien. Je dois rester ici avec mes parents.

Mais la jeune fille continuait à entendre les voix. C'était au moment où les Anglais allaient attaquer Orléans.

—Jeanne, Jeanne, va sauver ton pays. Ton roi a besoin de toi.

Jeanne a demandé à un de ses oncles de la conduire à Vaucouleurs. Le gouverneur de cette ville était là. Elle irait[1] à Orléans avec lui.

Quand la jeune fille s'est trouvée devant le gouverneur, il ne voulait pas l'écouter. Mais Jeanne n'était pas découragée.

—Il faut que je trouve le gentil dauphin.[2] C'est le Ciel qui m'envoie pour sauver mon pays. J'irai à mon roi même s'il faut faire tout le chemin à genoux.

Le gouverneur a hésité, mais après quelques moments il lui a donné son épée. Habillée en (*as a*) garçon, sur un beau cheval, elle est partie avec six cavaliers trouver le roi à Chinon.

[1] *would go*

[2] Title of the eldest son of a French king

II. Jeanne et son roi

C'était l'hiver de l'année 1429.[1] L'ennemi infestait le pays; mais Jeanne n'avait pas peur. Après dix jours elle est arrivée à Chinon, où était son roi.

Elle est entrée dans une grande salle où brûlaient des torches. Il y avait beaucoup de monde dans la salle. Jeanne n'avait jamais vu le roi, mais elle l'a reconnu tout de suite. Elle s'est mise à genoux devant lui, et lui a dit:

—Gentil dauphin, j'ai nom Jeanne la Pucelle.[2] C'est le Ciel qui m'envoie pour délivrer Orléans et pour vous conduire à Reims pour être sacré.

Quelques jours après Jeanne est partie pour Orléans à la tête d'une armée. Les soldats anglais entouraient la ville d'Orléans où tout le monde était découragé. Jeanne et ses soldats ont attaqué le château. On dressait des échelles contre les murs pour y monter. Les soldats étaient courageux à cause de la bravoure de la jeune fille, et Orléans fut delivrée.[3]

III. A Reims

Le roi ne voulait pas aller à Reims. Enfin il s'est mis en marche vers la ville, où, pendant une belle cérémonie, l'archevêque allait mettre[4] la couronne sur la tête du roi. La cathédrale était bondée. Il y avait là des évêques et des grands seigneurs. Jeanne, la petite paysanne, était contente. Le moment attendu avec tant d'impatience était arrivé. Son roi était sacré.

IV. La Mort de Jeanne d'Arc

A partir de ce moment le malheur semblait guetter la jeune fille.

Les jours heureux de Jeanne étaient passés. Elle voulait encore attaquer Paris pour le sauver de l'ennemi. Pendant le combat elle est blessée. Son roi avait peur. Il est retourné à Chinon. Jeanne a continué à se battre. A Compiègne elle est tombée entre les mains des Anglais. Ils riaient, ils se moquaient de la jeune fille, et ils l'insultaient même.

La jeune fille qui avait délivré son pays est condamnée à être brûlée. On l'appelait la sorcière.

C'est à Rouen qu'elle a été brûlée en 1431[5] par les Anglais. Si vous y allez un jour on vous montrera la place où Jeanne d'Arc, après avoir sauvé son pays, a trouvé la mort.

Vocabulaire

la **bravoure** [bravuːr], *bravery*

l'**échelle** [leʃɛl] (f.), *ladder*

la **sorcière** [sɔrsjɛːr], *witch*

les **Anglais** [ãglɛ] (m. pl.), *Englishmen*

affliger [afliʒe], *to afflict*

brûler [bryle], *to burn*

dresser [drɛse], *to raise*

entourer [ãture], *to surround, to encompass, to inclose*

guetter [gɛte], *to be on the watch for*

se mettre en marche [sə mɛtrã marʃ], *to set out, to start*

se moquer de [sə mɔke də], *to make fun of, to laugh at*

sembler [sãble], *to seem*

bondé [bõde], *crowded*

sacré [sakre], *crowned*

à partir de [a partiːr də], *from*

English Equivalents

le **cavalier** [kavalje], *horseman, rider*

le **dauphin** [dofɛ̃], *dauphin*

la **torche** [tɔrʃ], *torch*

délivrer [delivre], *to free*

infester [ɛ̃fɛste], *to infest*

insulter [ɛ̃sylte], *to insult*

découragé [dekuraʒe], *discouraged*

[1] quatorze cent vingt-neuf
[2] *Joan, the maid*
[3] *was delivered*

[4] *would put*
[5] quatorze cent trente et un

CENT VINGT-SIXIÈME LEÇON

Encore des voyages

—Moi, je demeure aux Etats-Unis, à Cincinnati.

—Et moi, je demeure aussi aux Etats-Unis, mais à Chicago qui est plus grand que Cincinnati.

—Oui, mais moi, j'ai un cousin au Canada. Il parle anglais et français.

—Mon oncle, lui, a voyagé au Mexique. Il sait l'espagnol, et il a parlé avec les Mexicains.

—Ma tante Louise ira au Japon cette année. Elle va y voir les cerisiers en fleur. On dit qu'ils sont très beaux, ces cerisiers. J'en ai vu à Washington.

—Quand je serai riche, j'irai aux Indes pour visiter les monuments célèbres de ce pays.

—Ah bah! Moi, j'irai au pôle nord. C'est là qu'on voit les Esquimaux et les icebergs.

—Oui, mais j'ai déjà été en France, en Angleterre, en Italie, en Hollande, en Belgique, en Turquie, en Russie, au Canada, au Mexique, au Japon, aux Indes, et . . .

—Vous racontez des histoires.

—Non, pas du tout. J'ai été partout—dans mes rêves.

Grammaire

A with Geographical Names

In Lesson 124 you learned that the preposition **en**, meaning *to* or *in*, is used before the names of countries that are feminine singular. Before all masculine names and those that are feminine plural the same meaning (*to* or *in*) must be expressed by **à** plus the definite article. These countries are masculine: **le Canada** (Canada), **le Mexique** (Mexico), **le Japon** (Japan), and **les Etats-Unis** (United States). **Les Indes** (India) is feminine plural. These five countries, according to the rule, require **à** and the definite article.

Je demeure aux Etats-Unis.
L'année dernière il a voyagé au Canada, au Mexique, et au Japon.
Ma tante ira aux Indes cette année.

The preposition **à** is used before the names of cities when *in* or *to* or *at* is meant.

Ils sont à Paris.   *They are in Paris.*
Elles vont à Chicago.   *They are going to Chicago.*

Vocabulaire

l'espagnol [lɛspaɲɔl] (m.), *Spanish*

l'iceberg [lisbɛrg] (m.), *iceberg*

le monument [mɔnymɑ̃], *monument, public building*

le pôle [poːl], *pole*

le rêve [rɛːv], *dream*

l'Esquimau [lɛskimo] (m.) (pl. les Esquimaux), *Eskimo*

Londres [lõːdr], *London*

les Mexicains [mɛksikɛ̃], *Mexicans*

se tirer d'affaire [sə tire dafɛːr], *to manage, to get along*

bah! [ba], *bah!*

Questionnaire

1. Dans quel pays et dans quelle ville demeurez-vous?
2. Avez-vous voyagé au Japon et au Canada?
3. Où demeure votre grand'mère?
4. Demeurez-vous aux Etats-Unis?
5. Avez-vous envie d'aller au Canada ou au Mexique?
6. Avez-vous des amis à New York ou à Washington?
7. Qu'a fait votre oncle au Mexique?
8. Pourquoi voulez-vous aller aux Indes?
9. Que voit-on au pôle nord?
10. Autrefois comment y allait-on? Et aujourd'hui?

Devoir

A. Replace the dash in each sentence by the correct preposition:

1. Quand nous serons riches, nous irons — Paris, — Londres, — Amsterdam, et — Montréal.
2. Paris est — France. Rome est — Italie.
3. Montréal est — Canada, n'est-ce pas?
4. Nous demeurons — Baltimore — Etats-Unis.
5. Tout d'abord, je crois que je n'irai jamais — Indes.
6. Je n'irai pas — Japon non plus. Je ne suis pas très riche.
7. Il se tirera d'affaire — Mexique et — Indes.
8. Nous débarquerons — Bordeaux.

B. Make the adjectives agree with the nouns and pronouns they modify:

1. Ils faisaient ensemble une (long) promenade à l'ombre.
2. Nous n'étions pas (fatigué) parce que la leçon était (intéressant).
3. Est-ce que sa voix est (doux)?
4. Marie est très (habile) de ses doigts.
5. Elles étaient très (heureux) de recevoir les (beau) fleurs.
6. Mon amie a de très (beau) cheveux (noir).

7. Je portais mes souliers (neuf) ce jour-là.
8. Encore une fois l'expression sur sa figure était (cruel).
9. Je m'occuperai des allées (étroit) et de la (merveilleux) fontaine.
10. Les marches de l'escalier devant la terrasse sont très (haut).
11. Nous sommes (rafraîchi) après notre courte promenade.
12. En mettant les (joli) fleurs dans l'eau, on les conservera.
13. Elle a pris des cravates (bleu), des cols (blanc), et des écharpes (jaune).
14. Je visiterai les pays (européen).
15. Le fromage est (nourrissant). Vendez m'en.
16. On peut trouver de la (beau) soie aux Indes.

Traduction:

We live in the United States. I have a cousin who lived in Canada. He has traveled in Japan and in India. He does not wish to go to Mexico. I have been in England and in France, but I have not been in Canada. When I return to France, I shall go to Bordeaux and to Orléans.

When you (on) go to France, you check your trunk; and when you return to the United States, they (on) inspect it.

THE MARSEILLAISE

In 1792 came the great moment in which there was to rise on the ruins of an old, outworn monarchy the new Republic of France. Troops from Marseilles had entered Paris and between the wildly cheering crowds were marching on the royal palace (the Tuileries). These were not soldiers forced into uniform by law, but volunteers who were hastening to aid in the struggle of bringing political equality to a nation. Suddenly, as at a given signal, the vast throng of onlookers ceased its cheering and stood silent. People wished to hear what these grim troops were shouting at the top of their lungs. Then for the first time broke upon the ears of the crowd the sublime patriotic hymn that was to become France's greatest national anthem—*La Marseillaise*.

For more than a hundred years now armies have marched to its music and its words. The hearts of those who sing it are mysteriously stirred. Battles have been won by it. One famous general wrote: "We are one to the enemy's ten. But the *Marseillaise* is fighting on our side to victory." Another wrote: "Send me a thousand men and a printed copy of the *Marseillaise*, and I shall shortly report to you a battle won."

The birth of this song and that of the French Republic are so closely connected that men always remember them together. They are two great symbols of liberty, one in song, and one in deed. It was near the end of the eighteenth century that French patriots began to wish for a republican form of government in place of the tyrannical monarchy that had stood so long.

Unfortunately, words alone could not grant them this wish. To gain it, they had to fight a bloody war called the French Revolution. The men who caused this war were named republicans, or revolutionists. Their battle-cry for freedom was the *Marseillaise*. It rang through the streets and lanes of France, a noble accompaniment to the marching feet of soldiers who thought their beloved land should be ruled by all her people, and not by only a few.

The story of the composing of the *Marseillaise* is an interesting one. In the Alsatian city of Strasbourg many young Frenchmen were preparing to hurry to the capital, where battalions were being formed. Dietrich, the mayor of Strasbourg, wished to show his sympathy with these volunteers, and so on the eve of their departure for Paris invited them to a fine dinner. Among the guests who sat at table with the mayor was a young captain named Rouget de Lisle, a talented musician. To this comrade Dietrich spoke the words that were to inspire the immortal marching song.

"Look here," he said to Rouget, "we simply must have a warlike hymn to stir the blood of the new recruits to the flag. The old choruses are as worm-eaten as the old monarchy. And what's more, we must have the thing at once! Now, here's the chance of a lifetime. You're a poet and you're a musician; so get us up something that's worth singing."

At midnight Rouget withdrew to his lodgings. He took up his violin and began his task. All through the night he worked to create the unforgetable words and melody of the hymn. At seven o'clock in the morning, Rouget visited Marclet, an officer of the general staff who had been at the dinner the night before.

From a painting by Pils

ROUGET DE LISLE SINGING THE MARSEILLAISE

"Dietrich's proposal murdered sleep for me," the young poet said, with a rueful grin; "so I put in the small hours trying to get him his war-song. Run your eye over it and see what you think."

"And you may well believe," wrote Marclet later to a friend, "that I read the score with admiration. And I thrilled to hear Rouget sing it from start to finish, the six stanzas just as they are sung today, with the sole exception of the last two lines, which were

And may the thrones of tyrants
Crash to the sound of our glory,

instead of the way they now run, as you know, with their tribute to Liberty:

And may thy dying enemies
See Thy triumph and our glory."

A few hours after his visit at Marclet's, the young author went to Dietrich's house. There, accompanied on the piano by one of the mayor's nieces, he sang his song. It was as if a star had fallen from the sky. Rouget's hearers were carried away by the stirring measures and hailed them with joy. They knew the song by heart when it had been sung through but once. From Strasbourg, the melody spread like wildfire far and near.

It was first sung in Paris by a body of troops from Marseilles, and the Parisians, ignorant of its origin, named it the *Marseillaise*. All Paris, all France have been singing it ever since.

LA MARSEILLAISE

Rouget de Lisle

CENT VINGT-SEPTIÈME LEÇON

Faut-il?

Il faut étudier.

Il faut faire attention en classe.

Il faut écouter ses parents.

Il faut que je finisse mes leçons.

Il faut que nous répondions en français.

Il faut que vous apportiez le livre demain.

Faut-il qu'ils restent à la maison?

Faut-il que nous soyons à l'école à neuf heures?

Il faut que vous fassiez une promenade dans la foule.

Il faut que l'enfant se couche de bonne heure (*early*).

Il faut que vous causiez avec elle.

Grammaire

More about *Il faut*

You already know that **il faut** means "it is necessary." The English expression is usually completed by an infinitive (It is necessary *to arrive* at eight o'clock). The same thing may be done in French also, provided the sentence does not relate to particular persons, but to a group in general, as is the case in the first three examples above. If, however, you wish to translate "It is necessary that *we* study," the sentence is no longer impersonal; "we" makes it personal. In the clause introduced by **que** after **il faut** the present subjunctive tense must be used, because **il faut** indicates obligation. A more common translation of **il faut** followed by a clause is *I must, you must, he must,* etc. Concentrate your attention on this new translation, because you are already familiar with the other.

The Present Subjunctive

To form the present subjunctive omit **-ant** from the present participle of a verb of any conjugation and add the present subjunctive endings. In reciting the present subjunctive place **que** before it to show that you know it introduces a clause.

PRESENT SUBJUNCTIVE

écouter, *to pay attention to*

écoutant, pres. part.

que j'écout **e**, *that I pay attention to*, etc.

que tu écout **es**, *that you pay attention*

qu'il écout **e**, *that he pay attention*

que nous écout **ions**, *that we pay attention*

que vous écout **iez**, *that you pay attention*

qu'ils écout **ent**, *that they pay attention*

choisir, *to choose*

choisissant, pres. part.

que je choisiss **e**, *that I choose*, etc.

que tu choisiss **es**, *that you choose*

qu'il choisiss **e**, *that he choose*

que nous choisiss **ions**, *that we choose*

que vous choisiss **iez**, *that you choose*

qu'ils choisiss **ent**, *that they choose*

répondre, *to reply*

répondant, pres. part.

que je répond **e**, *that I reply*, etc.

que tu répond **es**, *that you reply*

qu'il répond **e**, *that he reply*

que nous répond **ions**, *that we reply*

que vous répond **iez**, *that you reply*

qu'ils répond **ent**, *that they reply*

Il faut que nous écoutions nos parents.
Il faut que je choisisse les meilleures choses.
Il faut que vous répondiez vite.

The present subjunctives of **être** and **faire** are irregular in that they are not formed from the present participles **étant** and **faisant**. Learn these two subjunctives carefully. Are the endings of the present subjunctive of **être** irregular? Of **faire**?

PRESENT SUBJUNCTIVE

être, *to be*	**faire,** *to do*
que je sois, *that I be*, etc.	que je fasse, *that I do*, etc.
que tu sois, *that you be*	que tu fasses, *that you do*
qu'il soit, *that he be*	qu'il fasse, *that he do*
que nous soyons, *that we be*	que nous fassions, *that we do*
que vous soyez, *that you be*	que vous fassiez, *that you do*
qu'ils soient, *that they be*	qu'ils fassent, *that they do*

Il faut que vous soyez à l'école à neuf heures.
Il faut que je fasse une promenade.

Devoir

A. Write out the present subjunctive of:

finir	faire
se laver	être
rendre	entendre

B. Change to the correct verb-forms:

1. Il faut que ma mère (préparer) le goûter aujourd'hui.
2. Il faut que Christophe (faire) une boîte pour les fleurs.
3. Il faut que nous (étudier) tout à l'heure.
4. Il faut que le boucher (répondre) poliment.
5. Il faut que vous (faire) attention en classe.
6. Il faut que la bonne (acheter) la viande encore une fois.
7. Il faut que vous (se dépêcher) chez le boucher.

C. Write six sentences, one for each of these tenses: present, future, past descriptive, present subjunctive, past indefinite, and pluperfect.

Traduction:

1. We must take (**porter**) this package to my aunt. She forgot it.
2. Christopher must work in the garden this afternoon. I will help him.
3. You must pay attention in class.
4. The children must finish their lessons. They will play afterwards (**après**).
5. We must be at school at a quarter to nine Friday, February 20.
6. She must study all her lessons while we are here.
7. We must put (**installer**) the best things there.
8. I must look for the advertisement.
9. When he arrives, he must work quickly.
10. You must be here when she comes.

CENT VINGT-HUITIÈME LEÇON

Luc-le-long

Un jour un homme a apporté du lin chez un tisserand. L'homme lui a dit: "Dans huit jours je veux ma toile. Je vous payerai bien. Si elle n'est pas prête, vous aurez de mes nouvelles.[1] Alors, attention!"

Le pauvre tisserand a travaillé nuit et jour, mais il voyait bien qu'il ne pourrait pas[2] finir la toile.

—Je suis perdu, a-t-il dit. Si seulement quelqu'un pouvait m'aider!

Comme le tisserand finissait de parler, un petit homme habillé de vert a ouvert la porte de la maison du tisserand.

—Je vais t'aider, a-t-il dit en entrant. Je commande que la toile soit achevée tout de suite.[3] En échange je prendrai ton âme, si dans trois jours tu ne me dis pas mon nom. Tu pourras dire trois noms.

Le petit homme vert est parti. Comment découvrir le nom de ce diable! Voilà une chose difficile.

Le lendemain l'homme est venu chercher sa toile. Il en était bien content, et il a bien payé.

Le pauvre tisserand est allé voir sa marraine, qui était fée.

—Va demain au bois, a-t-elle dit. Cache-toi bien et écoute tous les bruits.

Le tisserand est allé au bois. Il a attendu toute la journée. Le soir il attendait encore. Tout à coup il a vu un grand diable noir dans un arbre. Le diable criait:—Luc-le-long! Luc-le-long! Ch'é mi nom![4]

Le diable répétait souvent ces mots que le tisserand ne comprenait pas. Il est allé trouver sa marraine.

—Qu'a dit le diable? a-t-elle dit.

—Il a dit: Luc-le-long, ch'é mi nom. Je ne comprends pas.

—Très bien, a dit la marraine. Le diable s'appelle Luc-le-long. Maintenant retourne chez toi.

Le tisserand attendait la visite du diable. Tout à coup il y eut[5] un grand bruit dans la cheminée, et le diable a sauté dans la chambre.

—Eh bien, mon nom, l'as-tu trouvé? demande-t-il. Dis-le vite!

—Est-ce Jean? demande le tisserand.

—Non, non, non.

—T'appelles-tu Pierre?

—Non.

—T'appelles-tu . . . peut-être Luc-le-long?

Le diable, en entendant son nom, a poussé un grand cri, et la maison du tisserand s'est remplie de fumée. Le tisserand était obligé de sortir dans la rue pendant quelques minutes.

Depuis ce temps on n'a jamais revu le diable Luc-le-Long.

Les trois fils du roi

Il y avait autrefois un grand roi qui avait trois fils; l'aîné s'appelait Robert, le deuxième, Louis, et le cadet, Philippe.

Dans le jardin du palais était un beau pommier que le roi aimait beaucoup parce que sa femme, maintenant morte, l'avait planté. Les pommes étaient belles, mais chaque année elles disparaissaient[6], et on ne savait pas qui les avait volées. Un jour le roi dit à son fils Robert:

---

[1] *you will hear from me*
[2] *would not be able*
[3] *I order the linen to be finished at once.*
[4] *That's my name!*
[5] *there was*
[6] *disappeared*

—Mon enfant, passe la nuit dans le jardin. Prends ton fusil. Si tu vois le voleur (*thief*), tue-le.

Robert passe la nuit au jardin, mais il est si fatigué qu'il s'endort. Le lendemain il manque des pommes.

La deuxième nuit le roi envoie Louis, mais c'est la même chose. Il ne voit rien, parce qu'il dort. Il manque trois pommes.

La troisième nuit Philippe prend son fusil et attend dans le jardin. Vers deux heures il entend un grand bruit et il voit un grand oiseau dans l'arbre. L'oiseau se met à manger des fruits.

Philippe le regarde. Il prend son fusil. L'oiseau pousse un grand cri et s'envole laissant une de ses plumes dans l'arbre. Philippe la prend.

Le lendemain Philippe montre la plume du voleur à son père.

—Que c'est extraordinaire, dit son père. Je donnerais[1] la moitié de mon royaume pour posséder cet oiseau rare.

Le roi tombe malade. Il pense aux plumes brillantes de l'oiseau. Les médecins déclarent que si on n'apporte pas cet oiseau au roi avant la fin de l'année il mourra.[2] Appelant ses fils dans sa chambre il leur dit:

—Il faut trouver l'oiseau de feu. Il faut l'enfermer dans une cage et me l'apporter. Robert va partir pour le chercher. Si dans un mois il n'est pas de retour, Louis partira.

Robert prend cent mille francs, s'habille richement, prend un bon cheval, et se met en route. Il rencontre une vieille femme.

—Une petite charité, monsieur, lui dit-elle.

—Mon argent n'est pas pour vous, répond Robert.

Robert s'arrête dans une auberge. Il est servi avec grand luxe. On lui réclame deux cent mille francs pour le dîner.

—Je n'ai pas même cent mille francs, proteste-t-il.

—Alors vous serez notre prisonnier jusqu'à ce que vous ayez de quoi payer votre repas.[3]

L'auberge était habitée par des voleurs.

Un mois après Louis part chercher son frère et l'oiseau de feu. Il lui arrive les mêmes aventures, et il est enfermé avec Robert.

Le roi appelle son dernier fils. Il ne veut pas le laisser partir, mais il le faut.

—Quelque chose me dit que je réussirai, dit Philippe, le cadet. Il met des habits modestes. Il monte sur un vieux cheval. Il rencontre la vieille femme.

—Mon bon monsieur, une petite charité, s'il vous plaît.

—Voilà du pain blanc et de l'argent.

—Je veux vous donner un bon conseil, lui dit la vieille femme. Ne vous arrêtez pas à l'auberge qui se trouve à quelque distance d'ici. Des voleurs y habitent. Ne vous y arrêtez pas.

Le prince continue son voyage. Il arrive devant l'auberge.

—Les voleurs lui demandent de venir dîner avec eux.

Sans regarder Philippe continue son chemin. Les voleurs montent à cheval et courent après lui, mais ne réussissent pas à le rejoindre. Le cheval de Philippe meurt de fatigue, et Philippe se trouve seul dans un bois inconnu. Il entend des cris de douleur derrière lui. C'est un serpent qui va tuer un loup tout blanc. Le prince prend son épée et coupe la tête du serpent.

—Je te remercie, prince, lui dit le loup. Je veux te donner un conseil. En sortant du bois tu trouveras un cheval tout en or. Jette-toi sur son

---

[1] *would give*
[2] *he will die*

[3] *until you have the wherewithal to pay for your meal*

PHILIP'S TRIUMPHANT ESCAPE

dos d'un seul bond. Ce cheval t'aidera à trouver l'oiseau de feu. Si tu as jamais besoin de mon aide, appelle-moi, et je viendrai.

Le prince trouve le cheval d'or, saute sur son dos, et le voilà parti pour le bord de la mer.

—Là dans cette grotte il y a un géant, lui dit le cheval. Il possède l'oiseau de feu. Propose-lui poliment de m'échanger contre l'oiseau.

Philippe frappe à la porte étroite de la grotte.

—Qui est là?

—C'est Moi-même, répond le prince sur le conseil du cheval d'or.

—Que me veux-tu, jeune homme?

—Vous avez l'oiseau de feu que mon père désire. Je vous propose de l'échanger contre ce cheval d'or.

—Ah, le bel animal! Certainement, mon ami, et je te donnerai encore un sac d'or et un sac de diamants.

Le géant va chercher l'oiseau dans sa cage. Il l'apporte tout de suite à Philippe.

—Adieu, crie Philippe; et il prend tout. Il saute sur son cheval d'or et le voilà parti aussi vite que possible.

—On m'a volé mon oiseau de feu, crie-t-il, le pauvre géant. Où est mon bel oiseau?

—Qui l'a volé? disent les voisins.

—C'est Moi-même. C'est Moi-même. C'est le méchant Moi-même.

—Alors pourquoi cries-tu?

* * * * *

Le prince arrive à l'auberge. Ses habits sont déchirés. Il a l'air pauvre. Il paye quatre cents mille francs pour délivrer ses frères. Ils partent ensemble. Philippe est fatigué. Il s'endort sur le cheval.

—Nous allons jeter Philippe dans un ravin, dit Louis. Nous ne l'aimons pas. Nous dirons qu'il est mort.

Voilà Philippe au fond du ravin.

—Comment sortirai-je, pense-t-il. Ah! je vais appeler mon ami le loup. Il m'aidera. J'en suis sûr.

Le loup blanc arrive.

—Je vais t'aider, dit-il. Je te descendrai une corde et tu remonteras.

Deux fois la corde se casse, et le pauvre Philippe retombe. La troisième fois il réussit à sortir du fond du ravin. Le loup lui dit de retourner vite au palais de son père.

Le roi n'était plus malade. Il était content de l'oiseau de feu. Il a donné la moitié du royaume à ses deux fils. Mais il n'a pas oublié Philippe.

Le prince veut entrer dans le palais.

—Que désirez-vous? lui disent les gardes.

—Rentrer chez moi! Je suis le fils du roi, le prince Philippe.

—Vous, le fils du roi, en habits déchirés? Ce n'est pas possible.

Philippe se jette sur les gardes. Ils comprennent très bien qui il est; mais ils ont parlé avec les autres fils et ont décidé de ne pas le laisser entrer. Le roi, entendant le bruit, demande ce qui se passe.[1]

—Comment, mon fils, mon Philippe!

Philippe raconte à son père comment ses frères l'ont jeté dans un ravin.

—Vite, commande le roi, enfermez mes deux fils dans la grande tour du palais.

Et maintenant Philippe et son père vivent fort heureux ensemble avec l'oiseau de feu et le cheval d'or.

Vocabulaire

l'aîné [lɛne] (m.), *first-born, eldest*

l'auberge [loberʒ] (f.), *inn*

le bond [bõ], *bound, leap*

le cadet [kadɛ], *younger or youngest son*

la cheminée [ʃəmine], *chimney, mantelpiece, fireplace*

le diable [djɑːbl], *devil*

la douleur [dulœːr], *pain*

l'échange [leʃɑ̃ːʒ] (m.), *exchange*

la fée [fe], *fairy*

le fond [fõ], *bottom, background*

la fumée [fyme], *smoke*

le fusil [fyzi], *gun*

les habits [lezabi] (m. pl.), *clothes*

le lin [lɛ̃], *flax*

le loup [lu], *wolf*

la marraine [mɑrɛn], *godmother*

la moitié [mwatje], *half*

le tisserand [tisrɑ̃], *weaver*

la toile [twal], *linen*

achever [aʃve], *to finish*

se cacher [sə kaʃe], *to hide oneself*

se casser [sə kɑse] *to get or to be broken*

chauffer [ʃofe], *to warm, to heat*

déchirer [deʃire], *to tear*

enfermer [ɑ̃fɛrme], *to lock up, to inclose*

s'envoler [sɑ̃vɔle], *to fly away*

réclamer [reklɑme], *to demand*

remonter [rəmõte], *to remount, to re-ascend*

revoir [rəvwaːr], *to see again*

inconnu [ɛ̃kɔny], *unknown*

contre [kõːtr], *against*

richement [riʃmɑ̃], *richly*

English Equivalents

la cage [kaːʒ], *cage*

la charité [ʃarite], *charity*

le diamant [djamɑ̃], *diamond*

la distance [distɑ̃ːs], *distance*

le géant [ʒeɑ̃], *giant*

la grotte [grɔt], *grotto*

le prince [prɛ̃ːs], *prince*

le ravin [ravɛ̃], *ravine*

le serpent [sɛrpɑ̃], *snake, serpent*

déclarer [deklare], *to declare*

descendre [desɑ̃ːdr], *to lower, to come or go down, to descend*

protester [prɔtɛste], *to protest*

rare [rɑːr], *rare, unusual, uncommon*

[1] *what the matter is*

CENT VINGT-NEUVIÈME LEÇON

Faut-il?

Il faut que je me lève à sept heures un quart. (*I must get up at a quarter after seven.*)

Il ne faut pas que je reste au lit.

Il faut que Marie aide sa mère.

Il ne faut pas que Marie joue.

Il faut que nous allions à la poste.

Il ne faut pas que nous allions à la gare.

Il faut qu'ils aient leurs livres de français.

Il ne faut pas qu'ils aient leurs livres d'anglais.

Il faut que vous vous amusiez.

Il ne faut pas que vous étudiiez ce matin.

Il faut dix minutes pour aller à l'école.

Il ne faut pas une heure pour aller chez ma grand'mère.

Faut-il quelques mois pour faire le tour du monde?

Grammaire

Il faut in a Negative Sentence

In Lesson 127 you learned a new translation for **il faut** followed by the present subjunctive, namely, *I must, you must*, etc. Notice carefully that to make a sentence containing **il faut** negative, the negative is attached to **il faut** and not to the verb in the subjunctive.

> Il ne faut pas que je reste au lit.
> Il ne faut pas que nous allions à la poste.

Il faut with Expressions of Time

Il faut has a third meaning. In expressions of time it means "it takes."

> Il faut dix minutes pour aller à l'école.
> Il ne faut pas une heure pour aller chez ma grand'mère.

The Present Subjunctive of *Aller* and *Avoir*

The present subjunctives of **aller** and **avoir** (like **être** and **faire**) are irregular in that they are not formed from the present participles. Learn these two subjunctives. Are the endings regular or irregular?

PRESENT SUBJUNCTIVE

aller, *to go*

que j'aille, *that I go*	que nous allions, *that we go*
que tu ailles, *that you go*	que vous alliez, *that you go*
qu'il aille, *that he go*	qu'ils aillent, *that they go*

avoir, *to have*

que j'aie, *that I have*	que nous ayons, *that we have*
que tu aies, *that you have*	que vous ayez, *that you have*
qu'il ait, *that he have*	qu'ils aient, *that they have*

Devoir

A. *Make the following sentences negative and change the infinitive to another form when necessary.*

1. Il faut que je (aller) chez le boucher chercher du veau.
2. Il faut que vous (rester) ici.
3. Il faut qu'ils (faire) attention.
4. Il faut six jours pour (aller) de New York à Paris.
5. Il faut que vous (avoir) les paniers demain.
6. Il faut que je (choisir) les cols.
7. Il faut dix minutes pour (faire) cette commission.
8. Il faut que nous (avoir) de l'argent pour aller en France.

B. *Replace the italicized words by pronouns:*

1. *Le petit homme habillé de vert* a ouvert *la porte.*
2. Tout à coup il a vu *un grand diable.*
3. Le pauvre tisserand est allé voir *sa marraine.*
4. Le diable a sauté encore une fois *dans le trou.*
5. Le tisserand répétait tristement *ces mots.*
6. Il est allé *chez sa marraine.*

7. Ce sont *les fils du roi* qui cherchent *l'or.*
8. Parlez *de cette affaire à votre oncle.*
9. Prêtez-moi *des livres.*

C. *Compare the following adjectives and adverbs:*

difficile	bien
heureux	vite
bon	souvent

Traduction:

1. It takes twenty hours to go from Chicago to New York, and it takes six days to go from New York to Paris.
2. We must go to France next summer if we can.
3. My friend must go to school this summer. She was sick during the winter.
4. You must not take a walk now.
5. Must I go to the post-office?
6. My friends must not return home. They must stay with us.
7. We have company for (à) dinner.
8. I must manage (**me tirer d'affaire**).

CENT TRENTIÈME LEÇON

Les Phrases avec *si*

Nous étudierions si nous avions nos livres. (*We should study if we had*, etc.)

Je serais content si je pouvais aller en France. (*I should be happy if I could go to France.*)

Si mon cousin avait de l'argent, il achèterait un auto.

Ma tante se lèverait de bonne heure si elle n'était pas malade.

Vous choisiriez un chapeau neuf si vous en désiriez un.

Nous répondrions en français si nous le pouvions.

Mes amis s'amuseraient s'ils avaient le temps.

Si mon père me donnait de l'argent, j'irais à Paris.

Vous feriez attention si vous étiez en classe.

Aimerait-il aller avec lui?

Auriez-vous l'obligeance de me faire une commission?

Grammaire

The Present Conditional

In this lesson you will learn how to form and use a new tense, known as the present conditional. This tense is often used in sentences containing si (*if*) clauses. The si clause, which states the condition, is put in the past descriptive tense, while the result clause is expressed by the present conditional. It is immaterial whether the sentence begins with the condition or the result.

Si mon cousin avait de l'argent (condition), il achèterait un auto (result).
If my cousin had money, he would buy an automobile.
Nous répondrions en français (result) si nous le pouvions (condition).
We should reply in French if we could.

The present conditional tense is formed by adding the past descriptive endings to the infinitive of the verb. You must pronounce the present conditional forms with special care, so that they will not be confused with the past descriptive.

PRESENT CONDITIONAL

regarder, *to look at*

je regarder **ais**, *I should look at*	nous regarder **ions**, *we should look at*
tu regarder **ais**, *you would look at*	vous regarder **iez**, *you would look at*
il regarder **ait**, *he would look at*	ils regarder **aient**, *they would look at*

finir, *to finish*

je finir **ais**, *I should finish*	nous finir **ions**, *we should finish*
tu finir **ais**, *you should finish*	vous finir **iez**, *you would finish*
il finir **ait**, *he would finish*	ils finir **aient**, *they would finish*

répondre, *to answer*

je répondr **ais**, *I should answer*	nous répondr **ions**, *we should answer*
tu répondr **ais**, *you would answer*	vous répondr **iez**, *you would answer*
il répondr **ait**, *he would answer*	ils répondr **aient**, *they would answer*

The verbs which are irregular in the future tense have the same irregularity of stem in the present conditional. The endings are those of the past descriptive.

avoir	faire	être	aller
j'aurais, *etc.*	je ferais	je serais	j'irais

Vocabulaire

l'obligeance [lɔbliʒãːs] (f.), *kindness*   de bonne heure [də bɔnœːr], *early*

Devoir

A. Write the present conditional negative of:

choisir	faire
aller	se coucher
pouvoir	s'amuser

B. Write five sentences containing si clauses. Use the following pronouns as subjects:

vous	elle	je
nous	ils	

C. *Change to the correct verb-forms. Remember that the condition is stated in the imperfect and the result in the conditional.*

1. Il (être) ici, s'il ne (être) pas malade.
2. Vous (jouer) avec vos petits amis s'ils (arriver), n'est-ce pas?
3. Je (aimer) voir Paris si je le (pouvoir).
4. S'ils (avoir) le temps, ils (finir) leurs leçons.
5. Nous ne (aller) pas à la campagne s'il ne (faire) pas beau.
6. Tu (faire) une promenade avec lui si tu le (pouvoir), n'est-ce pas?

D. *Conjugate these sentences:*

1. Je viendrais le remercier si je le pouvais.
2. Tout d'abord je pourrais chercher la malle.

3. Je me tirerai d'affaire.
4. Je me suis habillé plus vite qu'elle.
5. Je n'ai eu ni écharpe ni col.

Traduction:

1. I should take a walk with you if I were free (libre).
2. If you had the time, would you go with him?
3. They would like to visit their uncle in the United States.
4. We should finish our lessons if we had our books.
5. My aunt would give you the books if she had them.
6. If you found the box, would you bring it to my brother?
7. If I had money, I should go to England and to France.
8. Would he have the kindness to bring these books to my sister?

CENT TRENTE ET UNIÈME LEÇON

Pierrette

Pierrette demeure à Tours dans une jolie maison qui donne sur le petit mail devant la cathédrale. Elle est très surexcitée aujourd'hui et ça se comprend (*can be understood*). Elle part par le train de quatre heures. On va l'amener à Paris passer une huitaine de jours chez sa grand'mère.

C'est toujours grand'mère qui vient passer l'été avec papa et maman. Elle aime tant Tours. Elle dit qu'il n'y a pas d'endroit au monde où les gens parlent un si joli français. Pierrette sait que c'est vrai. Elle sait aussi que la Touraine est le Jardin de la France—on le lui a assez dit— et que nulle part les châteaux sont plus beaux que dans la vallée de la Loire. Elle les a vus.

Papa aussi aime beaucoup Tours.

Il fait voir (*shows*) à Pierrette, chaque fois qu'ils descendent la rue Nationale, la maison où est né Balzac, le grand romancier. Elle ne sait pas très bien qui est Balzac ni que c'est un grand romancier, mais elle sait bien que c'est quelque chose dont (*of which*) on doit être fier, et elle en est fière, très fière.

Il y a une chose qu'elle sait très bien, notre petite Pierrette, et ça sans qu'on ait jamais eu besoin de le lui dire.[1] C'est qu'il n'y a pas de pâtisseries pareilles à celles[2] de Tours. L'oncle Roger vante toujours les macarons de Nancy, mais les gâteaux et les petits fours, les tartes aux amandes, de Tours! Rien qu'à les voir dans les vitrines, on en a l'eau à la bouche (*makes one's mouth water for them*).

[1] *and that, without being told*   [2] *those*

From a painting by Puvis de Chavannes

ST. GENEVIEVE WATCHING OVER PARIS

Néanmoins elle est radieuse à l'idée d'aller à Paris. Elle y est déjà allée une fois. C'était pour la fête du quatorze juillet.

Elle se rappelle seulement comme un éblouissement—les maisons toutes pavoisées de drapeaux, les bannières au vent, partout des mâts avec le drapeau tricolore qui flottait et des guirlandes de lumière comme de grandes oranges en festons, et à tous les coins de rue de la musique et du monde qui dansait. L'après-midi on était allé à Versailles voir jouer les grandes eaux (*fountains*). C'était une merveille.

Cette fois elle va rester toute une semaine à Paris. Quelle joie! Elle va tout voir, tout. Pas la Tour Eiffel. Oh, non! Pierrette l'aime, la Tour Eiffel, mais papa dit que c'est une horreur, et qu'il n'y a que les gens sans goût qui aiment ça.

Ce qu'elle désire voir le plus, c'est la châsse de Sainte-Geneviève. Elle a dans sa petite chambre deux jolies photographies de Sainte-Geneviève, l'une où elle est petite fille, aux champs, et l'autre où elle est bien, bien vieille

et regarde sa chère ville de Paris la nuit. Comme ça va être beau de (*How wonderful it will be*) voir cette belle châsse toute en or et couverte de cierges allumés.

On la conduira aussi à l'Arc de Triomphe voir le tombeau du Soldat Inconnu. Papa était là le jour où on a allumé la flamme qui ne doit jamais s'éteindre. Il a voulu raconter ça à maman à son retour, mais il n'a pas pu. Chaque fois il s'est arrêté tout court.

Son grand frère Maurice a vu ça aussi. Il était avec papa. Voilà quatre ans qu'il est à Paris, lui, au lycée. Elle va aller le voir avec grand'-mère jeudi. C'est jeudi le jour des visites au Lycée Henri IV. Maurice va lui montrer la Tour de Clovis, qui est si vieille. Dire (*To think*) qu'elle va voir toutes ces belles choses! Elle ne peut pas tenir en place (*keep still*). Elle trépigne de joie et d'impatience. Il ne sera donc[1] jamais quatre heures (*It will never be four o'clock*)! Le temps passe si lentement quand on a envie de partir.

Giraudon, Paris

THE TOWER OF CLOVIS
A view from the court of the Lycée Henri IV

---

[1] donc for emphasis; not to be translated.

François Ier

François Ier aimait les arts italiens, et parce qu'il voulait développer les arts français, il faisait venir des poètes à sa cour. Ce roi était beau et brave, et il brillait par son esprit. Les poètes travaillaient dur pour plaire à leur roi.

Les grands seigneurs et les grandes dames vivaient dans des châteaux. C'était le roi qui en a donné l'exemple. Il passait une partie de l'année au château de Fontainebleau. Ensuite il allait à ses châteaux au bord de la Loire, à Blois, ou à Chambord.

Les châteaux du moyen âge ressemblaient à de véritables forteresses. Ils étaient tristes, presque sans fenêtres, et entourés de murs très hauts. Quels changements on remarque dans les châteaux construits au seizième siècle! Ils sont situés au milieu d'un beau parc. Les fenêtres sont très hautes et très larges. On a mis de beaux meubles, des tapisseries, des tableaux, et des statues dans les immenses salles. Le roi connaissait les artistes et commandait les œuvres.

Le roi donnait souvent des distractions à toutes les personnes qui vivaient à la cour. On donnait des spectacles. Le roi jouait souvent un rôle. Les costumes étaient magnifiques. En automne c'était la chasse qui était le passe-temps favori des courtisans. On chassait le sanglier, le cerf, et le renard dans les domaines qui appartenaient au roi. En hiver on donnait des fêtes où on entendait de la belle musique. On dansait aussi. Tout le monde portait des vêtements de soie et de velours. Les courtisans aimaient le roi, parce qu'il donnait de si belles fêtes; mais pour payer ces fêtes on avait besoin d'argent. C'étaient les paysans qui payaient tout ce plaisir au roi.

C'est la vallée de la Loire que le roi et les grands seigneurs ont choisie comme site de leurs châteaux. Ils comprenaient tout le charme naturel de la Touraine et des bords du magnifique fleuve. La Touraine, "le jardin de la France," est couverte de paisibles campagnes et de riches prairies. Sans exagérer c'est un paradis terrestre.

Levasseur, Paris

THE COURTYARD OF THE CHÂTEAU OF BLOIS

Vocabulaire

le cerf [sɛːr], *stag*
la châsse [ʃɑːs], *shrine*
le cierge [sjɛrʒ], *candle, taper*
la distraction [distraksjõ], *amusement*
l'éblouissement [lebluismã] (m.), *dazzling vision*
le goût [gu], *taste*
la guirlande [girlãːd], *garland*
la huitaine de jours [ɥitɛn də ʒuːr], *about a week*
le lycée [lise], *high school*
le mail [maːj], *promenade*
le mât [mɑ], *mast, pole*
le meuble [mœbl], *piece of furniture*
le moyen âge [mwajɛ̃nɑːʒ], *the Middle Ages*
l'œuvre [lœːvr] (f.), *work*
le passe-temps [pɑstã], *pastime*
la pâtisserie [pɑtisri], *pastry*

les petits fours [pti fuːr] (m. pl.), *small fancy cakes*
le romancier [rɔmãsje], *novelist*
le siècle [sjɛkl], *century*
le tableau [tablo], *picture*
la tapisserie [tapisri], *tapestry*
les tartes aux amandes [tart ozamãːd] (f. pl.), *almond cakes, pastry*
le velours [vluːr], *velvet*
Pierrette [pjɛrɛt], no English equivalent
Versailles [vɛrsɑːj], *Versailles*, a city about twelve miles from Paris
amener [amne], *to take (someone to a place), to lead*
appartenir [apartəniːr], *to belong*
briller [brije], *to be distinguished, to shine*

s'éteindre [setɛ̃ːdr], *to go out*
plaire [plɛːr], *to please*
trépigner [trepiɲe], *to tap one's foot*
vanter [vãte], *to praise*
allumé [alyme], *lighted*
entouré [ãture], *surrounded, inclosed*
paisible [pɛzibl], *peaceful*
pareil, -le [parɛːj], *as good as, equal, like, similar*
pavoisé [pavwaze], *festooned*
radieux, -se [radjø, radjøːz], *radiant*
surexcité [syrɛksite], *nervous, excited*
terrestre [tɛrɛstr], *terrestrial, earthly*
nulle part [nyl paːr], *nowhere*
néanmoins [neãmwɛ̃], *nevertheless*
rien que [rjɛ̃ kə], *only*

English Equivalents

le courtisan [kurtizã], *courtier*
le domaine [dɔmɛːn], *land, estates*
l'exemple [legzãːpl] (m.), *example*
le feston [fɛstõ], *wreath, festoon*

la forteresse [fɔrtərɛs], *fortress*
l'horreur [lɔrœːr] (f.), *horror*
le macaron [makarõ], *macaroon*
le parloir [parlwaːr], *parlor*
la prairie [prɛri], *meadow, field*

le site [sit], *site, situation*
la statue [staty], *statue*
exagérer [egzaʒere], *to exaggerate*
favori, favorite [favɔri, favɔrit], *favorite*
véritable [veritabl], *real, true, veritable*

Photo A. Breger Frères, Paris

THE PEACEFUL TOURAINE COUNTRYSIDE

CENT TRENTE-DEUXIÈME LEÇON

Encore des phrases avec *si*

1. Nous resterons à la maison si nous sommes malades.

Je pourrai étudier si j'ai mes livres.

Ils feront une promenade s'il fait beau.

Vous irez au parc si votre ami arrive.

Nous donnerions une montre à Jean s'il n'en avait pas.

Je ferais le tour du monde si j'avais beaucoup d'argent.

Les enfants chercheraient quelque chose à manger s'ils avaient faim.

2. Je pourrais étudier si j'avais mes livres.

Ils feraient une promenade s'il faisait beau.

Vous iriez au parc si votre ami arrivait.

Marie achèterait les petits pains si la boulangerie était ouverte.

3. Nous regarderions les livres si le professeur les avait apportés.

Elles feraient une promenade si leurs amies étaient venues.

Vous iriez au Canada si votre père vous avait donné de l'argent.

Si je m'étais levé à sept heures un quart, je ne serais pas en retard.

Grammaire

Conditional Sentences

Conditional sentences are not only expressed by the present conditional and the past descriptive tenses, but also by other fixed combinations of tenses. Learn these combinations so as to prevent mistakes in giving sentences containing *if* clauses. Remember that it is immaterial whether you begin your sentence with the independent clause (the result) or with the dependent *if* clause (condition).

Here are the combinations of tenses corresponding to the groups given above.

1. Fut. Indicative (independent cl.)   Pres. Indicative (dependent cl.)
2. Pres.* Conditional (independent cl.)   Past Descriptive (dependent cl.)
3. Pres. Conditional (independent cl.)   Pluperfect (dependent cl.)

Devoir

A. *Write six French sentences, two for each combination of tenses given above.*

B. *Complete these sentences, using one of these forms:* **de, de l', du, de la, des.**

1. Je n'aurai pas —— canif.
2. Elle a beaucoup —— bas et —— jolies robes.
3. En voyant mon embarras, il viendra me donner —— argent.
4. Elle commandera —— veau, —— poulet, et —— navets.

5. Dans les pays européens on voit —— statues merveilleuses.
6. Il pourra voir peu — monde.
7. Offrez-leur —— argent.
8. Ils ont tant —— fleurs.

Traduction: (Determine the combinations of tenses before translating the sentences below.)

1. I shall ask my father for (*omit*) the money if he comes early.
2. If she had the time, she would like to go to the country.

* *Note to the Teacher:* The use of the past conditional will be given in Book II.

3. If they had been there, they would speak of it.

4. Would you work in the garden if you were not going to the city?

5. If my cousin arrives from Boston, we shall not go to New York.

6. If Christopher had not brought the flowers, I should buy some.

7. We shall stay with him if he is here at a quarter after two.

8. The children would give the boxes to their cousins if they had them.

9. If her hair were not very pretty, we should not admire it so much.

CENT TRENTE-TROISIÈME LEÇON

Review

A

1. Explain how the pluperfect tense is formed.

2. How is it translated?

3. Why is this tense easy to use?

4. In the negative of the past indefinite or the pluperfect where is **ne** placed? Where are **pas** or **rien** to be placed?

5. What is the past descriptive of s'occuper.

6. Give the pluperfect of **se lever**.

7. What must be remembered about the conjunction **quand**?

8. How is *in* or *to* translated before the names of countries? of cities?

9. How may **il faut** be translated when followed by a dependent clause?

10. What form must be used in a dependent clause after **il faut**?

11. Explain how the present subjunctive is formed.

12. Mention three irregular subjunctives.

13. What special meaning has **il faut** in expressions involving time?

14. Explain how the conditional tense is formed.

15. What irregular conditional tenses do you recall? Are these verbs irregular in the same manner in any other tense?

16. How can you distinguish the conditional from the imperfect of first, second, and third conjugation verbs?

B

I. Conjugate:

1. Je n'étais pas allé en France.

2. Quand j'irai en Europe, je visiterai l'Italie et la France.

3. Si j'ai de l'argent, j'irai au Mexique.

4. Je n'avais rien planté.

5. Si j'avais de l'argent, je pourrais faire ce voyage à Paris.

II. Change to the correct verb-forms:

1. Il faut que j'y (être) bientôt.

2. Il ne faut pas que vous (faire) un voyage en Grèce.

3. Faut-il qu'ils (répondre) vite?

4. Il faut que nous (enregistrer) les bagages.

5. Il ne faut pas qu'elle (aller) au Canada.

III. Change the present to the past descriptive, and the future to the conditional:

1. Si nous trouvons les mouchoirs, nous vous les montrerons.

2. Si elle finit avant onze heures moins le quart, elle partira.

3. Si je réponds en français, mon professeur sera content.

4. S'ils se couchent à dix heures, ils ne seront pas fatigués.

5. Si je vais au Canada, je pourrai voir les Esquimaux et les icebergs.

By Ewing Galloway, N. Y.

A SCENE IN THE NATIVE SECTION OF TUNIS

THE FRENCH IN ALGERIA

More than any other great nation of Europe, the French have been slow to leave their mother country to settle permanently elsewhere. This clinging to their own homeland has kept them from being such born builders of empire overseas as are the English. It is true that devotion to France has led the French to explore and travel for her, but when it came to settling down and making a French colony far from the continent of Europe, there were few volunteers.

Thus, the tale of French colonization is not as stirring a one as those of some other nations. In America, France sufficiently proved herself a nation of bold explorers and brave men, especially when under the spur of religion or of political necessity. But she established no permanent colonies.

Before the London Company had founded its first English settlement at Jamestown, the father of New France,

Samuel de Champlain, was living among the Indians of Canada, in one hand his crucifix, in the other his sword. Before the Pilgrim Fathers established themselves at Plymouth, Champlain had explored New England, discovered the beautiful lake that bears his name, founded Quebec, and published two great volumes of his *Voyages*. Two generations after him, La Salle, Marquette, and Joliet were living symbols of the French spirit of adventure and religious zeal in America. Their forts and trading posts dotted the banks of the Mississippi, as they courageously drove their way into a strange, new land. But the colonies that were founded as a result of their prodigious labors were fated soon to pass into the hands of Englishmen or Americans. A similar destiny awaited every French settlement in the western world, until finally French colonies became little more than a vague and dim memory.

Fortunately for France, there is a different story to tell of her settlement to the southward. One wealthy and colorful colony saves France in the eyes of her neighbors who attach great importance to the ownership of foreign empire. In 1830 France took possession of her African colony, Algeria, with its domain of nearly one million square miles.

The history of Algeria had been a checkered one. Its most ancient inhabitants were of unknown descent, a race called Berbers. Long before the Christian era, Algeria had fallen a prey to those fiercest enemies of Rome, the Carthaginians, but it was wrested from them in turn by Rome as a result of the three exhausting Punic wars. When Rome fell in the fifth century of our era, the Vandals, a Germanic tribe, poured into northern Africa from Spain and successfully seized the reins of Algerian government. After a hundred fifty years of Vandal rule, soldiers of the Eastern Roman Empire, Byzantines by name, gained possession of this oft-contested prize.

They had held it for but a few generations, however, when they were forced to yield the ownership of Algeria to the Arabs. Moslem administration under Arab sway lasted until the fourteenth century, when the Turks proved their right to the country through conquest. Thereafter for a long time Algeria became a headquarters for pirates and buccaneers, who preyed upon the commerce of all the world of that time. Charles V of Spain and Louis XIV of France carried on campaigns against these miscreants, but largely in vain, for the chief offenders—the brothers Barbarossa—proved too slippery to be caught and held. Algeria remained under the rule of the Turkish sultan, until a decision was reached in favor of France, one hundred years ago.

This vast French empire in Africa is divided into three departments: Algeria, Oran, and Constantine. Each of these sends representatives and a senator to the law-making bodies in France. This direct representation of the French colonies undoubtedly accounts in large part for the con-

By Burton Holmes from Ewing Galloway

THE MODERN PORT OF ALGIERS

GAMES IN AN ALGERIAN OASIS

tentment felt by the natives. Of the three departments, Algeria has the largest number of French settlers, and is therefore given the precedence in the French legislature. By no means all Algerians are naturalized French citizens, for the rights of citizenship are granted the natives only as an especial honor, so that the great majority of them are without a voice in national affairs. France has tried to keep her colonies closely united to her, not by demanding that the natives become Frenchmen, but by striving to make them fitter representatives of their own race.

The most important city of this African district is of course Algiers, a town of nearly two hundred thousand people, beautifully situated on the Mediterranean. Arrival there by boat is a matter not easily forgotten. Hardly are the tourist's feet firmly planted on the pier of pontoons that stretches from the ship to the shore, when the Arabs are upon him—not "silently folding their tents" but shrilly crying their wares: beads of gaudy hues; purses of hand-tooled leather; knick-knacks of beaten silver, amber, and brass; and vivid scarfs.

On the broad stairway that leads up from the waterfront to the modern town, the tourist passes figures that seem to have stepped out of *The Arabian Nights:* huge Ethiopians, swarthy beak-nosed sheiks, Nubians from the native quarter, Oriental and Jewish peddlers such as have haunted this very spot for more than two thousand years. But in only another moment of walking, the visitor from the west is in Government Square. And here he feels at home, for the setting is less Oriental. Here are bazaars and cafes, where officers of the Foreign Legion and Zouaves rub shoulders with dark Arabs in fezzes and gay sightseers from America. Shrouded ladies are here, whose eyes gleam through slits in their veils, whose hennaed finger nails lend a tinge of savagery to their mysterious persons; but everywhere, too, are smartly-gowned Parisian women and English girls on holiday. Toward dusk the tourist grows more conscious of the banked palm trees and slender minarets that wall in this modern scene, and before long he hears the voice of the muezzin calling the Faithful to prayer. Lights then begin to lead the eye away from the gay square, down passages so narrow that opposite houses meet in an archway above them. A visit to this native quarter is not lightly to be undertaken except by the stout soul in search of adventure, and by one who can endure such smells as exist in absolutely no other corner of the habitable globe.

The African natives show genuine affection for France, because it has brought education and modern ways into their land. During the years of French occupation, Algeria has made long strides toward progress. Many miles of railroad are in operation, roads and bridges have been built, tens of thousands of acres of idle land thrown open to tillage. Native schools are well taught. Local laws, and not the French code, deal justice to the offender.

To the east of Algeria, France governs the domestic affairs of Tunis, and on the west those of Morocco. To the south, France controls also the Sahara, including Senegal. The government of these territories is very difficult, for the natives live mostly in tribes and speak many different dialects. Tribal wars are of constant occurrence.

But at the outbreak of the Great War in 1914, France learned the high regard her colonial subjects felt for her. At this time there was not the least sign of rebellion in the colonies; the dusky natives flocked to the French colors to defend them. They fought without fear, often winning the military cross for distinguished service to the flag. Most of them had never before been away from their native villages, but in the unknown land of Europe they bled and died like heroes. Those who lived to return to their families must have brought back strange tales of the country which is helping them to lead a fuller and a nobler life!

CROSSING THE SAHARA DESERT

FRENCH VERBS

NOTE: In this section are given models for the regular conjugations, followed by the important irregular verbs that are used in this book, including those with orthographic irregularities, which are treated separately. Only the tenses used in the book are here given. This section is not intended to be a complete guide to French verbs. Such a guide would not be suitable for first-year work.

NOTE: When two verbs are given with one page reference, it means that the forms of the second verb appear on that page and that the first is conjugated in like manner.

REGULAR VERBS

FIRST CONJUGATION

Infinitive TROUVER

Future (88)[1]
je trouverai

Present Conditional (130)[1]
je trouverais

Present Participle (100)[1]
trouvant

Past Descriptive (106)[1]
je trouvais

Present Subjunctive
que je trouve
que tu trouves
qu'il trouve
que nous trouvions
que vous trouviez
qu'ils trouvent

Present Indicative
je trouve
tu trouves
il trouve
nous trouvons
vous trouvez
ils trouvent

Imperative
trouve
trouvons
trouvez

Past Participle (41)[1]
trouvé

Past Indefinite (41)[1]
j'ai trouvé

Pluperfect (119)[1]
j'avais trouvé

Perfect Infinitive
avoir trouvé

SECOND CONJUGATION

Infinitive FINIR

Future
je finirai

Present Conditional
je finirais

Present Participle
finissant

Past Descriptive
je finissais

Present Subjunctive
que je finisse
que tu finisses
qu'il finisse
que nous finissions
que vous finissiez
qu'ils finissent

Present Indicative
je finis
tu finis
il finit
nous finissons
vous finissez
ils finissent

Imperative
finis
finissons
finissez

Past Participle
fini

Past Indefinite
j'ai fini

Pluperfect
j'avais fini

Perfect Infinitive
avoir fini

THIRD CONJUGATION

Infinitive VENDRE

Future
je vendrai

Present Conditional
je vendrais

Present Participle
vendant

Past Descriptive
je vendais

Present Subjunctive
que je vende
que tu vendes
qu'il vende
que nous vendions
que vous vendiez
qu'ils vendent

Present Indicative
je vends
tu vends
il vend
nous vendons
vous vendez
ils vendent

Imperative
vends
vendons
vendez

Past Participle
vendu

Past Indefinite
j'ai vendu

Pluperfect
j'avais vendu

Perfect Infinitive
avoir vendu

[1] These numbers refer to the lessons in which the formation of the tenses is explained.

REFLEXIVE

Infinitive **SE LEVER**

Future	*Present Participle*	*Present Indicative*	*Past Participle*
je me lèverai[1]	se levant	je me lève	levé
		tu te lèves	
Present Conditional	*Past Descriptive*	il se lève	*Past Indefinite*
je me lèverais	je me levais	nous nous levons	je me suis levé
	Present Subjunctive	vous vous levez	*Pluperfect*
	que je me lève	ils se lèvent	je m'étais levé
	que tu te lèves		
	qu'il se lève	*Imperative*	*Perfect Infinitive*
	que nous nous levions	lève-toi	s'être levé
	que vous vous leviez	levons-nous	
	qu'ils se lèvent	levez-vous	

REGULAR VERBS WITH ORTHOGRAPHIC CHANGES

Part I. *Verbs with Stem Vowel **e** or **é***

I. The verbs in this group have no irregularities as far as the tense-endings are concerned. The cases in which the irregularity occurs, (1) the addition of a grave accent, (2) the doubling of the final consonant, or (3) the changing of an acute accent to a grave accent, are always the same. The change occurs only in the entire future and conditional (except in Group C) and before the mute endings **-e, -es, -ent.**

A. The commonest verbs in (1) above, are **lever, se lever, acheter, mener, racheter.**

B. In (2), **appeler, s'appeler, se rappeler, jeter.**

C. In (3), **espérer, répéter, célébrer, préférer, régner, posséder, libérer, suggérer.**

In the following examples the only forms of each tense given are those in which the change occurs.

A. *Future*	**B.** *Future*	**C.** *Future*
j'achèterai	je jetterai	j'espérerai
Present Conditional	*Present Conditional*	*Present Conditional*
j'achèterais	je jetterais	j'espérerais
Present Indicative	*Present Indicative*	*Present Indicative*
j'achète	je jette	j'espère
tu achètes	tu jettes	tu espères
il achète	il jette	il espère
ils achètent	ils jettent	ils espèrent
Present Subjunctive	*Present Subjunctive*	*Present Subjunctive*
que j'achète	que je jette	que j'espère
que tu achètes	que tu jettes	que tu espères
qu'il achète	qu'il jette	qu'il espère
qu'ils achètent	qu'ils jettent	qu'ils espèrent

[1] See I, A, below.

Part II. Verbs Ending in cer and ger

I. Verbs ending in -cer, like **commencer, lancer, placer,** require the s sound of c throughout the conjugation. Consequently c becomes c cedilla (ç) before the vowels **a** or **o** in any tense. The c becomes (ç) in the following cases only:

Present	*Past Descriptive*
nous commençons	je commençais
	tu commençais
	il commençait
	ils commençaient

II. Verbs ending in -ger, like **manger, voyager, juger,** require the sound [ʒ], soft g, throughout the conjugation. Consequently g becomes **ge** before the vowels **a** or **o** in any tense. The following are the only forms requiring this change:

Present	*Past Descriptive*
nous mangeons	je mangeais
	tu mangeais
	il mangeait
	ils mangeaient

Part III. Verbs Ending in yer

III. Verbs ending in **uyer** and **oyer**, like **s'ennuyer** and **employer**, change **y** to **i** before a mute **e**. This change occurs, consequently, in the entire future and present conditional, and in the present indicative and subjunctive before the endings -e, -es, -ent, as follows:

Infinitive s'ennuyer

Future	*Present Indicative*
je m'ennuierai	je m'ennuie
	tu t'ennuies
Present Conditional	il s'ennuie
je m'ennuierais	ils s'ennuient
	Present Subjunctive
	que je m'ennuie
	que tu t'ennuies
	qu'il s'ennuie
	qu'ils s'ennuient

Infinitive employer

Future	*Present Indicative*
j'emploierai	j'emploie
	tu emploies
Present Conditional	il emploie
j'emploierais	ils emploient
	Present Subjunctive
	que j'emploie
	que tu emploies
	qu'il emploie
	qu'ils emploient

THE AUXILIARY VERBS

Infinitive AVOIR

Future	*Present Participle*	*Present Indicative*	*Past Participle*
j'aurai	ayant	j'ai	eu
Present Conditional	*Past Descriptive*	tu as	*Past Indefinite*
j'aurais	j'avais	il a	j'ai eu
		nous avons	
	Present Subjunctive	vous avez	*Pluperfect*
	que j'aie	ils ont	j'avais eu
	que tu aies		*Perfect Infinitive*
	qu'il ait	*Imperative*	avoir eu
	que nous ayons	aie	
	que vous ayez	ayons	
	qu'ils aient	ayez	

Infinitive ETRE

Future	*Present Participle*	*Present Indicative*	*Past Participle*
je serai	étant	je suis	été
Present Conditional	*Past Descriptive*	tu es	*Past Indefinite*
je serais	j'étais	il est	j'ai été
		nous sommes	
	Present Subjunctive	vous êtes	*Pluperfect*
	que je sois	ils sont	j'avais été
	que tu sois		*Perfect Infinitive*
	qu'il soit	*Imperative*	avoir été
	que nous soyons	sois	
	que vous soyez	soyons	
	qu'ils soient	soyez	

IRREGULAR VERBS

Infinitive ALLER

Future	*Present Participle*	*Present Indicative*	*Past Participle*
j'irai	allant	je vais	allé (e) (s) (es)
Present Conditional	*Past Descriptive*	tu vas	*Past Indefinite*
j'irais	j'allais	il va	je suis allé (e)
		nous allons	
	Present Subjunctive	vous allez	*Pluperfect*
	que j'aille	ils vont	j'étais allé (e)
	que tu ailles		*Perfect Infinitive*
	qu'il aille	*Imperative*	être allé (e) (s) (es)
	que nous allions	va	
	que vous alliez	allons	
	qu'ils aillent	allez	

Infinitive S'ASSEOIR

Future	*Present Participle*	*Present Indicative*	*Past Participle*
je m'assiérai	s'asseyant	je m'assieds	assis (e) (s) (es)
Present Conditional	*Past Descriptive*	tu t'assieds	*Past Indefinite*
je m'assiérais	je m'asseyais	il s'assied	je me suis assis(e)
		nous nous asseyons	
	Present Subjunctive	vous vous asseyez	*Pluperfect*
	que je m'asseye	ils s'asseyent	je m'étais assis(e)
	que tu t'asseyes		*Perfect Infinitive*
	qu'il s'asseye	*Imperative*	être assis (e) (s) (es)
	que nous nous asseyions	assieds-toi	
	que vous vous asseyiez	asseyons-nous	
	qu'ils s'asseyent	asseyez-vous	

Infinitive BATTRE

Future	Present Participle	Present Indicative	Past Participle
je battrai	battant	je bats	battu
Present Conditional	*Past Descriptive*	tu bats	
je battrais	je battais	il bat	*Past Indefinite*
		nous battons	j'ai battu
	Present Subjunctive	vous battez	
	que je batte	ils battent	*Pluperfect*
	que tu battes		j'avais battu
	qu'il batte	*Imperative*	*Perfect Infinitive*
	que nous battions	bats	avoir battu
	que vous battiez	battons	
	qu'ils battent	battez	

Infinitive BOIRE

Future	Present Participle	Present Indicative	Past Participle
je boirai	buvant	je bois	bu
Present Conditional	*Past Descriptive*	tu bois	
je boirais	je buvais	il boit	*Past Indefinite*
		nous buvons	j'ai bu
	Present Subjunctive	vous buvez	
	que je boive	ils boivent	*Pluperfect*
	que tu boives		j'avais bu
	qu'il boive	*Imperative*	*Perfect Infinitive*
	que nous buvions	bois	avoir bu
	que vous buviez	buvons	
	qu'ils boivent	buvez	

Infinitive CONDUIRE

Future	Present Participle	Present Indicative	Past Participle
je conduirai	conduisant	je conduis	conduit
Present Conditional	*Past Descriptive*	tu conduis	
je conduirais	je conduisais	il conduit	*Past Indefinite*
		nous conduisons	j'ai conduit
	Present Subjunctive	vous conduisez	
	que je conduise	ils conduisent	*Pluperfect*
	que tu conduises		j'avais conduit
	qu'il conduise	*Imperative*	*Perfect Infinitive*
	que nous conduisions	conduis	avoir conduit
	que vous conduisiez	conduisons	
	qu'ils conduisent	conduisez	

Infinitive CONNAÎTRE

Future	Present Participle	Present Indicative	Past Participle
je connaîtrai	connaissant	je connais	connu
Present Conditional	*Past Descriptive*	tu connais	
je connaîtrais	je connaissais	il connaît	*Past Indefinite*
		nous connaissons	j'ai connu
	Present Subjunctive	vous connaissez	
	que je connaisse	ils connaissent	*Pluperfect*
	que tu connaisses		j'avais connu
	qu'il connaisse	*Imperative*	*Perfect Infinitive*
	que nous connaissions	connais	avoir connu
	que vous connaissiez	connaissons	
	qu'ils connaissent	connaissez	

Infinitive COURIR

Future	*Present Participle*	*Present Indicative*	*Past Participle*
je courrai	courant	je cours	couru
Present Conditional	*Past Descriptive*	tu cours	*Past Indefinite*
je courrais	je courais	il court	j'ai couru
		nous courons	
	Present Subjunctive	vous courez	*Pluperfect*
	que je coure	ils courent	j'avais couru
	que tu coures		*Perfect Infinitive*
	qu'il coure	*Imperative*	avoir couru
	que nous courions	cours	
	que vous couriez	courons	
	qu'ils courent	courez	

Infinitive CROIRE

Future	*Present Participle*	*Present Indicative*	*Past Participle*
je croirai	croyant	je crois	cru
Present Conditional	*Past Descriptive*	tu crois	*Past Indefinite*
je croirais	je croyais	il croit	j'ai cru
		nous croyons	
	Present Subjunctive	vous croyez	*Pluperfect*
	que je croie	ils croient	j'avais cru
	que tu croies		*Perfect Infinitive*
	qu'il croie	*Imperative*	avoir cru
	que nous croyions	crois	
	que vous croyiez	croyons	
	qu'ils croient	croyez	

Infinitive DEVOIR

Future	*Present Participle*	*Present Indicative*	*Past Participle*
je devrai	devant	je dois	dû (*m.*) due (*f.*)
Present Conditional	*Past Descriptive*	tu dois	*Past Indefinite*
je devrais	je devais	il doit	j'ai dû
		nous devons	
	Present Subjunctive	vous devez	*Pluperfect*
	que je doive	ils doivent	j'avais dû
	que tu doives		*Perfect Infinitive*
	qu'il doive	*Imperative*	avoir dû
	que nous devions	dois	
	que vous deviez	devons	
	qu'ils doivent	devez	

Infinitive DIRE

Future	*Present Participle*	*Present Indicative*	*Past Participle*
je dirai	disant	je dis	dit
Present Conditional	*Past Descriptive*	tu dis	*Past Indefinite*
je dirais	je disais	il dit	j'ai dit
		nous disons	
	Present Subjunctive	vous dites	*Pluperfect*
	que je dise	ils disent	j'avais dit
	que tu dises		*Perfect Infinitive*
	qu'il dise	*Imperative*	avoir dit
	que nous disions	dis	
	que vous disiez	disons	
	qu'ils disent	dites	

Infinitive DORMIR

Future	Present Participle	Present Indicative	Past Participle
je dormirai	dormant	je dors	dormi
Present Conditional		tu dors	
je dormirais	*Past Descriptive*	il dort	*Past Indefinite*
	je dormais	nous dormons	j'ai dormi
	Present Subjunctive	vous dormez	*Pluperfect*
	que je dorme	ils dorment	j'avais dormi
	que tu dormes		
	qu'il dorme	*Imperative*	*Perfect Infinitive*
	que nous dormions	dors	avoir dormi
	que vous dormiez	dormons	
	qu'ils dorment	dormez	

Infinitive ECRIRE

Future	Present Participle	Present Indicative	Past Participle
j'écrirai	écrivant	j'écris	écrit
Present Conditional		tu écris	
j'écrirais	*Past Descriptive*	il écrit	*Past Indefinite*
	j'écrivais	nous écrivons	j'ai écrit
	Present Subjunctive	vous écrivez	*Pluperfect*
	que j'écrive	ils écrivent	j'avais écrit
	que tu écrives		
	qu'il écrive	*Imperative*	*Perfect Infinitive*
	que nous écrivions	écris	avoir écrit
	que vous écriviez	écrivons	
	qu'ils écrivent	écrivez	

Infinitive ENVOYER

Future	Present Participle	Present Indicative	Past Participle
j'enverrai	envoyant	j'envoie	envoyé
Present Conditional		tu envoies	
j'enverrais	*Past Descriptive*	il envoie	*Past Indefinite*
	j'envoyais	nous envoyons	j'ai envoyé
	Present Subjunctive	vous envoyez	*Pluperfect*
	que j'envoie	ils envoient	j'avais envoyé
	que tu envoies		
	qu'il envoie	*Imperative*	*Perfect Infinitive*
	que nous envoyions	envoie	avoir envoyé
	que vous envoyiez	envoyons	
	qu'ils envoient	envoyez	

Infinitive FAIRE

Future	Present Participle	Present Indicative	Past Participle
je ferai	faisant	je fais	fait
Present Conditional		tu fais	
je ferais	*Past Descriptive*	il fait	*Past Indefinite*
	je faisais	nous faisons	j'ai fait
	Present Subjunctive	vous faites	*Pluperfect*
	que je fasse	ils font	j'avais fait
	que tu fasses		
	qu'il fasse	*Imperative*	*Perfect Infinitive*
	que nous fassions	fais	avoir fait
	que vous fassiez	faisons	
	qu'ils fassent	faites	

Infinitive FALLOIR[1]

Future	*Present Participle*	*Present Indicative*	*Past Participle*
il faudra	*lacking*	il faut	fallu
Present Conditional	*Past Descriptive*	*Imperative*	*Past Indefinite*
il faudrait	il fallait	*lacking*	il a fallu
	Present Subjunctive		*Pluperfect*
	qu'il faille		il avait fallu
			Perfect Infinitive
			avoir fallu

[1] **Falloir** is an impersonal verb, i. e., it is used only in the third person singular.

Infinitive LIRE

Future	*Present Participle*	*Present Indicative*	*Past Participle*
je lirai	lisant	je lis	lu
Present Conditional	*Past Descriptive*	tu lis	
je lirais	je lisais	il lit	*Past Indefinite*
		nous lisons	j'ai lu
	Present Subjunctive	vous lisez	
	que je lise	ils lisent	*Pluperfect*
	que tu lises		j'avais lu
	qu'il lise	*Imperative*	*Perfect Infinitive*
	que nous lisions	lis	avoir lu
	que vous lisiez	lisons	
	qu'ils lisent	lisez	

Infinitive METTRE

Future	*Present Participle*	*Present Indicative*	*Past Participle*
je mettrai	mettant	je mets	mis
Present Conditional	*Past Descriptive*	tu mets	
je mettrais	je mettais	il met	*Past Indefinite*
		nous mettons	j'ai mis
	Present Subjunctive	vous mettez	
	que je mette	ils mettent	*Pluperfect*
	que tu mettes		j'avais mis
	qu'il mette	*Imperative*	*Perfect Infinitive*
	que nous mettions	mets	avoir mis
	que vous mettiez	mettons	
	qu'ils mettent	mettez	

Infinitive MOURIR

Future	*Present Participle*	*Present Indicative*	*Past Participle*
je mourrai	mourant	je meurs	mort(e)(s)(es)
Present Conditional	*Past Descriptive*	tu meurs	
je mourrais	je mourais	il meurt	*Past Indefinite*
		nous mourons	je suis mort(e)
	Present Subjunctive	vous mourez	
	que je meure	ils meurent	*Pluperfect*
	que tu meures		j'étais mort(e)
	qu'il meure	*Imperative*	*Perfect Infinitive*
	que nous mourions	meurs	être mort(e)(s)(es)
	que vous mouriez	mourons	
	qu'ils meurent	mourez	

Infinitive OFFRIR

Future	Present Participle	Present Indicative	Past Participle
j'offrirai	offrant	j'offre	offert
Present Conditional	**Past Descriptive**	tu offres	
j'offrirais	j'offrais	il offre	**Past Indefinite**
		nous offrons	j'ai offert
	Present Subjunctive	vous offrez	
	que j'offre	ils offrent	**Pluperfect**
	que tu offres		j'avais offert
	qu'il offre	**Imperative**	**Perfect Infinitive**
	que nous offrions	offre	avoir offert
	que vous offriez	offrons	
	qu'ils offrent	offrez	

Infinitive OUVRIR

Future	Present Participle	Present Indicative	Past Participle
j'ouvrirai	ouvrant	j'ouvre	ouvert
Present Conditional	**Past Descriptive**	tu ouvres	
j'ouvrirais	j'ouvrais	il ouvre	**Past Indefinite**
		nous ouvrons	j'ai ouvert
	Present Subjunctive	vous ouvrez	
	que j'ouvre	ils ouvrent	**Pluperfect**
	que tu ouvres		j'avais ouvert
	qu'il ouvre	**Imperative**	**Perfect Infinitive**
	que nous ouvrions	ouvre	avoir ouvert
	que vous ouvriez	ouvrons	
	qu'ils ouvrent	ouvrez	

Infinitive PARTIR

Future	Present Participle	Present Indicative	Past Participle
je partirai	partant	je pars	parti(e)(s)(es)
Present Conditional	**Past Descriptive**	tu pars	
je partirais	je partais	il part	**Past Indefinite**
		nous partons	je suis parti(e)
	Present Subjunctive	vous partez	
	que je parte	ils partent	**Pluperfect**
	que tu partes		j'étais parti(e)
	qu'il parte	**Imperative**	**Perfect Infinitive**
	que nous partions	pars	être parti(e)(s)(es)
	que vous partiez	partons	
	qu'ils partent	partez	

Infinitive PLEUVOIR[1]

Future	Present Participle	Present Indicative	Past Participle
il pleuvra	pleuvant	il pleut	plu
Present Conditional	**Past Descriptive**	**Imperative**	**Past Indefinite**
il pleuvrait	il pleuvait	lacking	il a plu
	Present Subjunctive		**Pluperfect**
	qu'il pleuve		il avait plu
			Perfect Infinitive
			avoir plu

[1] **Pleuvoir** is an impersonal verb, i. e., it is used only in the third person singular.

Infinitive POUVOIR

Future	Present Participle	Present Indicative	Past Participle
je pourrai	pouvant	je peux, puis	pu
Present Conditional	**Past Descriptive**	tu peux	**Past Indefinite**
je pourrais	je pouvais	il peut	j'ai pu
		nous pouvons	
	Present Subjunctive	vous pouvez	**Pluperfect**
	que je puisse	ils peuvent	j'avais pu
	que tu puisses		
	qu'il puisse	**Imperative**	**Perfect Infinitive**
	que nous puissions	lacking	avoir pu
	que vous puissiez		
	qu'ils puissent		

Infinitive PRENDRE

Future	Present Participle	Present Indicative	Past Participle
je prendrai	prenant	je prends	pris
Present Conditional	**Past Descriptive**	tu prends	**Past Indefinite**
je prendrais	je prenais	il prend	j'ai pris
		nous prenons	
	Present Subjunctive	vous prenez	**Pluperfect**
	que je prenne	ils prennent	j'avais pris
	que tu prennes		
	qu'il prenne	**Imperative**	**Perfect Infinitive**
	que nous prenions	prends	avoir pris
	que vous preniez	prenons	
	qu'ils prennent	prenez	

Infinitive RECEVOIR

Future	Present Participle	Present Indicative	Past Participle
je recevrai	recevant	je reçois	reçu
Present Conditional	**Past Descriptive**	tu reçois	**Past Indefinite**
je recevrais	je recevais	il reçoit	j'ai reçu
		nous recevons	
	Present Subjunctive	vous recevez	**Pluperfect**
	que je reçoive	ils reçoivent	j'avais reçu
	que tu reçoives		
	qu'il reçoive	**Imperative**	**Perfect Infinitive**
	que nous recevions	reçois	avoir reçu
	que vous receviez	recevons	
	qu'ils reçoivent	recevez	

Infinitive RIRE

Future	Present Participle	Present Indicative	Past Participle
je rirai	riant	je ris	ri
Present Conditional	**Past Descriptive**	tu ris	**Past Indefinite**
je rirais	je riais	il rit	j'ai ri
		nous rions	
	Present Subjunctive	vous riez	**Pluperfect**
	que je rie	ils rient	j'avais ri
	que tu ries		
	qu'il rie	**Imperative**	**Perfect Indefinite**
	que nous riions	ris	avoir ri
	que vous riiez	rions	
	qu'ils rient	riez	

Infinitive SAVOIR

Future	Present Participle	Present Indicative	Past Participle
je saurai	sachant	je sais	su
Present Conditional	**Past Descriptive**	tu sais	**Past Indefinite**
je saurais	je savais	il sait	j'ai su
		nous savons	
	Present Subjunctive	vous savez	**Pluperfect**
	que je sache	ils savent	j'avais su
	que tu saches		
	qu'il sache	**Imperative**	**Perfect Infinitive**
	que nous sachions	sache	avoir su
	que vous sachiez	sachons	
	qu'ils sachent	sachez	

Infinitive SENTIR

Future	Present Participle	Present Indicative	Past Participle
je sentirai	sentant	je sens	senti
Present Conditional	**Past Descriptive**	tu sens	**Past Indefinite**
je sentirais	je sentais	il sent	j'ai senti
		nous sentons	
	Present Subjunctive	vous sentez	**Pluperfect**
	que je sente	ils sentent	j'avais senti
	que tu sentes		
	qu'il sente	**Imperative**	**Perfect Infinitive**
	que nous sentions	sens	avoir senti
	que vous sentiez	sentons	
	qu'ils sentent	sentez	

Infinitive SORTIR

Future	Present Participle	Present Indicative	Past Participle
je sortirai	sortant	je sors	sorti(e)(s)(es)
Present Conditional	**Past Descriptive**	tu sors	**Past Indefinite**
je sortirais	je sortais	il sort	je suis sorti(e)
		nous sortons	
	Present Subjunctive	vous sortez	**Pluperfect**
	que je sorte	ils sortent	j'étais sorti(e)
	que tu sortes		
	qu'il sorte	**Imperative**	**Perfect Infinitive**
	que nous sortions	sors	être sorti(e)(s)(es)
	que vous sortiez	sortons	
	qu'ils sortent	sortez	

Infinitive SUIVRE

Future	Present Participle	Present Indicative	Past Participle
je suivrai	suivant	je suis	suivi
Present Conditional	**Past Descriptive**	tu suis	**Past Indefinite**
je suivrais	je suivais	il suit	j'ai suivi
		nous suivons	
	Present Subjunctive	vous suivez	**Pluperfect**
	que je suive	ils suivent	j'avais suivi
	que tu suives		
	qu'il suive	**Imperative**	**Perfect Infinitive**
	que nous suivions	suis	avoir suivi
	que vous suiviez	suivons	
	qu'ils suivent	suivez	

Infinitive VENIR

Future	*Present Participle*	*Present Indicative*	*Past Participle*
je viendrai	venant	je viens	venu(e)(s)(es)
Present Conditional	*Past Descriptive*	tu viens	*Past Indefinite*
je viendrais	je venais	il vient	je suis venu(e)
		nous venons	
	Present Subjunctive	vous venez	*Pluperfect*
	que je vienne	ils viennent	j'étais venu(e)
	que tu viennes		
	qu'il vienne	*Imperative*	*Perfect Infinitive*
	que nous venions	viens	être venu(e)(s)(es)
	que vous veniez	venons	
	qu'ils viennent	venez	

Infinitive VIVRE

Future	*Present Participle*	*Present Indicative*	*Past Participle*
je vivrai	vivant	je vis	vécu
Present Conditional	*Past Descriptive*	tu vis	*Past Indefinite*
je vivrais	je vivais	il vit	j'ai vécu
		nous vivons	
	Present Subjunctive	vous vivez	*Pluperfect*
	que je vive	ils vivent	j'avais vécu
	que tu vives		
	qu'il vive	*Imperative*	*Perfect Infinitive*
	que nous vivions	vis	avoir vécu
	que vous viviez	vivons	
	qu'ils vivent	vivez	

Infinitive VOIR

Future	*Present Participle*	*Present Indicative*	*Past Participle*
je verrai	voyant	je vois	vu
Present Conditional	*Past Descriptive*	tu vois	*Past Indefinite*
je verrais	je voyais	il voit	j'ai vu
		nous voyons	
	Present Subjunctive	vous voyez	*Pluperfect*
	que je voie	ils voient	j'avais vu
	que tu voies		
	qu'il voie	*Imperative*	*Perfect Infinitive*
	que nous voyions	vois	avoir vu
	que vous voyiez	voyons	
	qu'ils voient	voyez	

Infinitive VOULOIR

Future	*Present Participle*	*Present Indicative*	*Past Participle*
je voudrai	voulant	je veux	voulu
Present Conditional	*Past Descriptive*	tu veux	*Past Indefinite*
je voudrais	je voulais	il veut	j'ai voulu
		nous voulons	
	Present Subjunctive	vous voulez	*Pluperfect*
	que je veuille	ils veulent	j'avais voulu
	que tu veuilles		
	qu'il veuille	*Imperative*	*Perfect Infinitive*
	que nous voulions	veuille, veux	avoir voulu
	que vous vouliez	veuillons, voulons	
	qu'ils veuillent	veuillez, voulez	

VOCABULARY NOTES

As a guide to the selection of vocabulary for *French Book One*, the authors have accepted as authority these two publications: the *French Word Book*, by G. E. Vander Beke, and the *French Idiom List*, compiled by F. D. Cheydleur.

The French-English Vocabulary of *French Book One*, pages 384 to 412, contains 180 idioms and 1970 words, 560 being cognates, which reduce the vocabulary load considerably. These 1970 words include: (1) articles, common prepositions, pronouns, adverbs derived from adjectives, and numerals; (2) 80 irregular verb-forms; (3) 40 proper nouns; (4) the 69 basic items in Part I of the *Word Book;* (5) 830 of the first thousand words of the *Word Book;* (6) 785 words of lower frequency in the Vander Beke list, the

largest group being from the second thousand words, the next largest group from the third thousand, etc.; and (7) 166 words not found in the Vander Beke list. Many of the words in groups 6 and 7 are the common environmental words relating to the schoolroom, the home, weather, time, travel, etc., which are of lower frequency or are omitted from the *French Word Book*, due to its having been chosen from printed sources of a wide range of categories of French prose. The remaining words in these two groups are required as part of the passive vocabulary of the twenty-six unit reading lessons. Approximately 1300 of the 1970 words comprise what may be called the active vocabulary, i.e., the words that appear in the eighty-five grammar lessons.

BASIC VOCABULARY AND IDIOM LIST

The list below, consisting of 992 basic words and idioms chosen from the final vocabulary on pages 384-412, makes available in alphabetical order (1) the 69 basic words, (2) words from the first thousand of the Vander Beke list, and (3) idioms from the Cheydleur list.

The list is of particular value to the pupil and to the teacher as it points out the permanent foundation of a reading vocabulary and offers in concise form a review list for

the preparation of final tests. Since *French Book Two* has this vocabulary as its nucleus, the more thoroughly it is mastered in the first year, the easier will be the transition in this skill to second-year work.

To make the list most useful, words and idioms are designated as follows: (1) Boldface words are the 69 basic words; (2) * indicates the words appearing in Lessons 1-59 (all unstarred words appear in Lessons 60-133); (3) † indicates the cognates.

*à, au, aux, à l'	†s'amuser	*†attention	†avril
*à midi	*an	attirer	bas (*n.*)
*à tantôt	*ancien, ancienne	au-dessus	en bas
†abandonner	Anglais (*n.*)	*aujourd'hui	bas, basse
*d'abord	*anglais (*n.*)	auprès de	*battre
tout d'abord	*anglais (*adj.*)	*aussi	se battre
†accepter	année	*aussi . . . que	*beau, bel, belle,
†accident	*†annoncer	aussitôt	beaux, belles
*†accompagner	appartenir	autant que	*beaucoup
*accorder	*appeler	autour de	*beaucoup de
*acheter	s'appeler	**autre**	†beauté
achever	s'appliquer	*autrefois	besoin
†acte	*apprendre	d'avance	bête
†admirable	†approcher	*†avancer	**bien**
*†admirer	s'approcher de	*avant	bientôt
*†affaire	*après	avant de	*blanc, blanche
afin de	*arbre	***avec**	blesser
*âge	argent	***avoir**	*†bleu
agir	†arme	*avoir l'air d'être	boire
agiter	†armée	*avoir l'air inquiet	*bois
†aide	arrêter	avoir besoin de	**bon, bonne**
*†aider	s'arrêter	*avoir chaud	bonheur
*aimer	*†arriver	avoir de la chance	*bord
*ainsi	*arriver à	*avoir envie de	*bouche
*†air	†art	*avoir faim	*bout
*ajouter	s'asseoir	*avoir froid	*au bout de
*aller	*assez	*avoir honte	*bras
s'en aller	*assis	*avoir peur	†brave
*allumer	assister à	*avoir raison	*bruit
*alors	†assurer	*avoir soif	*ça
âme	*†attacher	*avoir sommeil	*c'est ça
amener	attendre	*il n'y a pas de quoi	cacher
*ami		avouer	*café

*†calme
*†camarade
*campagne
†capable
car
†caractère
cas
à cause de
causer, *to chat*
†causer, *to cause*
*ce, cet, cette, ces
*ceci
*c'est-à-dire
*cela
celle, celles
celui
cent
certainement
†cesser
ceux
chacun, chacune
*chaise
*†chambre
*champ
†chance
†changer
*chanter
*chapeau
*chaque
†charger
†charmant
*chaud
chef
chemin
cher, chère
*chercher
cheval
à cheval
cheveux
*chez
*choisir
*chose
*ciel
cinq
cinquante
clair
*†classe
*cœur
*coin
colère
*combien
comme
*†commencer
*comment
*commun
complet
†composer
*comprendre
†compter
†condition
*conduire
*connaissance
connaître
conseil
†conserver
†considérer
†constituer
contenir

*†content
*†continuer
contre
*†conversation
*corps
côte
côté
*à côté de
*de côté
se coucher
*†couleur
*coup
*couper
cour
†courage
courant
*courir
court
coûter
couvrir
*†cri
*†crier
croire
je crois bien
*dame
dans
davantage
*de, du, de l', de
  la, des
débuts
†décider
†déclarer
découvrir
défaut
défendre
†degré
dehors
*déjà
*demain
*†demander
demeurer
demi, demie
†départ
dépasser
*depuis
*dernier, dernière
*derrière
dès que
*†descendre
†désir
*†désirer
†détail
deux
*deuxième
*devant
*devenir
deviner
devoir (*n.*)
devoir (*v.*)
Dieu
*†différence
†différent
*†difficile
*†difficulté
dimanche
*†dîner (*n.*)
*†dîner (*v.*)
dire

se diriger vers
disparaître
divers
*dix
*doigt
*donc
donner
dont
*dormir
*dos
*doucement
douleur
*doute
sans doute
*doux, douce
*douze
dresser
se dresser
droit (*n.*)
droit (*adj.*)
à droite
*dur
*eau
échapper
éclairer
*école
*écouter
*écrire
*égal
église
*élever
elle, elles
s'éloigner
*†embrasser
*†employer
emporter
en (*prep.*)
en (*pron.*)
*encore
encore un (e)
*endroit
enfant
enfermer
*enfin
†engagé
enlever
†ennemi
énorme
*ensemble
ensuite
*entendre
bien entendu
entourer
*entre
*†entrer
envie
envoyer
épaule
époque
†erreur
*espérer
espoir
*esprit
essayer
*est-ce que
†estimé
*et
*†établir

*état
s'éteindre
éteint
†étrange
étranger (*n.*)
étranger (*adj.*)
être (*v.*)
étroit
*étudier
eux
éviter
exactement
†examiner
*†excellent
†exemple
*par exemple
†exercer
†exister
*expliquer
†exposer
*†expression
exprimer
en face
*facile
façon
faible
faire
*faire attention
*faire une
  promenade
il fait beau
il fait chaud
il fait froid
fallu
*†famille
†fatigue
faudra
*faut
*faute
faux, fausse
†faveur
femme
*fenêtre
*fermer
fête
*feu
feuille
*fier, fière
*figure
*fille
*fils
*fin (*n.*)
fin (*adj.*)
*†finir
†fixer
*fleur
foi
*fois
fond
*†force
*†forme
*†former
*fort
†fortune
foule
fournir
†franc
*Français (*n.*)

*français (n.)
*français (adj.)
*frapper
*frère
froid
*front
gagner
*garçon
*garder
gauche
à gauche
*†général (n.)
†général (adj.)
*genre
gens
se glisser
goût
*†gouvernement
†grâce
grâce à
*grand
*†grave
*gros, grosse
*†groupe
guerre
s'habiller
*habiter
habitude
*haut
*†hésiter
*heure
*à la bonne heure
de bonne heure
*heureux
*hier
*†histoire
hiver
*homme
†honneur
*†hôtel
*huit
*†humain
*ici
†idée
*il, ils
†s'imaginer
†immense
*†important
†impossible
†impression
inconnu
*†indiquer
*inquiet
†installer
s'installer
*†instant
†intention
†intéresser
s'intéresser à
*†intérêt
†intérieur
*†inviter
*jamais
*jambe
*jardin
*je
*jeter
jeu

*jeune
*jeunesse
*†joie
*joli
*jouer
*jour
*journal
*journée
juger
*jusqu'à
juste
*là
*là-bas
*laisser
*lancer
*langue
*large
*le, la, l', les
léger, -ère
lendemain
*lentement
lequel
*†lettre
*leur (s)
*lever
*se lever
*lèvre
†liberté
*libre
lieu
au lieu de
*ligne
*lire
*lit
*livre
*loin
au loin
*†long, longue
le long de
*longtemps
lorsque
*lourd
*lui
*lumière
lutte
*madame
magnifique
*main
*maintenant
*mais
mais non
*maison
*maître
mal (n.)
mal (adj.)
*malade
malgré
malheur
malheureusement
malheureux, -se
*manger
manière
*manquer
marche
*marché
*†marcher
mari
*matin

*mauvais
*me
médecin
meilleur
*même
†menacer
*mener
mer
*mère
*mettre
se mettre à
se mettre en route
mieux
milieu
mille
†million
*†minute
*†moderne
*moi
moindre
moins
mois
moitié
*†moment
*mon, ma, mes
monde
*monsieur,
   messieurs
*monter
*montrer
se moquer de
*morceau
mort (n.)
*mot
*mourir
†mouvement
moyen
mur
*naître
†nature
†naturel, -le
*†naturellement
*ne . . . jamais
*ne . . . pas
*ne . . . personne
*ne . . . plus
ne . . . que
*ne . . . rien
†nécessaire
*n'est-ce-pas?
*ni
*ni . . . ni
†noble
*noir
*nom
†nombre
nombreux, -se
†nommer
*non
*non plus
*notre, nos
*nous
*nouveau,
   nouvelle
de nouveau
nouvelle (n.)
*nuit
nul, -le

†obéir
*†objet
†obliger
†obscur
†observer
obtenir
†occasion
s'occuper de
*œil
œuvre
*offrir
ombre
*on
*or (n.)
or (conj.)
†ordinaire
†ordre
*oreille
oser
*ou
*où
*oublier (de)
*oui
*ouvert
*ouvrier
*ouvrir
*pain
*paix
†pâle
*papier
*par
paraître
*parce que
pareil, -le
*†parent
parfait
parfaitement
*parler
*parole
†part
de la part de
*partie
*partir
à partir de
*partout
*pas (n.)
*pas (neg. adv.)
*pas encore
†passage
†passer
pauvre (n.)
*pauvre (adj.)
†payer
pays
*paysan,
   paysanne
peine
*pendant
pendant que
†pénétrer
*pensée
*penser
*perdre
*père
†permettre
†personnage
*†personne (n.)
*†personne

†personnel
*petit
*peu
à peu près
peu à peu
†peuple
peur
*peut-être
*†phrase
pièce
*pied
*†place
†placer
plaire
*s'il vous plaît
plaisir
*avec plaisir
plein
pleurer
plume
plupart
*plus (adv.)
*plus de
*plusieurs
*plutôt
poche
†politique
*porte
*porter
*poser
*poser une
   question
†posséder
*†possible
*pour
*pourquoi
*pourtant
*pousser
*pouvoir (v.)
*†précéder
se précipiter
†précis
*†préférer
*premier,
   première
*prendre
*†préparer
*près de
†présence
†présenter
*presque
*prêt
prêter
prier
*†principal
prix
*prochain
produire
†projet
se promener
†promettre
*†prononcer
†proposer
propre
*†public, -que
*puis

puisque
*quand
quant à
*quarante
quart
quatre
*que (rel. pron.)
*que (int. pron.)
*que (conj.)
*qu'il est facile
*quel, quelle
*quelque
*quelque chose à
   manger
*quelqu'un
*qu'est-ce que
   c'est
*qu'est-ce que
   c'est que
*†question
*qui (rel. pron.)
*qui (int. pron.)
quinze
*quitter
quoi
*raconter
*raison
ramener
†rapide
se rappeler
*rapporter
†rare
recevoir
réclamer
†recommencer
reconnaître
réduire
*réfléchir
†refuser
*†regard
*†regarder
*règle
*†regretter
rejoindre
se relever
*†remarquer
remercier
remonter
remplacer
remplir
†rencontrer
*rendre
*rentrer
†répéter
*†répondre
*†se reposer
†représenter
†reprocher
†réserver
†ressembler à
†reste
†rester
†résultat
*en retard
*retenir
*retour

†retourner
*retrouver
réunir
réussir
rêve
*revenir
*revoir
*au revoir
†riche
*rien
*rire
*†robe
*roi
†rôle
*rouge
rouler
†route
*en route pour
*rue
saisir
*salle
*salon
*saluer
*sans
*sauter
*sauter de joie
sauver
*savoir (v.)
†scène
†science
*se
†second
secours
†secret
*semaine
sembler
†sentiment
†sentir
*séparé
sept
†sérieux
†service
*†servir
*seul
*seulement
*si (so, if)
siècle
siège
*†silence
†simple
simplement
*†singulier
*†six
†société
*sœur
*soir
soixante
soixante-dix
*†soldat
soleil
sombre
somme
*son, sa, ses
*sonner
†sorte
*sortir

souffrir
soumettre
sourire (v.)
*sous
soutenir
*souvent
*soyez
*soyons
*spécial
†spectacle
†succès
suffire
suite
suivre
*†sujet
†supérieur
†supporter
*sur
*†sûr, bien sûr
surprendre
*†surprise
surtout
tâcher
*†table
*tableau
taisez-vous
tandis que
*tant
tant mieux
tant pis
*tard
tel, telle
*temps
tenez
tenir
†terme
*terminer
*terre
*par terre
†terrible
*tête
*†théâtre
*tiens
*tirer
titre
tomber
†ton (n.)
tôt
*†toucher
*toujours
*tour
*†tourner
*tout, toute, tous,
   toutes
*tout à coup
*(pas) tout à fait
tout à l'heure
tout de suite
tout en
*tout le monde
*(pas) du tout
*tous les deux
*†train
trait (n.)
†traître
*†tranquille

*travail
*travailler
*à travers
*traverser
†trembler
trente
*très
*triste
*trois
troisième
se tromper (de)
*trop
*trop tard
*trouver
*tu, te, toi
tuer
*un, une (art., num.)
†unique
*valeur
valoir
il vaut mieux
*vendre
*venir
vent
véritable
vérité
*verre
*vers
†vertu
vêtements
je veux bien
†victime
vie
*vieux, vieille
*vif, vive
*†village
*ville
vingt
visage
†visite
†visiter
*vite
vivre
*voici
*voilà
*voilà pourquoi
*voir
*voisin,
   voisine (n.)
*voisin,
   voisine (adj.)
voiture
*voix
à voix basse
*votre, vos
*vouloir
vous voulez dire
*vous
†voyage
voyageur
vrai
*vraiment
*y
il y a
*yeux

FRENCH-ENGLISH VOCABULARY

A

il, elle, a [il, ɛl, a], he, she, has

à [a], at, to, on, with, for, of

à la bonne heure [a la bɔ nœːr], good! *or* that's good!

à cause de [a koːz də], because of

à cheval [a ʃəval], on horseback

à côté de [a kote də], beside

à droite [a drwɑt], at the right, to the right

à l'heure [a lœːr], on time

à la maison [a la mezõ], at home

à midi [a midi], I'll see you at noon

à partir de [a partiːr də], from

à peu près [a pø prɛ], about, approximately

à tantôt [a tɑ̃to], good-by (*for a short time*), "so long"

à travers [a travɛːr], across, through

à voix basse [a vwa bɑːs], in a low voice

à vous [a vu], you next

abandonner [abɑ̃dɔne], to abandon

abîmer [abime], to ruin, to spoil

d'abord [dabɔːr], at first; tout d'abord [tu dabɔːr], first of all

aboyer [abwaje], to bark

absence [apsɑ̃ːs] (*f.*), absence

accent [aksɑ̃] (*m.*), accent

accepter [aksɛpte], to accept

accident [aksidɑ̃] (*m.*), accident

accompagner [akõpaɲe], to accompany, to go with

il s'accorde [il sakɔrd], it agrees

accorder [akɔrde], to accord, to grant

accoutumé [akutyme], accustomed

achat [aʃa] (*m.*), purchase

acheter [aʃte], to buy

achever [aʃve], to finish

acte [akt] (*m.*), act, deed

addition [adisjõ] (*f.*), bill (*in a restaurant or hotel*), addition

adieu [adjø], good-by, adieu

adjectif [adʒɛktif] (*m.*), adjective

admirable [admirabl], admirable, fine

admiratrice [admiratris] (*f.*), admirer

admirer [admire], to admire

adorer [adɔre], to adore, to love

adresse [adrɛs] (*f.*), address

aéroplane [aerɔplan] (*m.*), airplane

affaire [afɛːr] (*f.*), matter, affair; tirer d'affaire [tire dafɛːr], to help out; se tirer d'affaire [sə tire dafɛːr], to manage, to get along.

affaires [afɛːr] (*f. pl.*), things, belongings, business

affiche [afiʃ] (*f.*), placard, poster

affliger [afliʒe], to afflict

afin de [afɛ̃ də], in order to

Afrique [afrik] (*f.*), Africa

âge [ɑːʒ] (*m.*), age; quel âge a-t-il? [kɛl ɑːʒ atil], how old is he?

âgé [ɑʒe], old

agent de police [aʒɑ̃d pɔlis] (*m.*), policeman

agile [aʒil], agile, active

agir [aʒiːr], to act

agiter [aʒite], to shake, to wave

agréable [agreabl], agreeable, pleasant

agrément [agremɑ̃] (*m.*), pleasure; jardin d'agrément [ʒardɛ̃ dagremɑ̃] (*m.*), flower garden, pleasure garden

j'ai [ʒe], I have, *etc.*; j'ai une question à vous poser [ʒe yn kɛstjõ a vu poze], I have a question to ask you

aide [ɛːd] (*f.*), help, aid, assistance

aider [ede], to aid, to help

aigu, aiguë [egy], sharp, acute

aiguille [egɥiːj] (*f.*), needle, hand of a clock

aile [ɛl] (*f.*), wing

aimable [ɛmabl], amiable, pleasant, kind

aimer [ɛme], to like, to love; j'aime [ʒɛːm], I like, love; il, elle, aime [il, ɛl, ɛm], he, she, likes, loves; nous aimons [nu zɛmõ], we like, love; vous aimez [vu zɛme], you like, love

aîné [ɛne] (*m.*), first-born, eldest

ainsi [ɛ̃si], thus, so, in this manner

air [ɛːr] (*m.*), air, look, manner; tune; avoir l'air d'être [avwaːr lɛːr dɛːtr], to seem to be, to look, to appear; avoir l'air inquiet [avwaːr lɛːr ɛ̃kje], to seem worried; en plein air [ɑ̃ plɛ̃ nɛːr], out of doors

ajouter [aʒute], to add

album [albɔm] (*m.*), album

algèbre [alʒɛbr] (*f.*), algebra

allée (ale) (*f.*), passage, path, walk

Allemagne [almaɲ] (*f.*), Germany

aller [ale] (*p.p.* **allé**), to go; **s'en aller** [sãnale], to go away, to go off

allumer [alyme), to light (*a fire*)

alors [alɔːr], then, now, so, at that time

âme [aːm] (*f.*), soul, mind, brains

amener [amne], to take (*someone to a place*), to bring about, to bring (*someone*) along

américain [amerikɛ̃], American

Amérique [amerik] (*f.*), America; **Amérique du Nord** [amerik dy nɔːr] (*f.*), North America; **Amérique du Sud** [amerik dy syd] (*f.*), South America

ami [ami] (*m.*), friend

amusant [amyzã], amusing

amuser [amyze], to amuse; **s'amuser** [samyze], to have a good time

an [ã] (*m.*), year

ancien, ancienne [ãsjɛ̃, ãsjɛn], ancient, former, old

ange [ãːʒ] (*m.*), angel

Anglais [ãglɛ] (*m.*), Englishman, Englishmen

anglais [ãglɛ] (*m.*), English (*language*)

anglais [ãglɛ], English

Angleterre [ãglətɛːr] (*f.*), England

animal [animal] (*m.*) (*pl.* **animaux**), animal

année [ane] (*f.*), year; **année bissextile** [ane bisɛkstil] (*f.*), leap year

anniversaire [anivɛrsɛːr] (*m.*), anniversary, birthday

annonce [anõːs] (*f.*), advertising, advertisement

annoncer [anõse], to announce, to portray, to advertise

antichambre [ãtiʃãːbr] (*f.*), entrance-hall, reception-room

août [u] (*m.*), August

appartement [apartəmã] (*m.*), suite of rooms, apartment

appartenir [apartəniːr] (*p.p.* **appartenu**), to belong

appel [apɛl] (*m.*), roll, roll-call; **il fait** (*inf.* **faire**) **l'appel** [il fɛ lapɛl], he calls the roll

appeler [aple], to call; **s'appeler** [saple], to be named, to be called

il appelle [il apɛːl] (*inf.* **appeler**), he calls

appétit [apeti] (*m.*), appetite; **de bon appétit** [də bõnapeti], with relish

applaudir [aplodiːr], to applaud

s'appliquer [saplike], to apply oneself

apporter [apɔrte], to bring, to take (*to someone*)

apprendre [aprãːdr] (*p.p.* **appris**), to acquire, to learn, to teach

approcher [aprɔʃe], to approach, to come near; **s'approcher de** [saprɔʃe də], to approach, to draw near

après [aprɛ], after, afterwards; **d'après** [daprɛ], adapted from

après-midi [apremidi] (*m.*), afternoon, in the afternoon

arbre [arbr] (*m.*), tree

archevêque [arʃəvɛːk] (*m.*), archbishop

architecture [arʃitɛktyːr] (*f.*), architecture

argent [arʒã] (*m.*), money, silver

arithmétique [aritmetik] (*f.*), arithmetic

armée [arme] (*f.*), army

armer chevalier [arme ʃəvalje], to make *or* dub (*one*) knight

armes [arm] (*f. pl.*), weapons, arms

arrangement [arãʒmã] (*m.*), arrangement

arrêter [arɛte], to arrest, to stop; **s'arrêter** [sarɛte], to stop, to pause

arrivée [arive] (*f.*), arrival

il arrive [il ariːv], there happens, there occurs

arriver [arive], to arrive, to come, to happen; **arriver à** [arive a], to reach

arroser [aroze], to water, to sprinkle

art [aːr] (*m.*), art

article [artikl] (*m.*), article; **article défini** [artikl defini] (*m.*), definite article; **article indéfini** [artiklɛ̃defini] (*m.*), indefinite article

artiste [artist] (*m. and f.*), artist

ascenseur [asãsœːr] (*m.*), elevator

Asie [azi] (*f.*), Asia

s'asseoir [saswaːr] (*p.p.* **assis**), to sit down

assez [ase], enough, well enough, rather, somewhat; **assez souvent** [ase suvã], fairly often, rather often, often enough

assiette [asjɛt] (*f.*), plate

assis [asi], seated

assister à [asiste a], to attend, to be present at

assurément [asyremã], surely, doubtless

assurer [asyre], to assure

attacher [ataʃe], to attach

attaquer [atake], to attack

attendre [atɑ̃:dr], to await, to wait for

attention [atɑ̃sjõ] (f.), attention, pay attention; faire attention [fɛːr atɑ̃sjõ], to pay attention

attirer [atire], to attract, to draw

attraper [atrape], to catch

au [o] (m. sing.), in the, to the

au bout de [o bu də], at the end of, at the bottom of

au lieu de [o ljø də], instead of

au loin [o lwɛ̃], in the distance

au revoir [o rəvwaːr], good-by

au salon [o salõ], in the living-room, to the living-room

au soleil [o sɔlɛ:j], in the sunshine

auberge [obɛrʒ] (f.), inn

au-dessus [odsy], above

aujourd'hui [oʒurdɥi], today

auprès de [oprɛ də], with, near (object of this preposition must be a person)

aussi [osi], also, too; aussi . . . que [osi kə], as . . . as

aussitôt [osito], immediately

Australie [ɔstrali] (f.), Australia

autant que [otɑ̃ kə], as much as

auteur [otœːr] (m.), author

auto [ɔto] (m. or f.), auto; faire une promenade en auto [fɛːr yn prɔmnad ɑ̃ nɔto], to take a ride

autobus [ɔtɔbys] (m.), autobus

automne [otɔn] (m.), autumn

automobile [ɔtɔmɔbil] (m. or f.), automobile

autoriser [ɔtɔrize], to authorize

autour de [otuːr də], about, around

autre [oːtr], other

autrefois [otrəfwa], formerly

aux [o] (pl.), of the, to the, with the

auxiliaire [ɔksiljɛːr] (m.), auxiliary

d'avance [davɑ̃:s], in advance

avancer [avɑ̃se], to advance

avant [avɑ̃], before (time)

avant de [avɑ̃ də], before (followed by an infinitive)

avant-garde [avɑ̃ gard] (f.), advance-guard

avec [avɛk], with

aventure [avɑ̃tyːr] (f.), adventure

vous avez [vu zave], you have, you are having, you do have

avoir [avwaːr] (p.p. eu), to have; avoir l'air d'être [avwaːr lɛːr dɛːtr], to seem

to be, to look, to appear; avoir l'air inquiet [avwaːr lɛːr ɛ̃kjɛ], to seem worried; avoir beaucoup de forces [avwaːr bokud fɔrs], to be strong, to be energetic, etc.; avoir besoin (de) [avwaːr bəzwɛ̃ də], to need; avoir de la chance [avwaːr də la ʃɑ̃:s], to be lucky; avoir chaud [avwaːr ʃo], to be warm, to be hot; avoir envie de [avwaːr ɑ̃vi də], to wish; avoir faim [avwaːr fɛ̃], to be hungry; avoir froid [avwaːr frwa], to be cold, to be cool; avoir honte [avwaːr õ:t], to be ashamed; avoir lieu [avwaːr ljø], to take place; avoir peur [avwaːr pœːr], to be afraid, to fear; avoir raison [avwaːr rezõ], to be right; avoir soif [avwaːr swaf], to be thirsty; avoir sommeil [avwaːr sɔmɛ:j], to be sleepy

avouer [avwe], to admit, to affirm, to avow

avril [avril] (m.), April

B

bagages [bagaːʒ] (m. pl.), baggage: salle des bagages [sal de bagaːʒ] (f.), baggage-room

baie [bɛ] (f.), bay

se baigner [sə bɛɲe], to bathe

bain [bɛ̃] (m.), bath; salle de bains [sal də bɛ̃] (f.), bathroom

baisser [bɛse], to lower; je baisse [ʒə bɛ:s], I lower, am lowering; nous baissons [nu bɛsõ], we lower, are lowering; vous baissez [vu bɛse], you lower, are lowering

balle [bal] (f.), ball (plaything)

ballon [balõ] (m.), balloon

banane [banan] (f.), banana

banc [bɑ̃] (m.), bench

bande [bɑ̃:d] (f.), band, group

bannière [banjɛːr] (f.), banner

barbe [barb] (f.), beard

barbet [barbɛ] (m.), water-spaniel

baron [barõ] (m.), baron

barrage [baraːʒ] (m.), signal (for the traffic to stop and the pedestrians to cross)

bas [bɑ] (m.) (pl. bas), stocking, bottom, lower part; en bas [ɑ̃ bɑ], downstairs, below

bas, basse [bɑ, bɑ:s], low, inferior

bassin [basɛ̃] (m.), pond

bataille [batɑ:j] (*f.*), battle

bateau [bato] (*m.*) (*pl.* bateaux), boat; bateau à voile [bato a vwal], sailboat

bâtiment [bɑtimɑ̃] (*m.*), building

bâton [bɑtõ] (*m.*), stick

battre [batr] (*p.p.* battu), to beat, to strike; se battre [sə batr], to fight

beau, bel, belle, beaux, belles [bo, bɛl, bɛl, bo, bɛl], beautiful, fine, handsome; il fait beau [il fɛ bo], it is pleasant (*weather*)

beaucoup [boku], very much, a great deal; beaucoup de [boku də], many

beauté [bote] (*f.*), beauty

bébé [bebe] (*m.*), baby

Belge [bɛlʒ] (*m.* and *f.*), Belgian

Belgique [bɛlʒik] (*f.*), Belgium

belle-sœur [bɛl sœ:r] (*f.*), sister-in-law

besoin [bəzwɛ̃] (*m.*), need; avoir besoin (de) [avwa:r bəzwɛ̃ də], to need

bête [bɛ:t] (*f.*), animal, beast

bête [bɛ:t], stupid

beurre [bœ:r] (*m.*), butter

bibliothèque [bibliɔtɛk] (*f.*), library, bookcase

bicyclette [bisiklɛt] (*f.*), bicycle

bien [bjɛ̃], well; c'est bien ça [sɛ bjɛ̃ sa], that's exactly right, that's very good; je crois bien [ʒə krwa bjɛ̃], I should say so; merci bien [mɛrsi bjɛ̃], thank you very much; bien entendu [bjɛ̃ nɑ̃tɑ̃dy], of course, naturally; je veux bien [ʒə vø bjɛ̃], willingly

bientôt [bjɛ̃to], soon

bifteck [biftɛk] (*m.*), beefsteak

billet [bijɛ] (*m.*), ticket, note

biscuit [biskɥi] (*m.*), biscuit, cracker

bizarre [biza:r], bizarre, strange, queer

blanc, blanche [blɑ̃, blɑ̃:ʃ], white

blanchisseuse [blɑ̃ʃisø:z] (*f.*), washerwoman, laundress

blancs [blɑ̃] (*m. pl.*), white men

blesser [blɛse], to wound

bleu [blø] (*m.*), blue

bleu [blø], blue

blouse [blu:z] (*f.*), blouse (*middy*), smock

bœuf [bœf] (*m.*) (*pl.* bœufs [bø]), ox, beef

boire [bwa:r] (*p.p.* bu), to drink

bois [bwɑ] (*m.*) (*pl.* bois), wood

boîte [bwa:t] (*f.*), box; boîte aux lettres [bwa:to lɛtr] (*f.*), letter-box

bon, bonne [bõ, bɔn], good; bon pour [bõ pu:r], good to; un bon moment [œ̃ bõ mɔmɑ̃], for some time; à la bonne heure [a la bɔ nœ:r], good! *or* that's good!; de bonne heure [də bɔ nœ:r], early, in good time

bonbons [bõbõ] (*m. pl.*), candy (*used only in the plural*)

bond [bõ] (*m.*), bound, leap

bondé [bõde], crowded

bondir [bõdi:r], to jump

bonheur [bɔnœ:r] (*m.*), happiness, good fortune

bonjour [bõʒu:r], good-morning, good-day

bonne [bɔn] (*f.*), maid

bonnet [bɔnɛ] (*m.*), bonnet, cap; bonnet de police [bɔnɛd pɔlis] (*m.*), informal military cap

bord [bɔ:r] (*m.*), shore, bank

bouche [buʃ] (*f.*), mouth

boucher [buʃe] (*m.*), butcher; chez le boucher [ʃe lə buʃe], to *or* at the butcher's

bouger [buʒe], to move, to budge

boulanger [bulɑ̃ʒe] (*m.*), baker

boulangerie [bulɑ̃ʒri] (*f.*), bakery

bouleau [bulo] (*m.*) (*pl.* bouleaux), birch

boulevard [bulva:r] (*m.*), boulevard

bout [bu] (*m.*), piece, end, bit; au bout de [o bu də], at the end of, at the bottom of; bout de ficelle [bud fisɛl] (*m.*), piece of string

boutique [butik] (*f.*), shop

bouton [butõ] (*m.*), button

branche [brɑ̃:ʃ] (*f.*), branch

bras [brɑ] (*m.*), arm

brave [bra:v], brave, good, fine

bravoure [bravu:r] (*f.*), bravery

Bretagne [brətaɲ] (*f.*), Brittany

brillant [brijɑ̃], brilliant, bright

brodé [brɔde], embroidered

brosse [brɔs] (*f.*), brush

brosser [brɔse], to brush; se brosser les dents [sə brɔse le dɑ̃], to brush the teeth

bruit [brɥi] (*m.*), noise

brûler [bryle], to burn

brun [brœ̃], brown

buffet [byfɛ] (*m.*), restaurant in a station

buffle [byfl] (*m.*), buffalo

bureau [byro] (*m.*) (*pl.* bureaux), office

C

ça [sa] (*contraction of* cela), that; c'est ça [sɛ sa], that is it, that is correct, that's right; c'est bien ça [sɛ bjɛ̃ sa], that's exactly right, that's very good

cacher [kaʃe], to hide; se cacher [sə kaʃe], to hide oneself

cadeau [kado] (*m.*) (*pl.* cadeaux), gift

cadet [kadɛ] (*m.*), younger *or* youngest son

café [kafe] (*m.*), coffee, café

cahier [kaje] (*m.*), notebook

caillou [kaju] (*m.*) (*pl.* cailloux), pebble

calendrier [kalãdrie] (*m.*), calendar

calme [kalm], calm, quiet, peaceful

camarade [kamarad] (*m.*), comrade

camembert [kamãbɛ:r] (*m.*), Camembert cheese

camion [kamjõ] (*m.*), truck, dray

campagne [kãpaɲ] (*f.*), country

canal [kanal] (*m.*), canal

caniche [kaniʃ] (*m.*), poodle

canif [kanif] (*m.*), penknife

capable [kapabl], able, fit, capable

cape [kap] (*f.*), cape

car [ka:r], for

caractère [karaktɛ:r] (*m.*), character

caramel [karamɛl] (*m.*), caramel; crème au caramel [krɛ:m o karamɛl] (*f.*), caramel pudding *or* custard

caresse [karɛs] (*f.*), caress

caresser [karɛse], to caress, to pet

carotte [karɔt] (*f.*), carrot

carte [kart] (*f.*), map, card; carte du jour [kart dy ʒu:r] (*f.*), menu, bill of fare

cas [kɑ] (*m.*) (*pl.* cas), case

casier [kɑzje] (*m.*), locker

casquette [kaskɛt] (*f.*), cap

se casser [sə kɑse], to get *or* be broken

catalogue [katalɔg] (*m.*), catalogue

cathédrale [katedral] (*f.*), cathedral

à cause de [a ko:z də], because of

causer [koze], to chat, to talk; to cause

cavalier [kavalje] (*m.*), horseman, rider

ce, cet, cette, ces [sə, sɛt, sɛt, se], this, that, these, those

ceci [səsi], this

cela [sla], that; c'est cela [sɛ sla], that's right

célèbre [selɛbr], celebrated

celle [sɛl] (*f. sing.*), this *or* that one, the one

celles [sɛl] (*f. pl.*), these *or* those, the ones

celui [səlɥi] (*m. sing.*), this *or* that one, the one

cent [sã], hundred

ce que [sə kə], what, that which

cérémonie [seremɔni] (*f.*), ceremony

cerise [səri:z] (*f.*), cherry; tarte aux cerises [tarto səri:z] (*f.*), cherry pie

cerisier [sərizje] (*m.*), cherry tree

certainement [sɛrtɛnmã], certainly

cesser [sɛse], to stop, to cease

c'est-à-dire [sɛ ta di:r], that is to say; c'est bien ça [sɛ bjɛ̃ sa], that's exactly right, that's very good; c'est ça [sɛ sa], that is it, that is correct, that's right; c'est cela [sɛ sla], that's right; c'est ce que je vais faire [sɛs kəʒ vɛ fɛ:r], that is what I am going to do; c'est fini [sɛ fini], that's the end of it, that's finished (*or* done)

ceux [sø] (*m. pl.*), these *or* those, the ones

chacun, chacune [ʃakœ̃, ʃakyn], each one, every one

chaise [ʃɛ:z] (*f.*), chair

chaleureusement [ʃalœrøzmã], warmly

chambre [ʃã:br] (*f.*), chamber, room; chambre à coucher [ʃã:bra kuʃe] (*f.*), bedroom; femme de chambre [fam də ʃã:br] (*f.*), chambermaid

champ [ʃã] (*m.*), field

champion [ʃãpjõ] (*m.*), champion

chance [ʃã:s] (*f.*), luck; avoir de la chance [avwa:r də la ʃã:s], to be lucky

changement [ʃãʒmã] (*m.*), change

changer [ʃãʒe], to change, to exchange

chanson [ʃãsõ] (*f.*), song, ballad

chanter [ʃãte], to sing

chapeau [ʃapo] (*m.*) (*pl.* chapeaux), hat

chapelle [ʃapɛl] (*f.*), chapel

chaque [ʃak], each, every

chargé [ʃarʒe], charged, burdened

charger [ʃarʒe], to charge, to load

charitable [ʃaritabl], charitable

charmant [ʃarmã], charming

charmé [ʃarme], charmed

chasse [ʃas] (*f.*), chase, hunting

chasser [ʃase], to drive out, to hunt, to chase

chat [ʃa] (*m.*), cat

château [ʃato] (*m.*) (*pl.* châteaux), château, castle

chaud [ʃo], warm, hot; **avoir chaud** [avwa:r ʃo], to be hot, to be warm; **il fait chaud** [il fɛ ʃo], it is hot

chauffeur [ʃofœ:r] (*m.*), engineer, chauffeur

chef [ʃef] (*m.*), chief, leader, head; **chef de gare** [ʃef də ga:r] (*m.*), station master

chef-d'œuvre [ʃedœ:vr] (*m.*), masterpiece

chemin [ʃəmɛ̃] (*m.*), way, road; **chemin de fer** [ʃmɛ̃ fɛ:r] (*m.*), railroad

chemise [ʃəmi:z] (*f.*), shirt

chêne [ʃɛ:n] (*m.*), oak

cher, chère [ʃɛ:r], dear, expensive

chercher [ʃɛrʃe], to look for, to search for; **je cherche** [ʒə ʃɛrʃ], I look for, I search for; **il cherche** [il ʃɛrʃ], he looks for, is looking for; **nous cherchons** [nu ʃɛrʃõ], we look for, are looking for; **vous cherchez** [vu ʃɛrʃe], you look for, search for

cheval [ʃəval] (*m.*) (*pl.* **chevaux**), horse; **à cheval** [a ʃəval], on horseback; **monter à cheval** [mõte a ʃəval], to ride horseback

chevalier [ʃəvalje] (*m.*), knight

cheveux [ʃəvø] (*m. pl.*), hair

chez [ʃe], at the house of, at the home of; **chez elle** [ʃe zɛl], at or to her house

chien, chienne [ʃjɛ̃, ʃjɛn] (*m., f.*), dog

chocolat [ʃɔkɔla] (*m.*), chocolate; **crème au chocolat** [krɛ:m o ʃɔkɔla] (*f.*), chocolate pudding or custard

choisir [ʃwazi:r], to choose

chose [ʃo:z] (*f.*), thing; **quelque chose à manger** [kɛlkə ʃo:z a mãʒe], something to eat

chou [ʃu] (*m.*) (*pl.* **choux**), cabbage

chrétien [kretjɛ̃] (*m.*), Christian

chrétien, -ne [kretjɛ̃, kretjɛn], Christian

christianisme [kristjanism] (*m.*), Christianity

ciel [sjɛl] (*m.*) (*pl.* **ciels** [*in paintings*], **cieux**), sky, heaven

cinéma [sinema] (*m.*), movies

cinq [sɛ̃:k], five

cinquante [sɛ̃kã:t], fifty

clair [klɛ:r], clear, bright; **il fait clair** [il fɛ klɛ:r], it is bright

classe [klɑ:s] (*f.*), class, session, school; **en classe** [ã klɑ:s], in class, to class; **salle de classe** [sal də klɑ:s] (*f.*), classroom

clef [kle] (*f.*), key

cloche [klɔʃ] (*f.*), bell

cœur [kœ:r] (*m.*), heart

coin [kwɛ̃] (*m.*), corner

col [kɔl] (*m.*), collar

colère [kɔlɛ:r] (*f.*), rage, anger

colis [kɔli] (*m.*), package

collé [kɔle], glued, fastened

coloniser [kɔlɔnize], to colonize

colonne [kɔlɔn] (*f.*), column

combat [kõba] (*m.*), combat

combien [kõbjɛ̃], how much, how many

comédie [kɔmedi] (*f.*), comedy

comédien [kɔmedjɛ̃] (*m.*), comedian

commander [kɔmãde], to order

comme [kɔm], like, as, how

commencer [kɔmãse], to begin

comment [kɔmã], how, in what manner, what

commercial [kɔmɛrsjal], commercial

commission [kɔmisjõ] (*f.*), errand; **faire des commissions** [fɛ:r de kɔmisjõ], to do some errands

commun [kɔmœ̃], common

compagnie [kõpaɲi] (*f.*), company

compagnon [kõpaɲõ] (*m.*), companion

compartiment [kõpartimã] (*m.*), compartment

complet [kõplɛ] (*m.*), suit

complet, complète [kõplɛ, kõplɛt], complete

complimenter [kõplimãte], to congratulate, to compliment

composer [kõpoze], to compose, to arrange

il comprend [il kõprã], he understands

comprendre [kõprã:dr] (*p.p.* **compris**), to understand

je comprends [ʒə kõprã], I understand

compris [kõpri] (*p.p. of* **comprendre**), understood

compter [kõte], to count, to intend

condamner [kõdane], to condemn

condition [kõdisjõ] (*f.*), condition, state, social class

conduire [kõdɥi:r] (*p.p.* **conduit**), to conduct, to drive, to take

confortable [kõfɔrtabl], comfortable

congé [kõʒe] (*m.*), day out, short holiday, leave

conjugaison [kõʒygɛzõ] (*f.*), conjugation

conjuguer [kõʒyge], to conjugate

je connais [ʒə kɔnɛ], I am acquainted with, know (*a person*)

tu connais [ty kɔnɛ], you are acquainted with, know (*a person*)

connaissance [kɔnɛsã:s] (*f.*), acquaintance

vous connaissez [vu kɔnɛse], you are acquainted with, know (*a person*)

nous connaissons [nu kɔnɛsõ], we are acquainted with, know (*a person*)

il connaît [il kɔnɛ], he is acquainted with, knows (*a person*)

connaître [kɔnɛ:tr] (*p.p.* **connu**), to be acquainted with, to know (*a person*)

connétable [kɔnetabl] (*m.*), commander-in-chief, constable

conquérant [kõkerã] (*m.*), conqueror

conseil [kõsɛ:j] (*m.*), advice

conserver [kõsɛrve], to save, to make last

considérer [kõsidere], to consider

constituer [kõstitɥe], to constitute

construire [kõstrɥi:r] (*p.p.* **construit**), to construct

consulter [kõsylte], to consult

conte [kõ:t] (*m.*), story, short story

contenant [kõtnã], containing

contenir [kõtni:r] (*p.p.* **contenu**), to contain

content [kõtã], happy, satisfied, glad

continuer [kõtinɥe], to continue

contre [kõ:tr], against

contrôleur [kõtrolœ:r] (*m.*), conductor, inspector

conversation [kõvɛrsasjõ] (*f.*), conversation

convertir [kõvɛrti:r], to convert

copier [kɔpje], to copy

copieux, -se [kɔpjø, kɔpjø:z], hearty, copious

corde [kɔrd] (*f.*), cord, rope

corne [kɔrn] (*f.*), horn

corps [kɔ:r] (*m.*) (*pl.* **corps**), body

corriger [kɔriʒe], to correct

costume [kɔstym] (*m.*), suit, dress, uniform

côte [ko:t] (*f.*), coast, low hill, elevation

côté [kote] (*m.*), side; **à côté de** [a kote də], beside; **de côté** [də kote], aside

côtelette [kotlɛt] (*f.*), chop, cutlet

se coucher [sə kuʃe], to go to bed; **chambre à coucher** [ʃã:bra kuʃe] (*f.*), bedroom

couleur [kulœ:r] (*f.*), color

couloir [kulwa:r] (*m.*), aisle (*of a train*), narrow corridor

coup [ku] (*m.*), blow, hit, punch; **coup de sifflet** [kud siflɛ] (*m.*), blowing of the whistle, sound of the whistle; **coup de téléphone** [kud telefɔn] (*m.*), ring of a telephone bell; **donner un coup de téléphone (à)** [dɔne œ̃ kud telefɔn a], to telephone (to)

coupable [kupabl], to blame, at fault

couper [kupe], to cut; **se couper** [sə kupe], to cut oneself

cour [ku:r] (*f.*), court, yard

courage [kura:ʒ] (*m.*), courage

courageux, -se [kuraʒø, kuraʒø:z], brave, courageous

courant [kurã] (*m.*), current

courir [kuri:r] (*p.p.* **couru**), to run

couronne [kurɔn] (*f.*), crown, wreath

court [ku:r], short

il court [il ku:r], he runs, is running

couru [kury] (*p.p. of* **courir**), run

cousin, cousine [kuzɛ̃, kuzin] (*m.*, *f.*), cousin

coussin [kusɛ̃] (*m.*), cushion

couteau [kuto] (*m.*) (*pl.* **couteaux**), knife

coûter [kute], to cost

couvert [kuvɛ:r] (*p.p. of* **couvrir**), covered

couvrir [kuvri:r] (*p.p.* **couvert**), to cover; **se couvrir** [sə kuvri:r], to cover oneself

craie [krɛ] (*f.*), chalk

cravate [kravat] (*f.*), necktie

crayon [krejõ] (*m.*), pencil

crème [krɛ:m] (*f.*), cream; **crème au caramel** [krɛ:m o karamɛl] (*f.*), caramel pudding *or* custard; **crème au chocolat** [krɛ:m o ʃɔkɔla] (*f.*), chocolate pudding *or* custard

crêpe [krɛ:p] (*m.*), crêpe

cri [kri] (*m.*), cry, shout

crier [krie], to cry

crime [krim] (*m.*), crime

critique [kritik] (*m.*), critic

croire [krwa:r] (*p.p.* **cru**), to believe; **je crois bien** [ʒə krwa bjɛ̃], I should say so

croisade [krwazad] (*f.*), crusade

croix [krwa] (*f.*) (*pl.* **croix**), cross

cruel, cruelle [kryɛl], cruel

cruellement [kryɛlmã], cruelly, sadly

cueillir [kœji:r] (*p.p.* **cueilli**), to pick, to gather cuillère [kɥijɛ:r] (f.), spoon

cuire [kɥi:r] (p.p. cuit), faire cuire [fɛ:r kɥi:r], to cook

cuisine [kɥizin] (f.), kitchen

cuisinière [kɥizinjɛ:r] (f.), cook

D

dame [dam] (f.), lady

danger [dãʒe] (m.), danger

dangereux, -se [dãʒrø, dãʒrø:z], dangerous

dans [dã], in, into, to

danser [dãse], to dance

danseur [dãsœ:r] (m.), dancer

date [dat] (f.), date

dauphin [dofɛ̃] (m.), dauphin (eldest son of a French king)

davantage [davãta:ʒ], more, any more

de [də], of, from, for, with, about; d'avance [davã:s], in advance; de côté [də kote], aside; de nouveau [də nuvo], again; de la part de [də la pa:r də], from, on behalf of

débarquer [debarke], to get off, to disembark, to debark

débarrasser [debarase], to free

débuts [deby] (m. pl.), first appearance

décembre [desã:br] (m.), December

déchiré [deʃire], torn

déchirer [deʃire], to tear

décider [deside], to decide, to persuade

déclarer [deklare], to declare

décoration [dekɔrasjõ] (f.), decoration (awarded for distinguished work)

découper [dekupe], to carve

découragé [dekuraʒe], discouraged

découverte [dekuvert] (f.), discovery

découvrir [dekuvri:r] (p.p. découvert), to discover

décrire [dekri:r] (p.p. décrit), to describe, to draw

dedans [dədã], within, inside

défaut [defo] (m.), failing, fault (of character)

défendre [defã:dr], to defend, to protect, to forbid

défini [defini], definite

degré [dəgre] (m.), degree, step

dehors [dəɔ:r], out of doors

déjà [deʒa], already

déjeuner [deʒœne] (m.), luncheon; petit déjeuner [pti deʒœne] (m.), breakfast

déjeuner [deʒœne], to have breakfast, to have lunch

délivrer [delivre], to deliver, to free

demain [dəmɛ̃], tomorrow

demander [dəmãde], to demand, to ask, to ask for

demeurer [dəmœre], to live (in a house, city, etc.), to remain

demi, demie [dəmi], half

démon [demõ] (m.), demon

démonstratif [demõstratif], demonstrative

dénouement [denumã] (m.), outcome

dent [dã] (f.), tooth

dentelle [dãtɛl] (f.), lace

départ [depa:r] (m.), departure

dépasser [depase], to surpass, to exceed

se dépêcher [sə depeʃe], to hasten, to hurry

déplorable [deplɔrabl], sad, deplorable

depuis [dəpɥi], since, for; depuis très longtemps [dəpɥi trɛ lõtã], for a long time

dernier [dɛrnje] (m.), the last, the latter

dernier, dernière [dɛrnje, dɛrnjɛ:r], last, final

dérouler [derule], to unroll

derrière [dɛrjɛ:r], behind

des [de], some

dès que [dɛ kə], when, as soon as

désagréable [dezagreabl], disagreeable

il descend [il desã] (inf. descendre), he descends, goes down

descendons [desãdõ] (inf. descendre), let's get out

descendre [desã:dr], to lower, to come or go down, to descend, to get off

désespoir [dezɛspwa:r] (m.), despair

se déshabiller [sə dezabije], to undress

désir [dezi:r] (m.), desire

désirer [dezire], to desire, to wish, to want

dessert [desɛ:r] (m.), dessert

dessiner [desine], to draw; se dessiner [sə desine], to stand out, to be traced

destination [dɛstinasjõ] (f.), destination

détail [deta:j] (m.) (pl. détails), detail

détester [detɛste], to detest

deux [dø], two; tous les deux, toutes les deux [tu le dø, tut le dø], both

deuxième [døzjɛm], second

devant [dəvã], before (place)

devenir [dəvniːr] (*p.p.* **devenu**), to become

il devient [il dəvjɛ̃] (*inf.* **devenir**), he becomes

deviner [dəvine], to guess

devoir [dəvwaːr] (*m.*), exercise, duty, work

devoir [dəvwaːr] (*p.p.* **dû**, *m.;* **due**, *f.*), should, must, ought, to owe, to be obliged

nous devons [nu dəvõ], we should, we must, we ought, we owe

dévorer [devɔre], to devour

diable [djɑːbl] (*m.*), devil

Dieu [djø], God, Lord

différence [diferɑ̃ːs] (*f.*), difference

différent [diferɑ̃], different

difficile [difisil], difficult, hard

difficulté [difikylte] (*f.*), difficulty

dimanche [dimɑ̃ːʃ] (*m.*), Sunday

dîner [dine] (*m.*), dinner; **au dîner** [o dine], at dinner

dîner [dine], to dine, to eat dinner

dire [diːr] (*p.p.* **dit**), to say, to tell; **c'est-à-dire** [sɛtadiːr], that is to say; **vous voulez dire** [vu vule diːr], you mean

direct [dirɛkt], direct

directeur [dirɛktœːr] (*m.*), principal, director, superintendent

se diriger vers [sə diriʒe vɛːr], to proceed, to go toward

discuter [diskyte], to discuss

nous disons [nu dizõ] (*inf.* **dire**), we say

disparaître [disparɛːtr] (*p.p.* **disparu**), to disappear

dispute [dispyt] (*f.*), dispute

distingué [distɛ̃ge], distinguished

distribuer [distribɥe], to distribute

il dit [il di], he says

dit [di] (*p.p. of* **dire**), said; **Maman a dit que non** [mɑmɑ̃ a di kə nõ], Mother said she didn't; Mother said no

dites-moi [dit mwa], tell me

divers [divɛːr], various, different

divisé [divize], divided

dix [dis] ([di] *before consonants*), ten

dix-huit [dizɥit], eighteen

dix-neuf [diznœf], nineteen

dix-sept [disɛt], seventeen

docteur [dɔktœːr] (*m.*), doctor

doigt [dwa] (*m.*), finger

je dois [ʒə dwa] (*inf.* **devoir**), I ought, should, must, owe; **il doit** [il dwa] (*inf.* **devoir**), he ought, should, must, owes

domestique [dɔmɛstik] (*m.*), servant

donc [dõːk], then, now

donner [dɔne], to give; **donner un coup de téléphone** (**à**) [dɔne ɛ̃ kud telefɔn a], to telephone (to); **donner sur** [dɔne syːr], to open upon, to face

donnez-moi [dɔne mwa], give me

dont [dõ], of which, in which, whose

dormir [dɔrmiːr] (*p.p.* **dormi**), to sleep

il dort [il dɔːr] (*inf.* **dormir**), he sleeps

dos [do] (*m.*), back

doucement [dusmɑ̃], gently, smoothly

douleur [dulœːr] (*f.*), pain

doute [dut] (*m.*), doubt; **sans doute** [sɑ̃ dut], without doubt, undoubtedly

doux, douce [du, dus], sweet, gentle; **il fait doux** [il fɛ du], it is mild (weather)

douze [duːz], twelve

douzième [duzjɛm], twelfth

drapeau [drapo] (*m.*) (*pl.* **drapeaux**), flag; **drapeau tricolore** [drapo tri-kɔlɔːr] (*m.*), tricolor

dresser [drɛse], to arrange, to prepare, to decorate, to raise; **se dresser** [sə drɛse], to rise, to stand

droit [drwa] (*m.*), right

droit [drwa], straight, right

à droite [a drwat], at the right

du [dy], of the, from the; **du matin jusqu'au soir** [dy matɛ̃ ʒysko swaːr], from morning till night; **du monde** [dy mõːd], company, guests; **du tout, pas du tout** [dy tu, pɑ dy tu], not in the least, not at all

duc [dyk] (*m.*), duke

dur [dyːr], hard

durer [dyre], to last

E

eau [o] (*f.*), water

échanger [eʃɑ̃ʒe], to exchange

échapper [eʃape], to escape

écharpe [eʃarp] (*f.*), scarf

échelle [eʃɛl] (*f.*), ladder

éclairer [eklɛre], to light up

école [ekɔl] (*f.*), school; **fête des écoles** [fɛːt de zekɔl] (*f.*), school holiday

économiser [ekɔnɔmize], to save, to economize

écouter [ekute], to listen to, to pay attention to

écraser [ekrɑze], to crush

écrire [ekriːr] (*p.p.* **écrit**), to write

écrit [ekri] (*p.p. of* **écrire**), written

écriteau [ekrito] (*m.*) (*pl.* **écriteaux**), sign, bill, poster

ils écrivent [ilzekriv] (*inf.* **écrire**), they write

effacer [efase], to erase

égal [egal], equal

égarer [egare], to mislay, to mislead

église [egliːz] (*f.*), church

électrique [elɛktrik], electric

élégant [elegɑ̃], elegant, fashionable

élément [elemɑ̃] (*m.*), element, metal

éléphant [elefɑ̃] (*m.*), elephant

élève [elɛːv] (*m.* and *f.*), pupil

élever [elve], to bring up, to raise

elle [ɛl], she, it

s'éloigner [selwaɲe], to go away

embarras [ɑ̃barɑ] (*m.*), embarrassment

embarrassé [ɑ̃barase], confused

embouchure [ɑ̃buʃyːr] (*f.*), mouth (*of a river*)

embrasser [ɑ̃brase], to kiss

empereur [ɑ̃prœːr] (*m.*), emperor

employé [ɑ̃plwaje] (*m.*), employee, clerk, conductor, official

employé [ɑ̃plwaje], used, employed

employer [ɑ̃plwaje], to use, to employ

emporter [ɑ̃pɔrte], to take away, to carry off

emprisonner [ɑ̃prizɔne], to imprison

en [ɑ̃], of, made of, in, of it, of them, some, any; (*with geog. names*) to, in; **en classe** [ɑ̃ klɑːs], in class, to class; **en face** [ɑ̃ fas], opposite; **en général** [ɑ̃ ʒeneral], in general; **en morceaux** [ɑ̃ mɔrso], in pieces; **en ordre** [ɑ̃ nɔrdr], in order; **en plein air** [ɑ̃ plɛ̃ nɛːr], out of doors; **en retard** [ɑ̃ rətaːr], late, tardy; **en route pour** [ɑ̃ rut puːr], on the way to; **tout en** [tu tɑ̃], while; **en train de** [ɑ̃ trɛ̃ də], in the act of; **en voiture!** [ɑ̃ vwatyːr], all aboard!

enchanté [ɑ̃ʃɑ̃te], delighted

encore [ɑ̃kɔːr], again, yet; **encore une fois** [ɑ̃kɔːr yn fwa], again, once again

encourager [ɑ̃kuraʒe], to encourage

encre [ɑ̃ːkr] (*f.*), ink

s'endormir [sɑ̃dɔrmiːr] (*p.p.* **endormi**), to fall asleep

endroit [ɑ̃drwa] (*m*), place

énergique [enɛrʒik], energetic

enfant [ɑ̃fɑ̃] (*m.* and *f.*), child; **enfant trouvé** [ɑ̃fɑ̃ truve] (*m.*), foundling

enfermer [ɑ̃fɛrme], to lock up, to inclose

enfilé [ɑ̃file], strung *or* threaded

enfin [ɑ̃fɛ̃], finally, at last, well

engagé [ɑ̃gaʒe], engaged, employed, enlisted

enlever [ɑ̃lve], to take away, to take off, to remove

ennemi [ɛnmi] (*m.*), enemy

ennui [ɑ̃nɥi] (*m.*), boredom, weariness; **quel ennui** [kɛl ɑ̃nɥi], what a bore, what a nuisance

s'ennuyer [sɑ̃nɥije], to be bored

ennuyeux, -se [ɑ̃nɥijø, ɑ̃nɥijøːz], boring, tiresome

énorme [enɔrm], enormous

énormément [enɔrmemɑ̃], greatly

enragé [ɑ̃raʒe], mad

enregistrer [ɑ̃rəʒistre], to check (*baggage*)

ensemble [ɑ̃sɑ̃ːbl], together

ensuite [ɑ̃sɥit], afterwards, then

entendre [ɑ̃tɑ̃ːdr], to hear, to listen to

bien entendu [bjɛ̃ nɑ̃tɑ̃dy], of course, naturally

entourage [ɑ̃turaːʒ] (*m.*), attendants, associates

entourer [ɑ̃ture], to surround

entre [ɑ̃ːtr], between, into

entreprendre [ɑ̃trəprɑ̃ːdr] (*p.p.* **entrepris**), to undertake

entrer [ɑ̃tre], to enter (requires **dans**)

envelopper [ɑ̃vlɔpe], to wrap

envie [ɑ̃vi] (*f.*), desire, envy; **avoir envie de** [avwaːr ɑ̃vi də], to wish

envoyer [ɑ̃vwaje], to send, to send away

épaule [epoːl] (*f.*), shoulder

épée [epe] (*f.*), sword

épicerie [episri] (*f.*), grocery store

épinards [epinaːr] (*m. pl.*), spinach

époque [epɔk] (*f.*), time, period, epoch

ermite [ɛrmit] (*m.*), hermit

errer [ɛre], to wander, to err

erreur [ɛrœːr] (*f.*), error, mistake

escalier [ɛskalje] (*m.*), stairs, staircase

Espagne [ɛspaɲ] (*f.*), Spain

espagnol [ɛspaɲɔl] (*m.*), Spanish (*language*)

espagnol [ɛspaɲɔl], Spanish

espérer [ɛspere], to hope

espoir [ɛspwaːr] (m.), hope

esprit [ɛspri] (m.), mind, spirit, intelligence

essayer [esɛje], to try, to try on

est [ɛ], is

est-ce que [ɛs kə], *no translation. It makes a declarative sentence interrogative.* (Est-ce que je regarde la page? Am I looking at the page?)

estimé [ɛstime], esteemed, prized

et [e], and

établir [etabliːr], to establish

état [eta] (m.), state, condition

Etats-Unis [etazyni] (m. pl.), United States

été [ete] (p.p. of être), been

été [ete] (m.), summer

s'éteindre [setɛ̃ːdr], to go out

éteint [etɛ̃] (p.p. of éteindre), extinguished, put out

étendu [etɑ̃dy], stretched out

vous êtes [vu zɛt] (inf. être), you are

Etienne [etjɛn], Stephen

étiquette [etikɛt] (f.), etiquette, ticket

étrange [etrɑ̃ːʒ], strange, odd, queer

étranger [etrɑ̃ʒe] (m.), stranger, foreigner; pour l'étranger [puːr letrɑ̃ʒe], for a foreign country

étranger [etrɑ̃ʒe], foreign

être [ɛːtr] (p.p. été), to be (very irreg.); avoir l'air d'être [avwaːr lɛːr dɛːtr], to seem to be, to look, to appear

étroit [etrwɑ], narrow

étude [etyd] (f.), study; faire ses études [fɛːr se zetyd], to pursue one's studies, to be studying

étudier [etydje], to study

eu [y] (p.p. of avoir), had

européen [œrɔpeɛ̃], European

eux [ø] (m. pl.), them, they

évêque [evɛːk] (m.), bishop

évidemment [evidamɑ̃], evidently

éviter [evite], to avoid, to escape

exact [egzakt], exact, punctual, accurate

exactement [egzaktəmɑ̃], exactly, punctually

examiner [egzamine], to examine

excellent [ɛksɛlɑ̃], excellent

excepté [ɛksɛpte], except

exception [ɛksɛpsjɔ̃] (f.), exception

s'exclamer [sɛksklame], to exclaim

excursion [ɛkskyrsjɔ̃] (f.), excursion

excuser [ɛkskyze], to excuse

exemple [egzɑ̃ːpl] (m.), example; par exemple [par egzɑ̃ːpl], as an illustration, for instance, for example

exercer [egzɛrse], to exercise; to practice

exercice [egzɛrsis] (m.), exercise

exigeant [egziʒɑ̃], strict, exacting

exiger [egziʒe], to require

exister [egziste], to exist

expédition [ɛkspedisjɔ̃] (f.), expedition

explication [ɛksplikasjɔ̃] (f.), explanation

expliquer [ɛksplike], to explain

explorateur [ɛksplɔratœːr] (m.), explorer

explorer [ɛksplɔre], to explore

exposer [ɛkspoze], to expose

expression [ɛksprɛsjɔ̃] (f.), expression

exprimer [ɛksprime], to express

extérieur [ɛkstɛrjœːr] (m.), outside, exterior

extraordinaire [ɛkstrɔrdinɛːr], extraordinary

F

fable [faːbl] (f.), fable, tale

fabrique [fabrik] (f.), factory

en face [ɑ̃ fas], opposite

fâché [faʃe], angry

facile [fasil], easy

facilement [fasilmɑ̃], easily

façon [fasɔ̃] (f.), way, fashion, manner

facteur [faktœːr] (m.), postman

faible [fɛːbl], feeble, weak

faim [fɛ̃] (f.), hunger; avoir faim [avwaːr fɛ̃], to be hungry

faire [fɛːr], to do, to make; faire attention [fɛːr atɑ̃sjɔ̃], to pay attention; faire des commissions [fɛːr de kɔmisjɔ̃], to do some errands; faire ses études [fɛːr se zetyd], to pursue one's studies, to be studying; faire le ménage [fɛːr lə menaːʒ], to do housework; faire de son mieux [fɛːr də sɔ̃ mjø], to do one's best; faire noir [fɛːr nwaːr], to be dark; faire nuit [fɛːr nɥi], to get dark; faire une promenade [fɛːr yn prɔmnad], to take a walk; faire une promenade en auto [fɛːr yn prɔmnad ɑ̃ noto], to take a ride; faire des tours [fɛːr de tuːr], to do tricks; faire venir [fɛːr vəniːr], to send for; faire un voyage [fɛːr œ̃ vwajaːʒ], to take a trip

je fais [ʒə fɛ] (*inf.* **faire**), I make, I do

fait [fɛ] (*p.p. of* **faire**), made, done

il, elle, fait [il, ɛl, fɛ], he, she, does, is doing, makes; **il fait beau** [il fɛ bo], it is pleasant; **il fait chaud** [il fɛ ʃo], it is hot; **il fait clair** [il fɛ klɛːr], it is bright; **il fait doux** [il fɛ du], it is mild; **il fait frais** [il fɛ frɛ], it is cool; **il fait froid** [il fɛ frwa], it is cold; **il fait mauvais** [il fɛ mɔvɛ], it is disagreeable; **il fait noir** [il fɛ nwaːr], it is dark (weather); **me fait penser** [mə fɛ pãse], makes me think; **il fait une promenade** [il fɛ tyn prɔmnad], he takes a walk

tout à fait [tu ta fɛ], completely, entirely; **pas tout à fait** [pɑ tu ta fɛ], not exactly, not altogether, not entirely

vous faites [vu fɛt], you make, you do

faites (*inf.* **faire**) **attention** [fɛt atãsjõ], pay attention

il a fallu [il a faly] (*past indefinite of* **il faut,** *inf.* **falloir**), it was necessary

famille [famiːj] (*f.*), family

fané [fane], faded

fatal [fatal], fatal

fatigant [fatigã], tiring

fatigue [fatig] (*f.*), fatigue

fatigué [fatige], tired

il faudra [il fɔdra] (*future of* **falloir**), it will be necessary, we must

il faut [il fo] (*present of* **falloir**), it is necessary, one has to, one must

faute [foːt] (*f.*), fault, mistake; **sans faute** [sã foːt], without fail

faux, fausse [fo, foːs], false

faveur [favœːr] (*f.*), favor

féliciter [felisite], to congratulate

féminin [feminɛ̃] (*m.*), feminine (*gender*)

femme [fam] (*f.*), woman, wife; **femme de chambre** [fam də ʃãːbr] (*f.*), chambermaid; **femme de ménage** [fam də menaːʒ] (*f.*), charwoman, cleaning-woman

fenêtre [fənɛːtr] (*f.*), window

fer [fɛːr] (*m.*), iron; **chemin de fer** [ʃmɛ̃ fɛːr] (*m.*), railroad

ferme [fɛrm] (*f.*), farm

ferme [fɛrm], hard, steadily

fermer [fɛrme], to close; **je ferme** [ʒə fɛrm], I close, I am closing; **il ferme** [il fɛrm], he closes, is closing; **vous fermez** [vu fɛrme], you close

fermier [fɛrmje] (*m.*), farmer

féroce [ferɔs], fierce, ferocious

fertile (en) [fɛrtil ã], fertile, full of

fête [fɛːt] (*f.*), holiday, birthday, birthday party, festival; **fête des écoles** [fɛːt de zekɔl] (*f.*), school holiday; **jour de fête** [ʒuːr də fɛːt] (*m.*), holiday

feu [fø] (*m.*) (*pl.* **feux**), fire

feuille [fœːj] (*f.*), leaf

feutre [føːtr] (*m.*), felt

février [fevrie] (*m.*), February

ficelle [fisɛl] (*f.*), string; **bout de ficelle** [bud fisɛl] (*m.*), piece of string

fidèle [fidɛl], faithful

fier, fière [fjɛːr], proud

fièrement [fjɛrmã], proudly

figure [figyːr] (*f.*), face

fil [fil] (*m.*), string, thread

fille [fiːj] (*f.*), daughter, girl; **jeune fille** [ʒœn fiːj] (*f.*), young girl, girl; **petite fille** [ptit fiːj] (*f.*), little girl

fils [fis] (*m.*) (*pl.* **fils**), son

fin [fɛ̃] (*f.*), end

fin [fɛ̃], clever, handsome, fine

c'est fini [sɛ fini], that's the end of it, that's finished (*or* done)

finir [finiːr], to finish

fixer [fikse], to fix, to fasten, to attach

flambeau [flãbo] (*m.*) (*pl.* **flambeaux**), torch, candlestick

flamme [flɑːm] (*f.*), flame

fleur [flœːr] (*f.*), flower; **fleur de lis** [flœːr də lis] (*f.*), fleur-de-lis, lily (*emblem*)

fleuri [flœri], in bloom

fleuve [flœːv] (*m.*), river (*that flows into the sea*)

flotter [flɔte], to float

foi [fwa] (*f.*), faith; **ma foi** [ma fwa], upon my word

fois [fwa] (*f.*), time (*in the sense of occurrence or repetition*); **encore une fois** [ãkɔːr yn fwa], again, once again

foncé [fõse], deep, dark (*of a color*)

fond [fõ] (*m.*), bottom, background, back

fonder [fõde], to found

ils font [il fõ], they make, they do, they take; **ils font des promenades** [il fõ de prɔmnad], they take walks

fontaine [fõtɛːn] (*f.*), fountain

football [futbaːl] (*m.*), football

force [fɔrs] (*f.*), force, strength; **avoir beaucoup de forces** [avwaːr bokud fɔrs], to be strong, to be energetic

forêt [fɔrɛ] (*f.*), forest

forme [fɔrm] (*f.*), form

former [fɔrme], to form, to make

fort [fɔːr], strong, hard; very (adv.)

fortune [fɔrtyn] (f.), fortune

fouet [fwɛ] (m.), whip

foule [ful] (f.), crowd

fourchette [furʃɛt] (f.), fork

fournir [furniːr], to furnish

fourrure [furyːr] (f.), fur

petits fours [pti fuːr] (m. pl.), small fancy cakes

frais, fraîche [frɛ, frɛːʃ], fresh, cool; il fait frais [il fɛ frɛ], it is cool

franc [frɑ̃] (m.), franc, French monetary unit (value about six cents)

Français [frɑ̃sɛ] (m.), Frenchman; Français [frɑ̃sɛ] (m. pl.), French people, Frenchmen

français [frɑ̃sɛ] (m.), French (language)

français [frɑ̃sɛ], French

frapper [frape], to strike, to hit, to knock

frère [frɛːr] (m.), brother

friandise [friɑ̃diːz] (f.), delicacy, dainty, tidbit

froid [frwɑ], cold; avoir froid [avwaːr frwɑ], to be cold, to be cool; il fait froid [il fɛ frwɑ], it is cold

fromage [frɔmaːʒ] (m.), cheese

front [frɔ̃] (m.), forehead

fruit [frɥi] (m.), fruit

fumée [fyme] (f.), smoke

fumer [fyme], to smoke

G

gagner [gaɲe], to earn, to gain, to win; gagner sa vie [gaɲe sa vi], to earn one's living

gai [ge], gay

galonné [galɔne], trimmed with gold braid or lace

garçon [garsɔ̃] (m.), boy, waiter

garder [garde], to hold, to keep, to watch, to guard

gare [gaːr] (f.), station; chef de gare [ʃef də gaːr] (m.), station master

gâteau [gato] (m.) (pl. gâteaux), cake; gâteau sec [gato sɛk] (m.), cooky

gauche [goːʃ], left, clumsy; à gauche [a goːʃ], to the left

Gauthier [gotje], Walter

geler [ʒəle], to freeze; geler vif [ʒəle vif], to freeze to death

général [ʒeneral] (m.) (pl. généraux), general

général [ʒeneral], general; en général [ɑ̃ ʒeneral], generally, in general, usually

généralement [ʒeneralmɑ̃], generally

généreux, -se [ʒenerø, ʒenerøːz], generous

genou [ʒənu] (m.) (pl. genoux), knee; à genoux [a ʒənu], on one's knees; se mettre à genoux [sə mɛtra ʒənu], to kneel down

genre [ʒɑ̃ːr] (m.), type, kind, manner

gens [ʒɑ̃] (m. and f. pl.), people

gentil, gentille [ʒɑ̃ti, ʒɑ̃tiːj], agreeable, kind, pleasant

gentillesse [ʒɑ̃tijɛs] (f.), pretty tricks, kindness

géographie [ʒeɔgrafi] (f.), geography

géranium [ʒeranjɔm] (m.), geranium

gibecière [ʒipsjɛːr] (f.), bag (slung over one's shoulder)

gilet [ʒilɛ] (m.), vest

glace [glas] (f.), ice, ice-cream, mirror, glass

glacière [glasjɛːr] (f.), refrigerator

se glisser [sə glise], to creep, to slip

gloire [glwaːr] (f.), glory

golfe [gɔlf] (m.), gulf; Golfe du Mexique [gɔlf dy mɛksik] (m.), the Gulf of Mexico

gomme [gɔm] (f.), rubber, eraser

gothique [gɔtik], Gothic

gourmand [gurmɑ̃], greedy

goût [gu] (m.), taste

goûter [gute] (m.), tea, snack, lunch between meals

goûter [gute], to have tea, to taste, to eat something

gouvernante [guvɛrnɑ̃ːt] (f.), governess

gouvernement [guvɛrnəmɑ̃] (m.), government

gouverneur [guvɛrnœːr] (m.), governor

grâce [graːs] (f.), grace, favor; grâce à [graːs a], thanks to

gracieux, -se [grasjø, grasjøːz], graceful, gracious

graine [grɛːn] (f.), seed

grammaire [gramɛːr] (f.), grammar

gramme [gram] (m.), gram

grand, grande [grɑ̃, grɑ̃ːd], large, big, tall, great, noble; le plus grand, la plus grande [lə ply grɑ̃, la ply grɑ̃ːd], largest

Grande-Bretagne [grɑ̃ːd brətaɲ] (f.), Great Britain

grand'chose [grãʃoːz] (f.), much, a great deal

grand'mère [grãmɛːr] (f.), grandmother

grand-père [grãpɛːr] (m.), grandfather

grave [graːv], grave, serious, solemn

Grèce [grɛːs] (f.), Greece

grillé [grije], toasted

gris [gri], gray

gronder [grõde], to scold

gros, grosse [gro, groːs], big (usually with the idea of fat or round)

groupe [grup] (m.), group

guerre [gɛːr] (f.), war

guetter [gɛte], to be on the watch for

guichet [giʃɛ] (m.), small window

H
*h = aspirate h[1]

habile [abil], clever

habillé [abije], dressed

s'habiller [sabije], to dress

habitant [abitã] (m.), inhabitant

habiter [abite], to inhabit, to live in

habits [abi] (m. pl.), clothes

habitude [abityd] (f.), custom, habit

*haricots [ariko] (m. pl.), beans

*harpe [arp] (f.), harp

*haut [o], high

hélas! [elɑːs], alas!

*héler [ele], to hail

herbe [ɛrb] (f.), grass, herb, plant

*héros [ero] (m.), hero

hésiter [ezite], to hesitate

heure [œːr] (f.), hour, time; à l'heure [a lœːr], on time; tout à l'heure [tu ta lœːr], a few minutes ago, in a few minutes; à la bonne heure [a la bɔ nœːr], good! or that's good!; de bonne heure [də bɔ nœːr], in good time, early; neuf heures [nœ vœːr], nine o'clock

heureux, -se [œrø, œrøːz], happy, fortunate

hier [jɛːr], yesterday

histoire [istwaːr] (f.), story, history

hiver [ivɛːr] (m.), winter

homme [ɔm] (m.), man

honnête [ɔnɛːt], honest

honneur [ɔnœːr] (m.), honor

honorable [ɔnɔrabl], honorable

avoir *honte [avwaːr õːt], to be ashamed

horloge [ɔrlɔːʒ] (f.), clock (on exterior of a building)

*hors-d'œuvre [ɔrdœːvr] (m.), hors-d'œuvre, appetizer

hospice [ɔspis] (m.), poorhouse, hospital

hôtel [ɔtɛl] (m.), hotel or large city residence, building

*huit [ɥit], eight

humain [ymɛ̃], human

I

iceberg [isbɛrg] (m.), iceberg

ici [isi], here

idée [ide] (f.), thought, idea

ignorant [iɲɔrã], ignorant, uneducated

il [il], he, it; il y a [il ja], there is, there are; il n'y a pas [il nja pa], there is not; il n'y a pas de quoi [il nja pɑd kwa], don't mention it, it's a pleasure, you are welcome

illustration [ilystrasjõ] (f.), picture in a newspaper, illustration

imagination [imaʒinasjõ] (f.), imagination

s'imaginer [simaʒine], to imagine

imiter [imite], to imitate

immédiatement [imedjatmã], immediately

immense [imãːs], immense, huge

impatience [ɛ̃pasjãːs] (f.), impatience

impatient [ɛ̃pasjã], impatient

important [ɛ̃pɔrtã], important

impossible [ɛ̃pɔsibl], impossible

impression [ɛ̃prɛsjõ] (f.), impression

inconnu [ɛ̃kɔny], unknown

indéfini [ɛ̃defini], indefinite

les Indes [le zɛ̃ːd] (f. pl.), India

indiquer [ɛ̃dike], to point to, to indicate

indulgent [ɛ̃dylʒã], indulgent, lenient

infester [ɛ̃fɛste], to infest, to overrun

infinitif [ɛ̃finitif] (m.), infinitive

innocent [inɔsã], innocent

inquiet [ɛ̃kjɛ], anxious, uneasy; avoir l'air inquiet [avwaːr lɛːr ɛ̃kjɛ], to seem worried

inquiétude [ɛ̃kjetyd] (f.), anxiety

insensé [ɛ̃sãse], foolish, senseless

inspecter [ɛ̃spɛkte], to inspect

installer [ɛ̃stale], to put, to place; s'installer [sɛ̃stale], to settle

---

[1]For an explanation of aspirate and inaspirate h, see page xxv.

instant [ɛ̃stɑ̃] (*m.*), instant

institut [ɛ̃stity] (*m.*), institute

instruction [ɛ̃stryksjɔ̃] (*f.*), instruction, direction

instruire [ɛ̃strɥiːr], to instruct

instruit [ɛ̃strɥi], learned, educated

insulter [ɛ̃sylte], to insult

intelligence [ɛ̃tɛliʒɑ̃ːs] (*f.*), intelligence

intelligent [ɛ̃tɛliʒɑ̃], intelligent

intention [ɛ̃tɑ̃sjɔ̃] (*f.*), intention

intéressant [ɛ̃teresɑ̃], interesting

intéresser [ɛ̃terese], to interest; s'intéresser à [sɛ̃terese a], to be interested in

intérêt [ɛ̃terɛ] (*m.*), interest

intérieur [ɛ̃terjœːr] (*m.*), interior, inside

invitation [ɛ̃vitɑsjɔ̃] (*f.*), invitation

inviter [ɛ̃vite], to ask, to invite

irrégulier, -ière [iregylje, iregyljeːr], irregular

Italie [itali] (*f.*), Italy

italien [italjɛ̃], Italian

J

Jacques [ʒɑːk], James

jamais [ʒamɛ], never, ever; ne . . . jamais [nə . . . ʒamɛ], never

jambe [ʒɑ̃ːb] (*f.*), leg

janvier [ʒɑ̃vje] (*m.*), January

Japon [ʒapɔ̃] (*m.*), Japan

jardin [ʒardɛ̃] (*m.*), garden; jardin d'agrément [ʒardɛ̃ dagremɑ̃] (*m.*), flower garden, pleasure garden; jardin potager [ʒardɛ̃ pɔtaʒe] (*m.*), vegetable garden, kitchen garden

jardinier [ʒardinje] (*m.*), gardener

jaune [ʒoːn], yellow

je [ʒə], I

Jean [ʒɑ̃], John

Jeanne [ʒɑːn], Joan, Jean, Jane

jésuite [ʒezɥit], Jesuit

jeter [ʒəte] (*p.p.* jeté), to throw, to throw away; il jette [il ʒɛːt], he hurls, throws

jeu [ʒø] (*m.*), play, game, fun

jeudi [ʒødi] (*m.*), Thursday

jeune [ʒœn], young; jeune fille [ʒœn fiːj] (*f.*), young girl, girl

jeunesse [ʒœnɛs] (*f.*), youth

joie [ʒwa] (*f.*), joy

joli [ʒɔli], pretty

joue [ʒu] (*f.*), cheek

jouer [ʒwe], to play

jour [ʒuːr] (*m.*), day; un jour [œ̃ ʒuːr], one day; jour de fête [ʒuːr də fɛːt] (*m.*), holiday; tous les jours [tu le ʒuːr], every day

journal [ʒurnal] (*m.*) (*pl.* journaux), newspaper

journée [ʒurne] (*f.*), day (*duration of time*)

jugement [ʒyʒmɑ̃] (*m.*), judgment

juger [ʒyʒe], to judge

juillet [ʒɥijɛ] (*m.*), July

juin [ʒɥɛ̃] (*m.*), June

jupe [ʒyp] (*f.*), skirt

jusqu'à [ʒyska], up to, until, as far as

juste [ʒyst], correctly, exactly, just, correct

K

képi [kepi] (*m.*), military cap

kilogramme, kilo [kilɔgram, kilo] (*m.*), kilogram, *about 35 ounces* (*weight used in France instead of the pound*)

L

la [la] (*f.*), the; her, it (*obj. pron.*)

là [la], there

là-bas [labɑ], down there, over there, yonder

laboratoire [labɔratwaːr] (*m.*), laboratory

lac [lak] (*m.*), lake

lâcher [lɑʃe], to let go, to loosen

laid [lɛ], ugly

laisser [lɛse], to let, to leave, to disregard

lait [lɛ] (*m.*), milk

laitue [lɛty] (*f.*), lettuce

lampe [lɑ̃ːp] (*f.*), lamp

lancer [lɑ̃se], to fling

langue [lɑ̃ːg] (*f.*), tongue, language

lapin, lapine [lapɛ̃, lapin] (*m.*, *f.*), rabbit

lard [laːr] (*m.*), bacon

large [larʒ], broad, large, wide

latin [latɛ̃] (*m.*), Latin

laver la vaisselle [lave la vɛsɛl], to wash the dishes

se laver [sə lave], to wash (*oneself*)

le [lə] (*m.*), the; him, it (*obj. pron.*)

leçon [ləsɔ̃] (*f.*), lesson

léger, -ère [leʒe, leʒeːr], light (*in weight*), slight

légume [legym] (*m.*), vegetable

lendemain [lᾰdmɛ̃] (*m.*), the next day

lent [lᾰ], slow

lentement [lᾰtmᾰ], slowly

lequel [ləkɛl], which, which one

les [le], the; them (*obj. pron.*)

lettre [lɛtr] (*f.*), letter; **boîte aux lettres** [bwaːto lɛtr] (*f.*), letterbox

leur [lœːr] (*pl.* **leurs**), their

leur [lœːr], to them, them

lever [ləve], to raise; **se lever** [sə ləve], to get up, to rise; **je lève** [ʒə lɛːv], I raise, am raising; **il lève** [il lɛːv], he raises, is raising; **vous levez** [vu ləve], you raise, are raising; **ils se lèvent** [il sə lɛːv] (*inf.* **se lever**), they get up, rise

lèvre [lɛːvr] (*f.*), lip

libérer [libere], to set free

liberté [libɛrte] (*f.*), liberty

librairie [librɛri] (*f.*), bookseller's shop, publishing-house

libre [libr], free

lieu [ljø] (*m.*) (*pl.* **lieux**), place, spot; **au lieu de** [o ljø də], instead of; **avoir lieu** [avwaːr ljø], to take place

ligne [liɲ] (*f.*), line

linge [lɛ̃ːʒ] (*m.*), linen (*household or personal*)

lion [ljõ] (*m.*), lion

lire [liːr] (*p.p.* **lu**), to read

lis [liːs] (*m.*), lily

je lis [ʒə li], I read

vous lisez [vu lize], you read

liste [list] (*f.*), list

lit [li] (*m.*), bed

il lit [il li], (*inf.* **lire**), he reads, is reading

livre [liːvr] (*m.*), book

livre [liːvr] (*f.*), pound

locomotive [lɔkɔmɔtiːv] (*f.*), locomotive

loin [lwɛ̃], far away; **au loin** [o lwɛ̃], in the distance, far off

long, longue [lõ, lõːg], long

le long de [lə lõ də], all along

longtemps [lõtᾰ], for a long time, long, a long time; **depuis très longtemps** [dəpɥi trɛ lõtᾰ], for a long time

lorsque [lɔrskə], when

louer [lwe], to rent

loup [lu] (*m.*), wolf

lourd [luːr], heavy

lu [ly] (*p.p. of* **lire**), read

lui [lɥi], him (*ind. obj.*)

lumière [lymjɛːr] (*f.*), light

lundi [lœ̃di] (*m.*), Monday

lunettes [lynɛt] (*f. pl.*), spectacles

lutte [lyt] (*f.*), struggle, fight

lutter [lyte], to fight

luxe [lyks] (*m.*), luxury, richness, splendor

M

M., *abbreviation for* **Monsieur**

ma [ma] (*f. sing.*), my

madame [madam], Mrs.; *abbreviation*, **Mme.; madame est servie** [madam ɛ sɛrvi], dinner is served

mademoiselle [madmwazɛl], Miss

magasin [magazɛ̃] (*m.*), store

magnifique [maɲifik], magnificent

mai [mɛ] (*m.*), May

main [mɛ̃] (*f.*), hand; **à la main** [a la mɛ̃], in one's hand

maintenant [mɛ̃tnᾰ], now

mais [mɛ], but; **mais non** [mɛ nõ], no, indeed! why no!

maison [mezõ] (*f.*), house; **à la maison** [a la mezõ], at home; **une drôle de petite maison** [yn droːl də ptit mezõ], a funny little house

maître [mɛːtr] (*m.*), master, teacher

maîtresse [mɛtrɛs] (*f.*), teacher, mistress

mal [mal] (*m.*), harm, evil, damage

mal [mal], bad, evil; badly

malade [malad], sick

maladie [maladi] (*f.*), illness

malgré [malgre], in spite of

malheur [malœːr] (*m.*), misfortune

malheureusement [malœrøzmᾰ], unhappily, unfortunately

malheureux, -se [malœrø, malœrøːz], unhappy, unfortunate

malle [mal] (*f.*), trunk

maltraiter [maltrɛte], to mistreat, to maltreat

maman [mamᾰ] (*f.*), mother

manger [mᾰʒe], to eat; **quelque chose à manger** [kɛlkə ʃoːz a mᾰʒe], something to eat; **salle à manger** [sal a mᾰʒe] (*f.*), dining-room

manière [manjɛːr] (*f.*), manner, way; **manières** [manjɛːr] (*f. pl.*), manners

manquer [mᾰke], to be absent from, to miss, to be lacking

manteau [mãto] (*m.*) (*pl.* **manteaux**), coat; **manteau de pluie** [mãtod plɥi] (*m.*), raincoat

marchand [marʃã] (*m.*), merchant, dealer, seller

marche [marʃ] (*f.*), step, track, walking; **se mettre en marche** [sə mɛtrã marʃ], to set out

marché [marʃe] (*m.*), market

marcher [marʃe], to walk; **se mettre à marcher** [sə mɛtra marʃe], to start to walk

mardi [mardi] (*m.*), Tuesday

mari [mari] (*m.*), husband

mariage [marjaːʒ] (*m.*), marriage

marier [marje], to marry, to join, to ally

marraine [marɛn] (*f.*), godmother

marronnier [marɔnje] (*m.*), French chestnut tree

mars [mars] (*m.*), March

masculin [maskylɛ̃] (*m.*), masculine (*gender*)

massacrer [masakre], to massacre

match [matʃ] (*m.*), match, game

mathématique [matematik] (*f.*), mathematics

matin [matɛ̃] (*m.*), morning; **du matin jusqu'au soir** [dy matɛ̃ ʒysko swaːr], from morning till night

matinée [matine] (*f.*), morning (*duration*), matinée

maussade [mosad], cross, disagreeable

mauvais [movɛ], bad; **il fait mauvais** [il fɛ movɛ], it is disagreeable (weather)

me [mə], me, to me

méchant [meʃã], bad, naughty, mischievous, wicked

médecin [mɛtsɛ̃] (*m.*), doctor

médecine [mɛtsin] (*f.*), medicine

méditer [medite], to meditate, to think of

meilleur [mɛjœːr], better, best

même [mɛːm], same, even

menacer [mənase], to menace, to threaten

faire le ménage [fɛːr lə menaːʒ], to do housework; **femme de ménage** [fam də menaːʒ] (*f.*), charwoman, cleaning-woman

mener [məne], to lead, to take, to drive

mentionner [mãsjɔne], to mention, to name

menton [mãtõ] (*m.*), chin

mer [mɛːr] (*f.*), sea

merci [mɛrsi] (*use the person's name or title*), thank you; **merci bien** [mɛrsi bjɛ̃], thank you very much

mercredi [mɛrkrədi] (*m.*), Wednesday

mère [mɛːr] (*f.*), mother

mériter [merite], to merit, to deserve

merveille [mɛrvɛːj] (*f.*), marvelous thing, marvel

merveilleux, -se [mɛrvɛjø, mɛrvɛjøːz], marvelous, wonderful

mes [me] (*pl.*), my

message [mesaːʒ] (*m.*), message

messe [mɛs] (*f.*), mass

il met [il mɛ] (*inf.* **mettre**), he puts; **il met de côté** [il mɛd kote], he puts aside *or* away

je mets [ʒə mɛ], I put, I place, I am putting, I am placing

vous mettez [vu mɛte], you put, you place, you are putting, you are placing

mettre [mɛtr] (*p.p.* **mis**), to put, to place; **se mettre** [sə mɛtr], to put, to place oneself, to go; **se mettre à** [sə mɛtra] (+*infinitive*), to begin; **se mettre à genoux** [sə mɛtra ʒənu], to kneel down; **se mettre à marcher** [sə mɛtra marʃe], to start to walk; **se mettre en marche** [sə mɛtrã marʃ], to set out; **se mettre en route** [sə mɛtrã rut], to start off

je meurs [ʒə mœːr] (*inf.* **mourir**), I am dying, I die

il meurt [il mœːr] (*inf.* **mourir**), he dies; **ils meurent** [il mœːr], they die

Mexicains [mɛksikɛ̃] (*m. pl.*), Mexicans

Mexique [mɛksik] (*m.*), Mexico

midi [midi] (*m.*), noon; **à midi!** [a midi], I'll see you at noon!

miette [mjɛt] (*f.*), crumb

mieux [mjø], better; **faire de son mieux** [fɛːr də sõ mjø], to do one's best; **tant mieux** [tã mjø], so much the better; **il vaut mieux** [il vo mjø] (*inf.* **valoir**), it is better

milieu [miljø] (*m.*) (*pl.* **milieux**), middle; **au milieu** [o miljø], in the middle

mille [mil], thousand

million [miljõ] (*m.*), million

mince [mɛ̃s], scanty, thin

minuit [minɥi] (*m.*), midnight

minute [minyt] (*f.*), minute

mis [mi] (*p.p. of* **mettre**), put

misérable [mizerabl], miserable, wretched

mission [misjõ] (*f.*), mission

moderne [mɔdɛrn], modern

modeste [mɔdɛst], modest, simple, plain

moi [mwa], I, me

moindre [mwɛ̃:dr], least, less

moine [mwan] (*m.*), monk

moineau [mwano] (*m.*) (*pl.* moineaux), sparrow

moins [mwɛ̃], less, to (*in telling time*); moins . . . que [mwɛ̃ kə], less . . . than

mois [mwa] (*m.*), month

moitié [mwatje] (*f.*), half

moment [mɔmã] (*m.*), moment; un bon moment [œ̃ bõ mɔmã], for some time

mon [mõ] (*m. sing.*), my; mon vieux [mõ vjø], old chap, old man, my dear fellow (*colloquial form of address used between men and boys*)

monarchie [mɔnarʃi] (*f.*), monarchy

monde [mõ:d] (*m.*), world, people; du monde [dy mõ:d], company, guests; tout le monde [tul mõ:d], everyone

monsieur [məsjø], Mr., sir

monsieur, messieurs [məsjø, mesjø] (*m.*), gentleman, gentlemen

montagne [mõtaɲ] (*f.*), mountain

monter [mõte], to go up, to rise; monter à cheval [mõte a ʃəval], to mount a horse, to ride horseback

montre [mõ:tr] (*f.*), watch

montrer [mõtre], to show, to point out; se montrer [sə mõtre], to show oneself

monument [mɔnymã] (*m.*), monument, public building

se moquer de [sə mɔke də], to make fun of, to laugh at

morceau [mɔrso] (*m.*) (*pl.* morceaux), piece; en morceaux [ã mɔrso], in pieces

mordre [mɔrdr], to bite

morsure [mɔrsy:r] (*f.*), bite

mort [mɔ:r] (*f.*), death

mort [mɔ:r] (*p.p. of* mourir), dead, died

mot [mo] (*m.*), word; petit mot [pti mo] (*m.*), note

mouchoir [muʃwa:r] (*m.*), handkerchief

mouette [mwɛt] (*f.*), sea gull

mouillé [muje], wet

mourir [muri:r] (*p.p.* mort), to die

moutarde [mutard] (*f.*), mustard

mouton [mutõ] (*m.*), sheep, mutton

mouvement [muvmã] (*m.*), movement, impulse

moyen [mwajɛ̃] (*m.*), means, way, middle

mur [my:r] (*m.*), wall

murmurer [myrmyre], to murmur

museler [myzle], to muzzle

musique [myzik] (*f.*), music

N

nager [naʒe], to swim

naître [nɛ:tr] (*p.p.* né), to be born

nation [nɑsjõ] (*f.*), nation

national [nasjɔnal], national

nature [naty:r] (*f.*), nature

naturel, -le [natyrɛl], natural

naturellement [natyrɛlmã], naturally, of course, certainly

navet [navɛ] (*m.*), turnip

ne . . . pas [nə . . . pɑ], not; ne . . . plus [nə . . . ply], no longer, no more; ne . . . que [nə . . . kə], only; ne . . . personne [nə . . . pɛrsɔn], nobody; ne . . . jamais [nə . . . ʒamɛ], never; ne . . . rien [nə . . . rjɛ̃], nothing

nécessaire [nesesɛ:r], necessary

négatif, -ve [negatif, negati:v], negative

neige [nɛ:ʒ] (*f.*), snow

neiger [nɛʒe], to snow

nerf [nɛ:r] (*m.*), nerve

n'est-ce pas? [nɛs pɑ], isn't it? isn't it so? doesn't one? (*Used after any statement.*)

neuf [nœf], nine; neuf heures [nœ vœ:r], nine o'clock

neuf, neuve [nœf, nœ:v], new

neveu [nəvø] (*m.*) (*pl.* neveux), nephew

nez [ne] (*m.*) (*pl.* nez), nose

ni [ni], nor; ni . . . ni [ni], neither, nor; ni moi non plus [ni mwa nõ ply], nor I either

niche [niʃ] (*f.*), kennel

nid [ni] (*m.*), nest

nièce [njɛs] (*f.*), niece

noble [nɔbl], noble, of noble descent

noir, noire [nwa:r], black; faire noir [fɛ:r nwa:r], to be dark

Noiraud [nwaro], Blackie

nom [nõ] (*m.*), name

nombre [nõ:br] (*m.*), number

nombreux, -se [nõbrø, nõbrø:z], numerous

nommer [nɔme], to name, to appoint

non [nõ], no (*adverb*); **mais non** [mε nõ], no, indeed! why, no!; **non plus** [nõ ply], neither, either

nord [nɔːr] (*m.*), north

Normandie [nɔrmãdi] (*f.*), Normandy

notre [nɔtr] (*pl.* **nos**), our

nourrir [nuriːr], to support, to nourish

nourrissant [nurisã], nourishing, nutritious

nourriture [nurityːr] (*f.*), food

nous [nu], we, us

nouveau, nouvelle [nuvo, nuvεl], new; **de nouveau** [də nuvo], again; **Nouveau Monde** [nuvo mõːd] (*m.*), New World, America

nouvelle [nuvεl] (*f.*), news

novembre [nɔvãːbr] (*m.*), November

nuit [nɥi](*f.*), night; **faire nuit** [fεːr nɥi], to get dark

nul, -le [nyl], nothing, no

numéral [nymeral] (*pl.* **numéraux**), numeral

numéro [nymero] (*m.*), number

O

obéir [ɔbeiːr], to obey

objet [ɔbʒε] (*m.*), object

obligeance [ɔbliʒãːs] (*f.*), kindness

obliger [ɔbliʒe], to oblige

obscur [ɔpskyːr], obscure, not clear, dark

observer [ɔpsεrve], to observe

obtenir [ɔptəniːr] (*p.p.* **obtenu**), to obtain

occasion [ɔkazjõ] (*f.*), bargain, occasion, opportunity, chance

occupé [ɔkype], busy, occupied

occuper [ɔkype], to occupy; **s'occuper de** [sɔkype də], to take care of

octobre [ɔktɔbr] (*m.*), October

œil [œːj] (*m.*) (*pl.* **les yeux** [lezjø]), eye

œuf [œf] (*m.*) (*pl.* **les œufs** [lezø]), egg

œuvre [œːvr] (*f.*), work; **chef-d'œuvre** [ʃedœːvr] (*m.*), masterpiece

office [ɔfis] (*f.*), pantry

offre [ɔfr] (*f.*), offer

il offre [il ɔfr] (*inf.* **offrir**), he offers

offrir [ɔfriːr] (*p.p.* **offert**), to offer

oie [wɑ] (*f.*), goose

oiseau [wazo] (*m.*) (*pl.* **oiseaux**), bird

olifant [ɔlifã] (*m.*), horn

ombre [õːbr] (*f.*), shade

on [õ], one, we, you, they (*indefinite reference*)

oncle [õːkl] (*m.*), uncle

onze [õːz], eleven

or [ɔːr] (*m.*), gold

or [ɔːr], well

orage [ɔraːʒ] (*m.*), storm

orange [ɔrãːʒ] (*f.*), orange

ordinaire [ɔrdinεːr], ordinary; **d'ordinaire** [dɔrdinεːr], ordinarily

ordinairement [ɔrdinεrmã], ordinarily

ordinal [ɔrdinal] (*pl.* **ordinaux**), ordinal

ordre [ɔrdr] (*m.*), order; **en ordre** [ã nɔrdr], in order

oreille [ɔrεːj] (*f.*), ear

oriflamme [ɔriflɑːm] (*f.*), *king's special banner* (flame of gold)

orné [ɔrne], ornamented

oser [oze], to dare

ôter [ote], to take off

ou [u], either, or

où [u], where, in which, when

oublier (de) [ublie də], to forget

oui [wi], yes

ours [urs] (*m.*), bear

ouverture [uvεrtyːr] (*f.*), opening

j'ouvre [ʒuːvr], I open, I am opening, I do open; **il ouvre** [il uːvr], he opens

vous ouvrez [vu zuvre], you open

ouvrier [uvrie] (*m.*), workman

ouvrir [uvriːr] (*p.p.* **ouvert**), to open; **s'ouvrir** [suvriːr], to disclose oneself, to open (*as of a flower*)

P

page [paːʒ] (*f.*), page

païen [pajε̃] (*m.*), pagan, unbeliever

nous paierons [nu pεjrõ] (*future of* **payer**), we shall pay

paille [pɑːj] (*f.*), straw

papa [papa] (*m.*), father, papa

pain [pε̃] (*m.*), bread, loaf of bread; **petit pain** [pti pε̃] (*m.*), roll

paire [pεːr] (*f.*), pair

paix [pε] (*f.*), peace

palais [palε] (*m.*), palace

pâle [pɑːl], pale

panier [panje] (*m.*), basket

pantalon [pãtalõ] (*m.*), pair of trousers, pantaloons

pantoufle [pãtufl] (*f.*), slipper

papa [papa] (*m.*), father, papa

papier [papje] (*m.*), paper

paquet [pakɛ] (*m.*), package, parcel, packet

par [paːr], by, with, through, by way of; **par exemple** [par egzãːpl], as an illustration, for instance, for example; **par terre** [par tɛːr], on the ground, on the floor

paradis [paradi] (*m.*), paradise

paraître [parɛːtr] (*p.p.* **paru**), to appear

parapluie [paraplɥi] (*m.*), umbrella

parc [park] (*m.*), park

parce que [parskə], because

pareil, -le [parɛːj], as good as, equal, like

parent [parã] (*m.*), relative, parent

paresseux, -se [parɛsø, parɛsøːz], lazy, idle

parfait [parfɛ], perfect

parfaitement [parfɛtmã], perfectly, exactly

parfum [parfœ̃] (*m.*), perfume

parisien [parizjɛ̃], Parisian

parler [parle], to speak, to talk; **il parle** [il parl], he speaks, is speaking; **nous parlons** [nu parlõ], we talk, are talking, speak

parole [parɔl] (*f.*), word; **paroles** [parɔl], talk, words

il part [il paːr] (*inf.* **partir**), he leaves

part [paːr] (*f.*), part; **de la part de** [də la paːr də], from, on behalf of

participe [partisip] (*m.*), participle

partie [parti] (*f.*), part, rôle, portion

partir [partiːr] (*p.p.* **parti**), to leave; **à partir de** [a partiːr də], from

partout [partu], everywhere

pas [pa] (*m.*), step

pas [pa], no, not; **pas du tout** [pa dy tu], not at all, not in the least; **pas encore** [pa zãkɔːr], not yet; **il n'y a pas** [il nja pa], there is not; **il n'y a pas de quoi** [il nja pad kwa], don't mention it, it's a pleasure, you are welcome; **pas tout à fait** [pa tu ta fɛ], not exactly, not altogether, not entirely

passage [pasaːʒ] (*m.*), passage

passé indéfini [pase ɛ̃defini] (*m.*), past indefinite

passer [pase], to pass, to go, to cross

Pataud [pato] (*from* **patte**), hence, "large paws"

pâté [pate] (*m.*), meat-pie

patiner [patine], to skate

patron [patrõ] (*m.*), employer

patte [pat] (*f.*), paw

pauvre [poːvr] (*m.* and *f.*), pauper, poor person; **les pauvres**, paupers, poor people

pauvre [poːvr], poor

payer [peje], to pay, to pay for

pays [pei] (*m.*), country

paysage [peizaːʒ] (*m.*), landscape

paysan [peizã] (*m.*), peasant; **paysanne** [peizan] (*f.*), peasant woman *or* girl

peau [po] (*f.*), skin; **peau de mouton** [pod mutõ] (*f.*), sheepskin; **Peaux-Rouges** [poruːʒ] (*m. pl.*), redskins

pêcher [pɛʃe], to fish, to catch fish

peindre [pɛ̃ːdr] (*p.p.* **peint**), to paint

peine [pɛːn] (*f.*), effort, difficulty, trouble

il peint [il pɛ̃] (*inf.* **peindre**), he paints

peintre [pɛ̃ːtr] (*m.*), painter, artist

pelouse [pluːz] (*f.*), lawn

pendant [pãdã], during; **pendant que** [pãdã kə], while

pendule [pãdyl] (*f.*), clock, timepiece

pénétrer [penetre], to penetrate

pensée [pãse] (*f.*), thought

penser [pãse], to think; **penser à** [pãse a], to think of; **me fait penser** [mə fɛ pãse], makes me think

perdre [pɛrdr] (*p.p.* **perdu**), to lose

père [pɛːr] (*m.*), father

permettre [pɛrmɛtr] (*p.p.* **permis**), to permit, to allow

permission [pɛrmisjõ] (*f.*), permission

personnage [pɛrsɔnaːʒ] (*m.*), personage, character

personne [pɛrsɔn] (*f.*), person

personne [pɛrsɔn], no one, nobody; **ne ... personne** [nə ... pɛrsɔn], nobody

personnel [pɛrsɔnɛl], personal

peser [pəze], to weigh

petit, petite [pəti, pətit], small, little; **petit déjeuner** [pti deʒœne] (*m.*), breakfast; **petite fille** [ptit fiːj] (*f.*), little girl; **petit mot** [pti mo] (*m.*), note; **petit pain** [pti pɛ̃] (*m.*), roll

petit-fils [ptifis] (*m.*), grandson

pétunia [petynja] (*m.*), petunia

peu [pø], a little, few; **peu à peu** [pø a pø], little by little, gradually; **petit peu** [pti pø], just a little

peuple [pœpl] (*m.*), people

peur [pœːr] (*f.*), fear; **avoir peur** [avwaːr pœːr], to be afraid, to fear

il peut [il pø] (*inf.* **pouvoir**), he can, may

peut-être [pøtɛːtr], perhaps, maybe

je peux [ʒə pø] (*inf.* **pouvoir**), I can, may; **tu peux** [ty pø], you can, may

pharmacie [farmasi] (*f.*), drug store

philosophe [filɔzɔf], philosophical

phoque [fɔk] (*m.*), seal

photographie [fɔtɔgrafi] (*f.*), photography

phrase [frɑːz] (*f.*), sentence

physicien [fizisjɛ̃] (*m.*), physicist

physiologie [fizjɔlɔʒi] (*f.*), physiology

piano [pjano] (*m.*), piano

pièce [pjɛs] (*f.*), piece, play

pied [pje] (*m.*), foot; **se promener à pied ou en auto** [sə prɔmne a pje u ɑ̃noto], to walk *or* to ride in a car

Pierre [pjɛːr], Peter

Pierrot [pjero], Peter (*diminutive*)

piéton [pjetɔ̃] (*m.*), pedestrian

pieux, -se [pjø, pjøːz], pious

pipe [pip] (*f.*), pipe

pique-nique [piknik] (*m.*), picnic

pittoresque [pitɔrɛsk], picturesque, beautiful

place [plas] (*f.*), place, seat, spot, position, employment

placer [plase], to place, to put, to invest

plafond [plafɔ̃] (*m.*), ceiling

plaine [plɛn] (*f.*), plain

plaire [plɛːr] (*p.p.* **plu**), to please

plaisir [pleziːr] (*m.*), pleasure; **avec plaisir** [avɛk pleziːr], with pleasure

s'il vous plaît [sil vu plɛ], if you please

plancher [plɑ̃ʃe] (*m.*), floor

planter [plɑ̃te], to plant

plein, -e [plɛ̃, plɛːn], full; **en plein air** [ɑ̃ plɛ nɛːr], out of doors

pleurer [plœre], to weep, to weep for

il pleut [il plø], it is raining

pleuvoir [plœvwaːr] (*p.p.* **plu**), to rain

plier [plie], to fold

pluie [plɥi] (*f.*), rain; **manteau de pluie** [mɑ̃tod plɥi] (*m.*), raincoat

plume [plym] (*f.*), feather

plupart [plypaːr] (*f.*), most part; **pour la plupart** [puːr la plypaːr], for the most part

pluriel [plyrjɛl] (*m.*), plural (*number*)

plus [ply], more; **plus de** [ply də], more than (*before numbers*); **plus . . . que** [ply . . . kə], more than; **le plus grand, la plus grande** [lə ply grɑ̃, la ply grɑ̃ːd], largest; **non plus** [nɔ̃ ply], neither, either; **ni moi non plus** [ni mwa nɔ̃ ply], nor I either; **ne . . . plus** [nə . . . ply], no longer, no more

plusieurs [plyzjœːr], several

plutôt [plyto], rather

poche [pɔʃ] (*f.*), pocket

poème [pɔɛːm] (*m.*), poem

poète [pɔɛːt] (*m.*), poet

poil [pwal] (*m.*), fur

pois [pwɑ] (*m.*), pea

poisson [pwasɔ̃] (*m.*), fish

poitrine [pwatrin] (*f.*), chest

poivre [pwaːvr] (*m.*), pepper

pôle [poːl] (*m.*), pole

poli [pɔli], polite

poliment [pɔlimɑ̃], politely

politique [pɔlitik], political

pomme [pɔm] (*f.*), apple; **pomme de terre** [pɔm də tɛːr] (*f.*), potato

pommier [pɔmje] (*m.*), apple-tree

pont [pɔ̃] (*m.*), bridge

population [pɔpylasjɔ̃] (*f.*), population

porte [pɔrt] (*f.*), door; **porte de service** [pɔrt də sɛrvis] (*f.*), back door

porter [pɔrte], to bear, to have, to wear, to strike

porteur [pɔrtœːr] (*m.*), porter

portière [pɔrtjɛːr] (*f.*), small door

poser [poze], to put

posséder [pɔsede], to possess

possible [pɔsibl], possible

poste [pɔst] (*m.*), station, body of men

poste [pɔst] (*f.*), post-office; **poste recommandée** [pɔst rəkɔmɑ̃de] (*f.*), registered mail; **poste restante** [pɔst rɛstɑ̃ːt] (*f.*), general delivery

Postes et Télégraphes [pɔst e telegraf], post and telegraph office

potage [pɔtaːʒ] (*m.*), soup

pouce [pus] (*m.*), thumb

poulet [pulɛ] (*m.*), chicken

poupée [pupe] (*f.*), doll

pour [puːr], for, in order to; **pour l'étranger** [puːr letrɑ̃ʒe], for a foreign country; **en route pour** [ɑ̃ rut puːr], on the way to

pourboire [purbwaːr] (*m.*), tip

pourquoi [purkwa], why; **voilà pourquoi** [vwala purkwa], that is the reason, that is why

pourtant [purtɑ̃], however

pousser [puse], to utter, to push, to thrust

vous pouvez [vu puve] (*inf.* **pouvoir**), you can, you may, you are able

pouvoir [puvwaːr] (*p.p.* **pu**), to be able, can, may

nous pouvons [nu puvõ] (*inf.* **pouvoir**), we can, we are able

précédent [presedɑ̃], preceding

précéder [presɛde], to precede

se précipiter [sə presipite], to rush

précis [presi], precise, exact

préférer [prefɛre], to prefer

premier, première [prəmje, prəmjɛːr], first

elle prend le thé [ɛl prɑ̃ lə te], she is having tea

prendre [prɑ̃ːdr] (*p.p.* **pris**), to take, to obtain

préparer [prepare], to prepare

près de [prɛ də], near; **à peu près** [a pø prɛ], about, approximately

présence [prezɑ̃ːs] (*f.*), presence

présent [prezɑ̃] (*m.*), present (*tense of verb*); present time

présenter [prezɑ̃te], to present

préserver [prezɛrve], to preserve, to protect

presque [prɛskə], almost, nearly

pressé [prɛse], in a hurry

prêt [prɛ], ready

prêter [prɛte], to lend

prêtre [prɛːtr] (*m.*), priest

prier [prie], to ask, to pray, to invite

principal [prɛ̃sipal], principal

printemps [prɛ̃tɑ̃] (*m.*), spring; **au printemps** [o prɛ̃tɑ̃], in spring

pris [pri] (*p.p. of* **prendre**), took

prison [prizõ] (*f.*), prison

prisonnier [prizɔnje] (*m.*), prisoner

prix [pri] (*m.*), price, prize

problème [prɔblɛːm] (*m.*), problem

prochain [prɔʃɛ̃], next

proche [prɔʃ], near

produire [prɔdɥiːr] (*p.p.* **produit**), to produce

professeur [prɔfɛsœːr] (*m.*), professor, teacher

profit [prɔfi] (*m.*), profit

projet [prɔʒɛ] (*m.*), project, plan

promenade [prɔmnad] (*f.*), walk, excursion; **faire une promenade** [fɛːr yn prɔmnad], to take a walk; **faire une promenade en auto** [fɛːr yn prɔmnad ɑ̃nɔto], to take a ride

se promener [sə prɔmne], to walk; **se promener à pied ou en auto** [sə prɔmne a pje u ɑ̃nɔto], to walk *or* to ride in a car

promesse [prɔmɛs] (*f.*), promise

promettre [prɔmɛtr] (*p.p.* **promis**), to promise

pronom [prɔnõ] (*m.*), pronoun

prononcer [prɔnõse], to pronounce

proposer [prɔpoze], to propose

propre [prɔpr], clean

protester [prɔtɛste], to protest

province [prɔvɛ̃ːs] (*f.*), country district, province

provision [prɔvizjõ] (*f.*), something to eat; **les provisions** [le prɔvizjõ], supplies, food

prudent [prydɑ̃], wise, prudent

public, -que [pyblik], public

puis [pɥi], then

puisque [pɥiskə], since, seeing that

punir [pyniːr], to punish

pupitre [pypitr] (*m.*), desk

Q

quai [ke] (*m.*), station platform, wharf

qualité [kalite] (*f.*), quality, good quality

quand [kɑ̃], when

quant à [kɑ̃ta], as for

quarante [karɑ̃ːt], forty

quart [kaːr] (*m.*), quarter

quartier [kartje] (*m.*), district, quarter

quatorze [katɔrz], fourteen

quatorzième [katɔrzjɛm], fourteenth

quatre [katr], four

quatre-vingts [katrəvɛ̃], eighty; **quatre-vingt-dix** [katrəvɛ̃dis], ninety

que [kə], whom, which, that, what; **ce que** [sə kə], what, that which; **qu'avez-vous?** [kavevu], what's the matter with you?

qu'est-ce que c'est? [kɛs kə sɛ], what is it? what is this?; **qu'est-ce que c'est que** [kɛs kə sɛ kə], what is; **qu'est-ce que c'est que ceci?** [kɛs kə sɛ kə səsi], what is this?; **qu'est-ce que c'est que cela?** [kɛs kə sɛ kə sla], what is that?

que [kə], how; **qu'il est facile** [kilɛ fasil], how easy it is; **que c'est bon** [kə sɛ bõ], how good this is, how good it is; **ne ... que** [nə ... kə], only

quel, quelle, quels, quelles [kɛl], what; **quel âge a-t-il?** [kɛl ɑ:ʒ atil], how old is he?; **quel ennui** [kɛl ãnɥi], what a bore, what a nuisance

quelque [kɛlkə], some; *pl.* **quelques** [kɛlkə], few; **quelque chose** [kɛlkə ʃo:z], something, anything; **quelque chose à manger** [kɛlkə ʃo:z a mãʒe], something to eat

quelquefois [kɛlkəfwa], sometimes

quelqu'un [kɛlkœ̃], someone, somebody

question [kɛstjõ] (*f.*), question; **j'ai une question à vous poser** [ʒe yn kɛstjõ a vu poze], I have a question to ask you

queue [kø] (*f.*), tail

qui [ki], who, which, that (*relative pronoun*)

qui [ki], who, whom (*interrogative pronoun*)

quinze [kɛ̃:z], fifteen

quitter [kite], to leave, to leave off

quoi [kwa], what, which

R

race [ras] (*f.*), race

racheter [raʃte], to buy back, to ransom

raconter [rakõte], to tell, to recount

radis [radi] (*m.*), radish

radium [radjɔm] (*m.*), radium

rafraîchir [rafreʃi:r], to refresh

ragoût [ragu] (*m.*), stew

raison [rɛzõ] (*f.*), reason; **avoir raison** [avwa:r rɛzõ], to be right

ramasser [ramase], to pick up, to collect

ramener [ramne], to bring, to bring out

ramer [rame], to row

Raoul [raul], Ralph

rapide [rapid], rapid, quick; express (*train*)

se rappeler [sə raple], to recall, to remember

rapporter [rapɔrte], to bring, to bring back

rare [rɑ:r], rare, unusual, uncommon

rarement [rɑrmã], rarely, seldom

ravageur [ravaʒœ:r] (*m.*), ravager, spoiler

rayon [rɛjõ] (*m.*), department (*of a store*), ray

recevoir [rəsəvwa:r] (*p.p.* **reçu**), to receive

recherche [rəʃɛrʃ] (*f.*), search

rechercher [rəʃɛrʃe], to seek again

récit [resi] (*m.*), tale, story, recital of facts

récite [resit], recites

réciter [resite], to recite

réclamer [reklame], to demand

il reçoit [il rəswa] (*inf.* **recevoir**), he receives

recommencer [rəkɔmãse], to recommence, to begin again

récompense [rekõpã:s] (*f.*), reward

reconnaissance [rəkɔnɛsã:s] (*f.*), gratitude, recognition

reconnaître [rəkɔnɛ:tr] (*p.p.* **reconnu**), to recognize

redouter [rədute], to dread, to fear

réduire [redɥi:r] (*p.p.* **réduit**), to reduce

réfléchir [refleʃi:r], to think, to ponder, to reflect

refuser [rəfyze], to refuse

regard [rəga:r] (*m.*), look, glance

regarder [rəgarde], to look at, to watch; **je regarde** [ʒə rəgard], I look at, I watch; **il regarde** [il rəgard], he looks at, he watches; **vous regardez** [vu rəgarde], you look at, you watch; **nous regardons** [nu rəgardõ], we look at, we watch

régime [reʒim] (*m.*), object (*grammatical*)

régional [reʒjɔnal] (*pl.* **régionaux**), regional, local

règle [rɛgl] (*f.*), rule, ruler

règne [rɛɲ] (*m.*), reign

régner [reɲe], to reign

regretter [rəgrɛte], to regret

régulier, -ière [regylje, regyljɛ:r], regular

rejoindre [rəʒwɛ̃:dr] (*p.p.* **rejoint**), to join, to rejoin, to catch up with

se relever [sə rəlve], to get up *or* to rise again

remarquer [rəmarke], to notice

remercier [rəmɛrsje], to thank

remonter [rəmõte], to remount, to reascend

remplaçant [rãplasã] (*m.*), substitute

remplacer [rãplase], to replace

remplir [rãpli:r], to fill, to fulfill

renard [rəna:r] (*m.*), fox

rencontrer [rãkõtre], to meet

rendre [rã:dr], to return (*something*), to give back, to render; **rendre visite** [rã:dr vizit], to visit

renfermer [rãfɛrme], to shut in

renseignement [rãsɛɲmã] (*m.*), information; **les renseignements,** pieces *or* bits of information

rentrer [rãtre], to re-enter, to return

repartir [rəparti:r] (*p.p.* **reparti**), to set out again

repas [rəpα] (*m.*) (*pl.* **repas**), meal

repasser [rəpαse], to go over, to review; to iron

répéter [repete], to repeat

répond [repõ], answers, responds, replies

répondre [repõ:dr], to answer, to reply

réponse [repõ:s] (*f.*), response, reply

repos [rəpo] (*m.*), rest

se reposer [sə rəpoze], to rest (*oneself*)

représentation [rəprezãtasjõ] (*f.*), performance

représenter [rəprezãte], to represent

reproche [rəprɔʃ] (*m.*), reproach

reprocher [rəprɔʃe], to reproach

reproduction [rəprɔdyksjõ] (*f.*), reproduction

républicain [repyblikɛ̃], of the republic

république [repyblik] (*f.*), republic

réservé [rezɛrve], reserved

réserver [rezɛrve], to reserve

résister [reziste], to resist

résoudre [rezudr], to solve

ressembler à [rəsãble a], to resemble

ressort [rəsɔ:r] (*m.*), spring (*used in upholstery*)

poste restante [pɔst rɛstã:t] (*f.*), general delivery

restaurant [rɛstɔrã] (*m.*), restaurant

reste [rɛst] (*m.*), remainder, rest

rester [rɛste], to remain, to stay

résultat [rezylta] (*m.*), result, answer to a problem, score

rétablir [retabli:r], to re-establish

retard [rəta:r] (*m.*), delay; **en retard** [ã rəta:r], late, tardy

retenir [rətni:r] (*p.p.* **retenu**), to retain, to keep in

retomber [rətõbe], to fall again, to sink

retour [rətu:r] (*m.*), return

retourner [rəturne], to return; **se retourner** [sə rəturne], to turn around

retrouver [rətruve], to find again, to rediscover

réunir [reyni:r], to collect, to join, to annex, to unite

réussir [reysi:r], to succeed

rêve [rɛ:v] (*m.*), dream

réveiller [revɛje], to wake; **se réveiller** [sə revɛje], to wake up

revenir [rəvni:r] (*p.p.* **revenu**), to come again, to return

il revient [rəvjɛ̃] (*inf.* **revenir**), he returns

revoir [rəvwa:r] (*p.p.* **revu**), to see again

au revoir [o rəvwa:r], good-by

révolution [revɔlysjõ] (*f.*), revolution

ri [ri] (*p.p. of* **rire**), laughed

riche [riʃ], rich, wealthy, sumptuous

richesse [riʃɛs] (*f.*), riches

rideau [rido] (*m.*) (*pl.* **rideaux**), curtain, hangings

rien [rjɛ̃] nothing; **je n'ai rien** [ʒə ne rjɛ̃], nothing is the matter with me; **je n'en sais rien du tout** [ʒə nã se rjɛ̃ dy tu], I know nothing at all about it

rire [ri:r] (*p.p.* **ri**), to laugh

rivière [rivjɛ:r] (*f.*), river (*that flows into a* **fleuve**)

robe [rɔb] (*f.*), dress, robe, frock

rocher [rɔʃe] (*m.*), rock

roi [rwα] (*m.*), king

rôle [ro:l] (*m.*), rôle, part

rond [rõ], round

ronger [rõʒe], to gnaw

roquefort [rɔkfɔ:r] (*m.*), Roquefort cheese

rose [ro:z] (*f.*), rose

rose [ro:z], pink

rôti [roti] (*m.*), roast

rouge [ru:ʒ], red

rouge-gorge [ru:ʒgɔrʒ] (*m.*) (*pl.* **rouges-gorges**), robin

rougir [ruʒi:r], to blush

rouler [rule], to roll along

route [rut] (*f.*), road; **en route pour** [ã rut pu:r], on the way to; **se mettre en route** [sə mɛtrã rut], to start off

royaliste [rwajalist] (*m.*), royalist

royaume [rwajo:m] (*m.*), kingdom

ruban [rybã] (*m.*), ribbon

rue [ry] (*f.*), street
Russie [rysi] (*f.*), Russia

S

sa [sa] (*f. sing. poss. adj.*), his, her, its
sac [sak] (*m.*), sack, bag
sacré [sakre], crowned, sacred
sage [sa:ʒ], good, wise
sain et sauf [sɛ̃ e soːf], safe and sound
je sais [ʒə se] (*inf.* **savoir**), I know, I know how; **tu sais** [ty se], you know, you know how; **je n'en sais rien du tout** [ʒə nɑ̃ se rjɛ̃ dy tu], I know nothing at all about it
saisir [sɛziːr], to seize
saison [sɛzõ] (*f.*), season
il sait [il se] (*inf.* **savoir**), he knows, he knows how
salade [saladɪ] (*f.*), salad
salle [sal] (*f.*), room; **salle d'attente** [sal datɑ̃ːt] (*f.*), waiting-room; **salle des bagages** [sal de bagaːʒ] (*f.*), baggage-room; **salle de bains** [sal də bɛ̃] (*f.*), bathroom; **salle de classe** [sal də klɑːs] (*f.*), classroom; **salle à manger** [sal a mɑ̃ʒe] (*f.*), dining-room; **salle de spectacle** [sal də spɛktakl] (*f.*), playhouse
salon [salõ] (*m.*), living-room, parlor, drawing-room; **au salon** [o salõ], in the living-room, to the living-room
saluer [salɥe], to greet
samedi [samdi] (*m.*), Saturday
sandwich [sɑ̃dwitʃ] (*m.*), sandwich
sanglier [sɑ̃glie] (*m.*), wild boar
sans [sɑ̃], without; **sans doute** [sɑ̃ dut], without doubt, undoubtedly; **sans faute** [sɑ̃ foːt], without fail
satisfaction [satisfaksjõ] (*f.*), satisfaction
sauf [sof], except
sauter [sote], to jump; **sauter de joie** [soted ʒwɑ], to jump for joy
sauvage [sovaːʒ], savage, wild
sauver [sove], to save
savant [savɑ̃] (*m.*), learned person, scholar
ils savent [il saːv] (*inf.* savoir), they know (*a fact*), they know how
vous savez [vu save] (*inf.* **savoir**), you know, you know how
savoir [savwaːr] (*p.p.* **su**), to know, to know how
scène [sɛːn] (*f.*), scene

science [sjɑ̃ːs] (*f.*), science
scolaire [skɔlɛːr], school (*adj.*), academic, of schools
se [sə], himself, herself, oneself, themselves
sébile [sebil] (*f.*), wooden bowl
second [səgõ], second
secours [səkuːr] (*m.*) (*pl.* **secours**), help
secret [səkrɛ] (*m.*), secret
seigneur [sɛɲœːr] (*m.*), lord, squire, nobleman
seize [sɛːz], sixteen
sel [sɛl] (*m.*), salt
semaine [səmɛn] (*f.*), week
sembler [sɑ̃ble], to seem
semé [səme] (*p.p. of* **semer**), covered (*with a pattern of small figures*), strewn
sentiment [sɑ̃timɑ̃] (*m.*), sentiment, feeling, opinion
sentir [sɑ̃tiːr] (*p.p.* **senti**), to smell, to feel
séparé [separe], separated, divided
sept [sɛ, sɛt *used alone or before a vowel*], seven
septembre [sɛptɑ̃ːbr] (*m.*), September
septième [sɛtjɛm], seventh
sérieux, -se [serjø, serjøːz], serious
service [sɛrvis] (*m.*), service, work; **porte de service** [pɔrt də sɛrvis] (*f.*), back door
madame est servie [madam ɛ sɛrvi], dinner is served
serviette [sɛrvjɛt] (*f.*), napkin; brief-case
servir [sɛrviːr] (*p.p.* **servi**), to serve
ses [se] (*pl.*), his, her, its
seul [sœl], alone, only; **tout seul** [tu sœl], of his own free will
seulement [sœlmɑ̃], only
sévère [sevɛːr], severe, stern
sévèrement [sevɛrmɑ̃], severely
si [si], so
si [si], yes (*as an affirmative answer to a negative question*); **mais si** [mɛ si], why yes
si [si], if; **s'il vous plaît** [sil vu plɛ], if you please
siècle [sjɛkl] (*m.*), century
siège [sjɛːʒ] (*m.*), siege, seat
siffler [sifle], to whistle, to whistle to
coup de sifflet [kud siflɛ] (*m.*), blowing of the whistle, sound of the whistle

signal [sinal] (m.) (pl. signaux), signal

signifier [sinifje], to signify; il signifie, it means

silence [silɑ̃:s] (m.), silence

silencieux, -se [silɑ̃sjø, silɑ̃sjø:z], silent

simple [sɛ̃:pl], simple, plain

simplement [sɛ̃pləmɑ̃], simply

singe [sɛ̃:ʒ] (m.), monkey

singulier [sɛ̃gylje] (m.), singular (number)

sire [si:r] (m.), sir, sire

situé [sitɥe], situated

six [sis] ([si] before consonants), six

société [sɔsjete] (f.), society

sœur [sœ:r] (f.), sister

sofa [sɔfa] (m.), sofa

soie [swɑ] (f.), silk

soierie [swɑri] (f.), silk material

soif [swaf] (f.), thirst; avoir soif [avwa:r swaf], to be thirsty

soigné [swane], taken care of, cared for

soigner [swane], to care for, to look after

soir [swa:r] (m.), evening; du matin jusqu'au soir [dy matɛ̃ ʒysko swa:r], from morning till night

soixante [swasɑ̃:t], sixty; soixante-dix [swasɑ̃tdis], seventy

soldat [sɔlda] (m.), soldier

soleil [sɔlɛ:j] (m.), sun; au soleil [o sɔlɛ:j], in the sunshine

sombre [sɔ̃:br], dark, gloomy

somme [sɔm] (f.), sum

sommeil [sɔmɛ:j] (m.), sleep; avoir sommeil [avwa:r sɔmɛ:j], to be sleepy

nous sommes [nu sɔm] (inf. être), we are

son [sɔ̃] (m. sing.), his, hers, its

on sonne [ɔ̃ sɔ:n], the bell rings, someone is ringing the bell

sonner [sɔne], to ring a bell, to ring; to sound, to blow (a horn); to strike (of clocks)

ils, elles, sont [il, ɛl, sɔ̃] (inf. être), they are

sorcière [sɔrsjɛ:r] (f.), witch

sorte [sɔrt] (f.), sort, kind

sortir [sɔrti:r] (p.p. sorti), to go out, to get out, to come out, to leave

sou [su] (m.), penny

souffrant [sufrɑ̃], ill, sick

souffrir [sufri:r] (p.p. souffert), to suffer

soulier [sulje] (m.), shoe

soumettre [sumɛtr] (p.p. soumis), to submit, to surrender

soupe [sup] (f.), soup

souri [suri] (p.p. of sourire), smiled

souriant [surjɑ̃], smiling

souricière [surisjɛ:r] (f.), mousetrap

sourire [suri:r] (p.p. souri), to smile

souris [suri] (f.), mouse

sous [su], under, on

soutenir [sutni:r] (p.p. soutenu), to sustain, to support; to uphold; to maintain; to protect

souvent [suvɑ̃], often; assez souvent [ase suvɑ̃], fairly often, rather often

soyeux, -se [swajø, swajø:z], soft, silky

soyez [swaje] (inf. être), be; soyez tranquille [swaje trɑ̃kil], don't worry

spécial [spesjal], special

spectacle [spɛktakl] (m.), spectacle, show, performance; salle de spectacle [sal də spɛktakl] (f.), playhouse

spectateur [spɛktatœ:r] (m.), spectator

sport [spɔ:r] (m.), sport; sports (m. pl.), athletics, sports

sportif, -ve [spɔrtif, spɔrti:v], sporting (news)

store [stɔ:r] (m.), window-shade

stupide [stypid], stupid

stupidité [stypidite] (f.), stupidity

stylo [stilo] (m.), fountain-pen

substantif [sypstɑ̃tif] (m.), substantive, noun

succès [syksɛ] (m.), success; avec succès [avɛk syksɛ], successfully

sud [syd] (m.), south

suffire [syfi:r] (p.p. suffi), to be enough, to suffice

suggérer [sygʒere], to suggest

je suis [ʒə sɥi] (inf. être), I am

suite [sɥit] (f.), attendants, retinue, followers; tout de suite [tut sɥit], immediately

suivre [sɥi:vr] (p.p. suivi), to follow

sujet [syʒɛ] (m.), subject

sultan [syltɑ̃] (m.), sultan

supérieur [syperjœ:r], superior, upper

supporter [sypɔrte], to put up with, to endure, to stand for

sur [sy:r], on, about

sûr, bien sûr [sy:r, bjɛ̃ sy:r], sure; of course, certainly

sûrement [syrmɑ̃], surely, certainly, to be sure

surprendre [syrprɑ̃:dr] (*p.p.* **surpris**), to surprise

surprise [syrpri:z] (*f.*), surprise

surtout [syrtu], above all, especially

système [sistɛ:m] (*m.*), system

T

tabac [taba] (*m.*), tobacco

table [tabl] (*f.*), table

tableau [tablo] (*m.*), blackboard

tablette [tablɛt] (*f.*), tablet, bar

tâcher (de) [tɑʃe də], to try, to endeavor

taisez-vous [tɛze vu] (*inf.* **se taire**), be quiet, hush, be silent

tandis que [tɑ̃di kə], while

tant [tɑ̃], so much, so many (*takes de when used before a noun*); **tant mieux** [tɑ̃ mjø], so much the better; **tant pis** [tɑ̃ pi], so much the worse, never mind

tante [tɑ̃:t] (*f.*), aunt

à tantôt [a tɑ̃to], good-by (*for a short time*), "so long"

tape [tap] (*f.*), tap, rap

tapis [tapi] (*m.*) (*pl.* **tapis**), carpet, rug

tard [ta:r], late; **trop tard** [tro ta:r], too late

tarte [tart] (*f.*), pie; **tarte aux cerises** [tart o səri:z] (*f.*), cherry pie

tartine [tartin] (*f.*), slice of bread and butter *or* jam

tasse [tɑ:s] (*f.*), cup

taxi [taksi] (*m.*), taxi

te [tə], you, to you

tel, telle [tɛl], such; **tel que, telle que** [tɛl kə], such as, like

téléphone [telefɔn] (*m.*), telephone; **coup de téléphone** [kud telefɔn] (*m.*), ring of a telephone bell; **donner un coup de téléphone (à)** [dɔne œ̃ kud telefɔn a], to telephone (to)

temps [tɑ̃] (*m.*), time, weather

tenez [təne] (*pres. imp. of* **tenir**), look here, I say, listen

tenir [təni:r] (*p.p.* **tenu**), to keep, to hold, to have

tennis [tɛnis] (*m.*), tennis

tentant [tɑ̃tɑ̃], tempting

terme [tɛrm] (*m.*), term, word, end

terminaison [tɛrminɛzɔ̃] (*f.*), ending, termination

il se termine [il sə tɛrmin], it ends

terminé [tɛrmine], finished

terminer [tɛrmine], to end, to finish

terrasse [tɛrɑs] (*f.*), terrace

terre [tɛ:r] (*f.*), earth, land, ground; **par terre** [pa:r tɛ:r], on the ground, on the floor

terrible [tɛribl], terrible

territoire [tɛritwa:r] (*m.*), territory

tête [tɛ:t] (*f.*), head

texte [tɛkst] (*m.*), text

thé [te] (*m.*), tea; **elle prend le thé** [ɛl prɑ̃ lə te], she is having tea

théâtral [teatral], theatrical

théâtre [teɑ:tr] (*m.*), theater

thermos [tɛrmɔs] (*m.*), Thermos bottle

tiens [tjɛ̃], say, look here, well

timbre-poste [tɛ̃brəpɔst] (*m.*) (*pl.* **timbres-poste**), postage stamp

timidement [timidmɑ̃], timidly

il tire [il ti:r], he draws, draws aside, takes

tirer [tire], to pull, to draw, to draw aside, to take, to pull back; **tirer d'affaire** [tire dafɛ:r], to help out; **se tirer d'affaire** [sə tire dafɛ:r], to manage, to get along

vous tirez [vu tire], you draw, take

tiroir [tirwa:r] (*m.*), drawer

tisserand [tisrɑ̃] (*m.*), weaver

titre [titr] (*m.*), title

toi [twa], you

toile [twal] (*f.*), linen

tombeau [tɔ̃bo] (*m.*) (*pl.* **tombeaux**), tomb

tomber [tɔ̃be] (*conj. with* **être**), to fall

ton [tɔ̃] (*m.*), color, tint, tone

torche [tɔrʃ] (*f.*), torch

tôt [to], soon, early

toucher [tuʃe], to touch, to affect

toujours [tuʒu:r], always, still

tour [tu:r] (*m.*), turn, trip, trick; **faire des tours** [fɛr de tu:r], to do tricks

tour [tu:r] (*f.*), tower

tourner [turne], to turn; **je tourne** [ʒə turn], I turn; **il tourne** [il turn], he turns; **vous tournez** [vu turne], you turn

tout, toute, tous, toutes [tu, tut, tu, tut], all; **tout d'abord** [tu dabɔ:r], first of all; **tout à coup** [tu ta ku], suddenly, all at once; **tout à fait** [tu ta fɛ], completely, entirely; **tout à l'heure** [tu ta lœ:r], a few minutes ago, in a few minutes; **tout le monde** [tul mɔ̃:d], everyone; **tout seul** [tu sœl], of his own free will; **tout de suite** [tut sɥit], immediately; **du tout, pas du tout** [dy tu, pɑ dy tu], not at all, not in the least; **pas tout à fait** [pɑ tu ta fɛ], not exactly, not entirely, not altogether; **je n'en sais rien du tout** [ʒə nɑ̃ se rjɛ̃ dy tu], I know nothing at all about it; **tous les deux** [tu le dø], both; **tous les jours** [tu le ʒuːr], every day; **toutes les deux** [tut le dø], both

tracer [trase], to trace

traduire [tradɥiːr] (*p.p.* **traduit),** to translate

train [trɛ̃] (*m.*), train; **en train de** [ɑ̃ trɛ̃ də], in the act of

trait [trɛ] (*m.*), trait, feature; **trait d'union** [trɛ dynjɔ̃] (*m.*), hyphen

traître [trɛːtr] (*m.*), traitor

trajet [traʒe] (*m.*), route, trip (*usually shorter than is implied by* **voyage)**

tranquille [trɑ̃kil], tranquil, calm, quiet; **soyez tranquille** [swaje trɑ̃kil], don't worry

travail [travaːj] (*m.*) (*pl.* **travaux),** work

travailler [travaje], to work

à travers [a travɛːr], across, through

traverser [travɛrse], to cross, to go across

treize [trɛːz], thirteen

treizième [trɛzjɛm], thirteenth

trembler [trɑ̃ble], to tremble

trente [trɑ̃ːt], thirty

très [trɛ], very

trésor [trezɔːr] (*m.*), treasure, riches

tricoter [trikɔte], to knit; **elle tricote** [ɛl trikɔt], she is knitting; **nous tricotons** [nu trikɔtɔ̃], we knit, are knitting

triste [trist], sad

tristement [tristəmɑ̃], sadly, sorrowfully

tristesse [tristɛs] (*f.*), sadness

trois [trwɑ], three

troisième [trwɑzjɛm], third

se tromper (de) [sə trɔ̃pe də], to be mistaken

trop [trɔ], too, too much; **trop tard** [trɔ taːr], too late

trottoir [trɔtwaːr] (*m.*), sidewalk

trou [tru] (*m.*), hole

troupe [trup] (*f.*), troop, band, company

trouver [truve], to find; **se trouver** [sə truve], to be, to be found; **vous trouvez** [vu truve], you find, you are finding; **nous trouvons** [nu truvɔ̃], we find, we are finding

T. S. F. [te ɛs ɛf] (*f.*), radio; **Télégraphie sans fil** [telegrafi sɑ̃ fil] (*f.*), wireless telegraphy

tu [ty], you

tuer [tɥe], to kill

Turc [tyrk] (*m.*), Turk

turc [tyrk] (*m.*), Turkish (*language*)

turc, -que [tyrk], Turkish

Turquie [tyrki] (*f.*), Turkey

U

un, une [œ̃, yn], a, an, one

unique [ynik], unique, only, sole

université [ynivɛrsite] (*f.*), university

utiliser [ytilize], to utilize, to use

V

il va [il va] (*inf.* **aller),** he goes

vacances [vakɑ̃ːs] (*f. pl.*), vacation, holidays

vache [vaʃ] (*f.*), cow

vague [vag] (*f.*), wave

je vais [ʒə vɛ] (*inf.* **aller),** I go, I am going

vaisseau [vɛso] (*m.*) (*pl.* **vaisseaux),** vessel, ship

laver la vaisselle [lave la vɛsɛl], to wash the dishes

valeur [valœːr] (*f.*), value, worth

valise [valiːz] (*f.*), valise, traveling bag

vallée [vale] (*f.*), valley

valoir [valwaːr] (*p.p.* **valu),** to be worth

valser [valse], to waltz

vanter [vɑ̃te], to praise

variété [varjete] (*f.*), variety

vaste [vast], vast

il vaut mieux [il vo mjø] (*inf.* **valoir),** it is better

veau [vo] (*m.*), calf, veal

vendre [vɑ̃ːdr], to sell

vendredi [vɑ̃drədi] (*m.*), Friday

venir [vəniːr] (*p.p.* **venu),** to come; **faire venir** [fɛːr vəniːr], to send for

vent [vɑ̃] (*m.*), wind

vente [vɑ̃ːt] (*f.*), sale

véranda [verɑ̃da] (*f.*), porch

verbe [vɛrb] (*m.*), verb

véritable [veritabl], real, true, veritable

vérité [verite] (*f.*), truth

verre [vɛːr] (*m.*), glass

vers [vɛːr] (*m.*) (*pl.* **vers),** verse

vers [vɛːr], toward, about

vert, verte [vɛːr, vɛrt], green

vertu [vɛrty] (*f.*), virtue

veston [vɛstõ] (*m.*), coat (*of a man's suit*)

vêtements [vɛtmã] (*m. pl.*), clothing

il veut [il vø] (*inf.* **vouloir**), he wishes; **il veut dire** [il vø diːr], he, it, means

veuve [vœːv] (*f.*), widow

je veux [ʒə vø] (*inf.* **vouloir**), I wish, I want; **je veux bien** [ʒə vø bjɛ̃], willingly

viande [vjãːd] (*f.*), meat

victime [viktim] (*f.*), victim

vider [vide], to empty

vie [vi] (*f.*), life, living; **gagner sa vie** [gaɲe sa vi], to earn one's living

vieillard [vjɛjaːr] (*m.*), old man

il vient [il vjɛ̃] (*inf.* **venir**), he comes, there comes

vieux, vieille [vjø, vjɛːj], old; **mon vieux** [mõ vjø], old chap, old man, my dear fellow (*colloquial form of address used between men and boys*)

vif, vive [vif, viːv], bright, clear, quick

vilain [vilɛ̃], ugly

village [vilaːʒ] (*m.*), village

ville [vil] (*f.*), city

vingt [vɛ̃], twenty

visage [vizaːʒ] (*m.*), countenance, face

visite [vizit] (*f.*), visit; **rendre visite** [rãːdr vizit], to visit

visiter [vizite], to visit

vite [vit], fast, quick, quickly

vitre [vitr] (*f.*), window-pane

vitrine [vitrin] (*f.*), shop-window, show-window

vivre [viːvr] (*p.p.* **vécu**), to live

vœu [vø] (*m.*) (*pl.* **vœux**), wish, vow

voici [vwasi], here is, here are

ils voient [il vwa] (*inf.* **voir**), they see

voilà [vwala], there is, there are; **les voilà** [le vwala], there they are, there they were; **voilà pourquoi** [vwala purkwa], that is the reason, that is why

voir [vwaːr] (*p.p.* **vu**), to see

je vois [ʒə vwa] (*inf.* **voir**), I see, I am seeing

voisin, voisine [vwazɛ̃, vwazin] (*m.* and *f.*), neighbor

voisin, voisine [vwazɛ̃, vwazin], neighboring

il voit [il vwa] (*inf.* **voir**), he sees

voiture [vwatyːr] (*f.*), carriage, vehicle, car; **en voiture!** [ã vwatyːr], all aboard!

voix [vwa] (*f.*), voice; **à voix basse** [a vwa baːs], in a low voice

voler [vɔle], to fly, to steal

voleur [vɔlœːr] (*m.*), thief

volontiers [vɔlõtje], freely, willingly, gladly

ils vont [il võ] (*inf.* **aller**), they go, they are going, they are on their way

vos [vo] (*pl.*), your

votre [vɔtr], your

vous voulez [vu vule] (*inf.* **vouloir**), you wish, you will; **vous voulez dire** [vu vule diːr], you mean

vouloir [vulwaːr] (*p.p.* **voulu**), to wish, to want

vous [vu], you; **à vous** [a vu], you next

voyage [vwajaːʒ] (*m.*), trip, traveling, journey; **faire un voyage** [fɛːr œ̃ vwajaːʒ], to take a trip

voyager [vwajaʒe], to travel, to take a trip

voyageur [vwajaʒœːr] (*m.*), traveler, voyager

voyelle [vwajɛl] (*f.*), vowel

vous voyez [vu vwaje] (*inf.* **voir**), you see

nous voyons [nu vwajõ] (*inf.* **voir**), we see

vrai [vrɛ], true, real

vraiment [vrɛmã], really, truly

vu [vy] (*p.p. of* **voir**), seen

W

wagon [vagõ] (*m.*), railroad car, coach

wagon-restaurant [vagõ rɛstɔrã] (*m.*), dining car

Y

y [i], there, in it, in them, at it, to it; **il y a** [ilja], there is, there are

yeux [jø] (*m. pl.*), eyes

ENGLISH-FRENCH VOCABULARY

Note: The following vocabulary is based on the English words used in the translation exercises. Only the meanings that apply in these exercises are here given. Consequently this vocabulary cannot be used as a dictionary, and care must be exercised in choosing words for original composition.

A

a, an, un, une

abbey, l'abbaye (*f.*); **abbey of St. Denis,** l'abbaye de Saint-Denis

to **be able,** pouvoir (*p.p.* pu)

about, de, sur

above, au-dessus

to accept, accepter

accustomed, habitué (à), accoutumé (à)

to **be in the act of,** être en train de

Adele, Adèle

to **admire,** admirer

to **adore,** adorer

adventure, l'aventure (*f.*)

advertisement, l'annonce (*f.*)

to **be afraid,** avoir peur; **I am afraid of dogs,** j'ai peur des chiens

after, après

afternoon, l'après-midi (*m.*); **in the afternoon,** l'après-midi

afterwards, après

again, de nouveau, encore

it agrees, il s'accorde

air, l'air (*m.*)

airplane, l'aéroplane (*m.*)

album, l'album (*m.*); **stamp album,** l'album de timbres

algebra, l'algèbre (*m.*); **algebra book,** le livre d'algèbre; **algebra class,** la classe d'algèbre; **algebra lesson,** la leçon d'algèbre

all, tout, toute, tous, toutes; **all day** toute la journée

almost, presque

alone, seul

along, le long de: **along the streets,** le long des rues

also, aussi

always, toujours

American, américain

to **amuse oneself,** s'amuser

and, et

another, un autre, une autre

to **answer,** répondre (à)

answers, répond

any, de, du, de l', de la, des, en (*pro.*)

anything, quelque chose; **not anything,** ne . . . rien

appetite, l'appétit (*m.*)

apple, la pomme

to **apply oneself,** s'appliquer

April, avril; **the twenty-first of April,** le vingt et un avril

they are, ils sont; **we are,** nous sommes; **you are,** vous êtes

aren't we, n'est-ce pas?

to **arise,** se lever

arithmetic, l'arithmétique (*f.*)

arm, le bras

to **arrive,** arriver

article, l'article (*m.*); **sporting articles,** les articles sur les sports

as, comme; **as . . . as,** aussi . . . que

to **be ashamed,** avoir honte

aside, de côté; **to put aside,** mettre de côté

to **ask,** demander; **to ask a question,** poser une question; **to ask someone something,** demander quelque chose à quelqu'un

to **fall asleep,** s'endormir

to **assure,** assurer; **I assure you,** je vous assure

at, à; **at home,** à la maison; **at Mrs. Gilbert's,** chez Mme. Gilbert

at first, d'abord, au commencement

athletics, les sports

attention, l'attention (*f.*); **to pay attention,** faire attention

August, août

aunt, la tante

automobile, l'automobile (*m. or f.*); **automobile ride,** une promenade en auto

B

bad, méchant, mauvais; **it is bad (weather),** il fait mauvais

bag, la gibecière

413

baggage, les bagages (*m. pl.*)

bakery-shop, la boulangerie

ball, la balle

banner, la bannière

bar, la tablette; **bar of chocolate,** la tablette de chocolat

basket, le panier

bathroom, la salle de bains

to be, être (*p.p.* été); **to be afraid,** avoir peur; **to be ashamed,** avoir honte; **to be careful,** faire attention; **to be cold,** avoir froid; **to be hot,** avoir chaud; **to be hungry,** avoir faim; **to be late,** être en retard; **to be thirsty,** avoir soif: **to be in the act of,** être en train de

beans, les haricots (*m. pl.*)

beautiful, beau, bel, belle, beaux, belles

because, parce que

bed, le lit; **to go to bed,** se coucher; **to jump out of bed,** sauter du lit

bedroom, la chambre à coucher

been, été (*inf.* être)

before, avant (+*noun or pronoun*), avant de (+*inf.*)

to begin, commencer (à)

behind, derrière

Belgium, la Belgique; **to, in, Belgium,** en Belgique

belongings, les affaires (*f. pl.*)

beside, à côté de

best (*adj.*), le meilleur, la meilleure, les meilleurs, les meilleures; **the best way,** la meilleure façon

better (*adj.*), meilleur, meilleure, meilleurs, meilleures

better (*adv.*), mieux

bicycle, la bicyclette

big, grand, gros, grosse

bill, l'addition (*f.*)

bird, l'oiseau (*m.*)

birthday, l'anniversaire (*m.*)

black, noir

blackboard, le tableau; **on the blackboard,** au tableau

we are to blame, nous sommes coupables

to blow (a whistle), siffler

blue, bleu

board (blackboard), le tableau

book, le livre

Bordeaux, Bordeaux; **to, in, Bordeaux,** à Bordeaux

bored, ennuyé; **to be bored,** s'ennuyer

boring, ennuyeux, -se

both, les deux, tous les deux (*m.*), toutes les deux (*f.*)

boulevard, le boulevard

box, la boîte

boy, le garçon

bread, le pain; **loaf of bread,** le pain

breakfast, le petit déjeuner

bright, brillant; **with bright eyes,** aux yeux brillants

to bring, apporter; **to bring back,** rapporter

Brittany, la Bretagne; **in Brittany,** en Bretagne

orother, le frère

brown, brun

building, le bâtiment

bus, l'autobus (*m.*)

business, les affaires (*f. pl.*)

but, mais

butcher-shop, at the butcher-shop chez le boucher

butter, le beurre

to buy, acheter

by, en, par

C

cabbage, le chou, les choux

cake, le gâteau, les gâteaux

calendar, le calendrier

to call, appeler

he came, il est venu

Camembert, le camembert.

can, pouvoir; **he can,** il peut; **I can,** je peux; **they can,** ils peuvent; **we can,** nous pouvons; **you can,** vous pouvez

Canada, le Canada; **to, in, Canada,** au Canada

cap, le bonnet; **boy's cap,** la casquette

car, le wagon

card, la carte; **to play cards,** jouer aux cartes

to be careful, faire attention

carpet, le tapis

carrot, la carotte

to carry, apporter, porter

to carve, découper

cat, le chat

to catch, attraper

chair, la chaise

chalk, la craie

Charles, Charles

check, enregistrer

cheek, la joue

cheese, le fromage

cherry, la cerise; **cherry pie,** la tarte aux cerises

chicken, le poulet

child, l'enfant (*m. or f.*)

chin, le menton

China, la Chine; **to, in, China,** en Chine

chocolate, le chocolat; **bar of chocolate,** la tablette de chocolat; **chocolate pudding,** la crème au chocolat

to choose, choisir

Christopher, Christophe

church, l'église (*f.*); **to church,** à l'église

city, la ville; **to the city,** en ville

class, la classe; **to, in, class,** en classe; **algebra class,** la classe d'algèbre; **English class,** la classe d'anglais

cleaning-woman, la femme de ménage

clear, clair; **it is clear weather,** il fait clair

click! clic!

clock, la pendule, l'horloge (*f.*)

I close, je ferme

to close, fermer

coach, le wagon

coat, le manteau

coffee, le café

cold, froid; **it is cold,** il fait froid; **to be cold,** avoir froid

collar (for an animal), le collier

color, la couleur

column, la colonne

to come, venir (*p.p.* venu*)*; **to come on time,** venir à l'heure

he comes, il vient

he will come, il viendra

common, commun

company, le monde; **to have company,** avoir du monde

containing, contenant

to continue, continuer (à)

conversation, la conversation

cook, la cuisinière

cool, frais; **it is cool,** il fait frais

corner, le coin, **at the corner,** au coin

corridor, le couloir

could, pouvoir (*past descriptive*)

to count, compter

country, (*region*) le pays; (*not* city) la campagne; **in, to the country,** à la campagne

cousin, le cousin, la cousine

covered with, couvert de

to cross, traverser

cross, maussade

cruel, cruel, cruelle

cup, la tasse

curtain, le rideau

to cut, couper

D

to dance, danser

dark, noir, sombre; **it is dark,** il fait noir

date, la date

day, le jour; **good-day,** bonjour; **the day before yesterday,** avant-hier; **every day,** tous les jours; **all day,** toute la journée

deal, a great deal, beaucoup

to decide, décider

delighted, enchanté

demon, le démon

desk, le pupitre

to devour, dévorer

did (*usually expressed by the past indefinite of the verb following* did)

difficult, difficile

difficulty, la difficulté

to dine, dîner

dining-room, la salle à manger

dinner, le dîner; **to have dinner,** dîner; **dinner is served,** Madame est servie

disagreeable, désagréable, mauvais; **it is disagreeable (weather),** il fait mauvais

discovery, la découverte

to discuss, discuter

distinguished, distingué

to do, faire (*p. p.* fait)

doctor, le docteur

dog, le chien

doll, la poupée

don't they? don't we? don't you? n'est-ce pas?

door, la porte

doubt, le doute; **without doubt,** sans doute

to draw, to pull, tirer

drawer, le tiroir

he draws, he pulls, il tire

dress, la robe

to dress oneself, s'habiller

during, pendant

E

each, chaque; **each time,** chaque fois; **each day,** chaque jour

ear, l'oreille (*f.*)

early, de bonne heure

to earn, gagner; **to earn one's living,** gagner sa vie

to eat, manger; **something to eat,** quelque chose à manger; **to eat with relish,** manger de bon appétit

egg, l'œuf (*m.*)

eight, huit; **eight minutes past one,** une heure huit; **a quarter to eight,** huit heures moins le quart

eighty, quatre-vingts

eighty-five, quatre-vingt-cinq

Emily, Emilie

employee, l'employé (*m.*)

employer, le patron

to empty, vider

it ends, il se termine

engineer, le chauffeur

England, l'Angleterre (*f.*); **to, in, England,** en Angleterre

English, anglais; **the English class,** la classe d'anglais

to enjoy oneself, to have a good time, s'amuser

enough, assez

to enter, entrer (dans)

eraser, la gomme

errand, la commission; **to go on errands,** faire des commissions

to establish, établir

esteemed, estimé; **highly esteemed,** très estimé

Europe, l'Europe (*f.*); **in, to, Europe,** en Europe

even, même

evening, le soir; **this evening,** ce soir

every, chaque; **every day,** tous les jours; **every evening,** tous les soirs

everybody, everyone, tout le monde

excellent, excellent

except, excepté, sauf

exercise, l'exercice (*m.*)

expensive, cher, chère

to explain, expliquer

expression, l'expression (*f.*)

eye, l'œil (*m.*); *pl.* les yeux; **with bright eyes,** aux yeux brillants

F

face, la figure

factory, la fabrique

faded, fané

fairly well, assez bien

to fall asleep, s'endormir

family, la famille

far, loin; **far away,** loin

farm, la ferme

farther, plus loin

fast, vite

fat, gros, grosse

father, papa, le père

February, février; **in February,** en février; **in the month of February,** au mois de février

few, a few, quelques, peu (de)

fierce, féroce

fifteen, quinze

fifth, cinquième

fifty, cinquante

to fill, remplir

finally, finalement, enfin

to find, trouver; **to be found,** se trouver

I find, je trouve

we find, nous trouvons

finger, le doigt

to finish, finir

first, premier, première; **the first of March,** le premier mars

first, at first, d'abord, au commencement

five, cinq; **five-thirty,** cinq heures et demie; **a quarter after five,** cinq heures et quart

flag, le drapeau; *pl.* les drapeaux

floor, le plancher

flower, la fleur

to fold, plier

food, la nourriture

foot, le pied; **on foot,** à pied

football, le football; **to play football,** jouer au football

for, pour, à

forehead, le front

foreign, étranger

foreigner, l'étranger (*m.*); **for a foreign country,** pour l'étranger

to forget, oublier

fork, la fourchette

former, ancien, ancienne

fountain, la fontaine

fountain-pen, le stylo

four, quatre; **half past four,** quatre heures et demie

fourteen, quatorze

fourth, quatrième

franc, le franc

France, la France; **to, in, France,** en France

Francis, François

free, libre

French, français; **in French,** en français; **French teacher,** le professeur de français; **French class,** la classe de français

French (people), les Français (*m. pl.*)

Friday, vendredi; **on Friday (every Friday),** le vendredi; **on Fridays,** le vendredi

friend, l'ami (*m.*), l'amie (*f.*)

from, de, de la part de

in front of, devant

G

garage, le garage

garden, le jardin; **in the garden,** dans le jardin; **vegetable garden, kitchen garden,** le jardin potager; **pleasure garden,** le jardin d'agrément

gardener, le jardinier

gate, le guichet

general, le général

geography, la géographie

to get, chercher

to get up, se lever

gift, le cadeau, *pl.* les cadeaux

girl, la fille; **little girl,** la petite fille; **young girl,** la jeune fille

to give, donner

he gives, il donne

glad, content

glass, le verre; **a glass of water,** un verre d'eau

to go, aller, passer; **to go home,** aller à la maison; **to go on errands,** faire des commissions; **to go to bed,** se coucher; **to go back,** retourner; **to go on foot,** aller à pied

goes, is going, va

I am going, je vais

we are going, nous allons

to go back, retourner

to go out, sortir

to go to bed, se coucher

to go to sleep, s'endormir

gold, l'or (*m.*); (*adj.*) doré; **gold lilies,** les lis d'or (*m. pl.*)

golf, le golf

good, bon, bonne; **good day,** bonjour; **to have a good time,** s'amuser

good-by, au revoir

good-night, bonne nuit

government, le gouvernement

grade, la note

grandfather, le grand-père

grandmother, la grand'mère; **to your grandmother's,** chez votre grand'mère

grass, l'herbe (*f.*)

gray, gris

a great deal, beaucoup

green, vert

to greet, saluer

grocery-store, l'épicerie (*f.*)

group, le groupe

gull, sea gull, la mouette

H

to hail, héler

hair, les cheveux (*m. pl.*)

half, demi; **half past four,** quatre heures et demie; **half past nine,** neuf heures et demie

hall, l'antichambre (*f.*)

handkerchief, le mouchoir

happy, content, heureux, -se; **to seem** or **to look happy,** avoir l'air heureux

hard (*adv.*), ferme

has, a

one has, on a

she has, elle a

hat, le chapeau

to have, avoir (*p.p.* eu); **to have tea,** prendre le thé

to have a good time, s'amuser

I have, j'ai

they have, ils ont

we have, nous avons

you have, vous avez

he, il (*subj.*); lui (*disj.*)

head, la tête

to hear, entendre

hearty, copieux, -se

to help, aider

Henrietta, Henriette

Henry, Henri

her, la (*dir. obj.*); lui (*ind. obj.*); elle (*disj.*); son, sa, ses (*poss.*)

here (is, are), voici

herself, se

high, haut

him, le (*dir. obj.*); lui (*ind. obj.*)

himself, se

Hippolyte, Hippolyte

his, her, its, son, sa, ses

Holland, la Hollande; to, in, Holland, en Hollande

home, la maison; at home, à la maison; at our home, chez nous; at her home, chez elle; to go home, aller à la maison; to come home, venir à la maison

to hope, espérer

hot, chaud; to be hot, avoir chaud; I am hot, j'ai chaud; it is hot, il fait chaud

hour, l'heure (*f.*)

house, la maison

how, comme, comment, que; how good the chocolate is! que le chocolat est bon!

how many, combien (de)

however, pourtant, cependant

hundred, one hundred, cent

to be hungry, avoir faim

hurriedly, vite

to hurry, se dépêcher

husband, le mari

I

I, je (*subj.*); moi (*disj.*)

if, si

ill, malade

illustration, l'illustration (*f.*)

immediately, tout de suite

impatient, impatient

important, important; less important, moins important

in, dans, à, de, en; in the, au, à la, à l', aux

India, les Indes (*f. pl.*); to, in, India, aux Indes

to indicate, indiquer

indulgent, indulgent

infinitive, l'infinitif (*m.*)

ink, l'encre (*f.*)

insect, l'insecte (*m.*)

to inspect, inspecter

intelligent, intelligent

interesting, intéressant

into, dans

invitation, l'invitation (*f.*)

to invite, inviter

is, est

isn't it? n'est-ce pas?

it, il, elle (*subj.*); le, la (*obj.*); ce, cela (*demonst.*); it is, (*before a noun*) c'est; (*before any other word*) il est, elle est

it is cold, il fait froid; it is hot, il fait chaud; it is mild, il fait doux; it is dark, il fait noir; it is bright, il fait clair; it is disagreeable, il fait mauvais; it is pleasant, il fait beau

it is necessary, il faut

Italian, italien, italienne

Italy, l'Italie (*f.*); to, in, Italy, en Italie

J

Jane, Jeanne

January, janvier; in January, en janvier

Japan, le Japon; in, to, Japan, au Japon

John, Jean

Joseph, Joseph

Josephine, Joséphine

joy, la joie; jumps for joy, saute de joie

July, juillet

to jump, sauter; to jump for joy, sauter de joie; to jump out of bed, sauter du lit

June, juin

K

to keep, garder

kilogram, le kilogramme

kindness, l'obligeance (*f.*); to have the kindness (to), avoir l'obligeance (de)

king, le roi

to kiss, embrasser

knife, le couteau

to knit, tricoter

she knits, elle tricote

is knitting, tricote

to know, to know how, savoir (*p.p.* su); to know (a person), connaître (*p.p.* connu)

I know, I know how, je sais

knows, knows how, sait

L

lake, le lac; lake shore, le bord du lac

lamp, la lampe

landscape, le paysage

large, grand, gros, grosse

last, dernier, dernière; **last year,** l'année dernière; **last Monday,** lundi dernier

late, tard, en retard

later, plus tard

to laugh, rire (*p.p.* ri)

to lay the cloth, mettre la nappe; **laid the cloth,** a mis la nappe

leap year, l'année bissextile (*f.*)

to learn, apprendre (*p.p.* appris)

he learns, il apprend

we learned, nous avons appris

to leave, partir, quitter; **to leave (something),** laisser

he left, il est parti

left, gauche; **at, to, the left,** à gauche

leg, la jambe

to lend, prêter

lenient, indulgent

less, moins

lesson, la leçon; **algebra lesson,** la leçon d'algèbre

letter, la lettre

letter-box, la boîte aux lettres

library, la bibliothèque

light, la lumière

like (*prep.*), comme

to like, aimer

I like, j'aime

we like, nous aimons

you like, vous aimez

likes, aime

lily, le lis (*pl.* les lis); **gold lilies,** les lis d'or

line, la ligne

to listen to, écouter

little, petit

a little, un peu; **a little longer,** un peu plus longtemps; **very little,** très peu

to live, demeurer

to earn one's living, gagner sa vie

living-room, le salon; **in, to, the living-room,** au salon

loaf (of bread), le pain

local, régional

locker, le casier

locomotive, la locomotive

long, long, longue, longtemps; **too long,** trop longtemps

longer, plus longtemps; **a little longer,** un peu plus longtemps

to look at, regarder

I look at, je regarde

you look at, vous regardez

to look for, chercher

I look for, je cherche

we look for, nous cherchons

you look for, vous cherchez

to look happy, avoir l'air heureux; **to look tired,** avoir l'air fatigué; **to look worried,** avoir l'air inquiet

looks into, regarde dans

to look like, ressembler (à), avoir l'air de

to lose, perdre

loss, la perte

Louise, Louise

to love, aimer

to lower, baisser

lunch, luncheon, le déjeuner

M

maid, la bonne

mail-carrier, mailman, le facteur

to make, faire (*p.p.* fait); **to make a mistake,** se tromper; **to make purchases,** faire des achats; **to make last,** conserver

man, l'homme (*m.*)

to manage, se tirer d'affaire

many, beaucoup, beaucoup de (*followed by noun*)

map, la carte

March, mars

market, le marché

Martha, Marthe

Mary, Marie; **at Mary's,** chez Marie

Mary Louise, Marie-Louise

what is the matter with you? qu'avez-vous?

may, pouvoir; **he may,** il peut; **I may,** je peux; **they may,** ils peuvent; **we may,** nous pouvons; **you may,** vous pouvez

Max, Max

me, me, moi (*disj.*); **with me,** avec moi

meal, le repas

meat, la viande

to meet, rencontrer

menu, la carte du jour

Mexico, le Mexique; **to, in, Mexico,** au Mexique

Michael, Michel

milk, le lait

minute, la minute

to mislay, égarer

Miss, mademoiselle

mistake, la faute; **to make a mistake,** se tromper

moment, le moment; **at that moment,** à ce moment

monarchy, la monarchie

Monday, lundi

money, l'argent (*m.*)

Mont Blanc, le Mont-Blanc

month, le mois; **in the month of,** au mois de; **in the months of,** aux mois de

more, plus

morning, le matin; **in the morning,** le matin; **all morning,** toute la matinée

most, le plus

mother, maman, la mère

mountain, la montagne

mouse, la souris; **Mr. Mouse,** Monsieur; **Mrs. Mouse,** Madame

mouse-trap, la souricière

mouth, la bouche

moving-pictures, le cinéma

Mr., Monsieur, M. (*abbr.*); **Mr. Baker,** M. Baker

much, beaucoup (de); **very much,** beaucoup (de); **so much,** tant (de)

music, la musique; **music lesson,** la leçon de musique

must, il faut que (+*subjunctive*)

my, mon, ma, mes

N

name, le nom

napkin, la serviette

narrow, étroit

near, près (de)

it is necessary, il faut

to need, avoir besoin (de)

we need, nous avons besoin (de)

neighbor, le voisin, la voisine

neighboring, voisin

nest, le nid

never, ne . . . jamais; **never again,** ne . . . plus

newspaper, le journal

next, prochain· **next summer,** l'été prochain (*m.*)

next to, à côté de

the next day, le lendemain

nine, neuf; **nine o'clock,** neuf heures; **a quarter to nine,** neuf heures moins un quart

nineteen, dix-neuf

no, non

nobody, no one, ne . . . personne

none, en; **he has none,** il n'en a pas

noon, midi; **at noon,** à midi; **see you at noon!** à midi!

nose, le nez

not, ne . . . pas; **not yet,** pas encore

note, le petit mot

nothing, ne . . . rien; **nothing to eat,** rien à manger

noun, le substantif

November, novembre

now, maintenant

number, le nombre

O

oak tree, le chêne

to obey, obéir (à)

object, l'objet (*m.*), la chose, le régime

obliged, obligé (de)

o'clock, l'heure (*f.*); **two o'clock,** *etc.,* deux heures, *etc.;* **at nine o'clock,** à neuf heures; **five o'clock P.M.,** cinq heures ou dix-sept heures

October, octobre

Odette, Odette

of, de

to offer, offrir (*p.p.* offert)

office, le bureau

often, souvent

old, âgé, vieux, vieille; **older,** plus âgé

on, sur, à; **on the blackboard,** au tableau; **on Thursday (every Thursday),** le jeudi

one, on (*pro.*), un, une (*art.*); **no one,** ne . . . personne

one's, son, sa, ses

only, seulement, ne . . . que

open, opened, ouvert

to open, ouvrir (*p.p.* ouvert)

open (*imper.*), ouvrez

I open, j'ouvre

you open, vous ouvrez

he opens, il ouvre

we opened, nous avons ouvert

the opening, l'ouverture (*f.*)

opportunity, l'occasion (*f.*)

or, ou

to order, commander

ordinarily, ordinairement, d'ordinaire

oriflamme, l'oriflamme (*f.*)

Orléans, Orléans; to, in, Orléans, à Orléans
other, autre; the others, les autres
our, notre, nos
out of doors, en plein air
outside, l'extérieur (m.): on the outside, à l'extérieur
over there, là-bas

P

package, le paquet, le colis
page, la page
pantry, l'office (f.)
paper, le papier; newspaper, le journal
parents, les parents (m. pl.)
Paris, Paris; to, in, Paris, à Paris
Parisian, parisien, parisienne
park, le parc; in the park, au parc
part, la partie
participle, le participe
to pass through, traverser
patience, la patience
to pay, to pay for, payer; to pay attention, faire attention
pedestrian, le piéton
fountain-pen, le stylo
pencil, le crayon
people, les gens, les personnes, on; many people, beaucoup de monde
person, la personne
Peter, Pierre, Pierrot
Philip, Philippe
to pick, cueillir
to pick up, ramasser
pick up (imper.), ramassez
picks up, ramasse
picture, le tableau
pie, la tarte; cherry pie, la tarte aux cerises
piece, bit, le morceau; piece of string, le bout de ficelle; a big piece, un gros morceau
pink, rose
place, la place; in place, en place
to place oneself, se mettre
I place myself, je me mets
to plant, planter
plate, l'assiette (f.)
to play, jouer; to play football, jouer au football; to play golf, jouer au golf; to play tennis, jouer au tennis

are playing, jouent
she plays, elle joue
you play, vous jouez
please, s'il vous plaît
pleasure garden, le jardin d'agrément
pocket, la poche
to point to, indiquer
possible, possible; as quickly as possible, aussi vite que possible
poster, l'affiche (f.)
postman, le facteur
post-office, la poste
potato, la pomme de terre
to prefer, préférer
prepare, préparer
pretty, joli
problem, le problème
pronoun, le pronom
proud, fier (de), fière (de)
chocolate pudding, la crème au chocolat
punctual, exact
pupil, l'élève (m. or f.)
purchase, l'achat (m.); to make purchases, faire des achats
to put, to put on, mettre (p.p. mis); to put aside, mettre de côté
he puts, il met
I put, je mets
she puts, elle met

Q

quarter, le quart; a quarter past two, etc., deux heures et quart, etc.; a quarter to two, etc., deux heures moins le quart, etc.; a quarter to two P.M., etc., deux heures moins le quart, etc., or quatorze heures moins le quart, etc.
question, la question; I have a question to ask you, j'ai une question à vous poser
quick, vite
quickly, vite; as quickly as possible, aussi vite que possible

R

radio, la T.S.F.
to rain, pleuvoir (p.p. plu)
it rains, it is raining, il pleut
to raise, lever
I raise, je lève
he raises, il lève
Ralph, Raoul

rapidly, vite; **too rapidly,** trop vite

rarely, rarement

to read, lire (*p.p.* lu)

he reads, il lit

is reading, lit

really, vraiment

to receive, recevoir (*p.p.* reçu)

to recite, réciter

red, rouge

to re-establish, rétablir

relative, le parent

with relish, de bon appétit

to remain, rester

to remember, se rappeler

Mr. Renaud, M. Renaud; **Mrs. Renaud,** Mme. Renaud; **the Renauds,** les Renaud

to repeat, répéter

to reply, répondre

reproduction, la reproduction

republic, la république

to require, exiger

to rest, se reposer

restaurant, le restaurant

to return, retourner, rentrer; **to return (something),** rendre

revolution, la révolution

ribbon, le ruban

rich, riche

ride, *see* **to take a ride**

right, droit; **at, to, the right,** à droite

roast, le rôti

robin, le rouge-gorge

roll, le petit pain

room, la chambre

Roquefort cheese, le roquefort

rose, la rose

to row, ramer

royalist, le royaliste

rug, le tapis

to run, courir (*p.p.* couru)

runs, court

Russia, la Russie; **to, in, Russia,** en Russie

S

he said, il a dit

Saint Denis, *see* **abbey**

salad, la salade

sale, la vente

same, même

sandwich, le sandwich

Saturday, samedi; **on Saturdays,** le samedi

we saw, nous avons vu

to say, dire (*p.p.* dit)

I say, je dis

says, dit

school, l'école (*f.*); **to, at, school,** à l'école

to scold, gronder

sea gull, la mouette

seat, la place

seated, assis

second, second, deuxième; **the second time,** la deuxième fois

to see, voir (*p.p.* vu)

he sees, il voit

I see, je vois

one sees, on voit

they see, ils voient

we see, nous voyons

see you at noon! à midi!

seed, la graine

to seem, avoir l'air; **to seem happy,** avoir l'air heureux

to sell, vendre

to send, envoyer

sentence, la phrase

September, septembre; **in September,** en septembre

to serve, servir

served, servi; **dinner is served,** madame est servie

to set the table, mettre le couvert

seven, sept

seventeen, dix-sept

seventh, septième

several, plusieurs; **several times,** plusieurs fois

shade, l'ombre (*f.*); **in the shade,** à l'ombre; **window-shade,** le store

she, elle

shoe, le soulier

butcher-shop, chez le boucher; **bakery-shop,** la boulangerie; **tobacco-shop,** chez le marchand de tabac

shop-window, la vitrine

shore, le bord; **lake shore,** le bord du lac; **on the shore,** au bord; **to the lake shore,** au bord du lac

short, court

to show, montrer

show-window, la vitrine

sick, malade

signal, le signal

to sing, chanter

sister, la sœur

situated, situé

six, six; six-twenty, six heures vingt

sixteen, seize; **sixteen minutes past seven**, sept heures seize

to skate, patiner

sky, le ciel

to sleep, dormir; **to go to sleep**, s'endormir

is sleeping, dort

to be sleepy, avoir sommeil

slowly, lentement

small, petit

smaller, plus petit

to smile, sourire (*p.p.* souri); **they were smiling**, ils souriaient

smiling, souriant

snow, la neige

so, si

sofa, le sofa

soldier, le soldat

"so long!" à tantôt!

some, de l', du, de la, des, quelque, en (*pro.*); **some day**, un jour

something, quelque chose; **something to eat**, quelque chose à manger

sometimes, quelquefois

son, le fils

sound, le bruit; **sound of the whistle**, le coup de sifflet

soup, la soupe

Spanish, espagnol

sparrow, le moineau, *pl.* les moineaux

to speak, parler; **to speak of**, parler de

spectacles, les lunettes (*f. pl.*)

spinach, les épinards (*m. pl.*)

spoon, la cuillère

sport, le sport; **winter sports**, les sports d'hiver; **sporting articles**, les articles sur les sports (*m. pl.*); **sporting news**, les nouvelles sportives (*f. pl.*)

spring, le printemps; **in spring**, au printemps

to sprinkle, arroser

stamp, le timbre-poste, *pl.* les timbres-poste; **stamp-book**, l'album de timbres (*m.*)

to stand, se mettre

I stand, je me mets

station, la gare

station master, le chef de gare

to stay, rester; **to stay in the woods**, rester au bois; **to stay out of doors**, rester en plein air, rester dehors

still (*adv.*), toujours

to stop, s'arrêter

store, le magasin; **grocery-store**, l'épicerie (*f.*)

story, l'histoire (*f.*), le conte

street, la rue

string, la ficelle; **piece of string**, le bout de ficelle

strong, fort

to study, étudier

subject, le sujet

successfully, avec succès

suggest, suggérer

summer, l'été (*m.*); **in summer**, en été; **all summer**, tout l'été

Sunday, dimanche; **on Sunday, Sundays**, le dimanche

sweet, doux, douce

to swim, nager

system, le système

T

table, la table; **at the table**, à table

to take, prendre (*p.p.* pris), apporter; **to take a walk**, faire une promenade; **to take an automobile ride**, faire une promenade en auto; **to take tea**, prendre le thé

it takes, il faut

we take tea, nous prenons le thé

to take off, ôter

tale, l'histoire (*f.*), le conte

to talk, parler

we talk, nous parlons

tall, grand

taxi, le taxi

tea, le thé; **to take tea**, prendre le thé; **to have tea**, prendre le thé

to teach, apprendre (*p.p.* appris)

teacher, le maître, la maîtresse, le professeur; **French teacher**, le professeur de français

to tell, raconter, parler, dire (*p.p.* dit); **to tell time**, dire l'heure

ten, dix; **ten o'clock**, dix heures; **ten-thirty**, dix heures et demie

tennis, le tennis

than, que

to thank, remercier

thank you, merci

that (*adj.*), ce, cet, cette, ce . . . -là, cet . . . -là, cette . . . -là

that (*conj.*), que

the, le, la, les (*see the noun in each case*)

theater, le théâtre

their, leur, leurs; **to their house,** chez eux

them, les (*dir. obj.*), leur (*ind. obj.*), eux, elles (*disj.*)

themselves, se

then, alors, puis, après, ensuite

there, là, y

there (is, are), voilà, il y a; **there will be,** il y aura

there they were, les voilà

these, ces, ces . . . -ci

they, ils, elles, on (*indefinite*)

thing, la chose

to think, penser, réfléchir, trouver

third, troisième

to be thirsty, avoir soif; **are you not thirsty?** n'avez-vous pas soif?

thirty, trente; **thirty-five,** trente-cinq; **thirty-one,** trente et un

this, ce, cet, cette; ce . . . -ci; cet . . . -ci; cette . . . -ci

Thomas, Thomas

those, ces, ces . . . -là

thought, la pensée

three, trois

to throw, jeter

Thursday, le jeudi; **on Thursday, every Thursday,** le jeudi

ticket, le billet

time, le temps, la fois, l'heure (*f.*); **to have a good time,** s'amuser; **several times,** plusieurs fois; **the second time,** la deuxième fois; **to tell time,** dire l'heure; **what time is it?** quelle heure est-il?; **at what time?** à quelle heure?; **to come on time,** venir à l'heure

tip, le pourboire

tired, fatigué

to, à, pour; **in order to,** pour; **up to,** jusqu'à

toasted, grillé

to the tobacco-shop, chez le marchand de tabac

today, aujourd'hui

together, ensemble

tomorrow, demain

too, aussi, trop, trop de; **too long,** trop longtemps; **too many,** trop, trop de

tooth, la dent

to touch, toucher

train, le train

mouse-trap, la souricière

to travel, voyager

tree, l'arbre (*m.*)

trick, le tour; **to do tricks,** faire des tours

tricolor, le drapeau tricolore

trunk, la malle

Tuesday, le mardi; **on Tuesdays,** le mardi

Turkey, la Turquie; **in, to, Turkey,** en Turquie

to turn, tourner

he turns, il tourne

I turn, je tourne

he turned back the covers, il a ouvert le lit

he turned out, il a éteint

turnip, le navet

twelve, douze; **twelve o'clock (noon),** midi **(midnight),** minuit

twenty, vingt

twenty-eight, vingt-huit

twenty-nine, vingt-neuf

twenty-one, vingt et un

twenty-seven, vingt-sept

twenty-three, vingt-trois

twenty-two, vingt-deux

two, deux; **a quarter after two,** deux heures et quart

U

ugly, vilain

umbrella, le parapluie

uncle, l'oncle (*m.*)

under, sous

to understand, comprendre (*p.p.* compris)

understands, comprend

to undress, se déshabiller

to unfasten, détacher

United States, les Etats-Unis; **in, to, the United States,** aux Etats-Unis

until, jusqu'à

upon, sur, en

us, nous

V

vacation, les vacances (*f. pl.*)

valise, la valise

value, la valeur

vegetable, le légume; **vegetable garden,** le jardin potager verb, le verbe

very, très; **very much**, beaucoup; **very long**, très longtemps

Virginia, Virginie

to visit, visiter

W

to wait, to wait for, attendre

waiter, le garçon

to wake, réveiller

to walk, marcher

walk, la promenade; **to take a walk**, faire une promenade

Walter, Gauthier

to want, vouloir (*p.p.* voulu), désirer, avoir envie (de)

I want, je veux, je désire

he wants, il veut

they want, ils veulent

warm, chaud; **it is warm**, il fait chaud

to wash oneself, se laver

to watch, regarder

watch, la montre

water, l'eau (*f.*)

to water, arroser

wave, la vague

way, la route, le chemin, la façon; **on his way**, en route (pour); **the best way**, la meilleure façon

we, nous

to wear, porter

week, la semaine

to weigh, peser

you are welcome, il n'y a pas de quoi

well, bien; **very well**, très bien; **fairly well**, assez bien

what (*int. adj.*), quel, quelle, quels, quelles

what, que, qu'est-ce que; **what is the matter with you?** qu'avez-vous?; **at what time?** à quelle heure?

what is it? qu'est-ce que c'est?

what is that? qu'est-ce que c'est que cela?

what is this? qu'est-ce que c'est que ceci?

when, quand

where, où

which, que, qui

while (*prep.*), en; (*conj.*), pendant que

whistle, le sifflet; **sound of the whistle**, le coup de sifflet

white, blanc, blanche

who, qui

whom, que, qui

why, pourquoi

wide, large

wife, la femme

window, la fenêtre; **shop-window**, la vitrine

window blind, le store

winter, l'hiver (*m.*); **in winter**, en hiver

to wish, désirer, vouloir (*p.p.* voulu), avoir envie (de)

I wish, je veux

he wishes, il veut, il désire, il a envie (de)

we wish, nous voulons

with, avec

without, sans; **without doubt**, sans doute

woman, la femme; **cleaning-woman**, la femme de ménage

woods, le bois; **in the woods**, au bois

word, le mot

to work, travailler

work, le travail

worried, inquiet, inquiète; **to look worried**, avoir l'air inquiet

to write, écrire (*p.p.* écrit)

he writes, il écrit

Y

year, l'année (*f.*); **last year**, l'année dernière; **leap year**, l'année bissextile

yellow, jaune

yes, oui

yesterday, hier; **day before yesterday**, avant-hier

you, vous

you are welcome, il n'y a pas de quoi

INDEX

(The numbers refer to pages.)

426